In Search of Democra

M000318033

This book evaluates the global status and prospects of democracy, with an emphasis on the quality of democratic institutions and the effectiveness of governance as key conditions for stable democracy. Bringing together a wide range of the author's work over the past three decades, it advances a framework for assessing the quality of democracy and it analyzes alternative measures of democracy. Drawing on the most recent data from Freedom House, it assesses the global state of democracy and freedom, as of the beginning of 2015, and it explains why the world has been experiencing a mild but now deepening recession of democracy and freedom since 2005.

A major theme of the book across the three decades of the author's work is the relationship between democratic quality and stability. Democracies break down, Diamond argues, not so much because of economic factors but because of corrupt, inept governance that violates individual rights and the rule of law. The best way to secure democracy is to ensure that democracy is accountable, transparent, genuinely competitive, respectful of individual rights, inclusive of diverse forms and sources of participation, and responsive to the needs and aspirations of ordinary citizens. Viable democracy requires not only a state that can mobilize power to achieve collective goals, but also one that can restrain and punish the abuse of power—a particularly steep challenge for poor countries and those with natural resource wealth.

The book examines these themes both in broad comparative perspective and with a deeper analysis of historical trends and future prospects in Africa and Asia. Concluding with lessons for sustaining and reforming policies to promote democracy internationally, this book is essential reading for students and scholars interested in democracy, as well as politics and international relations more generally.

Larry Diamond is senior fellow at the Hoover Institution and at Stanford University's Freeman Spogli Institute, where he directs the Center on Democracy, Development, and the Rule of Law.

Presenting decades of accumulated insight, wisdom, and constructive provocation, this volume is not only an irreplaceable account of the global state of democracy but also a remarkable testament to the power and value of one original, rigorous mind taking on an entire field of study across a defining generation of landmark events and trends.

Thomas Carothers, *Carnegie Endowment for International Peace*

In Search of Democracy brings together some of the seminal writings of Larry Diamond that have made him a pre-eminent figure among scholars of democracy and comparative democratic development. The essays in this twenty-three chapter volume are typically comprehensive and brim with insights, thanks in no small measure to the equal emphasis he places on the factors of structure, culture, state, society, politics, and political economy, backed by sound empirical data and appropriate illustrations. The unique combination of hard-headed analysis, passionately delivered in accessible prose, should make the collection indispensable to all students and policy actors in the field of comparative democratization and accountable governance.

E. Gyimah-Boadi, *Executive Director of the Ghana Center for Democratic Development and the Afrobarometer, and retired professor of political science at the University of Ghana, Legon*

Larry Diamond is the foremost scholar in fostering and guiding the burgeoning field of democratization over the past three decades. This collection includes the bulk of his most illuminating works of agenda-setting significance. The book cannot be ignored by anybody wanting a full grasp of all the most important intellectual debates over problems and opportunities of emerging democracies, especially during the critical phase of democratic consolidation, and the complex strategic issues as well as difficult policy choices surrounding democracy promotion.

Yun-han Chu, *Distinguished Research Fellow of the Institute of Political Science, Academia Sinica*

In Search of Democracy

Larry Diamond

Routledge
Taylor & Francis Group

LONDON AND NEW YORK

First published 2016
by Routledge
2 Park Square, Milton Park, Abingdon, Oxon OX14 4RN

and by Routledge
711 Third Avenue, New York, NY 10017

Routledge is an imprint of the Taylor & Francis Group, an informa business

© 2016 Larry Diamond

British Library Cataloguing-in-Publication Data
A catalogue record for this book is available from the British Library

Library of Congress Cataloging in Publication Data
Diamond, Larry.
In search of democracy / Larry Diamond.
pages cm
ISBN 978-0-415-78127-5 (hardback) – ISBN 978-0-415-78128-2 (pbk.)
– ISBN 978-1-315-68517-5 (e-book) 1. Democracy. 2. Comparative government. I. Title.
JC423.D655 2015
321.8–dc23
2015003888

ISBN: 978-0-415-78127-5 (hbk)
ISBN: 978-0-415-78128-2 (pbk)
ISBN: 978-1-315-68517-5 (ebk)

Typeset in New Baskerville
by GreenGate Publishing Services, Tonbridge, Kent

For Linda, my twin and first fan

Contents

Figures

Tables

Acknowledgments

When one gathers together for publication work that spans a career, it is difficult to resist the temptation to thank everyone who has been helpful along the way. Many people are thanked specifically in the essays that follow. But I would like to begin here by expressing some deep and overarching gratitude. As I explain in the introduction, I owe a huge intellectual debt—and a personal one larger than I can acknowledge—to Seymour Martin Lipset, who was one of my Ph.D. thesis advisors and whose writing and thinking did much to attract me to this field and shape my approach to it. It was Marty Lipset who introduced me three decades ago to the president of the new National Endowment for Democracy (NED), Carl Gershman. Since then, my friendship and interaction with Carl and the NED have been one of the key factors informing and inspiring my scholarship on and engagement with democratic development around the world.

Ten of the essays in this volume originally appeared in the journal published by NED, the *Journal of Democracy*, which I have had the privilege of coediting with Marc F. Plattner since it was launched in 1990. It is fitting that this book goes to press as we celebrate the 25th anniversary of the *Journal*. It not only has provided a periodic outlet for the kind of writing I have wanted to do on democracy, but it has also been for me a leading source of illumination and stimulation about evolving democratic ideas, theories, and empirical trends. I am deeply grateful to Marc for his intellectual and editorial leadership of the *Journal,* and for being a forthright but sympathetic and supportive critic. I also want to thank the editorial staff who I have worked with most closely: our long-time executive editor, Phil Costopoulos, who, along with Marc, has done so much over the years to make my work more lively and readable; our senior editor, Tracy Brown, a gifted and meticulous editor; our creative managing editor, Brent Kallmer; and other editorial staff who have helped me, including Zerxes Spencer, Nate Grubman, and Marta Kalabinski. Thanks also to NED staff—too numerous to mention—who have helped me understand the challenges and opportunities confronting democracy around the world, and who have done so much to support democratic change.

I want to thank the Hoover Institution, and its director, John Raisian, for providing me a supportive academic home on the Stanford University campus to research and write about democratic development, and more recently the Center for Democracy, Development and the Rule of Law (CDDRL) and its parent institute, the Freeman Spogli Institute for International Studies (FSI), where I have also been a senior fellow for the last decade (and director of CDDRL since 2009). I have learned a great deal from my faculty colleagues at CDDRL, and I thank in particular my fellow CDDRL scholars of democracy and political development, Michael McFaul (now director of FSI), Lisa Blaydes, Joshua Cohen, Alberto Diaz-Cayeros, Erik Jensen, Francis Fukuyama, Stephen Krasner, Beatriz Magaloni, Stephen Stedman, Kathryn Stoner, and Jeremy Weinstein.

I have had the benefit of support from some exceptional Stanford student research assistants who helped me prepare this volume for publication. Jack Mosbacher (who also coauthored one of the essays in this book) gave me intelligent, energetic, and unflagging assistance in organizing the book for publication, reviewing each final chapter, researching recent global trends, and helping to prepare the introduction. Jack's discipline, sense of humor, and quiet but relentless persistence help explain how this book finally got finished amid the crush of heavy competing obligations of institutional leadership at Stanford and travel outside it. With admirable skill and attention to detail, Alex Mayyasi tackled the initial task of transforming a number of my previous journal articles into a consistent form suitable for this book, and in editing and streamlining some of the material. Anne Sophie Lambert helped me compile the comprehensive database classifying regimes (as liberal democracies, electoral democracies, or autocracies) that underlies much of the empirical analysis in Chapter 4. Emily Green and William Gallery's work with me in assembling freedom and democracy data and comparing and assessing different measures of democracy was so outstanding that I invited them to coauthor the essay that appears as Chapter 3 of this book. At the time, they were both M.A. students in the Stanford program in International Policy Studies (IPS), and over the subsequent three years I had the pleasure of working with three other research assistants from the IPS program, Lukas Friedemann, Emma Farrario, and Erin Connors. I am deeply grateful to all three of these talented individuals for their skillful and committed support, particularly in updating and analyzing the data on democracy and freedom. As last in the line of succession in the run-up to publication, Erin Connors bore the brunt of the burden of managing the data and generating and updating the figures and tables for Chapter 4 of this book. I am particularly grateful to Erin for working so effectively and under significant time pressure to help me update my analysis of trends in freedom and democracy, especially with the new Freedom House data that was made available to us at the beginning of 2015.

I am deeply grateful to Arch Puddington, vice-president for research at Freedom House, for his leadership of the "Freedom in the World" annual survey, his openness over the years to my comments and research questions, his willingness to share the Freedom House data with me, and for providing me the detailed 2015 country scores immediately after they were finalized so they could be incorporated into this book without delay. Thanks also to Aili Piano and Bret Nelson at Freedom House for their help in recent years in providing data and answering my questions.

I once again heartily thank my long-time personal assistant, Alice Carter, for her devoted and cheerful support of my professional work, especially during the past six years of multiple professional roles, chaotic schedules, and ridiculous hours.

I am very grateful to Craig Fowlie, global editorial director for social and political sciences at Routledge, for recruiting this book and then for his patience in waiting for it as a succession of completion dates were defeated by the death of my mother and the accumulation of conflicting institutional obligations at Stanford. Finally I would like to thank Emma Chappell, who efficiently and gracefully managed the production process at Routledge, Carrie Baker, my production editor at GreenGate Publishing, and Cathryn Pritchard for the preparation of the index.

I extend my heartfelt appreciation to one of my most remarkable former students, Jared Cohen, founder and director of Google Ideas, for permitting me to use his painting on the cover of this book. Professors often recognize the impact their students have had in extending their knowledge and opening their minds to new ways of thinking. But Jared, an innovator and change maker from his earliest days as an undergraduate, was and is special. His extraordinary honors thesis on the U.S. failure to intervene in the Rwandan genocide was published as a book, *One Hundred Days of Silence: America and the Rwandan Genocide*, and his path-breaking work to advance liberation technology in both government and the private sector has established him as one of the most dynamic thinkers and practitioners working on governance reform. A gifted artist in addition, Jared gave me, upon graduating from Stanford, his stunning painting, "Mugonero," which depicts the moment when several Tutsi pastors of the Seventh-Day Adventist Church wrote to their senior pastor in a desperate appeal: "We wish to inform you that tomorrow we will be killed with our families." (The appeal brought no relief, the Tutsi faithful who had taken refuge in Mugonero's Adventist hospital were killed, and nine years later the senior pastor was convicted of genocide by the International Criminal Tribunal for Rwanda.) The painting is not only profoundly moving but underscores an important lesson about the stakes in institutionalizing democracy and decent governance.

Many academicians who have assumed significant administrative responsibilities will sympathize with the challenge I faced in completing this book amid the intense daily pressures of administration, teaching, student advising, meetings, seminars, conferences, and so on. In these circumstances, it helps to have a place to retreat to, where one can write and think, away from the relentless churn. My sister, Linda Raznick, and brother-in-law, Rob Raznick, have long provided me such a retreat in their beautiful home in rustic Hidden Hills, California, and it was in that idyllic location that I was able to finish writing this book. I would also like to thank Linda, my twin, for being (literally) a lifelong friend and supporter, and for her career-long dedication to educating and advancing the rule of law. I am so pleased to finally have this opportunity to dedicate a book to her.

The work in this collection has been published previously in a variety of different forms. We would like to thank the publishers for granting permission to use the following copyright material:

Larry Diamond and Leonardo Morlino, "The Quality of Democracy: An Overview," copyright © 2004 National Endowment for Democracy and the Johns Hopkins University Press. This article first appeared in *Journal of Democracy* 15 (October 2004), pp. 20–31. Reprinted with permission of Johns Hopkins University Press.

Larry Diamond, "Why Democracies Survive," copyright © 2011 National Endowment for Democracy and the Johns Hopkins University Press. This article first appeared in *Journal of Democracy* 22 (January 2011), pp. 17–30. Reprinted with permission of Johns Hopkins University Press.

Larry Diamond, "Rethinking Civil Society: Toward Democratic Consolidation," copyright © 1994 National Endowment for Democracy and the Johns Hopkins University Press. This article first appeared in *Journal of Democracy* 5 (July 1994), pp. 4–17. Reprinted with permission of Johns Hopkins University Press.

Larry Diamond, "Liberation Technology," copyright © 2010 National Endowment for Democracy and the Johns Hopkins University Press. This article first appeared in *Journal of Democracy* 21 (July 2010), pp. 69–83. Reprinted with permission of Johns Hopkins University Press.

Larry Diamond, "Elections without Democracy: Thinking about Hybrid Regimes," copyright © 2002 National Endowment for Democracy and the Johns Hopkins University Press. This article first appeared in *Journal of Democracy* 13 (April 2002), pp. 21–35. Reprinted with permission of Johns Hopkins University Press.

Larry Diamond, "Why Are There No Arab Democracies?" copyright © 2010 National Endowment for Democracy and the Johns Hopkins University Press. This article first appeared in *Journal of Democracy* 21 (January 2010), pp. 93–104. Reprinted with permission of Johns Hopkins University Press.

Larry Diamond, "Class Formation in the Swollen African State," copyright © 1988 Cambridge University Press. This article first appeared in *Journal of Modern African Studies* 26 (March 1988), pp. 567–596. Reprinted with permission of Cambridge University Press.

Larry Diamond, "Class, Ethnicity and the Democratic State: Nigeria, 1950–66," copyright © 1983 Cambridge University Press. This article first appeared in *Comparative Studies in Society and History* 25 (July 1983), pp. 457–489. Reprinted with permission of Cambridge University Press.

Larry Diamond, "Issues in the Constitutional Design of a Third Nigerian Republic," copyright © 1987 Oxford University Press. This article first appeared in *African Affairs* 86 (April 1987), pp. 209–226. Reprinted with permission of Oxford University Press.

Larry Diamond "Progress and Retreat in Africa: The Rule of Law versus the Big Man" copyright © 2008 National Endowment for Democracy and the Johns Hopkins University Press. This article first appeared in *Journal of Democracy* 19 (April 2008), pp. 138–149. Reprinted with permission of Johns Hopkins University Press.

Larry Diamond, "Promoting Real Reform in Africa," copyright © 2004 Lynne Rienner Publishers, Inc. This article first appeared in E. Gyimah-Boadi, ed., *Democratic Reform in Africa: The Quality of Progress* (2004), pp. 263–292. Reprinted with permission of Lynne Rienner Publishers.

Larry Diamond and Jack Mosbacher, "Petroleum to the People: Africa's Coming Resource Curse, and How to Avoid It," copyright © 2013 the Council on Foreign Relations, Inc. www.ForeignAffairs.com. This article first appeared in *Foreign Affairs* 92(5) (September/October 2013), pp. 86–98. Reprinted with permission of Foreign Affairs.

Larry Diamond, "The Coming Wave of East Asian Democracy," copyright © 2012 National Endowment for Democracy and the Johns Hopkins University Press. This article first appeared in *Journal of Democracy* 23 (January 2012), pp. 5–13. Reprinted with permission of Johns Hopkins University Press.

Larry Diamond, "Why China's Democratic Transition Will Differ From Taiwan's," copyright © 2008 Lynne Rienner Publishers, Inc. This article first appeared in Bruce Gilley and Larry Diamond, eds., *Political Change in China: Comparisons with Taiwan* (2008), pp. 243–257. Reprinted with permission of Lynne Rienner Publishers.

Larry Diamond, "A Comparative Perspective on Hong Kong Democratization: Prospects Toward 2017/2020," copyright © 2008 City University of Hong Kong Press. This article first appeared in Ming K. Chan, ed., *China's Hong Kong Transformed: Retrospect and Prospects* (2008), pp. 315–333. Reprinted with permission of City University of Hong Kong Press.

Larry Diamond, "Indonesia's Place in Global Democracy," copyright © 2010 Institute of Southeast Asian Studies. This article first appeared in Edward Aspinall and Marcus Mietzner, eds., *Problems of Democratisation in Indonesia: Elections, Institutions and Society* (2010), pp. 21–49. Reprinted with permission of the Institute of Southeast Asian Studies.

Larry Diamond, "Burma's Political Opening," copyright © 2012 National Endowment for Democracy and the Johns Hopkins University Press. This article first appeared in *Journal of Democracy* 23 (October 2012), pp. 135–146. Reprinted with permission of Johns Hopkins University Press.

Larry Diamond, "Empowering the Poor: What Does Democracy Have to Do with It?" copyright © 2005 The International Bank for Reconstruction and Development, The World Bank. This article first appeared in Deepa Narayan, ed., *Measuring Empowerment: Cross-Disciplinary Perspectives* (2005), pp. 403–425. Reprinted with permission of the World Bank.

Larry Diamond, "Promoting Democracy in Post-Conflict and Failed States," copyright © 2006 Taiwan Foundation for Democracy. This article first appeared in *Taiwan Journal of Democracy* 2 (December 2006), pp. 93–116. Reprinted with permission of Taiwan Foundation for Democracy.

1 Introduction

In search of democracy

Most careers owe much to chance, and mine as a scholar has been no exception. My entry in 1975 into the Ph.D. program in sociology at Stanford University coincided with the beginning of what Samuel P. Huntington would dub, a decade and a half later, the "third wave" of global democratization.[1] I did not choose to study democracy because it was fashionable at the time. In fact, during the second half of the 1970s, socioeconomic development was the predominant focus of comparative politics and sociology, and the most popular theories of the day explained underdevelopment in terms of economic dependence or structural inequality in the "world system," using neo-Marxist frameworks. While this drew my interest briefly late in my undergraduate career and early in my graduate career, I was always suspicious of structurally deterministic theories that appeared to absolve political and social actors of responsibility for their choices and behavior. Moreover, my moral and intellectual passion had always revolved around democracy, and although it was something of a passé subject in sociology in the late 1970s, I nevertheless resolved that that is what I wanted to study.

As I began in 1977 to formulate a dissertation topic, one fundamental and timeless issue gripped me: Why do some countries have democratic forms of government and others not? Embedded in this question were many others. From my childhood, which coincided with the decolonization of Africa, I had a long-standing interest in the politics of developing countries. In particular, I wondered: What explains the relative success of democracy in some postcolonial countries and its failure in others?

My starting point in attacking this question was to read widely and distill a substantial literature on what could loosely be called "the conditions for democracy."[2] I was deeply influenced by classic works such as Seymour Martin Lipset's *Political Man*, Robert Dahl's *Polyarchy*, Almond and Verba's *The Civic Culture*, and Juan Linz's *The Breakdown of Democratic Regimes*, as well as the work of Alex Inkeles on political culture and modernization, particularly his pathbreaking *Becoming Modern*.[3] All of these were reflective to one degree or another of the liberal, pluralist tradition, which viewed democracy as a political system of competition that required not only active citizen participation but also moderation, compromise, and restraint. Of course, this perspective stood diametrically opposed to the Marxist emphasis on "heightening the contradictions" and thus the necessity of class conflict and even violent revolution. My philosophical commitment to liberalism and my intellectual commitment to pluralism were viewed by many of my social science peers in graduate school and in my early academic career as quaint and naive at best (some no doubt saw them as reactionary). The prevailing thrust of theorizing about developing countries at the time took one of two forms. The first affirmed the need for a modernizing "developmental dictatorship," like that in South Korea and Taiwan, to manage and steer development without the supposed handicaps of a free press, a demanding civil society, a mobilized trade union movement, and so on. The second asserted the need for revolutionary withdrawal from the economic and political structures of the global capitalist system, which were seen as determined to, or even needing to, repress, distort, and extract wealth from the periphery of the world system in order to sustain the dominance of its capitalist core (mainly the United States and Western Europe).

I went in a different direction. I developed a comprehensive theoretical inventory of the "conditions for democracy." Some of these were economic and social, relating to the level of development, the extent of inequality, the size of the middle class, the class structure more broadly, and the availability of a wide range of autonomous intermediate groups, in essence a civil society. Some of these had to do with the broader structure of cleavages in society, the extent of ethnic, linguistic and other identity conflicts, and whether cleavages coincided with and reinforced one another or instead cut across and softened one another (the latter being one of Lipset's most important theories). Some of the variables concerned political structure and institutions—the structure of the party system (and how it mapped on to social cleavages), the degree of party system institutionalization, the role of the electoral system in shaping the party system and the political incentive structure, and (following Lipset, and in a different way Arend Lijphart[4]) whether power was decentralized, particularly in some kind of federal structure that was capable of managing identity cleavages and inhibiting the excessive concentration of power. Deeply influenced by Linz's study of democratic breakdowns, and subsequently by the work of G. Bingham Powell,[5] I looked for institutional arrangements that could preempt political polarization and extremism (as in the rise of antisystem parties and what Linz called the "politics of outbidding"). Given the prominent role of the military in ending many fragile democracies and then slowing democracy's return, I found it necessary to learn something about the military as an institution, and the way that militaries varied in their norms, structures, and incentives either to intervene or to remain aloof from politics.

I was fascinated and even consumed by this rich literature on what I came to term years later "the facilitating and obstructing conditions for democracy." However, I also continued to be uneasy with purely deterministic approaches. Studying the cases of democratic breakdown in the Linz and Stepan four-volume series on democratic breakdowns,[6] I became (and remain to this day) convinced that the failure of democracy is not foreordained, and that within the various social and institutional constraints, actors act, making choices that can doom or possibly sustain democracy. This underscored for me the importance of studying political culture to glean some further understanding of the norms and behavioral orientations that might shape the choices of political elites as well as mass actors. And it propelled me in my own research toward mostly qualitative work—grounded in historical analysis and field research—to attempt to understand and reconstruct the actors, processes, incentives, and constraints that shaped democratic success or failure.

For my doctoral dissertation I decided to assess and in a certain way "test" theories of the causal determinants for democracy. I proposed to my thesis advisors a comparative historical analysis of three different national experiences with democracy: one where democracy had been successful for some time and then failed (Chile); one where it emerged after decolonization and took root, however imperfectly (India); and one where it crashed and burned a few years after independence (Nigeria). My advisors persuaded me that three historical cases would be too much for one dissertation, and so I reluctantly dropped the Chilean case and wrote a thesis prospectus scoping out what I expected would be a comparative analysis of India and Nigeria. When that paper reached 140 pages, my thesis advisors persuaded me that I had better drop down to one case, or I would wind up with a 1,000-page dissertation. Very reluctantly again (as I had become thoroughly engrossed in India's political development), I shed another case. And then I wrote a 1,200-page dissertation on Nigeria. Thus was launched, for a time at least, my career as a Nigeria expert, and the special fascination and affection I have developed with the African continent.[7]

Why—when forced to choose—did I settle on the Nigerian case? One reason is that I had spent a month in Nigeria (in December 1974) on a six-month study trip throughout the developing world, in the year between my undergraduate and graduate study. I was instantly drawn to the country: its openness and dynamism, its formidable complexity, its boundless possibilities, and yet the scarring legacy of a ghastly civil war that had followed the breakdown of its constitutional democracy in January 1966. The largest country in Africa (with more than a fifth of the entire population of Sub-Saharan Africa), it was also in the midst of an oil boom that was lifting it up to regional leadership as one of Africa's richest countries. Just before I began graduate school in the fall of 1975, a group of military officers overthrew the sitting (and by then sit-tight) ruling general, Yakubu Gowon, and announced a program of transition back to civilian democratic rule. I felt it was crucial to understand why democracy had failed in Nigeria's First Republic if the Second Republic was to have a chance of succeeding. And there was no existing academic study that systematically analyzed the whole experience of the First Republic in order to explain its failure.

As I began reading about Nigeria's political history, I encountered a remarkable book, *Nigerian Political Parties: Power in an Emergent African Nation*, by the political scientist Richard L. Sklar.[8] A riveting and deeply informed account of the emergence of political parties during the final decade of colonial rule (the 1950s) in Nigeria, the book was significant most of all for its theoretical perspective, which built on the work of the Italian political theorist Gaetano Mosca and his concept of a "political class." For Sklar (and before him Mosca) the political class was not what it is glibly perceived to be in the news media today, as simply the collection of rotten and self-interested politicians (though rotten many of them were in Nigeria, and self-interested they always are everywhere to some degree). Rather, the emerging dominant class was "political" in the sense that government power became the primary instrument for the accumulation of personal wealth and status, so that even those outside of government office, in "private" business, needed access to government licenses and contracts in order to thrive. The state dominated the economy and held all the keys to the golden kingdom; thus the immortal phrase of Ghana's founding president, Kwame Nkrumah, "seek ye the kingdom of politics and all else shall be added unto you."

In researching the emergent structure of political alignment and conflict during the last decade of colonial rule and then the succession of polarizing political crises that rocked and destroyed the First Republic (1960–1966), I found affirmation for many elements of the pluralist theoretical tradition in which I was trained. Nigeria's First Republic was crippled with a famously unworkable federal system, with only three (later four) constituent units. Moreover, the regional boundaries were drawn in such a way that a different ethnic group was dominant in each region, and each dominant ethnic group then formed its own political party. As a result, the cleavages of ethnicity, region, and party—which intelligent institutional design could have steered into crosscutting currents—fell into one broad chasm of bitterly reinforcing antagonism. Any conflict involving one of these three cleavages almost immediately invoked the other two, and the succession of conflicts along this grand line of cleavage progressively polarized politics to the point of total distrust and dysfunction.

But there was still another puzzle to resolve. Why were Nigerian politicians so intent on winning and retaining political office that they would use any methods, embrace any allies, destroy any opponents, and impose any price on society in order to ensure their "victory" at the polls? To simply say that there had not yet emerged a culture of compromise and tolerance, or what Dahl called a "system of mutual security,"[9] was hardly a satisfying answer. Neither was I ready to rest content with the simplistic but popular notion at the time that democracy was doomed in Nigeria, and in most of Africa, because of its primordial ethnic differences (in a word, "tribalism"). Here is where class analysis and the concept of "political class" became essential to comprehending the trajectory of Nigeria, and indeed of postcolonial Africa more broadly. Because the colonial legacy was heavily statist (and perverse in many other respects that I documented), and because the economy was so poorly developed, the state controlled or regulated virtually all the means for social advancement and wealth accumulation. It was not just the salaries and perquisites of elective office. The bulk of the country's cash income flowed through the state. Winning elections meant controlling who would get access to this wealth; who would get appointive government jobs, military commissions, scholarships, contracts, loans, and licenses. Government office also provided the leverage to ensure admission of one's children to elite schools, and thus the transmission of membership in the dominant class to the next generation. The alternative to being at the table for this distribution of state booty was not a quiet, comfortable middle-class life, but rather grinding poverty. This explained much of the desperation of political life.

Utilizing the state to accumulate wealth and enter the dominant class was not limited in time and place to postcolonial Africa. It must have figured prominently in the state formation process in late nineteenth-century Italy, for example, because the Italian political scientist Gaetano Mosca was heavily preoccupied with the process as he wrote these memorable lines in his 1896 classic, *The Ruling Class:*

> If all moral and material advantages depend on those who hold power, there is no baseness that will not be resorted to in order to please them; just as there is no act of chicanery or violence that will not be resorted to in order to attain power, in other words, in order to belong to the number of those who hand out the cake rather than to the larger number of those who have to rest content with the slices that are doled out to them.[10]

This dependence of class on power had two huge and destructive consequences for Nigeria's tentative democracy. First, no party or indeed individual could afford to lose an election. As the late Claude Ake put it in his extraordinary presidential address to the 1981 conference of the Nigerian Political Science Association, "a desperate struggle to win control of state power ensues since this control means for all practical purposes being all powerful and owning everything. Politics becomes warfare, a matter of life or death."[11] And second, that warfare took the form of ethnic and regional conflict, not only because these lines of cleavage tapped people's most strongly felt identity, but also because politicians recognized that these identities could be easily mobilized on the path to power, and that doing so would distract attention from the politicians' own self-interested behavior. Thus the second consequence: the pervasive use of political office for personal and group enrichment bred a pattern of endemic corruption that gradually alienated the public as a whole even as it mobilized specific constituencies. As I showed in my study of the First Republic, resentment of corruption was an important parallel narrative sapping and ultimately destroying the legitimacy of the First Republic.

In search of big comparisons

I had never wanted or intended to be an Africanist per se. While I became deeply caught up with the drama and promise of Sub-Saharan Africa, I had always viewed my core intellectual interest as the one I had hoped to pursue for my doctoral dissertation—the comparative study of democratic success and failure. Early in my postdoctoral career, while I was finishing up an intense and formative year in Nigeria as a Fulbright Visiting Lecturer at Bayero University, Kano, I sketched a plan to return, in what I thought would be a manageable way, to the book I had wanted to write from the beginning. By then it was clear to me that I would not have the time—or in any case, as a young (untenured) professor, I could not assume the risk—of writing by myself a multicountry (and certainly very multiyear) comparative study of experiences with democracy. So instead I drafted a vision and a framework for an edited project that would recruit prominent country experts to write chapters tracing and explaining different national experiences with democracy in Asia, Africa, and Latin America. As I was preparing to leave Nigeria amid the chaos of another rigged election, and shortly in advance of another military coup that I was privately and grimly expecting, I sent my plan to my former dissertation advisor, Marty Lipset. I sought his comments, and more importantly his collaboration with me on this new project. Lipset loved the idea, and asked me if I would mind his making it a troika by drawing in one of his first graduate students, Juan Linz. Having been so deeply influenced by Linz's classic study of democratic breakdowns, I was thrilled.

So began the most rewarding and impactful intellectual collaboration of my life. Over the subsequent year Lipset and Linz and I met, reflected, debated and refashioned the framework into a rigorous and comprehensive conceptual, theoretical, and methodological agenda. We laid out a definition of regime types (including the important category of pseudo-democracy, or what are now called "hybrid regimes") and we offered an inventory of potentially relevant theoretical variables. We asked each case study author first to recount the major experiences with democratic and nondemocratic government in each country, and the characteristic conflicts and tensions in each regime; then to explain the fate of each regime, why it persisted or fell; then (third) to offer a summary theoretical judgment of the most important factors explaining the experience with democracy in the country; and then finally to ponder the future prospects for democracy in the country. In all, 26 case studies were produced in three regional volumes covering Africa, then Asia, then Latin America.[12]

The project yielded one of the greatest successes but also the most acute embarrassment of my scholarly career. The three regional volumes had a considerable impact on the discipline of comparative politics, focusing attention back from time-bound political processes (of breakdown and transition) to the longer-term historical legacies, structural conditions, as well as political and institutional choices that have shaped democratic outcomes over the long run. The volumes, which had been supported by what turned out to be the only purely research grant made within the United States by the National Endowment for Democracy, also spawned the launch in January 1990 of the *Journal of Democracy*, which went on to produce hundreds of new articles and more than 30 other edited volumes. Yet, aiming as it did to be comprehensive, covering so much variation across 26 countries, and publishing case study authors who had different theoretical proclivities, the project (predictably) identified a large number of distinct causal factors, with different ones emerging as important in different cases. Robert Dahl hit the mark when he observed, at a scholarly meeting where our work was discussed, that after a generation of work on democracy that featured a paucity of comparative evidence relative to the abundance of theorizing, we were probably entering an era when the abundance of evidence would, at least for a time, outrun and overwhelm theorizing.[13]

A political outcome as big and consequential as democracy was bound to have multiple sources of causation, and there was no shame in contributing such an infusion of carefully structured and systematically comparative case studies, even if the theoretical conclusions were mixed and middle-range. But there was a more basic problem with our project: The concluding theoretical volume (which we had subtitled "Persistence, Failure, and Renewal") was never published. And to make matters worse, we had numbered it volume one! To some extent, this problem was alleviated in 1995 when we published an updated collection of ten country case studies, with a theoretical introduction based on the evidence and entitled "What Makes for Democracy?" This lengthy chapter drew together the theoretical architecture and findings of the project, reviewing a number of "facilitating and obstructing" conditions for democracy: the crucial importance of democratic legitimacy; its strong relationship to the performance of the regime, not only in generating economic growth but in controlling corruption; the style and democratic commitment of political leadership, and underlying that the larger political culture; the benefit of economic development, the costs of extreme inequality, and the implications of the class structure; the role of civil society and of state-society relations; the role of democratic institutions and party systems in structuring and managing conflict; and the impact of the international community in pressuring for or undermining democracy.[14]

In one sense I was returning to basically the same inventory of theoretical variables with which I had started my own comparative study of democracy nearly 20 years before. But two things were different for me. First, we had a rich and compelling base of historical evidence to justify the generalizations and conclusions we were forging. And second, a unifying thread was beginning to emerge for me.

As I read through the cases and began as well to steep myself in the gathering flood of public opinion survey data from new democracies, I was becoming impressed not only with the core relationship between regime performance and democratic legitimacy—as close to a fundamental principle as I could think of in this field—but also with the role of what I would come to call "political performance." The survey evidence was showing (and it has continued to show across the different countries and regions where these public opinion polls have repeatedly been done, first in southern Europe, then in Asia, Africa, Latin America and the postcommunist states) that people do not only value economic performance. They also care about good governance: transparency and accountability, control of corruption, a rule of law and respect for civil liberties. Fidelity to the law, the constitution, and basic principles of decent governance is the least that democratically elected officeholders can do for democracy. If democracy cannot even be democratic, what use is it? In my 1999 book, *Developing Democracy: Toward Consolidation*, I stressed the vital importance of good governance in developing and sustaining democracy. And I posited a relationship between the quality of democracy and the stability of democracy. The democracies that seemed to be in trouble, or prone to failure, were virtually all *illiberal democracies*, in which one could show (using Freedom House and other data) there was a weak rule of law, extensive violation of human rights by police and other state and nonstate actors, political violence, and widespread political corruption, with little in the way of an independent and effective judicial system to rein in these problems.[15]

Now, I really had come full circle. This realization united the earlier phase of my work, on Nigeria and Sub-Saharan Africa, with my more recent comparative work, including the extended study I began of Taiwan's new democracy during a year of leave there in 1997–1998. Whatever their other flaws, the new democracies of Taiwan, South Korea, and much of Europe had developed or were quickly able to construct reasonably effective rule-of-law institutions to control corruption and abuse of power, while also generating effective and increasingly neutral state bureaucracies. If states were going to develop immunity against democratic breakdown, they had to achieve democratic consolidation, such that the broad bulk of people and groups in the society became unconditionally committed to democracy as the best form of government. That is very unlikely to happen unless there is a reasonably well-functioning state and judicial system that can restrain corruption, protect people's rights, and ensure decent and fair government—most especially, free and fair elections. Having participated in a *Journal of Democracy* conference and co-edited a book advancing the concept of "horizontal accountability" and examining its specific institutional expressions and dynamics, I became convinced that these different means of checking and restraining the abuse of government power (especially by executives) were vitally important to ensuring quality democracy, and therefore durable democracy.[16]

Thus, I became more and more concerned to get beyond issues of democratic persistence and failure to examine the quality and depth of democracy. This was necessary for two reasons. First, it was not only competitive, free and fair elections that people wanted—and had a right to expect. Democratic publics wanted, and too often were not getting, truly free, accountable, honest, just, inclusive, and responsive government. And second, if they did not get accountable and just governance, democracy in any form was going to be vulnerable to breakdown. Indeed, as I studied the trajectory of democracies around the world after 1990, an alarming pattern became evident: Many democracies in Africa, Asia, Latin America, and the postcommunist states were being degraded and even extinguished by the actions of their own democratically elected executives.

The dynamics and foundations of democracy

To assess the relationship between democratic quality and democratic stability, we had to find ways of conceptualizing and measuring the former. Fortunately, at the very time I was struggling with this conceptual issue, one of my intellectual homes at Stanford, the Center on Democracy, Development and the Rule of Law, had the good fortune to host the great Italian political scientist (later to become president of the International Political Science Association), Leonardo Morlino. He was then in the thick of thinking about how to delineate distinct dimensions of democratic quality, and our collaboration on that gave fruit to a coauthored essay on the quality of democracy, which opens the first part of this book as Chapter 2. Originally published in the *Journal of Democracy*, it was then extended to serve as the introduction to a book volume that elaborates the different conceptual dimensions of democratic quality and then applies them to a set of six paired comparisons in Western Europe, Eastern Europe, Latin America, East Asia, South Asia, and Africa.[17] We conceptualize the quality of democracy as having procedural dimensions (competition, participation, rule of law, and vertical and horizontal accountability); substantive dimensions (freedom and equality); and a results dimension, responsiveness of the political system to the expectations, interests, and demands of citizens. Of course, these dimensions interact and overlap in intricate ways, and some of these dimensions (for example, responsiveness) are hard to maximize, since they must weigh and reconcile competing interests. Nevertheless, our contribution provides a conceptual framework for evaluating the quality of democracy.

The next step beyond conceptualizing the quality of democracy is of course to measure it. This had been a long-standing interest of mine since I first began studying democracy, not long after Freedom House launched its annual survey of "Freedom in the World" in the early 1970s. As a Ph.D. student, I had taken an interest in quantitative efforts to measure democracy in order to study its relationship to economic development. But most of these sociological measures did not leave me very satisfied. In order to develop a highly continuous (and thus in one limited sense "precise") measure of democracy, they often heavily weighted rates of political participation (voter turnout), which struck me as putting too much stress on the data that was available rather than on the intrinsic conceptual structure of democratic quality. In 1988 I helped my former mentor, Alex Inkeles, organize a conference on measuring democracy, which led to an edited book of that title.[18] But I was left wanting a more systematic approach to comparing different measures of democracy. In 2011–2012, as I was working on this book, I had the benefit of an outstanding pair of research assistants in Emily Green and William Gallery. I enlisted them to help me compare systematically four different measures of democracy now in vogue—the Freedom House scales, the Polity IV scale, the Economist Democracy Index, and the Bertelsman Transformation Index. This is published here for the first time as Chapter 3.

Chapter 3 analyzes and compares the different components of these democracy measures and seeks to cut through some of the methodological clutter by finding more meaningful ways to compare them. It proposes a revision of the Freedom House methodology by reorganizing the two scales (of Political Rights and Civil Liberties) into three, with the third independently measuring transparency and the rule of law. We argue that transparency, control of corruption, and the rule of law are distinct from the extent and quality of political competition and participation, and of individual and civil freedom. And as I have already suggested theoretically, transparency and the rule of law form a particularly important dimension (and I believe a substantively coherent one), as this is the dimension that is most often wanting in practice. The data in the subsequent chapter in fact show this to be the case.

Chapter 4 was the last chapter to be written for this book and represents my most current effort to assess the state of democracy globally. The data—and the trends behind the numbers—suggest that the world has been in a mild democratic recession since around 2006, when the progress of democracy and freedom leveled off and began to decline. Since then, there has been an accelerating pace of democratic breakdown. The recession of freedom and democracy has been particularly apparent in lower-income countries (mainly in Sub-Saharan Africa), but it has also afflicted middle-income countries like Thailand and Turkey and oil-rich states like Russia and Venezuela. The common denominator in most of these cases has been a weak rule of law and the abuse of power by ruling executives who originally came to office via competitive democratic elections. Adding to the worrisome picture has been the rising skill and power projection of authoritarian regimes and the lackluster performance of the established democracies, not least the United States. As I stress in the concluding chapter as well, nothing is more important to the future of democracy globally than the capacity and resolve of the United States to promote democracy effectively.

Chapter 5 shifts the analysis from the trends and causes of democratic recession and breakdown to the dynamics of democratic resilience. Following the September 2008 financial crash that began on Wall Street, the world suffered a major economic recession, and many countries were buffeted by some of the most vicious economic storms since the Great Depression. Given what happened to democracy during that previous calamitous period, one might have expected the post-2008 economic crises to drag down many new or tentative democracies. Yet the economic crisis itself appears to have had relatively little impact on democracy in this period. Why? Examining the fate of governments and political systems in the two years following the onset of the economic crisis, we find two patterns. First, in the reasonably well-established democracies in Asia, Africa, Latin America and postcommunist Europe, voters responded to the economic downturn by using democratic institutions rather than subverting them. Where economic performance declined precipitously, voters punished the incumbents at the polls. Where the economic downturn was more modest, voters were more discriminating in their judgments. And second, where democracy did break down, economic growth was often fairly good, and democracy broke down for other reasons, having to do with deficiencies in the political dimensions of performance, particularly the quality of governance. All of this underscores the arguments in previous chapters (and, implicitly at least, throughout this book) about the intimate relationship between the quality and stability of democracy, with good governance as a critical intervening variable.

One bulwark of a quality democracy is a vigorous, resourceful, and pluralistic civil society. Comprehending what civil society is and what contributions it can make to the development and consolidation of democracy is the task of Chapter 6. Of course, a mobilized civil society with democratic norms and aspirations can play a crucial role in helping to bring about democracy in the first place, as Chapter 6 notes. But civil society is no less important after the transition in helping to entrench and consolidate democracy. It does so by performing a number of functions, many of which reinforce and leverage (but certainly cannot replace) the role of political institutions, such as parties, legislatures, and agencies of horizontal accountability. These functions include monitoring and checking the exercise of state power; stimulating and informing political participation; promoting a democratic culture of moderation, tolerance, and willingness (and ability) to compromise; helping aggregate and represent different political interests; generating crosscutting social cleavages that moderate the intensity of political conflict; recruiting and training new political leaders; and helping to deepen and reform the quality of democratic institutions and practices. I stress that while civil society typically acts to constrain the power of the state, it may also, in performing these various functions above, also strengthen the state by enhancing its legitimacy. I then review the features of a democratic civil society and the potential downside of a hyperactive, intensely demanding and politically polarizing civil society, which, rather than deepening democracy could potentially fragment or overwhelm it.

Over the past decade, democratic civil societies have increasingly utilized information and communication technology to perform many of the above functions for democracy. Chapter 7 surveys these and other means by which digital technologies and social media serve as instruments of "liberation technology" to extend and defend political and civic freedom, participation, and accountability. Here, I sound a cautionary note from the prior history of infatuation with the democratizing potential of information and communication technologies, but I also examine case studies in which new technologies have had such an effect. "Liberation technology," I argue, "enables citizens to report news, expose wrongdoing, express opinions, mobilize protest, monitor elections, scrutinize government, deepen participation, and expand the horizons of freedom." But it also can be censored and controlled by authoritarian regimes, and in fact these regimes are increasingly using these tools not just to thwart civil society but to monitor and repress it as well. And of course, terrorists and hatemongers also use digital tools as weapons for their own destructive ends. Thus, we must see technology as an instrument that can be used for good or for ill. Autocrats censoring and limiting access to the digital sphere are locked in a race with democrats trying to circumvent constraints and monitor and challenge authoritarian abuses. Liberal democracies need to stand up energetically for Internet access and freedom, and defend the users of liberation technology.

Chapter 8 offers a more detailed specification of the minimum requirements of electoral democracy, but mainly it shifts the analytic focus from democracy to the rise of authoritarian regimes that seek to masquerade as democracies. While allowing multiparty electoral competition, they so dominate the electoral playing field (and typically the administration and counting of the vote) and so abridge the exercise of democratic rights that they cannot be described as even electoral democracies. Rather, they fall into one or another form of hybrid regimes. They may encompass reasonably vigorous multiparty competition, with opposition parties gaining significant shares of the vote and the seats in parliament. Or they may be more thinly pseudodemocratic—electoral authoritarian in the shallow sense of having multiparty elections, but with a hegemonic ruling party that does not allow much real political pluralism. To complete the continuum of regime types, Chapter 8 also acknowledges the continued existence of politically closed authoritarian regimes that do not allow any form of electoral competition, and it identifies 17 regimes that were (when I performed the classification at the beginning of 2002) "ambiguous," lying somewhere along the boundary between (illiberal) electoral democracy and competitive authoritarianism. Today, my inclination is to classify all such regimes as competitive authoritarian, and this informs my judgments in Chapter 4 and in the Appendix, which classifies all regimes in the world at the beginning of 2015. Wherever one draws the line, the increase in the number of regimes that utilize the formal architecture of constitutional democracy, even though they do not in practice honor its norms, has been at least as striking a phenomenon of the third wave as the growth of democracy itself. Hence, there has been a dramatic contraction in the proportion of regimes that are unabashedly authoritarian—that do not allow multiparty electoral competition of any kind. And even military rulers these days feel the need to take on the fig leaf of electoral (and party-based) legitimacy if they intend to stay in power for the long run.

Part I concludes, in Chapter 9, by addressing the puzzle of why the Arab world has been the one broad cultural region of the world not touched by the third wave of democracy. The timing of this essay, which was originally published in the *Journal of Democracy* in January 2010, was rather ironic, as the Arab world began to erupt by the end of that year in a wave of pro-democracy protests that came to be known as "the Arab Spring" or (perhaps more appropriately) "the Arab awakening." As this book appears five years after the original publication of that article, the question in the title is no longer fitting in the literal sense, since Tunisia has emerged as the first Arab democracy (in at least four decades). This is a development of enormous historical and geopolitical significance, one that the established democracies in Europe and North America should place an extremely high priority on assisting. Yet, of the six Arab countries that experienced significant uprisings during the period from December 2010 through 2012 (Tunisia, Egypt, Libya, Yemen, Bahrain, and Syria), only Tunisia has achieved electoral democracy. As I note in Chapter 4, four years after mass popular protests for democratic change began to sweep through the Arab world, most of the region's regimes are either as authoritarian as they were in 2010, or more so. So the fundamental question persists: Why has the Arab world been so resistant to democratic change?

I dispute in Chapter 9 the common instinct to blame the absence of Arab democracy on religion. The mere fact of Islam being the dominant religion of the Arab world cannot be the cause, because a number of Muslim-majority countries have had significant experience with democracy elsewhere in the world (most especially Indonesia, the largest Muslim-majority country, but also, off and on, Bangladesh and Pakistan, and in Africa countries like Senegal, Mali, and Niger). Neither does culture seem a very satisfying explanation, at least if we examine the manifestations of it in public opinion surveys such as the Arab Barometer, which were showing when I wrote the essay in 2009, and which continue to show, widespread Arab public support for democracy as a system of government. It seems implausible to blame the democracy deficit on economic development, since there are a number of rich Arab oil states, and even the non-oil states have levels of development that have permitted democratic development elsewhere in the world.

The more convincing explanations, I argue, have to do with geopolitics, statecraft, and the strength of the repressive apparatuses of the Arab state. Oil wealth has given many Arab states the wherewithal to fund massive and sophisticated security apparatuses and to buy off societal discontent with lavish benefits for ordinary citizens. Many of the non-oil states (particularly since the fiscal crises associated with the Arab Spring) have benefited from substantial financial assistance from the Gulf states, and in addition have become adroit at using a combination of repression and co-optation to maintain political control. Thus, most Arab authoritarian regimes have not been entirely politically closed, but as in Morocco, Jordan, Yemen, and Kuwait, have allowed and co-opted political opposition in order to ease societal frustration.

Islam has entered into the picture in a peculiar sense: The fear of radical Islam has induced many middle-class Arab professionals who would be liberal democrats in other regional settings to back these largely secular authoritarian regimes as the lesser of two evils. This, unfortunately, has been an important factor explaining the failure of democracy in Egypt after the fall of Mubarak: Under President Mohamed Morsi, the Muslim Brotherhood tried to aggrandize its power, rather than reaching out (as its sister party, Ennahda, did in Tunisia) to form a broader coalition that would cooperate with liberal and secular elements of society, while adhering to the rules of the democratic game. More or less unquestioning Western support has added further ballast to Arab authoritarian regimes, helping to sustain them and insulate them from societal pressures. That changed when a number of Arab societies rose up in protest in 2010 and 2011, but unfortunately the destabilization and near state collapse in Libya, the debacle of Muslim Brotherhood rule in Egypt and the intense polarization of Egyptian society, along with the rise of the Islamic State and the ongoing chaos and violence in the region, have all combined to enervate the resolve of the West to support democratic principles and groups in the Arab world. As a result, authoritarianism has gained a new lease on life in that region, and perhaps so have my arguments explaining it in Chapter 9. Yet I think this lease is bound to be temporary, because Arab societies are undergoing fundamental change, and the old ruling bargains based on repression, co-optation, and intimidation cannot address the fundamental challenges these societies confront.

In search of democracy in Africa

Part II of this book begins with two articles that elucidate the founding themes of my work on Nigeria. Chapter 10 explores the general phenomenon of "class formation in the swollen African state," noting four means by which the state has served as the basis for forming, sustaining, and reproducing dominant classes in Africa. And Chapter 11 offers a summary analysis of the fatal interplay of class, ethnicity, and democratic politics during Nigeria's First Republic. Although Chapter 11 (published in 1983) was written several years prior to Chapter 10 (published in 1988), I have chosen to begin this section with the latter, more general treatment. This is because Chapter 10 shows that the mobilization of "tribalism" and the rigging of elections in order to conquer and loot the resources mediated by the state was not a peculiarly Nigerian problem but rather reflected the general pattern in postcolonial Africa.

Very early in my career, it became clear to me that the pervasive use of the state for personal and group enrichment is the core problem confronting democracy and development in Africa. One could call this simply corruption, clientelism, prebendalism (see below), or what was termed at the time by a number of scholars, following the work of Max Weber, "neopatrimonialism" (a concept signifying informal, personalized, corrupt rule, which, as I note in Chapter 4, Francis Fukuyama has favored in his magisterial new volume on *Political Order and Political Decay*[19]). But the processes I trace in Chapter 10 involve more than just looting or abusing state power for personal gain. They have encompassed a larger process of formation and reproduction of a dominant political class in most African states. And their impact on the emergent politics of postcolonial Africa was deeply toxic for two big reasons. First they prevented the development of strong, legitimate, and effective states, and second, in the context of competitive, multiparty politics, they provided politicians with regular means and incentives to mobilize ethnic identity in order to distract public attention (or at least anger) away from the scale of the corruption. Although there has been a heavy donor and international policy emphasis for three decades now on trying to shrink or limit the state sector in Africa, the neopatrimonial dynamic continues to dominate in too many states: Patron–client networks compete for state power and then bleed its resources away until there is far too little left for real development or state building. Africa cannot develop politically and economically until this fundamental problem is addressed.

In the quest to control corruption and achieve greater accountability and transparency, democracy can be a vital resource. But the problem is fiercely circular: If predatory dynamics infect competitive politics from the beginning, they will likely preempt and punish efforts by democratic actors (in the party system and civil society, and even the judiciary) to transform the system in a better direction. But unless those democratic institutions can somehow be leveraged for political reform, it is hard to see how lasting improvements in governance can be achieved in most countries.

This is the fundamental quandary that has confronted Nigeria for several decades, and it plagued Nigeria's First Republic. Chapter 11 traces the rise of competitive politics in Nigeria during the 1950s, the final decade of colonial rule, and through the crisis-ridden five-plus years of the postindependence democracy. It shows how class, ethnicity and party failed to cut across one another as organizing cleavages in politics but rather all flowed into a single and synthetic new grand cleavage, dominated by ethnic conflict between the three big groups, Hausa-Fulani (in the north), Yoruba (in the West), and Igbo (in the East). Political conflict became intensely polarized along this highly inflamed ethnoregional fault line, and the federal system, as noted above, only reinforced the problem. It was a dauntingly formidable structural problem, but by the time Nigeria passed into statehood, no one could figure out how to start over with a more viable institutional structure. Some progressives did lobby for change in the federal system (and other reforms), but the most the system could produce was a rather anemic (and cynical) move to create a fourth region out of the two smaller ones (East and West). Political conflict sometimes gravitated toward more explicit expressions of class tension, but for the most part politics became a desperate struggle for dominance among competing identity groups, with one group (the northerners) intrinsically advantaged by the federal system and pushing their advantage relentlessly until the whole system collapsed, first in a military coup, and then 18 months later, in civil war.

When the military-appointed constitution-makers, many of them lawyers and academics, set about designing a new constitutional structure for democracy in Nigeria in the mid-1970s, they resolved to create a more viable federation that would necessitate the formation of cross-ethnic alliances. The military had already gotten the ball rolling some years before, when it broke up the four-region structure into 12 states (six in the north and six in the south). As a result, new crosscutting cleavages began to be generated, as each of the three major ethnic groups was divided into different states. The constitution of the Second Republic (1979–1983) went further, splitting the country into 19 states, banning ethnic and regional parties, swapping the parliamentary for a presidential system, and requiring that a successful presidential candidate show some breadth of support around the country. These and other innovations made some impressive strides in generating more fluid and decentralized politics in Nigeria, the importance of which many scholars of federalism and ethnic conflict stressed.[20] Thus they went some distance to relieving one of the two key problems of the First Republic, the incessant polarization of ethnic conflict, as it merged with regional and partisan conflict. But the Constitution of the Second Republic did little in practice or design to address the other big cause of democratic failure in Nigeria, what Richard Joseph, the premier scholar of that period of Nigerian politics, called "prebendalism."[21] This is a term borrowed from the work of Max Weber to signify the practice of dispensing public offices in the expectation that they would be milked for personal and group gain, and that one's political clients and supporters would not only tolerate the predation but expect it.

Chapter 12 reprints a paper (first published in 1988) that sought to engage the emerging constitutional debate on how to design a better set of rules for a third Nigerian republic. The leitmotif of my effort was Nigeria's compelling need "to check, balance, and decentralize political power as extensively and innovatively as possible, and hence to reduce both the stakes in any electoral contest and the scope for behavioral abuses." While praising the logic of the existing federal system, I warned of the dangers of unchecked proliferation of the subfederal units (particularly the states), as there was then intense mobilization in Nigeria by many ethnic and subethnic groups for the creation of more states. In Nigeria's statist and prebendal system, every state capital became a magnet for the cornering and corrupt distribution of public wealth, and so the pursuit of one set of goals (decentralization and inclusion) had to wrestle with and be disciplined by an equally important goal, good governance. Thus I argued here not only for fiscal and political prudence in the creation of further states, but also for the maintenance of a reasonably strong central government that would be checked and balanced but not eviscerated by federalist design.

I was particularly concerned in this essay to stimulate thought about how institutions might be designed more effectively to monitor and control corruption. The Second Republic had formal government instruments (the Code of Conduct Bureau and Tribunal) for these purposes, but they never functioned, because the appointment and funding of these bodies were dependent on the very politicians whom they were to regulate. The same problems of political capture and subversion plagued other crucial regulatory institutions like the electoral commission and the judicial service commissions. When I wrote this essay a quarter-century ago, I strongly believed—and have continued to believe and argue ever since—that any effective system of horizontal accountability must find some way to insulate the appointment and oversight of these regulatory bodies so that they are able to become serious, purposeful, and resourceful. Chapter 12 advanced some innovative ideas on how to do so, by constituting a national oversight authority for these accountability institutions drawn substantially from civil society. But any exercise in constitutional design is merely a theoretical exercise unless it engages political leaders who have the will to achieve the underlying purposes of better, more democratic and responsible governance. This has been lacking in Nigeria under both military and civilian leadership, and civil society (which is much more open to such outside-the-box thinking about institutions) has been too weak to impose institutional reforms of the kind I outline here.

Chapter 13 shifts the focus back to Sub-Saharan Africa in general, as it probes the enduring tension between the aspiration for fair and open government under a rule of law and the reality of neopatrimonial distortion of governance through what is sometimes termed the "big man" syndrome. This more recent treatment does not employ the same language of class formation and class domination as Chapter 10, but two decades later, it underscores how tenacious those dynamics have been. The good news is that a new generation of African political reformers and civil society activists and organizations has been fighting back against the persistent patterns of clientelism, "tribalism," and neopatrimonial rule. The tools of liberation technology have aided their efforts, as have diplomacy, conditional aid, and democratic assistance grants from the international community. Democratic consciousness spread across the continent, and by 2008 Freedom House was classifying fully half the 48 states of the region as democracies. As the Afrobarometer surveys demonstrate, new norms have been taking hold, such as the momentum to limit presidents to two terms in office, and there have been more serious efforts to prosecute and combat corruption. Yet already (some seven years before the publication of this book) I was detecting vulnerability and erosion in Africa's democratizing trend, as some presidents were eviscerating term limits and others were undermining accountability in other ways. Neopatrimonial tendencies were beginning to reassert themselves, as African presidents overran constitutional constraints with increasing abandon, and the quality of governance (while improving in some countries) remained poor. Consequently, Africans perceive a significant gap between their own demand for democracy and the supply of it that they are getting from their leaders. Only strong countervailing institutions of horizontal accountability (following the logic of what I had recommended for Nigeria two decades before, in Chapter 12) can constrain these neopatrimonial tendencies. But particularly in an era when China is giving African autocrats the option of unconditional aid and support, the African reform agenda requires much more energetic support from the West.

Chapter 14 (initially published in 2004) ponders more systematically the links between democracy, good governance, and economic development in Africa. Although the story is somewhat different a decade later, when a number of African countries have been recording more impressive economic development, I think my theoretical argument here remains valid, because it has mainly been the African countries with democracy and more responsible governance that have been achieving the best rates of economic growth. The key point of Chapter 14 is that governance really does matter for development performance, and if Africa is going to climb out of its deep, debilitating cycles of poverty and instability, governance reform must be in the lead. Better governance, the evidence shows (at least for Africa), fosters more rapid and sustainable development in at least three ways. First, it inclines toward economic policies that are friendlier to the market and more conducive to rapid economic growth. Second, it reins in corruption, focusing the expenditure of public resources on generating public goods to improve human wellbeing. And third, it creates a more peaceful, consensual and predictable political order, in contrast to the cycles of coups, civil wars, and widespread violence that have ravaged so many African countries. To advance and consolidate the tentative progress toward better governance in some African countries, I urge efforts to break the continent's addiction to massive flows of unconditional aid that merely prop up corrupt dictatorships. International assistance can be a transformative partner *for* development in Africa, but only if it imposes conditions and expectations for decent governance. This is the new international grand bargain that could help to lift Africa out of poverty. Generating the political will to make this happen requires coalitions for reform pairing actors from below, in civil society, from within the political systems and governments of these African states, and from the international donor community. I conclude with a number of specific guidelines for reforming development assistance that I had helped to introduce into a 2002 review of our development assistance strategy by the U.S. Agency for International Development.[22]

Not just in Africa but around the world oil-rich countries in particular have seen their development hopes dashed by staggering corruption and debilitating economic distortions. Chapter 15, which I published with Jack Mosbacher in a 2013 issue of *Foreign Affairs*, explains why this is going to become an even more pressing problem for development in Africa over the next decade, as another dozen or more countries on the continent become significant oil exporters. After surveying the likely extent of this new oil boom in Africa, we explore the feasibility and implications of a potentially powerful policy innovation to fight the "resource curse": the distribution of state-accrued valuable natural resource revenues directly to citizens through cash transfers. We argue that direct distribution of oil revenues would attack the causes of the "resource curse" at their roots, challenging the pervasive disconnect between the state and its citizens. By handing a large share of the new revenues directly to the people as taxable income, it would reduce the amount of money sloshing around unaccountably in state coffers while also giving citizens a much stronger incentive to monitor how government spends what resources it has. However "oil to cash" is not a panacea. It must be accompanied by other measures to ensure fiscal and budget transparency and to compel extractive industries to publish what they pay to governments and government officials.

In search of democracy in Asia

Part III turns our attention from Africa to Asia. I argue in Chapter 16 that the best prospect for a new wave of democratic change in the coming decade lies in East Asia, given its rapid pace of economic development and the fact that it already has several robust electoral democracies and two of the most successful third-wave democracies, Korea and Taiwan. Yet it also contains some anomalies, including the richest autocracy in the history of the world (outside the oil states), Singapore, and another competitive authoritarian regime, Malaysia, that by now has a higher per capita income than most of the prominent third-wave countries had when they made their transitions to democracy. Both of these countries are experiencing growing support for opposition parties and rising pressures for democratic change, and when democracy does emerge in Singapore and Malaysia, it will be doing so in well-educated, middle-class societies that will have excellent prospects for sustaining it. The truly epic change, however, will come in China, where three decades of rapid economic development have generated a much better educated, more pluralistic society that is showing growing signs of independence from the party and the state. The Chinese communist regime, I stress, faces the classic dilemma of all modernizing dictatorships: It is damned if it does keep delivering development, and damned if it doesn't. Continued rapid development will accelerate the rise of civil society as well as liberalizing value change that seeks greater personal freedom and autonomy. However, a serious interruption in economic growth (and there are growing structural contradictions challenging that growth) risks undermining the legitimacy of communist rule, which in recent decades has increasingly depended on short-term performance. Either way, fundamental political change is coming to China, and I predict, "within a generation or so, most of East Asia will be democratic."

How—by what path or sequence—will China's democratization take place? China is undergoing the same extended run of rapid economic growth that Taiwan experienced, and so it is reasonable to expect that China's transition might replicate Taiwan's. Yet I argue in Chapter 17 that this is unlikely. While China's growth has seen similar positive social consequences as in Taiwan—better education, wider information, and a more pluralistic civil society with a gradual shift to more liberal values, especially among the young—it has also harbored a dark side, including a predatory state, rising inequality, and corruption that along with government unresponsiveness threatens the country's political stability. Moreover, while the ruling Kuomintang (KMT) gradually introduced competitive elections (though without opposition parties) early on in its rule, China's Communist Party has resisted moving the process of competitive elections up from the relatively minor level of village elections. KMT leaders envisioned an eventual transition to democracy, while most of China's communist rulers do not seem to have envisioned evolution beyond a Singaporean-style regime of "rule by law." Then, too, China is unlikely to face consequential external pressure to democratize of the type that weighed heavily on Taiwan, especially during the 1980s and early 1990s. These differences "do not imply that China will not become a democracy. But they do imply that China's transition to democracy will take longer, be driven by somewhat different logics, and will be more fraught with internal and, potentially, international peril than was Taiwan's."

While China as a whole is still a very long distance from democracy, there is one small part of China that is not: Hong Kong. I argue in Chapter 18 that Hong Kong's high level of economic development, strong rule of law institutions, significant experience with electoral competition, and prevalence of democratic values belie Beijing's repeated claim that the Special Administrative Region is "not yet ready" for democracy. Indeed, there are very few nondemocratic political systems that are *more* ready for democracy today than Hong Kong is. Six years after I first published this essay (in 2008), Hong Kong exploded in mass public protests in late 2014 over Beijing's refusal to deliver on its implicit promise that the people of Hong

Kong would be able to democratically elect their chief executive through universal-suffrage elections by 2017. Instead, what the National People's Congress Standing Committee (NPCSC) delivered in a decision at the end of August 2014 was a framework for an Iranian-style sham election in which up to three candidates chosen by the Beijing-dominated nominating committee would compete for the people's support.

Chapter 18 provides a historical and institutional context for understanding this ongoing dilemma of thwarted constitutional development in one of East Asia's most vibrant and pluralistic societies. I weigh here possible models of transition and constitutional compromises that might permit democratic development in Hong Kong to proceed. But the cold hard fact then and now is that the ultimate power to determine (or block) Hong Kong's democratic development lies not with the people or even the elites of Hong Kong but rather the authorities in Beijing. And gripped with insecurity about the stability of their rule in China generally, they show no sign of being willing to tolerate even "gradual and orderly progress" (as promised in the 1997 Basic Law) toward democracy in Hong Kong. Unfortunately, these fears of China's leaders about Hong Kong becoming a possible model for the mainland are the one anxiety that Hong Kong's democrats can do little to allay. And so, democracy in Hong Kong remains on hold.

Though it is still classified only as a lower middle-income country by the World Bank, Indonesia has made somewhat surprising progress in developing and sustaining democracy, which I explore in Chapter 19. During the first decade following the collapse of the Suharto dictatorship in 1997 and then the rise of democracy, Indonesia achieved reasonably good economic growth (better than most of its big emerging-market peers) and it also made significant progress in human development, improving at a faster clip that most of its regional neighbors. Its percentile ranks on the different World Bank measures of governance also improved appreciably, but they still fell well behind most of Indonesia's peers in the region or among large third-wave democracies. Extensive corruption and a weak rule of law thus remained by 2008 a significant challenge to the stability of democracy in Indonesia. Yet Indonesia's levels of political rights and civil liberties gradually improved, to the point where Indonesia became in 2006 (and remained until recently) a "free" state in the Freedom House framework. Indonesians seem to have embraced and supported the democratic experiment. Indonesia's levels of public support for democracy, satisfaction with the way it is working, and trust in its institutions in Indonesia are some of the highest in East Asia, and even support for basic liberal values is substantial, considering the middling level of economic development and the presence of Islam as the predominant religion. It is too early to say that democracy is consolidated in Indonesia, that it has become "the only game in town," but the values and institutions of democracy have at least become more rooted, and the country has not been plagued by the levels of political polarization that have repeatedly derailed democracy in Thailand and Bangladesh, for example. What we see in Indonesia instead is a vivid example of the global relationship between democratic quality and democratic stability. To become consolidated and thus stable for the long run, Indonesia needs deeper progress in reducing corruption, providing a rule of law, and modernizing and professionalizing the overall architecture of the state.

Chapter 20 examines the incipient transition in Asia's most recent aspirant for democratic change, Burma. It was published in 2012, when a "new and more hopeful mood" was dawning in Burma and there was still a certain euphoria in the West about the political opening following half a century of insular and deadening authoritarian rule. However, my analytic thrust here is mainly sobering. I note a number of respects in which the 2008 constitution of Burma—which serves as the basis for the transition and the new political system that is unfolding—puts formidable obstacles in the way of democracy and will, if it is not amended, result in nothing more than a competitive authoritarian regime. While this would still be better—freer and more pluralistic—than the single-party, military-dominated, and highly repressive regime that has preceded it, it would severely disappoint the majority of the Burmese people, who clearly aspire for genuine democratic change. Reviewing the major constitutional impediments to true democracy, I then consider how a genuine democratic transition might be facilitated, through the negotiation of a political pact between regime and opposition. Such a pact would no doubt have to make some familiar but painful concessions to the ruling elites, in terms of amnesty for their past crimes and security for their ill-gotten property, but if the result were removal of the constitutional impediments to democracy (such as the guarantee to the military of a quarter of all the seats in the parliament), most people in Burma might judge the compromise worth it. When I wrote this article two years ago, I was somewhat hopeful that a constitutional bargain might be forged as part of a larger political pact. But as international investors and donors rush in to do business and offer aid, Burma's rulers (a complex mix of serving and retired former military officers in the Army and the ruling party) no longer feel the heat of international pressure to deliver democracy. Hence, they have stood pat in refusing to consider constitutional reform. The result of the transition is thus likely to be a hybrid regime that combines a multiparty electoral system—in which the principal opposition party, the National League for Democracy will have substantial representation in parliament—with the reality of continued but more subtle military domination.

Promoting democracy: policy implications

Chapter 21 begins Part IV by looking at the relationship between democracy and poverty reduction. In keeping with the central theme of this book,

I argue here that the obstacles to ending poverty are political; democracy should in theory do much to address these obstacles, but often its record is disappointing because of bad governance. While distinctive circumstances (such as relative ethnic homogeneity and strong states) have enabled developmental authoritarian regimes in East Asia, I explain why the model of "developmental authoritarianism" is unlikely to work in Africa or in most of the rest of the less developed world. The key to sustainable poverty reduction is a political context of accountability, transparency, and rule of law, where the poor can have effective voice and use that voice (and vote) to hold their leaders accountable. Crucially, that requires as well an effective state which is not only able to deliver education, health services and physical infrastructure, but which can also maintain public security and safety without abusing citizens' rights. Electoral democracy can thus be an important instrument for achieving policies—and policy implementation—to level power disparities and reduce poverty, but democracy will only deliver in this way if it is paired with decent governance that is actually able to produce and distribute these public goods for development. The quality of democracy is thus strongly related not only to the stability of democracy but to economic development and the reduction of poverty as well. The more that the basic framework of electoral democracy is wedded to vigorous channels for grassroots participation in civil society, a strong rule of law, and a robust architecture of horizontal accountability to control corruption and abuse of power, the better the prospects for achieving brisk and lasting reductions in poverty. And of course, the more the progress in reducing poverty, the more sustainable will be the democracy. There is thus a powerful virtuous circle here between democracy, good governance, and poverty reduction. This compels a change in the logic of development assistance, toward an integrated and more *political* strategy that views the development and deepening of democracy, accountability, and the rule of law as key instruments in the overall campaign to reduce poverty.

Chapter 22 ponders the difficult challenge of promoting democracy after the state has collapsed into violent conflict. This is a challenge that I struggled with personally during a brief stint as a senior advisor to the Coalition Provisional Authority in Iraq during the first three months of 2004, and my arguments here are shaped by America's bitter disappointments during that fateful experience. Iraq and Afghanistan are unlikely to be the last two instances where the international community intervenes in some way to assist democratic development following war and state collapse, so it is important to examine carefully the lessons of these and other recent experiences.

The first lesson of the recent experiences in Iraq and Afghanistan is the first rule of all theorizing about democracy: In order to have a democratic state, a country must first have a state. And that requires an effective monopoly over the means of organized violence. However, when states have collapsed, often the only way to reestablish this monopoly quickly is through some kind of international military or peacekeeping intervention. Such an intervention must be prepared to use force even after the end of war to rein in spoilers and implement a plan for the disarmament, demobilization, and reintegration of combatants into a new national army and police. But a foreign intervention, particularly one that seeks to forge a certain kind of peace, may become the target of violent resistance. Moreover, when the international community intervenes to impose order, it also typically assumes responsibility for interim administration of the country, or at least for resurrecting some kind of indigenous government. Such an interim government may be able to gain public acquiescence for a time (partly in gratitude for the reduction of fear and violence). If it lacks any clear basis of representativeness, however, it may quickly find its legitimacy challenged. Increasingly, the response has been to rush to elections to fill the legitimacy void, but this may only make matters worse if elections are not well prepared and if there has not been time for a representative plurality of parties to form, organize, and begin to canvas public support. The bulk of Chapter 22 offers guidelines for democracy promoters in postconflict situations. Among these: study closely the local context; commit adequate military and financial resources (and prior to that, assess carefully the difficulty of the task in order to judge the level of commitment necessary); establish international legitimacy and support for the postconflict intervention; generate legitimacy and trust within the postconflict country; organize local elections before national ones; promote knowledge of democratic norms and institutional choices; disperse economic reconstruction funds and democratic assistance as widely as possible; and promote local participation and ownership, not least in constitution-making.

Postconflict interventions constitute only a small slice of international efforts to promote democracy. The last chapter (Chapter 23) surveys more broadly U.S. and international policies to promote democracy—their priority, their various tools, their achievements and shortcomings, and how they might become more effective. I argue there are not only compelling moral grounds to elevate the priority of democracy promotion in American foreign policy, but strong practical reasons as well. Real democracies make for more reliable long-term allies, do not threaten our security interests, and are not the sources of famine or other complex emergencies. The problem is that policymakers tend to have short time horizons, and thus, when confronted with tough choices, they take a predominantly realist approach to advance national interests in the short run, giving short shrift to human rights and democracy concerns.

Chapter 23 makes clear that the case against democracy promotion can't be made out of budgetary concerns, since the total cost of all democracy assistance programs is only a small percentage even of the international affairs budget of the United States. Neither can it be justified as an unwarranted intrusion, given the strong and growing demand for democracy in so many developing and postcommunist countries, and the urgent appeals of civil society actors in these countries not only for increased financial and technical assistance, but for more resolute and consistent diplomatic and moral support as well. Many Americans now shy away from "democracy promotion" because they associate it with the use of force and the subsequent beleaguered effort to "impose" democracy in Iraq. But as I explain in this chapter, force is only one instrument for trying to spread democracy around the world; it is not the most important and effective tool; and democracy promotion should never be the main motive for going to war. Much more effective are the use of various diplomatic tools to pressure autocrats and provide symbolic and political support to democrats (short of backing particular political parties and leaders); sanctions and aid conditionality as a way of bringing pressure on autocrats to loosen up and allow democratic change, and of rewarding governments that implement democratic reforms; targeted sanctions as a way of changing the calculus and shaping the choices of specific authoritarian regime leaders; and grants and training to political parties, independent media, think tanks, human rights and women's groups, NGOs, trade unions, and business associations. Fortunately, donors have increasingly come to appreciate the importance of advancing not just the formal institutions of democracy but the deep structures and norms that ensure good governance as well. This requires a flexible, steadfast, and country-specific approach that works on both the supply side—to strengthen accountability and the rule of law—and the demand side of public pressure for good-governance reforms. Steadfastness requires patience and a long-term commitment. One of the biggest mistakes democracy promoters make is to "graduate" new democracies from assistance programs well before the institutions and norms of liberal democracy have truly been consolidated.

What is at stake?

Imagine a world in which all states were democracies. Given the progress of the past four decades, it is no longer unthinkable. A world of universal democracy would not be a perfect world. Many democracies would no doubt still be illiberal, but the framework of democracy and an open society would generate public pressure to gradually move them in a more liberal direction. There would still be abuses of power by people in authority, from the local police to high-level officials. But these would be more often detected, punished, and deterred. It would be a world of dramatically fewer human rights abuses, greater personal and press freedom, less corruption, less violent conflict, and quite conceivably a world that had put an end to interstate war. It would be a world that no longer sponsored or tolerated mass killings like the Rwandan genocide, depicted on the cover of this book. It would be a world without famine; a world of states that were responsible to and could be held accountable by their own people. It would be a more just world.

Now ponder the real, measurable difference that a decently governed democracy can make. Compare (as I did in a public lecture in Nigeria in 2014) the experiences of Nigeria, where democracy has repeatedly been disfigured by corruption and electoral fraud, and Ghana, one of the most liberal democracies in Africa.[23] These are two countries from the same region of West Africa that achieved independence with the same British parliamentary model at roughly the same time.

Four decades ago, in the wake of the first oil boom, Nigeria was a much wealthier country than Ghana. Its per capita income was about 40 percent higher than Ghana's.[24] Since the darkest days of military rule and partial state collapse in Ghana, that country has moved forward to develop democracy and lift up state capacity and performance. Nigeria has not. As a result, Ghana has significantly improved its rankings on the quality of governance, while Nigeria's have remained miserable. In control of corruption, Ghana is now in the 56th percentile worldwide, Nigeria is in the 11th percentile. On rule of law, Ghana is in the 50th percentile. Nigeria is in the bottom 10 percent. Similar gaps characterize the two countries' rankings on other dimensions of good governance.[25] As a consequence of all of this, Ghana ranks in the 50th percentile in terms of political stability, and Nigeria is in the 3rd percentile, down in the neighborhood of Iraq, Afghanistan, and the DRC. And this was before Boko Haram abducted some 276 schoolgirls in Chibok in mid-2014, as part of its ruthless and escalating terrorist rampage.

To appreciate what a difference decent governance makes, consider the two countries' mortality rates for children under age five. Ghana has reduced this grim statistic since 1980 by 57 percent; Nigeria by only 42 percent. Today about 7.2 percent of Ghanaian children under age five die each year—a horrible statistic, but much better than the Nigerian rate, which is 12.4 percent. Nigeria has the ninth worst child death rate in the world, of the 196 countries for which UNICEF presents data. The difference between Nigeria and Ghana is the difference between one out of 14 kids dying a year versus one of out eight. UNICEF estimates that 827,000 Nigerian children under age five died in 2012, about one of every eight such deaths in the entire world. Now imagine for a moment that Nigeria had Ghana's under-five mortality rate of 7.2 percent. The number of Nigeria's child deaths in 2012 would have been about 347,000 fewer. Multiply that figure, or some large portion of it, by ten or 20 years (or more), and the number of children who have died because Nigeria's child death rate is larger than Ghana's runs well into the millions. In the last decade alone, it has surely been over two million (probably over three million) Nigerian children. That is many more deaths than in the Nigerian civil war. It is more than three times as many deaths as in the Rwandan genocide, and comparable to the number of Cambodians murdered by the Khmer Rouge in the 1970s. It is hard to see what can possibly account for the difference in child death rates between Nigeria and Ghana except the demonstrably worse governance in Nigeria.[26]

Fifty-three years after independence, an estimated half of Nigerian adults are illiterate, 70 percent lack access to improved sanitation facilities, a quarter of all children are underweight, and over a third of them are not being immunized.[27]

Who will be held accountable for these developmental failures, and for the roughly three million children who would not have died if Nigeria's Fourth Republic had managed to improve the quality of governance—not to the level of Sweden, just to the level of Ghana? When political leaders murder a million of their own people, we call it genocide. We do not have a term for the crime that is inflicted when egregious corruption and mismanagement cause the needless death of three million children over an extended period of time.

No one ever said that democracy brings nirvana or relieves its citizens of the need to be vigilant and work for institutional reform. Perhaps the most famous contemporary quotation about democracy is this one from a 1947 speech by Winston Churchill on the floor of the House of Commons:

> Many forms of Government have been tried, and will be tried in this world of sin and woe. No one pretends that democracy is perfect or all-wise. Indeed, it has been said that democracy is the worst form of Government except for all those other forms that have been tried from time to time.[28]

Democracy does not eliminate all forms of corruption and injustice. In fact, inequality is now increasing alarmingly around the world, and most democracies, not least the United States, are struggling to deal with this issue. All democracies are vulnerable to the relentless ambition of powerful interests to corner and entrench advantage and to capture or suborn the state. And as we see in the U.S. and elsewhere, democracies can also be prone to political polarization. But the great promise and redeeming advantage of democracy is its capacity for self-correction. Democracy provides citizens the freedom to expose and denounce unjust and unwise policies. It gives them the institutional tools to bring about change. It affirms the dignity and worth of the individual, and it at least gives individuals the means to secure their rights.

These are the reasons why more and more citizens around the world are saying that they want to live in a democratic system, and that they want their existing democracies to be more open and accountable. This is why we in the established democracies have an obligation to help other people achieve a decent, well-governed democracy. And it is why we owe it to ourselves and the world to ensure that our own democracies sustain, or renew, the levels of freedom, equality, participation, competition, accountability, responsiveness, and rule of law that will mark them as quality democracies, worthy of emulation.

Notes

1 Samuel P. Huntington, *The Third Wave: Global Democratization in the Late Twentieth Century* (Norman: University of Oklahoma Press, 1991).
2 Then it was possible to master the available social science literature on democratic development; now it is so voluminous that it would be an impossible task for any one scholar.
3 Seymour Martin Lipset, *Political Man: The Social Bases of Politics* (New York: Doubleday, 1960); Robert A. Dahl, *Polyarchy: Participation and Opposition* (New Haven, CT: Yale University Press, 1971); Gabriel Almond and Sidney Verba, *The Civic Culture: Political Attitudes and Democracy in Five Nations* (Princeton, NJ: Princeton University Press, 1965); Juan J. Linz, *The Breakdown of Democratic Regimes: Crisis, Breakdown, and Reequilibration* (Baltimore, MD: Johns Hopkins University Press, 1978); Alex Inkeles and David H. Smith, *Becoming Modern: Individual Change in Six Developing Countries* (Cambridge, MA: Harvard University Press, 1974).
4 Arend Lijphart, *Democracy in Plural Societies: A Comparative Exploration* (New Haven, CT: Yale University Press, 1977).
5 G. Bingham Powell, Jr., *Contemporary Democracies: Participation, Stability, and Violence* (Cambridge, MA: Harvard University Press, 1982).
6 Juan J. Linz and Alfred Stepan, eds, *The Breakdown of Democratic Regimes*, volumes I–IV (Baltimore, MD: Johns Hopkins University Press, 1978).
7 I still believe that there is an important comparative study to be written of Britain's most important postcolonial legacies in Asia and Africa, namely, India and Nigeria. Each inherited, at least formally, the British parliamentary and rule-of-law traditions, and each had to struggle with formidable ethnic complexity in the context of an emergent federal system. While the success of India relative to Nigeria may appear "overdetermined," in the sense that it has too many favorable factors relative to Nigeria, this is more obvious in historical retrospect than it was at the time. Yet I am not aware of a book explicitly comparing the two.
8 Richard L. Sklar, *Nigerian Political Parties: Power in an Emergent African Nation* (Princeton, NJ: Princeton University Press, 1963).
9 Dahl, *Polyarchy*, Chapter 1.
10 Gaetano Mosca, *The Ruling Class: Elementi di scienza politica* (New York: McGraw-Hill, 1936), 143–144.
11 Claude Ake, Presidential Address to the 1981 Conference of the Nigerian Political Science Association, *West Africa*, May 25, 1981, 1162.
12 Larry Diamond, Juan J. Linz, and Seymour Martin Lipset, *Democracy in Developing Countries: Africa, Asia, and Latin America* (Boulder, CO: Lynne Rienner Publishers, 1988, 1989).
13 Ibid., Preface, xiv.
14 Larry Diamond, Juan J. Linz, and Seymour Martin Lipset, "Introduction: What Makes for Democracy?" in Diamond, Linz, and Lipset, eds, *Politics in Developing Countries: Comparing Experiences with Democracy* (Boulder, CO: Lynne Rienner Publishers, 1995), 1–66.
15 Larry Diamond, *Developing Democracy: Toward Consolidation* (Baltimore, MD: Johns Hopkins University Press, 1999).
16 Andreas Schedler, Larry Diamond, and Marc F. Plattner, eds, *The Self-Restraining State: Power and Accountability in New Democracies* (Boulder, CO: Lynne Rienner Publishers, 1999).
17 Larry Diamond and Leonardo Morlino, *Assessing the Quality of Democracy* (Baltimore, MD: Johns Hopkins University Press, 2005).
18 Alex Inkeles, *On Measuring Democracy: Its Consequences and Concomitants* (New Brunswick, NJ: Transaction, 1991).

19 Francis Fukuyama, *Political Order and Political Decay: From the Industrial Revolution to the Globalization of Democracy* (New York: Farrar, Straus and Giroux, 2014).

20 See in particular Donald L. Horowtiz, *Ethnic Groups in Conflict* (Berkeley: University of California Press, 1985).

21 Richard A. Joseph, *Democracy and Prebendal Politics in Nigeria: The Rise and Fall of the Second Republic* (Cambridge and New York: Cambridge University Press, 1987).

22 *Foreign Aid in the National Interest* (Washington, DC: U.S. Agency for International Development, 2000).

23 The following is drawn from "The Governance Predicament: Poverty, Terrorism and Democracy," the 2014 Tinubu Lecture, Freedom House, Lagos, Nigeria, June 30, 2014; published as "Nigeria: Anatomy of a Feckless State," *Premium Times*, June 30, 2014, www.premiumtimesng.com/opinion/164182-nigeria-anatomy-of-a-feckless-state-by-larry-diamond.html.

24 Nigerian per capita GDP was $528, Ghanaian was $379.

25 Here are the other comparative rankings: State effectiveness: Ghana 52, Nigeria 16. Voice and accountability: Ghana 60, Nigeria 27. Regulatory quality: Ghana 56, Nigeria 25. http://data.worldbank.org/data-catalog/worldwide-governance-indicators.

26 UNICEF statistics, www.unicef.org/infobycountry/nigeria_statistics.html.

27 UNICEF statistics, www.unicef.org/infobycountry/ghana_statistics.html.

28 Winston Churchill speech in the House of Commons, November 11, 1947, www.goodreads.com/work/quotes/1716637-churchill-speaks-1897-1963-collected-speeches-in-peace-war.

Part I

The dynamics and foundations of democracy

2 The quality of democracy[1]

With Leonardo Morlino

As democracy has spread to a majority of the world's states over the past three decades, many scholars, politicians, activists, and aid administrators have gone from asking *why* transitions happen to asking *what* the new regimes are like. How can we evaluate—and if need be, help to improve—their quality (or any regime's quality) both as governments and as *democratic* governments? This stream of theory, methodological innovation, and empirical research flows from the notions that:

1 deepening democracy is a moral good, maybe even an imperative;
2 reforms to improve democratic quality are essential if democracy is to achieve the broad and durable legitimacy that marks consolidation; and
3 long-established democracies must also reform if they are to solve their own gathering problems of public dissatisfaction and even disillusionment.

There is plainly room for controversy here. Who, after all, is to say just what makes a "good" or "high-quality" democracy? Is a universal conception of democratic quality even possible? How can efforts to think about democratic quality avoid becoming paternalistic exercises in which the older democracies take themselves for granted as models and so escape scrutiny? How can quality assessments be made useful for political reformers, civil society activists, international donors, and others hungry for practical ways to make democracies better? These are only some of the questions that pervade this growing subfield of study.

This chapter summarizes and elaborates on five essays that were part of a collaborative effort, launched at a conference at Stanford University, to elaborate and refine the concept of democratic quality and to apply it to a series of six paired country comparisons.[2] We asked each author to discuss a particular dimension of the quality of democracy such as freedom, the rule of law, vertical accountability, responsiveness, and equality (our own list, and by no means exhaustive). We wanted each author to explain how the dimension in question relates to other dimensions in our framework, to suggest possible indicators for measuring the dimension, to identify ways in which this element of democratic quality is subverted in the real world, and to offer (where possible) policy recommendations. Our full framework features eight dimensions: the five outlined above, plus participation, competition, and horizontal accountability. Other dimensions might include transparency and the effectiveness of representation. The different aspects of democratic quality overlap, however, and we choose to treat these latter two as elements of our principal dimensions.

We attempt here to identify some of the ways in which the different elements of democracy not only overlap, but also depend upon one another, forming a system in which improvement along one dimension (such as participation) can have beneficial effects along others (such as equality and accountability). At the same time, however, there can be trade-offs between the different dimensions of democratic quality, and it is impossible to maximize all of them at once. In this sense at least, every democratic country must make an inherently value-laden choice about what *kind* of democracy it wishes to be.

Talk of a "good" or "better" democracy implies knowing what democracy is. At a minimum, democracy requires:

1   universal, adult suffrage;
2   recurring, free, competitive, and fair elections;
3   more than one serious political party; and
4   alternative sources of information.[3]

If elections are to be truly meaningful, free, and fair, there must be some degree of civil and political freedom beyond the electoral arena so that citizens can articulate and organize around their political beliefs and interests. Once a country meets these basic standards, further empirical analysis can ask how well it achieves the three main goals of an ideal democracy—political and civil freedom, popular sovereignty (control over public policies and the officials who make them), and political equality (in these rights and powers)—as well as broader standards of good governance (such as transparency, legality, and responsible rule).[4] In addition to "democracy," we must define "quality" clearly. A survey of the use of the term in the industrial and marketing sectors suggests three different meanings of quality (each with different implications for empirical research):

- *procedure:* a "quality" product is the result of an exact, controlled process carried out according to precise, recurring methods and timing;
- *content:* quality inheres in the structural characteristics of a product, such as its design, materials, or functioning;
- *result:* the quality of a product or service is indirectly indicated by the degree of customer satisfaction with it, regardless of how it is produced or its actual content.

What is a "quality" democracy?

The definitions above imply that a good democracy accords its citizens ample freedom, political equality, and control over public policies and policymakers through the legitimate and lawful functioning of stable institutions. Such a regime will satisfy citizen expectations regarding governance (*quality of results*); it will allow citizens, associations, and communities to enjoy extensive liberty and political equality (*quality of content*); and it will provide a context in which the whole citizenry can judge the government's performance through mechanisms such as elections, while governmental institutions and officials hold one another legally and constitutionally accountable as well (*procedural quality*).

With the above in mind—and remembering that there is no absolutely objective way of laying out a single framework for gauging democratic quality—we identify eight dimensions on which democracies vary in quality. The rule of law, participation, competition, and vertical plus horizontal accountability are content-relevant but mainly procedural, concerned mostly with rules and practices. The next two dimensions are substantive: respect for civil and political freedoms, and the progressive implementation of greater political (and underlying it, social and economic) equality. Our last dimension, responsiveness, bridges procedure and substance by providing a basis for measuring how much or little public policies (including laws, institutions, and expenditures) correspond to citizen demands and preferences as aggregated through the political process.

Each of these dimensions may vary as to form of institutional expression and degree of development. Capturing and explaining this variation require indicators that reveal how and to what degree each dimension is present in different countries (and in different models of good democracy). The resulting empirical data will also make it possible to track trends in the quality of democracy in individual countries over time, including the effectiveness of institutional reforms.[5]

The multidimensional nature of our framework, and of the growing number of democracy assessments that are being conducted, implies a pluralist notion of democratic quality. As we explain below, there are not only dense linkages but also trade-offs and tensions among the various dimensions of democratic quality, and democracies will differ in the normative weights they place on these various dimensions (for example, freedom versus responsiveness). There is no objective way of deriving a single framework of democratic quality, right and true for all societies.

We are now ready to explore more concretely our eight dimensions of democratic quality in three respects: the empirical definition, the conditions for the dimension to develop and thrive, and the means by which it is commonly subverted. We begin with the five procedural dimensions.

The rule of law

As Guillermo O'Donnell explains, under a rule of law all citizens are equal before the law, which is fairly and consistently applied to all by an independent judiciary, and the laws themselves are clear, publicly known, universal, stable, and nonretroactive. What makes a rule of law *democratic,* argues O'Donnell, is that the legal system defends the political rights and procedures of democracy, upholds everyone's civil rights, and reinforces the authority of other agencies of horizontal accountability that ensure the legality and propriety of official actions.[6]

The rule of law is the base upon which every other dimension of democratic quality rests. There are, to be sure, several dozen "illiberal democracies" in the world today where competitive elections and popular participation coexist with considerable lawlessness and abuse of power. Yet the very illiberalism of such regimes (including their lack of truly law-based rule) imperils their democratic character. A weak rule of law will likely mean that participation by the poor and marginalized is suppressed, individual freedoms are insecure, many civic groups are unable to organize and advocate, the resourceful and well-connected are unduly favored, corruption and abuse of power run rampant, political competition is unfair, voters have a hard time holding rulers to account, and overall democratic responsiveness is gravely enfeebled.

The most important conditions aiding the development of law-based rule are the diffusion of liberal and democratic values at both popular and elite levels; strong bureaucratic traditions of competence and impartiality; and adequate institutional and economic means. These conditions are uncommon and hard to create from scratch—hence the weakness of the rule of law in many recently established democracies (and some older ones as well). The best approach is probably to work first on gradually building up the independence, capacity, and authority of the courts. But the research literature is sobering: No amount of money and training (including generous external assistance) will suffice unless democratic leaders show both political will and appropriate self-restraint. This in turn requires a mobilized and aware civil society as well as efficient tools of democratic competition so that voters can remove officials who block reform.

Participation

No regime can be a democracy unless it grants all of its adult citizens formal rights of political participation, including the franchise. But a good democracy must ensure that all citizens are in fact able to make use of these formal rights to influence the decision-making process: to vote, to organize, to assemble, to protest, and to lobby for their interests. With regard to participation, democratic quality is high when we in fact observe extensive citizen participation not only through voting, but in the life of political parties and civil society organizations, in the discussion of public policy issues, in communicating with and demanding accountability from elected representatives, in monitoring official conduct, and in direct engagement with public issues at the local level.

Participation in these respects is intimately related to political equality. Even if everyone's formal rights of participation are upheld, inequalities in political resources can make it harder for lower-status individuals to exercise those rights. Thus a fundamental condition for widespread participation in a good democracy is broad diffusion of basic education and literacy, and with it a modicum of knowledge about government and public affairs. Important again, as a supporting condition, is the political culture, which should value participation and the equal worth and dignity of all citizens. The latter implies as well tolerance of political and social differences, and thus acceptance by groups and individuals that others (including weaker parties and one's adversaries) also have equal rights under law.

Competition

In order to be a democracy at all, a political system must have regular, free, and fair electoral competition between different political parties. But democracies vary in their degree of competitiveness—in the openness of access to the electoral arena by new political forces, in the ease with which incumbents can be defeated, and in the equality of access for competing political parties to the mass media and campaign funding. Depending on the type of electoral system, democracies may allow for more or less decisive electoral alternation as well. Here we confront a trade-off within the overall goal of competition. Electoral systems based on proportional representation (PR) score well on one element of competitiveness—ease of access to the electoral arena and parliament on the part of multiple political parties—but at the expense of another element of competitiveness, namely the ease of alternation of power (or the efficiency of the electoral process), since the presence of multiple parties with relatively defined shares of the vote tends to produce a succession of coalition governments with considerable continuity in party composition over time.[7] There is no objective, *a priori* way to determine which system produces a higher quality of democracy (though Arend Lijphart argues that PR does a better job of fulfilling other dimensions of democratic quality, such as the more equal representation of women and minorities).

One condition for vigorous competition is the legal and constitutional order. In contemporary democracies, funding for parties and campaigns is so vital for electoral viability that newer parties and candidates cannot seriously compete without some fair minimum in this regard. While there is considerable skepticism about the efficacy of laws that limit campaign spending—in part because of how easily circumvented they are in new and old democracies alike—some floor of public funding for significant parties and robust requirements for the full and rapid reporting of all contributions to parties and campaigns do seem to promote greater electoral fairness and competitiveness.[8] In first-past-the-post systems, the means by which electoral districts are drawn also heavily shape competitiveness. Where partisan bodies are able to draw electoral districts to their own advantage (as in the United States), they are likely to do so in ways that will promote partisan and incumbency advantage. Of course, electoral competitiveness also depends on fairness in access to the mass media, pluralism in media ownership (and viewpoints), some dispersion of economic resources in society, and the enforcement of political rights by an independent judiciary. There is also an important linkage with horizontal accountability, because the single most important institutional guarantee of freedom and fairness (and hence competitiveness) in elections is an independent and authoritative electoral commission.[9]

Vertical accountability

Accountability is the obligation of elected political leaders to answer for their political decisions when asked by voters or constitutional bodies. Andreas Schedler suggests that accountability has three main features: information, justification, and punishment (or compensation).[10] These roughly describe the stages in which citizens learn of public actions, hear the reasons for those actions presented by leaders, and decide whether to punish the leaders or reward them (most often by either turning them out of or continuing them in their offices).

This type of accountability is called vertical because it seems to run "upward" from citizens to leaders. As Philippe C. Schmitter notes, in modern democracies, representatives (elected and otherwise) play a crucial mediating role in the accountability relations between citizens and rulers.[11] Political competition and participation are crucial conditions for vertical accountability. So are fairly robust levels of voter interest, information, and turnout. At the same time, vertical accountability requires political competition and power distributions that are fair enough to allow for genuine electoral alternatives at the various levels of government, and that can produce turnover or at least a serious prospect thereof. The ongoing process of monitoring, questioning, and demanding justification through the work of civil society (the media, interest groups, think tanks, and so on) requires freedom for these groups to function and a rule of law that protects them from intimidation and retribution.

Horizontal accountability

Democratic quality—including the processes through which vertical accountability operates—also requires that officeholders must either behave lawfully and properly or answer for the contrary not only to voters, but also to other officials and state institutions that possess the expertise and legal authority needed for such a monitory role. Since one official or arm of government is answering to another in a roughly lateral way rather than as part of a regular "command-and-obedience" relationship, this is called horizontal accountability. Examples of horizontal-accountability institutions could include the legislative opposition, specific investigative committees formed by the legislature, the courts, audit agencies, a countercorruption commission, a central bank, an independent electoral administration, a state ombudsman, or various other bodies whose mission is to scrutinize and limit the power of those who govern.[12]

The vitality of horizontal accountability hinges most of all on a legal system that provides for the exertion of checks and balances by other public entities that are independent of the government, and not competing as an alternative to it. But the agencies of horizontal accountability constitute a system of their own, and if this system is to work it must have institutional capacity, training, and leadership that are at once capable, vigorous, and responsible. Like the law itself, the agencies of horizontal accountability can be used as a weapon against political opponents, but only at the possible cost of undermining the credibility enjoyed by the entire institutional network.

Freedom, equality, and responsiveness

Freedom

Freedom can be seen to consist of three types of rights: political, civil, and social (or socioeconomic). Political rights include the rights to vote, to stand for office, to campaign, and to organize political parties. These rights make possible vigorous political participation and competition, and hence vertical accountability.

Essential civil rights include personal liberty, security, and privacy; freedom of thought, expression, and information; freedom of religion; freedom of assembly, association, and organization (including the right to form and join trade unions and political parties); freedom of movement and residence; and the right to legal defense and due process. There are also a number of what could be called "civil economic rights," including not only the rights to private property and entrepreneurship, but also the rights associated with employment, the right to fair pay and time off, and the right to collective bargaining.

Assuring political and civil rights requires many of the institutional conditions of fairness and horizontal accountability discussed above with respect to participation, competition, and vertical accountability. First and foremost among these institutions is an independent, capable, and constitutionally authoritative judiciary, along with a broader legal system (and culture) that ensures a rule of law. Finally, if, as Benjamin Franklin said, "vigilance is the eternal price of liberty," then citizens themselves—organized outside the state in civil society and assisted by institutions such as the media—must care about and stand ready to defend rights, liberties, and the integrity of the electoral process.

Equality

Many of the previous dimensions imply or require—and the very word democracy commonly symbolizes—the formal political and legal equality of all citizens. A good democracy ensures that every citizen and group has the same rights and legal protections, and also meaningful, reasonably prompt access to justice and to power. Active prohibitions against unfairness must check all efforts to discriminate invidiously on the basis of gender, race, ethnicity, religion, political orientation, or other extraneous conditions.

Equality is an ideal that is never perfectly achieved, even in strictly political terms. As Dietrich Rueschemeyer observes, individuals and groups with better education, more information, and more resources will inevitably have more power to shape public debate and preferences and to determine the choice of leaders and policies.[13] While democracy does not demand a certain set of substantive social or economic policies, it does in practice presuppose a degree of political equality that is virtually impossible if wealth and status inequalities become too extreme. One increasingly popular solution—if newer democratic constitutions are any indication—is to mitigate inequalities by declaring that certain goods (health, education, a minimal income, and perhaps others) are "social" rights. The rub is that unlike "first-generation" political and civil rights, which can mainly be secured by the "negative" means of the state leaving people alone and staying within the limits of the law, social and economic rights burden the government with heavy positive demands to achieve costly material goals.

Political will aside, the main prerequisites for the furtherance of social rights are sufficient affluence to fund social policies and wise strategies to achieve egalitarian policy goals without destroying the freedom and efficiency that make prosperity possible in the first place. Efficiency requires that the available resources go as much as possible toward investments in physical infrastructure and especially human capital (public health and education) that will raise the productivity of the poor over time. This in turn necessitates the control of corruption, and hence strong institutions of horizontal accountability.

The key to promoting reasonable equality-enhancing measures, as Rueschemeyer notes, has historically been autonomous groups and parties committed to representing lower class and status groups. In particular, unified and strong trade unions have played an important role in winning the extension of many economic and social rights.[14] But it is also vital that the legal system protect the political and civic rights of subordinate and vulnerable groups to organize, assemble, protest, lobby, campaign, and vote.

Responsiveness

Responsiveness is akin to vertical accountability (and hence to participation and competition), and in turn influences the degree to which citizens will be satisfied with the performance of democracy and view it as legitimate. As G. Bingham Powell, Jr., explains, democratic governments are responsive when the democratic process induces them "to make and implement policies that the citizens want." Powell sees three links in the chain of democratic responsiveness. First, choices are structured in a way that distills citizens' diverse, multidimensional policy preferences into more coherent national policy choices offered by competing political parties. Second, citizens' electoral preferences are aggregated (by varying means from one country to another) into a government of policymakers. And third, elected officials (and their appointees) then translate policy stances and commitments into actual policy outcomes.[15]

In the real world, however, responsiveness is more complex and difficult to assess. Even well-educated and informed citizens may not always be able to identify their interests when policy choices require technical expertise to evaluate. Policymakers sometimes must weigh trade-offs between short-term preferences and long-term citizen interests. And as Powell explains, when campaign issues fall on multiple dimensions, it can be difficult for a victorious party to infer a clear policy mandate.

The conditions favoring responsiveness are similar to those that support vertical accountability—that is, a robust civil society, a functional party system, and the like. Also helpful is a government that can translate preferences, once aggregated, into policies and programs. This requires, as Powell notes, a public bureaucracy that is both skilled and honest. Strong horizontal accountability will obviously be helpful.

There are at least three orders of objective limits on responsiveness. Leaders seek to maximize their autonomy and to shape citizens' perceptions of interest in ways that are sometimes highly manipulative or even demagogic. Second, public resources may be too limited. Governing responsibly—as opposed to purely responsively—involves setting priorities and making difficult choices. Even the most committed and well-meaning democratic leaders will not be able to please everyone. Finally, globalization imposes its own constraints on popular sovereignty. Some of these are the immediate work of supranational governance institutions such as the European Union, while others (particularly in the developing world) come from the International Monetary Fund, the World Bank, the World Trade Organization, and foreign investment capital generally.

The system of democratic qualities

We have presented here eight different dimensions of democratic quality. In one sense, we can speak of different "qualities" of democracy, and assess the level of development of each one individually. But as we emphasize, these different dimensions densely interact and reinforce one another, ultimately converging into a system. Although it is possible to identify different types of lower-quality democracy, which are deficient in different qualities, the various dimensions are closely linked and tend to move together, either toward democratic improvement and deepening or toward decay. Where we find democracies very weak on some dimensions, such as freedom and the rule of law, they tend to be noticeably deficient on others as well.

The linkages among the different elements of democracy are so densely interactive and overlapping that it is sometimes difficult to know where one dimension ends and another begins. Without extensive protection for and facilitation of civil and political rights, many citizens will not have the ability to participate in the political process, both in the electoral arena and outside it. Unless there is fair and unimpeded access to the electoral arena, vertical accountability may be greatly diminished. This requires not only the prevention of electoral fraud, and of violence and intimidation against voters, candidates, and parties, but also—as David Beetham argues—the prevention of more subtle denigrations of electoral rights, including rights to (some measure of) equality in access to political finance and to the mass media.[16] If, because of the accumulated unfair advantages that the ruling party enjoys, voters are not able to convert their dissatisfaction with the incumbents into electoral support for the opposition; or if any party (ruling or not) overwhelms its opponents and drowns out their messages with vastly superior funding and media access, the electoral dimension of vertical accountability may be vitiated. And if voters cannot effectively hold their rulers accountable at the polls—and put in office an opposition whose policy promises they prefer—then a crucial link will have broken in the chain of responsiveness that Powell defines.

Civil and political rights are thus critical to the vigorous participation and competition of parties, interests, and organizations that make for vertical accountability and responsiveness. They are necessary as well for horizontal accountability, in that these state agencies become more active and effective when they are reinforced, beseeched, and informed by agents of vertical accountability, particularly mass media, NGOs, and other actors in civil society.

But none of this is possible without a rule of law, wherein an impartial judiciary affirms rights and penalizes and prohibits violations of the institutional safeguards for vertical and horizontal accountability. Neither can a rule of law be sustained and the abuse of power preempted and contained without strong institutions of horizontal accountability, which also ensure that the electoral instruments of competition and vertical accountability will not be abused. At the same time, participatory citizens, voting at the polls and acting in various organized ways in civil society, are the last line of defense against potential executive efforts to subvert rule-of-law and good-governance institutions.

To be sure, all good things do not go together smoothly. A government highly responsive to majority wishes, for instance, may be tempted to brush aside minority concerns or even deprive minorities of equal rights. Maximizing the procedural dimensions of popular sovereignty—participation, competition, and vertical accountability—may sometimes be bad for freedom and equality. A high-quality democracy thus does not rate infinitely high on every measure of democratic quality, but instead represents a balancing of virtues that lie in tension. As Guillermo O'Donnell has suggested, polyarchies (or by implication, good, robust democracies) "are the complex synthesis of three historical currents or traditions: democracy, liberalism, and republicanism."[17] Seen in this way, citizens and their organizations participate and compete to choose and replace their leaders and obtain responsiveness from them. That is the democratic element. But the liberal element protects the rights of all individuals and groups under the law, while the republican element (through unelected instruments of horizontal accountability) enforces the supremacy of law and ensures that public officials serve the public interest. Good democracies balance and integrate these three distinct traditions. Yet they do so with distinctive mixes and institutional designs, reminding us that democratic quality is a flexible and pluralistic concept, shaped by the normative choices of society.

Of course, vexing philosophical as well as empirical questions remain. Will a high-quality democracy necessarily produce high-quality results and citizen satisfaction? Will improvements in quality relieve the apparently growing disaffection of democratic citizens in many countries? A government may score generally well on our eight dimensions of quality—including responsiveness—yet still not entirely satisfy most citizens. This may be true for several reasons. First, as we suggested earlier, citizens do not always know what policies will produce even the sorts of outcomes that all tend to agree on, such as economic prosperity and stability with something close to full employment. Second, we live in an era when news and information reach citizens with unprecedented speed and competition for attention, generating a tendency toward sensationalism and negative exposure in the mass media. This makes the failings of democracy appear more scandalous, more often, than they would have in a previous era. Third, as we have noted, responsiveness in a democracy is intrinsically complex and multidimensional. With so many different interests in society, capable of aggregating in so many different ways, it is impossible for government to be responsive to all interests and concerns. Democracy is about competition and choice, and losers are bound to be dissatisfied, at least temporarily.

That said, we still think that at least part of the present disenchantment with democracy does concern procedures and institutions, and stems not only from more information about the failings of government, but also from higher citizen expectations of what democracy can deliver procedurally and substantively, as well as in terms of results. We believe that it is fitting for democratic citizens, who are increasingly informed and aware, to want more scope for participation; greater accountability, transparency, and competitiveness; a stronger rule of law; more freedom and equality; and more responsive—or at least reasonably responsive—government. In fact, we think the long historical evolution of democracy suggests that if citizens mobilize effectively, these aspirations for a higher quality of democracy can gradually, if still imperfectly, be achieved.

Notes

1 Originally published as Larry Diamond and Leonardo Morlino, "The Quality of Democracy: An Overview," *Journal of Democracy* 15 (October 2004): 20–31.

2 The conference on the Quality of Democracy was held October 10–11, 2003 at Stanford University's Center on Democracy, Development, and the Rule of Law. This essay, the five essays summarized here, and a sixth, more skeptical essay (all published in the same October 2004 issue of the *Journal of Democracy*), as well as six paired case-study comparisons, were published in Larry Diamond and Leonardo Morlino, eds, *Assessing the Quality of Democracy* (Baltimore, MD: Johns Hopkins University Press, 2005).

3 See for example, among a myriad of possible sources, Robert A. Dahl, *Polyarchy: Participation and Opposition* (New Haven, CT: Yale University Press, 1971).

4 For a related approach, see David Beetham, "Towards a Universal Framework for Democracy Assessment," *Democratization* 11 (April 2004): 1–17.

5 These are among the purposes of a formal democracy assessment. See David Beetham et al., eds, *International IDEA Guide to Democracy Assessment* (New York: Kluwer Law International, 2001), available at www.idea.int/ideas_work/14_political_state.htm.

6 Guillermo O'Donnell, "Why the Rule of Law Matters," *Journal of Democracy* 15 (October 2004).

7 See the debate among Arend Lijphart, Guy Larderet, and Quentin L. Quade in Larry Diamond and Marc F. Plattner, eds, *The Global Resurgence of Democracy* (Baltimore, MD: Johns Hopkins University Press, 1993).

8 Michael Pinto-Duschinsky, "Financing Politics: A Global View," *Journal of Democracy* 13 (October 2002): 69–86; U.S. Agency for International Development, *Money and Politics: A Guide to Increasing Transparency in Emerging Democracies,* November 2003, www.usaid.gov/our_work/democracy_and_governance/publications/pdfs/pnacr223.pdf.

9 Robert Pastor, "A Brief History of Electoral Commissions," in Andreas Schedler, Larry Diamond, and Marc F. Plattner, eds, *The Self-Restraining State: Power and Accountability in New Democracies* (Boulder, CO: Lynne Rienner, 1999), 75–82.

10 Andreas Schedler, "Conceptualizing Accountability," in Andreas Schedler, Larry Diamond, and Marc F. Plattner, eds, *The Self-Restraining State.*

11 Philippe C Schmitter, "The Ambiguous Virtues of Accountability," *Journal of Democracy* 15 (October 2004).

12 Andreas Schedler, Larry Diamond, and Marc F. Plattner, eds, *The Self-Restraining State.*

13 Dietrich Rueschemeyer, "Addressing Inequality," *Journal of Democracy* 15 (October 2004).

14 Dietrich Rueschemeyer, Evelyne H. Stephens, and John D. Stephens, *Capitalist Development and Democracy* (Chicago: University of Chicago Press, 1992).

15 G. Bingham Powell, "The Chain of Responsiveness," *Journal of Democracy* 15 (October 2004).

16 David Beetham, "Freedom as the Foundation," *Journal of Democracy* 15 (October 2004).

17 Guillermo O'Donnell, "Horizontal Accountability in New Democracies," in Andreas Schedler, Larry Diamond, and Marc F. Plattner, eds, *The Self-Restraining State*, 31.

3 Measuring democracy

With Emily C. Green and William Gallery

One of the most vexing challenges in the study of democracy over the last several decades has been a methodological one: How should we "measure" democracy? If we are simply trying to determine whether a country can be called a "democracy," it is enough to apply a relatively parsimonious set of criteria and ask whether a political system meets all of them. For many years, this has been the approach that many social scientists and a few independent assessment efforts have utilized to determine which countries were democracies in any given year.

"Minimalist" definitions have built on Joseph Schumpeter's concept of democracy as a system "for arriving at political decisions in which individuals acquire the power to decide by means of a competitive struggle for the people's vote."[1] In his seminal 1959 article, "Some Social Requisites of Democracy," Seymour Martin Lipset drew on Schumpeter's definition and the work of Max Weber to define democracy as a "political system which supplies regular constitutional opportunities for changing the governing officials, and a social mechanism which permits the largest possible part of the population to influence major decisions by choosing among contenders for political office." Specifically, he asserted, this also requires supporting legitimate institutions, like a competitive party system and a free press, as well as a political opposition to the party in power.[2] In his classic work on global democratization, *The Third Wave*, Samuel P. Huntington, similarly counted as democracies those systems in which the "most powerful collective decision makers are selected through fair, honest, periodic elections in which candidates freely compete for votes and in which virtually all the adult population is eligible to vote."[3] Adam Przeworski and his colleagues settled, for their ambitious quantitative analysis, on an even more parsimonious definition of democracy as "a regime in which those who govern are selected through contested elections." But they proceed to specify as well that those elected must have authority to govern "free of having to respond to a power not constituted as a result of the electoral process," which is another way of insisting, as Juan J. Linz and Alfred Stepan have long done, that in a democracy "the executive, legislative, and judicial power" generated (directly or indirectly) by free and popular elections has "*de facto* authority to generate new policies" and "does not have to share power with other bodies *de jure*."[4] In other words, the system is free of "reserved domains of authority and policy-making."[5] Przeworski and his colleagues go further, however, scoring as democracies "only those systems in which incumbent parties actually did lose elections" at some point in the time frame of their study (1950– 1990).[6] Some years ago, Freedom House began systematically identifying the electoral democracies of the world with a methodology that stressed four criteria: a competitive multiparty system, universal adult suffrage, free and fair elections "that yield results that are representative of the public will," and "significant public access of major political parties to the electorate through the mass media and through generally open public campaigning."[7]

There is a long and effective tradition in comparative politics of treating democracy as a binary concept, present or absent. But we know that democracies vary considerably in their quality. This raises two eternal questions. First, how "minimal" should our definitional standards for democracy be? Where do we draw the line between democracy and "pseudodemocracy" or even "near democracy"—hybrid or competitive authoritarian regimes that have the institutional form of electoral democracy but fail in practice to meet the minimum conditions for it (as are addressed in Chapter 8).[8] In his classic 1971 work, *Polyarchy*, Robert Dahl advanced a somewhat more demanding conceptual framework for democracy, requiring not simply universal suffrage in free and fair elections between competing political parties to determine who rules, but also freedom of the press, freedom of association, and institutions—such as interest aggregation by the legislature and horizontal power distribution—"for making government policies depend on votes and other expressions of preference."[9] Dahl's emphasis on freedom as an integral component of democracy heavily influenced the definitional approach of Diamond, Linz, and Lipset in their comparative study of democracy in developing countries, where they stressed that democracy required not just competition and participation but "a level of civil and political liberties ... sufficient to ensure the integrity of political competition and participation."[10]

The second question is more basic. Is it meaningful to make this binary distinction between democracies and nondemocracies, or shouldn't we be trying to measure the *degree* of democracy? Of course, doing the one does not preclude doing the other. Freedom House has been measuring the extent of political rights and civil liberties since 1973, and only much later (1989) did it begin to identify which countries were democracies. It is possible—and, we would argue, necessary—to identify and track, as in Chapter 4, the trends both in electoral democracy and in a higher threshold of democracy, which may be termed liberal democracy. The line between electoral and liberal democracy (how high to draw the bar) is inevitably arbitrary. However, it clearly requires not only robust and unambiguous electoral competition and participation but also a substantial presence of the other qualities of democracy—such as civic and personal freedom, the rule of law, vertical and horizontal accountability, political equality, and responsiveness—outlined in the previous chapter.[11]

Efforts to measure the *qualities* of democracy can lead in two directions: toward aggregation or disaggregation. The quest for a definitive aggregate measure of the extent of democracy across countries has been the methodological holy grail of comparative political studies in recent decades, spawning a number of measurement enterprises that we discuss and compare below. And pressure to use or develop aggregate measures of democracy has increased as democracy promotion has become a more explicit goal in the foreign policies and the foreign aid priorities of many established democracies. Increasingly, policymakers are searching for more meaningful and sensitive metrics to evaluate the extent of a country's democratic progress. Thus, two highly aggregated measures of the extent of democracy or freedom, the Polity Index and the Freedom House measures of Political Rights and Civil Liberties, are still widely used in both academic research and policy assessments, despite the many conceptual and methodological criticisms that have been leveled against them.

Yet many scholars question the very effort to arrive at a single, unified measure of the extent of democracy. Richard L. Sklar questioned the tendency toward "whole-system" thinking about democracy and stressed instead a developmental view of democracy as emerging in fragments or parts, by no fixed sequence or timetable.[12] Philippe Schmitter similarly urged that we conceptualize modern democracy "not as 'a regime,' but as a composite of 'partial regimes,' each … institutionalized around distinctive sites for the representation of social groups and the resolution of their ensuring conflicts."[13] This view has gained adherents during an era when there is increasingly broad recognition that the quality of governance (which overlaps with but is also distinct from the quality of democracy) has significant implications for economic development. For the past decade and a half, the World Bank Institute has sought to measure six dimensions of the quality of governance, including "voice and accountability," which overlaps with electoral democracy, and two key components of liberal democracy, rule of law and control of corruption.

Given the complex, evolving nature of political systems, it is not surprising that consensus on the very definition of democracy is elusive. Similarly, there is no agreement on the best way to measure this multidimensional, qualitative concept. Theoretical and methodological debates continue despite the development of numerous cross-national quantitative measures of democracy, and the relatively high correlations between them. The considerable level of agreement across numerous measures with diverse conceptual and methodological underpinnings does suggest that some fundamental characteristic of democracy is consistently captured. But some scholars emphasize that the differences are greater than they appear, and furthermore that they can have considerable implications for the policy decisions and empirical work that rely on them.[14]

There is a considerable body of literature devoted to addressing these conceptual and methodological disagreements. While most scholars now agree that moving beyond a minimalist, procedural definition of democracy is warranted, the highly aggregated, conceptually narrow indices of Polity and Freedom House are still widely utilized, in part because of their extensive temporal coverage. On the other hand, many of the newer indices that claim to address the shortcomings of these "thin" definitions employ an all-encompassing approach, including numerous indicators that are either redundant, of limited relevance to democracy's core features, or relate to outputs of, rather than inputs to, democracy. Still others simply suffer from inappropriate organization or aggregation of attributes.

We argue that a middle way can achieve reasonable conceptual coherence and clarity without sacrificing robustness. Furthermore, such an approach can improve the utility of democracy measures, both as a research tool and as a guide to policymakers and democracy assistance practitioners. Much previous literature shows that the different components of democracy are correlated. The countries that are most politically closed also most wantonly abuse the civil liberties of their citizens. By the same token, where free and fair elections are most institutionalized, liberties are best protected and the rule of law is strongest. The notion of "liberal autocracy" is a mirage. No country lacking free and fair elections has a very good record in providing civil liberties or a rule of law. Yet the correlations among these dimensions of democracy are far from perfect. There *is* a phenomenon of *illiberal* democracy. Countries can have quite competitive elections with considerable uncertainty of outcome and alternation in power, yet still badly abuse the rights of their citizens while drowning in corruption and abuse of power.[15] In fact, as the various chapters in this book show, it is precisely the lowest-quality democracies that face the greatest risk of breaking down. Finding more effective and discriminating ways of measuring democratic quality could therefore serve an important diagnostic function in identifying democracies at risk—and the failings that put them at risk. Excessive aggregation of data can obscure these problems and distinctions. Yet excessive disaggregation can overload scholars and policymakers with so much data that they can't see the forest for the trees. Without some meaningful aggregation, we miss the bigger picture—which is vitally important in studying democracy. Hence the pursuit of a "middle way."

This chapter therefore advances an alternative formulation of four widely utilized democracy indices in order to better reflect the core conceptual features of democracy contained in each measure. We do not aim to critique the methodological construction of existing efforts, or create an entirely new measurement of democracy—those tasks have been ably performed by other scholars, and there is particular promise in the new Varieties of Democracy measurement project.[16] We instead focus on the conceptual shortcomings of the Freedom House, Polity, Economist Intelligence Unit (EIU), and Bertelsmann Stiftung democracy indices, and through a simple rearrangement of their respective components and indicators we seek to generate a more straightforward and internally consistent formulation of the existing data. We find that once the subcategories of each index are arranged in a conceptually coherent fashion, high correlations across indices are achieved at the disaggregated level in addition to the overall level of agreement often highlighted when comparing democracy measures. We also provide comparative analysis of the newly conceived and rescaled indices by subcategory, both globally and for a region, in the hope of providing more straightforward, direct comparisons for those who regularly rely on such data.

Measuring democracy

While the study of democratic polities extends back millennia, many modern efforts to measure the degree of democracy have their roots in Robert Dahl's quintessential *Polyarchy* in which he distinguishes two fundamental features of democracy: public contestation or competition, and inclusiveness/participation.[17] Raymond Gastil adapted this formulation to create the two dimensions of democracy that form the basis of the well-known Freedom House survey of "Freedom in the World": political rights and civil liberties.[18] Similarly, the Polity scale first developed by Ted Gurr and his associates and later adapted is concerned with the competitiveness of executive recruitment and the inclusiveness of that competition.[19] Kenneth Bollen's index, advanced in 1980, based on political liberties and popular sovereignty, is also grounded in Dahl's conceptualization, as is Coppedge and Reinicke's Polyarchy Scale, among others.[20] Many of these early efforts are discussed in Alex Inkeles's edited volume, *On Measuring Democracy*, which summarizes the indices developed up until 1990.[21]

As data improved and the Third Wave reinvigorated the study of democracy and democratization, scholars responded with more geographically and conceptually comprehensive and diverse measurements of democracy.[22] Furthermore, with mounting empirical evidence and a broadening consensus by the mid-1990s that governance matters for economic growth, the World Bank and other international institutions previously more concerned with economic policy developed their own measurements of government quality and democracy.[23]

Many, though not all, of these more recent measurement efforts have gone beyond procedural definitions to include assessments of the effective exercise of democracy rather than solely its *de jure* articulation. As a criticism of "thin" conceptualizations based on electoral rights alone, authors have included various socioeconomic rights, levels of electoral or civil society participation or activity, cultural elements, freedom from violence/stability, and/or the efficacy, transparency, responsiveness, or impartiality of state institutions and agents, as additional criteria against which the degree of democracy in a polity ought to be assessed. Significant debate continues as to the theoretical justification for these "thicker" definitions of democracy. Similarly, how to address the practical and methodological challenges associated with quantifying such inherently qualitative concepts is likewise widely contested.

In addition to the theoretical questions surrounding appropriate conceptualization, the methodological construction of various democracy indices, as well as the suitability and implications of creators' underlying assumptions and judgments, has been the subject of various critiques.[24] In the most systematic and comprehensive of these, Munck and Verkuilen develop a framework to evaluate nine extant indices based on how each grapples with the issues of conceptualization, measurement, and aggregation. They determine that no existing effort adequately addresses the complex theoretical and practical questions inherent in all three challenges of index construction, although some perform better than others.[25]

Partially in response to such critiques, Pemstein et al. and Coppedge et al. have developed additional indices that seek to address Munck and Verkuilen's index construction challenges, albeit with different approaches.[26] The former combines ten extant scales to produce one "Unified Democracy Score (UDS)" with the goal of simplifying "the difficult—and often arbitrary—decision to use one existing democracy scale over another."[27] They also provide a measure of reliability for each measurement. The authors argue such an approach combines the strengths of individual indices while diminishing their idiosyncrasies, allowing researchers to capitalize on the advantages of all previous efforts. Coppedge et al.'s Varieties of Democracy project (V-Dem) develops an entirely new index based on a "historical, multidimensional, disaggregated, and transparent" approach that is perhaps the most conceptually, temporally, and geographically comprehensive measurement of democracy to date.[28] To do so it utilizes seven "principles," dozens of components, and literally hundreds of indicators. Beyond measuring many more distinct dimensions of democracy, and offering data at an unprecedented level of disaggregation, the V-Dem project extends much further back in time (to 1900) than most data sets, and enlists multiple country experts to code independently each subjective indicator.[29]

The aforementioned works have all dramatically advanced the study of both democracy and social science methods. However, despite the proliferation of measurement efforts and accompanying critiques, there has been little effort to develop a "middle way" between thick and thin conceptualizations, or to identify a simple, straightforward methodological approach to that path. Most critiques have resulted in yet another new index, adding to an already crowded field while failing to resolve fundamental theoretical debates or facilitate practical decisions of measurement choice and comparison. The problem is not simply one of insufficient or unreliable data or a weakness in measurement tools. No less serious—and much easier to fix—is the poorly conceived arrangement of existing information.

In the immediate future, a modest way forward can be found in simply rearranging the components or indicators of existing indices. We elaborate this process below, first discussing the existing formulation of the four indices examined and their shortcomings.

Methodology and data

Index selection

Of the large number of currently available democracy indices, we examine here the following four: Freedom House's Freedom in the World Index, the Polity IV project, the Economist Intelligence Unit's (EIU) Democracy Index and the Democracy Status component of the Bertelsmann Transformation Index (BTI) developed by the Bertelsmann Stiftung, a German think tank. While each index suffers from various shortcomings, many of which are detailed in the literature above and our discussion below, we believe that their common usage and consultation by scholars, policymakers, and civil society more broadly makes them most relevant for analysis.

The above four indices also share some other features that facilitate comparison. First, though they are conceptualized distinctly, each aggregate index seeks to measure the extent of democracy (or in the case of Freedom House, political and civil freedom) in a given polity, rather than related concepts like institutional quality or government performance. Second, all four indices use numeric scales to assess the degree of democracy in a given polity, not simply its presence or absence. Third, expert opinion is an important source of the primary data source in three of the four indices (less so in Polity IV), although the experts employed vary in expertise, as do the number of individual contributors. Furthermore, each index relies mainly on the judgments, opinions, or codings of its own research team and country experts rather than a combination or aggregation of multiple sources, as is the case for the World Bank's Governance Indicators. (The one exception is the EIU index, which also uses public opinion results.[30]) Lastly, the geographic coverage of each index is extensive, with 123 countries around the world covered by all four (see the appendix on page 71 for a complete list).

There are of course some important methodological differences between the indices as well. They vary considerably in temporal coverage, from a few years to a few decades (Freedom House) to more than two centuries (Polity IV). One of the great advantages of a long historical time series is the ability to put recent trends into a more meaningful context, which underscores the value of the retrospective assessments that the V-Dem project is now undertaking. The EIU index incorporates public opinion survey results. Polity IV relies on indicators that are so close to being objective that they require relatively little judgment from their coders. The upside of this is greater reliability in the scores; the downside is a very narrow measure of "democracy" that we think misses a number of important dimensions.[31]

Freedom in the World

Developed by Raymond Gastil in 1972 and published annually by Freedom House in almost every year since, the Freedom in the World Index measures the extent of political rights and civil liberties in now 194 countries and 14 (mostly disputed) territories of the world. It employs a 1–7 scale where 1 is considered most free (or democratic) and 7 least free (or most authoritarian). Based on seven subcategories and 25 indicators, individual scores are derived and presented separately for political rights and civil liberties, which can be averaged together to form an aggregate Freedom score. Figure 3.1 shows how the Freedom score is constructed. The Political Rights score is based on three subcategories, Electoral Process, Political Pluralism and Participation, and Functioning of Government. The remaining four subcategories, Freedom of Expression and Belief, Associational and Organizational Rights, Rule of Law, and Personal Autonomy and Individual Rights, make up the Civil Liberties score. Each subcategory is based on three or four indicators, each scored on a scale of 1 to 4, meaning that the maximum score for each subcategory is either 12 or 16. The maximum score attainable for the 10 Political Rights indicators is 40, and for the 15 Civil Liberties indicators the maximum score is 60. From these two sets of raw point scores, Freedom House then derives an overall rating of 1–7 on its twin scales of Political Rights and Civil Liberties, using the formula in Table 3.1.[32]

The raw point scores for the individual subcategories have only been publicly available since 2006. Prior to that, the information sources and coding rules used by Freedom House to derive its political rights and civil

Table 3.1 Freedom House scoring rubric

Political rights (PR)		Civil liberties (CL)	
Total scores	PR rating	Total scores	CL rating
36–40	1	53–60	1
30–35	2	44–52	2
24–29	3	35–43	3
18–23	4	26–34	4
12–17	5	17–25	5
6–11	6	8–16	6
0–5 *	7	0–7	7

Source: www.freedomhouse.org/report/freedom-world-2011/checklist-questions-and-guidelines; and Freedom House, *Freedom in the World 2013* (New York: Freedom House, 2013), p. 858.

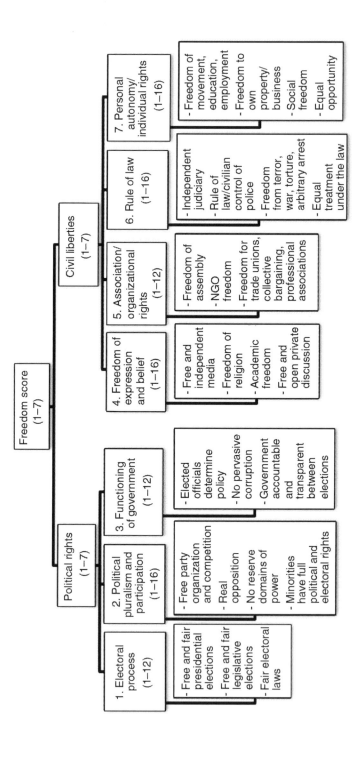

Figure 3.1 Current composition of Freedom in the World survey

liberties scores were unclear.[33] Furthermore, both conceptualization and the methodological organization of underlying attributes have varied somewhat over the lifetime of the index. Moreover, and perhaps more seriously for the purposes of longitudinal analysis across the 40 years of the survey, the neutrality and rigor of measurement have improved over the last 20 years, particularly with the end of the Cold War. This makes it very difficult to compare the trends in freedom scores over time, something that Freedom House freely concedes.[34]

Conceptually, the current organization of subcategories in the Freedom House survey suffers from a conflation of concepts. Two elements of organization are particularly suspect from a theoretical and conceptual standpoint. The survey includes Functioning of Government (which mostly measures government transparency, the extent of corruption, and the presence of independent institutions to control it) as a component of Political Rights. Political Rights otherwise measures the extent of electoral democracy—the ability of citizens to choose their leaders and representatives through free, fair, well-administered elections, with widespread participation. The only element of Functioning of Government that fits with this concept is the item measuring whether those who win elections are really able to determine government policies. The inclusion of Rule of Law in the scale of Civil Liberties score is similarly confusing. The Rule of Law category measures the independence and professionalism of the judiciary, police and other legal and security institutions. The rest of the Civil Liberties score is based on freedoms of expression, assembly, and various other individual liberties. The Rule of Law category and its components have more to do with *how* a government functions rather than the individual rights of its citizens. It therefore has more in common with the Functioning of Government category.

There are two other potential problems with the Freedom House survey, only one of which can be blamed on the survey itself. One is the common practice (to which the lead author of this chapter pleads guilty) of averaging the two scales to derive a rough overall measure of the extent of democracy, which has been criticized for going beyond the original purposes of the index and combining indicators that are probably best treated on distinct dimensions.[35] The other is the Freedom House practice of using the average scores to derive three categories of countries: "Free," "Partly Free," and "Not Free."[36] While the "Free" category identifies generally more robust democracies, which Dahl would probably have classified as "polyarchies," and the "Not Free" category is composed of quite authoritarian regimes, the "Partly Free" category is a bewilderingly mixed bag, including both democracies and nondemocracies, and political systems as diverse as Mexico, the Philippines, Pakistan, and Venezuela. Even the "Free" category includes not only very liberal democracies like Sweden but countries like India and Peru with quite significant problems of human rights and the rule of law (and thus a 3 on the Civil Liberties scale). Fortunately, this problem is incidental to our purposes of quantitative measurement here (though it has led some scholars, most recently Levitsky and Way, to simply take the category of "free" as a measurement of democracy in the world).[37]

EIU Democracy Index

Since 2007 (country year 2006), the Economist Intelligence Unit has published its *Democracy Index* on a biannual basis. It covers 167 countries and territories, excluding those with populations under one million.[38] Scores range from 0–10, with ten being most democratic, and are based on the simple average of five subcategories:

1   Electoral Process and Pluralism;
2   Civil Liberties;
3   Functioning of Government;
4   Political Participation; and
5   Democratic Culture (Figure 3.2).

Sixty indicators make up these five components.

The EIU claims that its "thicker" definition of democracy makes it a more robust measure than earlier attempts like Freedom House or the Polity index (discussed below). However, as discussed above, disaggregating too much, or incorporating too much, can present its own perils for conceptual coherence and practicality. In particular, the measure of Democratic Culture fits oddly with the other scales, since it is a measure not of the structure and functioning of government but of the individual attitudes and values toward democracy of its citizens. In most analyses of the dynamics of democracy, the extent of normative belief in and commitment to democracy is an important independent variable affecting the durability and depth of democracy (and may also be seen and studied in part as a consequence of the successful functioning of democracy). If we incorporate political culture into the conception of democracy, then we are unable to study the relationship between the two and we now have a much more diffuse, incoherent measure, conceptually and methodologically.[39] One can also question the treatment of political participation as a separate index, apart from electoral pluralism. The indicators here are based on the percentage of citizens that vote, belong to political parties, demonstrate for political causes, and even claim to follow politics in the news. Most of this is based on survey data, sometimes with limited coverage for countries or years, and there are other methodological problems (for example, the difficulty of comparing countries with and without mandatory voting laws—or even judging whether those laws intrinsically represent more democracy or less). The fact that these two categories contribute considerably (40 percent) to the EIU's overall democracy score raises serious doubts about the index's conceptual coherence and comparative utility.

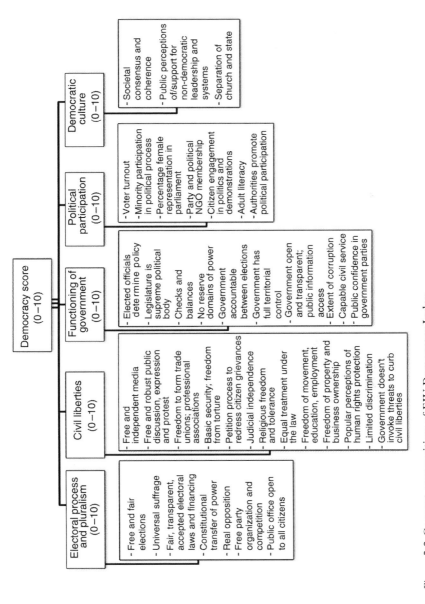

Figure 3.2 Current composition of EIU Democracy Index

These issues underscore a central point of this chapter: the need to dis-aggregate these various indices and consider how they are differently combining and weighting similar concepts, so that we might arrive at more comparable measures.

BTI Democracy Status

The Bertelsmann Stiftung created the Bertelsmann Transformation Index in 2003, and since 2006 has published it biannually. Its Status Index seeks to measure both economic and political openness, simultaneously tracking progress toward market liberalization and democratization. Its measure of political transformation, also called "democracy status," is only combined with that of economic transformation at the final stage of aggregation, thus providing a separate, independent measure of democracy that we examine here. Given its concern with transition, the BTI does not include the advanced market democracies of Western Europe, North America, Japan, Australia, and New Zealand, and like the EIU, also leaves out countries with less than one million people. These exclusions result in a total sample of 128 countries.

Democracy Status is the simple average on a 1–10 scale of five subcategories (also scored from 1–10), which are in turn composed of 18 component indicators (also with 1–10 scores). Ten indicates the highest level of democracy, one the lowest. The indicators are organized into the following five subcategories (see Figure 3.3):

1   Stateness;
2   Political Participation;
3   Rule of Law;
4   Stability of Democratic Institutions; and
5   Political and Social Integration.

Similar to the EIU Democracy Index, the Bertelsmann Democracy Status Index moves beyond the more procedural criteria employed by Freedom House and Polity. However, several BTI subcategories are of secondary importance to the fundamental definitional features of democracy, while others have misleading or inappropriate titles. Furthermore, many of the underlying indicators are poorly grouped, lacking relevance to the component to which they are assigned. For example, Association and Assembly Rights is grouped together with Free and Fair Elections under the heading of Political Participation. Freedoms of association and assembly are civil liberties, related to but also conceptually distinct from free and fair elections (in part because they help to determine the quality of democracy in between elections). Similarly, placing the question, "Are civil rights ensured?" under the Rule of Law subcategory makes comparison difficult (in that Freedom House pursues exactly the reverse methodological strategy). Although this

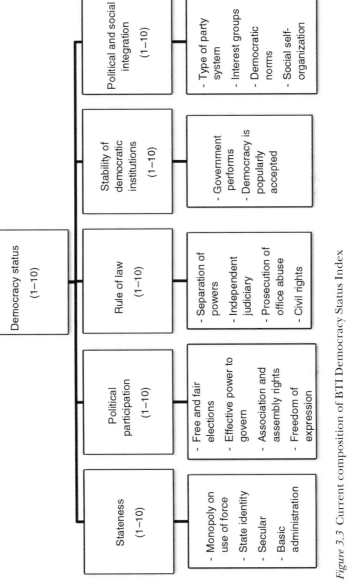

Figure 3.3 Current composition of BTI Democracy Status Index

index contains many of the individual pieces of democracy measurement, its hodgepodge approach to assembling them again undermines conceptual coherence and practical utility.

Polity IV

The Polity project, originally conceived by Ted Robert Gurr in 1974 and now in its fourth iteration, classifies regimes and regime change for 162 countries based on a polity's institutionalized "authority patterns." It excludes states with a population under 500,000, but is the only index included here that takes a historical approach in its temporal coverage: for those states with sufficient longevity, Polity scores are assessed retroactively to the year 1800.

"Authority patterns" can be either autocratic, democratic, or share aspects of both. They are quantified on a scale of –10 to 10, with the former indicating complete autocracy and the latter fully institutionalized democracy. A polity's democratic characteristics are assessed separately from its autocratic characteristics and each are assigned a score out of a maximum possible of 10. The autocracy score is then subtracted from the democracy score to arrive at the aggregate Polity score.

The Polity democracy score is derived by adding differentially weighted scores assigned to four component indicators:

1   Competitiveness of Participation;
2   Openness of Executive Recruitment;
3   Competitiveness of Executive Recruitment; and
4   Constraints on the Executive.

The autocracy score is composed of the same four components with one additional category, Regulation of Participation. The conceptual structure of Polity's Democracy measure is depicted in Figure 3.4.

All Polity subcategories therefore assess only formal political and electoral rights and functioning. At a gross level of generalization, the index provides some measure of horizontal accountability (constraints on the executive), but it neglects important other dimensions of democracy, for example, the extent of civic freedom or citizen political participation. This is particularly odd because the project leaders acknowledge that these are important conceptual elements of democracy:

> Democracy is conceived as three essential, interdependent elements. One is the presence of institutions and procedures through which citizens can express effective preferences about alternative policies and leaders. Second is the existence of institutionalized constraints on the exercise of power by the executive. Third is the guarantee of civil liberties to all citizens in their daily lives and in acts of political participation.

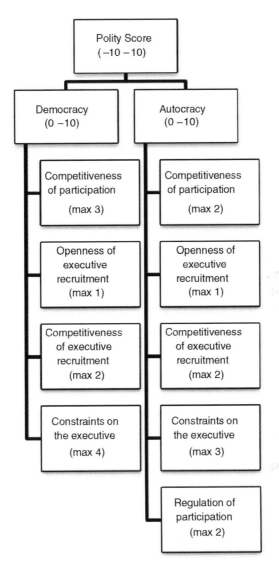

Figure 3.4 Current composition of Polity IV

Other aspects of plural democracy, such as the rule of law, systems of checks and balances, freedom of the press, and so on are means to, or specific manifestations of, these general principles. We do not include coded data on civil liberties.[40]

One reason why so many of the scores for Polity's Democracy Index bunch up at the maximum level of 10 is the limited scope of phenomena it examines, neglecting explicit measures of freedom and the rule of law (which we consider crucial elements of democracy), while measuring other dimensions at a high degree of abstraction. Moreover, for any citizen whose rights have been violated *in between elections,* civil liberties and the rule of law are not just "means to, or ... manifestations of" other principles. The bunching of Polity's Democracy scores at the maximum end of the scale is also a problem of the Freedom House indices of political rights and civil liberties, because of their aggregation into seven-point scales. But unlike Polity, Freedom House derives its aggregate indices from more detailed scores that permit finer distinctions to be made.

Reformulating the indices

The problems of conceptualization and organization described above should and can be addressed. One possible response is to simply start from scratch to develop a new scale, or collection of scales, that avoid the deficiencies in the existing scales identified above. The most ambitious of these new or recent efforts is the "Varieties of Democracy" project, led by Michael Coppedge, John Gerring, Staffan I. Lindberg, and Jan Teorrel. "V-Dem," as it is known, has mobilized extensive intellectual, organizational, and financial resources (including 15 project managers, 30 regional managers, and almost 200 country coordinators) to collect and code data for some 329 indicators, 175 of which require judgments by coders.[41] The latter items are organized into 12 sections and four clusters, which deal with:

1   elections, parties, and direct democracy;
2   the executive, the legislature, and deliberation;
3   the judiciary, civil liberties, and sovereignty; and
4   civil society, the mass media, and political equality.

V-Dem explicitly eschews the quest for a grand measure of democracy. Instead, it "has the modular quality of a Lego set": it seeks to generate indicators for a variety of principles and components, and then allow different researchers to "assemble and dis-assemble these parts in whatever fashion suits their needs and objectives."[42] Once the data is in hand, the project will experiment with multiple methods of aggregating the data, rather than simply using the additive approach of most of the existing indices, or attempting to aggregate into a single grand measure of "democracy." The data collection for this ambitious project is ongoing, and it proceeds with exceptional methodological rigor and consciousness. For example, V-Dem seeks five independent coders for every indicator—currently about 3,000 country experts. This is a much larger number (and probably with a higher percentage of experts who are nationals or residents of each country) than the Freedom House, EIU or BTI projects employ.[43] By extending its data gathering back to 1900 ("whenever possible"), V-Dem also aims to transcend the temporal limitations of the above three measures, which (unlike Polity) are only available for recent years, or in the case of the Freedom House scales, since 1972.

The V-Dem project may ultimately provide the best, most meaningful and reliable source of data on democratic trends, levels, and types. However, at the time of this writing, the V-Dem data was not available comprehensively for most countries across multiple years. And it will no doubt be some time before scholars and analysts settle on a few approaches for aggregating all this data that have broad acceptance for particular kinds of purposes. For the near term, at least, it may be helpful to attempt to clarify some of the conceptual and methodological clutter in the existing range of measures. Divergent approaches are unavoidable in a field where, as the V-Dem principal investigators acknowledge, there will never be consensus on how to conceptualize democracy, and thus even the V-Dem project will never yield—and most certainly does not intend to yield—a unified approach. Thus, there will always be value in having not only multiple measures but also multiple measurement efforts. And we think there is value now in a middle way between the radically ambitious innovation of V-Dem and the passive acceptance of (and disarticulation among) the existing measures.

We pursue below a simple strategy of rearranging the existing publicly available data from each democracy (or freedom) index to produce new subcategories with more conceptual coherence and, as a result, more practical utility, in part because they are more comparable to one another. Conceptually and theoretically, we suggest that the different elements and attributes of democracy can be grouped into three broad categories or domains:

1 **Political and electoral rights**: to contest for power in free, fair, and competitive elections; to form a government with effective authority, based on those elections; to ensure effective representation of citizen interests in the legislature produced by those elections; to provide for representative government at subnational levels of authority; and to form, join, and mobilize for political parties.
2 **Civil liberties**: freedoms of belief, religion, expression, association, assembly, and movement, including freedom of the press and Internet freedom, as well as personal autonomy and other individual rights.

3   **Rule of law (and the functioning of government)**: equality of all citizens before the law; neutrality, authority, and capacity of the judiciary to enforce the law and constrain the power of the executive and state security agencies; protection of citizens from arbitrary arrest and punishment, including torture and murder; elected civilian control of the military, intelligence agencies, and law enforcement; and transparency and control of corruption in the functioning of government.

Essentially, this reconfigures the existing Freedom in the World indices by pulling elements from the first two to create an additional third category that is more conceptually coherent. Each of these is a core component of a quality democracy, and each is conceptually distinct from the others and deserves to be measured as such.

We will see vividly in the next chapter the value of creating these new categories. Figure 4.7 on page 89 depicts the new categories for Sub-Saharan Africa using Freedom House data from 2005 to 2014. While the three categories follow similar trends during this time period, they differ significantly in their scores. In particular, Rule of Law/Transparency, which Freedom House does not treat separately, scores consistently lower than the other two. This is not just a casual finding. It strikingly supports a wealth of analysis over many years—including the chapters in Part II of this book—suggesting that the core problem confronting democracy in Africa and many other lower-income regions has been corruption and a weak rule of law. In other words, this is the true lagging indicator. Moreover, as we see in Figure 3.5, every region of the developing and postcommunist world ranks lower on rule of law (including transparency) than on political rights and civil liberties.

For each index, creating the new categories involved different manipulations, which are summarized in Table 3.2. Unfortunately, due to its narrow

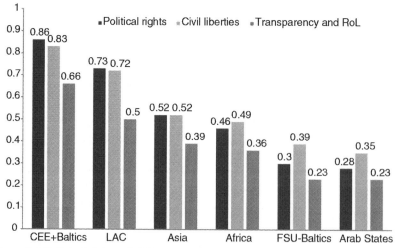

Figure 3.5 Political rights, civil liberties, and transparency/rule of law, 2014

focus on electoral processes Polity IV cannot be rearranged in this manner. But for each of the other three indices it is possible to create three coherent subcategories that integrate most or all of the scores from the original index. Beginning with the Freedom House data, we noted above that it includes Functioning of Government and Rule of Law subcategories under Political Rights and Civil Liberties, respectively. Given that these represent a distinct concept, we chose to simply remove them from the existing categories and average them to create their own category. For greater consistency we divided the scores Freedom House assigned to all seven of its subcategories by the maximum score available (either 12 or 16). We then combined subcategories 1 and 2 to make up Political and Electoral Rights; 4, 5, and 7 to comprise Civil Liberties; and 3 and 6 to form Rule of Law and Functioning of Government (see Figure 3.1 again for the seven subcategories). The new scores were calculated by simple average, rather than simply adding the numerical scores (which overweights indicators with four questions as opposed to three).[44]

EIU's Democracy Index is adjusted to take account of the critiques above. We used the Electoral Process and Pluralism to form Political and Electoral

Table 3.2 Components of reformulated democracy categories

	Political and electoral rights	*Civil liberties*	*Rule of law and functioning of government*
Freedom House	• Electoral process • Political pluralism and participation	• Freedom of expression and belief • Associational and organizational rights • Personal autonomy and individual rights	• Functioning of government • Rule of law
EIU Democracy Index	• Electoral process and pluralism • Political participation	• Civil liberties	• Functioning of government
BTI Democracy Status	• Free and fair elections (Q2.1)	• Association/ assembly rights (Q2.3) • Freedom of expression (Q2.4) • Civil rights (Q3.4)	• Effective power to govern (Q2.2) • Separation of powers (Q3.1) • Independent judiciary (Q3.2) • Prosecution of office abuse (Q3.3) • Performance of democratic institutions (Q4.1)

Rights, while we dropped the Political Culture and Political Participation measures, due to the conceptual and methodological issues we noted above. The other two EIU subcategories are internally coherent and thus require no manipulation. Their respective scores are used directly for the Civil Liberties and Rule of Law/Functioning of Government subcategories.

BTI's Democracy Status required the most reorganization for the reasons described above. Given the confused structure of its subcategories, we moved to the indicator level in order to rearrange the index's core attributes. Therefore Free and Fair Elections (Q2.1) is the sole indicator of Political and Electoral Rights. Scores for Association/Assembly Rights (Q2.3), Freedom of Expression (Q2.4), and Civil Rights (Q3.4) are averaged to comprise the Civil Liberties subcategory, while those for Effective Power to Govern (Q2.2), Separation of Powers (Q3.1), Independent Judiciary (Q3.2), Prosecution of Office Abuse (Q3.3), and Performance of Democratic Institutions (Q4.1) all make up the Rule of Law/Functioning of Government component, again by simple average. The index's remaining indicators were dropped due to redundancy or relation to questions of democratic culture.

Improved comparison

Such a reformulation allows us to move beyond comparisons and correlations of aggregate democracy scores. Instead, we can see how different observers assess countries' democratic performance against three broad and logical components of democracy, revealing potentially important variations in actual country status or expert opinion that are masked at the aggregate level. And crucially, we can gain a quick initial indication of where countries lag behind in their level of democracy. With a more conceptually coherent arrangement of index components and indicators, we also can have greater confidence that we are comparing apples to apples instead of apples to oranges. This offers users a clearer picture of whether and how the main measures of democracy differ in their assessments of democracy in their country or region of interest.

In comparing the new subcategories for Freedom House, EIU, and BTI, we use data from 2010 and for all 123 countries measured by all three surveys that year. The more limited country coverage is due to BTI's exclusion of the developed democracies of Western Europe, North America, Japan, Australia, and New Zealand and to the exclusion by both EIU and BTI of states with populations less than one million.

Interpreting comparatively the different measures of democracy is confounded by their use of different numerical scaling. To facilitate comparative analysis we converted each index to a 1 to 10 scale (with 10 being the most democratic), meaning all indices except BTI required rescaling.[45] This standardization provides an improved understanding of "overall measure congruence."[46] But due to the different coding methodologies employed by each index, it does little to reveal whether, for example, the difference between a 4 and a 7 on Freedom in the World is equivalent to the difference between a 4 and a 7 on the EIU's Democracy Index, even when both indices are converted to the same scale. Unfortunately, this inherent uncertainty is difficult to resolve.[47]

Figure 3.6 shows the reformulated subcategory scores on the three principal dimensions of democracy we have identified, and Figure 3.7 depicts all of our data on these three dimensions by region. The scores suggest some congruence across indices. It is difficult to say how significant the differences are. However, simple correlation coefficients of the new components for the Freedom House, EIU and BTI indices, shown in Table 3.3, support the reliability of the reformulation. Correlations are high for each index and subcategory—particularly given the fact that the established democracies are excluded from the analysis.[48] This suggests that the three measurement projects, despite their reliance on experts, are perceiving relatively similar underlying phenomena, and that if their component indicators within the three categories were more identical, so would be their scores. The lowest Pearson's R corresponds to the Rule of Law/Functioning of Government component, particularly between EIU and the other two indices. At 0.77 and 0.72 these correlations are still considerable, but a detailed examination of the indicators making up each subcategory provides some explanation. As shown in Figure 3.2, EIU's original Democracy Index has a separate Functioning of Government category, but it includes several Rule of Law questions in its Civil Liberties category. But because the EIU does not publish the scores assigned to individual questions, it is not possible to move these Rule of Law questions out of the Civil Liberties subcategory. Therefore, the new EIU subcategories are still measuring somewhat different concepts, despite the reformulation. Here again, greater transparency in coding would aid consumers' ability to utilize existing data for a wider variety of ways and means.

Previous critiques of democracy measures have emphasized that high correlations at the aggregate level (also found for these three indices)[49]

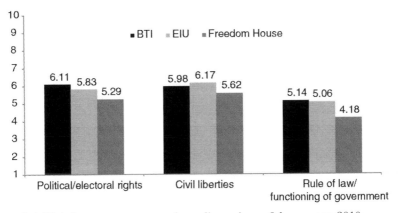

Figure 3.6 Global average scores on three dimensions of democracy, 2010

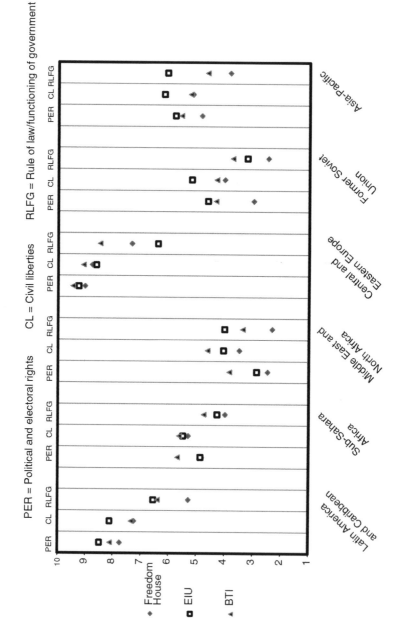

Figure 3.7 Comparison of democracy indices on three scales, 2010

Table 3.3 Reformulated subcategory correlation coefficients

	Political/electoral rights			Civil liberties			Rule of law/functioning of government		
	FH	EIU	BTI	FH	EIU	BTI	FH	EIU	BTI
FH	1.00			1.00			1.00		
EIU	0.93	1.00		0.90	1.00		0.77	1.00	
BTI	0.90	0.89	1.00	0.94	0.87	1.00	0.92	0.72	1.00

mask considerable differences in their underlying components. However Table 3.3 demonstrates that even at the disaggregated level, once subcategories are appropriately arranged into conceptually and theoretically consistent groupings, strong correlations across indices also prevail at more disaggregated levels. In other words, when one is comparing apples to apples, there is greater likelihood of agreement.

The same analysis can be conducted at the regional or even country level. Figure 3.8 provides the data for our three dimensions of democracy from each of the democracy indices (as we have reformulated them) for Latin America and the Caribbean. The reformulated subcategories allow us to observe subtle differences in assessment across indices as to Latin American

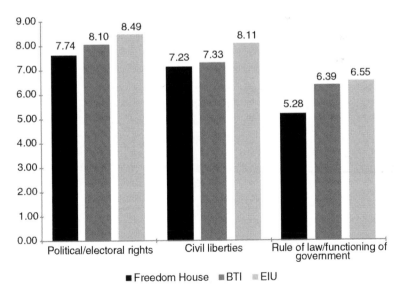

Figure 3.8 Scores on three dimensions of democracy, for Latin America and the Caribbean, 2010

countries' performance on each of these three dimensions of democracy, rather than merely overall. And we can see more clearly where the most serious democratic deficiencies are in the region. As with Africa, the lagging dimension in Latin America is very clearly the Rule of Law (including the control of corruption and abuse of power). What is even more striking is that all three measurement efforts—Freedom House, EIU, and BTI—agree on the step pattern: political rights are best protected in the region, then civil liberties, with rule of law doing worst.

Conclusion

Many valid conceptual and methodological critiques have been leveled against both the long-standing and newer indices of democracy. New and more rigorous measurements will generate deeper insights and more sensitive means for comparing specific attributes of democracy across countries, particularly if these indices can be sustained annually over time. But the above findings suggest that the current array of measures do not provide as disappointing a terrain of data as some criticisms suggest. It is important to understand conceptually precisely what each index is measuring and how each differs from the others. And it is vitally important to know their component scores, so that we can break down and reassemble their categories to achieve better, more conceptually valid comparisons. As we do that, we may well discover that expert annual assessments of specific features of democracy can be relatively robust, and that the key is in how we put the different component measures and scales together.

Every index has its strengths and weaknesses, and there are multiple ways to disaggregate their component scales, because, as Michael Coppedge has noted, each one contains "multiple partially overlapping concepts."[50] Yet, despite the methodological criticisms to which it has been subjected, the Freedom House scale actually appears to perform best of the four established indices of democracy reviewed here. It not only has the most robust correlations with the other scales, but it also has the broadest and most appropriate conceptual coverage of the relevant dimensions of democracy. Breaking its data into three scales rather than two can provide an even more useful and revealing picture of the comparative levels and trends not just of freedom but of democracy in the world as well.

Appendix: countries included in all four indices

Albania	Czech Republic	Macedonia	Saudi Arabia
Algeria	Dominican	Madagascar	Senegal
Angola	Republic	Malawi	Serbia
Argentina	Ecuador	Malaysia	Sierra Leone
Armenia	Egypt	Mali	Singapore
Azerbaijan	El Salvador	Mauritania	Slovakia
Bahrain	Eritrea	Mauritius	Slovenia
Bangladesh	Estonia	Mexico	South Africa
Belarus	Ethiopia	Moldova	South Korea
Benin	Georgia	Mongolia	Sri Lanka
Bhutan	Ghana	Montenegro	Sudan
Bolivia	Guatemala	Morocco	Syria
Botswana	Guinea	Mozambique	Taiwan
Brazil	Honduras	Namibia	Tajikistan
Bulgaria	Hungary	Nepal	Tanzania
Burkina Faso	India	Nicaragua	Thailand
Burma	Indonesia	Niger	Togo
Burundi	Iran	Nigeria	Tunisia
Cambodia	Iraq	North Korea	Turkey
Cameroon	Jamaica	Oman	Turkmenistan
Central African	Jordan	Pakistan	Uganda
Republic	Kazakhstan	Panama	Ukraine
Chad	Kenya	Papua New	UAE
Chile	Kuwait	Guinea	Uruguay
China	Kyrgyzstan	Paraguay	Uzbekistan
Colombia	Laos	Peru	Venezuela
Congo (DRC)	Latvia	Philippines	Vietnam
Congo (Rep.)	Lebanon	Poland	Yemen
Costa Rica	Lesotho	Qatar	Zambia
Côte d'Ivoire	Liberia	Romania	Zimbabwe
Croatia	Libya	Russia	
Cuba	Lithuania	Rwanda	

Notes

We are grateful to Michael Coppedge and Staffan Lindberg for their comments on a draft of this chapter.

1 Joseph A. Schumpeter, *Capitalism, Socialism, and Democracy*, 2nd ed. (New York: Harper, 1947), 269.

2 Seymour Martin Lipset, "Some Social Requisites of Democracy: Economic Development and Political Legitimacy," *American Political Science Review* 53 (1959): 69–105.

3 Samuel P. Huntington, *The Third Wave: Democratization in the Late Twentieth Century* (Norman: University of Oklahoma Press, 1991).

4 Adam Przeworski, Michael E. Alvarez, José Antonio Cheibub, and Fernando Limongi, *Democracy and Development: Political Institutions and Well-Being in the World, 1950–1990* (Cambridge: Cambridge University Press, 2000), 15; Juan J. Linz and Alfred Stepan, *Problems of Democratic Transition and Consolidation:*

Southern Europe, South America, and Post-Communist Europe (Baltimore, MD: Johns Hopkins University Press, 1996).

5 J. Samuel Valenzuela, "Democratic Consolidation in Post-Transitional Settings: Notion, Process and Facilitating Conditions," Working Paper #150, Kellogg Institute, Notre Dame University, December 1990 (no page numbers).

6 Przeworski et al., *Democracy and Development*, 16.

7 The last condition is really an elaboration of the minimum requirement for free and fair elections. Freedom House, *Freedom in the World 2013* (New York: Freedom House, 2013), 845. Although the four conditions represent a categorical rather than continuous approach to measuring democracy, Freedom House uses a numerical threshold to distinguish between democracies and nondemocracies. It classifies as "electoral democracies" those regimes that obtain a subtotal score of 7 or better (out of a possible total score of 12) on the Political Rights subcategory of Electoral Process, and an overall score on Political Rights of at least 20 (out of a possible total score of 40). While Freedom House takes into account certain other conditions as well, this leads to a somewhat expansive count of the number of democracies. See Chapter 2 of this volume for further discussion.

8 Robert A. Dahl identified several "near-polyarchies" in his study of the world's polyarchies, his term for a robust electoral democracy. See *Polyarchy: Participation and Opposition* (New Haven, CT: Yale University Press, 1971), 248, A-3.

9 Dahl, *Polyarchy*, 3, 236.

10 Larry Diamond, Juan J. Linz, and Seymour Martin Lipset, *Democracy in Developing Countries: Africa* (Boulder, CO: Lynne Rienner Publishers, 1989), xvi.

11 For a more extensive definition of liberal democracy, see Larry Diamond, *Developing Democracy: Toward Consolidation* (Baltimore, MD: Johns Hopkins University Press, 1999), 10–12, and Diamond, *The Spirit of Democracy: The Struggle to Build Free Societies through the World* (New York: Times Books, 2008), 22.

12 Richard L. Sklar, "Developmental Democracy," *Comparative Studies in Society and History* 29, no. 4 (1987): 686–714.

13 Philippe C. Schmitter, "Interest Systems and the Consolidation of Democracies," in Gary Marks and Larry Diamond, eds, *Re-Examining Democracy: Essays in Honor of Seymour Martin Lipset* (Newbury Park, CA: Sage, 1992), 160.

14 Zachary Elkins, "Gradations of Democracy? Empirical Tests of Alternative Conceptualizations," *American Journal of Political Science* 44 (2000): 193–200; Gretchen Casper and Claudiu Tufis, "Correlation versus Interchangeability: The Limited Robustness of Empirical Findings on Democracy Using Highly Correlated Data Sets," *Political Analysis* 11 (May 2003): 196–203; Gerardo L. Munck and Jay Verkuilen, "Conceptualizing and Measuring Democracy: Evaluating Alternative Indices," *Comparative Political Studies* 35 (February 2002): 5–34; Axel Hadenius and Jan Teorell, "Assessing Alternative Indices of Democracy," *C&M Working Papers* 6 (August 2005).

15 Diamond, *Developing Democracy*, 42–49.

16 See in particular Munck and Verkuilen, "Conceptualizing and Measuring Democracy."

17 Dahl, *Polyarchy*.

18 Raymond Gastil, "The Comparative Study of Freedom," Freedom House, *Freedom at Issue* (1972); the survey first appeared in book form in 1978, see Raymond Gastil, *Freedom in the World: Political Rights and Civil Liberties* (New York: Freedom House, 1978).

19 Ted Gurr and Harry Eckstein, *Patterns of Authority: A Structural Basis for Political Inquiry* (New York: John Wiley & Sons, 1975).

20 Kenneth A. Bollen, "Issues in the Comparative Measurement of Political Democracy," *American Sociological Review* 45 (1980): 370–390; Michael Coppedge

and Wolfgang Reinicke, "Measuring Polyarchy," in *On Measuring Democracy: Its Consequences and Concomitants*, ed. Alex Inkeles (New Brunswick, NJ: Transaction, 1991), 47–68.

21 Alex Inkeles, ed., *On Measuring Democracy: Its Consequences and Concomitants* (New Brunswick, NJ: Transaction Publishers, 1991).

22 See Zehra F. Arat, *Democracy and Human Rights in Developing Countries* (Boulder, CO: Lynne Rienner Publishers, 1991); Axel Hadenius, *Democracy and Development* (New York: Cambridge University Press, 1992); Keith Jaggers and Ted Robert Gurr, "Tracking Democracy's Third Wave with the Polity III Data," *Journal of Peace Research* 32 (1995): 469–482; Michael Alvarez, Michael, José Cheibub, Fernando Limongi and Adam Przeworski, "Classifying Political Regimes," *Studies in Comparative International Development* 31 (Summer 1996): 1–37; Tatu Vanhanen, "A New Dataset for Measuring Democracy, 1810–1998," *Journal of Peace Research* 37 (March 2000): 251–265.

23 See Daniel Kaufmann, Aart Kraay, and Pablo Zoido-Lobaton, "Governance Matters: From Measurement to Action," *Finance & Development* 37 (June 2000); Bertelsmann Stiftung, ed., "Bertelsmann Transformation Index 2003: Towards Democracy and a Market Economy" (Gütersloh, Germany: Verlag Bertelsmann Stiftung, 2005); Laza Kekic, "The Economist Intelligence Unit's index of democracy," *The World in 2007*, The Economist Intelligence Unit (2006).

24 Kenneth A. Bollen and Pamela Paxton, "Subjective Measures of Liberal Democracy," *Comparative Political Studies* 33 (February 2000): 58–86; Munck and Verkuilen, "Conceptualizing and Measuring Democracy"; Hadenius and Teorell, "Assessing Alternative Indices of Democracy."

25 The three they cite as performing better are Alvarez et al., "Classifying Political Regimes"; Coppedge and Reinicke, "Measuring Polyarchy"; and Hadenius, *Democracy and Development*.

26 Daniel Pemstein, Stephen Meserve, and James Melton, "Democratic Compromise: A Latent Variable Analysis of Ten Measures of Regime Type," *Political Analysis* 18 (2010): 426–449; Michael Coppedge and John Gerring, with David Altman, Michael Bernhard, Steven Fish, Allen Hicken, Matthew Kroenig, Staffan I. Lindberg, Kelly McMann, Pamela Paxton, Holli A. Semetko, Svend-Erik Skaaning, Jeffrey Staton, and Jan Teorell, "Conceptualizing and Measuring Democracy: A New Approach," *Perspectives on Politics* 9 (2011): 247–267.

27 Pemstein et al., "Democratic Compromise," 427.

28 Coppedge et al., "Conceptualizing and Measuring Democracy," 257.

29 Staffan I. Lindberg, Michael Coppedge, John Gerring, and Jan Teorell et al., "V-Dem: A New Way to Measure Democracy," *Journal of Democracy* 25 (July 2014): 159–169.

30 However, because public opinion data is missing for many (often half) of the countries in the EIU Index, the Index has to rely heavily on statistical interpolation to fill in the gaps, which then undermines the precision of the data. This is also true of the World Bank governance indicators.

31 We thank Michael Coppedge for sharing this insight with us.

32 For a comprehensive explanation of the methodology, see Freedom House, *Freedom in the World 2013* (New York: Freedom House, 2013): 840–858.

33 For more in-depth discussion, see Munck and Verkuilen, "Conceptualizing and Measuring Democracy," 20–21.

34 In the last 20 years the consistency over time of the Freedom House methodology and standards has improved, mitigating this problem for more recent comparisons.

35 Without explicit reference to Freedom House, the V-Dem scholars note, "However, as with Polity, aggregate scores are reflections of underlying components that can be quite different (and therefore are obscured by averaging)."

Michael Coppedge, John Gerring, and Staffan I. Lindberg, "Global Standards, Local Knowledge: The Varieties of Democracy" October 22, Varieties of Democracy Institute (2012), 13. Available at: https://v-dem.net/DemoComp/en/V_DemProjDescrv1_022Oct2012.pdf. In a separate communication with us, however, Coppedge expressed skepticism that the two Freedom House scales are really measuring separate phenomena, given how highly correlated they are; if that is the case, it may be just as well (or better) to simply average them into a single scale.

36 Countries with an average Freedom Score of 1 to 2.5 are designated "Free," 3–5 as "Partly Free," and 5.5–7 as "Not Free."

37 Steven Levitsky and Lucan Way, "The Myth of Democratic Recession," *Journal of Democracy* 26 (January 2015): 45–58.

38 The exclusion of small countries is common but unfortunate, since these countries have distinctive features, including being disproportionately liberal and democratic.

39 Another indication of the distinctiveness of this measure is its relatively low correlation (Pearson's R does not exceed 0.5) with all aggregate democracy scores considered here as well as the other subcategories contained within the EIU index itself.

40 Monty G. Marshall, Keith Jaggers, and Ted Robert Gurr, The Polity IV Project: Political Regime Characteristics and Transitions, 1800–2010: Dataset Users' Manual, Center for Systemic Peace, November 12, 2010, www.systemicpeace.org/inscr/p4manualv2010.pdf, p. 14.

41 See https://v-dem.net/DemoComp/en/about.

42 Coppedge, Gerring and Lindberg, "Global Standards, Local Knowledge," 26.

43 Coppedge, Gerring and Lindberg, "Global Standards, Local Knowledge," 41. The Polity project has also made a point over the years of seeking intercoder reliability for its much more limited set of judgments about political systems, but there is no indication as to whether Freedom House conducts these tests.

44 In the analyses and figures that follow, the category of "Rule of Law/Functioning of Government" was created from the Freedom House data by taking the "Functioning of Government" scale (C) out of Political Rights and the "Rule of Law" scale (F) out of Civil Liberties. All of our comparisons here with the EIU and Bertelsman indices use this method. In Chapter 4, however, the "rule of law/transparency" index removes from the Political Rights measure not the entire "functioning of government" measure but only its second and third components, dealing with corruption, accountability and transparency. The first item (measuring whether freely elected executives and representatives actually determine the policies of government) is left in the Political Rights category, creating a somewhat more precise measure. The differences in scores by the two methods on this third scale are in any case slight.

45 This was done according to the following formulas:
Freedom in the World: (original score × −1.5) + 11.5
Polity IV: (original score × 0.45) + 5.5
Democracy Index: (original score × 0.9) + 1

46 Daniel Pemstein, Stephen Meserve, and James Melton, "Democratic Compromise: A Latent Variable Analysis of Ten Measures of Regime Type," *Political Analysis* 18 (2010): 442.

47 And admittedly, as Michael Coppedge noted to us, this same problem applies (though we think to a lesser extent) in comparing the now three scales from the Freedom House data.

48 Coppedge, Gerring, and Lindberg find that the correlation between the Polity2 and Freedom House Political Rights scales declines precipitously when the

high-scoring countries on the Freedom House scale are eliminated ("Global Standards, Local Knowledge," 18). It is somewhat reassuring that we have obtained fairly high correlations between the more specific FH, EUI, and BTI scales, even when eliminating the advanced industrial democracies and the small countries, which also tend to be disproportionately liberal democracies.

49 Correlation coefficients for the aggregate global democracy scores of the three indices range from 0.92 to 0.96 with Polity's Pearson's R ranging from 0.83 to 0.86.

50 Private communication.

4 Is democracy in decline?[1]

The year 2014 marked the fortieth anniversary of Portugal's Revolution of the Carnations, which inaugurated what Samuel Huntington dubbed the "third wave" of global democratization. Any assessment of the state of global democracy today must begin by recognizing—even marveling at— the durability of this historic transformation. When the third wave began in 1974, only about 30 percent of the world's independent states met the criteria of electoral democracy—a system in which citizens, through universal suffrage, can choose and replace their leaders in regular, free, fair, and meaningful elections.[2] At that time, there were only about 46 democracies in the world. Most of those were the liberal democracies of the rich West, along with a number of small island states that had been British colonies. Only a few other developing democracies existed—principally, India, Sri Lanka, Costa Rica, Colombia, Venezuela, Israel, and Turkey.

In the subsequent three decades, democracy had a remarkable global run, as the number of democracies essentially held steady or expanded every year from 1975 until 2007. Nothing like this continuous growth in democracy had ever been seen before in the history of the world. During this period democracy became the only broadly legitimate form of government in the world, the predominant form of government in several regions of the world, and a viable option in every region of the world except the Middle East. While a number of these new "democracies" were quite illiberal—in some cases, so much so that Steven Levitsky and Lucan Way regard them as "competitive authoritarian" regimes[3]—the positive three-decade trend was paralleled by a similarly steady and significant expansion in levels of freedom (political rights and civil liberties, as measured annually by Freedom House). In 1974, the average level of freedom in the world stood at 4.38 (on the two seven-point scales, where 1 is most free and 7 is most repressive). It then gradually improved during the 1970s and 1980s, though it did not cross below the 4.0 midpoint until the fall of the Berlin Wall, after which it improved to 3.85 in 1990. In 25 of the 32 years between 1974 and 2005, average freedom levels improved in the world, peaking at 3.22 in 2005.

And then, around 2006, the expansion of freedom and democracy in the world came to a prolonged halt. From 2006 through 2013, there was no net expansion in the number of electoral democracies, which oscillated between 114 and 119 (about 60 percent of the world's states). At the end of 2014, Freedom House noted the birth of five new democracies that year (in Fiji, Kosovo, Madagascar, the Maldives, and the Solomon Islands). In Figure 4.1, the uptick in democracies in 2014 reflects these changes (as well as the failures of democracy in Bangladesh, Thailand and Turkey). However, each of the five new "democracies" is fragile and ambiguous, and four of the five new democracies are in very small states. Thus, if we examine only countries with populations over one million, we see a continued democratic recession, with the percentage of democracies peaking in 2006 at 58 percent and then declining slightly, down to 55 percent at the end of 2014. As we see in Figures 4.1 and 4.2, 2006 was also the high-water mark for the global presence of liberal democracy, which peaked that year at 41 percent of all states and 34 percent of states with more than one million people.[4] Since 2006, the average level of freedom in the world has also deteriorated slightly, leveling off at about 3.30 (Figure 4.3).

There are two ways to view these empirical trends. One is to see them as constituting a period of equilibrium; freedom and democracy have not continued gaining, but neither have they experienced net declines. One could even celebrate this as an expression of the remarkable and unexpected durability of the democratic wave. Given that democracy expanded to a number of countries where the objective conditions for sustaining it are unfavorable, due either to poverty (for example, in Liberia, Malawi, and Sierra Leone) or to strategic pressures (for example, in Georgia and Mongolia), it is impressive that reasonably open and competitive political systems have survived (or revived) in so many places, with roughly 60 percent of the world's states remaining democratic. As Marc F. Plattner has noted, democracy has become consolidated or at least endures in most of the important emerging market countries that have become members of the G20: India, Brazil, Mexico, Argentina, South Korea, Indonesia, Turkey, and South Africa; only China and Saudi Arabia among this group are authoritarian.[5] As we see in Figure 4.4, there was at the beginning of 2015 a critical mass of democracies in every region of the world except the Middle East. Latin America and the Caribbean had the most robust presence of democracy—and liberal democracy—of any major region in the developing world. But even in the poorest region, Sub-Saharan Africa, a little more than a third of all the states were electoral democracies, and about one in five were liberal democracies. The percentages were much higher in the postcommunist states, but mainly because virtually all of the states of Central and Eastern Europe were democracies, and most of them (including all of those that had been integrated into the European Union) were liberal democracies, while most of the post-Soviet states (save for the Baltics) were moving in the opposite direction.

A variant of this perspective affirms the resilience of democracy's third wave in a different and less celebratory way. Levitsky and Way argue that

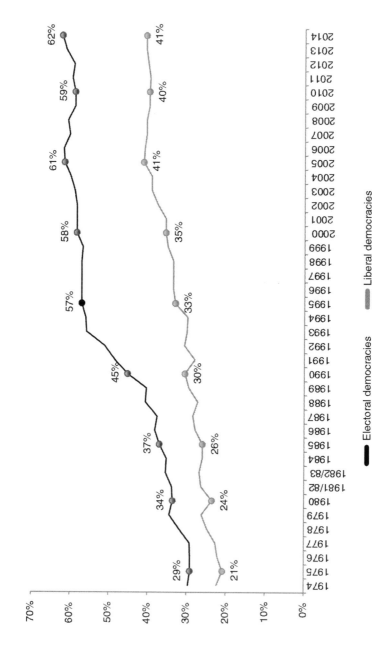

Figure 4.1 The growth of democracy in the world, 1974–2014 (all states)

Electoral democracies ⎯⎯ Liberal democracies

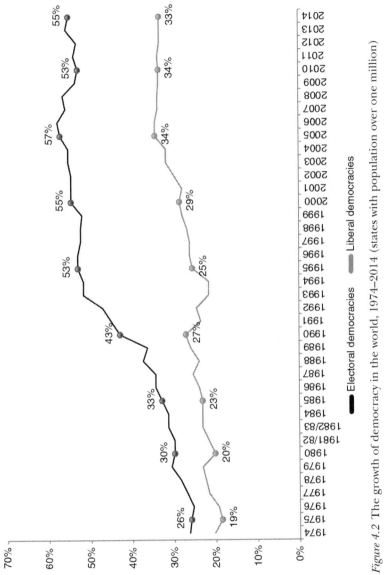

Figure 4.2 The growth of democracy in the world, 1974–2014 (states with population over one million)

Electoral democracies   Liberal democracies

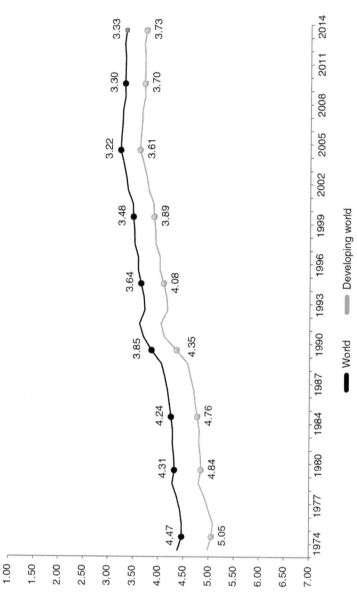

Figure 4.3 Global trends in freedom, 1974–2014

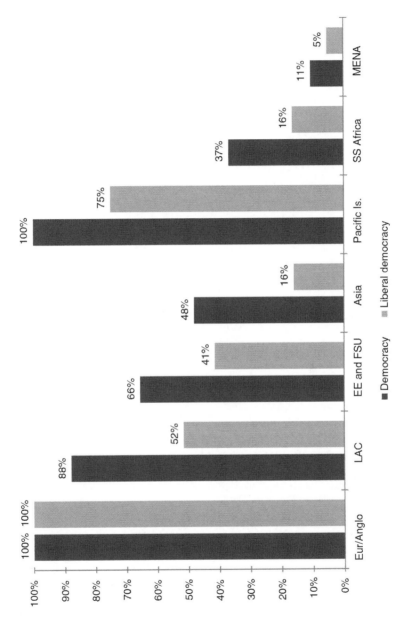

Figure 4.4 Democracy by region, January 2015

democracy never actually expanded as widely as Freedom House perceived in the first place. Thus, they contend, many of the seeming failures of democracy in the last 10–15 years were really deteriorations or hardenings of what had been from the beginning authoritarian regimes, however competitive.[6]

Alternatively, one can view the last decade as a period of at least incipient decline in democracy. To make this case, we need to examine not only the instability and stagnation of democracies, but also the incremental decline of democracy in what Thomas Carothers has termed the "gray zone" countries (which defy easy classification as to whether or not they are democracies),[7] the deepening authoritarianism in the nondemocracies, and the decline in the functioning and self-confidence of the world's established, rich democracies. This will be my approach in what follows.

The debate about whether there has been a decline in democracy turns to some extent on how we count it. It is one of the great and probably inescapable ironies of scholarly research that the boom in comparative democratic studies has been accompanied by significant disagreement over how to define and measure democracy, as the previous chapter demonstrated. I have never felt that there was—or could be—one right and consensual answer to this eternal conceptual challenge. Most scholars of democracy have agreed that it makes sense to classify regimes categorically—and thus to determine which regimes are democracies and which are not. But democracy is in many ways a continuous variable. Its key components—such as freedom of multiple parties and candidates to campaign and contest, opposition access to mass media and campaign finance; inclusiveness of suffrage, fairness and neutrality of electoral administration; and the extent to which electoral victors have meaningful power to rule—vary on a continuum (as do other dimensions of the quality of democracy, such as civil liberties, rule of law, control of corruption, vigor of civil society, and so on). This continuous variation forces coders to make difficult judgments about how to classify regimes that fall into the gray zone of ambiguity, where multiparty electoral competition is genuine and vigorous but flawed in some notable ways. No system of multiparty competition is perfectly fair and open. Some multiparty electoral systems clearly do not meet the test of democracy. Others have serious defects that nevertheless do not negate their overall democratic character. Thus hard decisions must often be made about how to weight imperfections and where to draw the line.

Most approaches to classifying regimes (as democracies or not) rely on continuous measurement of key variables (such as political rights, in the case of the Polity scale, or both political rights and civil liberties, in the case of Freedom House), along with a somewhat arbitrary cutoff point for separating democracies from nondemocracies.[8] My own method has been to accept the Freedom House coding decisions except where I find persuasive contradictory evidence. This has led to my counting two to five fewer democracies than Freedom House does for most years since 1989; for some years, the discrepancy is much larger.[9]

The democratic recession: breakdowns and erosions

The world has been in a mild but protracted democratic recession since about 2006. Beyond the lack of improvement or modest erosion of global levels of democracy and freedom, there have been several other causes for concern. First, there has been a significant and, in fact, accelerating rate of democratic breakdown. Second, the quality or stability of democracy has been declining in a number of large and strategically important emerging-market countries, which I call "swing states." Third, authoritarianism has been deepening, including in big and strategically important countries. And fourth, the established democracies, beginning with the United States, increasingly seem to be performing poorly and to lack the will and self-confidence to promote democracy effectively abroad. I explore each of these in turn.

First, let us look at rates of democratic breakdown. Between 1974 and the end of 2014, 30 percent of all the democracies in the world broke down (among non-Western democracies, the rate was 37 percent).[10] In the first decade and a half of this new century, the failure rate (17.6 percent) has been substantially higher than in the preceding 15-year period (12.7 percent). Alternatively, if we break the third wave up into its four component decades, we see a rising incidence of democratic failure per decade since the mid-1980s. The rate of democratic failure, which had been 15 percent in the first decade of the third wave (1974–1983), fell to 7 percent in the second decade (1984–1993), but then climbed to 10 percent in the third decade (1994–2003), and most recently to 14 percent (2004–2014) (see Figure 4.5).

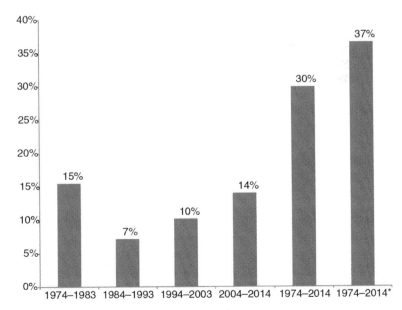

Figure 4.5 Rates of democratic breakdown, 1974–2014

* Rate for non-Western democracies only.

Table 4.1 Breakdowns of democracy, 2000–2014

Year of breakdown	Country	Year of return	Type of breakdown
2000	Fiji		Military coup
2000	Russia		Executive degradation, violation of opposition rights
2001	Central African Republic		Military rebellion, violence, human rights abuses
2002	Guinea Bissau	2005	Executive degradation, violation of opposition rights (military coup the following year)
2002	Nepal	2013	Rising political instability, monarchical coup
2004	Venezuela		Executive degradation, violation of opposition rights
2005	Thailand	2011	Military coup, then military constraint
2006	Solomon Islands		Decline of democratic process
2007	Bangladesh	2008	Military "soft coup"
2007	Philippines	2010	Executive degradation
2007	Kenya		Electoral fraud and executive abuse
2008	Georgia	2012	Electoral fraud and executive abuse
2009	Honduras	2013	Military intervention
2009	Madagascar	2014	Unconstitutional assumption of power by opposition; suspension of elected parliament
2009	Niger	2011	Presidential dissolution of Constitutional Court and National Assembly to extend his rule
2010	Burundi		Electoral fraud, opposition boycott, political closure
2010	Sri Lanka	2015	Executive degradation
2010	Guinea Bissau		Military intervention, weakening civilian control, deteriorating rule of law
2012	Maldives		Forcible removal of democratically elected president
2012	Mali	2014	Military coup
2011	Nicaragua		Executive degradation
2012	Ukraine	2014	Electoral fraud (parliamentary elections), executive abuse
2014	Turkey		Executive degradation, violation of opposition rights
2014	Bangladesh		Breakdown of electoral process
2014	Thailand		Military coup

Since 2000, I count 25 breakdowns of democracy in the world—not only through blatant military or executive coups, but also through subtle and incremental degradations of democratic rights and procedures that finally push a democratic system over the threshold into competitive authoritarianism (see Table 4.1). Some of these breakdowns occurred in quite low-quality democracies; yet in each case, a system of reasonably free and fair multiparty electoral competition was either displaced or degraded to a point well below the minimal standards of democracy.

One methodological challenge in tracking democratic breakdowns is to determine a precise date or year for a democratic failure that results from a long secular process of systemic deterioration and executive strangulation of political rights, civil liberties, and the rule of law. No serious scholar would consider Russia today a democracy. But many believe that it was an electoral democracy (however rough and illiberal) under Boris Yeltsin. If we score 1993 as the year when democracy emerged in Russia (as Freedom House does), then what year do we identify as marking the end of democracy? In this case (and many others), there is no single obvious event—like Peruvian president Alberto Fujimori's 1992 *autogolpe*, dissolving Congress and seizing unconstitutional powers—to guide the scoring decision. I postulate that Russia's political system fell below the minimum conditions of electoral democracy during the year 2000, as signaled by the electoral fraud that gave Vladimir Putin a dubious first-ballot victory and the executive degradation of political and civic pluralism that quickly followed. (Freedom House dates the failure to 2005.)

The problem has continuing and quite contemporary relevance. For a number of years now, Turkey's ruling Justice and Development Party (AKP) has been gradually eroding democratic pluralism and freedom in the country. The overall political trends have been hard to characterize, because some of the AKP's changes have made Turkey more democratic by removing the military as an autonomous veto player in politics, extending civilian control over the military, and making it harder to ban political parties that offend the "deep state" structures associated with the intensely secularist legacy of Kemal Atatürk. But the AKP has gradually entrenched its own political hegemony, extending partisan control over the judiciary and the bureaucracy, arresting journalists and intimidating dissenters in the press and academia, threatening businesses with retaliation if they fund opposition parties, and using arrests and prosecutions in cases connected to alleged coup plots to jail and remove from public life an implausibly large number of accused plotters.

This has coincided with a stunning and increasingly audacious concentration of personal power by Turkey's long-time prime minister Recep Tayyip Erdoğan, who was elected president in August 2014. The abuse and personalization of power and the constriction of competitive space and freedom in Turkey have been subtle and incremental, moving with nothing like the speed of Putin in the early 2000s. But by now, these trends appear to have crossed a threshold, pushing the country below the minimum standards of democracy. If this has happened, when did it happen? Was it in 2014, when the AKP further consolidated its hegemonic grip on power in the March local-government elections and the August presidential election? Or was it, as some liberal Turks insist, several years before, as media freedoms were visibly diminishing and an ever-wider circle of alleged coup plotters was being targeted in the highly politicized Ergenekon trials?

A similar problem exists for Botswana, where a president (Ian Khama) with a career military background evinces an intolerance of opposition and distaste for civil society beyond anything seen previously from the long-ruling Botswana Democratic Party (BDP). Increasing political violence and intimidation—including assaults on opposition politicians, the possible murder of a leading opposition candidate three months before the October 2014 parliamentary elections, and the apparent involvement of the intelligence apparatus in the bullying and coercion of the political opposition—have been moving the political system in a more authoritarian direction. Escalating pressure on the independent media, the brazen misuse of state television by the BDP, and the growing personalization and centralization of power by President Khama (as he advances his own narrow circle of family and friends while splitting the ruling party) are further signs of the deterioration, if not crisis, of democracy in Botswana.[11] Again, Levitsky and Way had argued a number of years ago that Botswana was not a genuine democracy in the first place.[12] Nevertheless, whatever kind of system it has been in recent decades, "respect for the rule of law and for established institutions and processes" began to diminish in 1998, when Khama ascended to the vice-presidency, and it has continued to decline since 2008, when the former military commander "automatically succeeded to the presidency."[13]

There are no easy and obvious answers to the conundrum of how to classify regimes in the gray zone. One can argue about whether these ambiguous regimes are still democracies—or even if they ever really were. Those who accept that a democratic breakdown has occurred can argue about when it took place. But what is beyond argument is that there is a class of regimes that in the last decade or so have experienced significant erosion in electoral fairness, political pluralism, and civic space for opposition and dissent, typically as a result of abusive executives intent upon concentrating their personal power and entrenching ruling-party hegemony. The best-known cases of this since 1999 have been Russia and Venezuela, where populist former military officer Hugo Chávez (1999–2013) gradually suffocated democratic pluralism during the first decade of this century. After Daniel Ortega returned to the presidency in Nicaragua in 2007, he borrowed many pages from Chávez's authoritarian playbook, and left-populist authoritarian presidents Evo Morales of Bolivia and Rafael Correa of Ecuador have been moving in a similar direction. Scott Mainwaring and Aníbal Pérez-Liñán assert that democratic erosion has occurred since 2000 in all four of these

Latin American countries (Venezuela, Nicaragua, Bolivia, and Ecuador), as well as Honduras, with Bolivia, Ecuador, and Honduras now limping along as "semi-democracies."[14]

Of the 25 breakdowns since 2000 listed in Table 4.1, 18 have occurred after 2005. Only eight of these 25 breakdowns came as a result of military intervention (and of those eight, only four took the form of a conventional, blatant military coup, as happened twice in Thailand). Two other cases (Nepal and Madagascar) saw democratically elected rulers pushed out of power by other nondemocratic forces (the monarch and the political opposition, respectively). The majority of the breakdowns—13—resulted from the abuse of power and the desecration of democratic institutions and practices by democratically elected rulers. Four of these took the form of widespread electoral fraud or, in the recent case of Bangladesh, a unilateral change in the rules of electoral administration (the elimination of the practice of a caretaker government before the election) that tilted the electoral playing field and triggered an opposition boycott. The other nine failures by executive abuse involved the more gradual suffocation of democracy by democratically elected executives (though that too was occurring in several of the instances of electoral fraud, such as Ukraine under President Viktor Yanukovich during 2010–2014). Overall, nearly one in every five democracies since the turn of this century has failed.

The decline of freedom and the rule of law

Separate and apart from democratic failure, there has also been a trend of declining freedom in a number of countries and regions since 2005. The most often cited statistic in this regard is the Freedom House finding that in each of the nine consecutive years from 2006 through 2014 more countries declined in freedom than improved. In fact, after a post-Cold War period in which the balance was almost always highly favorable—with improvers outstripping the decliners by a ratio of two to one (or greater)—the balance simply inverted beginning in 2006. In Figure 4.6, we see the ratio abruptly dipping well below 1 (parity) in 2006 and never rising much above one-half after that. But this does not tell the whole story.

Two important elements are noteworthy, and they are both especially visible in Africa. First, the declines have tended to crystallize over time. Thus, if we compare freedom scores at the end of 2005 and the end of 2013, we see that 29 of the 49 Sub-Saharan African states (almost 60 percent) declined in freedom, while only 15 (30 percent) improved and five remained unchanged. Moreover, 20 states in the region saw a decline in political rights, civil liberties, or both that was substantial enough to register on the seven-point scales (while only 11 states saw such a visible improvement). The larger states in Sub-Saharan Africa (those with a population of more than ten million) did a bit better, but not much: Freedom deteriorated in 13 of the 25 of them, and improved in only eight.

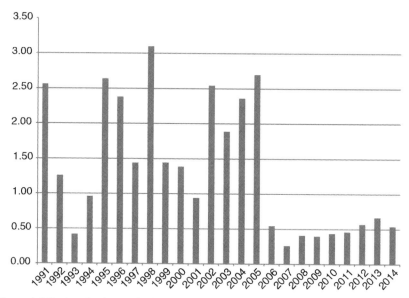

Figure 4.6 Ratio of gains to declines in freedom, 1991–2014

Another problem is that the pace of decay in democratic institutions is not always evident to outside observers. In a number of countries where we take democracy for granted, such as South Africa, we should not. In fact, there is not a single country on the African continent where democracy is firmly consolidated and secure—the way it is, for example, in such third-wave democracies as South Korea, Poland, and Chile. In the global democracy-promotion community, few actors are paying attention to the growing signs of fragility in the more liberal developing democracies, not to mention the more illiberal ones.

Why have freedom and democracy been regressing in many countries? The most important and pervasive answer is, in brief, bad governance. As noted in the previous chapter, the Freedom House measures of political rights and civil liberties both include subcategories that directly relate to the rule of law and transparency (including corruption). If we remove these subcategories from the Freedom House political-rights and civil-liberties scores and create a third distinct scale with the rule-of-law and transparency scores, the problems become more apparent. African states (like most others in the world) perform considerably worse on the rule of law and transparency than on political rights and civil liberties.[15] Moreover, rule of law and political rights have both declined perceptibly across Sub-Saharan Africa since 2005, while civil liberties have oscillated somewhat more. These empirical trends are shown in Figure 4.7, which presents the Freedom House data for these three reconfigured scales as standardized scores, ranging from 0 to 1.[16]

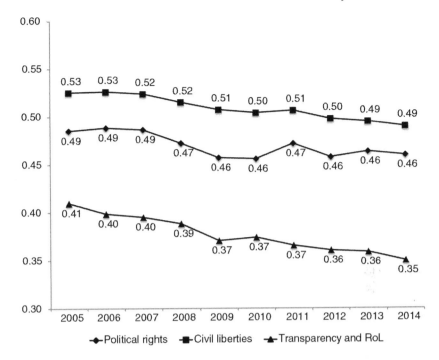

Figure 4.7 Freedom and governance trends in Africa, 2005–2014

The biggest problem for democracy in Africa is controlling corruption and abuse of power. The decay in governance has been visible even in the best-governed African countries, such as South Africa, which suffered a steady decline in its score on rule of law and transparency (from .79 to .63) between 2005 and 2013. And as more and more African states become resource-rich, with the onset of a second African oil boom, the quality of governance will deteriorate further. This has already begun to happen in one of Africa's most liberal and important democracies, Ghana.

The problem is not unique to Africa. As we saw in Figure 3.5, every region of the world scores worse on the standardized scale of transparency and the rule of law than it does on either political rights or civil liberties. In fact, transparency and the rule of law trail the other two scales even more dramatically in Latin America, postcommunist Europe, and Asia than they do in Africa. Moreover, in the postcommunist states there has also been a visible (if modest) decline in transparency and the rule of law, similar in extent to that observed in Africa since 2005 (Figure 4.8). Many democracies in lower-income and even middle- or upper-middle-income countries (notably, Argentina) struggle with the resurgence of what Francis Fukuyama calls "neopatrimonial" tendencies.[17] Leaders who think that they can get away with it are eroding democratic checks and balances, hollowing

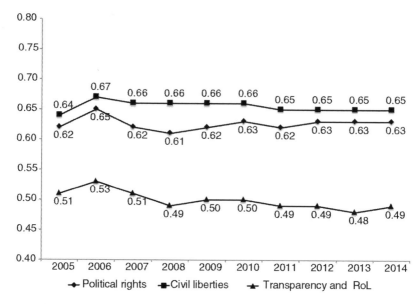

Figure 4.8 Freedom and governance trends in postcommunist states, 2005–2014

out institutions of accountability, overriding term limits and normative restraints, and accumulating power and wealth for themselves and their families, cronies, clients, and parties.

In the process, they demonize, intimidate, and victimize (and occasionally even jail or murder) opponents who get in their way. Space for opposition parties, civil society, and the media is shrinking, and international support for them is drying up. Ethnic, religious, and other identity cleavages polarize many societies that lack well-designed democratic institutions to manage those cleavages. State structures are too often weak and porous—unable to secure order, protect rights, meet the most basic social needs, or rise above corrupt, clientelistic, and predatory impulses. Democratic institutions such as parties and parliaments are often poorly developed, and the bureaucracy lacks the policy expertise, and even more so the independence, neutrality, and authority, to effectively manage the economy. Weak economic performance and rising inequality exacerbate the problems of abuse of power, rigging of elections, and violation of the democratic rules of the game.

Undoubtedly, these problems all tend to be worse in lower-income countries, and not only in Africa. It is not that middle-income (and even some upper-income countries) do not struggle with corruption, clientelism and weak state capacity, but the quality of governance simply tends to be poorer in lower-income countries, and this in itself makes democracy more vulnerable. And in addition, other dimensions of the quality of democracy, such as participation, civil society, and the fairness and transparency of elections themselves, also tend to be weaker in lower-income countries. Thus, this is where the disproportionate share of the democratic erosion has been during the third wave, and this is where the greatest challenge of deepening and consolidating democracy lies.

The strategic swing states

A different perspective on the global state of democracy can be gleaned from a focus not on regional or global trends, but on the weightiest emerging-market countries. These are the ones with large populations (say, more than 50 million) or large economies (over US$200 billion). I count 27 of these (Table 4.2).[18] Twelve of these 27 swing states had worse average freedom scores at the end of 2013 than they did at the end of 2005. These declines took place across the board: in fairly liberal democracies (South Korea, Taiwan, and South Africa); in less liberal democracies (Colombia, Ukraine, Indonesia, Turkey, Mexico, and Thailand before the 2014 military coup); and in authoritarian regimes (Ethiopia, Venezuela, and Saudi Arabia). In addition, three other countries appear distinctly less free at the end of 2014 than they were in 2005: Russia, where the noose of repressive authoritarianism has clearly been tightening since Vladimir Putin returned to the presidency in early 2012; Egypt, where the new military-dominated government under former general Abdel Fattah al-Sisi is more murderous, intolerant, and domineering than even the Mubarak regime (1981–2011); and Bangladesh, where (as noted above) democracy broke down early in 2014. Only two countries (Singapore and Pakistan) were freer in 2014 (and only modestly so) than in 2005. Some other countries have at least remained stable. Chile continues to be a liberal-democratic success story; the Philippines has returned to genuine democracy after an authoritarian interlude under President Gloria Macapagal-Arroyo (2001–2010); and Brazil and India have preserved robust democracy, albeit with continuing challenges. But overall, among the 27 (which also include China, Malaysia, Nigeria, and the United Arab Emirates) there has been scant evidence of democratic progress.[19] In terms of democracy, the most important countries outside the stable democratic West have been either stagnating or slipping backward.

Another way of putting global democracy trends in perspective is to break them down by country size. As noted above, there is a substantial difference between small countries (under one million population) and the rest in terms of the probability of being a democracy and also the (lower) probability of being a liberal democracy. This has long been the case, but the divergence has sharpened over the last 20 years, and especially since the onset of the democratic recession in 2005. Three of the five countries that Freedom House classified as new democracies in 2014 (Fiji, the Maldives, and the Solomon Islands) are under one million population, and a fourth, Kosovo, has barely over two million. Overall, the percentage of democracies

Table 4.2 Regime types in swing states, 2015

Country	2012 GDP (billions US$)	2012 GDP per capita (US$)	Population in 2012 (millions)	2014 average freedom score	Regime type
China*	8,227.10	6,091	1,351	6.5	Authoritarian
Brazil*	2,252.70	11,340	199	2	Liberal democracy
India*	1,858.70	1,503	1,237	2.5	Democracy
Russia*	2,014.80	14,037	144	5.5	Electoral authoritarian
Mexico*	1,178.10	9,749	120	3	Democracy
South Korea*	1,129.60	22,590	50	2	Liberal democracy
Turkey*	789.3	10,666	74	3.5	Competitive authoritarian
Indonesia*	878	3,557	247	3	Democracy
Saudi Arabia*	711	25,136	28	7	Authoritarian
Taiwan	473.9	20,930	23	1.5	Liberal democracy
Argentina*	475.5	11,573	41	2	Democracy
South Africa*	384.3	7,352	51	2	Liberal democracy
Venezuela	381.3	12,729	30	5	Electoral authoritarian
Iran	552.4	7,228	76	6	Electoral authoritarian
UAE	383.8	41,692	9	6	Authoritarian
Thailand	366	5,480	67	5.5	Authoritarian
Colombia	369.6	7,748	48	3.5	Democracy
Malaysia	305	10,432	29	4	Competitive authoritarian
Singapore	274.7	51,709	5	4	Competitive authoritarian
Egypt	262.8	3,256	81	5.5	Competitive authoritarian
Chile	269.9	15,452	17	1	Liberal democracy
Philippines	250.1	2,587	97	3	Democracy
Pakistan	225.1	1,257	179	4.5	Democracy

Country	2012 GDP (billions US$)	2012 GDP per capita (US$)	Population in 2012 (millions)	2014 average freedom score	Regime type
Nigeria	262.6	1,555	169	4.5	Competitive authoritarian
Ukraine	176.3	3,867	46	3	Democracy
Bangladesh	116.4	752	155	4	Competitive authoritarian
Ethiopia	41.6	454	92	6	Electoral authoritarian

Sources: 2012 GDP (current US$) and 2012 GDP per capita (current US$)—World Bank.

* G20 country.

among states with populations over one million barely changed between 1995 and 2014; in fact since 2005, it has declined from 55 to 53 percent. All of the growth of democracy has been among countries with less than one million people, which increased from 79 percent democracies in 2005 to 90 percent in 2014 (Figure 4.9). Between 2005 and 2014, the percentages of liberal democracies in each population group hardly changed at all, but among small states it was more than twice as high (69 percent) as it was among larger states (33 percent) (Figure 4.10).

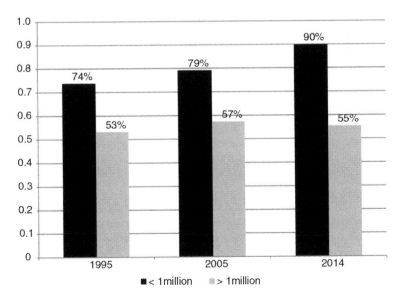

Figure 4.9 Electoral democracy by population

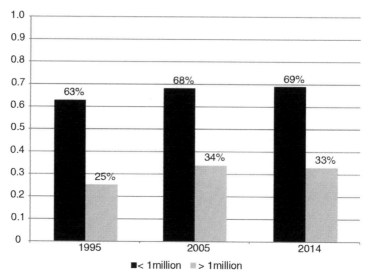

Figure 4.10 Liberal democracy by population

The authoritarian resurgence

An important part of the story of global democratic recession has been the deepening of authoritarianism. This has taken a number of forms. In Russia, space for political opposition, principled dissent, and civil society activity outside the control of the ruling authorities has been shrinking dramatically.[20] In China, human-rights defenders and civil society activists have faced mounting harassment and victimization. The (mainly) postcommunist autocracies of the Shanghai Cooperation Organization, centered on the axis of cynical cooperation between Russia and China, have become much more coordinated and assertive. Russia and China have both been aggressively flexing their muscles in dealing with their neighbors on territorial questions. And increasingly they are pushing back against democratic norms by also using instruments of soft power—international media (such as RT, Russia's slick 24/7 global television "news" channel), Confucius Institutes, lavish conferences, and exchange programs—to try to discredit Western democracies and democracy in general, while promoting their own models and norms.[21] This is part of a broader trend of renewed authoritarian skill and energy in using state-run media (both traditional and digital) to air an eclectic mix of proregime narratives, demonized images of dissenters, and illiberal, nationalist, and anti-American diatribes.[22]

African autocrats have increasingly used China's booming aid and investment (and the new regional war on Islamist terrorism) as a counterweight to Western pressure for democracy and good governance. And they have been only too happy to point to China's formula of rapid state-led development without democracy to justify their own deepening authoritarianism. In Venezuela, the vise of authoritarian populism has tightened and the government's toleration (or even organization) of criminal violence to demobilize middle-class opposition has risen. The "Arab Spring" has imploded in almost every state that it touched save Tunisia, leaving in most cases even more repressive states or, as in the cases of Libya and increasingly Yemen, hardly a state at all.

The resurgence of authoritarianism over the past eight years has been quickened by the diffusion of common tools and approaches. Prominent among these have been laws to criminalize international flows of financial and technical assistance from democracies to democratic parties, movements, media, election monitors, and civil society organizations in authoritarian regimes, as well as broader restrictions on the ability of NGOs to form and operate and the creation of pseudo-NGOs to do the bidding (domestically and internationally) of autocrats.[23] One recent study of 98 countries outside the West found that 51 of them either prohibit or restrict foreign funding of civil society, with a clear global trend toward tightening control; as a result, international democratic-assistance flows are dropping precipitously where they are needed most.[24] In addition, authoritarian (and even some democratic states) are becoming more resourceful, sophisticated, and unapologetic in suppressing Internet freedom and using cyberspace to frustrate, subvert, and control civil society.[25]

Western democracy in retreat

Perhaps the most worrisome dimension of the democratic recession has been the decline of democratic efficacy, energy, and self-confidence in the West, including the United States. Amid the protracted economic and political woes of Europe, Japan, and the United States, there is emerging a new rhetoric of skepticism (if not outright pessimism) about the capacity of democratic institutions to solve the fundamental problems of aging populations and physical infrastructure, rising dependency ratios, spiraling debt burdens, and declining economic competitiveness. The moment is not unlike the mid-1970s, when the Trilateral Commission produced its famous report on "The Crisis of Democracy" (the focus of which was heavily on "governability.")[26] Perhaps most damaging is the growing sense, both domestically and internationally, that democracy in the United States has not been functioning effectively enough to address the major challenges of governance. The diminished pace of legislation, the vanishing ability of Congress to pass a budget, and the 2013 shutdown of the federal government are only some of the indications of a political system (and a broader body politic) that appears increasingly polarized and deadlocked. As a result, both public approval of Congress and public trust in government are at historic lows. The ever-mounting cost of election campaigns, the surging role of nontransparent money in politics, and low rates of voter participation are additional signs of democratic ill health. Internationally, promoting democracy abroad scores close to the bottom of the public's foreign-policy priorities. And the international perception is that democracy promotion has already receded as an actual priority of U.S. foreign policy.

The world takes note of all this. Authoritarian state media gleefully publicize these travails of American democracy in order to discredit democracy in general and immunize authoritarian rule against U.S. pressure. Even in weak states, autocrats perceive that the pressure is now off: They can pretty much do whatever they want to censor the media, crush the opposition, and perpetuate their rule, and Europe and the United States will swallow it. Meek verbal protests may ensue, but the aid will still flow and the dictators will still be welcome at the White House and the Elysée Palace.

It is hard to overstate how important the vitality and self-confidence of U.S. democracy has been to the global expansion of democracy during the third wave. While each democratizing country made its own transition, pressure and solidarity from the United States and Europe often generated a significant and even crucial enabling environment, which helped to tip finely balanced situations toward democratic change, and then in some cases gradually toward democratic consolidation. If this solidarity is now greatly diminished, so will be the near-term global prospects for reviving and sustaining democratic progress. This is why it is so important that the United States continue to play a leadership role in the promotion of democracy, as I discuss in the concluding chapter of this book.

A brighter horizon?

Democracy has been in a global recession for most of the last decade, and there is a growing danger that the recession could deepen and tip over into something much worse. Many more democracies could fail, not only in poor countries of marginal strategic significance, but also in big swing states such as Indonesia and Ukraine (again). There is little external recognition yet of the grim state of democracy in Turkey, and there is no guarantee that democracy will return any time soon to Thailand or Bangladesh. Apathy and inertia in Europe and the United States could significantly lower the barriers to new democratic reversals and to authoritarian entrenchments in many more states.

Yet the picture is not entirely bleak. Despite having passed through the most challenging economic period since the Great Depression, the world has not experienced "a third reverse wave" of democratic breakdowns. Globally, average levels of freedom have ebbed a little bit, but not calamitously. Most important, there has not been significant erosion in public support for democracy. In fact, what the Afrobarometer has consistently shown is a gap—in some African countries, a chasm—between the popular demand for democracy and the supply of it provided by the regime.[27] This is not based just on some shallow, vague notion that democracy is a good thing. Many Africans understand the importance of political accountability, transparency, the rule of law, and restraint of power, and they would like to see their governments manifest these virtues.

While the performance of democracy is failing to inspire, authoritarianism faces its own steep challenges. There is hardly a dictatorship in the world that looks stable for the long run. The only truly reliable source of regime stability is legitimacy, and the number of people in the world who believe in the intrinsic legitimacy of any form of authoritarianism is rapidly diminishing. Economic development, globalization, and the information revolution are undermining all forms of authority and empowering individuals. Values are changing, and while we should not assume any teleological path toward a global "enlightenment," generally the movement is toward greater distrust of authority and more desire for accountability, freedom, and political choice. In the coming two decades, these trends will challenge the nature of rule in China, Vietnam, Iran, and the Arab states much more than they will in India, not to mention Europe and the United States. Already, democratization is visible on the horizon of Malaysia's increasingly competitive electoral politics, and it will come in the next generation to Singapore as well.

As I suggest in Chapter 16, China is likely to experience growing pressures for democratic change as the legitimacy of Chinese communist rule erodes. Communist rule in China is trapped in a contradiction it cannot resolve. Economic growth is slowing down, probably permanently, from its torrid pace of 8–10 percent per year, as the society ages and the economy matures. China is now facing significant developmental challenges, in the form of an overheated real estate market, a potentially vulnerable banking sector, a looming severe labor shortage, and massive unaddressed environmental stresses. If the Chinese leadership cannot find ways to address these daunting challenges, a crisis of performance will gather and quite possibly swallow the regime, despite all of its sophisticated authoritarian controls. But even if the regime does parry these threats for a time and sustain a relatively brisk pace of economic growth, the resulting social and cultural change will pose its own severe predicament for authoritarian rule. China has already long since entered the famous "political zone of transition" that Samuel P. Huntington identified as the likeliest developmental zone for democratic transitions.[28] In fact, by now China has already exceeded the per capita income level (in purchasing power parity dollars) that South Korea had in 1987 when it made its transition to democracy.[29] One does not need to be a modernization theorist to have difficulty imagining that a China with as large a middle class, in proportional terms, as South Korea had in 1987—and in an era with increasing access to independent (or at least pluralistic) sources of information and communication through the Internet and social media—will continue to accept the unaccountable, one-party hegemony of Communist rule. One way or another, through continued rapid development or a sudden bursting of the development bubble, through incremental political reform or through another eruption of mass protest from below, China is headed for a whopping political transformation in the next generation. Without major political reforms, it is unlikely that communist rule can survive in China beyond Xi Jinping's two five-year terms as president. Democracy is not the inevitable outcome, but it will inevitably be widely demanded.

The key imperative in the near term is to work to reform and consolidate the democracies that have emerged during the third wave—the majority of which remain illiberal and unstable, if they remain democratic at all. With more focused, committed, and resourceful international engagement, it should be possible to help democracy sink deeper and more enduring roots in countries such as Indonesia, the Philippines, South Africa, and Ghana. It is possible and urgently important to help stabilize the new democracies in Ukraine and Tunisia (whose success could gradually generate significant diffusion effects throughout the Arab world). It might be possible to nudge Thailand and Bangladesh back toward electoral democracy, though ways must be found to temper the awful levels of party polarization in each country. With time, the electoral authoritarian project in Turkey will discredit itself in the face of mounting corruption and abuse of power, which are already growing quite serious. And the oil-based autocracies in Iran and Venezuela will face increasingly severe crises of economic performance and political legitimacy.

It is vital that democrats in the established democracies not lose faith. Democrats have the better set of ideas. Democracy may be receding somewhat in practice, but it is still globally ascendant in peoples' values and aspirations. This creates significant new opportunities for democratic growth. If the current modest recession of democracy spirals into a depression, it will be because those of us in the established democracies were our own worst enemies.

Notes

I would like to thank Erin Connors, Emmanuel Ferrario, and Lukas Friedemann for their excellent research assistance on this chapter.

1 An abbreviated form of this chapter was published as "Facing up to the Democratic Recession," *Journal of Democracy* 26 (January 2015): 140–154.
2 For an elaboration of this definition, see Larry Diamond, *The Spirit of Democracy* (New York: Times Books, 2008), 20–26.
3 Steven Levitsky and Lucan Way, *Competitive Authoritarianism: Hybrid Regimes After the Cold War* (New York: Cambridge University Press, 2010); see also their essay, "The Myth of Democratic Recession," *Journal of Democracy* 26 (January 2015): 45–58.
4 I count as liberal democracies all those regimes that receive a score of 1 or 2 (out of 7) on *both* political rights and civil liberties. These are the higher-quality democracies as manifested on the dimensions outlined in Chapter 2.

5 Marc F. Plattner, "The Impact of the Economic Crisis: From the G-8 to the G-20," *Journal of Democracy* 22 (January 2011): 31–38. As I argue below, however, I think it is no longer accurate to describe Turkey as a democracy.

6 Levitsky and Way, "The Myth of Democratic Recession."

7 Thomas Carothers, "The End of the Transition Paradigm," *Journal of Democracy* 13 (January 2002): 5–21.

8 Freedom House classifies all the world's regimes as democracies or not from 1989 to the present based on whether they (a) score at least 7 out of 12 on the "electoral process" dimension of political rights; (b) score at least 20 out of 40 overall on the raw point scale for political rights; (c) their most recent parliamentary and presidential elections were reasonably free and fair; (d) there are no significant hidden sources of power overriding the elected authorities; and (e) there are no recent legal changes abridging future electoral freedom. In practice, this has led to a somewhat expansive list of democracies—rather too generous in my view, but at least a plausible "upper limit" of the number of democracies every year. Levitsky and Way suggest that a better standard for democracy would be the Freedom House classification of Free, which requires a minimum average score of 2.5 on the combined scales of political rights and civil liberties. But I think this standard excludes many genuine but illiberal democracies.

9 During 1998 to 2002, my count of electoral democracies was lower than that of Freedom House by 8 to 9 countries, and in 1999, by 11 countries. For example, I dropped from this category Georgia in 1992–2002, Ukraine in 1994–2004, Mozambique in 1994–2008, Nigeria in 1999–2003, Russia in 2001–2004, and Venezuela in 2004–2008.

10 This counts regimes, not countries, so some countries, such as Thailand, experienced multiple breakdowns of democracy.

11 Amy R. Poteete, "Democracy Derailed? Botswana's Fading Halo," AfricaPlus, October 20, 2014, http://africaplus.wordpress.com/2014/10/20/democracy-derailed-botswanas-fading-halo.

12 Levitsky and Way, *Competitive Authoritarianism*, 20.

13 Kenneth Good, "The Illusion of Democracy in Botswana," in Larry Diamond and Marc F. Plattner, eds, *Democratization in Africa: Progress and Retreat* (Baltimore, MD: Johns Hopkins University Press, 2010), 281.

14 Scott Mainwaring and Aníbal Pérez-Liñán, "Cross-Currents in Latin America," *Journal of Democracy* 26 (January 2015): 114–127.

15 The comparisons here and in Figure 4.7 are with the reconfigured political-rights and civil-liberties scales, after the subscales for transparency and rule of law have been removed.

16 I created the scale of transparency and rule of law by drawing subscales C2 (control of corruption) and C3 (accountability and transparency) from the political-rights scale and the four subscales of F (rule of law) from the civil-liberties scale. For the specific items in these subscales, see the Freedom in the World methodology, www.freedomhouse.org/report/freedom-world-2014/methodology#. VGww5vR4qcI.

17 Francis Fukuyama, *Political Order and Political Decay: From the Industrial Revolution to the Globalization of Democracy* (New York: Farrar, Straus and Giroux, 2014).

18 The 27 include including Ukraine, which does not quite reach either measure, but is of immense strategic importance.

19 As this book was going to press, Nigeria confounded the odds by holding, for the first time in its 55-year history, national elections in which the incumbent party was defeated. The 2015 elections appear to mark a return to democracy for Nigeria, but unfortunately they came too late to be analyzed in this book.

20 On Russia, see Miriam Lanskoy and Elspeth Suthers, "Putin versus Civil Society: Outlawing the Opposition," *Journal of Democracy* 24 (July 2013): 74–87.
21 Andrew Nathan, "China's Challenge," *Journal of Democracy* 26 (January 2015): 156–170.
22 Christopher Walker and Robert W. Orttung, "Breaking the News: The Role of State-Run Media," *Journal of Democracy* 25 (January 2014): 71–85.
23 Carl Gershman and Michael Allen, "The Assault on Democracy Assistance," *Journal of Democracy* 17 (April 2006): 36–51; William J. Dobson, *The Dictator's Learning Curve: Inside the Global Battle for Democracy* (New York: Doubleday, 2012).
24 Darin Christensen and Jeremy M. Weinstein, "Defunding Dissent: Restrictions on Aid to NGOs," *Journal of Democracy* 24 (April 2013): 77–91.
25 See the essays in Larry Diamond and Marc F. Plattner, *Liberation Technology: Social Media and the Struggle for Democracy* (Baltimore, MD: John Hopkins University Press, 2012) and the ongoing trailblazing work of the Citizen Lab, https://citizenlab.org.
26 Michel Crozier, Samuel P. Huntington, and Joji Watanuki, *The Crisis of Democracy: Report on the Governability of Democracies to the Trilateral Commission* (New York: New York University, 1975).
27 Michael Bratton, "Trends in Popular Attitudes To Multiparty Democracy in Africa, 2000–2012," Afrobarometer Briefing Paper No. 105, October 2012, www.afrobarometer.org/files/documents/briefing_papers/afrobriefno105a.pdf.
28 Samuel P. Huntington, *The Third Wave: Democratization in the Late 20th Century* (Norman: University of Oklahoma Press: 1991).
29 China's per capita income in purchasing power parity dollars was estimated at about $11,907 in 2013 (http://data.worldbank.org/indicator/NY.GDP.PCAP.PP.CD). In 2009 dollars, this is about $11,000, well above the roughly $9,000 per capita income (in 2009 dollars) that South Korea had when it transitioned to democracy in 1988. See Table 16.1.

5 Why democracies survive[1]

It is a cardinal principle of empirical democratic theory that hard economic times are supposed to mean hard times for democracy, particularly when it is new and fragile. As Seymour Martin Lipset argued in his 1960 classic *Political Man*, when democratic regimes lack intrinsic legitimacy (what is often now called democratic "consolidation"), their survival depends precariously on effective performance—a concept that is measured primarily in economic terms. If no crisis supervenes, democracies with weak legitimacy may muddle along for some time, but when they lose their effectiveness, they collapse—as did shaky democratic governments in Austria, Germany, and Spain in the 1930s, following the onset of the Great Depression.[2] In fact, the economic disarray of the late 1920s and 1930s swallowed up a number of other democracies as well in Europe and Latin America, even though the origin of the "first reverse wave" of global democratization can be traced further back to the March on Rome by Benito Mussolini's Fascists in October 1922.[3]

During the second half of the twentieth century, there was a strong relationship between economic performance and the survival of regimes, particularly democracies. Analyzing data covering the years from 1950 to 1990, Adam Przeworski and his colleagues found that when democracies face a decline in income, they are three times more likely to disappear than when they experience economic growth. When they looked at longer-term trajectories, the impact of economic performance became even more striking: "The chance that a democracy will die is 1 in 135 when incomes grow during any three or more consecutive years, and 1 in 13 when incomes fall during any two consecutive years."[4] More than two-thirds of the democratic failures that Przeworski and his colleagues documented in their 40-year period of analysis were accompanied by a fall in income in one or both of the preceding years. Thus, "deaths of democracies follow a clear pattern: They are more likely when a country experiences an economic crisis, and in most cases they are accompanied by one."[5]

Yet the current period in world history defies these patterns. By all accounts, the global financial crisis that began in September 2008 has triggered the worst economic downturn since the Great Depression. Yet it appears to have had little effect on the survival of democracy so far, for three reasons. First, the countries hardest hit economically by the financial crisis have mostly been the wealthy, industrialized democracies and the new European market economies. As Przeworski and his colleagues also showed, democracy has never broken down in a wealthy country, and after many decades of successful functioning, these democracies are now consolidated and deeply institutionalized. The postcommunist democracies of Central and Eastern Europe that have recently been admitted into the European Union (and would face enormous economic costs for abandoning democracy) also now appear to be consolidated. Second, in the newer and weaker democracies (including both the upper-middle-income ones in Eastern Europe and the less developed ones), the effect of economic turbulence has been the defeat of democratically elected governments but not the demise of democracy. And third, the breakdowns of democracy that have been occurring largely predate the onset of the global recession and are due to bad internal governance, not unfavorable global conditions. In fact, in a surprising number of instances, democratic breakdowns occurred while aggregate rates of economic growth were fairly robust.

The analysis that follows should not be read as implying that economic circumstances make no difference to the fate of fragile democracies. On the contrary, the data from recent decades suggest that such circumstances do matter—*especially* for younger and lower-income democracies.[6] But where governance is bad—in particular, where corruption and abuse of power are rampant, and where inequality is extreme and intensifying—it may not much matter much for democracy that the economy as a whole is expanding. To the extent that democracies depend for their survival on the support or at least acquiescence of the governed, bad governance undermines that support and inclines at-risk democracies toward calamity. Both survey data and objective trends suggest that in the short run, political factors may be more important than economic ones in determining the fate of new and fragile democracies. Thus, even if the world economy recovers quickly and vigorously from the current recession, more democracies will fail if they do not improve their quality of governance and rein in abuse of power.

The causes of recent democratic failures

One of the most remarkable features of the "third wave" of global democratic expansion that began in 1974 has been its persistence. Unlike the relatively short "second wave" that began after World War II and began running into difficulties in the early 1960s, the third wave has not yet met with a decisive "reverse wave" of democratic breakdowns. Yet, as the previous chapter shows, there has been a leveling off of democratic progress and a rising incidence of democratic breakdown since around 2006 and we are now in an extended period of at least mild—and potentially deepening—democratic recession.

What is striking, however, is how small a role overall economic performance appears to have played in the breakdowns of democracy in this new century. As Table 5.1 shows, many of the failed democracies since the Pakistan coup in 1999 had positive economic growth rates in the year or two before their collapse.[7] In fact, some of the democracies had quite good—even startlingly good—economic performance around the time they failed, with annual growth rates topping 6 percent. Generally, those democracies that were extinguished as a result of mounting executive abuses of power were experiencing robust economic growth at the time. This was particularly true of the oil-exporting countries. Rising oil prices produced growth in the year before and the year of democratic demise of 6.4 and 10 percent in Russia and 18.3 and 10.5 percent in Venezuela. A weaker version of the same pattern held in non-oil countries such as Kenya and the Philippines, while in Georgia and Niger growth was outstanding in the year before

Table 5.1 Recent cases of loss of democracy

Country, year of reversal	Freedom scores, year before democratic reversal (political rights, civil liberties)	Economic growth rate (%), year before reversal	Economic growth rate (%), year of reversal	Per capita GDP in PPP, year of reversal, 2010 $US (IMF)
Pakistan 1999	4, 5	2.6	3.7	1,698
Fiji 2000	2, 3	9.2	−1.8	3,402
Nepal 2002	3, 4	5.6	0.1	832
Venezuela 2005	3, 4	18.3	10.5	9,992
Solomon Islands 2006	3, 3	5.4	6.9	2,540
Thailand 2006	3, 3	4.6	5.2	7,404
Bangladesh 2007	4, 4	6.0	6.3	1,325
Philippines 2007	3, 3	5.3	7.1	3,383
Kenya 2007	3, 3	6.4	7.1	1,672
Georgia 2008	4, 4	12.3	2.0	4,907
Honduras 2009	3, 3	4.0	−2.0	4,344
Madagascar 2009	4, 3	−0.4	7.1	945
Niger 2009	3, 4	9.5	1.0	712

Freedom scores are from the annual surveys of "Freedom in the World," by Freedom House, www.freedomhouse.org, for the year before the democratic breakdown. Scores range from 1 to 7 with 1 being most free and 7 most repressive.

Economic data are from the World Bank and the IMF World Economic Outlook Database, October 2010, www.imf.org/external/pubs/ft/weo/2010/02/weodata/index.aspx.

the reversal but slight in the year during which the democratic reversal occurred. In the case of the oil countries, it is even plausible that the boom in this commodity created an additional incentive to strangle democracy. To be sure, it is hard to pinpoint a "time of death" for democracy when it dies by inches rather than perishing in a putsch, but the pattern is striking. Even in some countries that did have military coups, such as Bangladesh and Thailand, the economy was clearly growing, even in per capita terms. Only in a few countries—Nepal in 2002, and more recently Honduras and Niger—did growth expire or swing negative in per capita terms during the year of reversal.[8]

As the previous chapter has argued, what has consistently plagued the failed and failing democracies of the past decade has been bad governance. Around the time most of these countries saw their democracies overthrown or strangled by executive abuse, they ranked in the bottom third on most of the World Bank's six indicators of the quality of governance. Of the 13 countries that experienced a reversal of democracy between 1999 and 2009, only two (Fiji and Thailand) were above the median on the rule of law, and only four on corruption. More typical was Kenya, which was in the 17th percentile on political stability, the 28th percentile in government effectiveness, the 21st in rule of law, and the 18th in control of corruption—in other words, stuck in the bottom quartile that contains the world's most poorly governed states (most of which, by the way, are authoritarian regimes).

To summarize, the troubled or outright failed democracies of the third wave share certain key characteristics. First, they tend (with exceptions such as Russia, Thailand, and Venezuela) to be poor or lower-middle-income, with per capita incomes (in purchasing power parity dollars) under $5,000. Second, they rank low on the World Bank's good-governance scale. Most of the current democracies that could be said to be severely at risk, if they are even still democracies (countries like Bolivia, Ecuador, East Timor, Liberia, Malawi, and Sierra Leone), fall into the bottom third of the world's states when it comes to controlling corruption. In addition, their governments are not very effective in terms of the quality and independence of the civil service, or of public services and policy formulation and implementation more generally.[9] Third, they are politically unstable, with significant levels of politically motivated violence, or still-fresh histories of such violence that have not been laid to rest, or a more general sense that their governments are fragile and could be overthrown. Fourth, they are deeply split along class, ethnic, or other lines (with interparty hostility sometimes part of the mix, as in Bangladesh), which is one reason why they suffer civil wars and high levels of political violence. Fifth, executive power is seriously abused.

Executive abuse of power has been a key factor in the demise of democracy in such countries as Georgia, Honduras, Niger, the Philippines, Russia, and Venezuela, and it has played a role in Kenya and Pakistan as well. Ethan

Kapstein and Nathan Converse find in their quantitative analysis that "effective constraints on executive power substantially increase the chances that democracy will survive" in posttransitional or otherwise fragile circumstances.[10] Several of the current democracies (if we can call them that) most at risk have presidents who embrace grandiose political projects that they believe require them to concentrate and aggrandize power. For Bolivia's Evo Morales and Ecuador's Rafael Correa, the goal is to remake their respective countries along left-wing populist lines, redistributing wealth and power to historically dispossessed indigenous majorities (and to themselves and their supporters). When this article was first written, that was also true for leftist Daniel Ortega in Nicaragua, who sought to restore the dominance of his Sandinista party and movement, as well as his own revolutionary authority and legacy—while digging into the same national trough of corruption at which previous presidents of the country have fed. Subsequently, he pushed the political system below the democratic threshold in Nicaragua. Until he was defeated in his quest for a third term in 2012, the increasingly obsessive goal of President Abdoulaye Wade of Senegal was to dominate the country's institutions and pass power on to his son. Since assuming his nation's highest office in 2005, and especially since his defeat of the Tamil Tigers in 2009 in one of the world's longest-running civil wars, Sri Lanka's President Mahinda Rajapaksa has pursued an ethnic-chauvinist agenda that has gone hand in hand with formidable concentration of power. As in Nicaragua, his abuses wound up degrading political pluralism and freedom below the threshold of democracy.

Significantly, none of these narratives of democratic struggle and crisis has been mainly about the stresses of imploding economic growth or spiraling unemployment. Certainly, economic and social injustice has formed the backdrop for the crises of social and political polarization that have long been gathering in the Andean region of South America as well as parts of Central America (Guatemala, Honduras, and Nicaragua). But some of these fragile or now failed democracies—Bangladesh, Burundi, Liberia, Malawi, Sierra Leone, and Sri Lanka—have been only lightly affected by the global *economic* recession. That is also true of a number of other African democracies that have been more liberal, including Benin, Ghana, Mali, and Zambia.[11] Mostly, these are poor countries that are not well integrated into world markets. In a few other vulnerable low-income countries, such as Ecuador, Guatemala, Nicaragua, and Senegal, the rate of economic growth plunged below that of population growth, meaning that per capita income shrank. In Bolivia and Ecuador, such slippage in prosperity could reinforce the leftist, antiglobalist narratives of presidents already inclined toward authoritarian populism. In short, it is too early to dismiss economic hardship as a factor that could undermine the stability of poor and lower-middle-income democracies, but at most its recent effects appear to have been secondary, reinforcing other negative trends.

The global recession's political impact

Not all developing and emerging-market economies have been spared the harsh impact of the Great Recession. Most countries have experienced some kind of downturn. In a great many of the more mature or middle-income, emerging-market countries, the IMF reported negative economic growth rates for 2009, though in most cases the 2010 figures were expected to reveal a return to (modest) positive growth. In some cases, the impact at the end of 2008 was brutal enough to wipe out all year-to-date growth. The drop from 2007's brisk growth was steep in far-flung places ranging from Argentina, the Baltic states, Botswana, Brazil, Colombia, and Poland to Romania, South Africa, South Korea, Taiwan, Ukraine, and Uruguay. Among developing and emerging-market democracies, it has generally been the poorer ones (Ghana, Indonesia, Mali, and Zambia, for instance) that have experienced the slightest effects.

What has been the political impact on democracy in the economically harder-hit countries? So far, surprisingly little: Governments have come and gone, but democracy has remained. Both effects—the instability of governments and the stability of democracy—have been quite striking. Among those democracies that were hit harder by the recession but were more strongly rooted as democracies, incumbents often took an electoral beating. In my count of the 29 major democratic elections that took place in these countries (where at least some portion of governing power was up for grabs) between October 2008 and October 2010, the party of the incumbent president or prime minister lost more than half the time (16 elections; for the details, see Table 5.2).[12] Adding in as well midterm elections in presidential systems, the parties of incumbent parties or presidents went down to defeat or suffered a setback in 19 out of 34 elections.[13] The impression of tough sledding for incumbents is intensified by the severe setbacks that ruling parties encountered in midterm elections held by the presidential systems in Argentina, Mexico, and Venezuela (and if one widens the optic to include the wealthier democracies, the United States as well).

A good example of electoral punishment came in Bulgaria, where in the July 2009 parliamentary election incumbent premier Sergey Stanishev's Socialist Party was able to garner only about 18 percent of the vote, down from 34 percent in 2005. Sofia mayor Boiko Borisov won nearly 40 percent and a near majority of seats by promising to tackle corruption and the economic downturn. It is possible that the first pledge mattered more than the second: In 2008, "Bulgaria lost access to more than 500m euros (£430m) of EU funding for failing to deal with corruption and organized crime."[14] This underscores a continual theme of democratic elections across the troubled landscape of the global recession: Particular national factors, often political, matter as much as if not more than economic distress. Often, the economic distress is a serious aggravating factor, but not the sole cause of electoral alternation.

Table 5.2 Election results in emerging-market democracies, October 2008–October 2010

Country and type of election	Date of election	GDP Growth rate in year of election	Change in % pts from previous year	Ruling party % of vote	Change in % pts from last election	Ruling party % of seats	Change in % pts from last election
Lithuania, Parliamentary	10/12–26/08	2.8%	-7.0%	9.0% D	-19.4%	7.1%[i]	-20.6%
Romania, Parliamentary	11/30/08	7.4%	1.1%	18.6%[ii]	—	19.5%	1.6%
Ghana, Legislative	12/7/08	7.2%	1.5%			46.9%	-8.7%
Presidential 1st round				49.1%	-3.4%		
Presidential runoff				49.7% D	—		
El Salvador, Presidential	3/15/09	2.4%	-1.9%	48.9% D	-8.8%		
Legislative				39.0%	0.0%	38.0%	0.0%
Slovakia, Presidential 1st round	4/4/09	-4.7%	-10.9%	46.7%	24.4%		
Presidential runoff				55.5%	-4.4%		
Macedonia, Presidential	4/5/09	-0.8%	-5.8%	36.9%[iii] D	-23.7%		
Moldova, Parliamentary	4/5/09	-6.5%	-14.3%	50.0%	4.0%	59.4%	4.0%
Parliamentary	7/29/09			44.7% D	-4.7%	47.5%	-11.9%
Indonesia, Legislative	4/9/09	4.5%	-1.5%	20.9%	13.4%	26.8%	16.8%
South Africa, Parliamentary	4/22/09	-1.8%	-5.5%	66.0%	-3.8%	65.9%	-3.8%
India, Parliamentary	April–May 09	5.7%	-0.7%	28.6%	2.0%	37.9%	11.2%
Panama, Presidential	5/3/09	3.0%	-7.1%	37.7% D	-9.7%		
Legislative				40.6%	-8.4%	38.0%	-19.6%

Table 5.2 Election results in emerging-market democracies, October 2008–October 2010, *continued*

Country and type of election	Date of election	GDP Growth rate in year of election	Change in % pts from previous year	Ruling party % of vote	Change in % pts from last election	Ruling party % of seats	Change in % pts from last election
Mongolia, Presidential	5/24/09	-1.6%	-10.5%	47.4% D	-6.8%		
Argentina, Legislative[iv]	6/28/09	0.9%	-5.9%	30.80% d	-12.2%	37.0%	-23.0%
Albania, Parliamentary	6/28/09	3.3%	-4.4%	47%		50.0%	-7.1%
Bulgaria, Parliamentary	7/5/09	-5.0%	-11.0%	17.7% D	-16.3%		
Mexico, Legislative	7/5/09	-6.5%	-8.0%	28.0% d	-5.4%	29.4%	-11.8%
Indonesia, Presidential	7/8/09	4.5%	-1.5%	60.8%	0.2%		
Romania, Presidential 1st round	11/22/09	-7.1%	-14.5%	32.4%	-1.5%		
Presidential runoff				50.3%	-0.9%		
Honduras, Presidential	11/29/09	-1.9%	-5.9%	38.1%D	-7.5%		
Parliamentary						35.2%	-13.3%
Bolivia, Presidential	12/6/09	3.4%	-2.7%	64.1%	10.4%		
Legislative						67.7%	12.30%
Croatia, Presidential[v]	12/27/09	-5.8%	-8.2%	7.3% D	-33.8%		
Chile, Presidential[vi]	1/17/10	-1.5%	-5.2%	29.6%	-16.4%		
Presidential runoff				48.4% D	-5.1%		
Legislative				44.4%	-7.4%	47.5%	-6.7%
Ukraine, Presidential[vii]	1/17/10	-15.1%	-17.2%	5.5% D	-34.4%		
Sri Lanka, Presidential	1/26/10	3.5%	-2.5%	57.9%	7.6%		

Table 5.2 Election results in emerging-market democracies, October 2008–October 2010, *continued*

Country and type of election	Date of election	GDP Growth rate in year of election	Change in % pts from previous year	Ruling party % of vote	Change in % pts from last election	Ruling party % of seats	Change in % pts from last election
Costa Rica, Presidential	2/7/10	-1.1%	-3.9%	46.8%	5.90%		-3.51%
Legislative				37.2%	0.70%	40.4%	
Hungary, Parliamentary	4/11–25/10	0.6%*	6.9%*	19.3% D	-22.7%	15.3%	-33.9%
Sri Lanka, Parliamentary	4/20/10	7.0%*	3.5%*	60.3%	14.7%	64%	17.3%
Mauritius, Parliamentary	5/5/10	3.6%*	1.1%*	49.7%	0.9%	66.1%	4.8%
Philippines, Presidential	5/10/10	7.0%*	5.9%*	11.3% D	-28.7%		
Legislative[viii]				38.5%		37.1%	-18.8%
Dominican Republic, Legislative	5/16/10	5.5%*	2.0%*	54.6%	8.2%	63.3%	7.1%
Trinidad and Tobago, Parliamentary	5/24/10	1.2%*	4.7%*	39.5% D	-6.4%	29.3%	-34.1%
Czech Republic, Parliamentary	5/28/10	2.0%*	6.1%*	20.2% D	-15.2%	26.5%	-14.0%
Colombia, Presidential 1st round[ix]	5/30/10	4.7%*	3.9%*	46.7%	-15.7%		
Presidential runoff			.	69.1%			
Legislative				25.9%	-1.5%	28.7%	0.3%
Poland, Presidential[x]	6/20/10	3.4%*	1.7%*	47% D?	-7.0%		
Slovakia, Parliamentary	6/12/10	4.1%*	8.8%*	34.8%	5.7%	41.3%	8.0%
Venezuela, Legislative	9/26/10	-1.3%*	2.0%*	48.2% d	-11.8%	57.5%	-12.0%
Brazil, Presidential 1st round	10/3/10	7.5%*	7.7%*	46.9%	-1.7%		
Presidential runoff				56.1%	-4.7%		
Legislative				16.9%	1.9%	17.1%	0.9%

* Signifies estimate. "D" signifies ruling party loss of power, here defined as losing the presidency in a presidential or semi-presidential system or losing parliamentary elections in a parliamentary or semi-presidential system. "d" indicates a setback for incumbents in legislative elections in a presidential system. Source for economic growth data: See Table 5.1 (p. 103). All legislative results presented are for the lower house. For elections held in the first three months of the year, the previous year's GDP growth is used.

i The Lithuanian election was extremely complicated, as the ruling coalition consisted of many parties. The largest party, Labor, is treated here as the "ruling" party, and it declined from 39 to 10 seats, although the party of the Prime Minister, the Social Democratic Party, gained five seats but lost the prime minister's post, as power shifted from a left to a right coalition. The Presidential election results are not listed because both the current and former presidents ran as independents.

ii Election results for former Prime Minister Popescu-Tariceanu's National Liberal Party (also supporting the incumbent president) are used, and for the lower house. Senate elections showed similar results.

iii Signifies 2nd round vote total.

iv Only 127 out of 257 seats were contested in Argentina's midterm elections. The figures are for the ruling Peronist party.

v For Croatia, results are presented for only the first round of elections since the incumbent was defeated in the first round.

vi Elections results from both the first round and runoff are presented and compared to results from the previous election's first round and runoff, respectively. The votes are for the coalition, Concert of Parties for Democracy, which includes the Socialist Party of Chile, Christian Democrat Party, Party for Democracy, and Social Democrat Radical. Economic growth numbers are for 2009 since first round of elections were held in 2009.

vii In Ukraine, the incumbent lost in the first round of elections, so results are presented for the first round.

viii Presented are the results of the lower house. Vote percentage and seats are of the Lakas-Kampi CMD coalition. For comparison with previous election, results of the Lakas-Kampi and CMD are aggregated.

ix Neither the incumbent (Alvaro Uribe) nor his party (Colombia First) ran in the 2010 elections. Presenting results of the Social Party of National Unity/Party of the U (which is composed of Uribe supporters) in 2010 and comparing it with the percentage of votes received by Colombia First in the 2006 elections. The previous election had only one round. The supporter of the incumbent won the second round as well. For the legislative elections, presenting total vote and seat percentages for the alliance of Party of the U in 2010 and comparing to the alliance of Party of the U and Radical Change in 2006. Results are only for the lower house—Chamber of Representatives.

x The results could be interpreted as either a defeat of the incumbent party holding the presidency or a victory for the incumbent party controlling the parliamentary coalition. To be consistent with the counting rules for this table, I score it as an incumbent defeat because Poland is a semi-presidential system.

In Panama, multimillionaire businessman Ricardo Martinelli recaptured the presidency for the political right with a thumping victory over the ruling party, which finished nearly 10 points below its 2004 mark. The left-of-center ruling coalition had "struggled to rein in crime and high prices" amid a sharp economic downturn that had slashed economic growth from 9.2 percent in 2008 to an estimated 1.8 percent in 2009.[15] Martinelli, leading a three-party coalition, won by 24 points—the biggest margin since the restoration of democracy in 1989. The center-right also made gains in other postcommunist elections in 2009, tossing out the former communists in presidential elections in Mongolia and in Macedonia, where the ruling Social Democratic Union went down to a crushing defeat with barely a third of the vote. In both countries, growth had plunged steeply into negative territory during the year of the election. In Moldova, the decline at the polls of the (still rather unreformed) Communist Party in mid-2009 was partly due to the parliamentary deadlock over the choice of a president, but this in turn was fallout from an intensely disputed and allegedly fraudulent election three months earlier in which the Communists had somehow managed to expand their majority despite poor governance and a plunging economy.[16] A free and fair election at that time might well have seen them booted out of power.

In Chile, the right returned to power after two decades in the political wilderness following the 1990 exit of military dictator Augusto Pinochet. After losing to center-left coalition candidate Michele Bachelet in January 2006, billionaire businessman Sebastián Piñera finally triumphed in a January 2010 runoff election against former president Eduardo Frei. Particularly striking was the improvement in Piñera's first-round vote. In 2005, he had won only 30 percent, but four years later this went up to 44 percent. To be sure, the long-ruling center-left coalition had achieved impressive results. "Booming copper revenues and prudent fiscal policies," along with innovative and targeted antipoverty programs, had "helped the government reduce poverty from 45 percent in 1990 to 13 percent today," while lifting per capita income to the level of a middle-income country, at about $14,000.[17] Although barred by law from running again, President Bachelet enjoyed a stratospheric 78 percent approval rating and had won widespread plaudits for her competent and effective economic management. But there was still considerable unease over the maldistribution of wealth, and the election was poorly timed for the ruling coalition, as 2009 had seen Chile's GDP decline by 1.5 percent, after years of 4 to 6 percent growth.

Electoral gains following the 2008 financial crisis were not solely the province of the right, however. In El Savador's March 2009 election, the ruling Arena party, after four terms and 20 years in power, finished 9 points down from its previous showing and lost the presidency to a moderate leftist. Although the economy contracted in 2009, it had recorded at least 3 percent annual growth in the preceding years, as "each successive Arena administration worked hard to improve the delivery of public services."[18] But economic inequality remained severe while poverty was reduced at only a modest pace. Moreover, the left had been gaining at the local level for some time, and many observers expected it to win the presidency once it transcended its divisions and fielded a less radical candidate. Arena's 2009 defeat was particularly noteworthy because it marked the first democratic and "peaceful turnover of power since the nation-state became independent in 1821," and because it brought to power the FMLN (Farabundo Martí National Liberation Front), a party whose origins lay in "a coalition of guerrilla groups that fought a bitter insurrection in the hope of ushering in revolutionary change."[19] But the FMLN's victory probably owes more to long-term and short-term political factors than to the immediate economic downturn. In Mexico, the ruling right-of-center National Action Party was also handed a setback in midterm legislative elections, falling from 40 percent of the seats in the lower house to less than 30 percent amid mounting problems of drug violence and an economy that shrank by 6.5 percent in 2009.

Elsewhere in 2009, left-of-center governments that had performed well or remained popular with voters were rewarded with strong votes of confidence. With India feeling the global recession only lightly, and the country coming off several years of exceptional economic growth under a very capable prime minister, Manmohan Singh, the Congress Party defied expectations and increased its share of seats in parliament by more than a third. In South Africa, where the electorate remains sharply divided along racial lines and the ruling African National Congress (ANC) still wears the mantle of liberation from apartheid, the incumbents held on to their nearly two-thirds majority in parliament. And with Indonesia enjoying greater stability and more decent governance than it had known since the fall of Suharto, incumbent president Susilo Bambang Yudhoyono coasted to reelection with more than 60 percent of votes in July 2009, a few months after his once-small party nearly tripled its share of the legislative vote. In Ghana, by contrast, the ruling party was not so fortunate. After eight years in power, and with the incumbent stepping down, the New Patriotic Party suffered an excruciatingly narrow defeat at the hands of the old ruling party of former authoritarian strongman Jerry Rawlings. The economy was not the reason for this setback: Ghana was still enjoying some of its most prosperous times since independence. Rather, voters seemed to be reacting against the familiar problem of rising corruption and arrogance in power.

As election results piled up in 2010, the pattern of retrospective voting— of voters in emerging-market democracies holding ruling parties and leaders accountable for their performance—continued. In several instances, voters punished incumbents for poor performance. With Ukraine reeling from a disastrous economic plunge and incessant squabbling between the two predominant factions born of the 2004 Orange Revolution, both of them paid the price. President Viktor Yuschenko's reelection bid was swept aside with barely 5 percent of the vote, while his erstwhile ally Yulia Tymoshenko lost the runoff to pro-Russian former premier Viktor Yanukovich. In April 2010, Hungary's ruling Socialists suffered a crushing defeat following a year (2009) in which the economy shrank by more than 6 percent. The election came while popular outrage was still simmering over the September 2006 leak of an audiotape on which the Socialist prime minister could be heard avowing that his party had "lied in the morning, in the evening, and at night" about the state of the country's finances in order to win the April 2006 parliamentary elections. Similarly, voters in the Philippines had been itching for years to punish incumbent president Gloria Macapagal Arroyo for her abuses of power, including possible tampering with results from the previous presidential election. In this case, it did not matter that the country's economy had come roaring back after a sharp dip in growth in 2009; Benigno Aquino III, son of the late and revered President Corazon Aquino, won easily in a verdict widely interpreted as a rejection of Arroyo (who was not on the ballot). In September 2010, after years of economic mismanagement and creeping authoritarianism, Venezuelan voters dealt a stinging setback to President Hugo Chávez in midterm National Assembly elections. Had Chávez not grossly rigged the electoral rules, his party would have lost control of the legislature.

By contrast, Sri Lanka's President Rajapaksa was decisively reelected in early 2010 after defeating the Tamil Tigers and maintaining decent economic growth. This came in a political system that was descending into electoral authoritarianism, but Rajapaksa was nevertheless popular with voters because of his achievements. Later in the year, Colombian voters gave a similar reward for perceived success. Juan Manuel Santos, the successor to highly successful and popular but term-limited President Alvaro Uribe, won an electoral landslide by pledging to build on Uribe's achievements in stimulating economic growth and defeating *narcotraficantes* and left-wing insurgents. However, no instance of reflected gratitude was more profound than in Brazil, where, after eight years of vigorous economic growth, significant reductions in poverty, and rising international prestige, voters convincingly elected President Lula da Silva's designated successor Dilma Rousseff, who had never before held elective office.

The resilience of democratic accountability

What do we learn from this review of electoral politics in a time of global economic turmoil? If there is a common thread running through all these cases, it is the resilience of democratic politics. Voters punished incumbent leaders and parties who performed poorly, either because they were dragged down into the global economic undertow or because they had otherwise done a poor job of meeting voters' expectations for good governance, or perhaps for both reasons. In most cases where economic downturns were severe, with the growth rate in the election year plummeting by at least 7 percentage points (as happened in Bulgaria, Mexico,

Mongolia, Panama, and Ukraine), incumbents took a beating. The only ruling party that defied this trend was the rather unreconstructed Communist Party of Moldova, which probably rigged the vote—and even then it was punished badly just three months later. One could also cite the narrow reelection of Romania's incumbent president in late 2009, but that came in a semipresidential system where governing power had shifted to a different ruling coalition after parliamentary elections the previous year.

The summary data can be viewed in Table 5.3. I sort elections going back to the fourth quarter of 2008 into two outcomes: whether the incumbent party retained power (or gained legislative ground), or whether it lost power (or suffered a midterm defeat). In addition, I distinguish three groups in terms of the impact of the economic recession: modest impact, with economic growth declining (or estimated to have declined) in the

Table 5.3 Economic performance and the fate of incumbents, 2008–2010

	Economic growth declines <3%		Economic growth declines 3–7%		Economic growth declines >7%		Total
Incumbent victory	9	56%	3	38%	3	30%	15
Incumbent defeat or setback	7	44%	5	62%	7	70%	19
Total	16	100%	8	100%	10	100%	34
Incumbent victory	Indonesia, India, Bolivia, Sri Lanka, Mauritius, Dominican Republic, Colombia, Brazil, Slovakia (2010)		South Africa, Albania, Costa Rica		Slovakia (09), Moldova (4/09), Romania (09)		
Incumbent defeat or setback	Ghana, El Salvador, Trinidad and Tobago, Hungary, Philippines, Czech Republic, Venezuela		Lithuania, Macedonia, Argentina, Honduras, Chile		Panama, Mongolia, Moldova (7/09), Bulgaria, Croatia, Mexico, Ukraine		

A country is counted twice if it had elections in separate calendar years. If elections were held simultaneously or in the same calendar year, then it is counted once.

Poland's 2010 presidential election was not included in this Table as it is difficult to determine whether the incumbent was defeated. The Prime Minister ran against the brother of the late President and won. While the party of the late president was defeated, the ruling party (and candidate) of the ruling coalition won. It could thus be scored as an incumbent victory or defeat. Romania's 2008 parliamentary election is also ambiguous due to coalitional politics and was excluded.

election year by fewer than 3 percentage points from the previous year; moderate impact (a decline of 3 to 7 points); and severe impact, with growth declining from the previous year by more than 7 points.[20] In seven of the ten "severe-impact" cases, the incumbents lost (this becomes seven of nine if we eliminate Moldova's questionable April 2009 balloting). Where economic growth declined sharply but not as drastically, incumbents lost five of eight times. Where economic performance was good or least not as bad, incumbents won a majority of the time, and where they lost they were being punished for other performance failures. In general, democratic elections have performed as intended in times of economic distress, providing a safety valve that allows voters to punish incumbents while preserving the system as a whole.

This may seem to suggest a somewhat sanguine view of the health of most existing democracies, but it requires some qualification. First, it is likely that a deeper, longer, and more pervasive global economic recession (not to mention a global depression) would probably exact a far more serious toll from the world's vulnerable democracies. At a minimum, illiberal populist and even extremist political parties could be expected to draw many more voters, even in some of the postcommunist countries that have joined the European Union. In some of these countries, the principal obstacle in the way of democratic breakdown might then be the EU itself, with its political conditionality and its transfer payments to buffer economic dislocation and social pain. Elsewhere, in parts of Asia, Latin America, and Africa, the pace of democratic breakdowns would surely accelerate and possibly gather into a potent and undeniable reverse wave, driven not only by the spread of economic crisis but also by the much deeper symbolic loss of democratic prestige in an era—were it to come—in which the rich, established, capitalist democracies proved powerless to turn back the tide of economic misfortune.

Fortunately, there are growing signs that the United States is (slowly) emerging from its own encounter with economic recession, and the more seriously affected countries will probably follow it as global demand gradually increases. And many of the emerging-market democracies are now doing extremely well economically. But if the good news is that emerging democracies are weathering an economic storm that is not of their own making, the bad news is that they are too often staggering under the weight of governance problems that *are* largely rooted in their own deficient political institutions and norms. In the long run, these democracies will need to improve the quality of their state institutions (both democratic and bureaucratic)—to boost accountability and bolster the rule of law—if they are to become secure against future challenges both economic and political.

Notes

I am grateful for the excellent research assistance of Aayush Man Sakya and Nashat Moin on this chapter.

1 Originally published as "Why Democracies Survive," *Journal of Democracy* 22 (January 2011): 17–30. Portions of that article have been deleted as they are superseded by the data and analysis in the previous chapter.
2 Seymour Martin Lipset, *Political Man: The Social Bases of Politics* (Baltimore, MD: Johns Hopkins University Press, 1981 [1960]), 68–70.
3 Samuel P. Huntington, *The Third Wave: Democratization in the Late Twentieth Century* (Norman: University of Oklahoma Press, 1991), 17–18.
4 Adam Przeworski, Michael E. Alvarez, José Antonio Cheibub, and Fernando Limongi, *Democracy and Development: Political Institutions and Well-Being in the World, 1950–1990* (New York: Cambridge University Press, 2000), 109.
5 Ibid., 11. More recently, with a different data set (covering 1960 through 2004) and methodology, Ethan Kapstein and Nathan Converse have found a similar effect for young and therefore fragile democracies: Higher GDP growth, particularly averaging over five years, "is significantly associated with a reduced probability of democratic reversal." *The Fate of Young Democracies* (New York: Cambridge University Press, 2008), 60.
6 That is the implication of the findings of both Przerworski et al. and Kapstein and Converse. As the latter show, for example, older and more economically developed democracies have greater ability to withstand the negative effects of poor economic performance.
7 In the original published version of this article, the table included four other cases of democratic breakdown: Kyrgyzstan in 2000, Nigeria in 2003, Mauritania in 2008, and Mozambique in 2009. In preparation for this book, I removed each of these cases, concluding that none of the prior regimes had met the test of electoral democracy.
8 And in these cases it is hard to distinguish cause from effect. It is possible that the sudden implosion of political stability might have contributed to the economic downturn (via the familiar route of loss of investor confidence).
9 The explanation for these measures of governance can be found in Daniel Kaufmann, Aart Kraay, and Massimo Mastruzzi, "Governance Matters VIII: Aggregate and Individual Governance Indicators, 1996–2008," World Bank Policy Research Working Paper No. 4978, June 29, 2009, http://papers.ssrn.com/sol3/papers.cfm?abstract_id=1424591#.
10 Kapstein and Converse, *Fate of Young Democracies*, 68.
11 As of October 2009, the IMF expected these economies to record positive per capita income growth in 2009, with overall GDP growth generally expected to top 4 percent in 2009 and perhaps hit 5 percent in 2010.
12 This counts both presidential and parliamentary election results in semipresidential systems such as Slovakia, but not concurrent or midterm legislative results in presidential systems such as those of Mexico or Venezuela. See Table 5.2 for more on the criteria for the elections included in this count.
13 This excludes a small number of elections in this period where it is difficult to interpret who the incumbent was or what fate they met, as in Poland's 2010 presidential election, or Bangladesh, which was returning to democracy after two years of military rule.
14 "Bulgaria Opposition Wins Election," BBC News, July 6, 2009, http://news.bbc.co.uk/2/hi/8134851.stm.

15 "Panama Election: Supermarket Millionaire Ricardo Martinelli Wins Presidency," *Telegraph* (London), May 4, 2009, www.telegraph.co.uk/news/worldnews/centralamericaandthecaribbean/panama/5270318/Panama-election-supermarket-millionaire-Ricardo-Martinelli-wins-presidency.html.

16 Alina Mungiu-Pippidi and Igor Munteanu, "Moldova's 'Twitter Revolution,'" *Journal of Democracy* 20 (July 2009): 136–142.

17 "Billionaire Beats Rivals in Chile's Presidential Election," CBC News, December 13, 2009, www.cbc.ca/world/story/2009/12/13/chile-election.html?ref=rss.

18 Forrest D. Colburn, "The Turnover in El Salvador," *Journal of Democracy* 20 (July 2009): 146.

19 Ibid., 144, 143.

20 For elections in the first quarter of a year, I took the economic-growth rate from the preceding year. If I had also done that for Hungary regarding its April 2010 elections, the results in Table 5.3 would have been even more striking, as the ruling party would have lost in a climate of sharp economic decline.

6 Civil society and democratic consolidation[1]

In this third wave of global democratization, no phenomenon has more vividly captured the imagination of democratic scholars, observers, and activists alike than "civil society." What could be more moving than the stories of brave bands of students, writers, artists, pastors, teachers, laborers, and mothers challenging the duplicity, corruption, and brutal domination of authoritarian states? Could any sight be more awe-inspiring to democrats than the one they saw in Manila in 1986, when hundreds of thousands of organized and peaceful citizens surged into the streets to reclaim their stolen election and force Ferdinand Marcos out through nonviolent "people power"?

In fact, however, the overthrow of authoritarian regimes through popularly based and massively mobilized democratic opposition has not been the norm. Most democratic transitions have been protracted and negotiated (if not largely controlled from above by the exiting authoritarians). Yet even in such negotiated and controlled transitions, the stimulus for democratization, and particularly the pressure to complete the process, have typically come from the "resurrection of civil society," the restructuring of public space, and the mobilization of all manner of independent groups and grassroots movements.[2]

If the renewed interest in civil society can trace its theoretical origins to Alexis de Tocqueville, it seems emotionally and spiritually indebted to Jean-Jacques Rousseau for its romanticization of "the people" as a force for collective good, rising up to assert the democratic will against a narrow and evil autocracy. Such images of popular mobilization suffuse contemporary thinking about democratic change throughout Asia, Latin America, Eastern Europe, and Africa—and not without reason.

In South Korea, Taiwan, Chile, Poland, China, Czechoslovakia, South Africa, Nigeria, and Benin (to give only a partial list), extensive mobilization of civil society was a crucial source of pressure for democratic change. Citizens pressed their challenge to autocracy not merely as individuals, but as members of student movements, churches, professional associations, women's groups, trade unions, human rights organizations, producer groups, the press, civic associations, and the like.

It is now clear that to comprehend democratic change around the world, one must study civil society. Yet such study often provides a one-dimensional and dangerously misleading view. Understanding civil society's role in the construction of democracy requires more complex conceptualization and nuanced theory. The simplistic antinomy between state and civil society, locked in a zero-sum struggle, will not do. We need to specify more precisely what civil society is and is not, and to identify its wide variations in form and character. We need to comprehend not only the multiple ways it can serve democracy, but also the tensions and contradictions it generates and may encompass. We need to think about the features of civil society that are most likely to serve the development and consolidation of democracy. And, not least, we need to form a more realistic picture of the limits of civil society's potential contributions to democracy, and thus of the relative emphasis that democrats should place on building civil society among the various challenges of democratic consolidation.

What civil society is and is not

Civil society is conceived here as the *realm of organized social life that is voluntary, self-generating, (largely) self-supporting, autonomous from the state, and bound by a legal order or set of shared rules.* It is distinct from "society" in general in that it involves citizens *acting collectively in a public sphere* to express their interests, passions, and ideas, exchange information, achieve mutual goals, make demands on the state, and hold state officials accountable. Civil society is an intermediary entity, standing between the private sphere and the state. Thus it excludes individual and family life, inward-looking group activity (for example, for recreation, entertainment, or spirituality), the profit-making enterprise of individual business firms, and political efforts to take control of the state. Actors in civil society need the protection of an institutionalized legal order to guard their autonomy and freedom of action. Thus civil society not only restricts state power but legitimates state authority when that authority is based on the rule of law. When the state itself is lawless and contemptuous of individual and group autonomy, civil society may still exist (albeit in tentative or battered form) if its constituent elements operate by some set of shared rules (which, for example, eschew violence and respect pluralism). This is the irreducible condition of its "civil" dimension.[3]

Civil society encompasses a vast array of organizations, formal and informal. These include groups that are:

1   *economic* (productive and commercial associations and networks);
2   *cultural* (religious, ethnic, communal, and other institutions and associations that defend collective rights, values, faiths, beliefs, and symbols);
3   *informational and educational* (devoted to the production and dissemination—whether for profit or not—of public knowledge, ideas, news, and information);

4   *interest-based* (designed to advance or defend the common functional or material interests of their members, whether workers, veterans, pensioners, professionals, or the like);

5   *developmental* (organizations that combine individual resources to improve the infrastructure, institutions, and quality of life of the community);

6   *issue-oriented* (movements for environmental protection, women's rights, land reform, or consumer protection); and

7   *civic* (seeking in nonpartisan fashion to improve the political system and make it more democratic through human rights monitoring, voter education and mobilization, poll-watching, anticorruption efforts, and so on).

In addition, civil society encompasses "the ideological marketplace" and the flow of information and ideas. This includes not only independent mass media but also institutions belonging to the broader field of autonomous cultural and intellectual activity—universities, think tanks, publishing houses, theaters, film production companies, and artistic networks.

From the above, it should be clear that civil society is not some mere residual category, synonymous with "society" or with everything that is not the state or the formal political system. Beyond being voluntary, self-generating, autonomous, and rule abiding, the organizations of civil society are distinct from other social groups in several respects. First, as emphasized above, civil society is concerned with *public* rather than private ends. Second, civil society *relates to the state* in some way but does not aim to win formal power or office in the state. Rather, civil society organizations seek from the state concessions, benefits, policy changes, relief, redress, or accountability. Civic organizations and social movements that try to change the nature of the state may still qualify as parts of civil society if their efforts stem from concern for the public good and not from a desire to capture state power for the group per se. Thus peaceful movements for democratic transition typically spring from civil society.

A third distinguishing mark is that civil society encompasses *pluralism* and diversity. To the extent that an organization—such as a religious fundamentalist, ethnic chauvinist, revolutionary, or millenarian movement—seeks to monopolize a functional or political space in society, claiming that it represents the only legitimate path, it contradicts the pluralistic and market-oriented nature of civil society. Related to this is a fourth distinction, *partialness*, signifying that no group in civil society seeks to represent the whole of a person's or a community's interests. Rather, different groups represent different interests.

Civil society is distinct and autonomous not only from the state and society at large but also from a fourth arena of social action, *political society* (meaning, in essence, the party system). Organizations and networks in civil society may form alliances with parties, but if they become captured by parties, or hegemonic within them, they thereby move their primary locus of activity to political society and lose much of their ability to perform certain unique mediating and democracy-building functions. I want now to examine these functions more closely.

The democratic functions of civil society

The first and most basic democratic function of civil society is to provide "the basis for the limitation of state power, hence for the control of the state by society, and hence for democratic political institutions as the most effective means of exercising that control."[4] This function has two dimensions: to monitor and restrain the exercise of power by democratic states, and to democratize authoritarian states. Mobilizing civil society is a major means of exposing the abuses and undermining the legitimacy of undemocratic regimes. This is the function, performed so dramatically in so many democratic transitions over the past two decades, that has catapulted civil society to the forefront of thinking about democracy. Yet this thinking revives the eighteenth-century idea of civil society as *in opposition* to the state and, as I will show, has its dangers if taken too far.[5]

Civil society is also a vital instrument for containing the power of democratic governments, checking their potential abuses and violations of the law, and subjecting them to public scrutiny. Indeed, a vibrant civil society is probably more essential for consolidating and maintaining democracy than for initiating it. Few developments are more destructive to the legitimacy of new democracies than blatant and pervasive political corruption, particularly during periods of painful economic restructuring when many groups and individuals are asked to sustain great hardships. New democracies, following long periods of arbitrary and statist rule, lack the legal and bureaucratic means to contain corruption at the outset. Without a free, robust, and inquisitive press and civic groups to press for institutional reform, corruption is likely to flourish.

Second, a rich associational life supplements the role of political parties in stimulating political participation, increasing the political efficacy and skill of democratic citizens, and promoting an appreciation of the obligations as well as the rights of democratic citizenship. For too many Americans (barely half of whom vote in presidential elections), this now seems merely a quaint homily. A century and a half ago, however, the voluntary participation of citizens in all manner of associations outside the state struck Tocqueville as a pillar of democratic culture and economic vitality in the young United States. Voluntary "associations may therefore be considered as large free schools, where all the members of the community go to learn the general theory of association," he wrote.[6]

Third, civil society can also be a crucial arena for the development of other democratic attributes such as tolerance, moderation, willingness to compromise, and respect for opposing viewpoints. These values and norms become most stable when they emerge through experience, and organizational participation in civil society provides important practice in political advocacy and contestation. In addition, many civic organizations (such as Conciencia, a network of women's organizations that began in Argentina and has since spread to 14 other Latin American countries) are working directly in schools and among groups of adult citizens to develop these elements of democratic culture through interactive programs that demonstrate the dynamics of reaching consensus in a group, the possibility for respectful debate between competing viewpoints, and the means by which people can cooperate to solve the problems of their own communities.[7]

A fourth way in which civil society may serve democracy is by creating channels other than political parties for the articulation, aggregation, and representation of interests. This function is particularly important for providing traditionally excluded groups—such as women and racial or ethnic minorities—access to power that has been denied them in the "upper institutional echelons" of formal politics. Even where (as in South America) women have played, through various movements and organizations, prominent roles in mobilizing against authoritarian rule, democratic politics and governance after transitions have typically reverted to previous exclusionary patterns. In Eastern Europe, there are many signs of deterioration in the political and social status of women posttransition. Only with sustained, organized pressure from below, in civil society, can political and social equality be advanced, and the quality, responsiveness, and legitimacy of democracy thus be deepened.[8]

Civil society provides an especially strong foundation for democracy when it generates opportunities for participation and influence at all levels of governance, not least the local level. For it is at the local level that the historically marginalized are most likely to be able to affect public policy and to develop a sense of efficacy as well as actual political skills. The democratization of local government thus goes hand in hand with the development of civil society as an important condition for the deepening of democracy and the "transition from clientelism to citizenship" in Latin America, as well as elsewhere in the developing and postcommunist worlds.[9]

Fifth, a richly pluralistic civil society, particularly in a relatively developed economy, will tend to generate a wide range of interests that may crosscut, and so mitigate, the principal polarities of political conflict. As new class-based organizations and issue-oriented movements arise, they draw together new constituencies that cut across long-standing regional, religious, ethnic, or partisan cleavages. In toppling communist (and other) dictatorships and mobilizing for democracy, these new formations may generate a modern type of citizenship that transcends historic divisions and contains the resurgence of narrow nationalist impulses. To the extent that individuals have multiple interests and join a wide variety of organizations to pursue and advance those interests, they will be more likely to associate with different types of people who have divergent political interests and opinions. These attitudinal cross-pressures will tend to soften the militancy of their own views, generate a more expansive and sophisticated political outlook, and so encourage tolerance for differences and a greater readiness to compromise.

A sixth function of a democratic civil society is recruiting and training new political leaders. In a few cases, this is a deliberate purpose of civic organizations. The Evelio B. Javier Foundation in the Philippines, for instance, offers training programs on a nonpartisan basis to local and state elected officials and candidates, emphasizing not only technical and administrative skills, but normative standards of public accountability and transparency.[10] More often, recruitment and training are merely a long-term byproduct of the successful functioning of civil society organizations as their leaders and activists gain skills and self-confidence that qualify them well for service in government and party politics. They learn how to organize and motivate people, debate issues, raise and account for funds, craft budgets, publicize programs, administer staffs, canvass for support, negotiate agreements, and build coalitions. At the same time, their work on behalf of their constituency, or of what they see to be the public interest, and their articulation of clear and compelling policy alternatives, may gain for them a wider political following. Interest groups, social movements, and community efforts of various kinds may therefore train, toughen, and thrust into public notice a richer (and more representative) array of potential new political leaders than might otherwise be recruited by political parties. Because of the traditional dominance by men of the corridors of power, civil society is a particularly important base for the training and recruitment of women (and members of other marginalized groups) into positions of formal political power. Where the recruitment of new political leaders within the established political parties has become narrow or stagnant, this function of civil society may play a crucial role in revitalizing democracy and renewing its legitimacy.

Seventh, many civic organizations have explicit democracy-building purposes that go beyond leadership training. Nonpartisan election-monitoring efforts have been critical in deterring fraud, enhancing voter confidence, affirming the legitimacy of the result, or in some cases (as in the Philippines in 1986 and Panama in 1989) demonstrating an opposition victory despite government fraud. This function is particularly crucial in founding elections like those which initiated democracy in Chile, Nicaragua, Bulgaria, Zambia, and South Africa. Democracy institutes and think tanks are working in a number of countries to reform the electoral system, democratize political parties, decentralize and open up government, strengthen the legislature, and enhance governmental accountability. And even after the transition, human rights organizations continue to play a vital role in the pursuit of judicial and legal reform, improved prison conditions, and greater institutionalized respect for individual liberties and minority rights.

Eighth, a vigorous civil society widely disseminates information, thus aiding citizens in the collective pursuit and defense of their interests and values. While civil society groups may sometimes prevail temporarily by dint of raw numbers (for example, in strikes and demonstrations), they generally cannot be effective in contesting government policies or defending their interests unless they are well-informed. This is strikingly true in debates over military and national security policy, where civilians in developing countries have generally been woefully lacking in even the most elementary knowledge. A free press is only one vehicle for providing the public with a wealth of news and alternative perspectives. Independent organizations may also give citizens hard-won information about government activities that does not depend on what government *says* it is doing. This is a vital technique of human rights organizations: by contradicting the official story, they make it more difficult to cover up repression and abuses of power.

The spread of new information and ideas is essential to the achievement of economic reform in a democracy, and this is a ninth function that civil society can play. While economic stabilization policies typically must be implemented quickly, forcefully, and unilaterally by elected executives in crisis situations, more structural economic reforms—privatization, trade, and financial liberalization—appear to be more sustainable and far-reaching (or in many postcommunist countries, only feasible) when they are pursued through the democratic process.

Successful economic reform requires the support of political coalitions in society and the legislature. Such coalitions are not spontaneous; they must be fashioned. Here the problem is not so much the scale, autonomy, and resources of civil society as it is their distribution across interests. Old, established interests that stand to lose from reform tend to be organized into formations like state-sector trade unions and networks that tie the managers of state enterprises or owners of favored industries to ruling party bosses. These are precisely the interests that stand to lose from economic reforms that close down inefficient industries, reduce state intervention, and open the economy to greater domestic and international competition. The newer and more diffuse interests that stand to gain from reform—for example, farmers, small-scale entrepreneurs, and consumers—tend to be weakly organized and poorly informed about how new policies will ultimately affect them. In Asia, Latin America, and Eastern Europe, new actors in civil society—such as economic-policy think tanks, chambers of commerce, and economically literate journalists, commentators, and television producers—are beginning to overcome the barriers to information and organization, mobilizing support for (and neutralizing resistance to) reform policies.

Finally, there is a tenth function of civil society—to which I have already referred—that derives from the success of the above nine. "Freedom of association," Tocqueville mused, may, "after having agitated society for some time ... strengthen the state in the end."[11] By enhancing the accountability, responsiveness, inclusiveness, effectiveness, and hence legitimacy of the political system, a vigorous civil society gives citizens respect for the state and positive engagement with it. In the end, this improves the ability of the state to govern, and to command voluntary obedience from its citizens. In addition, a rich associational life can do more than just multiply demands on the state; it may also multiply the capacities of groups to improve their own welfare, independently of the state. Effective grassroots development efforts may thus help to relieve the burden of expectations fixed on the state, and so lower the stakes of politics, especially at the national level.

Features of a democratic civil society

Not all civil societies and civil society organizations have the same potential to perform the democracy-building functions cited above. Their ability to do so depends on several features of their internal structure and character. One concerns the goals and methods of groups in civil society. The chances to develop stable democracy improve significantly if civil society does not contain maximalist, uncompromising interest groups or groups with anti-democratic goals and methods. To the extent that a group seeks to conquer the state or other competitors, or rejects the rule of law and the authority of the democratic state, it is not a component of civil society at all, and may do much damage to democratic aspirations. Powerful, militant interest groups pull parties toward populist and extreme political promises, polarizing the party system, and are more likely to induce state repression that may have a broad and indiscriminate character, weakening or radicalizing the more democratic elements of civil society.

A second important feature of civil society is its level of organizational institutionalization. As with political parties, institutionalized interest groups contribute to the stability, predictability, and governability of a democratic regime. Where interests are organized in a structured, stable manner, bargaining and the growth of cooperative networks are facilitated. Social forces do not face the continual cost of setting up new structures. And if the organization expects to continue to operate in the society over a sustained period of time, its leaders will have more reason to be account-able and responsive to their constituency, and may take a longer-range view of the group's interests and policy goals, rather than seeking to maximize short-term benefits in an uncompromising manner.

Third, the internally democratic character of civil society itself affects the degree to which it can socialize participants into democratic—or undemo-cratic—forms of behavior. If the groups and organizations that make up civil society are to function as "large free schools" for democracy, they must function democratically in their internal processes of decision-making and leadership selection. Constitutionalism, representation, transparency, accountability, and rotation of elected leaders within autonomous associa-tions will greatly enhance the ability of these associations to inculcate such democratic values and practices in their members.

Fourth, the more pluralistic civil society can become without fragmenting, the more democracy will benefit. Some degree of pluralism is necessary by definition for civil society. Pluralism helps groups in civil society survive, and encourages them to learn to cooperate and negotiate with one another. Pluralism within a given sector, like labor or human rights, has a number of additional beneficial effects. For one, it makes that sector less vulnerable (though at the possible cost of weakening its bargaining power); the loss or repression of one organization does not mean the end of all organized representation. Competition can also help to ensure accountability and representativeness by giving members the ability to bolt to other organizations if their own does not perform.

Finally, civil society serves democracy best when it is dense, affording individuals opportunities to participate in multiple associations and informal networks at multiple levels of society. The more associations there are in civil society, the more likely it is that they will develop specialized agendas and purposes that do not seek to swallow the lives of their members in one all-encompassing organizational framework. Multiple memberships also tend to reflect and reinforce crosscutting patterns of cleavage.

Some important caveats

To the above list of democratic functions of civil society we must add some important caveats. To begin with, associations and mass media can perform their democracy-building roles only if they have at least some autonomy from the state in their financing, operations, and legal standing. To be sure, there are markedly different ways of organizing the representation of interests in a democracy. Pluralist systems encompass "multiple, voluntary, competitive, nonhierarchically ordered and self-determined [interest associations] which are not specially licensed, recognized, subsidized, created or otherwise controlled ... by the state." Corporatist systems, by contrast, have "singular, noncompetitive, hierarchically ordered, sectorally compartmentalized, interest associations exercising representational monopolies and accepting (de jure or de facto) governmentally imposed limitations on the type of leaders they elect and on the scope and intensity of demands they routinely make upon the state."[12] A number of northern European countries have operated a corporatist system of interest representation while functioning successfully as democracies (at times even better, economically and politically, than their pluralist counterparts). Although corporatist arrangements are eroding in many established democracies, important differences remain in the degree to which interest groups are competitive, pluralistic, compartmentalized, hierarchically ordered, and so on.

While corporatist-style pacts or contracts between the state and peak interest associations may make for stable macroeconomic management, corporatist arrangements pose a serious threat to democracy in transitional or newly emerging constitutional regimes. The risk appears greatest in countries with a history of authoritarian *state corporatism*—such as Mexico, Egypt, and Indonesia—where the state has created, organized, licensed, funded, subordinated, and controlled "interest" groups (and also most of the mass media that it does not officially own and control), with a view to co-optation, repression, and domination rather than ordered bargaining. By contrast, the transition to a democratic form of corporatism "seems to depend very much on a liberal-pluralist past," which most developing and postcommunist states lack.[13] A low level of economic development or the absence of a fully functioning market economy increases the danger that corporatism will stifle civil society even under a formally democratic framework, because there are fewer autonomous resources and organized interests in society.

By co-opting, preempting, or constraining the most serious sources of potential challenge to its domination (and thus minimizing the amount of actual repression that has to be employed), a state-corporatist regime may purchase a longer lease on authoritarian life. Such regimes, however, eventually come under pressure from social, economic, and demographic forces. Successful socioeconomic development, as in Mexico and Indonesia, produces a profusion of authentic civil society groups that demand political freedom under law. Alternatively, social and economic decay, along with massive political corruption, weakens the hold of the authoritarian corporatist state, undermines the legitimacy of its sponsored associations, and may give rise to revolutionary movements like the Islamic fundamentalist fronts in Egypt and Algeria, which promise popular redemption through a new form of state hegemony.

Societal autonomy can go too far, however, even for the purposes of democracy. The need for *limits* on autonomy is a second caveat; paired with the first, it creates a major tension in democratic development. A hyperactive, confrontational, and relentlessly rent-seeking civil society can overwhelm a weak, penetrated state with the diversity and magnitude of its demands, leaving little in the way of a truly "public" sector concerned with the overall welfare of society. The state itself must have sufficient autonomy, legitimacy, capacity, and support to mediate among the various interest groups and balance their claims. This is a particularly pressing dilemma for new democracies seeking to implement much-needed economic reforms in the face of stiff opposition from trade unions, pensioners, and the state-protected bourgeoisie, which is why countervailing forces in civil society must be educated and mobilized, as I have argued above. In many new democracies there is a deeper problem, stemming from the origins of civil society in profoundly angry, risky, and even anomic protest against a decadent, abusive state. This problem is what the Cameroonian economist Célestin Monga calls the "civic deficit":

> Thirty years of authoritarian rule have forged a concept of indiscipline as a method of popular resistance. In order to survive and resist laws and rules judged to be antiquated, people have had to resort to the treasury of their imagination. Given that life is one long fight against the state, the collective imagination has gradually conspired to craftily defy everything which symbolizes public authority.[14]

In many respects, a similar broad cynicism, indiscipline, and alienation from state authority—indeed from politics altogether—was bred by decades of communist rule in Eastern Europe and the former Soviet Union, though it led to somewhat different (and in Poland, much more broadly organized) forms of dissidence and resistance. Some countries, like Poland, Hungary, the Czech Republic, Slovakia, and the Baltic states, had previous civic traditions that could be recovered. These countries have generally made the most progress (though still quite partial) toward reconstructing state authority on a democratic foundation while beginning to constitute a modern, liberal-pluralist civil society. Those states where civic traditions were weakest and predatory role greatest—Romania, Russia, the post-Soviet republics of Central Asia, and most of Sub-Saharan Africa—face a far more difficult time, with civil societies still fragmented and emergent market economies still heavily outside the framework of law.

This civic deficit points to a third major caveat with respect to the positive value of civil society for democracy. Civil society must be autonomous from the state, but not alienated from it. It must be watchful but respectful of state authority. The image of a noble, vigilant, organized civil society checking at every turn the predations of a self-serving state, preserving a pure detachment from its corrupting embrace, is highly romanticized and of little use in the construction of a viable democracy.

A fourth caveat concerns the role of politics. Interest groups cannot substitute for coherent political parties with broad and relatively enduring bases of popular support. For interest groups cannot aggregate interests as broadly across social groups and political issues as political parties can. Nor can they provide the discipline necessary to form and maintain governments and pass legislation. In this respect (and not only this one), one may question the thesis that a strong civil society is strictly complementary to the political and state structures of democracy. To the extent that interest groups dominate, enervate, or crowd out political parties as conveyors and aggregators of interests, they can present a problem for democratic consolidation. To Barrington Moore's famous thesis, "No bourgeois, no democracy," we can add a corollary: "No coherent party system, no stable democracy." And in an age when the electronic media, increased mobility, and the profusion and fragmentation of discrete interests are all undermining the organizational bases for strong parties and party systems, this is something that democrats everywhere need to worry about.[15]

Democratic consolidation

In fact, a stronger and broader generalization appears warranted: the single most important and urgent factor in the consolidation of democracy is not civil society but political institutionalization. *Consolidation* is the process by which democracy becomes so broadly and profoundly legitimate among its citizens that it is very unlikely to break down. It involves behavioral and institutional changes that normalize democratic politics and narrow its uncertainty. This normalization requires the expansion of citizen access, development of democratic citizenship and culture, broadening of leadership recruitment and training, and other functions that civil society performs. But most of all, and most urgently, it requires political institutionalization.

Despite their impressive capacity to survive years (in some cases, a decade or more) of social strife and economic instability and decline, many new democracies in Latin America, Eastern Europe, Asia, and Africa will probably break down in the medium to long run unless they can reduce their often appalling levels of poverty, inequality, and social injustice and, through market-oriented reforms, lay the basis for sustainable growth. For these and other policy challenges, not only strong parties but effective state institutions are vital. They do not guarantee wise and effective policies, but they at least ensure that government will be able to make and implement policies of some kind, rather than simply flailing about, impotent or deadlocked.

Robust political institutions are needed to accomplish economic reform under democratic conditions. Strong, well-structured executives, buttressed by experts at least somewhat insulated from the day-to-day pressures of politics, make possible the implementation of painful and disruptive reform measures. Settled and aggregative (as opposed to volatile and fragmented) party systems—in which one or two broadly based, centrist parties consistently obtain electoral majorities or near-majorities—are better positioned to resist narrow class and sectoral interests and to maintain the continuity of economic reforms across successive administrations. Effective legislatures may sometimes obstruct reforms, but if they are composed of strong, coherent parties with centrist tendencies, in the end they will do more to reconcile democracy and economic reform by providing a political base of support and some means for absorbing and mediating protests in society. Finally, autonomous, professional, and well-staffed judicial systems are indispensable for securing the rule of law.

These caveats are sobering, but they do not nullify my principal thesis. Civil society can, and typically must, play a significant role in building and consolidating democracy. Its role is not decisive or even the most important, at least initially. However, the more active, pluralistic, resourceful, institutionalized, and democratic is civil society, and the more effectively it balances the tensions in its relations with the state—between autonomy and cooperation, vigilance and loyalty, skepticism and trust, assertiveness and civility—the more likely it is that democracy will emerge and endure.

Notes

This essay evolved from a two-year research project on "Economy, Society, and Democracy" supported by the Agency for International Development, and from lectures and conference papers presented at the Kennedy School of Government, the Gorée Institute in Senegal, the Human Sciences Research Council in South Africa, and the Institute for a Democratic Alternative, also in South Africa. I am grateful to all those who made comments at these gatherings, as well as to Kathleen Bruhn for research assistance on an earlier draft.

1 Originally published as "Rethinking Civil Society: Toward Democratic Consolidation," *Journal of Democracy* 5 (July 1994): 4–17.
2 Guillermo O'Donnell and Philippe C. Schmitter, *Transitions from Authoritarian Rule: Tentative Conclusions about Uncertain Democracies* (Baltimore, MD: Johns Hopkins University Press, 1986), ch. 5.
3 This conceptual formulation draws from a number of sources but has been especially influenced by Naomi Chazan. See in particular Chazan, "Africa's Democratic Challenge: Strengthening Civil Society and the State," *Worm Policy Journal* 9 (Spring 1992): 279–308. See also Edward Shils, "The Virtue of Civil Society," *Government and Opposition* 26 (Winter 1991): 9–10, 15–16; Peter Lewis, "Political Transition and the Dilemma of Civil Society in Africa," *Journal of International Affairs* 27 (Summer 1992): 31–54; Marcia A. Weigle and Jim Butterfield, "Civil Society in Reforming Communist Regimes: The Logic of Emergence," *Comparative Politics* 25 (October 1992): 3–4; and Philippe C. Schmitter, "Some Propositions about Civil Society and the Consolidation of Democracy," *HIS Reihe Politikwissenschaft* 10 (September 1993).
4 Samuel P. Huntington, "Will More Countries Become Democratic?" *Political Science Quarterly* 99 (Summer 1984): 204. See also Seymour Martin Lipset, *Political Man* (Baltimore, MD: Johns Hopkins University Press, 1981), 52.
5 Bronislaw Geremek, "Civil Society Then and Now," *Journal of Democracy* 3 (April 1992): 3–12.
6 Alexis de Tocqueville, *Democracy in America,* 2 vols. (New York: Vintage Books, 1945 [1840]), vol. 2, p. 124.
7 Marfa Rosa de Martini and Soffa de Pinedo, "Women and Civic Life in Argentina," *Journal of Democracy* 3 (July 1992): 138–146; and Maria Rosa de Martini, "Civic Participation in the Argentine Democratic Process," in Larry Diamond, ed., *The Democratic Revolution: Struggles for Freedom and Pluralism in the Developing World* (New York: Freedom House, 1992), 29–52.
8 Georgina Waylen, "Women and Democratization: Conceptualizing Gender Relations in Transition Politics," *World Politics* 46 (April 1994): 327–354. Although Waylen is correct that O'Donnell and Schmitter speak to the dangers of excessive popular mobilization during the transition, her criticism of the democracy literature as a whole for trivializing the role of civil society is unfairly overgeneralized and certainly inapplicable to work on Africa. Moreover, accepting her challenge to treat civil society as a centrally important phenomenon in democratization does not require one to accept her insistence on *defining* democracy to include economic and social fights as well as political ones.
9 Jonathan Fox, "Latin America's Emerging Local Politics," *Journal of Democracy* 5 (April 1994): 114.

10 Dette Pascual, "Organizing People Power in the Philippines," *Journal of Democracy* 1 (Winter 1990): 102–109.
11 Tocqueville, *Democracy in America,* vol. 2, p. 126.
12 Philippe C. Schmitter, "Still the Century of Corporatism?" in Wolfgang Streeck and Schmitter, eds, *Private Interest Government: Beyond Market and State* (Beverly Hills, CA: Sage Publications, 1984), 96, 99–100.
13 Ibid., 126. See ibid., 102–108 for the important distinction between societal (democratic) and state corporatism.
14 Célestin Monga, "Civil Society and Democratization in Francophone Africa," paper delivered at Harvard University, 1994, and now available in the same author's French-language work, *Anthropologie de la colère: Societé et démocratie en Afrique Noire* (Paris: L'Harmattan, 1994).
15 Juan J. Linz, "Change and Continuity in the Nature of Contemporary Democracies," in Gary Marks and Larry Diamond, eds, *Reexamining Democracy: Essays in Honor of Seymour Martin Lipset* (Newbury Park, CA: Sage Publications, 1992), 184–190.

7   Liberation technology[1]

In March 2003, police in Guangzhou (Canton), China, stopped 27-year-old Sun Zhigang and demanded to see his temporary living permit and identification. When he could not produce these, he was sent to a detention center. Three days later, he died in its infirmary. The cause of death was recorded as a heart attack, but the autopsy authorized by his parents showed that he had been subjected to a brutal beating.

Sun's parents took his story to the liberal newspaper *Nanfang Dushi Bao* (Southern Metropolis Daily), and its investigation confirmed that Sun had been beaten to death in custody. As soon as its report appeared on April 25, "newspapers and Web sites throughout China republished the account, [Internet] chat rooms and bulletin boards exploded with outrage," and it quickly became a national story.[2] The central government was forced to launch its own investigation and on June 27, it found 12 people guilty of Sun's death.

Sun's case was a rare instance in China of official wrongdoing being exposed and punished. But it had a much wider and more lasting impact, provoking national debate about the "custody and repatriation" (C&R) measures that allowed the police to detain rural migrants (typically in appalling conditions) for lacking a residency or temporary-living permit. In the outrage following Sun's death, numerous Chinese citizens posted on the Internet stories of their own experiences of C&R, and the constitutionality of the legislation became a hotly debated topic in universities. An online petition asking the Standing Committee of the National People's Congress to reexamine C&R quickly garnered widespread popular support, and in June 2003 the government announced it would close all of the more than 800 C&R detention centers.[3]

Sun's case was seen as a watershed—the first time that a peaceful outpouring of public opinion had forced the communist Chinese state to change a national regulation. But it also soon became the case of muckraking editor Cheng Yizhong, whom local officials jailed (along with three of his colleagues) in retaliation for their efforts to ferret out the wrongdoing that led to Sun's death. The legal defense that Xu Zhiyong mounted on behalf of the four journalists itself became a *cause célèbre*. As their fellow journalists launched an unprecedented campaign for their release, using among other means an Internet petition, Xu established a website, the Open Constitutional Initiative, to post documents and legal arguments about the case. All of this reflected a burgeoning *weiquan* ("defend-rights") movement. But while Cheng and his deputy editor were released from prison without charge, they lost their jobs and the authorities closed down Xu's site. Xu continued his work in defense of rights until July of last year, when his organization was shut down and he was arrested on politically motivated charges of tax evasion.

Optimists discern in these events a striking ability of the Internet—and other forms of "liberation technology"—to empower individuals, facilitate independent communication and mobilization, and strengthen an emergent civil society. Pessimists argue that nothing in China has fundamentally changed. The Chinese Communist Party (CCP) remains firmly in control and beyond accountability. The *weiquan* movement has been crushed. And the Chinese state has developed an unparalleled system of digital censorship.

Both perspectives have merit. Liberation technology enables citizens to report news, expose wrongdoing, express opinions, mobilize protest, monitor elections, scrutinize government, deepen participation, and expand the horizons of freedom. But authoritarian states such as China, Belarus, and Iran have acquired (and shared) impressive technical capabilities to filter and control the Internet, and to identify and punish dissenters. Democrats and autocrats now compete to master these technologies. Ultimately, however, not just technology but political organization and strategy and deep-rooted normative, social, and economic forces will determine who "wins" the race.

New era or false hope?

Liberation technology is any form of information and communication technology (ICT) that can expand political, social, and economic freedom. In the contemporary era, it means essentially the modern, interrelated forms of digital ICT—the computer, the Internet, the mobile phone, and countless innovative applications for them, including "new social media" such as Facebook and Twitter. Digital ICT has some exciting advantages over earlier technologies. The Internet's decentralized character and ability (along with mobile-phone networks) to reach large numbers of people very quickly are well suited to grassroots organizing. In sharp contrast to radio and television, the new ICTs are two-way and even multiway forms of communication; with tools such as Twitter (a social-networking and micro-blogging service allowing its users to send and read messages with up to 140 characters), a user can instantly reach hundreds or even thousands of "followers." Users are thus not just passive recipients but journalists, commentators, videographers, entertainers, and organizers. Although most of this use is not political, the technology can empower those who wish to become political and to challenge authoritarian rule.

It is tempting to think of the Internet as unprecedented in its potential for political progress. History, however, cautions against such hubris. In the fifteenth century, the printing press revolutionized the accumulation and dissemination of information, enabling the Renaissance, the Protestant Reformation, and the scientific revolution. On these foundations, modern democracy emerged. But the printing press also facilitated the rise of the centralized state and prompted the movement toward censorship.[4] A century and a half ago, the telegraph was hailed as a tool to promote peace and understanding. Suddenly, the world shrank; news that once took weeks to travel across the world could be conveyed instantly. What followed was not peace and freedom but the bloodiest century in human history. Today's enthusiasts of liberation technology could be accused of committing the analytic sins of their Victorian forebears, "technological utopianism" and "chronocentricity"—that is, "the egotism that one's own generation is poised on the very cusp of history."[5]

In the end, technology is merely a tool, open to both noble and nefarious purposes. Just as radio and TV could be vehicles of information pluralism and rational debate, so they could also be commandeered by totalitarian regimes for fanatical mobilization and total state control. Authoritarian states could appropriate digital ICT to a similar effect. Yet to the extent that innovative citizens can improve and better use these tools, they can bring authoritarianism down—as in several cases they have.

Mobilizing against authoritarian rule represents only one possible "liberating" use of digital ICT. Well before mobilization for democracy peaks, these tools may help to widen the public sphere, creating a more pluralistic and autonomous arena of news, commentary, and information. The new ICTs are also powerful instruments for transparency and accountability, documenting and deterring abuses of human rights and democratic procedures. And though I cannot elaborate here, digital ICT is also liberating people from poverty and ill health: conveying timely information about crop prices, facilitating microfinance for small entrepreneurs, mapping the outbreaks of epidemics, and putting primary healthcare providers in more efficient contact with rural areas.[6]

Malaysia: widening the public sphere

A crucial pillar of authoritarian rule is control of information. Through blogs (there are currently more than 100 million worldwide), blog sites, online chat rooms, and more formal online media, the Internet provides dramatic new possibilities for pluralizing flows of information and widening the scope of commentary, debate, and dissent.

One of the most successful instances of the latter type is *Malaysiakini*, an online newspaper that has become Malaysia's principal alternative source of news and commentary.[7] As Freedom House has documented, Malaysia lacks freedom of the press. The regime—both the state and the ruling Barisan Nasional (BN) coalition—dominates print and broadcast media through direct ownership and monopoly practices. Thus it can shape what Malaysians read and see, and it can punish critical journalists with dismissal. Repressive laws severely constrain freedom to report, publish, and broadcast. However, as a rapidly developing country with high literacy, Malaysia has witnessed explosive growth of Internet access (and, recently, broadband access), from 15 percent of the population in 2000 to 66 percent in 2009 (equal to Taiwan and only slightly behind Hong Kong).[8] The combination of tight government control of the conventional media, widespread Internet access, and relative freedom on the Internet created an opening for online journalism in Malaysia, and two independent journalists—Steven Gan and Premesh Chandran—ventured into it. Opponents of authoritarian rule since their student days, Gan and Chandran became seized during the 1998 *reformasi* period with the need to reform the media and bring independent news and reporting to Malaysia. Using about US$9,000 of their own money (a tiny fraction of what it would take to start a print newspaper), they launched *Malaysiakini* in November 1999. Almost immediately, they gained fame by exposing how an establishment newspaper had digitally cropped jailed opposition leader (and former deputy prime minister) Anwar Ibrahim from a group photo of ruling-party politicians.

From its inception, *Malaysiakini* has won a loyal and growing readership by providing credible, independent reporting on Malaysian politics and governance. As its readership soared, that of the mainstream newspapers fell. Suddenly, Malaysians were able to read about such long-taboo subjects as corruption, human-rights abuses, ethnic discrimination, and police brutality. Now the online paper posts in English about 15 news stories a day, in addition to opinion pieces, letters, readers' comments, and daily satire (in *Cartoonkini*), plus translations and original material in Chinese, Malay, and Tamil. *Malaysiakini* reports scandals that no establishment paper would touch, such as massive cost overruns related to conflicts of interest at the country's main port agency and ongoing financial misconduct at the government-supported Bank Islam Malaysia. With the regime's renewed legal assault on Anwar Ibrahim, *Malaysiakini* is the only place where Malaysians can turn for independent reporting on the legal persecution of the opposition leader. In July 2008, it became Malaysia's most visited news site with about 2.5 million visitors per month. Yet, like many online publications worldwide, it still strives for financial viability.

While Malaysia today is no less authoritarian than when *Malaysiakini* began publishing a decade ago, it is more competitive and possibly closer to a democratic breakthrough than at any time in the last four decades. If a transition occurs, it will be mainly due to political factors—the coalescence of an effective opposition and the blunders of an arrogant regime. In addition, economic and social change is generating a better-educated and more diverse population, less tolerant of government paternalism and control. Polling and other data show that young Malaysians in particular support the (more democratic) opposition. But it is hard to disentangle these political and social factors from the expansion of the independent public sphere that *Malaysiakini* has spearheaded. In March 2008, the BN made its worst showing at the polls in half a century, losing its two-thirds parliamentary majority for the first time since independence. Facilitating this was the growing prominence of online journalism, which diminished the massive BN advantage in media access and "shocked the country" by documenting gross police abuse of demonstrators, particularly those of Indian descent.

Malaysiakini and its brethren perform a number of democratic functions. They report news and convey images that Malaysians would not otherwise see. They provide an uncensored forum for commentary and debate, giving rise to a critical public sphere. They offer space and voice to those whose income, ethnicity, or age put them on the margins of society. They give the political opposition, which is largely shut out of the establishment media, a chance to make its case. In the process, they educate Malaysians politically and foster more democratic norms. Many online publications and Internet blog sites perform similar functions in other semiauthoritarian countries, such as Nigeria, and in emerging and illiberal democracies. But is it possible for these functions to take root in a country as authoritarian as China is today?

Opening a public sphere in China

The prevailing answer is no: China's "Great Firewall" of Internet filtering and control prevents the rise of an independent public sphere online. Indeed, China's policing of the Internet is extraordinary in both scope and sophistication. China now has the world's largest population of Internet users—more than 380 million people (a number equal to 29 percent of the population, and a 16-fold increase since the year 2000). But it also has the world's most extensive, "multilayered," and sophisticated system "for censoring, monitoring, and controlling activities on the Internet and mobile phones."[9] Connection to the international Internet is monopolized by a handful of state-run operators hemmed in by rigid constraints that produce in essence "a national intranet," cut off from anything that might challenge the CCP's monopoly on power.

Access to critical websites and online reporting is systematically blocked. Google has withdrawn from China in protest of censorship, while YouTube, Facebook, and Blogspot, among other widely used sites, are extensively blocked or obstructed. Chinese companies that provide search and networking services agree to even tighter self-censorship than do international companies. When protests erupt (as they did over Tibet in 2008, for instance) or other sensitive political moments approach, authorities preemptively close data centers and online forums. Now the party-state is also trying to eliminate anonymous communication and networking by requiring registration of real names to blog or comment and by tightly controlling and monitoring cybercafés. Fifty thousand Internet police prowl cyberspace removing "harmful content"—usually within 24 to 48 hours. Students are recruited to spy on their fellows. And the regime pays a quarter of a million online hacks (called "50-centers" because of the low piece rate they get) to post favorable comments about the party-state and report negative comments.

Such quasi-Orwellian control of cyberspace is only part of the story, however. There is simply too much communication and networking online (and via mobile phones) for the state to monitor and censor it all. Moreover, Chinese "netizens"—particularly the young who are growing up immersed in this technology—are inventive, determined, and cynical about official orthodoxy. Many constantly search for better techniques to circumvent cyber-censorship, and they quickly share what they learn. If most of China's young Internet users are apolitical and cautious, they are also alienated from political authority and eagerly embrace modest forms of defiance, often turning on wordplay.

Recently, young Chinese bloggers have invented and extensively lauded a cartoon creature they call the "grass mud horse" (the name in Chinese is an obscene pun) as a vehicle for protest. This mythical equine, so the narrative goes, is a brave and intelligent animal whose habitat is threatened by encroaching "river crabs." In Chinese, the name for these freshwater crustaceans (*hexie*) sounds very much like the word for Hu Jintao's official governing philosophy of "harmony"—a label that critics see as little more than a euphemism for censorship and the suppression of criticism. Xiao Qiang, editor of *China Digital Times,* argues that the grass mud horse "has become an icon of resistance to censorship. The expression and cartoon videos may seem like a juvenile response to unreasonable rule. But the fact that the vast online population has joined the chorus, from serious scholars to usually politically apathetic urban white-collar workers, shows how strongly this expression resonates."[10]

In order to spread defiance, Chinese have a growing array of digital tools. Twitter has become one of the most potent means for political and social networking and the rapid dissemination of news, views, and withering satire. On April 22 at People's University in Beijing, three human-rights activists protested a speech by a well-known CCP propaganda official, Wu Hao. Showering him with small bills, they declared, "Wu Hao, wu mao!" ("Wu Hao is a fifty-center!"). Twitter flashed photographs of the episode across China, delighting millions of students who revel in mocking the outmoded substance, tortured logic, and painfully crude style of regime propagandists.

When Google announced in late March 2010 that it was withdrawing its online search services from mainland China (after failing to resolve its conflict with the government over censorship and cyber-attacks), the Chinese

Twitter-sphere lit up. Many Chinese were upset that Google would abandon them to the more pervasive censorship of the Chinese search-engine alternatives (such as Baidu), and they worried that the Great Firewall would block other services such as Google Scholar and Google Maps. Others suspected Google of doing the U.S. government's bidding. But the company's decision provoked a wave of sympathy and mourning, similar to what happened in January when Google first announced that it was considering withdrawing:

> Citizen reporters posted constant updates on … Twitter, documenting the Chinese netizens who endlessly offered flowers, cards, poems, candles, and even formal bows in front of the big outdoor sign "Google" located outside the company's offices in Beijing, Shanghai and Guangzhou.[11]

Security guards chased the mourners away, declaring the offerings "illegal flower tributes." The term quickly spread in China's online forums, symbolizing the suppression of freedom.

The public sphere in China involves much more than "tweets," of course. Those often link to much longer blogs, discussion groups, and news reports. And many thought-provoking sites are harder to block because their critiques of CCP orthodoxy are subtler, elucidating democratic principles and general philosophical concepts, sometimes with reference to Confucianism, Taoism, and other strains of traditional Chinese thought that the CCP dares not ban. Full-scale blog posts (not subject to Twitter's severe length limits) are far likelier to criticize the government (albeit artfully and euphemistically). Rebecca Mackinnon finds that China's blogosphere is a "much more freewheeling space than the mainstream media," with censorship varying widely across the 15 blog-service providers that she examined. Thus, "a great deal of politically sensitive material survives in the Chinese blogosphere, and chances for survival can likely be improved with knowledge and strategy."[12]

Despite the diffuse controls, China's activists see digital tools such as Twitter, Gmail, and filtration-evading software as enabling levels of communication, networking, and publishing that would otherwise be unimaginable in China today. With the aid of liberation technology, dissident intellectuals have gone from being a loose assortment of individuals with no specific goal or program to forming a vibrant and increasingly visible collaborative force. Their groundbreaking manifesto—Charter 08, a call for 19 reforms to achieve "liberties, democracy, and the rule of law" in China—garnered most of its signatures through the aid of blog sites such as *bullog.cn*. When Charter 08 was released online on 10 December 2008, with the signatures of more than 300 Chinese intellectuals and human-rights activists, the government quickly moved to suppress all mention of it. But then, "something unusual happened. Ordinary people such as Tang [Xiaozhao] with no history of challenging the government began to circulate the document and declare themselves supporters," shedding their previous fear. Within a month, more than 5,000 other Chinese citizens had signed the document. They included not just the usual dissidents but "scholars, journalists, computer technicians, businessmen, teachers and students whose names had not been associated with such movements before, as well as some on the lower rungs of China's social hierarchy—factory and construction workers and farmers."[13]

Officials shut down Tang's blog soon after she signed the Charter, and did the same to countless other blogs that supported it (including the entire *bullog.cn* site). But the campaign persists in underground salons, elliptical references, and subversive jokes spread virally through social media and instant messaging. One imagines a testy Chinese president Hu Jintao complaining about the Charter's democratic concepts such as federalism, opposition parties, and freedom of association. "Where do they all come from?" he demands. His minions run down the sources and bring him the bad news: The troublesome notions can be traced to Mao Zedong, Zhou Enlai, the CCP, the official newspaper (the *Xinhua Daily*), and the constitution of the People's Republic itself. A flustered Hu wonders what to do. His staff suggests banning all mention of these names. "You idiots!" shouts Hu. "If you ban them, you might as well ban me too!" "Well," his staff retorts, "People do say that if they ban you, at least the Charter will be left alone."[14]

Monitoring governance, exposing abuses

Liberation technology is also "accountability technology," in that it provides efficient and powerful tools for transparency and monitoring. Digital cameras combined with sites such as YouTube create new possibilities for exposing and challenging abuses of power. Incidents of police brutality have been filmed on cellphone cameras and posted to YouTube and other sites, allowing bloggers to call outraged public attention to them. Enter "human rights abuses" into YouTube and you will get roughly 10,000 videos of everything from cotton-growers' working conditions in Uzbekistan, to mining practices in the Philippines, to human-organ harvesting in China, to the persecution of Bahá'ís in Iran. A YouTube video of a young Malaysian woman forced by the police to do squats while naked forced the country's prime minister to call for an independent inquiry. When Venezuelan president Hugo Chávez forced Radio Caracas Television off the air in May 2007, it continued its broadcasts via YouTube. No wonder, then, that authoritarian states such as Iran and Saudi Arabia completely block access to the site.

Across much of the world, and especially in Africa, the quest for accountability makes use of the simplest form of liberation technology: text messaging via mobile phone. (Mobile phone networks have proven particularly useful in infrastructure-starved Africa since they can cover vast areas without requiring much in the way of physical facilities beyond some cell towers.) Around the world, the reach and capabilities of cellphones are being dramatically expanded by open-source software such as FrontlineSMS, which enables large-scale, two-way text messaging purely via mobile phones. In recent years, the software has been used over mobile-phone networks to monitor national elections in Nigeria and Ghana, to facilitate rapid reporting of human-rights violations in Egypt, to inform citizens about anti-corruption and human-rights issues in Senegal, and to monitor and report civil unrest in Pakistan. A Kenyan organization, Ushahidi (Swahili for "testimony"), has adapted the software for "crisis-mapping." This allows anyone to submit crisis information through text messaging using a mobile phone, e-mail, or online-contact form, and then aggregates the information and projects it onto a map in real time. Citizen journalists initially developed it to map reports of postelection violence in Kenya in early 2008, drawing some 45,000 Kenyan users. It has since been used to report incidents of xenophobic violence in South Africa; to track violence and human-rights violations in the Democratic Republic of Congo; and to monitor elections in Afghanistan, India, Lebanon, and Mexico.

The largest funder of both Ushahidi and FrontlineSMS is the Omidyar Network (ON), a philanthropic investment firm established six years ago by eBay founder Pierre Omidyar and his wife Pam. It extends the eBay approach—giving everyone equal access to information and the opportunity to leverage the potential of individuals and the power of markets—into the worlds of political and social innovation. This innovative effort—which comprises both a venture-capital fund directed at for-profit start-ups and a nonprofit grant-making fund—has committed more than US$325 million in investments and grants in two broad areas: "access to capital" (microfinance, entrepreneurship, and property rights), and "media, markets, and transparency" (which supports technology that promotes transparency, accountability, and trust across media, markets, and government). The ON supports national partners in Nigeria, Ghana, and Kenya that are using information technology to improve governance and free expression. These include Infonet, a web portal that provides citizens, media, and NGOs easy-to-access information on national and local government budgets in Kenya; and Mzalendo, a comprehensive site that enables Kenyans to follow what their members of parliament are doing.

The ON's support for transparency initiatives also extends to other countries and to U.S.-based organizations. These include Global Integrity, which harnesses the Internet and other sources of information in order to generate detailed assessments of corruption in more than 90 countries; and the Sunlight Foundation, which utilizes the Internet and related technology in order to make information about federal-government spending, legislation, and decision making more accessible to U.S. voters.

Mobilizing digitally

One of the most direct, powerful, and—to authoritarian regimes—alarming effects of the digital revolution has been its facilitation of fast, large-scale popular mobilizations. Cellphones with SMS text messaging have made possible what technology guru Howard Rheingold calls "smart mobs"—vast networks of individuals who communicate rapidly and with little hierarchy or central direction in order to gather (or "swarm") at a certain location for the sake of protest. In January 2001, Philippine president Joseph Estrada "became the first head of state in history to lose power to a smart mob," when tens of thousands and then, within four days, more than a million digitally mobilized Filipinos assembled at a historic protest site in Manila.[15] Since then, liberation technology has been instrumental in virtually all of the instances where people have turned out *en masse* for democracy or political reform.

Liberation technology figured prominently in the Orange Revolution that toppled the electoral authoritarian regime in Ukraine via mass protests during November and December 2004. The Internet newspaper *Ukrainskaya Pravda* provided a vital source of news and information about both the regime's efforts to steal the presidential election and the opposition's attempts to stop it. By the revolution's end, this online paper had become "the most widely read news source of any kind in Ukraine."[16] Website discussion boards gave activists a venue for documenting fraud and sharing best practices.[17] Text messaging helped to mobilize and coordinate the massive public protests—bringing hundreds of thousands to Kiev's Independence Square in freezing weather—that ultimately forced a new runoff election, won by the democratic opposition. These digital tools also facilitated the 2005 Cedar Revolution in Lebanon (which drew more than a million demonstrators to demand the withdrawal of Syrian troops); the 2005 protests for women's voting rights in Kuwait; the 2007 protests by Venezuelan students against the closure of Radio Caracas Television; and the April 2008 general strike in Egypt, where tens of thousands of young demonstrators mobilized through Facebook.[18] In September 2007, the "Internet, camera phones, and other digital networked technologies played a critical role" in Burma's Saffron Revolution, so called because of the involvement of thousands of Buddhist monks. Although digital technology did little directly to mobilize the protests, it vividly informed the world of them, and revealed the bloody crackdown that the government launched in response: "Burmese citizens took pictures and videos, many on their mobile phones, and secretly uploaded them from Internet cafes or sent digital files across the border to be uploaded." This international visibility may have saved many lives by inhibiting the military from using force as widely and brutally as it had in 1988.[19]

In China, pervasive text messaging has been a key factor in the mushrooming of grassroots protests. In 2007, an eruption of hundreds of thousands of cellphone text messages in Xiamen, a city on the Taiwan Strait, generated so much public dismay at the building of an environmentally hazardous chemical plant that authorities suspended the project.[20] The impact of the text messages was magnified and spread nationally as bloggers in other Chinese cities received them and quickly fanned the outrage. The technology is even seeping into North Korea, the world's most closed society, as North Korean defectors and South Korean human-rights activists entice North Koreans to carry the phones back home with them from China and then use them to report what is happening (via the Chinese mobile network).[21] In the oil-rich Gulf states, text messaging allows civic activists and political oppositionists "to build unofficial membership lists, spread news about detained activists, encourage voter turnout, schedule meetings and rallies, and develop new issue campaigns—all while avoiding government-censored newspapers, television stations, and Web sites."[22]

The most dramatic recent instance of digital mobilization was Iran's Green Movement, following the egregious electoral malpractices that appeared to rob opposition presidential candidate Mir Hosein Musavi of victory on June 12, 2009. In the preceding years, Iran's online public sphere had been growing dramatically, as evidenced by its more than "60,000 routinely updated blogs," exploring a wide range of social, cultural, religious, and political issues;[23] the explosion of Facebook to encompass an estimated 600,000 Persian-language users;[24] and the growing utilization of the Internet by news organizations, civic groups, political parties, and candidates. As incumbent president Mahmoud Ahmedinejad's election victory was announced (complete with claims of a 62 percent landslide) on June 13, outraged accounts of vote fraud spread rapidly on Internet chatrooms, blogs, and social networks. Through Twitter, text messaging, Facebook, and Persian-language social-networking sites such as Balatarin and Donbleh, Iranians quickly spread news, opinions, and calls for demonstrations. On June 17, Musavi supporters used Twitter to attract tens of thousands of their fellow citizens to a rally in downtown Tehran. Internet users organized nationwide protests throughout the month including more large demonstrations in the capital, some apparently attended by two to three million people. YouTube also provided a space to post pictures and videos of human-rights abuses and government crackdowns. A 37-second video of the death of Neda Agha-Soltan during Tehran's violent protests on June 20 quickly spread across the Internet, as did other images of the police and regime thugs beating peaceful demonstrators. Neda's death and the distressing images of wanton brutality decimated the remaining legitimacy of the Islamic Republic domestically and internationally.

To date, the Green Movement illustrates both the potential and limits of liberation technology. So far, the Islamic Republic's reactionary establishment has clung to power through its control over the instruments of coercion and its willingness to wield them with murderous resolve. Digital technology could not stop bullets and clubs in 2009, and it has not prevented the rape, torture, and execution of many protestors. But it has vividly documented these abuses, alienating key pillars of the regime's support base, including large segments of the Shia clergy. While the regime has tortured dissidents to get their e-mail passwords and round up more opponents, the Internet has fostered civic and political pluralism in Iran; linked the opposition within that country to the Iranian diaspora and other global communities; and generated the consciousness, knowledge, and mobilizational capacity that will eventually bring down autocracy in Iran. A key factor affecting when that will happen will be the ability of Iranians to communicate more freely and securely online.

Breaking down the walls

Even in the freest environments, the new digital means of information and communication have important limits and costs. There are fine lines between pluralism and cacophony, between advocacy and intolerance, and between the expansion of the public sphere and its hopeless fragmentation. As the sheer number of media portals has multiplied, more voices have become empowered, but they are hardly all rational and civil. The proliferation of online (and cable) media has not uniformly improved the quality of public deliberation, but rather has given rise to an "echo chamber" of the ideologically like-minded egging each other on. And open-access facilitates much worse: hate-mongering, pornography, terrorism, digital crime, online espionage, and cyberwarfare. These are real challenges, and they require careful analysis—prior to regulation and legislation—to determine how democracies can balance the great possibilities for expanding human freedom, knowledge, and capacity with the dangers that these technologies may pose for individual and collective security alike.

Still, the overriding challenge for the digital world remains freedom of access. The use of Internet filtering and surveillance by undemocratic regimes is becoming both more widespread and more sophisticated. And some less-sophisticated efforts, using commercial filtering software, may block sites even more indiscriminately. Currently, more than three dozen states filter the Internet or completely deny their citizens access.[25] Enterprising users can avail themselves of many circumvention technologies, but some require installation of software and so will not be available if the Internet is accessed from public computers or Internet cafes; many of the Web-based applications are blocked by the same filters that block politically sensitive sites; and most of these means require some degree of technical competence by the user.[26] Not all circumvention methods protect netizens' privacy and anonymity, which can be a particularly acute problem when state-run companies provide the Internet service. The free software Tor, popular among Iranians, promises anonymity by "redirecting encrypted traffic through multiple relays ... around the world," making it difficult for a regime to intercept a transmission.[27] But if it effectively monopolizes the provision of Internet service, a desperate regime such as

Burma's in 2007 can always respond by shutting down the country's Internet service or, as did Iran's government, by slowing service to a paralyzing crawl while authorities search electronic-data traffic for protest-related content.[28]

Even in liberal democracies, issues of access arise. Recently netizens worldwide—and the U.S. government—became concerned over excessively broad legislative proposals in Australia that would force Internet service providers to blacklist a large number of sites for legal and moral considerations (including the protection of children). The Chinese practice of forcing Internet providers to assume liability for the content to which they provide access is seeping into European legal and regulatory thinking on the Internet.[29]

There is now a technological race under way between democrats seeking to circumvent Internet censorship and dictatorships that want to extend and refine it. Recently, dictatorships such as Iran's have made significant gains in repression. In part, this has happened because Western companies like Nokia-Siemens are willing to sell them advanced surveillance and filtering technologies. In part, it has also been the work of dictatorships that eagerly share the ways, means, and "how-to's" of their worst practices with one another. A host of new circumvention technologies are coming onto the market, and millions of Chinese, Vietnamese, Iranians, Tunisians, and others fervently want access to them. Rich liberal democracies need to do much more to support the development of such technologies, and to facilitate (and subsidize) their cheap and safe dissemination to countries where the Internet is suppressed. More could be done to improve encryption so that people in authoritarian regimes can more safely communicate and organize online. Breakthroughs may also come with the expansion of satellite access that bypasses the national system, if the cost of the satellite dishes and monthly usage rates can be reduced dramatically. Western governments can help by banning the export of advanced filtering and surveillance technologies to repressive governments, and by standing behind Western technology companies when dictatorships pressure them "to hand over Internet users' personal data."[30] And finally, liberal democracies should stand up for the human rights of bloggers, activists, and journalists who have been arrested for peacefully reporting, networking, and organizing online.

It is important for the United States to have declared, as Secretary of State Hillary Clinton did in a historic speech on January 21, 2010, "We stand for a single internet where all of humanity has equal access to knowledge and ideas."[31] But the struggle for electronic access is really just the timeless struggle for freedom by new means. It is not technology, but people, organizations, and governments that will determine who prevails.

Notes

The author thanks Anna Davies, Blake Miller, and Astasia Myers for their truly superb research assistance on this article; and also Lian Matias, Galen Panger,

Tucker Herbert, Ryan Delaney, Daniel Holleb, Sampath Jinadasa, and Aaron Qayumi for their prior research assistance on this project.

1 Originally published as "Liberation Technology," *Journal of Democracy* 21 (July 2010): 69–83.
2 Sophie Beach, "The Rise of Rights?" *China Digital Times*, http://chinadigital-times.net/2005/05/rise-of-rights.
3 Yongnian Zheng, *Technological Empowerment: The Internet State and Society in China* (Stanford, CA: Stanford University Press, 2008), 147–151.
4 Ithiel de Sola Pool, *Technologies of Freedom* (Cambridge, MA: Belknap Press, 1983), 251.
5 Tom Standage, *The Victorian Internet* (New York: Berkley, 1998), 210, 213.
6 For various accounts, see http://fsi.stanford.edu/research/program_on_liberation_technology.
7 This account draws heavily from a student research paper conducted under my supervision: Astasia Myers, "*Malaysiakini:* Internet Journalism and Democracy," Stanford University, June 4, 2009.
8 Figures on the growth of Web use in Malaysia and China are available at www.internetworldstats.com/stats3.htm.
9 Freedom House, "Freedom on the Net: A Global Assessment of Internet and Digital Media," April 1, 2009, 34. Available at www.freedomhouse.org/uploads/specialreports/NetFreedom2009/FreedomOnTheNet_FullReport.pdf.
10 Private e-mail message from Xiao Qiang, May 2009. Quoted with permission.
11 S. L. Shen, "Chinese Forbidden from Presenting Flowers to Google," UPI Asia Online, January 15, 2010. Available at www.upiasia.com/Politics/2010/01/15/chinese_forbidden_from_presenting_flowers_to_google/4148.
12 Rebecca Mackinnon, "China's Censorship 2.0: How Companies Censor Bloggers," *First Monday,* February 2, 2009. Available at http://firstmonday.org/htbin/cgiwrap/bin/ojs/index.php/fm/article/view/2378/2089. See also Ashley Esarey and Qiang Xiao, "Below the Radar: Political Expression in the Chinese Blogosphere," *Asian Survey* 48 (September–October 2008): 752–772.
13 Ariana Eunjung Cha, "In China a Grassroots Rebellion," *Washington Post,* January 29, 2009.
14 "Charter 08 Still Alive in the Chinese Blogosphere," *China Digital Times,* February 9, 2009.
15 Howard Rheingold, *Smart Mobs: The Next Social Revolution* (New York: Basic: 2003), 158.
16 Michael McFaul, "Transitions from Postcommunism," *Journal of Democracy* 16 (July 2005): 12.
17 Robert Faris and Bruce Etling, "Madison and the Smart Mob: The Promise and Limitations of the Internet for Democracy," *Fletcher Forum of World Affairs* 32 (Summer 2008): 65.
18 Cathy Hong, "New Political Tool: Text Messaging," *Christian Science Monitor,* June 30, 2005; Jose de Cordoba, "A Bid to Ease Chavez's Power Grip; Students Continue Protests in Venezuela; President Threatens Violence," *Wall Street Journal,* June 8, 2007.
19 Mridul Chowdhury, "The Role of the Internet in Burma's Saffron Revolution," Berkman Center for Internet and Society, September 2008, 14 and 4. Available at http://cyber.law.harvard.edu/sites/cyber.law.harvard.edu/files/Chowdhury_Role_of_the_Internet_in_Burmas_Saffron_Revolution.pdf_0.pdf.
20 Edward Cody, "Text Messages Giving Voice to Chinese," *Washington Post,* June 28, 2007.

21 Choe Sang-Hun, "North Koreans Use Cell Phones to Bare Secrets," *New York Times*, March 28, 2010. Available at www.nytimes.com/2010/03/29/world/asia/29news.html.

22 Steve Coll, "In the Gulf, Dissidence Goes Digital; Text Messaging Is the New Tool of Political Underground," *Washington Post*, March 29, 2005.

23 John Kelly and Bruce Etling, "Mapping Iran's Online Public: Politics and Culture in the Persian Blogosphere," April 2008, Berkman Center for Internet and Society. Available at http://cyber.law.harvard.edu/sites/cyber.law.harvard.edu/files/Kelly&Etling_Mapping_Irans_Online_Public_2008.pdf.

24 Omid Habibinia, "Who's Afraid of Facebook?" September 3, 2009. Available at http://riseoftheiranianpeople.com/2009/09/03/who-is-afraid-of-facebook.

25 In addition to Freedom House, "Freedom on the Net," see Ronald Deibert, John Palfrey, Rafal Rohozinski, and Jonathan Zitrain, *Access Denied: The Practice and Policy of Global Internet Filtering* (Cambridge, MA: MIT Press, 2008). For the ongoing excellent work of the OpenNet Initiative, see http://opennet.net.

26 University of Toronto Citizen Lab, "Everyone's Guide to By-Passing Internet Censorship," September 2007, www.civisec.org/guides/everyones-guides.

27 Center for International Media Assistance, National Endowment for Democracy, "The Role of New Media in the 2009 Iranian Elections," July 2009, 2. Available at http://cima.ned.org/wp-content/uploads/2009/07/cima-role_of_new_media_in_iranian_elections-workshop_report.pdf.

28 Rory Cellan-Jones, "Hi-Tech Helps Iranian Monitoring," *BBC News,* June 22, 2009. *news.bbc.co.uk/2/hi/technology/8112550.stm.*

29 Rebecca MacKinnon, "Are China's Demands for Internet 'Self-Discipline' Spreading to the West?" McClatchy News Service, January 18, 2010. Available at www.mcclatchydc.com/2010/01/18/82469/commentary-are-chinas-demands.html.

30 Daniel Calingaert, "Making the Web Safe for Democracy," *ForeignPolicy.com*, January 19, 2010. Available at www.foreignpolicy.com/articles/2010/01/19/making_the_web_safe_for_democracy.

31 See www.state.gov/secretary/20092013clinton/rm/2010/01/135519.htm.

8 Hybrid regimes[1]

Is Russia a democracy? What about Ukraine, Nigeria, Indonesia, Turkey, or Venezuela? There was a time when these were simple questions of regime classification. But the empirical reality in these countries is a lot messier than it was two decades ago, and so, in a way, is the never-ending dialogue on how to think about and classify regimes.

Few conceptual issues in political science have been subjected to closer or more prolific scrutiny in recent decades than this problem of "what democracy is ... and is not,"[2] and which regimes are "democracies" and which not. We are replete with definitions and standards and tools of measurement. But the curious fact is that—a quarter-century into the "third wave" of democratization and the renaissance it brought in comparative democratic studies—we are still far from consensus on what constitutes "democracy." And we still struggle to classify ambiguous regimes.

Some insist on a fairly robust (though still procedural) definition of democracy, like Robert Dahl's "polyarchy." By this conception, democracy requires not only free, fair, and competitive elections, but also the freedoms that make them truly meaningful (such as freedom of organization and freedom of expression), alternative sources of information, and institutions to ensure that government policies depend on the votes and preferences of citizens. Some measure democracy by a "minimalist" standard like Joseph Schumpeter's: a political system in which the principal positions of power are filled "through a competitive struggle for the people's vote."[3] Yet contemporary applications of this electoral conception heavily overlap with Dahl's polyarchy by also implying the civil and political freedoms necessary for political debate and electoral campaigning.

Even if we agree to apply a minimalist, electoral standard for democracy, vexing questions remain. If, following Samuel Huntington, a system is democratic when "its most powerful collective decision makers are selected through fair, honest, and periodic elections in which candidates freely compete for votes,"[4] what constitutes "fair, honest, and free" elections? How can we know that parties have had a fair chance to campaign and that voters around the country (especially countries as large and diverse as Russia, Nigeria, and Indonesia) have been able to exercise their will freely?

How—especially where elections do not benefit from parallel vote tabulations[5]—can we know that the reported results accurately reflect the votes that were cast? And how do we know that the officials elected are really the "most powerful decision makers," that there are not significant "reserved domains" of military, bureaucratic, or oligarchical power?[6]

These questions have taken on a heightened relevance in recent years for several reasons. First, more regimes than ever before are adopting the *form* of electoral democracy, with regular, competitive, multiparty elections. Second, many of these regimes—indeed, an unprecedented proportion of the world's countries—have the form of electoral democracy but fail to meet the substantive test, or do so only ambiguously. And third, with heightened international expectations and standards for electoral democracy, including the rise of international election observing, there is closer international scrutiny of individual countries' democratic practices than ever before.

Yet even with this closer scrutiny, independent observers do not agree on how to classify regimes. Freedom House classified all six regimes mentioned at the beginning of this essay as democracies (in January of 2002). Yet by the reasoning of scholars of "competitive authoritarianism,"[7] they are all (or mostly) something less than electoral democracies: competitive authoritarian systems, hegemonic-party systems, or hybrid regimes of some kind. At best, Ukraine, Nigeria, and Venezuela are *ambiguous* cases. We may not have enough information now to know whether electoral administration will be sufficiently autonomous and professional, and whether contending parties and candidates will be sufficiently free to campaign, thus giving the political opposition a fair chance to defeat the government in the next elections. Regime classification must, in part, assess the previous election, but it must also assess the intentions and capacities of ambiguously democratic ruling elites, something that is very hard to do. Increasingly, independent observers view Russia as an electoral authoritarian regime. Many so view Nigeria as well, given the massive (and quite characteristic) fraud in the 1999 elections. Indonesia's constitutional assignment of some parliamentary seats to unelected military representatives contradicts a basic principle of democracy. But even if that provision were removed, the military would remain a major veto player (like the Turkish military, which has repeatedly forced the disqualification of a popular, moderately Islamist party).

These are hardly the only issues or anomalies in regime classification. In the 1970s and 1980s, scholars and observers debated whether Mexico, Senegal, and Singapore were really democracies (as their governments insisted). These debates fizzled once other countries in their respective regions began to experience true democratization and the democratic deficiencies of these one-party hegemonies became more blatantly apparent. More recently, a growing number of scholars are questioning the tendency to classify regimes as democratic simply because they have multiparty elections with some degree of competition and uncertainty. In an important conceptual contribution focused on Eurasia and Latin America, Steven

Levitsky and Lucan Way argue that regimes may be *both* competitive *and* authoritarian.[8]

We are thus witnessing a new wave of scholarly attention to the varieties of nondemocratic regimes and to the rather astonishing frequency with which contemporary authoritarian regimes manifest, at least superficially, a number of democratic features. This new intellectual upsurge partly reflects the exhaustion of the "third wave" of democratic transitions, which essentially crested in the mid-1990s.[9] For some years now, it has been apparent that a great many of the new regimes are not themselves democratic, or any longer "in transition" to democracy. Some of the countries that fall into the "political gray zone ... between full-fledged democracy and outright dictatorship" are in fact electoral democracies, however "feckless" and poorly functioning, but many fall below the threshold of electoral democracy and are likely to remain there for a very long time.[10]

A historical perspective

Hybrid regimes (combining democratic and authoritarian elements) are not new. Even in the 1960s and 1970s, there existed multiparty, electoral, but undemocratic regimes. Of these electoral autocracies—Mexico, Singapore, Malaysia, Senegal, South Africa, Rhodesia, and Taiwan (which allowed *dangwai,* or "outside the party," competitors)—only the Malaysian and Singaporean regimes survive today. Historically, there have also been numerous cases in Europe and Latin America of limited (elite) party competition with a limited franchise. In Latin America, these nineteenth-century and early-twentieth-century "oligarchical" democracies "contributed to the ultimate development of full democracy" by establishing some of its major political institutions, as well as the principles of limitation and rotation of power.[11] Thus these countries epitomized Dahl's optimal path to stable polyarchy, with the rise of political competition preceding the expansion of participation, so that the culture of democracy first took root among a small elite and then diffused to the larger population as it was gradually incorporated into electoral politics.[12] In the contemporary world of mass participation, this gradualist path has been closed off, and anxious elites have thus sought out other ways to limit and control competition.

Until the past decade or two, most efforts at political control included a ban on opposition political parties (if not on electoral competition altogether) and severe limits on the organization of dissent and opposition in civil society as well. Thus Juan Linz's encyclopedic *Totalitarian and Authoritarian Regimes* (originally published in 1975) contains barely a mention of multiparty electoral competition *within* authoritarian regimes. Party politics figures within the framework of a single (typically mobilizational) party, and only brief mention is made of "pseudo-multiparty systems."[13] Certainly Linz does not identify, among his seven principal authoritarian regime types, anything like the "competitive authoritarian" regime type discussed by Levitsky and

Way—and for good reason. This type of hybrid regime, which is now so common, is very much a product of the contemporary world.

One term for this phenomenon is "electoral authoritarianism." However, the term "pseudodemocracy" resonates distinctively with the contemporary era, in which democracy is the only broadly legitimate regime form, and regimes have felt unprecedented pressure (international and domestic) to adopt—or at least to mimic—the democratic form. Virtually all hybrid regimes in the world today are quite deliberately *pseudodemocratic*, "in that the existence of formally democratic political institutions, such as multiparty electoral competition, masks (often, in part, to legitimate) the reality of authoritarian domination."[14] All such regimes lack an arena of contestation sufficiently open, free, and fair so that the ruling party can readily be turned out of power if it is no longer preferred by a plurality of the electorate. While an opposition victory is not impossible in a hybrid regime, it requires a level of opposition mobilization, unity, skill, and heroism far beyond what would normally be required for victory in a democracy. Often, too, it requires international observation and intervention to preempt and prevent (as in Nicaragua in 1990) or to expose and delegitimate (as in the Philippines in 1986) the electoral manipulations and fraud of the authoritarian regime.

If scholarly treatment of hybrid or "electoral authoritarian" regimes is relatively new, it is not without some intellectual foundations in the transitions paradigm and in other earlier comparative work on democracy. Guillermo O'Donnell and Philippe Schmitter emphasized the inherent uncertainty and variation in the outcomes of regime transitions. A transition from authoritarian rule could produce a democracy, or it could terminate with a liberalized authoritarian regime *(dictablanda)* or a restrictive, illiberal democracy *(democradura)*.[15] During the early wave of enthusiasm over the spread of democracy in Latin America, Terry Karl criticized the tendency to equate democracy with competitive multiparty elections. She argued that military domination and human rights abuses rendered the Central American regimes of the 1980s and early 1990s "hybrid regimes," not democracies.[16] Robert Dahl classified (circa 1969) as "near polyarchies" six competitive electoral regimes.[17] Juan Linz, Seymour Martin Lipset, and I labeled "semidemocratic" those regimes:

> where the effective power of elected officials is so limited, or political party competition so restricted, or the freedom and fairness of elections so compromised that electoral outcomes, while competitive, still deviate significantly from popular preferences; and/or where civil and political liberties are so limited that some political orientations and interests are unable to organize and express themselves.[18]

Among our 26 cases, Senegal, Zimbabwe, Malaysia, and Thailand (during 1980–1988, when the government was led by an unelected prime minister) fell into the category that Levitsky and Way call "competitive authoritarian."[19] Mexico fit the model of a hegemonic party system, in which a relatively institutionalized ruling party monopolizes the political arena, using coercion, patronage, media control, and other means to deny formally legal opposition parties any real chance of competing for power.[20] Singapore remains a classic example of such a system.

The rise of pseudodemocracy

One of the most striking features of the "late period" of the third wave has been the unprecedented growth in the number of regimes that are neither clearly democratic nor conventionally authoritarian. If we use a very demanding standard of democracy, encompassing not only democratic elections but solid protection of civil liberties under a strong rule of law, then the proportion of intermediate regimes truly swells because so many of the new "democracies" of the third wave are "illiberal."[21] However, I believe a more analytically fruitful approach is to measure separately both *electoral democracy,* in the minimalist terms that Schumpeter, Huntington, and others have used, and *liberal democracy.*[22] We can also divide nondemocratic regimes into those with multiparty electoral competition of some kind (variously termed "electoral authoritarian," "pseudodemocratic," or "hybrid") and those that are *politically closed.* We can further divide electoral authoritarian regimes into the *competitive authoritarian* (following Levitsky and Way's formulation) and the uncompetitive or (following Schedler,[23] and before him Giovanni Sartori) *hegemonic.* Table 8.1 sorts the world's regimes (at the end of 2001) into these five categories, plus the residual category of *ambiguous regimes.*

Table 8.1 Regime types and frequencies, end 2001

Regime types	Countries over one million population N (%)	Countries under one million population N (%)	All countries N (%)
Liberal democracy (FH Score 1.0–2.0)	45 (30)	28 (66.7)	73 (38.0)
Electoral democracy	29 (19.3)	2 (4.8)	31 (16.1)
Ambiguous regimes	14 (9.3)	3 (7.1)	17 (8.9)
Competitive authoritarian	19 (12.7)	2 (4.8)	21 (10.9)
Hegemonic authoritarian	22 (14.7)	3 (7.1)	25 (13.0)
Politically closed	21 (14)	4 (9.5)	25 (13.0)
Total	150 (100)	42 (100)	192 (100)

During the third wave, both the number and proportion of democracies in the world have more than doubled. We find 105 regimes in the world that were clearly democracies at the end of 2001, 17 fewer than Freedom House counts[24] but well over twice the number of democracies at the start of the third wave; this accounts for 54 percent of the world's regimes (Table 8.1). About seven in ten of these democracies may be considered liberal (in that they have a fairly liberal Freedom House score of 2.0 or lower on the seven-point scale averaging political rights and civil liberties). Another 31 democracies are electoral but not liberal; some are clearly illiberal, with no more than a middling score on civil liberties. I consider 17 regimes "ambiguous" in the sense that they fall on the blurry boundary between electoral democracy and competitive authoritarianism, with independent observers disagreeing over how to classify them.[25] Virtually all 17 could be classified as "competitive authoritarian." Doing so would raise the number of such regimes from 21 to as many as 38, and the proportion from 11 to 20 percent—quite a significant phenomenon. Another 25 regimes are electoral authoritarian but in a more hegemonic way. They do not exhibit the degrees and forms of competitiveness elucidated by Levitsky and Way and illustrated as well by some of the African cases discussed by van de Walle.[26] Their elections and other "democratic" institutions are largely facades, yet they may provide some space for political opposition, independent media, and social organizations that do not seriously criticize or challenge the regime. Finally, 25 regimes do not have any of the architecture of political competition and pluralism. These remain politically closed regimes.

The data in Table 8.1 and the underlying scheme of classification raise a number of interesting points and issues. The most stunning is the dwindling proportion of politically closed regimes in the world. This transformation is partly reflected in the steady overall rise of freedom in the world (with the average score on the combined seven-point Freedom House scale improving from 4.47 in 1974 to 3.47 in 2001). And it is partly seen in the shrinking number and proportion of states with the two most repressive average freedom scores of 6.5 and 7.0. These most repressive regimes declined from 29 in 1974 to 21 in 2001, and as a proportion of all states, they shrank from one-fifth to barely a tenth (11 percent).

Thus the trend toward democracy has been accompanied by an even more dramatic trend toward pseudodemocracy. Only about half a dozen regimes in 1974 (less than 5 percent) would have met Schedler's criteria of electoral authoritarianism: undemocratic but with multiparty elections and some degree of political pluralism.[27] The rest were all military, one-party, or personalist regimes. Today, at least 45 (and perhaps as many as 60) are electoral authoritarian—roughly between a quarter and a third of all states. In proportional terms, authoritarian forms of multiparty electoral competition have increased during the third wave much more rapidly than democratic ones.

At the same time, military regimes have virtually disappeared as anything more than a transitional type of rule. Today, ambitious soldiers either legitimize their rule by running for president in contested, multiparty elections (however fraudulent, coerced, and manipulated), or they carve out large, autonomous spheres of political influence and economic domination behind the veil of civilian, multiparty rule. The first path has been taken by a number of African military strongmen, such as Jerry Rawlings in Ghana and most recently Yahya Jammeh in the Gambia. Nigerian dictator Sani Abacha was engaged in such a maneuver when he was struck dead by a "heart attack" in 1998. General—now President—Pervez Musharraf may yet pursue a similar conversion in Pakistan, albeit perhaps with considerably more genuine popular support. The second course has been taken by the military in Indonesia, and to a lesser degree still characterizes the military in Turkey, Thailand, Nigeria, and parts of Latin America.

There is also a striking correlation between country size and regime type. As I noted a few years ago,[28] countries with populations under one million are much more likely to be both democracies and liberal democracies. Two-thirds of these countries are liberal democracies, while only 30 percent of countries with populations over one million are. Among the 150 countries over one million population, 49 percent are democracies (liberal or illiberal), but 72 percent of countries under one million population are. The countries with populations over one million are about twice as likely as small states to have an electoral authoritarian regime and half again as likely to have a closed authoritarian regime.

Electoral democracy vs. electoral authoritarianism

Interesting issues revolve around the boundaries between regime types, which all the authors in this issue recognize to be blurry and controversial. When fitting messy and elusive realities against ideal types, it cannot be otherwise. This is why I classify so many regimes as ambiguous—a judgment, however, that only addresses the border between democracy and electoral authoritarianism. The distinctions between liberal and electoral democracy, and between competitive and hegemonic electoral authoritarianism, can also require difficult and disputable judgments. Thus the country classifications in the Appendix to this volume—which updates this analysis to the end of 2014—are offered more in an illustrative than a definitive spirit.

As Schedler elaborates, the distinction between electoral democracy and electoral authoritarianism turns crucially on the freedom, fairness, inclusiveness, and meaningfulness of elections.[29] Often particularly difficult are judgments about whether elections have been free and fair, both in the ability of opposition parties and candidates to campaign and in the casting and counting of the votes. Hence the frequency with which the validations by international observer missions of elections in ambiguous or electoral authoritarian regimes are, often convincingly, criticized as superficial, premature, and politically driven.

Elections are "free" when the legal barriers to entry into the political arena are low, when there is substantial freedom for candidates and supporters of different political parties to campaign and solicit votes, and when voters experience little or no coercion in exercising their electoral choices. Freedom to campaign requires some considerable freedom of speech, movement, assembly, and association in political life, if not fully in civil society. It is hard, however, to separate these two spheres, or to weigh the significance of particular violations. How many opposition candidates and supporters must be killed or arrested before one discerns a blatantly undemocratic pattern? Typically more than one murder is necessary, but fewer than the 21 deadly assaults committed during the two months prior to Cambodia's 1998 elections.[30] In India, election-related killings have a long history and have recently risen to alarming levels in some states. No major observer denies that India is a democracy, but particularly in states (like Bihar) where corruption, criminality, murder, and kidnapping heavily taint the electoral process, it is an illiberal and degraded one. A crucial consideration in assessing a regime is whether political violence is clearly and extensively organized by the state or ruling party as a means of punishing, terrorizing, and demoralizing opposition.

Assessments about whether elections are free or not thus require careful and nuanced judgments about the scale, pattern, and context of violations. The same is true for the dimension of electoral fairness. Levitsky and Way argue that political systems descend into electoral authoritarianism when violations of the "minimum criteria for democracy" are so serious that they create "an uneven playing field between government and opposition."[31] Yet even in many liberal and established democracies, there is not a truly level playing field. Often, governing parties or executives enjoy advantages of incumbency—readier access to the media, an easier time raising money from business, and the ability (strictly legal or not) to use government transport and staff while campaigning. No system is a perfect democracy, all require constant vigilance, and scattered violations do not negate the overall democratic character of elections.

When evaluating elections, it is crucial to examine their systemic character. We have by now elaborate criteria to judge the fairness of elections. Elections are fair when they are administered by a neutral authority; when the electoral administration is sufficiently competent and resourceful to take specific precautions against fraud in the voting and vote counting; when the police, military, and courts treat competing candidates and parties impartially throughout the process; when contenders all have access to the public media; when electoral districts and rules do not systematically disadvantage the opposition; when independent monitoring of the voting and vote-counting is allowed at all locations; when the secrecy of the ballot is protected; when virtually all adults can vote; when the procedures for organizing and counting the vote are transparent and known to all; and when there are clear and impartial procedures for resolving complaints and disputes.[32] This is a long list, but serious efforts to compromise the freedom and fairness of elections form a pattern (beginning well before election day) that is visible across institutional arenas. The institutional biases and misdeeds are there for international observers to see if those observers have the time, experience, courage, and country expertise to do so.[33]

Degrees of authoritarian competitiveness

No less difficult is the challenge of distinguishing between competitive authoritarian regimes and hegemonic electoral authoritarian ones. Levitsky and Way posit four arenas in which "opposition forces may periodically challenge, weaken, and occasionally even defeat autocratic incumbents."[34] While contestation in the judiciary and the mass media is hard to quantify, contestation in elections and legislatures does allow for more structured comparison.

In classifying regimes by the framework of Table 8.1, regimes are considered democratic if they have free, fair, and open elections for all the principal positions of political power, as defined above and by Schedler.[35] In addition to the Freedom House scores, three types of data are drawn upon in my classification of nondemocratic regimes: the percentage of legislative seats held by the ruling party, the percentage of the vote won by the ruling party presidential candidate, and the years the incumbent ruler has continuously been in power. The latter, as van de Walle shows for Africa, can be a telling indicator of the degree to which a country has opened up, as well as a predictor of its future openness to democratic change.[36] Although I do not use any mathematical formulae to combine these three indicators and the Freedom House scores, a formal index of authoritarian competitiveness is worth developing.

One defining feature of competitive authoritarian regimes is significant parliamentary opposition. In regimes where elections are largely an authoritarian facade, the ruling or dominant party wins almost all the seats: repeatedly over 95 percent in Singapore, about 80 percent in Egypt in 2000 and Mauritania in 2001, 89 percent in Tanzania in 2000, and repeatedly over 80 percent in Tunisia during the 1990s. In Cambodia, the hegemonic character of rule by Hun Sen's Cambodian People's Party (CPP) was not apparent in the bare majority of parliamentary seats it won in 1998, but it became more blatant in early 2002 when the CPP won control of about 99 percent of the 1,621 local communes with about 70 percent of the vote. Where, as in Kazakhstan and Kyrgyzstan, parties are so poorly developed that it is difficult to interpret legislative election results, presidential election returns offer other evidence of hegemony. After winning a presidential referendum with a 95 percent "yes" vote in 1995, Kazakhstan's President Nursultan Nazarbayev was reelected with 80 percent of the vote in 1999. In 1995 and again in 2000, Kyrgyz president Askar Akayev, in whom the

West placed early (and naive) hopes for democratic progress, was ree-lected with 75 percent of the vote. One clear sign of hegemony is when the president "wins" three-quarters or more of the popular vote. This also hap-pened in Algeria in 1999, in Azerbaijan in 1998, in Burkina Faso in 1998, in Cameroon (with an opposition boycott) in 1997, in Djibouti in 1999, and in Tanzania in 2000.

At the extreme end of the continuum, the presidents of Egypt, Tunisia, and Yemen were all "reelected" in the 1990s with well over 90 percent of the vote. By the beginning of 2002, these men had been in power for 21, 15, and 12 years, respectively, pointing to another sign of authoritarian hegemony: prolonged presidential tenure. Other examples of protracted presidential tenure include 23 years in Angola, 20 years in Cameroon, 35 years in Gabon, 18 years in Guinea, and 16 years in Uganda. Yet some long-ruling autocrats have had to fight for their political lives in the 1990s. Daniel arap Moi (who finally pledged to step down in 2002 after 24 years in power) was reelected twice during the 1990s with less than 42 percent of the vote. Zimbabwe's President Robert Mugabe, in power for 22 years, resorted to mass violence and intimidation in his unpopular 2002 presiden-tial reelection bid. His ruling party won only a bare majority of seats in a rough 2000 election that marked a breakthrough from numbing hegemony to competitive authoritarianism.

These data become more revealing when weighed with the annual Freedom House ratings of political rights and civil liberties. Generally, electoral authoritarian regimes range from 4.0 to 6.0 on the combined seven-point scale. Regimes closer to the less repressive score (4.0) allow more political pluralism and civic space, and hence are more likely to be competitive authoritarian. Some examples include Peru under Fujimori (4.5 in 1995), Senegal under the hegemonic Socialist Party (which aver-aged 4.0 or 4.5 during the 1990s), and Côte d'Ivoire (4.5 today, with competitive presidential and legislative elections in 2000). Many observ-ers consider Tanzania a democracy, with its relatively benign regime (4.0), despite persistent electoral irregularities. Yet if one traces its pedigree back to President Julius Nyerere's original TANU party, the Chama Cha Mapizindi (CCM) is the only ruling party Tanzanians have known in nearly 40 years of independence.

The reason we must examine several variables is that levels of freedom and levels of electoral competitiveness do not always neatly align. Indeed, when long-time authoritarian rulers face serious challenges (as in Malaysia and Zimbabwe recently), they may turn to their nastiest levels of repression, deploying levels of violence and intimidation that are unnecessary when political domination can be more subtly secured at the ballot box. Tracking the interplay between changes in political competition and changes in political repression may thus help us understand when and how moments of possible transition open and close in electoral authoritarian regimes.

Black and white or shades of gray?

Comparative politics is returning with new concepts and data to a very old issue: the forms and dynamics of authoritarian rule. As democracies differ among themselves in significant ways and degrees, so do contemporary authoritarian regimes, and if we are to understand the contemporary dynamics, causes, limits, and possibilities of regime change (including possible future democratization), we must understand the different, and in some respects new, types of authoritarian rule.

At the same time, we must appreciate that classificatory schemes impose an uneasy order on an untidy empirical world. We should not ignore the critics of "whole system" thinking, who eschew efforts at regime classification altogether and seek to identify the ways in which each political system combines democratic and undemocratic features.[37] These approaches remind us that most regimes are "mixed" to one degree or another.[38] Even many politically closed regimes have quasi-constitutional mechanisms to limit power and consult broader opinion. For example, although China lacks competitive elections at any significant level, it has taken some steps to rotate power and to check certain abuses of corrupt local and provincial officials. Every step toward political liberalization matters, both for the prospect of a transition to democracy and for the quality of political life as it is daily experienced by abused and aggrieved citizens. As Levitsky and Way imply, significant steps toward a more open, competitive, pluralistic, and restrained authoritarian system can emerge in arenas other than electoral ones.[39]

Democratic regimes are also "mixed" forms of government, not only in the ways they empower institutions intentionally placed beyond the reach of elected officials (such as constitutional courts or central banks), but in less desirable respects as well. In their constant struggles to restrain corruption, and in their ongoing frustration in trying to contain the role of money in politics, even the world's most liberal democracies exhibit the pervasive imperfections of responsiveness that led Robert Dahl to adopt the term "polyarchy" instead of "democracy" for his seminal study. As we add the forms and dynamics of electoral authoritarianism to our long list of issues in comparative democratic studies, we should not neglect these imperfections in our own systems. The transformations of Taiwan, Mexico, and Senegal in the 1990s show that competitive authoritarian regimes can become democracies. But democracies, new and old, liberal and illiberal, can also become more democratic.

Notes

I am grateful to Terrence Blackburne for his research assistance and to Andreas Schedler, Steven Levitsky, and Nicolas van de Walle for their constructive comments.

1 Originally published as "Elections Without Democracy: Thinking about Hybrid Regimes," *Journal of Democracy* 13 (April 2002): 21–35.
2 Philippe C. Schmitter and Terry Lynn Karl, "What Democracy Is ... and Is Not," *Journal of Democracy* 2 (Summer 1991): 75–88.
3 Joseph Schumpeter, *Capitalism, Socialism, and Democracy,* 2nd ed. (New York: Harper, 1947), 269.
4 Samuel P. Huntington, *The Third Wave: Democratization in the Late Twentieth Century* (Norman: University of Oklahoma Press, 1991), 7.
5 Larry Garber and Glenn Cowan, "The Virtues of Parallel Vote Tabulations," *Journal of Democracy* 4 (April 1993): 95–107.
6 J. Samuel Valenzuela, "Democratic Consolidation in Post-Transitional Settings: Notion, Process, and Facilitating Conditions," in Scott Mainwaring, Guillermo O'Donnell, and J. Samuel Valenzuela, eds, *Issues in Democratic Consolidation: The New South American Democracies in Comparative Perspective* (Notre Dame, IN: University of Notre Dame Press, 1992), 64–66.
7 Steven Levitsky and Lucan A. Way, "The Rise of Competitive Authoritarianism," *Journal of Democracy* 13 (April 2002): 51–66. See also the other essays in the "Elections Without Democracy" cluster of that issue of the *Journal of Democracy*: Andreas Schedler, "The Menu of Manipulation," 36–50, and Nicolas van de Walle, "Africa's Range of Regimes," 66–80. This chapter was originally published as the lead article in that cluster. Subsequent to the original publication of this article, Freedom House downgraded Russia, Nigeria, and Venezuela to nondemocratic status.
8 Levitsky and Way, "The Rise of Competitive Authoritarianism." Subsequent to the original publication of their essay and mine in the April 2002 *Journal of Democracy*, their arguments and analysis were greatly elaborated in their seminal book, *Competitive Authoritarianism: Hybrid Regimes After the Cold War* (New York: Cambridge University Press, 2010).
9 Larry Diamond, *Developing Democracy: Toward Consolidation* (Baltimore, MD: Johns Hopkins University Press, 1999), ch. 2.
10 Thomas Carothers, "The End of the Transition Paradigm," *Journal of Democracy* 13 (January 2002): 5–21, quoted from pp. 9 and 18.
11 Larry Diamond and Juan J. Linz, "Introduction: Politics, Society, and Democracy in Latin America," in Larry Diamond, Juan J. Linz, and Seymour Martin Lipset, eds, *Democracy in Developing Countries: Latin America* (Boulder, CO: Lynne Rienner, 1989), 8.
12 Robert Dahl, *Polyarchy: Participation and Opposition* (New Haven, CT: Yale University Press, 1971), 33–36.
13 Juan J. Linz, *Totalitarian and Authoritarian Regimes* (Boulder, CO: Lynne Rienner, 2000), 60.
14 Diamond, Linz, and Lipset, *Democracy in Developing Countries*, xviii.
15 Guillermo O'Donnell and Philippe C. Schmitter, *Transitions from Authoritarian Rule: Tentative Conclusions about Uncertain Democracies* (Baltimore, MD: Johns Hopkins University Press, 1986), 9.
16 Terry Lynn Karl, "The Hybrid Regimes of Central America," *Journal of Democracy* 6 (July 1995): 72–86. See also Terry Lynn Karl, "Dilemmas of Democratization in Latin America," *Comparative Politics* 23 (October 1990): 14–15.
17 Dahl, *Polyarchy*, 248.
18 Diamond, Linz, and Lipset, *Democracy in Developing Countries*, xvii.
19 Levitsky and Way, "The Rise of Competitive Authoritarianism."
20 Giovanni Sartori, *Parties and Party Systems: A Framework for Analysis* (Cambridge: Cambridge University Press, 1976): 230–238.
21 Guillermo O'Donnell, "Delegative Democracy," *Journal of Democracy* 5 (January 1994): 55–69; Larry Diamond, "Democracy in Latin America: Degrees, Illusions,

and Directions for Consolidation," in Tom Farer, ed., *Beyond Sovereignty: Collectively Defending Democracy in the Americas* (Baltimore, MD: Johns Hopkins University Press, 1996), 52–104; Diamond, *Developing Democracy,* 42–50; Fareed Zakaria, "The Rise of Illiberal Democracy," *Foreign Affairs* 76 (November-December 1997): 22–43.

22 Liberal democracy extends freedom, fairness, transparency, accountability, and the rule of law from the electoral process into all other major aspects of governance and interest articulation, competition, and representation. See Diamond, *Developing Democracy,* 10–13.

23 Schedler, "The Menu of Manipulation."

24 See Adrian Karatnycky, "The 2001 Freedom House Survey," *Journal of Democracy* 13 (January 2002): 99.

25 The only exception in this ambiguous group is Tonga, the lone "liberal autocracy"—a nondemocracy with a Freedom House score on civil liberties better than the midpoint of 4—and thus difficult to classify in this framework.

26 Levitsky and Way, "The Rise of Competitive Authoritarianism," and van de Walle, "Africa's Range of Regimes."

27 Schedler, "The Menu of Manipulation."

28 Diamond, *Developing Democracy,* 117–119.

29 Schedler, "The Menu of Manipulation."

30 Freedom House, *Freeedom in the World: The Annual Survey of Political Rights and Civil Liberties, 2000–2001* (New York: Freedom House, 2001), 121.

31 Levitsky and Way, "The Rise of Competitive Authoritarianism," 53.

32 This draws from Jørgen Elklit and Palle Svensson, "What Makes Elections Free and Fair?" *Journal of Democracy* 8 (July 1997): 32–46. See also the essays on electoral administration in Andreas Schedler, Larry Diamond, and Marc F. Plattner, eds, *The Self-Restraining State: Power and Accountability in New Democracies* (Boulder, CO: Lynne Rienner, 1999), 75–142.

33 For a thoughtful critique of international election observation, see Thomas Carothers, "The Rise of Election Monitoring: The Observers Observed," *Journal of Democracy* 8 (July 1997): 16–31.

34 Levitsky and Way, "The Rise of Competitive Authoritarianism," 54–58.

35 Schedler, "The Menu of Manipulation."

36 Van de Walle, "Africa's Range of Regimes."

37 For a classic critical treatment in this vein, see Richard L. Sklar, "Developmental Democracy," *Comparative Studies in Society and History* 29 (October 1987): 686–724.

38 For an Africanist perspective, see Richard L. Sklar, "The Significance of Mixed Government in Southern African Studies: A Preliminary Assessment," in Toyin Falola, ed., *African Politics in Postimperial Times: The Essays of Richard L. Sklar* (Trenton, NJ: Africa World Press, 2002), 479–487.

39 Levitsky and Way, "The Rise of Competitive Authoritarianism."

9 Why are there no Arab democracies?[1]

During democratization's third wave, democracy ceased being a mostly Western phenomenon and "went global." When the third wave began in 1974, the world had only about 40 democracies, and only a few of them lay outside the West. By the time the *Journal of Democracy* began publishing in 1990, there were 76 electoral democracies (accounting for slightly less than half the world's independent states). By 1995, that number had shot up to 117—three in every five states. By then, a critical mass of democracies existed in every major world region save one—the Middle East.[2] Moreover, every one of the world's major cultural realms had become host to a significant democratic presence, albeit again with a single exception—the Arab world.[3] Fifteen years later, this exception still stands.

The continuing absence of an Arab democracy is a striking anomaly—the principal exception to the globalization of democracy. Why is there no Arab democracy? Indeed, why is it the case that among the 16 independent Arab states of the Middle East and coastal North Africa, Lebanon is the only one to have *ever* been a democracy?

The most common assumption about the Arab democracy deficit is that it must have something to do with religion or culture. After all, the one thing that all Arab countries share is that they are Arab. They speak the same language (at least to the extent that they share the *lingua franca* of classical Arabic), and it is often suggested that there are cultural beliefs, structures, and practices more or less common to all countries of the region. Moreover, they share the same predominant religion, namely Islam—though Lebanon has historically been about half (though it is now less than half) Christian, and other countries, such as Egypt, also have significant Christian minorities. But as I will show, neither culture nor religion offers a convincing explanation for the Arab democracy deficit. Maybe countries such as Egypt, Jordan, Morocco, and Yemen are not democracies because they are not yet economically developed. Yet this argument fails once one compares the development levels of Arab and non-Arab states, as I will shortly do. Perhaps the perverse sociopolitical effects of being so awash in petrochemical deposits (the so-called oil curse) is the reason—but how does that explain the lack of democracy in non-oil-rich Egypt, Jordan, Morocco, and Tunisia?

As I will explain, answering the riddle of the Arab democracy deficit does involve political economy—as well as geopolitics. And it demands analysis of the internal political structures of Arab states. But first it requires dispensing with assumptions that cannot stand the test of evidence.

Religion and culture

As Alfred Stepan and Graeme Robertson have shown, there is a big "democracy gap" among states in the world, but it is an Arab much more than a "Muslim" gap. Comparing the 16 Muslim-majority countries that are predominantly Arab with 29 other Muslim-majority countries, Stepan and Robertson find among the latter a number (including Albania, Bangladesh, Malaysia, Senegal, and Turkey) with significant records of extending reasonably democratic political rights to their citizens. Among the Arab countries, the only one that meets this description is Lebanon before the civil war that began in 1975. Moreover, taking account of the level of political rights one might predict from the level of per capita income, they find numerous "electoral overachievers" among the Muslim-majority states that are not predominantly Arab, and none among the Arab states.[4]

My own further and more recent analysis uncovers the following additional points. First, if we ask whether regimes meet the minimum test of electoral democracy (free and fair elections to determine who rules), then there are eight non-Arab Muslim-majority states rated by Freedom House as democracies today and zero Arab ones.[5] Second, there is a big "freedom gap" between the Arab and non-Arab Muslim-majority states. At the end of 2008, the 16 Arab states of the Middle East had an average score across the two Freedom House scales of 5.53 (the worst possible score is a 7, signaling "least free"). The other 30 Muslim-majority states had an average freedom score of 4.7.[6] A difference between two such groups of nearly a full point on a seven-point scale is substantial. Moreover, while 11 of the non-Arab countries (about a third) are at the midpoint (4) or better on the average freedom scale, among the Arab states only Kuwait rates that well.

So much for religion, what about culture? One could argue, as the late British historian Elie Kedourie did in 1992, that there is "nothing in the political traditions of the Arab world—which are the political traditions of Islam—which might make familiar, or indeed intelligible, the organizing ideas of constitutional and representative government."[7] But outside the Arab world, a number of countries with Muslim political traditions have had some significant experiences with democracy. And even if one omitted Kedourie's equation of Arab and Islamic political traditions, one would still need to explain why the alien "organizing ideas" of modern democracy have taken hold in a number of countries in Africa and Asia for which there really were no prior precedents, but not in the Arab world. If the problem, as Kedourie went on, is that Arab countries "had been accustomed to ... autocracy and passive obedience," why has this remained an insurmountable obstacle in the Arab world while it has not prevented democratization in large swaths of the rest of the world that had once also known only authoritarian domination?

It could also be argued—and has been regarding both Iraq and Lebanon—that sectarian and ethnic divisions run too deep to permit democracy in these countries. Yet Iraq and Lebanon—for all their fractious, polarized divisions—are the two Arab countries closest to full electoral democracy today, while two of the most homogeneous countries, Egypt and Tunisia, are also two of the most authoritarian. In fact, ethnic or religious differences hardly pose a more severe obstacle to democracy in the Arab world than they do in countries such as India, Indonesia, South Africa, and Ghana. Again, something else must be going on.

Maybe it is that Arab populations simply do not want or value electoral democracy the way mass publics have come to desire and value this form of self-government in other regions of the world.[8] But then how do we account for the overwhelming shares of Arab publics—well over 80 percent in Algeria, Jordan, Kuwait, Morocco, the Palestinian Authority, and even Iraq—who agree that "despite drawbacks, democracy is the best system of government," and that "having a democratic system would be good for our country"?[9] Not only is support for democracy very broad in the Arab world, but it doesn't vary by degree of religiosity. "In fact, more religious Muslims are as likely as less religious Muslims to believe that democracy, despite is drawbacks, is the best political system."[10] Look at the way Iraqis turned out to vote *three* times in 2005, amid widespread and dire risks to their physical safety, and it is hard to conclude that Arabs do not care about democracy. By contrast, when elections (as in Egypt) offer little meaningful choice, or where (as in Morocco) they are of little consequence in determining who will really rule, it is not surprising that most people become disillusioned and opt not to vote.

Beneath the aggregate figures of Arab support for democracy, however, lies a more complex story. In five countries surveyed between 2003 and 2006 by the Arab Barometer, 56 percent of respondents agreed that "men of religion should have influence over government decisions."[11] A survey done in 2003 and 2004 also found half or more of four Arab publics agreeing that the government should implement as law nothing but Islamic sharia. When support for democracy and support for some kind of Islamic form of government are cross-tabulated, the generic pattern is something like this: 40–45 percent of each public supports secular democracy while roughly the same proportion backs an Islamic form of democracy; meanwhile 5–10 percent of the public supports secular authoritarianism and the same proportion supports Islamic authoritarianism.[12]

Here is where religion and attitudes do enter in as relevant factors. We do not yet know, on the basis of the Arab Barometer data to date, what proportion of those who opt both for "democracy" *and* for Islamic influence in government favor an understanding of democracy that affirms not only majority rule but also minority rights—including the right of the minority to try to become the majority in the next election. The evidence examined by Amaney Jamal and Mark Tessler suggests that proponents of secular democracy vary little from their compatriots who back Islamic democracy when it comes to support for democratic values such as openness, tolerance, and equality, with the qualification that secular democrats seem modestly more liberal when it comes to racial tolerance and the rights of women. Jamal and Tessler conclude hopefully that Arabs value democracy, even if their concern for stability leads them to want it to come only gradually, and that neither religious politics nor personal religiosity pose a major obstacle.

But there remains one problem. Among the secular democrats in the Arab world are the kinds of middle-class liberal intellectuals, professionals, and businessmen who have pressed for democracy elsewhere around the globe. Many of these secular democrats (some of whom are also members of religious or ethnic minorities) are not sifting through Arab Barometer survey data regarding what their fellow citizens believe. These democrats are instead imagining what the imminent political alternative would be to the authoritarian regime they dislike. They fear that it would not be some modestly Islamist version of a resolutely constitutional democracy, but rather a regime dominated by the Egyptian Muslim Brotherhood, the Jordanian Islamic Action Front, or some other hard-line and antidemocratic Islamist political force—a new and more ominous hegemony. Further, they fear that this Islamist alternative would produce "one person, one vote, one time" before hijacking an electoral democratic revolution, much as Ayatollah Khomeini hijacked the Iranian Revolution in 1979. Or they fear that a last-minute effort to prevent that prospect would plunge their country into the horrific scenario of Algeria in 1991, when the military seized control to stop the Islamic Salvation Front from winning national elections, touching off an almost decade-long civil war that claimed perhaps 150,000 lives. One need not justify the choice made by Algeria's political and military elites then, and in the brutal years that followed, in order to recognize the obstacle to democratization inherent in the fear of radical Islam as the alternative waiting just offstage should a current regime collapse. In recent decades, there has been only one parallel elsewhere: the fear of a radical left-wing or "communist" electoral takeover. It is no coincidence that in those countries (in Latin America, and South Africa) where this fear gripped authoritarian rulers *and* some of their liberal opponents, elites proved willing to negotiate transitions to democracy only when the prospect of the antidemocratic left coming to power had dissipated as a result of brutal suppression or the end of the Cold War.

Economic development and social structure

It remains the case, as Seymour Martin Lipset argued 50 years ago, that the more well-to-do a country is, the better will be its prospects for gaining and keeping democracy. By now, however, many Arab countries are quite "well-to-do." If we compare per capita income levels (in 2007 purchasing power parity dollars), Kuwait is nearly as rich as Norway, Bahrain is on a par with France, Saudi Arabia with Korea, Oman with Portugal, and Lebanon with Costa Rica. Only Egypt, Jordan, Morocco, Syria, and Yemen fall toward the lower end, but still these countries are no poorer in per capita terms than India or Indonesia, where democracy functions despite a lack of broad prosperity.

Of course, per capita income figures can be deceiving. The distribution of income can be badly skewed—and it is in the Arab world. Moreover, oil countries in particular look on the surface much more developed than they are. Most rank much lower on "human development" than they do in per capita money income (Saudi Arabia ranks 31 places lower; Algeria, 19). Still, when we look at levels of human development (which take into account education and health as well), the richest Arab oil states are at least on a par with Portugal and Hungary, while Saudi Arabia ranks with Bulgaria and Panama. And turning to Arab states with little or no oil to export, we see that Egypt still ranks with Indonesia, and Morocco with South Africa. In other words, one can find at any level of development, and by any measure, numerous democracies that are about as developed as the respective Arab nondemocracies.

If the problem is not economic level, maybe it is economic structure. Of the 16 Arab countries, 11 are "rentier" states in the sense that they depend heavily on oil and gas rents (in essence, unearned income) to keep their states afloat. These 11 states derive more than 70 percent (in some cases more than 90 percent) of their export earnings from oil and gas. Most are so awash in cash that they do not need to tax their own citizens. And that is part of the problem—they fail to develop the organic expectations of accountability that emerge when states make citizens pay taxes. As Samuel P. Huntington observed in *The Third Wave*:

> Oil revenues accrue to the state: they therefore increase the power of the state bureaucracy and, because they reduce or eliminate the need for taxation, they also reduce the need for the government to solicit the acquiescence of its subjects to taxation. The lower the level of taxation, the less reason for publics to demand representation. "No taxation without representation" was a political demand; "no representation without taxation" is a political reality.[13]

There is much more to the oil curse than just big states and apathetic citizens. Oil states are not merely big—they are heavily centralized too, since oil wealth accrues to the central state. They are usually also intensely policed, since there is plenty of money to lavish on a huge and active state-security apparatus. They are profoundly corrupt, because the money pours into central-state coffers as rents, and it is really "nobody's money" (certainly no one's tax money), so it is—in a warped normative sense—free for the taking. In these systems, the state is large, centralized, and repressive. It may support any number of bloated bureaucracies as de facto jobs programs meant to buy political peace with government paychecks. Civil society is weak and co-opted. And what passes for the market economy is severely distorted. Real entrepreneurship is scarcely evident, since most people in "business" service the state or its oil sector, or otherwise feed off government contracts or represent foreign companies.

Where oil dominates, there is little wealth creation through investment and risk-taking, for why take risks when there are steady profits to be made at no risk? And then there are the other grim dimensions of the "paradox of plenty," such as the boom-and-bust cycles that go with dependence on primary commodities, as well as the more general tendency for windfall mineral rents to smother or preempt the development of industry and agriculture (the so-called Dutch disease). These consequences are only avoided when vigorous market economies and well-developed, accountable states and taxation systems are in place *before* oil revenues flood in (as for example in Norway and Britain).[14]

There is, then, an economic basis for the absence of democracy in the Arab world. But it is structural. It has to do with the ways in which oil distorts the state, the market, the class structure, and the entire incentive structure. Particularly in an era of high global oil prices, it is relentless: not a single one of the 23 countries that derive most of their export earnings from oil and gas is a democracy today. And for many Arab countries, the "oil curse" will not be lifted any time soon: Five of the eight countries with the largest proven reserves of oil are in the Arab Middle East.[15]

Authoritarian statecraft

Two key pillars of Arab authoritarianism are political. They encompass the patterns and institutions by which authoritarian regimes manage their politics and keep their hold on power, along with the external forces that help to sustain their rule. These authoritarian structures and practices are not unique to the Arab world, but Arab rulers have raised them to a high pitch of refinement, and wield them with unusual skill. Although the typical Arab state may not be efficient in everyday ways, its *mukhabarat* (secret-police and intelligence apparatus) is normally amply funded, technically sophisticated, highly penetrating, legally unrestrained, and splendidly poised to benefit from extensive cooperation with peer institutions in the region as well as Western intelligence agencies. More broadly, "these states are the world leaders in terms of proportion of GNP spent on security."[16]

Yet most Arab autocracies do not rely on unmitigated coercion and fear to survive. Rather, repression is selective and heavily mixed with (and thus often concealed by) mechanisms of representation, consultation, and co-optation. Limited pluralistic elections play an important role in about half the 16 Arab autocracies. As Daniel Brumberg wrote, "liberalized autocracy has proven far more durable than once imagined. The trademark mixture of guided pluralism, controlled elections, and selective repression in Egypt, Jordan, Morocco, Algeria, and Kuwait is not just a 'survival strategy' adopted by the authoritarian regimes, but rather a *type* of political system whose institutions, rule, and logic defy any linear model of democratization."[17] Indeed, in such systems even liberalization is not linear but rather cyclical and adaptive. When pressure mounts, both from within the society and from outside, the regime loosens its constraints and allows more civic activity and a more open electoral arena—until political opposition appears as if it may grow too serious and effective. Then the regime returns to more heavy-handed methods of rigging elections, shrinking political space, and arresting the usual suspects. The electoral arena in these states is thus something like a huge pair of political lungs, breathing in (at times deeply and excitedly) and expanding, but then inevitably exhaling and contracting when limits are reached.

The political trajectory that Egypt followed in 2004 and 2005 was a perfect illustration of this dynamic. The aging autocrat, President Hosni Mubarak, was coming under growing domestic pressure from the unusually broad opposition coalition known as Kifaya (meaning "enough"—which succinctly summed up the country's mood), as well as from U.S. president George W. Bush, who was also pushing for more open and competitive presidential and legislative elections. Reluctantly, Mubarak agreed to allow a contested presidential election and then more transparent legislative elections in 2005. But the presidential "contest" was still grossly unfair, and within three months of the vote (which official figures claim was won by the incumbent with 88.6 percent), Mubarak's opponent, Ayman Nour, was sentenced to five years in prison. By then, the regime had also intervened in the second and third rounds of the parliamentary elections to undermine independent administration of the vote, neutralize civil society monitors, and halt the tempo of opposition victories by Muslim Brotherhood candidates running as de jure "independents." Not long thereafter, the ruling party embarked on a campaign of constitutional "reform" to ensure against any political "accidents" in the future, while a demoralized and divided opposition, weakened by arrests and intimidation, watched helplessly with little in the way of concrete support from the Bush Administration. The institutional maneuver was part of a general Arab pattern of "managed reform," in which Arab autocracies adopt the language of political reform in order to avoid the reality, or embrace limited economic and social reforms to pursue modernization without democratization.[18]

To the extent that political competition and pluralism are allowed in these Arab regimes (which include Algeria, Jordan, Kuwait, and Morocco as well as Egypt), it is within rules and parameters carefully drawn to ensure that regime opponents are disadvantaged and disempowered. Electoral practices (such as Jordan's use of the single non-transferrable vote) are chosen and tilted to privilege personal ties and tribal candidates over organized political parties, especially Islamist ones.[19] Parliaments that result from these limited elections have no real power to legislate or govern, as more or less unlimited authority continues to reside with hereditary kings and imperial presidents. Yet opposition parties face serious costs whether they boycott these semi-charades or take part in them. If oppositionists participate in elections and parliament, they risk becoming co-opted—or at least being seen as such by a cynical and disaffected electorate. Yet if they boycott the "inside game" of electoral and parliamentary politics, the "outside game" of protest and resistance offers little realistic prospect of influence, let alone power. Caught on the horns of such dilemmas, political oppositions in the Arab world become divided, suspicious, and torn from within. They are damned if they do and damned if they don't. Even the Islamists in countries such as Egypt, Kuwait, and Morocco are fragmented into different camps, along moderate and militant (as well as other tactical and factional) lines. Islamist parties that stand resolutely outside the system, while building up social-welfare networks and religious and ideological ties at the grassroots, garner long-term bases of popular support. Secular parties, by contrast, look marginal, halting, and feckless. "Caught between regimes that allow little legal space ... and popular Islamist movements that are clearly in the ascendancy ... they are struggling for influence and relevance, and in some cases even for survival."[20]

The coils of geopolitics

The unfavorable geopolitical situation confronting Arab democracy extends well beyond the overwhelming factor of oil, though oil drives much of the major powers' interest in the region. External support for Arab regimes, historically coming in part from the Soviet Union but now mainly from Europe and the United States, confers on Arab autocracies crucial economic resources, security assistance, and political legitimacy. In these circumstances, for non-oil regimes such as Egypt, Jordan, and Morocco, foreign aid is like oil: another source of rents that regimes use for survival. Like oil, aid flows into the central coffers of the state and helps to give it the means *both* to co-opt and to repress. Since 1975, U.S. "development" assistance to Egypt has totaled more than $28 billion, not including the nearly $50 billion that has flowed to that country in unconditional military aid since the 1978 Camp David Peace Accords.[21] Less well known is the huge flow of U.S. economic and military aid to the much less populous state of Jordan, which has taken in an average of $650 million since 2001. "Western aid makes possible the regime's key political strategy of spending massively on public jobs without imposing steep taxes. From 2001 through 2006, the foreign assistance that Jordan raked in accounted for 27 percent of all domestic revenues."[22]

Two other external factors further reinforce the internal hegemony of Arab autocracies. One is the Arab–Israeli conflict, which hangs like a toxic miasma over Middle Eastern political life. It provides a ready and convenient means of diverting public frustration away from the corruption and human-rights abuses of Arab regimes, turning citizen anger outward to focus on what Arab private and state-run media alike depict emotively as Israeli oppression of the Palestinians, and by symbolic extension, the entire Arab people. Protests over the failings of Arab regimes themselves—the poor quality of education and social services, the lack of jobs, transparency, accountability, and freedom—are banned, but Arab publics can vent their anger in the press and on the streets in the one realm where it is safe, condemnation of Israel.

The second external factor is the other Arab states themselves, who reinforce one another in their authoritarianism and their techniques of monitoring, rigging, and repression, and who over the decades have turned the 22-member Arab League into an unapologetic autocrats' club. Of all the major regional organizations, the Arab League is the most bereft of democratic norms and means for promoting or encouraging them. In fact, its charter, which has not been amended in half a century, lacks any mention of democracy or individual rights. Beyond all this is the lack of even a single clear example of Arab democracy, which means that there is no source of democratic diffusion or emulation anywhere inside the Arab world. Even in a globalized era, this matters: Throughout the third wave, demonstration effects have been "strongest among countries that were geographically proximate and culturally similar."[23]

Will anything change?

Is the Arab world simply condemned to an indefinite future of authoritarian rule? I do not think so. Even the beginnings of a change in U.S. foreign policy during the years from 2003 to 2005 encouraged political opening and at least gave space for popular democratic mobilization in countries such as Egypt, Lebanon, and Morocco, as well as the Palestinian Authority. Although most of these openings have partly or fully closed for the time being, at least Arab oppositions and civil societies had some taste of what democratic politics might look like. Opinion surveys suggest that they clearly want more, and new social-media tools such as Facebook, Twitter, the blogosphere, and the mobile-phone revolution are giving Arabs new opportunities to express themselves and to mobilize.

Three factors could precipitate democratic change across the region. One would be the emergence of a single democratic model in the region, particularly in a country that might be seen as a model. That role would be difficult for Lebanon to play, given its extremely complicated factions and consociational fragmentation of power, as well as the continuing heavy involvement of Syria in its politics. But were Iraq to progress politically, first by democratically electing a new government this year and then by having it function decently and peacefully as U.S. forces withdraw, that could gradually change perceptions in the region. Egypt also bears watching, as the sun slowly sets on the 81-year-old Hosni Mubarak's three decades of personal rule. Whether or not his 46-year-old son Gamal succeeds him, the regime will experience new stresses and needs for adaptation when this modern-day pharaoh passes from the scene.

Second would be a change in U.S. policy to resume principled engagement and more extensive practical assistance to encourage and press for democratic reforms, not just in the electoral realm but with respect to enhancing judicial independence and governmental transparency as well as expanding freedom of the press and civil society. If this were pursued in a more modest tone, and reinforced to some degree by European pressure, it could help to rejuvenate and protect domestic political forces that are now dispirited and in disarray. But to proceed along this path, the United States and its European allies would have to overcome their undifferentiated view of Islamist parties and engage those Islamist actors who would be willing to commit more clearly to liberal-democratic norms.

The biggest game changer would be a prolonged, steep decline in world oil prices (say to half of current levels). Although the smallest of the Gulf oil kingdoms would remain rich at any conceivable price, the bigger countries such as Saudi Arabia (population 29 million) would find it necessary to broach the question of a new political bargain with their own burgeoning (and very young) publics. Algeria and Iran would come under even greater pressure, and while Iran is not an Arab state, it has an Arab minority, and one should not underestimate the felicitous impact on Arab democratic prospects of a democratic transition in a major Middle Eastern country that also contains the region's only example of a full-blown Islamist regime. When one looks at what has happened to democracy in Nigeria, Russia, and Venezuela as the price of oil has soared in recent years, the policy imperative for driving down the price of oil becomes even more compelling. Before too much longer, however, accelerating climate change is likely to compel a much more radical response to this challenge. When the global revolution in energy technology hits with full force, finally breaking the oil cartel, it will bring a decisive end to Arab political exceptionalism.

Notes

I am grateful for the many valuable comments offered to me when versions of this paper were presented in 2009 at Stanford University, Indiana University, and the Ash Institute for Democratic Governance and Innovation at Harvard University.

1 Originally published as "Why Are There No Arab Democracies?" *Journal of Democracy* 21 (January 2010): 93–104.
2 By "Middle East," I mean the 19 states of the Middle East and North Africa (MENA). When I refer to the Arab world I mean the 16 Arab states of this region, namely Algeria, Bahrain, Egypt, Iraq, Jordan, Kuwait, Lebanon, Libya, Morocco, Oman, Qatar, Saudi Arabia, Syria, Tunisia, the United Arab Emirates, and Yemen.

3 There are 22 members of the Arab League, though one of them (Palestine) is not yet a state. Of the other 21, five are better analyzed within the context of Sub-Saharan Africa: Comoros, Djibouti, Mauritania, Somalia, and Sudan. Of these, Comoros is the only democracy today. Mauritania was briefly a democracy not long ago, and Sudan has seen two failed democratization attempts.

4 Alfred Stepan and Graeme B. Robertson, "An 'Arab' More than 'Muslim' Electoral Gap," *Journal of Democracy* 14 (July 2003): 30–44.

5 The eight democracies are Albania, Bangladesh, Comoros, Indonesia, Mali, Senegal, Sierra Leone, and Turkey.

6 Of the 47 countries that Stepan and Robertson list as Muslim-majority, I exclude from my analysis only Nigeria, where no one really knows what the overall population is or what the balance is between religious groups. And I have included two countries (Brunei and Maldives) for which they did not have data.

7 Elie Kedourie, *Democracy and Arab Culture* (Washington, DC: Washington Institute for Near East Policy, 1992), 5–6.

8 These broad levels of support have been documented in numerous *Journal of Democracy* articles over the past decade, some of which were gathered together in Larry Diamond and Marc F. Plattner, *How People View Democracy* (Baltimore, MD: Johns Hopkins University Press, 2008).

9 Mark Tessler and Elearnor Gao, "Gauging Arab Support for Democracy," *Journal of Democracy* 16 (July 2005): 82–97, and Amaney Jamal and Mark Tessler, "The Democracy Barometers: Attitudes in the Arab World," *Journal of Democracy* 19 (January 2008): 97–110.

10 Jamal and Tessler, "The Democracy Barometers," 101.

11 Ibid., 102. See www.arabbarometer.org for more details about the Arab Barometer.

12 See for example the table in Tessler and Gao, "Gauging Arab Support for Democracy," 91.

13 Samuel P. Huntington, *The Third Wave: Democratization in the Late Twentieth Century* (Norman: University of Oklahoma Press, 1991), 65.

14 Terry Lynn Karl, *The Paradox of Plenty: Oil Booms and Petro-States* (Berkeley: University of California Press, 1997), 5–6, 15–17, 213–221, 236–242.

15 Saudi Arabia, Iraq, Kuwait, UAE, and Libya. Iran ranks second behind Saudi Arabia.

16 Eva Bellin, "Coercive Institutions and Coercive Leaders," in Marsha Pripstein Posusney and Michele Penner Angrist, eds, *Authoritarianism in the Middle East: Regimes and Resistance* (Boulder, CO: Lynne Rienner, 2005), 31. Middle Eastern countries spent on average 6.7 percent of GNP on defense in 2000, compared with a global average of 3.8 percent. Bellin sees Arab regimes in the Middle East as being unusually "robust," in that they are "exceptionally able and willing to crush reform initiatives from below" (ibid., 27). But this is true of many authoritarian regimes. Arab autocracies have also proven more supple and adept than others.

17 Daniel Brumberg, "Democratization in the Arab World? The Trap of Liberalized Autocracy," *Journal of Democracy* 13 (October 2002): 56.

18 Michele Dunne and Marina Ottaway, "Incumbent Regimes and the 'King's Dilemma' in the Arab World: Promise and Threat of Managed Reform," in Marina Ottaway and Amr Hamzway, eds, *Getting to Pluralism: Political Actors in the Arab World* (Washington, DC: Carnegie Endowment for International Peace, 2009): 13–40.

19 Julia Choucair, "Illusive Reform: Jordan's Stubborn Stability," Carnegie Papers No. 76, Democracy and Rule of Law Project, Carnegie Endowment for International Peace, December 2006, 7. www.carnegieendowment.org/files/cp76_choucair_final.pdf.

20 Marina Ottaway and Amr Hamzawy, "Fighting on Two Fronts: Secular Parties in the Arab World," in Ottaway and Hamzaway, *Getting to Pluralism*, 41.

21 See www.usaid.gov/our_work/features/egypt and www.fas.org/asmp/profiles/egypt.htm. The latter source reports $38 billion in military aid through 2000, but each additional year has brought $1 billion more.

22 Sean Yom, "Jordan: Ten More Years of Autocracy," *Journal of Democracy* 20 (October 2009): 163.

23 Huntington, *Third Wave*, 102.

Part II

In search of democracy in Africa

10 Class formation in the swollen African state[1]

As the state has moved back to the center of analysis of political change and conflict, increasing attention has focused on its role in forming new classes and in structuring the possibilities of class action. As Nelson Kasfir notes, both Marx and Weber "saw the vital role the state could play in consolidating the class position of a dominant social group."[2] Neither, however, saw the state as the inherent locus of the process of class formation and of class domination. For Marx, the state was typically the instrument of a ruling class whose origin and basis was in control over the means of production. For Weber, power, class, and status were potentially independent dimensions of stratification.

A more powerful, and in a sense radical, theory of the state's central role in the generation of class domination is to be found in Gaetano Mosca's classic work, *The Ruling Class,* first published in 1896. For Mosca, there is in every society a minority that constitutes a ruling class, which may be termed a "political class," because it is formed through and based upon monopoly control over the instruments of power. He insisted, as did Marx, that "all ruling classes tend to become hereditary in fact if not in law." But this does not make them permanent. When social change produces a demand for different capacities in the management of the state, "then the manner in which the ruling class is constituted also changes." If the practical importance of wealth, or knowledge, or religion, or ideology dramatically increases, "far-reaching dislocations ... in the ruling class" will occur.

With particular prescience in relation to Africa, Mosca observed that "rapid restocking of ruling classes is a frequent and very striking phenomenon in countries that have been recently colonized." In the wake of sweeping social change,

> there comes a period of renovation ... during which individual energies have free play and certain individuals, more passionate, more energetic, more intrepid or merely shrewder than others, force their way from the bottom of the social ladder to the topmost rungs.

Eventually, those who have gained admittance to this new ruling class

> will begin to acquire a group spirit. They will become more and more
> exclusive and learn better and better the art of monopolizing to their
> advantage the qualities and capacities that are essential to acquiring
> power and holding it.

When the monopoly of political power is so securely established that possession of it is transmitted by inheritance, the ruling class is firmly in place.[3]

Mosca's theory offers the most insightful and revealing understanding of the origins of dominant classes in the new nations of Africa. Its application to contemporary Africa follows upon the pathbreaking work of Richard L. Sklar, whose study, *Nigerian Political Parties,* traced the emergence of a "new and rising class ... engaged in class action and characterized by a growing sense of class consciousness." Admittance into this new class was on the basis of four socioeconomic criteria (high-status occupation in the modern sector, high income, superior education, and ownership or control of business enterprise, with aristocratic status the leading element in the north), but the instrument of its rise to dominance and its social fusion was the modern political party, through which control of the state was obtained and the resources of the state were appropriated for the purposes of class formation.[4] In a subsequent work, Sklar followed Mosca explicitly in naming this class the "political class," noting the particular value of this term in analyzing "a developing country, like Nigeria, where it may serve to suggest that political power is the primary force that creates economic opportunity and determines the pattern of social stratification."[5]

The nomenclature of this politically based dominant class has since become a matter of considerable confusion and debate (with Sklar subsequently abandoning the term "political class" because it was mistakenly interpreted as denoting only politicians).[6] And arguments about nomenclature are not without theoretical implications. These notwithstanding, students of African national development have become increasingly sensitive to the role of the modern state as an autonomous force in shaping the class structure. The most forceful and seminal formulation of this perspective comes, again, from Sklar. In contradistinction to the Marxist conception of the economic determinants of class formation, he asserts that "the exertion of political power in the form of state action appears to overtake and outweigh more gradual processes of economic and social change" in the formation of dominant classes in Africa, and not simply because of extensive state control over economic resources, but because "class relations, at bottom, are determined by relations of power, not production."[7]

This chapter outlines four ways in which the state may serve as the basis of dominant-class formation: through its legitimate employment and expenditures; through its development plans and strategy; through the manipulation of patronage and ethnic ties to inhibit the development of lower-class consciousness and organization; and finally, through the illegitimate accumulation of public wealth, i.e. political corruption. It then briefly considers the nature and means of class consolidation. In conclusion, it offers some reflections on the implications and consequences of these processes of stratification.

Before proceeding, however, we must be clear on what is meant by the crucial terms "class" and "dominant class." I conceive of class here both in the Marxian sense of relationship to the means of production, and in the Weberian sense of income or consumptive power in relation to the market. Put more broadly, class may be understood "as a category encompassing those who have similar economic motivation because they have similar economic opportunities, even if class consciousness, class solidarity, or class action do not exist."[8] A class may be considered socially dominant if it owns or controls the most productive assets, appropriates the bulk of the most valued consumption opportunities, and commands a sufficient monopoly over the means of coercion and legitimation to sustain politically this cumulative socio-economic preeminence.[9] Necessarily, the members of such a class will have "controlling positions in the dominant institutions of society."[10] They will also have high degrees of class consciousness and social coherence—constituting in the Marxian sense a "class-for-itself"—as this is a precondition for the class action necessary to preserve and extend class domination. Finally, following in the tradition of both Marx and Mosca, the transmission of this status across generations will be seen as a particular mark of the consolidation of class domination.

The state as employer and consumer

Among the most significant legacies of colonial rule—and probably the most decisive in shaping the pattern of national development, even after independence—has been the modern state. To be sure, the colonial bureaucracy was much smaller, and the mission of the colonial state was much more limited, than their successors after independence.[11] Moreover, in British territories, in particular, the power of the colonial state was checked to some extent by the metropolitan and local press, the overseas parliament, financial constraints, and the small size of the coercive apparatus.[12] Nevertheless, it was not simply that the European conquerors constructed for the first time the infrastructure of a large-scale and complex state; in fact, this was already in place, at least to some degree, in several African nations at the time of conquest. Nor was it just that a modern state system was forcibly imposed over diverse peoples within arbitrary boundaries, though surely this has heavily shaped the subsequent pattern of political conflict. Most significantly, these new state structures dwarfed in wealth and power both existing social institutions and various new fragments of modern organization.

As Crawford Young has observed, the need for domination over a subject population left no room for the transfer to the new colonial states of the "state-limiting doctrines ... constitutionalism, civil liberties, liberalism" that had evolved in Europe. Rather, "the colonial state sought to equip itself with a mythology of irresistible power and force ... in order to impose its hegemony and simultaneously find means to extract from peasant economies the fiscal resources to pay for conquest and for its own institutionalization." After World War II, "the notions of 'development' and 'welfare' were added to the public doctrine of the state, and given concrete embodiment in a ramifying state infrastructure to provide these services," which necessitated breathtaking rates of growth in state expenditures.[13]

Both the extractive purposes of the colonial state, and later (under the pressure of nationalist demands and incipient political-party mobilization) its development and welfare functions, required it to become the dominant factor in the emerging modern economy. Establishing control over the primary means of production, peasant agriculture, was essential for obtaining the needed revenue and raw materials. Hence, "the colonial state quickly became committed to the promotion of cash export agriculture."[14] Through the establishment of statutory marketing boards as monopsony purchasers for all export crops, private investment in agriculture was discouraged in most places, and the state gained direct control over the greatest source of cash revenue in the colony. Rather than supporting agricultural development and farm income, marketing-board funds became a primary source of state revenue and the leading factor in its expansion during the commodities boom of the 1950s.[15]

Similar control was established over the development of infrastructure and, in some countries, the mining of minerals. In Nigeria, indigenous mining activity was eliminated and state mining corporations were introduced for tin and coal,[16] setting a precedent for petroleum after independence. There and elsewhere, public corporations were established in transportation (road, rail, sea, and air) and other public utilities. Significantly, the colonial state also discouraged the development of indigenous private enterprise by preempting local capital accumulation in cash-crop agriculture, favoring the foreign firms and industrial exports of the metropolis, and curtailing individual access to the land.[17]

Ironically, however, while colonial rule rapidly established state structures, it did little to develop their *indigenous* capacities, but rather "restricted and even widely prevented the involvement of Africans in higher, non-clerical levels of administration."[18] When Africanization of the bureaucracy was undertaken, it began "too late to enable Africans to fill most senior government posts at the time of independence."[19] This legacy weakened the authority and effectiveness of the new states, and encouraged them to embark on "rapid and wholesale Africanization" after independence, which deflated rather than enhanced their governmental capacity and, in the absence of established traditions of probity and accountability, fostered the growth of corruption.[20] Thus was spawned the distinctive and enduring feature of postindependence African states: they have been, as Naomi Chazan has said of Ghana's civil service, "overestablished, but underbureaucratized."[21]

The nationalist inheritors of these colonial states, being frequently committed to socialist ideologies and more so to neomercantilist development strategies, dramatically expanded state control over the economy. Such was the ideology of "developmentalism," the passionate impatience for economic growth, that even the capitalist orientation was "deeply tinged with statism."[22] As explained by Sayre Schatz:

> [Recognizing] that indigenous business was not yet able to provide the initiative, leadership, or managerial and technological expertise needed to generate substantial modern-sector economic development, government assumed an increasingly active role in the directly productive sector of the economy.[23]

Virtually everywhere in Africa the parastatal sector mushroomed, often through the nationalization of productive assets owned by expatriates. According to David B. Abernethy, "Zambia had 134 parastatal bodies by 1970, Nigeria about 250 by 1973, Tanzania about 400 by 1981."[24] A recent World Bank study found an average of about 100 public enterprises in the 20 Sub-Saharan African countries for which data were available (in the late 1970s and early 1980s). And these raw figures typically understate the importance of public enterprises in the modern sector, where they may account for as much as 40–50 percent of manufacturing value-added and of modern-sector employment, and 20–40 percent of gross fixed-capital formation and total domestic credit.[25] In Nigeria, where indigenous private enterprise is more developed than in much of the rest of Africa, statutory corporations at both the federal and state level came to figure in or dominate not only petroleum, but almost every aspect of production and distribution: mining, steel, agriculture, printing, banking, insurance, shipping, supplying, hotels, electricity, construction, telecommunications, radio, and television, to offer a partial list.[26]

This sweeping expansion, which has accelerated since independence, has established the state as the primary wage employer in Africa. Citing a recent IMF study, Abernethy estimates that government at all levels in Sub-Saharan Africa accounted for 15–20 percent of wage employment outside agriculture in 1960 and 30–35 percent by 1980. Considering as well non-financial public enterprises, "A rough estimate is that total public sector employment accounted for 40–45 percent of non-agricultural wage employment in 1960 and 50–55 percent in 1980."[27] The latter compares with an average of 36 percent in Asia, 27 percent in Latin America, and 24 percent in the OECD industrial countries.[28] Clearly, the state dominates modern-sector jobs in Africa to an unprecedented degree. And typically, the bulk of wage labor in the private sector is accounted for by foreign corporations. In Nigeria in 1964, for example, 54 percent of wage earners were employed by government and 38 percent by foreign capital; thus, less than a tenth worked for private Nigerian companies.[29] In many African countries today, the proportion is probably even less. The implication of this juxtaposition of statism and economic dependence is transparent: the space for upward social mobility, and even more so for dominant-class formation, in indigenous private enterprise is low throughout Africa and often effectively nil.

In similar fashion, the consumptive power of the state in Africa has also grown, in both absolute and relative terms. In some instances these have reached extraordinary proportions. "Public expenditures totalled 59 percent of gross domestic product (GDP) in 1974 in Zaïre; in Tanzania, the fraction of GDP collected by the state increased from 15 percent in 1961 to nearly 35 percent in 1974."[30] In Nigeria, federal expenditures are estimated to have risen from 12 percent of GDP in 1966 to 36 percent of a 1977 GDP that was many times larger.[31] Throughout Africa, the growth rate of public expenditures has far outstripped that for private consumption, averaging about 8 percent during the 1960s and 1970s. This was twice the rate of growth of private consumption in 1960–1965, "and almost three times the private sector growth rate in the 1970s."[32]

Given the role of the state as the primary wage employer, it is not surprising that a huge and often staggering proportion of these swelling expenditures are claimed by "administration"—essentially, the pay and support of state personnel. The trend has been trenchantly summarized by Irving Markovitz:

> The steady growth of the "public sector," the continual expansion of government expenditures for administration, and the rising costs of maintaining political officialdom at ever higher levels of "comfortable" living are among the most striking phenomena of the postindependence period. In a searching look at the budgets of new states, Gerard Chaliand reveals that almost half (47.2 percent) of Senegal's budget for 1964–65 was devoted to administrative salaries; not a single dollar was spent on direct investment. The administration in the Cameroons absorbed eighteen times as much money as capital expenditure. The civil service in the Central African Republic absorbed 81 percent of the budget.[33]

Nor did the trend abate in the 1970s. Nigerian civil servants received wage increases of as much as 133 percent in 1974. "In the Ivory Coast, wages and salaries rose by over 16% a year between 1966 and 1975, absorbing 43.5% of current expenditure in 1966 and 50.9% in 1975."[34] Excepting the oil-exporting countries, African states during the 1970s devoted on average about twice as much (roughly 30 percent) of their total expenditures to wages and salaries as did the nations of any other region (save those of Latin America, which they exceeded by a factor of 50 percent).[35] Only in the past two or three years—under the pressure of crushing fiscal crises and harsh austerity programs encouraged or imposed by the IMF and the international banking community—have this and related trends in state expansion begun to abate.

These figures imply more than a burden of overheads that sap the potential for productive investment and genuine development (about which more later). They suggest that the state—through its administrative expenditures alone—has become a major engine of social differentiation in Africa, and further, that unless there is a relatively egalitarian distribution of income among the employees of the state, the salaries and benefits paid to senior staff and officials may constitute an important mechanism of dominant-class formation. If the "legitimate" remuneration of higher-level public servants is large enough in relation to other possible sources of income in society, it can represent a virtual guarantee of upper-class standing. Given that the proportion of the gross domestic product captured by African states is typically as high as—or much higher than—in Western nations, and that incomes *per capita* are pervasively low, one would logically expect the salaries and wages of state employees to be considerably higher than what could typically be earned in the private economy. In fact, this is the case in the extreme. The ratio of the average central government wage to the GDP *per capita* is roughly six to one in Africa, twice as high as in Latin America or Asia, and almost four times the ratio in OECD countries.[36]

But it is the salaries at the top of the civil-service scale that have the most significant implications for class formation, and these

are even more strikingly elevated above per capita GDP. As of 1963–4 the ratio of the former to the latter was 73:1 in Malawi, 82:1 in Kenya, 96:1 in Tanganyika, 118:1 in Nigeria, and 130:1 in Uganda. This pattern is in sharp contrast to that of the United States, where the ratio is well under 10:1—most likely under 8:1. If we translate African ratios at independence into contemporary American terms—admittedly a procedure of dubious validity—a top American civil servant earning one hundred times U.S. per capita income would now receive a salary (in 1985 dollars) of over $1.7 million a year![37]

These figures do not include the enviable perquisites (subsidized housing, transportation, medical care, pensions) that usually accompany these hefty salaries. The situation in Nigeria's First Republic was typical of what came to prevail in many African states, whether parliamentary or military. There the salaries and perquisites of high public office became a ticket of admission into the emergent dominant class. A new university graduate *began* in the civil service at a salary 20 times the annual earnings of the average farmer.[38] Legislators, ministers, and high-ranking civil servants could expect to earn from 7 to 30 times the pay of an ordinary government laborer, and still quite a bit more after car allowances, housing subsidies, and other emoluments were included.[39] In such circumstances, members of the state elite became "the beneficiaries of a process of rapid class formation."[40]

In a sense, then, the African political class was the offspring of the colonial state. As a matter of nationalist and (ironically) egalitarian principle, the rising elite of African politicians and bureaucrats demanded the same career opportunities, and the same salaries and benefits for the same work, as European officials of the colonial state whose high standards of remuneration had been set by market conditions in the metropolis.[41] But of course, this was also a matter of self- and incipient class-interest. Using the advantage of a Western education and the literacy in a European language it conferred, which were the prerequisites for white-collar employment in the colonial bureaucracy or auxiliary institutions, the new African elite sought to turn the system to their own advantage at the same time as they struggled to free it from colonial domination.

As the European colonial elites departed, the new African elites sought to emulate their standard of living. They imbibed their materialist values and sought eagerly to accumulate and display the modern consumer goods that had symbolized Western affluence and now became the mark of rising-class status in Africa.[42] As they accepted power from rulers who had never been responsible to the masses, "the new elite accepted the same remoteness from the popular will as their natural and proper role."[43] Throughout Africa, the members of this emergent class became visibly distinguishable from the rest of society, not only by their strategic locations in the structure of power—which enabled them "to derive their livelihood from the 'national income,' from the productive efforts of others"—but also

> by their general health, height and weight, the chances of survival of their children, their manner of speech, their leisure activities, their eating habits ... their means of transportation, the games they play, the conversation of their wives, the work habits and values they attempt to inculcate in their children—every aspect of their existence.[44]

No less significant than its provision of elite employment and salaries has been the African state's preeminent role in consumption. The large proportion of national wealth captured and expended by the state in Africa is more significant than its face value because it is derived mainly from the money economy, and so constitutes a much larger proportion of the type of wealth most instrumental to modern class formation.[45] Because the state is the most important source of expenditure in the modern economy, even those who do not hold any formal office in the public sector (or in the party apparatus that controls it) must depend for their success on state largesse. In such circumstances, the indigenous bourgeoisie typically becomes, as in the case of Morocco, "a parasitic bourgeoisie that lives off privileged access to state-controlled resources or the differential application of state regulations."[46]

To return again to the Nigerian example, state office in the First Republic

> could deliver or block the licenses, the contracts and the public loan
> and investment funds that could make a new enterprise or quick for-
> tune; the scholarships that could launch a bureaucratic career; the
> bureaucratic positions and military commissions that offered a coveted
> livelihood and status.[47]

This did not change with the petroleum boom or the introduction of the
ill-fated Second Republic. Private business success remained heavily dependent upon government contracts, consultancies, agencies, commissions,
fees, licenses, loans, land allocations, and so on.[48] Still relatively backward
in finance and technology, and caught between the leviathans of the state
on the one hand and of foreign capital on the other, the Nigerian bourgeoisie came to specialize in linking the one to the other, in finding roles
as gatekeepers and middlemen, ways to make profits quickly and surely by
selling influence or by mediating in the distribution of goods and services
rather than in their production.

Indeed, the tendency to rely on the manipulation of the state rather
than productive investment has heightened considerably since the petroleum boom and what Schatz describes as the shift "from nurture capitalism
to pirate capitalism."[49]

> With the recent utter predominance of "government" as a source of for-
> tune, a new stage has been reached ... For the most vigorous, capable,
> resourceful, well-connected, and "lucky" entrepreneurs (including pol-
> iticians, civil servants, and army officers), productive economic activity
> ... has faded in appeal. Access to, and manipulation of, the govern-
> ment-spending process has become the golden gateway to fortune.[50]

The Nigerian example is only one of many suggesting the validity of Kasfir's
proposition that "the presence of a bonanza, particularly one creating no
productive linkages with the rest of the economy, will only increase the
dependence of incipient entrepreneurs on the largesse of the state."[51] As
the state becomes wealthier, especially in a rapid or sudden fashion, its centrality in the process of dominant-class formation will increase.

Political corruption as class action

To speak of the kind of state manipulation entailed in "pirate capitalism" is
to go well beyond the state's legitimate and legal expenditures for salaries,
benefits, goods, and services. Despite the African state's enormous financial
burden of remunerating its officials, this is everywhere supplemented and
in many countries dwarfed by political corruption. Following Joseph Nye,

political corruption is here defined as behavior by a state official for self
or group benefit that violates legal rules about official conduct or formal
duties of the office.[52] This encompasses the illicit manipulation of public
political resources (for example, the powers and influence of political
office) and/or appropriation of public political goods (government funds,
jobs, licenses, and so forth) for ends that are either self-serving or that serve
some individuals, clique, community, party, or other constituency or clien-
tele of the officeholder.[53]

The scale of political corruption in many African states is by now legendary, and increasingly well documented. In the majority, it is manifestly the
primary mechanism of dominant-class formation. Certainly, this is the case
in Zaire, where the political class of Mobutu's patrimonial, absolutist state
has relentlessly bled into bankruptcy a nation endowed with great natural
wealth. Thomas Callaghy has conveyed some sense of the systematic character and incredible scale of this means of accumulation in Zaire:

> The line between private and state property is almost nonexistent.
> Embezzlement, fraud, theft, illicit economic ventures of all kinds,
> including widespread smuggling and export-import swindles, are all
> common, and external efforts to control them have all failed ... One
> estimate puts the amount of revenue lost or diverted at roughly 60 per-
> cent of each annual operating budget. In 1975 the Shaba Regional
> Commissioner was reportedly grossing $100,000 a month, of which
> only 2 percent was his salary. Also in 1975 a prominent general was
> reputed to have a monthly salary of 45,000 Zaïres plus numerous infor-
> mal payments, including 8,000 Zaïres a month paid to him out of a
> special account in the Banque de Kinshasa ... Each newly appointed
> member of the Political Bureau or the Executive Council would receive
> a 17,000 Zaïre "settling-in allowance" to allow him to purchase some
> of the "essentials" needed to maintain the life-style expected of a high
> member of the political aristocracy.[54]

In Nigeria (even with its far more complicated political system and more
pluralistic economic structure), corruption has grown over the past two
decades into the primary means for accumulation of wealth. During late
colonial rule and the period of the First Republic, it became rampant at
first in the local and then at the regional and federal levels. At perhaps
its most sophisticated, in the cocoa-rich Western Region, an investigation
revealed that the corrupt machinations of a small circle of ruling-party politicians and businessmen had drained the region's Marketing Board of more
than £10 million, essentially bankrupting it in seven years.[55] Throughout
that period, government contracts, purchases, and loan programs were
systematically manipulated to enrich political officials and the politically
well connected,[56] and public disgust with the growth of this venality figured
prominently in the downfall of the Republic.[57]

But those amounts were dwarfed by the level of corrupt appropriation during Nigeria's oil boom, which saw a "frantic grab of the well-placed for easy wealth" and "hideous displays of affluence" amid appalling poverty.[58] Following the 1975 coup that toppled the regime of General Yakubu Gowon, a commission of inquiry found ten of the 12 State Governors guilty of corruption and misuse of funds totaling over 16 million naira.[59] And this, in turn, became a pittance relative to the corrupt profits from the politics of the Second Republic. During those four years (1979–1983), scandals in the tens of millions, and even billions, dominated the headlines. These included the illicit auction of much of the $2,500 million annual allocation of import licenses; the arrest of several top officials of the Federal Capital Development Authority in Abuja over an alleged $820 million fraud; and the revelation by a federal minister that Nigeria was losing $50 million a month to ghost workers and other forms of payroll fraud.[60] That these were not just rumors was demonstrated by the findings of the subsequent military regime's tribunals, which convicted numerous former high elected and appointed officials of corrupt accumulation, and sentenced them to long prison terms.

In absolute terms, Zaire and Nigeria have probably witnessed the largest scale of corrupt accumulation in Africa. But political corruption has been widespread (if not endemic) and often massive in other African countries as well. Ghana's descent into instability and ungovernability cannot be understood apart from the increasing privatization and plundering of state resources by successive regimes, both democratic and authoritarian.[61] In Zambia, widespread political graft has been a critical factor in the formation of an indigenous propertied class.[62] Recent evidence from Kenya indicates that the friends and clients of President Daniel arap Moi have amassed fortunes from their political jobs and connections, while Moi himself is alleged to have built a personal economic empire that is reported by *Africa Confidential* to include $100 million of prime real estate in Nairobi, a transport corporation, the oil company which bought out Mobil's interests in Kenya, and a cinema chain with monopoly control over the distribution of films.[63]

While every society has its share of venality, there is a tendency to view corruption on such a mammoth scale as an aberration of a particular regime or set of rotten personalities. This is a serious fallacy. Both the pervasiveness of the phenomenon throughout Africa (and other weakly institutionalized political systems) and its growth through different types of political regimes suggest a far more systemic and deeply rooted character. It is not an aberration, but rather the way the system works in the typical African state.

Recent research on African political systems has refocused attention on the pivotal role of patron–client relations in structuring access both to power and the resources of class formation that depend upon power.[64] In the absence of meaningful and effective political institutions and of viable channels of upward mobility outside the state, politics becomes the means for personal and group accumulation, and the competition to accumulate gets organized into hierarchical networks of patrons and clients. Unconstrained by the hollow formalities of laws and constitutions, these networks use the state to appropriate its wealth (and that of other social groups and organizations) for their own enrichment. State office is awarded primarily as an entitlement to accumulate personal wealth. And when such a system of clientelism is wedded to a structure of political party competition and mass political participation, it must greatly expand, since the maintenance of power then requires distribution to a much larger load of clients, especially at the bottom levels of the system.[65]

Robert Jackson and Carl Rosberg term this system "personal rule," because it is commonly dominated by an individual ruler who relies on his personal skills and acumen to manipulate and retain control of the state. But arbitrary and personalistic relations of power prevail at every level of the system, since adherence to rules is everywhere absent. Hence the polity shrinks to "a system of relations linking rulers not with the 'public' or even with the ruled (at least not directly), but with patrons, associates, clients, supporters, and rivals, who constitute the 'system.'"[66]

Political corruption is essential to the survival of this clientelistic system, not only because of the huge and increasing scale of patronage resources required to maintain lengthening and proliferating lines of clientage, but also because clientelism can only function if officeholders are free to allocate political resources and goods to their clients irrespective of rules that demand distribution by impersonal, bureaucratic criteria. Once such rules are routinely ignored, state offices become "entitlements," giving incumbents immense discretion to use the patronage resources of office not only to enrich themselves, but "to assist clients and followers and thereby maintain— and perhaps enlarge—their political base."[67] In such a system, the public offices are themselves the most dearly desired type of patronage resource.

Because Jackson and Rosberg center their model on a single dominant leader, they limit its utility for polities like Nigeria, where power relations are more complicated and dispersed. Here Richard Joseph has offered a more useful conceptual framework in applying Max Weber's model of the "prebendal" state. In Weber's analysis of traditional authority, prebends are entitlements to income dispensed by the patrimonial ruler to his political retainers and administrative staff, frequently as a way of "routinizing" authority that was originally charismatic in nature.[68] "In patrimonial systems generally, and particularly in those of the decentralized type, all governmental authority and the corresponding economic rights tend to be treated as privately appropriated economic advantages."[69] Joseph thus uses the term "prebendal" to denote "patterns of political behavior which reflect as their justifying principle that the offices of the existing state may be competed for and then utilized for the personal benefit of officeholders as well as that of their reference or support groups," irrespective of the laws and regulations concerning conduct in state offices.[70]

In a typology closer to the concept of "personal rule," Callaghy conceptualizes a "patrimonial administrative state" in which officials who owe their positions (more or less) to the personal ruler are granted what is in effect a prebend—an entitlement to appropriate for personal benefit the resources of the offices in the inherited colonial administrative apparatus and the more recent state-party structures.[71] Callaghy as well traces this phenomenon to the state's predominance as "the major avenue of upward mobility, status, power and wealth,"[72] and to the statist views and policies which further enlarge access to appropriable wealth within the state arena.

Where all of these theories are misleading and excessively pessimistic, however, is in their implication that corruption, clientelism, and abuse of power are inherent in the operation of the African state at this stage of national development. They *are* inherent in the politics of personalistic or prebendal states, to be sure, but these—to reiterate—emerge in the absence first of effective institutions to check the abuse of power and to ensure administrative accountability, and second of alternative channels for the accumulation of wealth. Where these other political and social structures develop, as they have to some extent in Botswana,[73] these pathologies can be substantially avoided.

Yet the challenge that such institutions of accountability face is underscored by the powerful socioeconomic motives for political corruption. Even in countries where the salaries of state officials account for over half the national budget, they may not be sufficient to achieve a level of consumption equivalent to real European standards. Hence, in Senegal, "The local bureaucrat, whose style of life is still modeled on that of his French predecessors, finds that he cannot hope to attain such relative luxury without systematically breaking the rules of his organization."[74] And perhaps more significantly, even though official salaries and benefits placed the African state elite right at or near the material level of the former European dominant class of the colony, it has since become apparent to this rising class that there is a far greater level of accumulation and domination to which to aspire. This is the lifestyle of the international bourgeoisie, and the security of social place that derives from the ownership of landed property.

As Africa's political classes have been drawn into a shrinking global society, the rich of Europe and North America have replaced middle-class colonial officials as the reference group for class aspirations. State salaries might set the higher bureaucrat or politician comfortably apart from the rest of his society, but they could hardly land him in a London town house or a Beverly Hills estate. They could guarantee his children a place in the elite schools of his own nation, but perhaps not at Eton or Choate, Cambridge or Harvard or the Sorbonne. When the "big man" syndrome became defined in material terms, there was no reason why it should stop at the boundaries of the continent. In the past decade or two in particular, the big men of Africa's political classes—indeed the higher and more cosmopolitan elements of dominant classes throughout the Third World—have sought wealth and prestige on an international scale. In Africa, this has generally been attainable only through massive illicit manipulation and diversion of state resources.

In these several respects, political corruption has been central to the process of dominant-class formation in Africa, and to the secure control of the state machinery that serves as the foundation for this process. Given this and earlier generalizations, it stands to reason that the larger the state—the greater the proportion of resources it controls and economic activity it regulates—the greater will tend to be the level of political corruption. Most recent studies of this phenomenon have advanced this proposition and provided considerable evidence in support of it. Victor LeVine heavily attributes the "increased incidence and generalization of corruption in the 1950s" in Ghana to "the growth of state corporations, secretariats, commissions, authorities, and the like," which "provided almost unlimited opportunities for the diversion of public goods to favourably placed entrepreneurs at all levels both within and without the formal polity."[75] Finding a similar effect for Morocco, John Waterbury concludes:

> [As] bureaucracies regulate and sanction ever wider spheres of social and economic behavior [and] influence and determine the allocation of desired resources on a hitherto unprecedented scale ... competition for privileged access to state services or relief from impositions has come to dominate political life; the scope for corrupt patronage has expanded with the state itself.[76]

Similarly, drawing from the Nigerian experience, Joseph argues that

> when the state itself becomes the key distributor of financial resources—and this in the absence of any socialist or even capitalist ideology—all governmental projects become the object of intense pressure to convert them into means of individual and group accumulation.[77]

Morris Sfetzel's analysis of Zambia points in the same direction, and Jackson and Rosberg find the pattern characteristic of Africa in general.[78]

If this proposition is correct, it implies an interesting and distressing circularity of causation: swollen states give rise to large-scale political corruption, which becomes a key factor in the birth of a dominant class. But this class, springing from and still largely dependent upon control of the state, has as one of its primary class interests the further expansion of the state—which tends to generate even greater political corruption to reinforce the dominance of the political class. This is why the cycle has been so difficult to break through the first two to three decades of African independence—and why it will remain difficult until the weight of crisis and stagnation compels some alteration in the relationship between state and society.

Politics as class diversion

A third way in which political power may contribute to dominant class formation is through a different consequence of the politics of clientage. State patronage may not only provide the resources for class formation, it may also purchase sufficient acceptance of, or even identification with, the system at the mass level to preempt any serious lower-class challenge. This need not be a deliberate strategy, but it does tend to be the inevitable by-product of patron–client relations in a poorly developed, multiethnic society.

Joseph stresses the "non-contradictory interplay between class formation and ethnic conflict via the mediating mechanism of clientelism."[79] From this perspective, pyramids of patron-client ties, cutting across the widening chasm between the political class and the mass, tend to legitimize the growing inequality by giving a wider share of society some small, immediate stake in the system, while also heightening the salience of ethnic ties in the struggle for socioeconomic rewards. More than two decades ago, Sklar took prominent note of this phenomenon in analyzing "the communal basis of democracy" in Nigeria. The politics of ethnic patronage functioned psychologically and to some extent materially to limit the economic and social distance between the "rising class" and the masses. Socially, the members of this class were found to

> retain a strong sense of identity with the people of their home towns and villages. A successful man of affairs is expected by his people to contribute to the improvement of his home community and to the education of its youth ... At home, the *arrive* is not regarded and does not regard himself as a member of the upper class; he is an eminent son of the soil, bound to the service of his people by traditional pressures and sentimental ties.[80]

In the framework of Peter Ekeh's valuable model of the "two publics," by distributing patronage to their ethnic communities, the members of the political class build support among the "primordial public" and so win toleration for corruption within the "civic public."[81] More fundamentally, perhaps, such a preoccupation with patronage completely defines the way that people perceive and think about politics.

> Through the conferral of divisible benefits, [African governments] make it in the interests of individual rural dwellers to seek limited objectives. Political energies, rather than focusing on the collective standing of the peasantry focus instead on the securing of particular improvements ... The politics of the pork barrel supplant the politics of class action.[82]

But the provision of patronage can only go so far in neutralizing potential disenchantment with the system. Appetites at the top of the hierarchy are too large to enable the incorporation of the whole population into the channels of distribution in any significant fashion or to leave much in the way of meaningful development resources for dispersion to communities. Hence, the positive element of ethnic patronage has had to be supplemented with a negative element of ethnic fear and suspicion in order to divert attention from the process of class formation and the deepening inequality it entails. This has been accomplished through the politics of "tribalism." By mobilizing political support on the basis of blatant appeals to ethnic chauvinism and resentment, the politicians of the African political class have helped to retard the development of lower-class consciousness, and have made it exceedingly difficult for political conflict to be organized on the basis of a deepening but not fully perceived class cleavage. In this sense, the politics of tribalism has functioned, to use Sklar's words, as "a mask for class privilege."[83]

The state as social architect

One reason why the state has expanded so rapidly in postindependence Africa is the universal hunger for rapid progress in development. Acutely aware of the huge gap in living standards that separates them from the more developed countries (including the former colonial powers), African political leaders have searched for ways to speed up the process of socioeconomic development.

> "Growth" is an imperative, and no one believes that it can be left to the beneficent workings of the invisible hand. State intervention and leadership are deemed critical by African capitalists as well as socialists.[84]

The more the state guides the process of development, the more heavily will the resulting patterns of social stratification be shaped by state policies and strategies. Since the latter are a product of a political process, it should not be surprising to find that state intervention in economic development frequently serves the interest of the rich and powerful. The more resourceful and better organized a group is, the more likely will its members be to benefit from the state's development plans and policies. Throughout Africa—and the Third World in general—this has meant a heavy bias in favor of urban dwellers, since they are (for logistical reasons alone) better organized, better educated and informed, more politically aware, and hence more of a political threat to those in power. In addition, of course, the political class, concentrated as it is in the nation's capital and perhaps a few regional centers, is largely an urban class.

Hence, state-pricing policies have served to extract enormous amounts of wealth from peasant agriculture and transfer it to urban populations in the form of underpriced foodstuffs and underpriced raw materials for local manufacturers. Cheap food has been a particular necessity for the survival of fragile African regimes. Only when the elite is itself engaged in the production of a food item do state policies not depress the price below—but rather, often inflate it considerably above—the world market level.[85] By the same logic of political survival, state expenditures on education, electricity, water, health care, and other amenities tend to be heavily concentrated in the cities, where reside both the political class and its most threatening rivals for power. In fact, however, some of this is due to the very momentum of state expansion: "The sheer scale of state consumption tended to direct resources to cities and towns associated with governmental apparatus, particularly the capital."[86]

State industrial policy may also favor dominant-class interests, particularly where there is some kind of bourgeoisie at least nominally involved in production. Both as an unintended consequence of the dense thicket of state regulations, which large and well-established firms are better equipped to negotiate, and by deliberate intention, state policies have promoted industrial concentration. In some instances, "the rights to import capital goods and inputs necessary for manufacturing a particular product have been purposefully restricted to particular enterprises." Tax credits and other subsidies and preferences have been used to attract large foreign investors.

In the extreme case, such preferential treatment by the state can confer an effective monopoly on a particular firm.[87] Frequently this firm is owned by the state or foreign capital, but in capitalist countries like Nigeria and Kenya, it has at times worked to the benefit of politically well-connected local entrepreneurs who either own their own business or have, as a result of indigenization decrees, acquired a piece of a foreign-owned enterprise. In any case, as industrial concentration is promoted by the state, the emergence of a more diversified, numerous, productive, and autonomous bourgeoisie—which might eventually rival the political class—is discouraged. Such local production as exists is dominated by a few monopolistic or oligopolistic businessmen whose fortunes are closely tied to state favors and to the continued domination of the political class of which they are a part.

Without in any way exhausting the variety of ways in which state policy and planning can shape the emerging pattern of class domination, we can note here in conclusion the state's role in guiding and regulating the pattern of consumption. This is done not only through direct state consumption but also through its power, pervasively exercised, to control imports and to allocate foreign exchange. In the typical African state, this power is used to service the wants of the dominant class rather than to meet basic needs. In 1964, in the 14 former French colonies,

> six times as much was spent in importing alcoholic drinks as in importing fertilizer. Half as much was spent on perfume and cosmetic imports as on machine tools. Almost as much went on importing petrol for

privately owned cars as on the purchase of tractors; and five times as much in importing private cars as on agricultural equipment. The resources of the new states were being devoured by a tiny group whose demands distorted the budgets and economies of the states they governed.[88]

The pattern is well known to observers of the Nigerian scene. When oil income dropped precipitously, foreign exchange could still be obtained by the privileged and well-connected to import champagne and Mercedes-Benzes, and to travel abroad in the finest style of the international bourgeoisie—while industries shut down for lack of raw materials and spare parts, and families searched the markets in vain for the most basic necessities of daily life.

The nature and means of dominant class consolidation

It is beyond the scope of this chapter to deal in any detail with the process of class consolidation, but the central role of the state must again be noted. According to Sklar, the members of the dominant class "reconstruct the existing organization of authority" in order to "protect and extend" their class interests.[89] This consists of extending and deepening dominant-class control over economic power (the means of production) and over political power (i.e. the state itself). Few would dispute Sklar's assertion that the most common strategy for the process of political consolidation has been authoritarian government. Again Zaire provides an extreme, in which Mobutu has sought to eliminate all potential rival sources of power. The elements of his "highly organic-statist" strategy of state formation include:

> the consolidation and use of coercive force (with considerable external assistance) to ... prevent or contain political unrest ... recentralisation of power along the lines of the authoritarian colonial state ... the emasculation or elimination of all alternative sources of autonomous authority, traditional or modern; the maintenance of severely constricted and channelled political participation (departicipation) in which a highly corporatist single state-party is recognized as the only legitimate political arena ... and neo-mercantilist economic policies designed to increase the economic and political power of the state, its ruler, and his political aristocracy.[90]

Such an authoritarian-corporatist strategy may provide the best immediate sense of political security but, as Sklar notes, it may entail greater risks in the long run, because "authoritarian rule virtually guarantees that political change will be eruptive and costly to privileged classes."[91] Class domination is most secure politically when it is buttressed by a system of political competition in which the rival parties fall within "acceptable" ideological boundaries, and when it is legitimated by a wide range of social institutions sympathetic to the existing social order. Such a situation of ongoing legitimation and renewal may be seen to operate in the advanced capitalist societies,[92] but is very difficult to construct in developing countries, where political institutions are poorly articulated, and where widespread poverty and inequality may generate support for radical political alternatives. Class domination might have been consolidated in Nigeria's Second Republic through democratic means but for two unfortunate facts: first, class formation was so dependent on state control that members of the political class became determined to preserve their position in, and access to, the state by any means necessary; and second, any limits on their appetites for accumulation and consumption evaporated in the heady atmosphere of the oil boom, and the climate persisted even after the boom collapsed.[93]

Economic consolidation of class domination requires a base of wealth outside the state, both as an additional means for accumulation and as a hedge against the possible loss of access to state wealth and to the state power that can be used to extract wealth from other sources. This means that the class which formed its domination through the state must secure its preeminence through the acquisition of wealth-producing assets outside the state. For this as well, state power is a crucial instrument. In Nigeria, state policies requiring the indigenization of foreign enterprise have generated a windfall of wealth and corporate ownership for members of the dominant class, especially politically well-connected businessmen, while doing relatively little to increase effective Nigerian control of the economy.[94] Indigenization was even more transparently a vehicle for the economic consolidation of class domination in Zaire, where it exemplified "the conversion of political power and position into economic wealth for the benefit of the few at the expense of the many."[95]

At any stage of development, the ownership of landed property is an important mark of class standing, and this is all the more so in African nations, where the most important productive activity is not industry but agriculture. A crucial element of economic consolidation has thus been the acquisition by members of the dominant class of large holdings of land. In many African countries, including Nigeria, Ghana, and the Sudan, state agricultural development policies have enabled politically influential urban elites to acquire substantial plots of land for the mechanized production of food and other commodities. These big commercial farmers have also been able to obtain privileged access to subsidized credit, fertilizer, equipment, and so on. In the process, small producers have been displaced, inequalities in the countryside have widened, and the structure of peasant-based agriculture has begun to undergo fundamental changes.[96] The great "land grab" proceeds in the cities as well, where "state sponsored credit and loan schemes" allow members of the dominant class to "to speculate in real estate at state expense."[97] In addition, state control over urban land was used pervasively in Nigeria's Second Republic to obtain, at little or no cost, choice urban plots, on which a portion of the corrupt fortunes of the political class was expended in the construction of palatial personal residences.

Finally, the importance of intergenerational transmission of class status should be noted. Class domination cannot be considered truly securely rooted until it is passed on to the next generation, which is one reason why the family must be considered the individual unit within the class. African elites have shown a manifest concern in this regard, and they have sought to use the state to ensure that the benefits of membership in the dominant class would be passed on to their children. For this, extensive education is, as we have seen, critical. As early as the 1960s, the rising class in Nigeria used the leverage of political and administrative office to obtain favored admission to elite schools for their children and extended relations, giving their next generation a competitive advantage for higher education and professional employment, and so shifting the basis of status attainment in southern Nigeria from achievement to ascription.[98] This phenomenon has been widespread through Africa. "Providing for the special education of their offspring has been a central preoccupation of every indigenous bourgeoisie in every country throughout the continent"[99]—and, indeed, of the dominant class in every country, capitalist and socialist, throughout the globe.

Consequences of the swollen state

The above analysis is not meant to suggest that class formation and social differentiation can be avoided in the process of socioeconomic development. All complex and large-scale societies have some degree of inequality and some degree of domination by a particular class. But it matters greatly how these phenomena are established, as well as how and whether they are attenuated and contained. The particular bane of African national development has not been the emergence of a dominant class, but rather its often parasitic character as a political class feeding off the revenue of a swollen state.

The oversized, overowning, overregulating African state, and the dependence of class formation upon it, have obstructed national development in many ways. Massive state overhead costs have preempted many of the investments that were needed in physical and human capital. Too many regulations have discouraged production, especially in agriculture, while overvalued local currencies have diminished exports and induced a squandering of foreign exchange on artificially cheap consumer imports. Proliferating state corporations crowded out private enterprise and—with their overemployment and weak discipline—often strained state finances by requiring continuous subsidies to make up for operating losses.

In addition, we have seen how the swollen state gives rise to systematic corruption on an unprecedented scale, and this has seriously retarded economic growth by reducing net investment, particularly through the diversion of state resources from productive investment to profligate consumption; by weakening administrative competence and compromising the state's ability to deal aggressively with foreign investors; by reducing the productivity of the state's development expenditures; and by inhibiting entrepreneurship.[100] The latter consequence, obstructing the emergence of a genuine, productive bourgeoisie, is perhaps the least appreciated and the most difficult to overcome. Why should any entrepreneur risk capital on a venture that is likely to be the object of extortion by a self-aggrandizing state elite, of suffocation by a ponderous and unwieldy bureaucracy, and of unfair competition by state-sanctioned oligopolies, when he or she can submit to the reality of state domination and join "the racket," which promises far greater rewards with far less risk?

If power replaces effort as the basis of social reward, as it has in much of Africa, then the ambitious, energetic, and talented will seek to manipulate power in pursuit of rewards, and "the embryonic capitalist class" will fail "to play its historical role of initiative, capital formation and increased production," to borrow from Joseph's analysis of the Nigerian predicament.[101] Kasfir puts the problem thus:

> If available wealth flows into society through the corridors of the state, the local capitalist class may have no interest in enterprises requiring high risks and hard work. If state officials also demand a slice from every pie, they render all business more marginal. Productive African bourgeoisies may emerge from those who have no state positions and can avoid the control of state officials.[102]

In fact, Kasfir's own research indicates that as state capacity and authority decline to the degree they have in Uganda (and in Ghana and many other parts of Africa), "a new potential route for class formation opens through the black market," or "*magendo*" as it is known in Uganda.[103] But even here, statist economic intervention—maintaining a grossly overvalued currency and undervalued fixed prices for scarce commodities—enables the huge black-market fortunes to be made, and the resulting *nouveau riches* can hardly be said to herald the emergence of capitalism in any real sense of the term.[104]

State policies can help to generate more opportunities for local entrepreneurs, and to nurture their development. In Nigeria, Biersteker finds that the indigenization decrees of the 1970s have begun to create a niche for local capital in low-technology manufacturing, and to propel the traditionally *comprador*, commercial bourgeoisie into more productive activity.[105] Nigerians with capital have also been moving into large-scale, mechanized agricultural production in recent years as the returns from investment in this sector have increased. However, state requirements for the participation of indigenous, private capital are quite different from state ownership and control.

If a productive entrepreneurial class is to develop in Africa, the size of the state and the scope of its economic intervention must be dramatically reduced. Freer rein must be given to the play of market forces and to competition between autonomous enterprises. Certainly, in the absence of any serious socialist commitment, a productive entrepreneurial class must emerge if African nations are to develop economically. And even socialist regimes must allow some play of market forces, and some scope for individual incentives, if they are to be able to sustain economic progress.[106]

The political consequences of the swollen state point in the same direction. Nigeria is only one of many countries where the breathtaking expansion of the state, and the consequent dependence of class formation and consolidation on state control has put an extraordinarily high premium on political power. As a result, "a desperate struggle to win control of state power ensues since this control means for all practical purposes being all powerful and owning everything. Politics becomes warfare, a matter of life or death."[107] Hence the swollen character of the state must be seen as one of the root causes of democratic failure in Nigeria, since it has done so much to generate the corruption, electoral fraud, political violence, ethnic chauvinism, and general desperation of political conflict that figured so prominently in the demise of both the First and Second Republics.[108]

More generally, this same factor may be seen as an important cause of the turmoil, violence, and desperation that have infused the struggle for power throughout independent Africa. Even as the European powers were scrambling for pieces of the African continent, Mosca anticipated this problem with striking clarity:

> One of the most important reasons for the decline of the parliamentary system is the relatively huge number of offices, contracts for public works and other favors of an economic character which the governing class is in a position to distribute either to individuals or to groups of persons; and the drawbacks of that system are the greater in proportion as the amount of wealth that the government or local elective bodies absorb and distribute is greater, and the harder it becomes, therefore, to secure an independent position and an honest living without relying in some respect or other upon public administration. If, then, all the instruments of production pass into the hands of the government, the officials who control and apportion production become the arbiters of the fortunes and welfare of all, and we get a more powerful oligarchy, a more all-embracing "racket," than has ever been seen in a society of advanced civilisation. If all moral and material advantages depend on those who hold power, there is no baseness that will not be resorted to in order to please them; just as there is no act of chicanery or violence that will not be resorted to in order to attain power, in other words, in order to belong to the number of those who hand out the cake rather than to the larger number of those who have to rest content with the slices that are doled out to them.[109]

To a significant degree, the economic stagnation and political decay of independent African nations may be traced to the inexorable expansion of a state structure that was oversized even at independence. Progress would now seem to require a reduction in the size of the state—in the scope of both its regulation and ownership—and at the same time an increase in the effectiveness of the functions it continues to perform. Indeed, it is difficult to see how African states can become more effective unless they become leaner and more efficient. This is not to suggest that the state can or should withdraw from the economy altogether. Nothing like a pure reliance on markets is feasible politically, and even a *laissez-faire* development strategy requires active and carefully directed government support—for example provision of credit, agricultural inputs, improved transport, and other infrastructure.[110] But if there is to be any basis for self-sustaining growth and peaceful, democratic politics, there must be a transition in the state's role from that of resource for a parasitic few to that of nurturant for a genuinely productive bourgeoisie—both *grande* and *petite,* agricultural and industrial—that will not be dependent on the state for its survival. This transition will be exceedingly difficult, because it threatens the interests of much of the existing dominant classes in Africa, and because the idea of the state as the engine of social progress retains considerable legitimacy among the intelligentsia in both socialist and "capitalist" African nations.

Yet, both statist ideologies, and the structures of privilege they have spawned, have come under intense challenge in recent years as a result of the crises of economic stagnation and external indebtedness. Literally and figuratively, Africa's swollen states are bankrupt. The momentum for a sharp departure comes not only from the IMF and the international banking community (public and private), but also increasingly from indigenous officials and intellectuals. Hence, in one of the more interesting and far-reaching instances of economic adjustment in Africa, Nigeria has begun to implement most of the IMF's standard program—devaluing the currency by two-thirds, eliminating the budget deficit, loosening state controls over external trade, and reducing civil-servant salaries and consumer subsidies—while declining to sign a formal agreement and to take an IMF loan.[111] Since the military returned to power at the end of 1983, agricultural-producer prices have been raised significantly and output has increased. Future plans call for a sharp pruning of parastatals in Nigeria, and if, indeed, a significant number of state corporations are sold off to the private sector, this could do much to advance the recent (and by no means irreversible) trend towards the emergence of a productive bourgeoisie.

Elsewhere in Africa as well, state controls are beginning to be lifted, and "privatization" is the new buzzword. But even in Nigeria (not to mention the more socialist African countries), it remains to be seen how serious and enduring will be this new policy direction. In Nigeria, it is vulnerable both to popular political backlash—especially if privatization gives rise to sudden, new concentrations of wealth, while failing to improve the overall economy—and to a possible new euphoric binge of state expansion should the global oil market start to boom again.

In most African countries, the greatest resistance to reduction in state control over the economy is likely to come not from the people, who have seen so little benefit from it, but from the political class, whose economic and social dominance depend on it. Is the situation now so desperate that this class will yield—with part of it seeking to reestablish its dominance as a genuine, productive bourgeoisie—or will its grip only be loosened through even more profound, and possibly more violent, crises?

Notes

1 Originally published as "Class Formation in the Swollen African State," *Journal of Modern African Studies* 26 (March 1988): 567–596.

2 Nelson Kasfir, "Introduction: Relating State to Class in Africa," *Journal of Commonwealth and Comparative Politics* 21 (November 1983): 2. This issue was also published as Nelson Kasfir, ed., *State and Class in Africa* (London: Frank Cass, 1984).

3 Gaetano Mosca, *The Ruling Class: Elementi di scienza politica* (New York: McGraw-Hill, 1936), 50–69.

4 Richard L. Sklar, *Nigerian Political Parties* (Princeton, NJ: Princeton University Press, 1963), 480–481.

5 Richard L. Sklar, "Contradictions in the Nigerian Political System," *Journal of Modern African Studies* 3 (August 1965): 203–204.

6 To overcome this confusion and to emphasize the role of the private and public business elite, Sklar adopted the term "managerial bourgeoisie," which encompasses as well other upper-level bureaucrats, members of the learned professions, and high government officials. See Richard L. Sklar, "Postimperialism: A Class Analysis of Multinational Corporate Expansion," *Comparative Politics* 9 (October 1976): 81 and 91 fn. 51. This term, like Irving L. Markovitz's "organizational bourgeoisie," is more broadly conceived than "bureaucratic" or "state" bourgeoisie, in that it seeks "to comprehend the dominant class as a whole" (to quote Sklar's later analysis), and is more precise than Peter Ekeh's simple designation of these groups as "bourgeois," which "connotes the newness of a privileged class which may yield much power but have little political acceptance." Precisely because this class forms and consolidates its social dominance through political power, I favor the term "political class." It has the advantage of avoiding the implication of a materially productive class that is suggested by the term "bourgeois," a consideration that led Thomas Callaghy to describe the Zairian ruling class as a "political aristocracy." This term, however, would also seem to be misleading, in that it implies familial inheritance as the primary mechanism of recruitment into the dominant class. See Irving Leonard Markovitz, *Power and Class in Africa* (Englewood Cliffs, NJ: Prentice-Hall, 1977), 198–229; Richard L. Sklar, "The Nature of Class Domination in Africa," *Journal of Modern African Studies* 17 (December 1979): 544–547; Peter Ekeh, "Colonialism and the Two Publics in Africa: A Theoretical Statement," *Comparative Studies in Society and History* 17 (January 1975): 93; and Thomas Callaghy, *The State–Society Struggle: Zaire in Comparative Perspective* (New York: Columbia University Press, 1984), 185–186.

7 Sklar, "The Nature of Class Domination in Africa," 536–537.

8 Kasfir, "Introduction: Relating State to Class in Africa," 5.

9 Cf. Ralph Miliband, *The State in Capitalist Society* (New York: Basic Books, 1969), and G. William Domhoff, *Who Rules America Now?* (Englewood Cliffs, NJ: Prentice Hall, 1983).

10 Sklar, "Contradictions in the Nigerian Political System," 204.

11 Peter Duignan, "Introduction," in Duignan and Robert H. Jackson, eds., *Politics and Government in African States, 1960–85* (Stanford, CA: Hoover Institution Press, 1986), 18–19.

12 I am grateful to Lewis H. Gann for his comments on this and related points.

13 Crawford Young, "Patterns of Social Conflict: State, Class and Ethnicity," *Daedalus* 111 (Spring 1982): 75–76.

14 Ibid., 78.

15 Robert H. Bates, *Markets and States in Tropical Africa* (Berkeley: University of California Press, 1981), 12–13; Claude Ake, *A Political Economy of Africa* (Harlow: Longman Group, 1981), 63–65; and Uyi-Ekpen Ogbeide, "The Expansion of the State and Ethnic Mobilization: The Nigerian Experience," (Ph.D. dissertation, Vanderbilt University, Nashville, TN, 1985), 37–40.

16 Ogbeide, "The Expansion of the State and Ethnic Mobilization," 42–44.

17 E. O. Akeredolu-Ale, *The Underdevelopment of Indigenous Entrepreneurship in Nigeria* (Ibadan, Nigeria: Ibadan University Press, 1975), 53–61; and Naomi Chazan, "Ghana: Problems of Governance and the Emergence of Civil Society," in Larry Diamond, Juan J. Linz, and Seymour Martin Lipset, eds., *Democracy in Developing Countries: Africa* (Boulder, CO: Lynne Rienner, 1988), 122.

18 Robert H. Jackson, "Conclusion," in Duignan and Jackson, eds., *Politics and Government in African States, 1960–85*, 411.

19 Duignan, *Politics and Government in African States*, 11.

20 Jackson, "Conclusion," 411.

21 Chazan, "Ghana: Problems of Governance and the Emergence of Civil Society," 129.

22 Crawford Young, *Ideology and Development in Africa* (New Haven, CT: Yale University Press, 1982), 189.

23 Sayre P. Schatz, "Economic Effects of Corruption," 12th Annual Meeting of the African Studies Association, Montreal, 1969, 5.

24 David B. Abernethy, "Bureaucratic Growth and Economic Decline in Sub-Saharan Africa," 26th Annual Meeting of the African Studies Association, Boston, 1983, an updated version of which is published as "Bureaucratic Growth and Economic Stagnation in Sub-Saharan Africa," in Stephen K. Commins, ed., *Africa's Development Challenges and the World Bank* (Boulder, CO: Lynne Rienner, 1988).

25 John R. Nellis, "Public Enterprise in Sub-Saharan Africa," World Bank Discussion Paper, Washington, DC, 1986, 4–12.

26 Richard A. Joseph, "Class, State and Prebendal Politics in Nigeria," *Journal of Commonwealth and Comparative Politics* 21 (November 1983): 23; and Larry Diamond, "Nigeria in Search of Democracy," *Foreign Affairs* 62 (Spring 1962): 921.

27 Abernethy, "Bureaucratic Growth and Economic Decline," 13.

28 Peter S. Heller and Alan A. Tait, "Government Employment and Pay: Some International Comparisons," International Monetary Fund Occasional Paper No. 24, Washington, DC, 1984, 7, table 1.

29 Larry Diamond, *Class, Ethnicity and Democracy in Nigeria: The Failure of the First Republic* (London: Macmillan Press, 1988), 178–179.

30 Young, "Patterns of Social Conflict," 81.

31 Joseph, "Class, State and Prebendal Politics in Nigeria," 23.

32 Abernethy, "Bureaucratic Growth and Economic Decline," 14.

33 Markovitz, *Power and Class in Africa*, 207–208.

34 Abernethy, "Bureaucratic Growth and Economic Decline," 14.

35 Ibid., table 5.

36 Ibid., table 4.

37 Ibid., 17. The latter income figure would be $3.6 million in 2012 dollars.

38 David B. Abernethy, *The Political Dilemma of Popular Education* (Stanford, CA: Stanford University Press, 1969), 243.

39 Richard L. Sklar and C. S. Whitaker, Jr, "The Federal Republic of Nigeria," in Gwendolyn M. Carter, ed., *National Unity and Regionalism in Eight African States* (Ithaca, NY: Cornell University Press, 1966), 112.

40 Abernethy, "Bureaucratic Growth and Economic Decline," 10.

41 Ibid., 23–25.

42 Hugh H. Smythe and Mabel M. Smythe, *The New Nigerian Elite* (Stanford, CA: Stanford University Press, 1960), 69.

43 Ibid., 132.

44 Markovitz, *Power and Class in Africa*, 205–206.

45 Kasfir, "Introduction: Relating State to Class in Africa," 8.

46 John Waterbury, "Endemic and Planned Corruption in a Monarchical Regime," *World Politics* 25 (July 1973): 543.

47 Larry Diamond, "Class, Ethnicity and the Democratic State: Nigeria, 1950–66," *Comparative Studies in Society and History* 25 (July 1983): 462.

48 Larry Diamond, "Cleavage, Conflict, and Anxiety in the Second Nigerian Republic," *Journal of Modern African Studies*, 20 (December 1982): 661.

49 Sayre P. Schatz, "Pirate Capitalism and the Inert Economy of Nigeria," *Journal of Modern African Studies*, 22 (March 1984): 54.

50 Ibid., 55.

51 Kasfir, "Introduction: Relating State to Class in Africa," 12.

52 Joseph S. Nye, "Corruption and Political Development: A Cost–Benefit Analysis," Arnold J. Heidenheimer, ed., *Political Corruption: Readings in Comparative Analysis* (New Brunswick, NJ: Holt, Rinehart and Winston, 1970), 566–567.

53 Victor T. LeVine, *Political Corruption: The Ghana Case* (Stanford, CA: Hoover Institute Press, 1975), 2–5; and James C. Scott, *Comparative Political Corruption* (Englewood Cliffs, NJ: Prentice Hall, 1972), 4–5.

54 Callaghy, *The State–Society Struggle*, 189–190.

55 Larry Diamond, "The Social Foundations of Democracy: The Case of Nigeria," (Ph.D. dissertation, Stanford University, 1980), 556–582.

56 Sayre P. Schatz, *Nigerian Capitalism* (Berkeley: University of California Press, 1977), 190–195, 208–209, 231–232, and 244–245; and Gerald K. Helleiner, "The Eastern Nigeria Development Corporation: A Study in Resources and Uses of Public Development Funds, 1949–62," *Nigerian Journal of Economic and Social Studies* 6 (1964): 98–123.

57 Diamond, *Class, Ethnicity and Democracy in Nigeria*, 126, 252–254, 288–289, and 311.

58 Richard A. Joseph, "Affluence and Underdevelopment: the Nigerian Experience," *Journal of Modern African Studies* 16 (June 1978): 238.

59 Victor A. Olorunsola, *Soldiers and Power: The Development Performance of the Nigerian Military Regime* (Stanford, CA: Hoover Institution Press, 1977), 127.

60 For a fuller list, see Larry Diamond, "The Political Economy of Corruption in Nigeria," 27th Annual Meeting of the African Studies Association, Los Angeles, 1984.

61 Chazan, "Ghana: Problems of Governance and the Emergence of Civil Society."

62 Morris Sfetzel, "Political Graft and the Spoils System in Zambia—the State as a Resource in Itself," *Review of African Political Economy* 24 (1982): 4–21.

63 *Africa Confidential* 27(8) (April 9, 1986): 3.

64 For example, Robert H. Jackson and Carl G. Rosberg, *Personal Rule in Black Africa: Prince, Autocrat, Prophet, Tyrant* (Berkeley: University of California Press, 1982); Joseph, "Class, State and Prebendal Politics in Nigeria"; Kasfir, "Introduction: Relating State to Class in Africa"; Callaghy, *The State–Society Struggle*; Callaghy, "External Actors and the Relative Autonomy of the Political Aristocracy in Zaire," *Journal of Commonwealth and Comparative Politics,* 21 (1983): 61–83.

65 Donal O'Brien, "Saints and Politicians," in Chris Allen and Gavin Williams, eds., *Sub-Saharan Africa* (New York: Monthly Review Press, 1982), 169; and Joseph, "Class, State and Prebendal Politics in Nigeria," 33.

66 Jackson and Rosberg, *Personal Rule in Black Africa,* 19.

67 Ibid., 42.

68 Max Weber, *The Theory of Social and Economic Organization* (New York: The Free Press, 1964), 351.

69 Ibid., 352–353.

70 Joseph, "Class, State and Prebendal Politics in Nigeria," 30–31; see also Waterbury, "Endemic and Planned Corruption in a Monarchical Regime," 538.

71 Callaghy, *The State–Society Struggle*; Callaghy, "Politics and Vision in Africa: The Interplay of Domination, Equality and Liberty," in Patrick Chabal, ed., *Political Domination in Africa: Reflections on the Limits of Power* (Cambridge: Cambridge University Press, 1986), 31–36.

72 Callaghy, *The State–Society Struggle,* 11.

73 John D. Holm, "Botswana: A Paternalistic Democracy," in Diamond, Linz, and Lipset, eds., *Democracy in Developing Countries: Africa.*

74 O'Brien, "Saints and Politicians," 168.

75 LeVine, *Political Corruption: The Ghana Case,* 17–18.

76 Waterbury, "Endemic and Planned Corruption in a Monarchical Regime," 539, 538.

77 Joseph, "Class, State and Prebendal Politics in Nigeria," 24.

78 Sfetzel, "Political Graft and the Spoils System in Zambia," and Jackson and Rosberg, *Personal Rule in Black Africa,* 46. See also Samuel P. Huntington, *Political Order in Changing Societies* (New Haven, CT: Yale University Press, 1968), 61; Scott, *Comparative Political Corruption,* 14; and Varda Eker, "On the Origins of Corruption: Irregular Incentives in Nigeria," *Journal of Modern African Studies* 19 (March 1981): 174.

79 Joseph, "Class, State and Prebendal Politics in Nigeria," 29.

80 Sklar, *Nigerian Political Parties,* 503.

81 Ekeh, "Colonialism and the Two Publics in Africa."

82 Bates, *Markets and States in Tropical Africa,* 117–118.

83 Richard L. Sklar, "Political Science and National Integration—a Radical Approach," *Journal of Modern African Studies* 5 (May 1967): 6.

84 Young, *Ideology and Development in Africa,* 188.

85 Bates, *Markets and States in Tropical Africa,* 188.

86 Young, "Patterns of Social Conflict," 83.

87 Bates, *Markets and States in Tropical Africa,* 67–70.

88 Ruth First, *The Barrel of a Gun: Political Power in Africa and the Coup D'État* (London: Penguin, 1970), 110.

89 Sklar, "The Nature of Class Domination in Africa," 358.

90 Callaghy, "External Actors and the Relative Autonomy of the Political Aristocracy in Zaire," 66.

91 Sklar, "The Nature of Class Domination in Africa," 552.

92 Miliband, *The State in Capitalist Society.*

93 Diamond, "Cleavage, Conflict and Anxiety in the Second Nigerian Republic"; and Diamond, "Nigeria in Search of Democracy."

94 Schatz, *Nigerian Capitalism*; Joseph, "Affluence and Underdevelopment," 227–230; Sklar, "The Nature of Class Domination in Africa," 538–540; and Thomas J. Biersteker, *Multinationals, the State and Control of the Nigerian Economy* (Princeton, NJ: Princeton University Press, 1987). However, Biersteker's work—by far the most extensive and imaginative research on the subject to date—does depart from previous analyses in its discovery that the two indigenization decrees of 1972 and 1977 (and related policies) have substantially increased Nigerian control of its own financial sector, while also advancing the promotion of those employed at middle/senior levels, and enabling Nigerian businessmen to consolidate their position throughout the commercial sector.

95 Callaghy, "External Actors and the Political Aristocracy in Zaire," 70.

96 Bates, *Markets and States in Tropical Africa*, 58–60; Sara Berry, "Rural Class Formation in West Africa," in Robert H. Bates and Michael Lofchie, eds., *Agricultural Development in Africa* (New York: Praeger, 1980), 414; and Michael Watts and Paul Lubeck, "The Popular Classes and the Oil Boom: A Political Economy of Rural and Urban Poverty," in I. William Zartman, ed., *The Political Economy of Nigeria* (New York: Praeger, 1983), 119–121, 124–126.

97 Watts and Lubeck, "The Popular Classes and the Oil Boom," 134; Joseph, "Affluence and Underdevelopment," 228.

98 Abernethy, *The Political Dilemma of Popular Education*, 244–249.

99 Markovitz, *Power and Class in Africa*, 215.

100 Schatz, "Economic Effects of Corruption"; Diamond, "The Political Economy of Corruption in Nigeria."

101 Joseph, "Affluence and Underdevelopment," 226.

102 Kasfir, "Introduction: Relating State to Class in Africa," 16.

103 Nelson Kasfir, "State, Magendo and Class Formation in Uganda," *Journal of Commonwealth and Comparative Studies* 2 (1983): 101.

104 Ibid., 99–101.

105 Biersteker, *Multinationals, the State and Control of the Nigerian Economy*, 271–276.

106 Goran Hyden, "Problems and Prospects of State Coherence," in Donald Rothchild and Victor A. Orunsola, eds., *State Versus Ethnic Claims: Africa Policy Dilemmas* (Boulder, CO: Westview Press, 1983), 77.

107 Claude Ake, Presidential Address to the 1981 Conference of the Nigerian Political Science Association, *West Africa*, May 25, 1981, 1162–1163.

108 Diamond, "The Political Economy of Corruption in Nigeria"; and Diamond, "Nigeria in Search of Democracy."

109 Mosca, *The Ruling Class*, 143–144.

110 Sayre P. Schatz, "Laissez-Faireism for Africa?" *Journal of Modern African Studies* 25 (March 1987): 29–38.

111 Larry Diamond, "Nigeria Between Dictatorship and Democracy," *Current History* 86 (May 1987): 201–204 and 222–224.

11 Class, ethnicity, and the democratic state
Nigeria, 1950–1966[1]

> Seek ye first the kingdom of politics and all else shall be added unto you.
>
> Kwame Nkrumah

Amid the disruption of rapid social and economic change in contemporary developing nations, political order has been a fragile commodity. The simultaneous, urgent demands of integrating nations, constructing states, institutionalizing participation, and satisfying revolutionary expectations have overwhelmed most Third World regimes, and liberal democratic ones in particular. The dependence of constitutional democracy on moderation, tolerance, and restraint in political behavior[2] has been especially difficult to reconcile with the desperate, consummatory character of politics in nations where public agendas and personal expectations grossly exceed available resources and rewards.

Where the legacy of colonialism has been not simply economic dependence but the arbitrary consolidation of diverse nations into territorial states, the pressures of political development have been sorely compounded. Thus we repeatedly find a strong association between ethnic pluralism and political instability,[3] and in particular, a powerful negative association between ethnic pluralism and the stability of pluralistic, competitive regimes.[4] In the context of economic development and state expansion, ethnic identities are widened and mobilized into competition for scarce and similarly valued resources and opportunities.[5] This ethnic competition—fierce, often violent, and inevitably political—has in turn been widely viewed as a fundamental cause of political disorder and decay in the multiethnic states of Asia and especially Sub-Saharan Africa.

Perhaps no nation has come more graphically to symbolize the political explosiveness and human tragedy of competitive ethnic mobilization than Nigeria in its first decade of independence. Though widely regarded in the West as Africa's best hope for parliamentary democracy, Nigeria labored from its birth in 1960 under immense structural burdens. The demographic distribution of ethnic groups into a "centralized" structure[6] meant that competition tended to center around the three major groups—the

Hausa–Fulani, the Yoruba, and the Igbo—which together comprised some two-thirds of the population. The political preference of the British for indirect rule—which won the cooperation of the powerful Fulani emirs by agreeing to block the penetration of modern forces in the North—gave the Yoruba, the Igbo, and other southern groups an enormous advantage in income, education, and modern professional training, stirring alarmist fears of southern domination among northern elites when independence approached.[7] Moreover, the three-region federal structure which the British imposed—and steadfastly retained in the face of vigorous agitation by minority groups for the creation of more states—reified the centralized character of the ethnic structure and, by giving the less-developed Northern Region a population (and hence parliamentary) majority, forged a hopeless contradiction between socioeconomic power and political power.[8] Finally, the organization of political parties along ethnic and regional lines, and the rapid drift to one-party rule in each region (developments hardly surprising, given the above), reinforced ethnicity as the fundamental cleavage in social and political life. From the inception of organized politics in Nigeria in 1951, ethnic competition found not only social and economic but incessant political expression as well, and ethnic conflict fell victim to the progressive polarization that is so difficult to prevent under the strain of accumulated cleavages.

Thus, in pre-civil war Nigeria we seem to have the classic case of society rent and liberal democracy destroyed by ethnic conflict. In its sophisticated form, this argument has traced the failure of the First Republic, and its descent into chaos and civil war, not to the mere fact of ethnic pluralism, nor to primordial cultural tensions or historical legacies of conflict, but rather to the ethnic competition that was generated by socioeconomic and political modernization.[9] The leading proponents of this explanation have also recognized the important contribution to ethnic polarization of a political structure that overlaid regional and party cleavages on the major, tripartite ethnic cleavage in coinciding fashion.

A variety of other historical explanations has been advanced. A related assessment attributes the primary responsibility for democratic failure to the strains and contradictions in the constitutional structure which—in generating coinciding cleavages, consolidating regional inequalities, and assigning such immense powers to so few regions—encouraged ethnic political mobilization, made regional dominance the prerequisite and the basis for intense national political competition, and so only heightened regional and cultural insecurity.[10] The above two theoretical perspectives are, in turn, woven together in a synthetic interpretation which emphasizes the failure of political integration—rooted in the colonial legacy of flawed institutional arrangements, regional disparities, and a restricted political process—but which conceptualizes "tribalism" somewhat distinctively as rooted in ethnic competition between elites.[11] All of these interpretations stand in contrast to the traditionalist perspective, locating the root cause of democratic failure in Nigeria's political culture—which had so little appreciation for "the conventions or rules on which the operation of western democratic forms depend" that "nothing the British could have done would have affected the introduction of Nigerian methods into public life"[12]—and the dependency perspective, which traces political instability to the social and economic contradictions imposed by colonial, and subsequently neocolonial, capitalist economic relations.[13]

Most of these interpretations bear important insights, but none of them adequately explains why elite ethnic competition consumed democracy in Nigeria. Least useful is the conception of a flawed political culture, which reduces in the end to a tendency toward antidemocratic behavior, and so only begs the question of what the forces were that pressed elites to trample constitutional limits. The focus on political structure alerts us to the constitutional flaws that enabled regional power elites to repress opposition and facilitated their ethnic political mobilization, but, again, informs us only very partially as to their motives for doing so. A step closer to meaningful historical explanation is taken by those synthetic interpretations which recognize the role of political elites in mobilizing mass ethnic conflict as part of their own competition for the resources of modernization, but these works as well stop short of a systematic analysis of the class forces motivating elite political behavior and shaping the pattern of political conflict. Of the above modes of explanation, the one that has most explicitly analyzed the development of class relations has misdirected attention to neocolonial economic relations as the essential determinant of class structure.

There exists another mode of analysis, overviewed in the previous chapter, which is genuinely class analytic. From this perspective, not only is "tribalism ... viewed as a dependent variable rather than a primordial political force," but it is seen as generated specifically "by the new men of power in furtherance of their own special interests which are, time and again, the constitutive interests of emerging social classes."[14] From this perspective, state power is the engine of class formation; the competition for it and the manipulation of it represent fundamentally class, not ethnic, action. Hence, the failure of Nigeria's first attempt at democracy must be understood in light of the distinctive interaction among ethnicity, in an ethnically plural and modernizing society; class action, in a dependent and highly underdeveloped economy; and political competition, in a democratic polity in which elite competition required mass mobilization. To understand the tragedy of Nigeria in the 1960s, we must understand the emergent class forces that expressed ethnicity in political terms and used it for class ends.

Class formation and consolidation in Nigeria, 1950–1966

Though the traditional class structures and the processes of class formation differed sharply between North and South in Nigeria, they shared one feature with diffuse implications for social and political development. In both southern and northern Nigeria, class structure and individual class standing came to be determined essentially by political power. Throughout Nigeria, personal income and occupational status, and the control and distribution of national wealth, came to depend heavily upon position in and access to the expanding state structures—a phenomenon characteristic of the development of a new dominant class in postcolonial Africa, as discussed in the previous chapter. Traditional Nigerian cultures did not value the personal accumulation of material wealth, ordinary people did not seek social mobility through it, and most of the traditional stratification systems had no ruling class or aristocracy. But with the penetration of Western education, administration, mass media, and market relations, materialist values diffused rapidly throughout the population. And in underdeveloped, postcolonial Nigeria, political power represented the only means to acquire and maintain wealth.

Socioeconomic consolidation

The desire to achieve elite status and to accumulate wealth thus motivated a fierce hunger for political power. This was accentuated by the pervasive poverty from which all Nigerians were struggling to escape. These were, for the most part, "first-generation educated and prosperous men, having emerged from very humble peasant and working-class stock and from the most grinding and dehumanizing poverty," to which they could not "with equanimity" contemplate returning.[15] For the typical incumbent, defeat meant the loss not simply of political office but of most of the economic and social progress one had achieved for one's self and family. That so much was at stake in every election—both the major channel of upward mobility and the primary insurance against downward mobility—explains both the bruising intensity of election campaigns and the increasingly ruthless repression of political opposition during the life of the First Republic.

Nowhere did political repression become more ruthless and systematic than in the North,[16] for there the stakes were even more important than the formation of a dominant class position by a new elite. In the Hausa-Fulani emirates of the North, electoral politics and socioeconomic change challenged a steeply hierarchical class structure of centuries' standing. There, power, wealth, and status were rigidly ascribed from birth to a titled aristocracy (*sarakuna*), which, under the dominance of the emirs, ruled in despotic fashion over the mass of commoners (*talakawa*). Validated by the religious authority of Islam and institutionalized through complex bureaucratic and judicial administrations and elaborate networks of clientage, the authority of the emirs was enormous and deeply based.[17] So long as their kingdoms were insulated from Western education and foreign ideas of democracy and egalitarianism, their feudalistic authority—and the entire, sharply graded structure of power and privilege which it protected—was stable. A common interest in the stability of this system was the basis for the highly successful compact between the British and the emirs through which the interests of each in northern Nigeria were advanced for half a century.

But the transition to independence in 1951 fundamentally threatened this dominance, forcing the Fulani aristocracy to choose between the rapid promotion of the Western education and economic modernization it had so far eschewed and the otherwise likely domination of the North by radical and culturally alien southerners. Given the southerners' stated intention to dismantle what they saw as a feudalistic and unjust social system in the North, and their political liaison with radical young northern *talakawa* similarly pledged to sweeping reform, the traditional aristocracy found itself forced to choose between adaptation and extinction. It had to control the pace of change in the North to preserve its social dominance, and to do this it had to control the emergent democratic state in the North. With a shrewdness and political skill never anticipated by southern elites, a new generation of northern aristocrats, educated in Western politics and culture, used the instrument of a modern political party to modernize, and so preserve, the structure of class dominance.[18] By delimiting the traditional authority of the emirs and subordinating it to that of the modern state, they sought to reconstitute the social and economic dominance of the aristocracy on a modern foundation.

From the lower ranks of the *sarakuna*—the clerks and officials of the emirates' native administrations—and the highest rank of the *talakawa*—the wealthy merchants, or *attajirai*—the Fulani aristocracy drew together in a political alliance the additional social segments it needed to reproduce and entrench its class dominance in northern Nigeria.[19] Herein lay the fundamental difference between North and South. In the North, power was used to preserve the position of a dominant class through a political alliance in which the traditional elite remained dominant. In the South, power was used to shape the position of a rising class through political parties which were inaugurated and controlled by modern professional and business elites, and into which traditional elites were integrated in a subordinate role.[20]

What these two processes had in common was a recognition that control of the state was the necessary foundation of class formation and consolidation. State power became the unifying force that drew together educated professionals, businessmen, and traditional elites in the ethnically based parties of the three regions. In each region, it was the party of the dominant ethnic group that captured regional power and welded the diverse elites into dominant regional classes. In each case, this was accomplished through the vast powers delegated to the regional governments in the sweeping regionalization of the 1954 constitution.[21]

Perhaps the most valuable of these regional powers (and crucial at the local and federal levels as well) was the commercial patronage vital to the formation of private wealth and business control. Government construction contracts were much less instruments for construction per se than for enrichment of the officials who awarded them and of the politically connected "contractors" who received them.[22] Purchases of all kinds by public corporations and government bodies were padded, inflated in cost, and otherwise manipulated for private gain.[23] Loan programs fostered not genuine agricultural and industrial development but, through favoritism in awards, security conditions, and repayment enforcement, the enrichment of the well connected.[24]

The largest source of commercial patronage was the finance capital held primarily in the reserves of the agricultural marketing boards and statutory corporations of each region. These strategic funds were placed under the direction of trusted operatives of the ruling parties and dispensed, under criteria defying economic rationality, to party-connected businesses and banks. In the wealthiest region, the cocoa-rich West, a 1962 corruption inquiry traced a dizzying hemorrhage of public resources to the ruling Action Group (AG) party and a small interlocking circle of its top politicians and businessmen, whose machinations and sheer recklessness and incompetence essentially bankrupted the Western Region Marketing Board in only seven years of operation.[25] This was not the only public institution so drained in the West, but it was by far the largest and most fundamental, for the regional marketing boards were expected to use the vast surpluses they accumulated from monopoly trade in commodity crops to support agricultural prices and foster economic development. As had happened in the Eastern Region five years earlier,[26] government purchase of majority control (with Marketing Board funds) rescued the major indigenous bank (and the party leaders who owned it) when, despite massive previous government deposits, it was threatened with financial collapse.[27]

Political consolidation

Control of the state was thus essential to the economic and social consolidation of class dominance—to the accumulation of wealth and ownership and to the social fusion of elites with common class interests and "a growing sense of class consciousness."[28] But it was equally vital to its political consolidation. For the state afforded the means to maintain class dominance and to induce support for, and punish opposition to, the party of the dominant class in each region. In an emergent capitalist society, where bourgeois dominance was not secured by the breadth of economic control and thick network of legitimating institutions that mark advanced capitalist societies,[29] a rising class risked its tenuous position if it allowed the possibility of rule by a party it did not control. Even for the much more deeply rooted structure of class dominance in the North, the context of sweeping social and economic change made the prospect of political defeat dangerously threatening. The democratic state thus had to be controlled directly by the dominant class. And in order to secure state control through "democratic" elections, nothing was more valuable than the state itself. The powers of incumbency thus took their place beside manipulation of ethnicity as primary electoral weapons of the regional ruling parties.

Each ruling party set about in the early 1950s to use the levers of state power—the control over patronage, coercion, and chieftaincy, in particular—to consolidate its political base and to suppress those elements that resisted consolidation. Rank favoritism in the awards of loans, contracts, bank credits, positions on public boards and corporations, and licenses to trade commodity crops gave rise in each region to a privileged group of entrepreneurs who came upon sudden and fantastic success and who, in return, "were expected to contribute substantially to party funds, use their wealth and influence to mobilize support for their parties in their various localities, and maintain unflinching loyalty to party leadership."[30]

In the North, such sweeping patronage was the primary instrument for inducting new social strata into the expanding class coalition of the Islamic aristocracy and into its party, the Northern Peoples' Congress (NPC). This instrument was focused on two critical strata: the *attajirai* and the traditional elites of northern minority ethnic groups outside the Fulani emirates. The *attajirai* were crucial to the dominance of the NPC not only because their wealth was a needed source of party finance but because, as Hausas, they were ideal candidates to turn back the challenge of the radical opposition party, the Northern Elements Progressive Union (NEPU), whose electoral strategy was to ignite ethnic resentment among the Hausa masses against the Fulani ruling class.[31] The ethnic minorities around the perimeter of the emirates were crucial because, while the NPC could control the regional government without their political support, it could not control the federal Parliament, which it needed to do to insure against any federal assault on the social structure of the North and the enormous regional autonomy that facilitated its preservation. Political and commercial patronage forged the horizontal integration of these elites into the dominant party under its banner of regional unity: "One North, one people, irrespective of religion, rank, or tribe."[32]

Patronage was also used to induce the electoral support of whole communities, as constituencies were explicitly warned during election campaigns that the provision of amenities depended on support of the ruling party. Even in federal elections, the ruling regional parties heavily exploited their capacity to deliver the stuff of popular aspirations—the roads, water, schools, health care, scholarships, and loans that were the lifeblood of development—and to deny them to constituencies which might by some "stroke of misjudgment" cast their votes for a "worthless [opposition] candidate."[33] For individuals, open support of the opposition could mean denial of whatever they might need from the expanding state: scholarships for their sons, loans for their farms, even their personal freedom.[34]

In all three regions, albeit differently in each, the power to regulate and depose chiefs was used to consolidate political domination. In the Western Region, the Action Group embarked from the very start on a strategy of integrating the culturally important Yoruba chiefs into its emergent class alliance. It exchanged formal political recognition of, and deference to, their honorary status for political support, but it also severely punished those who resisted.[35] In the North, the new generation of aristocrats who vaulted into party leadership used the power of the modern state to effect needed reforms in local government and judicial administration, and did not hesitate to punish traditional rulers whose resistance to change appeared to threaten the interests of the dominant class as a whole.[36] In the East, chieftaincy was not a significant tradition, but the ruling party, the National Council of Nigeria and the Cameroons (NCNC), yielded in 1959 to minority demands for a House of Chiefs at least partly out of a desire "to use the institution for partisan advantage, as in the North and West."[37]

The power of the state was also used effectively to entice ethnic and radical (usually young) opposition politicians to "cross the carpet" in regional legislatures and otherwise transfer their allegiance to the ruling parties. As "many of the radicals acquired attitudes and interests akin to those of a privileged class,"[38] they were gradually co-opted. Those who resisted co-optation were repressed. During the 1950s, and especially after independence, control over the judiciary (in the North), the local police (in the North and West), and tax assessment were used to intimidate and thwart political opposition. Opposition candidates and supporters were jailed on trumped-up charges, while their campaign rallies were denied permits or banned by new regulations.[39] And when massive repression and frenetic manipulation of patronage became insufficient to assure the election of an unpopular ruling party, as they did in the West in 1965, there was always the final instrument of wholesale electoral fraud.

Finally, corruption was an important means not only of enrichment but entrenchment. By appropriating huge sums of public funds, the ruling regional party was able to amass a formidable campaign treasury. In combination with the other advantages of incumbency, this was normally sufficient to guarantee it a huge margin of victory at the polls.

Class action and ethnic conflict

The abuse of public responsibilities and resources for personal enrichment was not the random expression of individual corruption and greed; it was the deliberate, systematic effort of a rising class to accumulate private wealth and to establish concentrated private control over the means of production, at public expense. Similarly, the use of state power by each regional party to entrench its rule must be seen in a context larger than the mere hunger for power. These processes of "enrichment" and "entrenchment"[40] were the primary forms of class action, where this is defined as "collective action ... to increase or reduce social inequality and domination, or to strengthen or weaken the means whereby the domination of a privileged stratum is maintained."[41] Because state power was the instrument of these processes, the resulting social formation has been given the name "political class."[42] The term reflects the preponderance of politicians among the emergent dominant class (one survey showing more than two-thirds of the nation's top elite to hold elected or appointed government office),[43] but its analytic logic derives precisely from the extent to which formally *nonpolitical* elites as well owed their class position to relations of power.

If control of the state was the basis of class formation and consolidation, then dominant class elements had to control the state at any price. In a democratic polity, this meant winning elections, and, in a largely illiterate, multiethnic society, where modernization was expanding popular expectations at a faster rate than resources, no electoral strategy seemed more assured of success than the manipulation of ethnic pride and prejudice. From the first significant elections in 1951 to the final, fraudulent and brutal confrontations in 1964 and 1965, the regional political classes used ethnicity as an electoral weapon against each other and against challengers from the classes below.

In doing so, they were not simply manufacturing ethnicity out of whole cloth but, rather, exploiting a profound cultural tendency for politics to be perceived and expressed in communal terms. The scope of the community varied across areas and over time. But be it a village, a ward in a town, a lineage, an entire town, or a whole ethnic nation, it was in terms of the subjective sense of community that the voters perceived political appeals and formulated their voting decisions. Especially in rural areas, where objective information was scarce and group pressure was strong, choice based on individual ideology or economic interest was unheard of; "for a man to support a political party different from the one supported by the rest of the community amounted almost to a repudiation of his own people."[44] Thus, it was through the familiar imagery of communal interests that local politicians and opinion leaders interpreted regional and national political struggle.

Major party newspapers and political leaders never failed to keep the local elites and candidates amply supplied with ethnic accusations and suspicions, however hysterical or malicious. The Action Group would ban Islam in the North. The NPC would force it upon the South. The NCNC would stack the whole bureaucracy with Igbos. Far-fetched in the extreme, such tactics nevertheless successfully transformed people's basest prejudices and wildest fears into resounding electoral mandates. The fact that "political constituencies were geographical in nature and ethnically homogeneous,"[45] and the prevailing tendency for opposition candidates to be nominees of parties associated with "foreign" ethnic groups, further heightened the utility of "tribalism" as an electoral vehicle for the entrenchment of each region's political class.

In a second sense as well, tribalism sprang from class action and became "a mask for class privilege."[46] As suggested by their aggressive forays into each other's political turf (a strategy eschewed only by the NPC, and there progressively less so after independence), the regional political classes were deeply divided among themselves, essentially on an ethnic basis. Despite their common interest in using the state to advance their class dominance, they could not agree on a sharing out of the national spoils. Bitterly and repeatedly they contested for control of the federal government and its resources, and, in the case of the two major southern parties, for control of the northern and other southern regions as well, since their own regions were insufficient bases for federal power. Increasingly, segments of these political classes also fought for control of major social and economic institutions.

Inevitably, such competition for limited resources and opportunities in Nigeria became organized along ethnic lines. When competition brought members of different ethnic groups into conflict, ethnic boundaries were pushed out to encompass a wider circle of commonality, which still contained the irreducible core of cultural unity, a common language of communication and understanding. It was around this cultural core that people rallied for mutual assistance in the competition for wealth and power, and it was precisely the real cultural content of ethnicity that made it "possible for class actions to be successfully dressed in ethnic garb."[47] Similarly, it was the real psychological force of cultural commitments that so disposed them to erupt in violent conflict and made this conflict so difficult to manage. Nevertheless, the roots of conflict lay not in cultural dissonance but in cultural similarity—in the common value placed on the expanding but still limited fruits of economic growth and state expansion. At the federal level in particular, elites of different ethnic groups desired and competed for the same base of national wealth and the same positions of power, prestige, comfort, and challenge. Their competitive mobilization of mass bases, and their resulting political conflicts, appeared sectional— ethnic and regional—in character, tapping and inciting mass sectional tensions. But what catalyzed these tensions into conflict was not sectionalism. It was class action.

Class, ethnicity, and political conflict, 1950–1960

At one level of analysis, political conflict in Nigeria during the 1950s may be seen as largely the product of the convergence of ethnic, regional, and political cleavage. All of the major conflicts of the decade tapped at least one of these cleavages directly, and inevitably involved the other two in some form. But, as was the case with the regional and federal elections of the decade, other conflicts that appeared sectional were significantly rooted in class action. For the most part, these were elite conflicts, even when they mobilized a mass base. They sprang from the struggle within the elite to control the narrow resource base of an underdeveloped economy and state, a struggle which, in becoming organized along ethnic and regional lines, ultimately infected the whole of political and social life in Nigeria.

Igbo versus Yoruba

The first ethnic struggle among emergent dominant-class elements grew out of the nationalist movement. The late 1930s and 1940s witnessed a sweeping movement for collective improvement among the Igbo people, both in Igboland itself and in the multiethnic towns abroad, Lagos in particular. Through amazingly rapid adoption of Western education and Christian religion, and determined communal organization, the Igbos closed by 1950 a substantial early Yoruba advantage in Western education and employment.[48] This sweeping social advance by the Igbo put them in competition with the Yoruba for the educational, economic, and political opportunities that were opening up to Nigerians. Alarmed by this challenge, the Yoruba elite organized politically and culturally in defense of their privileged position, and there ensued in the 1940s a struggle for socioeconomic power between the Yoruba and Igbo "new men" that permanently split the nationalist movement along largely ethnic lines.[49]

The competition reached its peak in 1948, when the rivalry between the two nationalist organizations erupted in a virulent press war between their respective newspapers. Though the Igbo-led organization, the NCNC, had sought with some success to construct a multiethnic base, the war of words featured an ugly outpouring of ethnic hatred that came very close to exploding into mass violence that summer.[50] The bitter confrontation permanently politicized Yoruba and Igbo cultural organizations[51] and produced an ethnic political tension that was never successfully eliminated. It sprang from years of competition within a rising elite for access to the limited tools of class formation—newspaper circulation, organizational membership, popular support, bureaucratic position, and local elective office.

Embittered by another sensational flash of press warfare and continuing streams of mutual vilification, and entrenched by successive failures of half-hearted attempts at reconciliation, this Yoruba–Igbo cleavage could not but assume a formal political character as well with the preparation for full-scale electoral politics during the constitutional review of 1949–1950. This process brought multiple conflicts not only between Yoruba and Igbo but also between northern and southern political elites over the distribution of power and revenue between the regions and territories they expected to control. As the first regional elections approached in 1951, openly regionalist parties were formed in the West and North out of existing cultural organizations for the express purpose of winning political control of those regions against the challenge of the better organized and more broadly based NCNC.

With the 1951 victory of each party in its home region, a rough identity was established between region, ethnicity, and party. The identity heightened over the course of the decade as the ruling parties tightened their grips on regional power and reached out to compete for national resources and power. Each of these cleavages contributed a real and distinctive dimension of strain to the resulting conflicts. The substantial disparity in level of development between North and South strained relations between the regions, as northern leaders demanded resources needed to catch up, while southern leaders argued for investment in demonstrated progress and bureaucratic placement strictly by merit. Social and political tension inhered in the enormous cultural distance between North and South, as reflected in their vastly different orientations to authority and structures of status, and in the fact that "the Christian South was looking toward England and Western Europe" while "the Islamic North fixed its gaze on Mecca."[52] But these groups were not without cultural similarities as well,[53] and, in any case, cultural distance did not keep the various ethnic elites from forming all manner of alliances when it served their interests to do so. It was the intersection of cultural and regional tensions with the emergent class structure that fixed party competition around these sectional tensions, and so substantially inflamed them.

North versus South

The close interaction between sectional conflict and class structure is illustrated even (perhaps especially) by those conflicts that appeared most purely ethnic, such as the tragic Kano riot of 1953. Early in 1953, a bitter political confrontation erupted in the Central House of Representatives with the introduction of a motion calling for self-government for Nigeria in 1956. This date, to which both southern parties had committed themselves in their competition for nationalist leadership, was bitterly opposed by northern politicians, who feared that self-government would mean government by southerners unless postponed until the North could to some degree catch up with the South in education, training, and political expertise, and free itself from the increasing control by southerners of its bureaucracy, commerce, and transportation system. When northern politicians blocked the motion, they were insulted and abused by street crowds in Lagos and subsequently by the southern press. The press condemnation escalated when, upon their return to the North, they announced a program for the virtual secession of their region from Nigeria. As the war of words was peaking, the two southern parties sent a series of delegations to the North to campaign directly for self-government. The arrival of one such delegation in Kano sparked four days of rioting in that city's Sabon Gari (strangers' quarters) that left more than 200 people injured and 36 dead, 21 of them Igbos.[54]

The 1953 Kano riot was an event of great historical significance. Though not the first instance of interethnic violence in the North, it was the bloodiest, and foreshadowed an even more traumatic confrontation in Kano 13 years later that would accelerate the slide toward civil war. Like the 1966 clash, the 1953 riot was essentially an outpouring of resentment by the indigenous Hausa population against the escalating preemption of commercial opportunities and modern clerical and semiskilled jobs by Igbo migrants to the city.[55] This mass-based social and economic competition, rubbing against sharply visible cultural differences, generated the necessary preconditions for violent ethnic conflict. But, as in 1966, these palpable tensions erupted into mass violence only in a climate of national political crisis created by competing elites, who fanned a conflict over the timing of self-government into a national confrontation by interpreting it to their constituencies as a threat to consummate cultural interests. This was not simply cynical manipulation, however. Southern elites sincerely saw the North as feudal and backward, a brake upon nationalist progress. And northern elites, both the reigning traditional rulers and the new generation of Western-educated nobility and allied commoners, sincerely perceived the prospect of southern domination as a threat to cherished cultural values and traditions and to the long-term socioeconomic interests of their people. But their attachment to Islamic values could not be separated from their commitment to the particular structure of power and privilege that Islam legitimated. Nor could their concern for their people's social and economic progress be divorced from their anxiety over the threat of southern penetration to their own careers. In short, the fuse for mass violence in Kano was elite conflict over not simply cultural and regional but also class interests. At stake in the timing of self-government was control over the basic instrument of class formation—the modern state.

For precisely this reason, northern political leaders resolved, soon after assuming office in 1952, that qualified northerners would be given explicit preference over southerners in hiring for the Northern Region's civil service, and that the development of modern education and training was now not a threat to emirate class structure but a condition essential for its preservation.[56] This strategy accelerated with the division of the unitary Public Service into regional branches in 1954. While the Eastern Region and Western Region raced to "indigenize" their bureaucracies, the North sought "northernization." Expatriates were actually preferred to southerners when no qualified northerner was available, while southerners were gradually driven out, and permanently excluded from the Northern Public Service.[57] Aside from engendering bitter southern resentment, this policy worked almost precisely as intended, purging the bureaucracy of all but one southerner by 1959, heavily disposing it toward manipulation and domination by the ruling NPC, and so further concentrating administrative and political power in the narrow dominant class of the North.[58]

The character of northernization as the confluence of ethnic and class action was apparent also in its other ramifications. During the final four years of colonial rule, northern businessmen used their growing prominence in the NPC to press for extension of northernization to the regional economy as well. Gradually, provisions accumulated excluding southerners from government contracts, retail trade, and ownership of land.[59] By 1958, northern Premier Sir Ahmadu Bello was boldly declaring that the goal of northernization was to have "northerners gain control of everything in the country."[60] Indeed, much of the turbulence of postindependence Nigerian politics revolved around the effort of the northern aristocracy to realize this ambition of national dominance—to consolidate its political control over the federation and its financial resources, to advance the position of northern elites in the federal bureaucracy, and so to secure and enhance its class interests in competition against the political classes of the Eastern and Western Regions.

Minorities and majorities

A third major ethnic cleavage in Nigeria found the various ethnic minority groups rising in opposition to the dominance in the West of the Yoruba, in the East of the Igbo, and in the North of the Hausa–Fulani. In each region, the political organization of ethnic minorities gathered momentum in the twilight of colonial rule, spurred by mounting apprehension of political repression, socioeconomic discrimination, and even cultural extinction by the majority groups when they took unfettered control of regional governments after independence. Seeking for their people safeguards against such abuse, and for themselves power and its material gains, minority-group politicians spawned movements for separate states that, if successful, would have totally transformed the existing regional structure.

As with the majority groups, the cultural mobilization of the ethnic minorities emanated from the intricate and volatile interaction between ethnicity and class. The chemistry of minority political ferment involved two familiar components: mass-based socioeconomic competition, grounded in real cultural attachments, and elite mobilization of these attachments for class ends.

Once again in Nigeria, ethnic consciousness and organization were stimulated by the expansion of the state and its social and economic activity, and by the expectation of further and more rapid expansion after independence. As outlined by a 1957 British colonial commission, ethnic minority fears and grievances centered around obtaining a fair share of the rewards and resources of an expanding economy and state: contracts, loans, scholarships, processing plants, water supplies, street lights, schools, and hydroelectric projects.[61] Minority demands for separate states were based on the belief, actively promoted by their leaders, that minorities were being cheated in the distribution of these resources by the majority-dominated regional governments, and that the existing modest restraints on this oppression would evaporate with the departure of the British. The root of ethnic mobilization in the competition for scarce resources was strikingly manifested in the extent to which communal groups fell back upon ethnicity to rationalize their setbacks. Time and again the commission heard that entrepreneurs could not obtain the loans, students the scholarships, and towns the amenities that others were getting because the others were of the region's majority ethnic group and they were not.[62]

It was not simply due to a lack of other lines of cleavage that socioeconomic competition was organized and perceived through the prism of ethnicity. The political mobilization and statehood demands of the minorities also reflected deep emotional attachment to their distinctive group values, symbols, languages, ways of life, and historical traditions, and genuine fear that these would be suppressed or obliterated. This cultural content of ethnicity mirrored that of the majority groups to the extent that, where minority cultural fears were most pronounced, in the Northern Region, they closely resembled the chief cultural fear of both the Yoruba and the Igbo—that the Fulani aristocracy would seek to impose upon them its authoritarian Islamic traditions.

If minority ethnic mobilization was based in social, economic, and cultural conflict at the mass level, the perceptions of conflicting interests were nevertheless heightened (if not largely generated), and their transformation into political movements achieved, by minority-group leaders who were significantly motivated by personal interests. Gifted and ambitious individuals of every ethnicity coveted political office for its sheer power, its income and perquisites, the "big man" status it conferred in their communities, and the vast wealth that could be accumulated in it through enterprising manipulation of the public trust. Just as shrewdly as the politicians of the ethnic majorities, minority-group politicians understood the relationship between class formation and state power, and the importance not simply of holding political office but of controlling the primary accumulations of public capital, the regional marketing boards and development corporations. This was one reason why minority movements demanded separate states: separate states would have separate marketing boards and public corporations, which their own parties would control.

Just as much as their Yoruba, Igbo, Hausa, and Fulani competitors, minority-group politicians found ethnicity the surest vehicle for their political ambitions. Thus they not only cast their electoral appeals quite blatantly in the language of ethnic pride, prejudice, and suspicion, but they organized ethnic political parties to fix the identity between their personal causes and their people's. At times, substantial cultural entrepreneurship was required to organize latent corporate feelings into a coherent identity that could be embodied in a political party, which the politician could then ride to power. The phenomenon was cogently summarized by the minorities' commission in its discussion of Muslim political organization in the Western Region:

> It can hardly be said too often that at the moment there is a general struggle for power in Nigeria and that any group with a corporate feeling can be the vehicle by which a politician reaches power; there is therefore a tendency on the part of the ambitious to work up party feeling where it was hardly formulated before.[63]

The description could also have been applied to the birth in ethnic consciousness of the AG in the Western Region and the NPC in the North,
and to the increasingly close association between the NCNC and the Igbo
State Union, but nowhere was it more graphically reflected than in the dizzying fluidity of minority politics: the formation and dissolution of parties
and alliances, and the movement in and out of them of young politicians,
searching for vehicles for political advancement, settling upon ethnicity
as the paramount instrument for rallying mass support.[64] In the energetic
maneuvering of these young ethnic elites may be found the most vivid
expression of the relationship between ethnicity, class action, and democratic politics.

Conflict, crisis and collapse, 1960–1966

The First Nigerian Republic was buffeted during its tumultuous five years
by an alternation and accumulation of two forms of political conflict.
One, the sectional rivalry between regional political classes for control of
national resources, was all too familiar. This rivalry had been substantially
heightened by the three-cornered contest for national political power,
culminating in the 1959 federal election campaign, in which the major parties, and in particular the Western-based AG, used the unrest of the ethnic
minorities to make inroads upon the political bases of the opposition. The
three ruling parties, viewing the capture of federal power, or at least some
piece of it, as essential to their survival, and the electoral support of their
own ethnic minorities as essential to this goal, each drew deep anxiety from
the incursion of one of its two main rivals into its electoral base. In the
North, the AG alliances with minority movements in the Middle Belt converged with aggressive challenges to its Hausa heartland by both the AG and
the NCNC (allied with the radical NEPU) to threaten seriously the political
domination of the Fulani aristocracy. This accounted for the substantial
political intimidation and repression with which the latter responded during the 1959 campaign. But the North was not unique. The huge stakes in
the election made it a fierce contest throughout the nation, pressing each
party to resort to fanatical tactics—vituperative personal condemnations,
hateful ethnic recriminations, official intimidation and obstruction, and
physical violence by party thugs. The extraordinary bitterness of the campaign did not destroy the tacit pre-election alliance between the NCNC and
the NPC, which afterward matured into a coalition government led by the
latter. But it did badly strain the nascent partnership and expose its shallow
foundation in the temporary convergence of strategic interests (not least,
the subjection of the AG).

The second form of political conflict, scarcely visible before independence, was essentially class in nature. It found a loose and shifting coalition
of lower-class groups and progressive educated elites opposing with increasing stridency and popular support the entire basis of dominant-class rule

in Nigeria. It tapped, within each of the two southern parties, the hitherto latent ideological tension between, on the one hand, radical and progressive elements—who were determined to smash the northern aristocracy's ever-tightening control of the federation and who understood the necessity, for this end, of dismantling the regional system—and, on the other, conservative, primarily business, elements whose primary concern was a stable regional distribution of the resources of class formation. These latter elements were led in the NCNC by the party's federal ministers, who forged comfortable relations with their NPC coalition partners based on a mutual recognition of common class interests, and in the AG by the party's deputy leader, Samuel Akintola, who replaced the dynamic leader Obafemi Awolowo as western premier when the latter resigned to lead the AG's ill-fated 1959 national campaign. Like other southern conservatives, Chief Akintola perceived the interests of the emergent southern bourgeoisie to lie in an accommodation with the politically dominant northern aristocracy based on the idea of "regional security."[65] Such an accommodation, to which NPC leaders were themselves increasingly attracted, would essentially have ended the socioeconomic and political competition between the regional political classes by respecting the dominance of each in its regional "sphere of influence" and dividing up the spoils of power at the center.

In the competition between regions and ethnic groups, which mobilized sectional passions for class ends, and the competition over regionalism, which embraced the conflict between opposing class forces, the First Republic reeled from one crisis to the next, and finally collapsed.

Class conflicts

The succession of political crises in the First Nigerian Republic involved essentially five major conflicts: the 1962 split within the AG and subsequent subjugation of that party; the regional confrontation over the 1962 census, which dominated politics until early 1964; the 1964 general strike; the federal election struggle of late 1964; and the final confrontation in the Western Regional election of 1965. It is beyond the scope of this paper to describe in detail the complex, overlapping character of these conflicts, or the manner in which they progressively polarized politics, sapped the legitimacy of the regime, and so paved the way for its overthrow. What can be demonstrated here is the significant contribution to each crisis of the emergent class structure.

Attempting to distinguish between class and communal conflict in the First Republic may be seen as a futile and misleading endeavor, since all conflicts were rooted in class action to one degree or another, and most also involved sectional competition and distrust. Still, it is valuable to distinguish between those conflicts in which the basic cleavage was class and those in which the cleavage was essentially sectional—ethnic, regional, or in some way communal. The first and last of the five conflicts mentioned above revolved most fundamentally around class cleavage, but they also heavily mobilized sectional cleavages, and became inextricably tangled in them. The 1964 general strike was almost purely a class cleavage—the only major political action in the First Republic that effectively transcended ethnicity. The census crisis and federal election were sectional conflicts rooted significantly, if not primarily, in class action.

The 1962 AG split was a boiling to the surface of the inevitable ideological tensions in a party that had originally been organized around ethnicity rather than ideology. Long committed to a moderate socialist program, Chief Awolowo moved increasingly, after the stunning 1959 defeat of the AG, to a much more explicitly and radically socialist program, vowing in general to dismantle the emergent structure of class privilege in Nigeria, and specifically to replace the regional system with a structure of multiple states; to sharply reduce ministerial salaries and political corruption and waste; to reorient development around the needs of farmers and workers; to strike a much more militantly nationalist stand in foreign affairs and against foreign capital; and to forge a political alliance of southern progressives against the NPC. The latter element (which Chief Awolowo had pursued unsuccessfully after the 1959 election in seeking an AG–NCNC coalition government) drove to the core aim of southern radicals and progressives—to smash the national political dominance of the Fulani aristocracy. The regional system was the keystone of this dominance, and the Middle Belt was perhaps the key to the regional system. Its retention in a Northern Region in which the NPC was tightening its grip enabled this party of the aristocracy to achieve by 1962 an outright majority in the federal parliament, and provided a buffer to keep the winds of radical change in the South from whipping up into the emirates, where the dominance of the aristocracy was less stable than it appeared.[66] Break-up of the regional system threatened the political classes in the Eastern and Western Regions as well, since smaller regions would mean smaller bases of patronage for ruling parties, and very likely different ruling parties in some of the new regions. For those reasons, regionalism went hand in hand with the conservatism of the Akintola faction in the 1962 conflict, while Awolowo's antiregionalism was the logical spearhead of his radical challenge to the status quo.[67]

For these reasons also, such a conflict within the AG and the Western Region could hardly remain internal for long. When it broke out into the open at the party's annual congress in February 1962, the Awolowo faction scored a resounding if bitter triumph, sweeping the elections for control of the party platform and machinery.[68] Three months later, it succeeded in deposing Chief Akintola as Western premier. This was more than the ruling federal coalition could stand. Affronted by the attacks of the Awolowo AG on political corruption and high living, fearful of its commitment to radical change, aggravated by its political forays into their minority areas, and resentful of its increasing attractiveness to educated Nigerian youth, the NPC and NCNC leaders sought to "consolidate and stabilize their control of the system" by placing "in power in the West individuals who would be content to limit themselves to that sphere."[69] Swiftly they seized upon the occasion of a riot in the Western Region House (staged by the Akintola faction for the purpose) to intervene in the West and prevent the Awolowo faction from taking power.[70] After six months of heavily biased emergency rule, Chief Akintola was reinstated as premier at the helm of a new party, and a government inquiry released its report attributing massive corruption to Chief Awolowo and his top aides while exonerating Chief Akintola. By the time the full effects of federal emergency rule had been felt, a fourth region had been created out of the West, weakening its original power in the federation; Chief Awolowo and his closest radical associates stood convicted of treason; the AG had been destroyed as a national political force; and a transethnic, transparty progressive alliance had begun to emerge from the wreckage, straining the unity of the NCNC.

While the long crisis in the West was colored by elite ethnic competition and intense cultural nationalism (stemming from a feeling among the Yoruba that they were being victimized as a people),[71] its basic cause was conflict over the future of class dominance in Nigeria, and its basic effect was (despite the conservative victory) to undermine this dominance, and the constitutional regime that sustained it. Disgust with the "gross materialism and corruption" of the political class was building among educated young professionals and workers, and it is likely that the sordid manner in which the radical challenge from the West was suppressed affected idealistic elements everywhere.[72] Moreover, the unseemly struggle for power and subsequent inquiry into corruption appeared to heighten popular cynicism toward the entire class of politicians.[73]

The 1964 general strike was the explosive expression of the swelling popular cynicism and resentment. More than just a strike by the nation's workers for higher wages, more even than a confrontation between organized labor and the nation's largest employer, the state, it was a sweeping challenge to the entire political class and its ruling authority. Uniting in protest against the federal government were virtually the entire population of organized labor in Nigeria (some 300,000 workers organized into about 300 active unions), most of the rest of the nation's one million wage laborers, both blue and white collar, and a large number of unemployed workers and urban sympathizers. For 13 days in June of 1964, the strike brought the economic life of the nation and most of its essential services to a virtual standstill, costing the economy between 4 and 14 million man-days.[74]

What united a hitherto badly fractured labor movement and inspired perhaps the most widespread transethnic organization the nation had ever seen was not simply personal economic discontent but outrage over the entire structure of inequality in Nigerian society. Union leaders fixed their protest not simply on the meager and declining real income of urban work-ers but on the enormous disparities in the official structure of wages and benefits and on the glaring levels of corruption and extravagant consump-tion by the nation's political elite. It was this larger issue that rallied the broad-based and spontaneous outpouring of popular support for the strike in most Nigerian cities.[75]

Understanding the centrality of the northern aristocracy in the national structure of class dominance they opposed, union leaders also pointedly attacked "northern feudalism" and evinced a special hostility to the NPC. This may explain why the strike drew support not only from left-wing Action Group intellectuals but from the more moderate progressives who led the NCNC and the Eastern Region government. Having just lost a bitter regional showdown over the census to the NPC, these NCNC leaders no doubt saw in the mass movement a vehicle for their increasingly desperate struggle for national power. But this was something of a miscalculation. For though the unions, youth groups, and other popular forces in the South would back the NCNC–AG coalition in the federal election confron-tation that December, their strike was an expression of disgust with the entire political class. This disgust could be submerged by the resurgence of sectional conflict, but it could not be dissipated. It soured popular com-mitment to the regime as a legitimate form of government, even as people rallied behind competing alliances in the struggle for regime control.

By the time the crisis over the 1964 federal election had subsided in 1965 and NPC control of the federation had been tightened, sectional conflict had come to merge almost indistinguishably with class conflict. Politics had been reduced to a bipolar confrontation between a progressive alliance led by the NCNC and a conservative one led by the NPC, and the long-standing sectional cleavage between eastern and northern elites for control of the federation had converged with the equally deep-seated ideological and class cleavage between regionalist and antiregionalist forces. How, then, is one to classify the final confrontation between these two alliances for con-trol of the Western Region in the October 1965 election? Perhaps the most meaningful way is according to popular perception. Just as the 1964 federal election was waged and perceived as primarily a sectional conflict, so the 1965 Western Regional election and subsequent rebellion were fought pri-marily as a class struggle within the Yoruba nation.

If the 1965 election in the Western Region was the stage for the final showdown between the bitterly opposed parties of the other two major regions and ethnic groups, and in particular a do-or-die struggle for the eastern party, it was even more so for opposing political forces within the West. If Chief Akintola's ruling party, the Nigerian National Democratic Party (NNDP), won a full five-year term, AG leaders knew it would continue to use regional power ruthlessly to extinguish their party. The Akintola forces, on the other hand, expected, in the case of defeat, to become the victims of their own methods, without a genuine base of popular support to sustain them. In fact, their manifest unpopularity was the key to the cleavage in the West. The fundamental issue in 1965 was a ruling political class whose corruption was so naked, whose coercion so ruthless, whose arrogance so total that it had come to be hated even by a people who expected a certain amount of corruption and coercion from their political leaders. In the orgy of personal greed and opportunism, development needs were denied attention, imagination, and funding in the West, as in the federation overall. Political greed did not begin with Chief Akintola's rule, but it was his special misfortune that it escalated during a horrendous slump in the world cocoa market, when the western economy could least afford it, and that it did so under a regime which, lacking Chief Awolowo's charismatic appeal and burdened with the popular resentment of his humiliation and imprisonment, had pervasively to employ coercion and intimidation as substitutes for legitimate authority.

Like the 1964 general strike, the 1965 Western Regional election was a conflict between a corrupt and oppressive political class and mass elements who felt themselves its victims. Hence, even though it had used every available instrument of regional power to intimidate and thwart the opposition campaign, the incumbent regime still had to resort to wholesale electoral fraud to salvage a claim to reelection. The claim was recognized as hollow. Upon its announcement, the region erupted into popular rebellion, with violence and destruction primarily taking the form not of rival party vengeance or indiscriminate anger but of a kind of traditional retribution "against the wealthy and arrogant," who, in using their position single-mindedly to enrich themselves, had offended against the community.[76]

The class conflict in the West followed a spate of exposés of federal scandal and corruption earlier in the year, and a growing consciousness of the degree to which not only corruption but swollen official salaries and allowances, ill-advised prestige projects, and financially draining, economically dislocating political crises were squandering the nation's resources and sapping its development potential. In the context of spreading popular rebellion and social chaos in the West, such consciousness led educated young elites in the intelligentsia, the civil service, and the military to reject utterly the legitimacy of the constitutional regime in Nigeria and inspired those among them with the power to do so to overthrow it.

Class action as ethnic conflict

In the early morning hours of January 15, 1966, a clique of young colonels and majors overthrew the First Nigerian Republic and arrested or assassinated its primary political leaders. That the oppressive, sclerotic dominance of a narrow political class was a basic motivation for their coup is strikingly revealed in their initial pronouncements, which pledged, typically, "to get rid of rotten and corrupt ministers ... to bring an end to gangsterism and disorder, corruption and despotism"[77] and to put the nation on the path to genuine development of its economic potential.[78] But equally prominent was their desire to free the nation from "tribalism" and the incessant, debilitating political conflict it had spawned.

The census and federal election crises were only the most prominent instances of ethnic, or "tribal," conflict. As we have seen, other conflicts had tribal implications, and there were also numerous, more limited contests for control of particular institutions, such as universities. But as was the case before independence, ethnic conflict in the First Republic was significantly rooted in the actions and competing aspirations of dominant-class elements.

The competitive mobilization of ethnic constituencies in the 1962 census was a classic expression of the interaction between ethnicity and emergent class. Political elites at all levels perceived in the census important class implications because resources of class formation such as legislative seats and revenue were apportioned between regions and districts on a per capita basis. To the extent that one region's population showed a larger percentage increase than another's, the political class of that region could expect a greater share of national resources and a greater prospect of winning national political control. Southern (especially eastern) political leaders hoped for sufficient southern gains to break the population majority of the North and so wrest control of the federal government from the NPC. Northern political leaders were determined that the census outcome not threaten this position of dominance.

Thus it was that the census was conducted in an atmosphere not so much of a count as a contest, with regional governments utilizing every medium of communication—pamphlets, posters, radio, schools, churches, word-of-mouth, and political campaigning—to mobilize their people for "a good result."[79] Owing perhaps to more intensive mobilization in the South, the initial results showed much larger increases there—sufficient to end the population majority of the North. In fact, the increases in some eastern districts were so large as to have been demographically impossible in the view of the professional census staff, which judged them "grossly inflated."[80] This revelation by the responsible federal minister, a northerner, unleashed a storm of partisan conflict late in 1962. There followed conflicting reports of the results, based on a "verification check" in the North that had somehow found eight and a half million northerners missed entirely in the count, thus producing a percentage increase just slightly higher than that claimed by the East. Public confusion and political deadlock abated only for a time when Prime Minister Abubakar Tafawa Balewa canceled the entire census early in 1963 and announced a new one for later that year.

The count resumed amid renewed mass mobilization by politicians and escalating distrust and tension, with one southern politician warning of secession by the South if the census collapsed as a result of "intrigue" by northern Nigerians.[81] Elaborate sampling and checking procedures did not prevent an even greater fiasco, with the final result an "altogether incredible" national increase of 83 percent in ten years and a continued Northern population majority.[82] Though completely rejected by the Eastern Region's NCNC government, which documented numerous census irregularities and flaws in the North, the figures stood because the NPC possessed sufficient parliamentary power to make them stand.[83]

This intransigence did not resolve the conflict, however. Once again, sectional conflict within the political class boiled over into mass-based tension. As political leaders traded ethnic recriminations in the wake of the census dispute, a chorus of demands poured forth in the Northern Region House of Assembly for expulsion of easterners (Igbos) from the North and confiscation of their wealth. Igbo traders were hastily evicted from a number of northern cities while the official northern newspaper published cartoons depicting Igbos as cannibals.[84] From the floors of their regional Houses, the politicians of each ethnic group charged the others with usurping national resources and bureaucratic patronage in a bitter month-long dispute which ran "till the tribal origins of virtually every government and corporation employee had been canvassed" and the federal prime minister forced to intervene to prevent actual violence.[85]

The census crisis marked the beginning of intense, polarized competition for national political power between the two federal coalition partners, the NPC and the NCNC. The lines of cleavage on which they fought were more ethnic and regional than political in character, but the origins of their competition were no less in their personal pursuit of class resources than in their defense of mass-based communal interests. Whatever their motives, *theirs* were the motives that counted, for the major ethnic and regional conflicts in Nigerian politics were rooted in *elite* conflict, as the census crisis so vividly demonstrated. It was the politicians, the competing factions of the dominant class, who campaigned for good results, who disputed and manipulated the results, who launched the bitter burst of ethnic recriminations, and who brought the nation to the brink of disaster. The elite basis of ethnic political conflict has been emphasized by the late B. J. Dudley:

> [R]eferences to the NPC, NCNC, AG ... and so on are not to the "total collective," the organizations which these symbols denote, but rather [to] "leaders of the NPC, NCNC, etc." ... Thus interpreted ... politics in Nigeria ... is not about *alternative policies* but about the *control over men and resources*. It is therefore incorrect to see politics in Nigeria, as in the other states of Africa, as simply "tribalism"—the competition of one "tribe" against the other.[86]

Elite conflict over the census polarized into the two competing political alliances of the NPC and NCNC, which in turn shaped the year-long struggle around the 1964 federal election. At one level, the election conflict was manifestly tribal. Ugly ethnic recriminations and violence burst into the open in the summer, even before the campaign began, and escalated thereafter. Politicians appealed for votes in blatant and vicious ethnic tones. Both NPC politicians in the North and, with special fury and crudity, NNDP politicians in the West, attacked the Igbo leaders of the NCNC for alleged ethnic imperialism and warned of Igbo domination if the AG–NCNC Progressive Alliance won. Eastern minority parties in the NPC alliance also played heavily on this ethnic fear. NCNC politicians urged Igbo constituencies to rally to the defense of their embattled people, and, with Action Group politicians, urged voters throughout the South to end the domination of the Hausa-Fulani and the unfair share of development resources they were appropriating to the North.[87] In the heat of such ethnic mobilization, the class consciousness of the June general strike was drowned in an emotional resurgence of communal attachments,[88] and the democratic character of the election was obliterated by waves of political violence and official obstruction and repression of opposition campaigns.[89]

So crippling was the official obstruction in the West and North that the AG–NCNC Progressive Alliance boycotted the election, provoking a tense showdown with NPC leaders in which, for several days, the specter of secession and possible civil war loomed large. Partly to avoid the prospect of imminent bloodshed, and partly because they could not gain assurances of military and police support, NCNC leaders finally yielded, in the guise of a hollow compromise that only tightened the grip of the NPC on federal power.

The 1964 federal election crisis, which carried tribalism to the brink of civil war, was the clearest expression yet of the potential mass consequences of elite ethnic mobilization, and a foreshadowing of the holocaust yet to come. Like previous major ethnic conflicts, it was the product of manipulation by political leaders, as repeatedly recognized by both Prime Minister Tafawa Balewa and President Nnamdi Azikiwe, who, in a stunning address to the nation two months before the election, condemned the Nigerian political leaders who took such delight "in beating the tom-tom of tribal hatred."[90] As in previous conflicts, the ethnic drum beating was the calculated strategy of dominant-class elements locked in bitter competition for control of state power and resources. If not consciously a mask for class action, such tribalism was certainly a manifestation and tragic consequence of it.

Conclusion: ethnicity, class, and the democratic state

Neither the persistence of strong ethnic identities nor the stimulus to ethnic competition of modernization can suffice in explaining the failure of democratic government and national unity in Nigeria in the 1960s. An important lesson of this experience is the distinction between the manifest and latent bases of conflict. What may seem on its face essentially an ethnic conflict may in fact have significant class causes. Thus, without diminishing the reality of cultural conflict and socioeconomic competition between ethnic groups, the origins of the census and federal election crises in elite competition for the resources of class formation must be acknowledged. Neither these specific crises nor the process of political decay that they advanced can otherwise be understood.

This underscores the distinctive interaction among ethnic structure, class structure, and the democratic state. In ethnically plural societies, especially those with centralized ethnic structures, political cleavage tends to flow heavily along ethnic lines. This is not necessarily inconsistent with reasonable social harmony and political order, so long as the competition between groups respects certain boundaries of tolerance, moderation, and elementary decency. Crippling polarization and animosity will be less likely to occur where ethnic cleavage is crosscut, and ethnic identities cross-pressured, by other types of cleavage—such as class, region, and, in a democratic system, political party.[91] Federalism in Nigeria served not to crosscut but to reinforce ethnicity. The class structure similarly failed to generate effective crosscutting cleavage for two reasons, both having to do with the highly underdeveloped state of the economy. Underdevelopment meant that few Nigerians held an occupation in the economic sector most conducive to development of functional or class identity, the urban wage economy. Most Nigerians farmed for a living in the villages where they were born—where cleavage was understood in terms of being in or outside the cultural community, where education and independent sources of information were limited and political participation was mobilized from above along communal lines. And underdevelopment also meant that the resource base of the emerging dominant class was too limited for it to be a transethnic class. Because the resources of class formation were far too scarce to accommodate all of those struggling for entrance into the emerging dominant class, intense competition was inevitable. Given the absence of crosscutting, functional cleavage, the presence of real ethnic and regional differences, and their substantial reinforcement by the federal structure, it was not surprising that resource competition became organized along communal lines.

A further feature of extreme underdevelopment was the enormous concentration of scarce resources in the control of the state. The near total absence of nonstate routes to the accumulation of wealth and achievement of status meant that those who aspired to high class standing and those who wished to consolidate it needed assured access to the state, if not position within it. Under an authoritarian state sympathetic to the dominant class, such access and support can be confidently secured. In a democratic state, and particularly in one lacking a social consensus legitimating the capitalist accumulation of wealth, it cannot. It is at risk in every election and must continually be renewed through elections. In ethnically plural societies, these elections, and the continual legislative and political conflict which is the stuff of democratic politics, become the vehicle not only for protecting the general process of capitalist accumulation but also for promoting accumulation by one cultural section of the elite in competition with others.

Thus they become a major expression of sectional conflict within the dominant class. And because manipulation of mass ethnic feeling is the surest instrument of electoral success for both the individual dominant-class member and the cultural section of the dominant class, democratic competition serves to fan ethnic conflict at the mass level as well.

Thus, ethnic division and competition, an emerging dominant-class structure in an underdeveloped economy, and a democratic state interact to produce an intense polarization of politics around ethnicity. Given the first two alone, elite ethnic competition would lack such regular political outlets and weapons. If elite access to state resources could be broadly assured, competition might be eliminated by some stable division of state resources like that sought by regionalist forces in the First Republic. Given the emergent class structure and democratic competition in a more ethnically homogeneous society, conflict might become intense and polarized, but not along ethnic lines. Given ethnic pluralism and democracy but a developed economic structure, where the position of the dominant class had either a secure base or at least ample opportunity for formation and consolidation outside the state, elites would not depend so desperately for their class position on political victory and so would not so demagogically manipulate ethnic tension and so systematically trounce democratic rules-of-the-game in the pursuit of victory.

The Nigerian case thus suggests several general propositions. First, in ethnically plural societies with low levels of socioeconomic development but relatively large state sectors, ethnicity is mobilized by elites as a tool in their competition for the scarce but expanding resources of class formation mediated by the state. Since these conditions are typical of Asian and especially African nations, this suggests that the ethnic conflict that has so commonly polarized their politics has been, to a significant degree, the product of the process of class formation, and cannot be explained simply by the stimulus to competition for new resources and rewards introduced by modernization. Second, in such a context, electoral competition may make mass ethnic conflict—and its polarization into violence and perhaps secession—more likely, by inducing politicians to mobilize mass constituencies along ethnic lines in their struggle for state control. Third, because such ethnic polarization is more a phenomenon of class than political structure, attempts to generate crosscutting cleavage through constitutional innovations, in the absence of changes in socioeconomic structure and in the nature of class formation, are likely to prove disappointing.

These propositions generate a mixed assessment of the prospects for the Second Nigerian Republic, inaugurated in 1979. Certainly the replacement of the acutely unstable regional system with a structure of multiple states, and the conscious constitutional efforts to eliminate sectional parties and generate crosscutting cleavage in politics, will reduce the structural conduciveness of the republic to ethnic polarization.[92] At the same time, the sweeping pace of social and economic change and the heightening inequalities and contradictions generated by the oil boom have thrust class-based cleavages into politics more resolutely than ever before.[93] Indeed, the major political conflicts of the Second Republic in its first two years have revolved primarily around class, not ethnicity, and have not consistently mobilized ethnicity even as a manifest or superficial cleavage.

But ethnicity is not the only mass-based cleavage that threatens democratic stability. Any line of cleavage may, in principle, do so if it sufficiently consumes political energy and tolerance and polarizes political alignments. Moreover, to the extent that political office and state power remain crucial to the formation and consolidation of class dominance, political competition may grow more intense and political methods more extreme than democratic order can long withstand.

It may further be hypothesized that the higher the level of economic development, the less directly does class position tend to depend on political power. In this respect, despite enormous oil wealth and a decade of rapid economic growth, the Nigerian economy has yet achieved only a very modest level of functional elaboration and only very limited independent bases for the accumulation of wealth. In fact, the Nigerian state has expanded even faster than the economy itself, and government scholarships, jobs, loans, contracts, consultancies, and licenses are no less vital to class formation and consolidation today than they were two decades ago.[94]

As economic development and social and political change temper the role of ethnicity in politics, continuing dominant-class action appears to be provoking more coherent class action by peasants and workers, and more explicit class-based appeals to them by progressive parties. As Nigerian society becomes more urban and its labor force more industrial, political competition may polarize around this class cleavage in a pattern more akin to the politics of Latin America than of Sub-Saharan Africa. Whether class becomes not simply a salient, crosscutting cleavage but a source of debilitating political polarization will depend significantly on the degree to which dominant-class action diverts the necessary resources for broad-based development and increases the nation's already substantial socioeconomic inequality.

Notes

1 Originally published as "Class, Ethnicity and the Democratic State: Nigeria, 1950–66," *Comparative Studies in Society and History* 25 (July 1983): 457–489.
2 Seymour Martin Lipset, *Political Man* (Baltimore, MD: Johns Hopkins University Press, 1981), 70–79; Gabriel Almond and Sidney Verba, *The Civic Culture* (Boston, MA: Little Brown and Co., 1963), 85–116, 354–360; Sidney Verba, "Conclusion: Comparative Political Culture," in *Political Culture and Political Development,* Lucian W. Pye and Sidney Verba, eds. (Princeton, NJ: Princeton University Press, 1965): 512–560; Robert Dahl, *Polyarchy* (New Haven, CT: Yale University Press, 1971), 150–162.
3 D. G. Morrison and H. M. Stevenson, "Cultural Pluralism, Modernization and Conflict: An Empirical Analysis of Sources of Instability in African Nations,"

Canadian Journal of Political Science 5(1) (1972); Michael T. Hannan and Glenn R. Carroll, "Dynamics of Formal Political Structure: An Event-History Analysis," *American Sociological Review,* 46 (February 1981): 19–35.

4 Dahl, *Polyarchy,* 107–112; Hannan and Carroll, "Dynamics of Formal Political Structure," 28–29. Hannan and Carroll's sophisticated analysis of rates of change between regime forms (military, one-party, and multiparty) during the period 1950–1975 shows multiparty regimes to be peculiarly sensitive to the destabilizing effects of ethnic diversity.

5 Donald Horowitz, "Ethnic Identity," in *Ethnicity: Theory and Experience,* Nathan M. Glazer and Daniel P. Moynihan, eds. (Cambridge, MA: Harvard University Press, 1975); Robert Melson and Howard Wolpe, "Modernization and the Politics of Communalism: A Theoretical Perspective," in *Nigeria: Modernization and the Politics of Communalism,* Robert Melson and Howard Wolpe, eds. (East Lansing: Michigan State University Press), 1–42; Crawford Young, *The Politics of Cultural Pluralism* (Madison: University of Wisconsin Press, 1976); Okwudiba Nnoli, *Ethnic Politics in Nigeria* (Enugu: Fourth Dimension Publishing Co., 1978); Michael T. Hannan, "The Dynamics of Ethnic Boundaries," in *National Development and the World System: Educational, Economic and Political Change, 1950–70,* John W. Meyer and Michael T. Hannan, eds. (Chicago, IL: University of Chicago Press, 1979), 253–275.

6 Donald Horowitz, "Three Dimensions of Ethnic Politics," *World Politics* 23 (January 1971).

7 The emergence of modern political organization and conflict is traced in two definitive studies: James S. Coleman, *Nigeria: Background to Nationalism* (Berkeley: University of California Press, 1958); and Richard L. Sklar, *Nigerian Political Parties* (Princeton, NJ: Princeton University Press, 1963).

8 Richard L. Sklar, "Contradictions in the Nigerian Political System," *Journal of Modern African Studies* 3(2) (1965): 201–213; B. J. Dudley, "Federalism and the Balance of Political Power in Nigeria," *Journal of Commonwealth Studies* 4(1) (1966): 16–29.

9 Melson and Wolpe, "Modernization and Politics of Communalism"; Young, *Politics of Cultural Pluralism,* 274–326.

10 C. S. Whitaker, Jr., "Second Beginnings: The New Political Framework," *Issue* 11:1/2 (1981): 2–13.

11 James O'Connell, "Political Integration: The Nigerian Case," in *African Integration and Disintegration,* Arthur Hazelwood, ed. (London: Oxford University Press, 1967), 129–184; O'Connell, "The Fragility of Stability: The Fall of the Nigerian Federal Government, 1966," in *Protest and Power in Black Africa,* Robert I. Rotberg and Ali A. Mazrui, eds. (New York: Oxford University Press, 1970), 1012–1034. For a similar synthesis of the political structure and competitive ethnic mobilization explanations that is particularly sensitive to the elite basis of the latter, see K. W. J. Post and Michael Vickers, *Structure and Conflict in Nigeria, 1960–65* (London: Heinemann, 1973).

12 John P. Mackintosh, *Nigerian Government and Politics* (Evanston, IL: Northwestern University Press, 1967), 617–618.

13 Gavin Williams, "Nigeria: A Political Economy," in *Nigeria: Economy and Society,* Gavin Williams, ed. (London: Rex Collings, 1976); Nnoli, *Ethnic Politics in Nigeria.*

14 Richard L. Sklar, "Political Science and National Integration—A Radical Approach," *Journal of Modern African Studies* 5(1) (1967): 1–11.

15 Segun Osoba, "The Nigerian Power Elite, 1952–65," in *African Social Studies,* Peter C. W. Gutkind and Peter Waterman, eds. (New York: Monthly Review Press, 1977), 378.

16 K. W. J. Post, *The Nigerian Federal Election of 1959* (London: Oxford University Press, 1963), 290–292; Frederick A. O. Schwarz, *Nigeria: The Tribes, the Nation or the Race—the Politics of Independence* (Cambridge, MA: Massachusetts Institute of Technology Press, 1965), 106–107; J. M. Dent, "A Minority Political Party—The United Middle Belt Congress" in *Nigerian Government and Politics,* Mackintosh, ed.

17 B. J. Dudley, *Parties and Politics in Northern Nigeria* (London: Frank Cass and Co., 1968), 49, 54; M. G. Smith, "The Hausa System of Social Status," *Africa,* 39 (July 1957); Victor N. Low, *Three Nigerian Emirates: A Study in Oral History* (Evanston, IL: Northwestern University Press, 1972).

18 This profoundly important historical process, which challenges the predominant conceptualization of modernization, is articulated in absorbing detail in the landmark study by C. S. Whitaker, Jr., *The Politics of Tradition: Continuity and Change in Northern Nigeria, 1946–66* (Princeton, NJ: Princeton University Press, 1970).

19 Coleman, *Nigeria: Background to Nationalism,* 353–368; Sklar, *Nigerian Political Parties;* Dudley, *Parties and Politics,* 134–152; Whitaker, *Politics of Tradition,* 313–354.

20 Coleman, *Nigeria: Background to Nationalism,* 284–291, 327–352; Sklar, *Nigerian Political Parties,* 485–494; Post, *Nigerian Federal Election of 1959,* 46–47.

21 Sklar, *Nigerian Political Parties.*

22 Sayre P. Schatz, *Nigerian Capitalism* (Berkeley: University of California Press, 1977), 190–195.

23 Ibid., 208–209.

24 Ibid., 231–232; Gerald K. Helleiner, "The Eastern Nigeria Development Corporation: A Study in Resources and Uses of Public Development Funds, 1949–62," *Nigerian Journal of Economic and Social Studies* 6 (March 1964): 98–123.

25 G. B. A. Coker, J. O. Kassim, and Akintola Williams, *Report of the Coker Commission of Inquiry into the Affairs of Certain Statutory Corporations in Western Nigeria* (Lagos: 1962), I, II, III. The flow of public funds through the various private business concerns of top Action Group politicians and supporters is reconstructed in Larry J. Diamond, "The Social Foundations of Democracy: The Case of Nigeria" (Ph.D. diss., Stanford University, 1980), 556–582.

26 Sir Stafford William Powell Foster-Sutton, *Report of the Tribunal Appointed to Inquire into Allegations Reflecting on the Official Conduct of the Premier of, and Certain Persons Holding Ministerial and Other Public Office in, the Eastern Region of Nigeria* (London: Her Majesty's Stationery Office, 1957); Sklar, *Nigerian Political Parties,* 161–185.

27 Coker et al., *Report,* I, pt. 3. For a summary of local and regional corruption and a provocative comparative analysis, see Ronald Wraith and Edgar Simpkins, *Corruption in Developing Countries* (New York: W. W. Norton and Co., 1963).

28 Sklar, *Nigerian Political Parties,* 480.

29 Ralph Miliband, *The State in Capitalist Society* (New York: Basic Books, 1969).

30 Osoba, "Nigerian Power Elite," 370; Sklar, *Nigerian Political Parties,* 501.

31 Whitaker, *Politics of Tradition,* 33.

32 Sklar, *Nigerian Political Parties,* 338–349.

33 Post, *Nigerian Federal Election of 1959,* 393.

34 Dent, "Minority Political Party"; Post, *Nigerian Federal Election of 1959,* 264.

35 Sklar, *Nigerian Political Parties,* 230–241.

36 Whitaker, *Politics of Tradition,* 279–282, 352; Dudley, *Parties and Politics,* 211–217.

37 Sklar, *Nigerian Political Parties,* 446.

38 Ibid., 481.

39 Post, *Nigerian Federal Election of 1959,* 66–71; Dent, "Minority Political Party"; Schwarz, *Nigeria: Tribes, Nation or Race,* 106.

40 This dual classification for political corruption and abuse of power is borrowed from Schatz, *Nigerian Capitalism.*

41 Sklar, "Nature of Class Domination," 547.

42 Sklar, "Contradictions in Nigerian Political System," 203–204.

43 Smythe and Smythe, *New Nigerian Elite*, 78–79.

44 Post, *Nigerian Federal Election of 1959*, 396.

45 Nnoli, *Ethnic Politics in Nigeria*, 152.

46 Sklar, "Political Science and National Integration," 6.

47 Nnoli, *Ethnic Politics in Nigeria*, 20.

48 Coleman, *Nigeria: Background to Nationalism*, 332–343.

49 Ibid., 343–352.

50 Ibid., 346.

51 Sklar, *Nigerian Political Parties*, 70.

52 H. O. Davies, *Nigeria: The Prospects for Democracy* (London: Weidenfeld and Nicolson, 1961), 92.

53 Nnoli, *Ethnic Politics in Nigeria*, 110–112.

54 Coleman, *Nigeria: Background to Nationalism*, 398–399.

55 John Paden, "Communal Competition, Conflict and Violence in Kano," in *Nigeria*, Melson and Wolpe, eds, 127.

56 I. Nicolson, "The Machinery of the Federal and Regional Government," in *Nigerian Politics and Government*, Mackintosh, ed., 171–173.

57 Ibid., 184; Dudley, *Parties and Politics*, 220.

58 Nicolson, "The Machinery of the Federal and Regional Government," 142, 220.

59 Sklar, *Nigerian Political Parties*, 328; Dudley, *Parties and Politics*, 232; Nnoli, *Ethnic Politics in Nigeria*, 194.

60 Dudley, *Parties and Politics*, 220.

61 Commission Appointed to Enquire into the Fears of Minorities and the Means of Allaying Them, *Report* (London: Her Majesty's Stationery Office, 1958).

62 Ibid.

63 Ibid., 26.

64 Ibid.; Sklar, *Nigerian Political Parties*, 119–124, 245–255, 296–302, 339–354; Post, *Nigerian Federal Election of 1959*. 78–98.

65 Sklar, "Contradictions in Nigerian Political System."

66 Stanley Diamond, "Notes for the Record," *Africa Today* (May 1964).

67 Richard L. Sklar, "Nigerian Politics: The Ordeal of Chief Awolowo, 1960–65," in *Politics in Africa: Seven Cases*, Gwendolen Carter, ed. (New York: Harcourt Brace and World, 1966), 156. See also Richard L. Sklar, "Nigerian Politics in Perspective," in *Nigeria: Modernization and Politics of Communalism*, Melson and Wolpe, eds, 47–48, for a brief historical synopsis of the issue of regionalism and its intimate relationship to tribalist ideology.

68 Sklar, "Nigerian Politics: Ordeal of Chief Awolowo," 130–131; Mackintosh, *Nigerian Government and Politics*, 444–446.

69 Post and Vickers, *Structure and Conflict in Nigeria*, 78.

70 Mackintosh, *Nigerian Government and Politics*, 448–458.

71 Post and Vickers, *Structure and Conflict in Nigeria*, 88, 90.

72 K. W. J. Post, "Nigeria Two Years after Independence," *The World Today* 18:11–12 (November–December, 1962); *West Africa* (June 16, 1982).

73 Post, "Nigeria Two Years After Independence"; James O'Connell, "Some Social and Political Reflections on the Plan," *Nigerian Journal of Economic and Social Studies* 4(2) (July 1962); Lloyd A. Free, *The Attitudes, Hopes and Fears of Nigerians* (Princeton, NJ: Institute for International Social Research, 1964).

74 Robert Melson, "Nigerian Politics and the General Strike of 1964," in *Protest and Power*, Rotberg and Mazrui, eds, 771–774, 785; Robin Cohen, *Labour and Politics in Nigeria, 1945–71* (London: Heinemann, 1974), 166.

75 Melson, "Nigerian Politics."
76 Post and Vickers, *Structure and Conflict in Nigeria,* 233.
77 N. J. Miners, *The Nigerian Army, 1956–66* (London: Methuen and Company, 1971), 177.
78 A. H. M. Kirk-Greene, *Crisis and Conflict in Nigeria* (London: Oxford University Press, 1971), I, 126–127, 145, 147.
79 Mackintosh, *Nigerian Government and Politics,* 547.
80 Ibid., 548.
81 *West Africa* (November 5, 1963), 1231.
82 Walter Schwarz, *Nigeria* (New York: Frederick A. Praeger, 1968), 158.
83 Mackintosh, *Nigerian Government and Politics,* 554–556.
84 Ibid., 556–558.
85 Ibid., 559.
86 B. J. Dudley, *Instability and Political Order* (Ibadan: Ibadan University Press, 1973), 76. The italics are Dudley's.
87 Post and Vickers, *Structure and Conflict in Nigeria,* 122–124; Mackintosh, *Nigerian Government and Politics,* 572–573.
88 Robert Melson, "Ideology and Inconsistency: The 'Cross-Pressured' Nigerian Worker," in *Nigeria: Modernization and Politics of Communalism,* Melson and Wolpe, eds, 581–605.
89 Post and Vickers, *Structure and Conflict in Nigeria,* 141–149; Mackintosh, *Nigerian Government and Politics,* 576–579.
90 *West Africa* (October 10, 1964).
91 Lipset, *Political Man,* 77.
92 For an analysis of the structure and politics of the Second Republic, see Larry Diamond, "Cleavage, Conflict and Anxiety in the Second Nigerian Republic," *Journal of Modern African Studies* 20:4 (1982).
93 Larry Diamond, "The Transformation of Political Conflict in Nigeria," paper presented to the Annual Meeting of the International Studies Association, March 1982.
94 Ibid., 40–43.

12 Issues in the constitutional design of a Third Nigerian Republic[1]

Reflective of its deep commitment to political freedom and popular, accountable government, Nigeria has recently been engaged in a vigorous and wide-ranging national debate on its constitutional future. The search for a fresh design for democracy in Nigeria comes less than three years after the overthrow of the failed Second Republic (on December 31, 1983). If a third attempt at democratic government is to be successful, it must tailor democratic institutions to fit Nigeria's unique heritage and to overcome the structural problems that have defeated democratic government in the past. As it was in the Second Republic, so it must be a premise of a Third Republic that "institutional architecture is a key to democratic viability."[2]

The focus in this chapter on constitutional structure should not be taken to suggest that a wisely tailored constitution can assure future democratic success in Nigeria. As has been argued elsewhere, the immense premium on political power must be diminished if the contest for power is not to become again a desperate, fraudulent, and violent struggle.[3] State control over economic resources and rewards must be reduced. Opportunities need to be generated for individuals to establish careers, accumulate wealth, and raise their social status outside of the state, through private initiative. Growing recognition of these imperatives heightens the pressure for privatization in Nigeria today. Similarly, the strong residue of support for the "War Against Indiscipline" launched by Generals Muhammadu Buhari and Tunde Idiagon reflects not an admiration of the unprecedented authoritarianism of that discredited military regime (December 31, 1983 to August 27, 1985), but rather a widespread sense that the construction of a democratic and decent society in Nigeria requires a transformation of values, greater political tolerance and civic responsibility. Economic structure and political values will take years to change and perhaps a generation or more to fully take root. Nevertheless, institutional innovations seem imperative if there is to be any real change soon in the way the democratic game is played in Nigeria.

Previous democratic failures in Nigeria have heavily involved the abuse of power and desecration of the rules of the democratic game (as demonstrated in the previous chapter).[4] A central purpose of constitutional design must therefore be to check, balance, and decentralize political power as extensively and innovatively as possible, and hence to reduce both the stakes in any electoral contest and the scope for behavioral abuses. Constitutional engineering should focus on this basic problem and not be misled into presuming either that everything about the Second Republic was misconceived or that *any* innovation must therefore represent improvement in the democratic prospect for Nigeria.

Federalism

A fundamental challenge to democracy in Nigeria, or any other country with such deep and volatile ethnic divisions, is to find means for managing, containing, and reducing ethnic conflict. The polarization of ethnic and regional conflict was a leading factor in the collapse of Nigeria's First Republic and a central concern in the design of the Second Republic. In the bitterness and disappointment over the failure of the Second Republic, there has not been adequate appreciation of the considerable progress achieved by the federal structure, as it has been evolving since 1966. The 19-state federal system and the federalist provisions in the 1979 Constitution functioned reasonably (even remarkably) well to break up the hegemony of Nigeria's largest ethnic groups, decentralize ethnic conflict, disperse development activity, foster crosscutting cleavages, expose intraethnic divisions, facilitate inter-ethnic alliances, and in general contain the powerful centrifugal forces inherent in Nigeria's ethnic composition.[5] Debate will (and should) persist over the proper balance of power and authority between federal, state and local government. This type of continuing adjustment and adaptation is necessary and inevitable in any federal system, including that of the United States.

But it is mistaken to think that, because the creation of 19 states succeeded in decentralizing power and distributing resources to some degree, these goals could be further advanced by doubling or tripling the number of states, as would have happened had the politicians given in to all the demands for new states during the Second Republic. Certainly anomalies exist in the structure and size of states; some are much larger, more populous and more ethnically heterogeneous than others. This may suggest the logic of breaking up a few of the largest and most deeply divided states to give the overall system a better population and ethnic balance. But wholesale state creation would probably not further decentralize power. On the contrary, the greater the number of states, the weaker and less viable individual states will become, with the direct consequence that the center would actually gather *more* powers and initiative. Neither would the creation of many new states necessarily transfer resources more effectively from the center to the periphery of the system. The doubling or tripling in the number of state governments and administrations (which was a major attraction for the political elites who led the movements for new states) would leave for distribution even fewer resources for genuine development. In Nigeria's current financial circumstances, such an expansion in the number of states would probably recreate the Second Republic's pathetic spectacle of teachers and civil servants around the country waiting months for their state governments to pay their salaries.

It is equally mistaken to imagine, as have a few prominent Nigerians publicly and many more privately, that a confederal system will solve the continuing problems of ethnic tension, distrust, and inequality. Aside from the fact that this would seem to many Nigerians to render tragically pointless the massive loss of life in a civil war that was believed at the time to have settled this question, the competition for limited resources would hardly disappear in a looser confederation. In fact, because the more autonomous units of a confederal system would probably have to be much larger than the current states (even if there were quasi-autonomous states within them), such an arrangement would tend to plunge Nigeria back to the days of the regional system of the First Republic—when ethnic conflict became a tripolar struggle between Hausa–Fulani, Yoruba, and Igbo (later reducing to a bipolar, North–South confrontation) and the interests of the country's ethnic minorities (almost half the population) got shortchanged.

Because ethnic identities are multiple and fluid, shifting up or down in scale depending on the political context, the problems of ethnic conflict in developing countries are rarely solved by changing the composition of the nation.[6] The challenge is to find institutional means to enable ethnic groups to live with one another in some degree of equity and mutual security. In this regard, the Second Republic made progress not only in its federalist distribution of power and resources between the three levels of government, but also in its imaginative provisions to distribute power and resources equitably among the major ethnic groups and to develop political institutions that cut across the major ethnic divisions. These should be preserved. For example, the requirement that presidential appointments "shall have regard to the federal character of Nigeria and the need to promote national unity"[7] has become a cornerstone of ethnic justice and fair government in Nigeria and should be retained in the next constitution. Similarly, if there are to be political parties (and I believe they are indispensable in a large-scale democracy, as I shall argue later), these should again be required, first, to have a broad base of organization in at least two-thirds (perhaps even three-quarters) of the states, and second, to eschew ethnic, regional, and religious mottos, emblems, and allusions.[8]

Despite the many forms of erosion of democratic faith and vitality during the Second Republic, the system did register continuing progress in the development of broad-based, ethnically heterogeneous parties with real strength in diverse regions of the country.[9] I think Donald Horowitz underestimates the progress toward cross-ethnic alliances and heterogeneous parties in the Second Republic before and during the 1983 election campaign. Nevertheless, his observations on the conflicting incentives for party consolidation and breadth in the Nigerian electoral system merit close attention. The proliferation of states and the first-past-the-post method for electing national legislators, from single-member districts, exerted countervailing pressures against the consolidation of the party system into just two or three broad, transethnic parties. The number of states will not be reduced in a Third Republic, nor is the single-member district model (with its closer identity between legislators and geographical communities) likely to be abandoned. But two alternatives mentioned by Horowitz might increase the incentives for multiethnic appeal and organization by the parties. One would be to raise the threshold requirement for direct election of the President on the first ballot, so that the victor would need, in addition to 25 percent of the vote in at least two-thirds of the states, something more than a simple plurality of the total vote, say, for example, 40 percent. Alternatively, a majority vote could be required, and a preferential or alternative vote system adopted, like that in Sri Lanka, in which voters would be required to rank their preferences among the candidates, so that the votes for losing candidates would be distributed among the higher finishers until one received a majority. This has the virtue of requiring interparty agreements in advance of the voting, and so encouraging "a politics of bargaining and moderation,"[10] but it would be difficult to conduct among an electorate of such limited literacy, where voting is done by thumbprinting beside a party symbol. It would also complicate the task of counting the ballots by hand at the polls, which is an important check upon electoral fraud in Nigeria. Nevertheless, if the sorts of provisions to which I have referred are retained, this progress toward a truly national party system is likely to continue in a Third Republic and to be a major foundation of its health.

Zoning: the quest for ethnic balance

If distribution and rotation of power among Nigeria's ethnic and regional groups is now an article of faith and a foundation of political stability, more thought must be given to how this can be prescribed and achieved. The current assumption that reflecting the federal character requires the representation of every state (or virtually every state) in federal bodies and batches of federal appointments is often cumbersome and unwieldy. This is especially the case where only a few people need to be appointed, or where it may be difficult to find persons of suitable professional training and experience from every state. Under such circumstances, there is a more general principle of distribution that has been implicit in political dialogue for a long time, and that was explicitly incorporated into the regulations for rotation of the Presidential nomination and other important offices of the most broad-based party in the Second Republic, the ruling National Party of Nigeria (NPN). This is the principle of zoning. It maintains that Nigeria's many states and ethnic groups can reasonably be aggregated into a smaller number of zones, roughly equal in their population size and number of states and reflecting more general divisions in the country. Distribution and rotation of power among these zones can ensure some ethnic balance even when it is unreasonable or impossible to mandate the representation of every state.[11]

A reasonable method for constructing such zones (not so different than how the NPN went about it) would first divide the country into an equal number of zones between north and south; let us say (as did the NPN) three each. Then, natural groupings could be sought within those divisions. In the south this is quite easy: there are four Yoruba states (Lagos, Ogun, Ondo, and Oyo), two Igbo (Imo and Anambra), and three minority (Bendel, Rivers, and Cross River). Moreover, these three zones probably would not vary too widely in their total population.[12] Similarly, the ethnic minority states of the "middle belt" in the north form a natural grouping (Kwara, Niger, Benue, and Plateau and perhaps Gongola). It is less clear how the states of the predominantly Muslim far north would be grouped, but, given the fact that Kano is by far the most populous state in the federation and Kano and Kaduna the most industrialized in the north, it might make sense to group these two together, leaving Sokoto, Bauchi, and Borno (the less developed states of the far north) as a sixth zone.[13]

Clearly, there are anomalies and problems with the above arrangement (as there would be with any other). The effort to devise an equitable zoning arrangement may pinpoint problems in the federal structure that may call for attention if any further states are to be created, but it may also help to assure those seeking new states of a fair share, even within the current arrangement. If, for example, the two Igbo states are made to constitute a single zone, equivalent to the four Yoruba states (especially since the two ethnic groups are fairly close in total population), and if Kano and Kaduna alone were to constitute a zone, the pressures in these four states for the creation of new states might dissipate significantly.

However it is structured, such a zoning system, codified in the constitution, would provide more flexibility in fulfilling the goal of ethnic balance and justice and so help to reconcile the demands of governmental efficiency and high professional standards, on the one hand, with those for ethnic harmony and fairness on the other.[14] At the same time, the preservation of the states as genuinely significant political units with real administrative authority and development powers would keep the zones from descending into just another synonym for "regions."

Decentralization

The search for a more effective federal system as a cornerstone of stable democracy in Nigeria should give high priority to strengthening the level at which democracy has historically evolved and operated in Nigeria: local government. Not only is local government a vital arena of initiative and action in a truly federal system, it can also be a school for the development

of citizen awareness and political skills. A strong system of local government can mobilize people into the political process because it is the level
of government to which ordinary people, especially those with little or no
education, can most easily relate. And in a truly federal system, it is also the
level that most immediately affects ordinary people's lives.

Thought must therefore be devoted to establishing appropriate electoral
structures for governments in the Local Government Areas. In addition to
some kind of executive office, perhaps there should be an elected assembly,
even a very large one, which would be paid only very modestly and would
meet only part-time, but would have as one of its purposes the development
of democracy at the grass roots. Such local assemblies, particularly if they
were accompanied by informal gatherings in towns and villages to discuss
major issues, would parallel in some ways the communal assembly that has
been a crucial building block of democracy in many of Nigeria's traditional
political systems. Consideration might also be given to the division of powers between federal, state, and local government. Are there functions and
responsibilities that can be transferred at least partially to local governments? Perhaps schools and community development projects would be
two such areas. In an era of drastically reduced federal resources, communities must expect to bear more of the responsibility for their own finance
as the price of greater political autonomy and power.

Checks and balances

As indicated above, the basic problem of democracy in Nigeria has been
the abuse of its powers and the corruption of its processes for the benefit
of private individuals and their friends and clients. In other words, the system has lacked accountability, both to the citizenry and to the premises of
the system itself.[15] In each of the first two republics, democracy was disfigured and robbed of legitimacy by massive and grave electoral fraud.[16] In
each instance, the system was further delegitimized by widespread political corruption, which reached truly devastating proportions in the Second
Republic.[17] The adverse consequences of corruption in office have been
especially diffuse. Not only does it give rise to extraordinary concentrations
of wealth and displays of affluence, which come to be bitterly resented,
but it destroys the efficiency and saps the resources of government, thus
eclipsing progress in socioeconomic development. It further destroys the
incentive structure of society, preempting productive entrepreneurial activity and intensifying the determination to get and keep political power at
any cost.[18]

While not diminishing the central role of values and social structure in
these problems, the failure of accountability implicates, inescapably, the
political institutions. Electoral administration at all levels has typically been
highly permeable to partisan manipulation. Similarly, the judiciary, while
blessed with some capable and courageous judges, has lacked vigor and

independence and hence has often bowed to political pressures. Ruling parties have tended to use the police, especially at election time, as their political security force. In the First Republic, ethnic parties made the census a part of their struggle for power. The 1979 Constitution established a Code of Conduct Bureau and Tribunal to monitor, investigate, and punish corruption in office, but it made its members' appointment, supervision, and funding dependent on the very politicians whom they were supposed to regulate. Not surprisingly, these two bodies never functioned as intended.[19] The repeated degradation and partisan manipulation of these crucial regulatory institutions underscores the need for original and more far-reaching mechanisms to check, balance and distribute power. The Constitution of the Second Republic attempted to ensure the independence of the federal executive bodies overseeing the elections, judiciary, police, census, and code of conduct by making the chairman and members of those bodies extremely difficult to remove and by articulating explicit guarantees of operational autonomy. But this was undermined by giving the president the power to appoint these bodies and by making them dependent in some cases on legislative funding and review.[20] As a result, the judicial service commissions, for example, were full of politicians and the judiciary itself was starved of adequate funds.[21]

The separation of powers between executive, legislative, and judicial branches has proved inadequate in Nigeria to ensure the integrity of the democratic process. Hence, what is needed is almost a fourth branch of government, truly autonomous from party politics in its origins, composition, and functioning. Such a new arm of government must have authority to oversee the appointment, funding, and operation of crucial procedural institutions. The latter would be defined as "those institutions that must remain above party conflict and independent of party control if the democratic process is to work."[22] In a previous analysis, I proposed five candidates for inclusion:

1   The Federal and State Electoral Commissions.
2   The Code of Conduct Bureau and Tribunal.
3   The Federal and State Judicial Service Commissions.
4   The Police Service Commission.
5   The National Population Commission.[23]

To this list of regulatory institutions could be added two new ones:

1   A network of federal and state ombudsmen.
2   A General Accounting Office, like the GAO of the United States Congress, to investigate and assess the efficiency and management of government.

No institution is more in need of independent control in Nigeria than the electoral administration. One useful model of autonomous electoral administration can be found in Costa Rica, where a Supreme Electoral Tribunal (TSE) exercises exclusive responsibility for the organization and administration of elections in a fashion similar to Nigeria's Federal Electoral Commission (known in the Second Republic as FEDECO). However, since its creation in 1949, Costa Rica's TSE has enjoyed powers far more sweeping and an autonomy far more secure than Nigeria's FEDECO. The TSE consists of three magistrates (expanded to five during elections) who are appointed to staggered six-year terms by the Supreme Court of Justice. It not only administers voter registration, balloting, and counting, but is also empowered to investigate charges of political bias by public employees, file criminal charges against persons violating electoral laws, control the police and other security forces during election periods, monitor executive neutrality in campaigns, and allocate the governmental subvention of campaign costs. The extensive authority and autonomy of this electoral tribunal has had much to do with Costa Rica's outstanding record of fairness and honesty in elections, which in turn has been a key foundation of stable democracy in that country.[24]

Similarly, an autonomous code of conduct machinery would permit the rigorous monitoring, investigation, and punishment of corrupt conduct in office. Like other forms of white-collar crime, political corruption can be deterred by exposure and punishment if such punishment is sufficiently likely, swift, and severe. Only with secure tenure in office, fully adequate staffs and funding, and complete freedom of action—beyond even the most indirect political pressure or influence—can the Code of Conduct Bureau and Tribunal perform their essential mission of vigilance and deterrence.

Independent control over the Judicial Service Commissions would enhance public confidence in the integrity of the judiciary and might help to remove it from the pressure and entanglements of partisan politics. But this step alone is unlikely to be sufficient. Under the 1979 Constitution, Justices of the Supreme Court and the Federal Court of Appeal were appointed by the President "on the advice of the Federal Judicial Service Commission," subject to approval by a majority of the Senate. Similar procedures applied at the state level for the appointment of High Court Justices.[25] In addition, "the constitution also empowers the other two branches of government to create courts and determine the number of judicial personnel for any particular court as well as the jurisdiction of the courts so created."[26] These provisions did not give the judiciary adequate autonomy from the other two branches of government. It may therefore be necessary to vest in the Federal and State Judicial Service Commissions sole authority for the appointment of appellate-level justices (perhaps requiring certification of their qualifications by the Bar Association) and for the organization and jurisdiction of the court system. In addition, these commissions should be given responsibility for the funding of the judiciary, which is now "made to beg for money for its services."[27] Since independence, the judiciary's financial dependence on the other two branches and its inadequate salaries, facilities, and staff have been important causes of its weakness and vulnerability, and hence its difficulty in fulfilling its mission "as the bulwark of democracy, the last hope of the common man."[28] Like the Federal Electoral Commission, the judiciary also needs its own permanent staff.[29]

As the hands-on regulators of political campaigns and demonstrations, the impartiality of the police is also vital to the democratic process. As the Police Service Commission appoints and exercises disciplinary control over all police officers, it too should be responsible to an independent authority. As for the census, insulating its administrative body from partisan political oversight and pressure would probably not eliminate fraud—and certainly not suspicion and controversy. But it might reduce them and at least limit the damage a conflict over the census would wreak upon the democratic system.

The last two functions above would be new ones in Nigeria. While some states began to appoint ombudsmen during the Second Republic, this would seem to be an idea whose time has arrived for the country as a whole. The ombudsman functions effectively in a growing number of countries to protect individual rights, investigate citizen complaints, and enhance the accountability, responsiveness, and fairness of government.[30] Similarly, there might be a role for an independent investigatory and analytical agency to assess the performance of government and weigh the advisability of potential future projects and contracts. Such independent, advance assessments might save the country considerable money by acting as an additional check on corruption, waste, and ineptitude in government.

The fundamental question, however, remains: How are these regulatory institutions to be protected from partisan interference and control? If there is to be an independent body to supervise the appointment, funding, and operation of these several procedural institutions, how should that body be constituted?

I have suggested elsewhere that the military somehow constitute this special branch of government, while all other political and governmental functions, including the funding and deployment of the military itself, would remain under civilian control.[31] Nigerian proposals for "diarchy" have gone much further, envisioning an extensive sharing of *substantive* authority between military and elected, civilian officeholders.[32] Recently, such proposals have formed a prominent theme among the submissions to the Political Bureau, appointed by President Babangida in January 1986 to stimulate debate and propose ideas for a new, participatory political system.[33] However, there are compelling reasons to argue that proposals for a permanent diarchy are inherently ill conceived and likely to prove counterproductive.

The experience of institutionalized military participation in political life elsewhere in the world, especially in Latin America and Asia, suggests that this is not a promising means to enhance the accountability of democratic government. To give the military as an institution substantive functions in government not only eclipses the electoral accountability of the rulers to the ruled, it also tends to give rise to a continuous and relatively enduring expansion in the military's role, responsibility, and self-conception. Moreover, it creates confusion about which is the real source of authority in the country—the law (the constitution) or armed force—and undermines civilian control over the military *qua* military, which is a critical feature of a democratic society. Perhaps most disturbing is the highly equivocal commitment of most military establishments in developing countries to democracy and human rights. The violations of civil liberties under the Buhari-Idiagbon dictatorship, as well as the real and alleged incidents of state violence under the Babangida regime,[34] raise grave doubts about the suitability of the Nigerian military as a partner in, or guarantor of, a new democratic system in Nigeria. Finally, the frequency of military coups against military governments, both in Nigeria and throughout Africa, contradicts the assumption, common to virtually all diarchy proposals, that military participation in government would make democracy more stable.

How, then, shall an independent oversight institution be constituted? A purely civilian institution is possible, and Nigeria could contribute significantly to the development of democracy worldwide by innovating in the construction of it. The challenge is to identify groups and organizations that are autonomous from party politics and command general respect in society. Such groups could then be asked to each nominate a member or officer to serve on a national oversight council, which would have as its sole and explicit purpose the supervision of the above-named regulatory bodies. Such a National Oversight Council would have the following responsibilities: appointing the members of the regulatory bodies, and having the sole authority to remove them, under certain explicitly stated circumstances, before the end of their terms; supervising the conduct of these bodies and checking any efforts to introduce partisan or other biased considerations into their deliberations; and determining their level of funding, which the National Assembly might then have the authority to review but to alter only by vote of a special majority.

A list of groups and associations from which such a National Council could be constituted might include: the Nigerian Bar Association; the Nigerian Medical Association; the Nigeria Labour Congress; the Nigerian Chamber of Commerce and/or the Nigerian Association of Manufacturers; the Academic Staff Union of Universities; the National Association of Nigerian Students; the Nigerian Union of Journalists; and women's organizations such as Women in Nigeria and the National Organization of Nigerian Women Societies. Admittedly, this group is overrepresentative of professionals and intellectuals, but this might be balanced by adding two or three traditional rulers and representatives from associations of peasants, market women, and traders. The body need not, and probably should not, be large. The key to its effectiveness would be its independence from partisan politics. For this reason, any group that agreed to be represented in this oversight council should have to surrender its right to endorse candidates for electoral office.[35]

Staggered elections

An important issue in the design of a new constitution is the length of term in office for major elected officials and how the expirations of those terms are timed. One unfortunate feature of the electoral structure in the Second Republic was that the terms of every state and national electoral office expired at precisely the same four-year interval, and so everything was contested simultaneously. While this economized on scarce resources of electoral administration, it also put too much pressure on these once-every-four-years contests. With everything up for grabs, it was highly likely that a failed and fraudulent election would bring the system crashing down.

Both for the efficiency of electoral administration and the civility and integrity of the electoral process, elections should be staggered in the future, so that only a portion of the offices are contested in any one election. There are several ways of doing this. Let us assume here that the system will again be a presidential one, given the contributions that presidentialism made in the Second Republic to crosscutting and balancing ethnic cleavages.[36] If all the executive and legislative offices have, as in the Second Republic, four year terms, half of them could be contested every two years, some coming in a Presidential election year and some in an off-year. Alternatively, if a single six-year term is chosen for the president (and perhaps the state governors), midterm elections could be held every two years or every three years. The combination of a six-year term for presidents and governors along with staggered legislative elections every two years would best diffuse the pressure of electoral competition.[37] Then, one-third of the state governors (and perhaps a third of the senators) would come up for election every two years. If the House of Representatives and state Houses of Assembly were given four-year terms, half of their members would contest elections every two years.

Beyond distributing the political stakes over more than one election, such a system of staggered elections would give the Federal Electoral Commission more experience in the conduct of elections. It would require a more continuous updating of the electoral register and would compel FEDECO to maintain a much larger and more professional permanent staff, independent of local and state elected officials and more partisan elements in the bureaucracy. These are important requirements for the integrity of the electoral process in Nigeria.[38]

The transition to democracy

One of the most profound and least appreciated flaws in the Second Republic was the chaotic state of the party system. Parties were continually feuding and rupturing internally. Politicians and elected officials moved from one party to another in a continuous stream of defections and realignments, open and de facto. In and of itself, this was not necessarily unhealthy for democracy, but the general situation it produced was one of constant political crisis, opportunism, and institutional weakness. Internally, the parties lacked substantive coherence and procedural consensus and had trouble as well developing organizational depth, complexity, and autonomy, since they were so much absorbed with their struggle to survive. Between them, the parties lacked any basis for mutual trust, largely because their only experience with one another was the struggle for power in 1979 and the bitterness of its aftermath. As a result, the parties lacked confidence both in themselves and in one another.

As was the case in the "Great Debate" over the structure of the Second Republic, many Nigerians today are questioning whether political parties are necessary and appropriate for democracy in their country.[39] In fact, the current political debate reflects a widespread popular cynicism with party politics, and more than a few influential political and military leaders have called for a zero- or one-party system as the solution to the political corruption, fraud, and violence that have attended party competition in Nigeria. But this is to mistake the framework for the cause. Party competition *per se* is not the cause of political instability in Nigeria. Rather, it is the enormous premium on power and the inadequacy of structural means to ensure accountability. Moreover, it is doubtful how genuine competition for national power can exist in the absence of multiple parties. The political party is the indispensable instrument for the articulation, aggregation, and representation of political interests and principles in a modern, large-scale democratic system. It is the primary vehicle for mobilizing new voters, linking the elite with the mass, and organizing the competition for power around common interests and policy preferences.[40] Hence, to ban political parties is to repress one of the primary instruments of democratic participation and one of the most basic elements of the freedom of association.

The challenge ahead for Nigeria is not to do away with parties (as if this could somehow banish the unseemly aspects of the struggle for power) but to enable them to develop those features that are the mark of institutional maturity and strength: coherence, complexity, autonomy, and adaptability.[41] Institutional development takes time and patience, as well as organizational skill and imagination.

Party leaders were not short of skill and creativity in the Second Republic, but they were desperately short of time. Although the transition from military rule to the Second Republic spanned four years, it was not until three of those years had passed that the ban on political parties was lifted. From 21 September 1978, aspiring political parties were given only three months to submit their registration forms to FEDECO. Given that political activities had been banned for 13 years and that the parties of the First Republic were to remain prohibited, this left little time to found "wholly 'new' parties … to establish followers throughout the country, and to satisfy the other stringent requirements … in the Constitution."[42] The compression of this period for party development and registration followed from the military's own deeply ambivalent attitude toward political parties, but it had precisely the opposite effect from that intended by the Supreme Military Council. Under the intense pressure of imminent elections, most truly fresh political formations either fractured into more familiar forms or died stillborn. Politicians tended to retreat into more convenient and familiar ethnic political alignments, and new political thinkers and activists were forced to draft old political warhorses to make their incipient parties viable. As a result, parties failed to develop the national breadth, fresh profiles, and new ideas they might have; instead, they were forced to swallow contradictions that were bound to explode at some point.[43]

The clear lesson is that parties need more time to develop, free from the pressures of an imminent election in which everything of political importance will be at stake. They need time not only to develop their organizational structures and political identities, but also to build relationships of mutual tolerance and trust with one another; only in this way can there develop the confidence that defeat will not mean political death and victory will be tempered by magnanimity. Such a system of "mutual security" can only grow gradually over many years and several elections.[44] This is one reason for staggering elections, so that everything is not at stake at once. It is also an argument for phasing in elections gradually, from the bottom up, so that parties can get accustomed to competing with one another and can internalize the rules of democratic competition, beginning at levels where the stakes are small and the risks low, while the military remains on hand as a referee of political competition. Finally, the need for time, experience, and political learning in developing party organizations and interparty trust argues against banning all politicians of the Second Republic from future political involvement, as President Ibrahim Babangida has done.[45]

All of this argues for a much longer and more methodically phased transition to fully competitive democracy than has typically been contemplated in Nigeria. Such a transition would restore electoral competition gradually, to successively higher levels of political authority. A possible scenario would begin with permission soon for the election of local government councils. This would begin to get people involved in the democratic process again and establish representative voices, old and new, at the grass roots. These new officials could not only regenerate democracy from the bottom up, they could also become influential in shaping the remaining phases of the transition process. This stage would be followed by the election of a nonpartisan constituent assembly, as in the Second Republic, to draft a constitution. The third development would lift the ban on the formation of political parties but allow a lengthy period of time, at least a year, before parties could begin to submit their applications for registration to FEDECO. This would give political leaders time to negotiate with one another and to canvass the nation, so as to develop more broadly based and original political parties.

Another long interval of time, at least another year, would then be allowed between the start of party registration and the date of the first partisan election, perhaps for state legislatures, which would serve for some period of time (between two and four years) alongside military governors. Thereafter a national assembly would be elected, which would serve alongside a military President for some transition period. Only after that would civilian governors be elected to replace the military governors, with terms of office of varied length to allow for staggered elections in the future; finally, at least two to four years after the national assembly had been elected, and perhaps as much as ten years after the transition had begun, would the national election of a president or prime minister be allowed.

Such a lengthy transition raises several serious concerns: that it would not only extend the period of arbitrary and authoritarian rule, but might tempt the military to try to institutionalize its political role and even to cancel the transition, while also threatening rivalry and turmoil within the military. These are legitimate concerns.

Preventing military abuse of power in this transitional period (including the corruption in office that might lead some officers to want to extend their stay as long as possible) requires that the military subject *itself* to the rule of law as a first step in its declared intention to build a more enduring democratic system. One condition in this regard would be a new or reactivated Bill of Rights, to which the Armed Forces Ruling Council (AFRC) could be held accountable in the courts of law. Another would be for the AFRC to put in place immediately the Code of Conduct Bureau and Tribunal to monitor the conduct of both military and civilian officeholders throughout the transition. At the same time, the independent National Oversight Council described above could be inaugurated to take responsibility for the code of conduct apparatus, perhaps the judiciary, and later the elections.

There is no inherent reason why a military government cannot take such steps. In fact, there is every reason to question its professed commitment to democracy and public accountability if it does not do so. If these lofty goals are ever to be institutionalized in Nigeria, some regime must take the first courageous step by allowing itself to be held accountable. No regime would be better positioned to establish this legacy than a military regime, such as President Babangida's, that has voluntarily committed itself to a democratic transition.

As for the probability of regime instability during this period or even the abortion of the whole transition process, the recent Brazilian transition to democracy suggests the value of clear and limited terms of office for military heads of state. This not only limits the personalization of, and rivalry for, power, but also establishes the principle of constitutional and orderly succession.

Perhaps the most serious problem with a long transition is the likely impatience of the people, and of course the politicians, for a full military withdrawal. This would be attenuated at least to some extent if procedural accountability were established soon, along with democratic elections for local governments that would have some real responsibility and autonomy. If the announced timetable were faithfully implemented, this would also enhance public confidence in, and commitment to, the process. But beyond this, Nigerians must now ponder frankly whether the speed of a transition to democracy is not inversely related to the prospects for consolidating democracy in their country. One may argue that it is better for a nation to take the time to build painstakingly the institutions and understandings that make democracy durable, even at the price of extending the period of semiauthoritarian rule, than to risk descent into a generation or more of repression and praetorianism.

Conclusion

Nigeria stands now at a crossroads. It cannot live with authoritarian rule and yet it has twice failed to make democratic government work. The overthrow of the repressive Buhari-Idiagbon dictatorship marked the beginning of the long road back to democracy. The current debate on the constitutional future marks another step along that path. But historically, in other nations, that path has been a long and painful one, often involving failures and sometimes repeated ones (France now has its Fifth Republic). Where democracy has finally been consolidated, these successes have been steered by skilled and creative political leaders who were willing to compromise, committed to the democratic process, and capable of innovating in the design of democratic institutions.

Constitutional innovations alone cannot solve the problems facing democracy in Nigeria. But they can compensate for some of the weaknesses in the social structure and political environment. Even the most imaginative constitutions may be relentlessly abused. But a shrewdly crafted constitution may reduce the scope for abuse and so tilt the odds in favor of those who are committed to the democratic process above any partisan, personal or ideological interest.

The Second Republic went an impressive distance in innovating in the "institutional architecture" of democracy. That it failed should not be cause for cynicism or despair. There was much about the design and performance of that system in which Nigerians may take pride. If the specific flaws of that experience can be corrected with equal boldness and imagination, a Third Republic can emerge from that foundation and endure.

Notes

This paper benefited from the very helpful comments of Professors Naomi Chazan, Uyi-Ekpen Ogbeide, Alaba Ogunsanwo, and Richard Sklar.

1 Originally published as "Issues in the Constitutional Design of a Third Nigerian Republic," *African Affairs* 86 (April 1987): 209–226.
2 C. S. Whitaker, Jr., "Second Beginnings: The New Political Framework," *Issue* 11 (Spring/Summer 1981): 2.

3 Claude Ake, "Presidential Address to the 1981 Conference of the Nigerian Political Science Association," *West Africa* (May 25, 1981): 1162–1163; and Larry Diamond, "Nigeria in Search of Democracy," *Foreign Affairs* 62 (1984): 905–927.

4 On the failure of the First Republic, see John P. Mackintosh, *Nigerian Government and Politics* (London: Allen and Unwin, 1966); K. W. J. Post and Michael Vickers, *Structure and Conflict in Nigeria 1960–66* (London: Heinemann, 1973); Richard L. Sklar, "Contradictions in the Nigerian Political System," *Journal of Modern African Studies* 3 (1965): 201–213; and Larry Diamond, *Class, Ethnicity and Democracy in Nigeria: The Failure of the First Republic* (London: Macmillan, 1988). On the decay and collapse of the Second Republic, see Diamond, "Nigeria in Search of Democracy"; Diamond, "Cleavage, Conflict and Anxiety in the Second Nigerian Republic," *Journal of Modern African Studies* 20 (December 1982): 629–668; Richard Joseph, "Class, State and Prebendal Politics," *Journal of Commonwealth and Comparative Politics* 21 (November 1983): 21–38; Joseph, "The Overthrow of Nigeria's Second Republic" *Current History* 83 (March 1984): 121–124, 138.

5 Donald Horowitz, *Ethnic Groups in Conflict* (Berkeley: University of California Press, 1985), 604–613; Diamond, "Nigeria in Search of Democracy," 921.

6 Horowitz, *Ethnic Groups in Conflict.*

7 The Constitution of the Federal Republic of Nigeria 1979 (Lagos), Section 157, 51. The President was also explicitly required to appoint "at least one minister from each state, who shall be an indigene of such State" (Section 135, 45).

8 1979 Constitution, Sections 202 and 203, 65.

9 Whitaker, "Second Beginnings," 10–12; Diamond, "Cleavage, Conflict and Anxiety in the Second Nigerian Republic," 652–668.

10 Horowitz, *Ethnic Group in Conflicts,* 635–638.

11 In an intriguing and controversial contribution to the current debate on Nigeria's constitutional future, Lt.-General T. Y. Danjuma (rtd.) has proposed that the presidency itself be rotated among five ethnic groups or zones: the Hausa–Fulani, Igbo, Yoruba, Northern minorities, and Southern minorities. This zonal scheme differs from that outlined below primarily in providing for only two northern zones rather than three (*West Africa,* September 8, 1986, 1875–1876).

12 Their estimated 1983 populations (projecting from the official 1979 statistics) would be something like 19.4 million, 13.3 million, and 13.1 million respectively, although the official figures must be taken with many grains of salt. Larry Diamond, "Free and Fair? The Administration and Conduct of the 1983 Nigerian Elections," paper presented to the Annual Meeting of the African Studies Association (USA), Boston, December 1983, table 1.

13 This northern breakdown has not only a certain political logic but also a relatively even population balance between the three zones, with the 1983 estimates being 17.1 million for the five minority states, 16.9 million for Kano and Kaduna and 17.1 million for Bauchi, Borno, and Sokoto.

14 On the trade-offs and options in structuring preferential and distributional provisions, see Horowitz, *Ethnic Groups in conflict,* 656–657.

15 I am grateful to Naomi Chazan for suggesting this formulation.

16 On the elections of the First Republic, see Mackintosh, *Nigerian Government and Politics,* and Post and Vickers, *Structure and Conflict in Nigeria,* 161–185, 219–232. On the rigging of the 1983 elections, see Diamond, "Free and Fair?" The controversy that tarnished the legitimacy of the 1979 Presidential election is discussed in Billy Dudley, *An Introduction to Nigerian Government and Politics* (Bloomington: Indiana University Press, 1982), 168–178; Richard A. Joseph, "Democratization Under Military Tutelage: Crisis and Consensus in the Nigerian 1979 Elections," *Comparative Politics* 14 (October 1981): 80–88; and Whitaker, "Second Beginnings," 13, fn. 1.

17 Sayre P. Schatz, *Nigerian Capitalism* (Berkeley: University of California Press, 1977), 190–195, 208–209, 231–232, 244–245; Diamond, "Nigeria in Search of Democracy," 905–910, and "The Political Economy of Corruption in Nigeria," paper presented to the Annual Meeting of the African Studies Association (USA), Los Angeles, October 1984.

18 Richard A. Joseph, "Affluence and Underdevelopment: The Nigerian Experience," *Journal of Modern African Studies* 16 (June 1978): 221–239, and "Class, State and Prebendal Politics," 21–38; Sayre Schatz, "Economic Effects of Corruption" (paper presented to the Annual Meeting of the African Studies Association (USA), 1969); Diamond, "Political Economy of Corruption."

19 Diamond, "Nigeria in Search of Democracy," 913.

20 1979 Constitution, Sections 140–145, 47–48, and Fifth Schedule, Part I, 112–113.

21 Funke Fagbohun, "The Quality of Justice," *Newswatch* (Lagos), May 26, 1986, 22; and Dan Agbese, "The Courts in the Dock," *Newswatch*, May 26, 1986, 18.

22 Diamond, "Nigeria in Search of Democracy," 916.

23 Ibid., 917–918.

24 John A. Booth, "Costa Rican Democracy," paper presented to the Conference on Democracy in Developing Countries, Hoover Institution, Stanford, California, December 1985, 17–19.

25 *1979 Constitution,* Sections 211, 218, and 235. In practice, the executive branch enjoyed the predominant initiative in the appointment of justices (Agbese, "The Courts in the Dock," 19).

26 Agbese, "The Courts in the Dock," 18.

27 Ibid.

28 The latter quotation is from Justice C. O. Oputa of the Nigerian Supreme Court (in Agbese, "The Courts in the Dock," 17). For an authoritative and penetrating analysis of the problems of partiality, uneven competence, and growing corruption in the Nigerian judiciary, see in its entirety, Agbese, "The Courts in the Dock," 15–21.

29 Judicial support staff are now accountable to the more politicized Civil Service Commission (Agbese, "The Courts in the Dock," 18). On the need for a larger permanent and professional staff for the Federal Electoral Commission, see below.

30 Richard L. Sklar, "Developmental Democracy," paper presented to the Annual Meeting of the American Political Science Association, New Orleans, August 1985, 15–16.

31 Diamond, "Nigeria in Search of Democracy," 914–919.

32 For the original proposal, see Nnamdi Azikiwe, *Democracy with Military Vigilance* (Nsukka, Nigeria: African Book Company, 1974). More recent proposals may be found in Arthur Nwankwo, *Civilianized Soldiers: Army/Civilian Government for Nigeria* (Enugu, Nigeria: Fourth Dimension Publishers, 1984) and S. G. Ikoku, *Nigeria's Fourth Coup: Options for Modern Statehood* (Enugu, Nigeria: Fourth Dimension Publishers, 1985). Reviews and critiques may be found in "The Diarchy Proposition," *West Africa* (April 1, 1985): 610–611, and "The Diarchy Debate," *West Africa* (May 13, 1985): 937–938.

33 "The Political Debate," *West Africa* (April 14, 1986): 768–769.

34 On the Buhari-Idiagbon regime, see Larry Diamond, "Nigeria Update," *Foreign Affairs* 64 (Winter 1985): 326–336. The concerns about the Babangida regime include the killing of several university students by police in May 1986 and the assassination by parcel bomb in October 1986 of Dele Giwa, editor-in-chief of *Newswatch* magazine. Circumstantial evidence links the latter incident to the state security services and, as of this writing, the government has ignored widespread calls for an independent commission of inquiry.

35 Another condition for this body's legitimacy and effectiveness would probably be some provision to ensure its representativeness of ethnic and regional diversity in the country. This could be achieved by applying a zoning system to its composition, such that each group would be requested to nominate a member from a particular zone in the country, with the zones rotating among the associations over time.

36 Horowitz, *Ethnic Groups in Conflict*, 635–638.

37 Three-year electoral intervals would make for less flexibility, since they would require that state and federal legislators either have six-year terms, in which case half of them would come up for election every three years, or else three-year terms, in which case all of them would contest every time, defeating the purpose of staggered elections.

38 Haroun Adamu and Alaba Ogunsanwo, *Nigeria: The Making of the Presidential System 1979 General Elections* (Kano, Nigeria: Triumph Publishing Co., 1983), 187.

39 W. Ibekwe Ofonagoro, Abiola Ojo, and Adele Jinadu, eds, *The Great Debate: Nigerian Viewpoints on the Draft Constitution, 1976–77* (Lagos: Daily Times, 1977), 390–408; and "The Political Debate," 768–769.

40 Gabriel Almond and G. Bingham Powell, *Comparative Politics: System, Process and Policy*, 2nd ed. (Boston, MA: Little, Brown & Co., 1978); Giovanni Sartori, *Parties and Party Systems* (Cambridge: Cambridge University Press, 1976), 18–29.

41 Samuel P. Huntington, *Political Order in Changing Societies* (New Haven, CT: Yale University Press, 1968), 12–14.

42 Claude S. Phillips, "Nigeria's New Political Institutions, 1975–9," *Journal of Modern African Studies* 18:1 (March 1980): 15.

43 Anthony Kirk-Greene, "The Making of the Second Republic," in Anthony Kirk-Greene and Douglas Rimmer, ed., *Nigeria Since 1970: A Political and Economic Outline* (London: Hodder and Stoughton, 1981), 31–37; Richard A. Joseph, "Political Parties and Ideology in Nigeria," *Review of African Political Economy* 13 (1978): 78–90, and "The Ethnic Trap: Notes on the Nigerian Campaign and Elections, 1978–79," *Issue* 11 (Spring/Summer 1981): 18; and Larry Diamond, "Social Change and Political Conflict in Nigeria's Second Republic," in I. William Zartman, ed., *The Political Economy of Nigeria* (New York: Praeger, 1983), 25–84.

44 Robert A. Dahl, *Polyarchy: Participation and Opposition* (New Haven, CT: Yale University Press, 1969), 10–16, 33–40.

45 *West Africa* (July 7, 1986): 1403–1406.

13 The rule of law versus the big man[1]

Governance in Africa is in a state of transition, or some would say suspension.[2] Two powerful trends vie for dominance. One is the long-standing organization of African politics and states around autocratic personal rulers; highly centralized and overpowering presidencies; and steeply hierarchical, informal networks of patron–client relations that draw their symbolic and emotional glue from ethnic bonds. The other is the surge since 1990 of democratic impulses, principles, and institutions. Of course, the formal institutions of democracy—including free, fair, and competitive elections—can coexist with the informal practices of clientelism, corruption, ethnic mobilization, and personal rule by largely unchecked presidents. Indeed, much of the story of African politics over the last two decades has been the contest between these two approaches to power—even in countries that are formally democratic. But slowly, democracy, with its norms of freedom, participation, accountability, and transparency, is giving rise to new and more vigorous horizontal forms of organization, in both the state and civil society.

According to Freedom House, fully half the 48 states of Sub-Saharan Africa (hereafter "Africa") are democracies today, but analysts will inevitably differ on whether the glass is half-full or half-empty. I am more worried than Richard Joseph that democratization is starting to lose momentum in Africa.[3] Certainly Kenya's calamitous December 2007 election, which triggered horrific violence and ethnic cleansing that few analysts fully anticipated, shows that nothing can be taken for granted. As Joseph and Kwasi Prempeh note, even the high-profile democracies in South Africa and Ghana are showing worrisome trends.[4] Moreover, it is possible to argue that a number of the African countries Freedom House classifies as electoral democracies are really better scored as "competitive authoritarian states."[5]

Nevertheless, even if some of Africa's "democracies" hover in a gray zone between democracy and pseudodemocracy, the larger picture still represents historic progress. In the half-century since decolonization began, there have never been so many democracies and so much public pressure on democracy's behalf. Civil society has never been stronger, mass publics have never been so questioning and vigilant, and the natural impulse toward the reassertion of predatory personal rule has never faced so many constraints. Prempeh is right that these constraints remain weak relative to their counterparts in Europe and now parts of Asia and Latin America that are much more economically developed and better educated.[6] Yet if we take Africa's history of abusive government as our measure, significant progress is evident.

Part of this progress is taking place at the level of specific democratic institutions. As Joel Barkan notes in his comparative analysis of six African legislatures, under certain circumstances, we see (even in Uganda's non-democracy) the emergence of legislative coalitions for reform.[7] These comprise legislators who (for varying motives) want to enhance their own branch's power relative to that of the executive. Doing so, he writes, entails institutional (and even constitutional) changes to give African legislatures significantly more resources, and more financial independence. The same is true for African judiciaries and other institutions of horizontal account-ability, such as ombudsmen and anticorruption commissions. When these bodies have serious leaders, significant resources, and independent legal authority, they can begin to cut away at seemingly impregnable dynamics of predatory corruption and abuse of power. With leadership, resources, and authority, Joseph notes, the Economic and Financial Crimes Commission of Nigeria made unprecedented progress in prosecuting venal governors and other prominent public officials—until the country's new president reassigned the Commission's chairman in late 2007.[8]

When Africa's "second liberation" began in 1990, the continent was home to just three countries that could be called democracies (Botswana, Mauritius, and the Gambia) with a total population of only about three million. Between that year and 2008, more than 20 African countries made transitions to democracy or something near it.[9] Today, of the 24 African countries that Freedom House rates as democracies, eight are relatively "liberal," meaning that they score no worse than a 2 on Freedom House's scales of political rights and civil liberties (where 1 is the most free and 7 the most repressive).

Between 2001 and 2007, 22 African countries experienced a net improve-ment in their freedom scores (though some were by a small margin from a very authoritarian starting point), while only nine countries suffered declines. In 2007, however, eight African countries declined in freedom while only four gained. The most recent trend is moving slightly downward, then, but over the last six years African countries have continued improv-ing in their levels of freedom and democracy, more than a decade after the onset of this democratic wave.

The picture looks worse, however, if we focus on Africa's biggest countries, the seven with populations above 30 million. South Africa is still a liberal democracy. None of the other six—Democratic Republic of Congo, Ethiopia, Kenya, Nigeria, Sudan, and Tanzania—can be said to be a democracy at all.

Still, the general transformation of African politics has been extraordi-nary. Many of the electoral democracies that emerged after 1990—such as those in Benin, Mali, and South Africa—have persisted for more than a decade. Following two decades of rule under coup-maker Jerry Rawlings, Ghana has emerged as one of Africa's most liberal and vibrant democracies, reclaiming a leading position like that of its early postindependence years.

The positive trend is all the more remarkable when one looks at the many unlikely democratizers. They include four of the six poorest countries on the Human Development Index (Mali, Mozambique, Niger, and Sierra Leone) and several others in the bottom 20 (such as Benin, Burundi, Malawi, and Zambia), as well as four countries (Burundi, Liberia, Mozambique, and Sierra Leone) where democratization followed murderous civil conflicts, including the one in Burundi that left 200,000 dead.

Across Africa, the formal constitutional rules governing how leaders acquire and leave power are coming to matter more than ever before. As Daniel Posner and Daniel Young have shown, Africa's politics have grown less violent and more institutionalized since 1990.[10] Between 1990 and 2005, six presidents, including Uganda's Yoweri Museveni, succeeded in eviscerating term limits. But these cases were the minority. Powerful presidents such as Ghana's Rawlings and Kenya's Daniel Arap Moi, joined eventually by ten others, ran into term-limit provisions that forced them to step down. After more than two decades in power, Rawlings and Moi were tempted to hang on, but yielded to domestic and international pressure. Three African leaders—including President Olusegun Obasanjo in Nigeria—tried hard and failed to extend their presidencies. Further, from the 1960s through the 1980s, more than two-thirds of African leaders left power violently—usually as a result of a coup or assassination. During the 1990s, Posner and Young find, peaceful exits—principally as a result of electoral defeat or voluntary resignation—became the norm. Between 2000 and 2005, roughly four out of five African leaders were replaced this way.

Even more decisive than the rise of democracy has been the end of the one-party state. Since the 1990s, African elections have become increasingly regular and frequent, and almost all of them have been contested. As has been the case in Nigeria—and in Ethiopia, the Gambia, Kenya, Uganda, and Zimbabwe, among others—many of these elections have been brutally fought and outrageously rigged. But the sight of a ruling party or a "big man" losing is no longer quite so odd. Whereas only one African president was defeated at the polls between 1960 and 1990, incumbent presidents lost one out of every seven tries at reelection between 1990 and 2005.[11] Moreover, electoral alternation has significant positive effects on public support for and confidence in democracy.[12]

Why do African presidents feel more constrained now? Posner and Young advance two intriguing explanations. One is greater sensitivity to international pressure. The median level of foreign aid (relative to the overall economy) in countries where presidents did not attempt to secure third terms was almost twice as high as in those countries where the presidents did (and often succeeded). The other explanation points to public opinion. The nine African presidents who declined to seek a third term had narrower electoral mandates than the nine who did, suggesting a greater sensitivity to public opinion.

Building from the bottom up

This points to another positive trend in Africa, with potentially lasting consequences: the growth of civil society.[13] As wide varieties of associations independent of ruling parties have begun to engage in political dialogue and advocacy, demands for increased political accountability gain force, challenging and at times even preempting presidents inclined to flirt with the idea of staying in power. Some of these organizations—including many student associations, trade unions, religious bodies, and interest groups based on commercial, professional, and ethnic solidarities—date back to colonial days or the era just after independence. Yet active as well is a new generation of groups devoted explicitly to promoting democracy and good governance: think tanks, bar associations, human rights organizations, women's and civic-education groups, election-monitoring networks, and local as well as national-level development organizations.

More than ever, the building of democracy in Africa is a bottom-up affair. Nongovernmental organizations are teaching people their rights and duties as citizens, giving them the skills and confidence to demand answers from their rulers, to expose and challenge corruption, to resolve conflicts peacefully, to promote accommodation among ethnic and religious groups, to monitor government budgets and spending, to promote community development, and to recruit and train new political leaders. Civic groups and think tanks are also working at the national level to monitor elections, government budgets, and parliamentary deliberations; to expose waste, fraud, and abuses of power; and to lobby for legal reforms and institutional innovations to control corruption and improve the quality and transparency of governance.

These organizations draw strength not only from the funding and advice that international foundations and donors give them, but more importantly from their increasingly dense interactions with one another. The African Democracy Forum now links dozens of organizations from 30 countries on the basis of a common desire to advance the related causes of democracy and good governance.[14] Some African civil society organizations, most notably the Institute for Democracy in South Africa (IDASA), have reached a point of institutional maturity where they are now assisting democratic development elsewhere on the continent.

Also significant has been the growth of independent media and new information and communication technologies in Africa. The long tradition of independent daily newspapers has been enriched by a proliferation of newsweeklies and community and cross-border radio stations. Many of the community stations focus on local development and health issues, from agriculture to HIV/AIDS, but they also address political issues and compensate for their low-wattage signals with high-voltage independence. And some broadcast from exile as the last sources of credible information about the deplorable conditions in their own home countries. One of the best is SW Radio Africa. Accurately self-billed as the "independent voice of Zimbabwe," it left the air when the Mugabe regime succeeded in suppressing its signal with Chinese-provided jamming gear. Undaunted, the station then turned to live streaming and posting on the Internet.

Perhaps most revolutionary are the ways that digital technology is being used in Africa, even where few computers (not to mention little broadband Internet access) can be found. One nonprofit organization, kiwanja.net, is making available free software—FrontlineSMS—that can be used by charities and NGOs to facilitate text-messaging via short-message service (SMS) on everything from crop, weather, and road conditions to health news and politics:

> Originally developed for conservationists to keep in touch with communities in National Parks in South Africa, the system allows mass-messaging to mobile phones and crucially the ability [for recipients] to reply to a central computer.[15]

Then there is the mobile phone, whose advantage is its versatility and astonishingly rapid empowerment of even poor individuals. Today, more than 30 million Nigerians (nearly one in every four) own a mobile phone. In Africa as a whole, the number of mobile users is believed to be approaching 300 million.[16] This rapid spread has enabled quantum leaps forward in election monitoring. In Nigeria in April 2007, millions of ordinary citizens instantly became election monitors by reporting what they saw (much of it bad, unfortunately) at the polls. The profusion of evidence did not stop massive rigging, but it may be helping to provide the legal basis for court challenges to overturn some of the cheating's effects.

The abovementioned FrontlineSMS technology is the brainchild of intrepid British anthropologist and programmer Ken Banks. Now being revised with support from the MacArthur Foundation, FrontlineSMS has also served to facilitate feedback to community radio programs in South Africa, to monitor voting in the Philippines, to send "security alerts to fieldworkers in Afghanistan [and] market prices to smallholder farmers in Aceh, and to circumvent government restrictions in countries including Zimbabwe and Pakistan."[17] Increasingly in Africa, and around the world, text-messaging will give citizens, NGOs, and community radio stations a powerful tool not only to extend their reach and connect people in ways that enhance development, but to monitor what governments do, document human rights abuses as they happen, and facilitate civic organization and demonstrations.

As text-messaging gains momentum in Africa, it will probably encounter a technological challenge from its biggest global nemesis, the communist regime in China. The rulers of the People's Republic are continually and desperately looking for ways to contain and disrupt any uncontrolled citizen activity that takes on a political edge. African dictatorships can be expected to call on Beijing for help in fighting this new tool for promoting democratic mobilization. African civil societies, meanwhile, can be expected to look for ways around the control mechanisms—one hopes with plenty of technical support from sympathetic actors in international civil society.[18]

Coinciding with the flowering of civil society has been a visible public demand for and appreciation of democracy. When surveyed by the Afrobarometer in 2005 and 2006, an average of 62 percent of the public in 18 countries said that "democracy is preferable to any other kind of government."[19] Levels of support for democracy ran as high as 75 percent in Ghana, Kenya, and Senegal, and reached 65 percent or higher in ten of the countries surveyed. In fact, in only a few African countries can one find much of an avowed appetite for any specific form of authoritarian rule, and never does it rise above a fifth of the population. Moreover, this is not just an abstract commitment to democracy in general. Four out of five Africans surveyed believe that "regular, open, and honest elections" are the only way to choose their country's leaders, and two-thirds agree that elected assemblies (not the president) should make the laws in the country, even if the president disagrees with them.[20] Only about one in six Africans, on average, expresses a positive preference for an authoritarian option such as military or one-party rule. And a slight majority (52 percent) actively rejects all three authoritarian options offered.

Africans' support for democracy seems to flow from something other than a naive sense that democracy must spell quick economic progress. When asked to define what democracy means to them, "a majority of Africans interviewed (54 percent) regard it in procedural terms by referring to the protection of civil liberties, participation in decision making, voting in elections, and governance reforms."[21] And when asked whether they felt that their system of electoral democracy "should be given more time to deal with inherited problems" or instead, if it "cannot produce results soon, we should try another form of government," 56 percent of Africans in 2005–2006 chose to give democracy more time. This represents a significant increase in patience with democracy since 2000.

Michael Bratton notes that while the demand for democracy is proving fairly resilient in Africa, the perceived supply is more questionable. For example, while 81 percent of Africans want free and fair elections that can remove incumbents, only 47 percent think they are getting this in their countries. Two-thirds of Africans want their president to be subject to the rule of law, but barely a third (36 percent) thinks that he is.[22] Clearly, Africans value and demand democracy—but African parties and politicians are not meeting citizens' aspirations.

Consequently, disillusionment is rising. Between 2000 and 2005, satisfaction with the way democracy works declined an average of 13 percentage points (from 58 to 45 percent) across the countries surveyed. While satisfaction rose in a few relatively well-functioning democracies such as Ghana and South Africa, it declined in eight of the twelve countries surveyed both times. Nevertheless, even on the supply side there are cautious grounds for optimism. The perception that one's own country is a democracy has held constant at around 50 percent, and 54 percent think it is likely that their country will remain a democracy.[23] Nor are the problematic numbers set in stone. On the contrary, there is evidence that actually delivering democracy can dramatically improve citizen attitudes and perceptions. Analyzing the 2005 data, Bratton found that respondents' perception of the most recent national election as free and fair was the most powerful predictor of their readiness to agree that their countries were democracies. In other words, the ruler's performance is no longer enough to satisfy the public—formal institutions are starting to matter more than informal ones.[24]

The deadening hand of personal rule

These trends, hopeful as they are, nonetheless tell only part of the story. Countries such as Cameroon, Eritrea, Ethiopia, Gabon, Sudan, and Togo remained trapped in long-standing patterns of authoritarian rule. Nigeria, Uganda under the increasingly corrupt Museveni, and now Kenya have been slipping backwards. And in Zimbabwe, deepening repression is morphing into a psychosis of authoritarian misrule under an aging dictator, Robert Mugabe, who seems increasingly detached from reality as his country's economy collapses amid hyperinflation that his policies have bred.

No less worrisome are the poor governance, persistent corruption, and stubborn personalism that so often continue to beset Africa's democracies. Of the six measures that the World Bank Institute uses to gauge the quality of governance in a country, the one known as "voice and accountability" (which includes freedom of expression and citizen participation in selecting the government) is a rough and partial surrogate for democracy. The others measure political stability and the absence of violence; the effectiveness of public services and administration; whether or not public regulations "permit and promote private sector development"; the rule of law (including the quality of policing and the courts); and control of corruption.

Africa does poorly on all these measures. On average, it ranks in the 30th percentile—a little better on the political measures of accountability and stability, but slightly worse on the measures of rule of law, corruption control, regulatory quality, and governmental effectiveness. On these latter four measures, which I collect together as a gauge of "state quality," Africa's mean percentile ranking, 28th, trails well behind Eastern Europe (59th), Latin America and East Asia (47th), the Middle East (42nd), and even South Asia (36th).

Save for South Africa, the other six largest countries in Africa rank very low in their quality of governance. Five of the six have worse governance than the continent as a whole, and three of them dismally so. Across all six measures, Nigeria ranks in the 13th percentile. On rule of law plus control of corruption and political stability plus control of violence, only 5 percent of countries score worse. Ethiopia ranks in the 18th percentile, Sudan in the 5th, Democratic Republic of Congo in the 3rd. Kenya and Tanzania do better, at the 26th and 36th percentiles, respectively, but Kenya still scores below the African average.

Underlying these painful figures is the continuing neopatrimonial character of politics in Africa. Experts call postcolonial African states *neo*patrimonial because they combine the forms of a modern bureaucratic state—constrained in theory by laws, constitutions, and other impersonal rules and standards—with the informal reality of personalized, unaccountable power and pervasive patron-client ties. These ties radiate out and down from the biggest "big man"—the autocratic president—to his lieutenants and allies, who in turn serve as patrons to lower-level power brokers, and down to the fragmented mass of ordinary citizens, who are trapped by their dependence on local political patrons.

In such systems, the informal always trumps the formal. Subordinates owe loyalty to their personal patrons, not to laws and institutions. Presidents and their minions use state resources as a personal slush fund to maintain political dominance, giving their clients state offices, jobs, licenses, contracts, vehicles, bribes, and other access to illicit rents, while getting unconditional support in return.[25] State offices at every level become permits to loot, either for an individual or a somewhat wider network of family members, ethnic kin, political clients, and business cronies.[26] Corruption, clientelism, and personal rule thus seep into the culture, making the system even more resilient. In Africa, contending patron–client networks organize along ethnic or subethnic lines, and the president sees his ethnic kin as the most reliable loyalists in the struggle for power. This makes the system particularly unstable, as conflicts over pelf, power, and identity mix in a volatile, even explosive brew.[27] The typical African pattern of concentrating extreme power in the presidency makes politics even more of a tense, zero-sum game. This helps to explain how a single rigged election can ignite the paroxysms of violence and ethnic cleansing that a horrified world has been watching lately in Kenya, where ethnic groups that have been shut out of the presidency ever since independence nurse deep anger.

The fundamental purpose of neopatrimonial governments is not to produce *public* goods—roads, bridges, markets, irrigation, education, health care, public sanitation, clean drinking water, effective legal systems—that increase productivity, improve human capital, stimulate investment, and generate development. The point of neopatrimonialism, rather, is to produce *private* goods for those with access to power. Contracts are granted not on the basis of who can deliver the best service for the lowest price, but rather on who will pay the biggest bribe. Budgets are steered to projects that can readily generate bribes. Government funds disappear into the overseas accounts of officeholders. Public payrolls are swollen with the ranks of phantom workers and soldiers whose pay goes into the pockets of higher-ups.

One thing that can arrest the decay and refresh the system is a change in leadership. But a key feature of the neopatrimonial system is the way the "king of the hill" hangs on and on. In 2005, Uganda's President Museveni, whose original claim to his office was being the top general of the strongest private army in his conflict-wracked homeland, "openly bribed members of parliament, blackmailed and intimidated others to amend the constitution and remove term limits on the presidency so that he can run again, and again, and again."[28] In the run-up to the February 2006 election, he stepped up his harassment of the independent media and those elements of civil society that he had not already co-opted. Then he jailed the main opposition presidential candidate, before finally claiming a highly suspect first-round victory through apparent manipulation of the vote count.[29]

Museveni's two decades in power hardly make him Africa's longest-serving president, however. Omar Bongo of small but oil-rich Gabon in West Africa has ruled for nearly four decades. Robert Mugabe's merciless reign in Zimbabwe has stretched past a quarter-century. In Angola, Cameroon, and Guinea, presidents have also ruled for well over 20 years, and in Burkina Faso for nearly that. Sudan's Hassan al-Bashir has held power for 18 years, and Meles Zenawi in Ethiopia and Yahya Jammeh in the Gambia for more than a decade each. None of them shows any sign of surrendering office. Of course, such prolonged personal reigns are hardly new in Africa—witness the late Mobutu Sese Seko's 32 years in power in Zaire, now Democratic Republic of Congo—but they have always been associated with national decline, if not disaster.

If Africa is now suspended between democracy and personal rule, what can tip it toward democracy? The deciding factor will not be economic development. For probably decades to come, much of Africa will remain well below the high level of development that seems to assure democratic survival. Steady economic growth can help to give people more confidence in democracy, building up its long-term legitimacy. But sustainable development has been stymied by the same factor that has undermined democracy itself: bad governance. If both democracy and development are to have a future in Africa, the core priority must be to improve the quality of governance.

Social scientists often lament their lack of adequate understanding of the policy challenges of our time, calling for more research. We do need to understand better how winning coalitions can be generated and sustained for the kinds of institutional reforms that will gain traction on Africa's core problem of bad, corrupt, abusive governance. But broadly, we know where the answers lie. Countervailing institutions of power—the judiciary, the legislature, and the whole apparatus of countercorruption, audit, human rights, and other oversight bodies that are sometimes called a "fourth branch of government"—must be greatly strengthened in their political autonomy, statutory authority, and financial and human resources. Power and resources must be decentralized down to elected lower levels of government, ideally (in any large country) through a federal system (the one saving grace that has held Nigeria together). Political parties must themselves be democratized internally and made more effective as organizations, independent of ethnicity or personal ties. Elections must be truly free and fair, and thus electoral administrations must be made up of career civil-service professionals who, as in India, have the training, resources, autonomy, and *esprit de corps* to resist partisan pressures. State economic ownership and control must be diminished, but the state must be strengthened in its capacity to deliver its essential mission of managing the economy and generating the public goods needed for development. And citizens must have the freedom to monitor and report on what government does, and to organize to challenge it and pursue their interests.

It is not difficult to find, in African civil societies and in the state itself, numerous actors ready to rise to the challenge. The problem is that African leaders are not generally to be found among these coalitions for reform, because they calculate that their own interests lie not in reform, but in building or reinforcing monopolies of power and wealth. Of course, in the absence of democracy, it is always the monopolists who triumph. But democracy in itself is no guarantee against the resurgence of many bad practices.

For much of the last half-century (and well before that, of course, under colonial rule), the missing link has been the international community, which has been only too happy to embrace any African despot in the quest for resources and strategic advantage. Idealists, by contrast, have thought that the answer lies in "foreign aid," which is supposed to make up for the vast shortages of financial resources needed to deliver health, education, and roads. About US$600 billion later, we know (or at least we *should* know) that pouring more aid unconditionally on bad governments is like pouring gasoline on a fire. In the circumstances of predatory rule in Africa, aid functions like the revenue that gushes in from oil exports— it is just another source of external rents that enables rulers to float on a cushion above their societies, controlling the state without having to answer to their own people.

Certainly Richard Joseph is correct that the entry of China into the "great game" of aid, investment, and resources in Africa creates a new context, in some ways akin to the superpower competition of the Cold War.[30] And the "new cold war" against international terrorism has not helped. Both developments have given African authoritarian regimes new alternatives and new forms of leverage against Western pressure for democratic reform. But this is not the 1960s or 1970s. African societies are informed and autonomously organized as never before. Africans are increasingly aware of their political rights and demanding of democracy. And together, Europe and the United States still provide the vast bulk of aid and investment in Africa.

Most of all, principled pressure is needed from international actors, tying substantial flows of development assistance to concrete institutional improvements in governance. Donors can also provide generous financial and technical assistance to the institutions of governance—African legislatures, judiciaries, countercorruption commissions, and other agencies of horizontal accountability—that must work well if the balance is to tip from autocracy to democracy. It is the very fluidity of things on the continent today—so powerfully evoked by Joseph's concept of "frontier Africa"—that makes so much possible.[31] From the experience of a small but growing number of better-functioning African democracies, we know that the continent is not condemned to perpetual misrule. The challenge now is for the international donors to join with Africans in demanding that their governments be truly accountable.

Notes

1 Originally published as "Progress and Retreat in Africa: The Rule of Law versus the Big Man," *Journal of Democracy* 19 (April 2008): 138–149.

2 This chapter was initially published as the conclusion to a cluster of articles, "Progress and Retreat in Africa," in the April 2008 issue of the *Journal of Democracy*. The other three articles in that cluster, by Richard Joseph, Kwasi Prempeh, and Joel D. Barkan, are cited below.

3 See Richard Joseph, "Progress and Retreat in Africa: Challenges of a 'Frontier' Region," *Journal of Democracy* 19 (April 2008).

4 Ibid.; H. Kwasi Prempeh, "Progress and Retreat in Africa: Presidents Untamed," *Journal of Democracy* 19 (April 2008).

5 Steven Levitsky and Lucan Way, *Competitive Authoritarianism: Hybrid Regimes After the Cold War* (New York: Cambridge University Press, 2010). They classify countries on the basis of their respective regimes during the period 1990–1995, and then track their evolution. On this basis, they classify Benin, Malawi, Mozambique, and Zambia all as competitive authoritarian regimes, whereas other analyses (including that of Freedom House) often have considered them democracies. I exclude the Central African Republic because of its very poor freedom score, average 5 on the two 7-point scales of Freedom House.

6 Prempeh, "Presidents Untamed."

7 Joel D. Barkan, "Progress and Retreat in Africa: Legislatures on the Rise?" *Journal of Democracy* 19 (April 2008).

8 Richard Joseph, "Challenges of a 'Frontier' Region."

9 The Gambia, whose politics had been dominated for almost 30 years by one leader and his party, slipped entirely from democratic ranks after a military coup in 1994. Retrospectively, some analysts have questioned just how democratic the Gambia was at that point.

10 Daniel Posner and Daniel Young, "The Institutionalization of Political Power in Africa," *Journal of Democracy* 18 (July 2007): 126–140.

11 Ibid., 131.

12 Michael Bratton, "The 'Alternation Effect' in Africa," *Journal of Democracy* 15 (October 2004): 147–158.

13 The evidence and arguments here are developed at greater length in Larry Diamond, *Developing Democracy: Toward Consolidation* (Baltimore, MD: Johns Hopkins University Press, 1999), ch. 6.

14 See www.africandemocracyforum.org.

15 "Texts Monitor Nigerian Elections," BBC News, April 20, 2007. Available at http://news.bbc.co.uk/2/hi/technology/6570919.stm.

16 This would probably represent something like 30 percent of the roughly 750 million people in Sub-Saharan Africa, even allowing for some people owning multiple devices.

17 From http://frontlinesms.kiwanja.net.

18 The potential and pitfalls of digital technology for global democratic progress is discussed further in Chapter 7.

19 Most of the data presented here from the Afrobarometer are available in the publications of the project, at www.afrobarometer.org/publications.html. See in particular, "The Status of Democracy, 2005–2006: Findings from Afrobarometer Round 3 for 18 Countries," Afrobarometer Briefing Paper no. 40, June 2006.

20 Michael Bratton, "Formal vs. Informal Institutions in Africa," *Journal of Democracy* 18 (July 2007): 96–110.

21 Michael Bratton, Robert Mattes, and E. Gyimah-Boadi, *Public Opinion, Democracy, and Market Reform in Africa* (Cambridge: Cambridge University Press, 2005), 69–70.

22 Bratton, "Formal vs. Informal Institutions," figure 2, 106.

23 Ibid., 102.

24 Ibid., table 2, 107.

25 Michael Bratton and Nicolas van de Walle, *Democratic Experiments in Africa: Regime Transitions in Comparative Perspective* (Cambridge: Cambridge University Press, 1997), 61–68; Robert H. Jackson and Carl G. Rosberg, *Personal Rule in Black Africa: Prince, Autocrat, Prophet, Tyrant* (Berkeley: University of California Press, 1982), 38–42.

26 Drawing on Max Weber, Joseph has called such systems "prebendal." Richard A. Joseph, *Democracy and Prebendal Politics in Nigeria: The Rise and Fall of the Second Republic* (Cambridge: Cambridge University Press, 1987), 6; see also ibid., 55–68 for elaboration of the concept and its relationship to clientelism.

27 Ibid., 8. This work develops these themes at length.

28 Andrew Mwenda, "Please Stop Helping Us," paper presented to the Novartis Foundation, August 12, 2006, 3.

29 Andrew Mwenda, "Personalizing Power in Uganda," *Journal of Democracy* 18 (July 2007): 23–37.

30 Joseph, "Challenges of a 'Frontier' Region."

31 Ibid.

14 Promoting real reform in Africa[1]

The statistics tell a grim story. Sub-Saharan Africa (which I will subsequently term "Africa") is trapped in the world's worst poverty and stagnation. Most African countries had lower per capita incomes (in constant 1995 dollars) at the end of the century than they had in 1980. Improvements in life expectancy have stagnated over the last two decades, and in many countries, the gains that had been made are rapidly eroding in the face of the HIV/AIDS pandemic. Progress in reducing illiteracy has been slow. Two in five Africans (and half of all African women) are illiterate; only South Asia has a worse rate. By comparison, only about one of every eight adults in East Asia or Latin America is illiterate. A clear reason why is that far fewer Africans are in school than are young people in other regions (see Table 14.1 for all the regional comparisons). Africa is the only region of the world where school enrollments have been declining at every level, and the only region where life expectancy has been declining, falling in 2000 to just 47 years. It is also the only region where average life expectancy is less than 60 years of age. Because so many African infants and young children die (Africa also has the highest infant and child mortality rates), women have more children to ensure that some survive to adulthood. Low levels of female literacy and formal employment also are associated with higher fertility. As a result, Africa also has the highest population growth rate—higher than the next fastest-growing region by half a percentage point.

Africa is the world's poorest region. Its average per capita national income, in purchasing power parity dollars, is a third lower than the next poorest region, South Asia (which has little in the way of oil or other mineral resources). Its ratio of external debt to annual national income is the worst of any region (about two-thirds of national income, on average). With 13 percent of the world's population, Africa accounts for only 1.6 percent of global trade and less than 1 percent of global investment, and it is the only major region where per capita investment and savings have declined since 1970. Overall, Africa has by far the worst average "human development" score (0.468) of any region of the world (see Table 14.1).[2] Indeed, the statistics suggest that Africa is virtually equivalent to "least developed countries" (which average 0.448 on the index). According to the United

Table 14.1 Relative development performance of Africa, 2001 and 2010

Development indicators	Year	SS Africa	East Asia/ Pacific	Latin America/ Caribbean	South Asia	Middle East/ North Africa
Gross national income per capita[i]	2001	1,358	5,014	6,962	1,525	7,230
	2010	2,148	9,618	11,136	3,068	10,856
Life expectancy	2001	49.7	71	71.6	61.9	69.8
	2010	54.2	73.3	74.1	65.3	72.5
Adult literacy[ii]	2000	57.4	91.5	89.7	58	70.4
	2010	62.6	94.3	91.4	61.6	77.6
Population growth rate	1990–2001	2.7	1.2	1.7	2	2.2
	2001–2010	2.5	0.7	1.2	1.6	2
Development assistance per capita[iii]	1990	53.4	9.8	62	15.6	51.2
	2000	29.8	6.4	38.2	9.3	41.3
	2010	52.2	20.3	75.7	41.3	25.8
School enrollment ratio[iv]	2001	28.8	56.8	62.3	40.8	57.2
	2007	35.4	63.1	67.5	48.4	61.5
Human Development Index[v]	2000	0.401	0.581	0.68	0.468	0.578
	2010	0.463	0.671	0.731	0.548	0.641
External debt[vi]	2001	65.4	28.8	40.2	25	36.8
	2011	24.8	13.5	22.7	20	15

All sources, unless otherwise noted, are gathered from the World Bank Data Set 2011: http://databank.worldbank.org/ddp/home.do?Step=2&id=4&DisplayAggregation=N&SdmxSupported=Y&CNO=2&SET_BRANDING=YES

i   PPP (Current International $)

ii Age 15 and above.

iii Net official development assistance per capita (constant 2010 US$).

iv Primary, secondary, and tertiary enrollment combined (net).

v   Source: Human Development Index. http://hdr.undp.org/en/media/HDR_2011_EN_Table2.pdf

vi Percentage of of Gross National Income.

Nations Development Programme (UNDP), 30 of the 34 countries that rank lowest in human development are in Sub-Saharan Africa, as are *all* of the bottom 25.[3] These are also, for the most part, the countries where the majority of the population lives in absolute poverty, forced to survive on less than $2 or even less than $1 per day. In fact, half of Africans live on less than a dollar per day.[4]

Yet Africa is hardly ignored by the international community. Historically, it has received far more per capita in official "development assistance" than any other region of the world.[5] By the late 1990s, well over half of all African states were deriving at least 10 percent of their gross national product (GNP) from foreign aid, which was also accounting (in the first half of the decade) for

> over 50 percent of African government revenues and 71 percent of their public investments. In many countries in the region, virtually the entire nonrecurrent component of the budget as well as large parts of the recurrent budget were financed by the donors.[6]

During the 1990s, Africa's ratio of official development assistance to GNP (13.4 percent) was three times higher than the next most aid-dependent region (South Asia, 4.7 percent), and total aid (including aid to nongovernmental organizations) averaged almost 80 percent of government expenditures (half again as high as South Asia and 15 times that of Latin America).[7] Even though Africa's total net official development assistance has declined in recent years from a high of $17 billion to $12 billion, in 1999, this was still two-thirds higher than its foreign direct investment (most of which was in the oil sector).[8] Leonard and Straus calculate that many African countries receive more in development assistance than they collect in tax revenue. An estimated half of this aid has been going to finance repayment of the most crushing external debt burdens of any region of the world.[9] Africa's external debt is now two-thirds of its annual income, a ratio much higher than any other "developing" region, despite far-reaching debt forgiveness (amounting to $13 billion of bilateral debt between 1988 and 1995).[10]

Aid flows to Africa—and to the developing world in general—have been driven by a long-standing theoretical model, which assumes the key missing ingredient for development is financing. If external donors could just provide enough foreign aid to fill the "financing gap" between a country's own savings and a determined necessary level of investment, economic growth would take place. International development economists and policymakers clung to this "financing gap" model even when it became apparent that it wasn't working, that more aid was not producing more economic growth, but often less, because the aid was not being used for productive investment and was not being accompanied by corresponding increases in a country's savings rate.[11]

The core problem obstructing economic development in Africa is not a lack of resources, though that is a serious constraint in many countries. Those African countries, such as Nigeria, Angola, Cameroon, and the Democratic Republic of the Congo (formerly Zaire) that are rich in oil and other natural resources have largely squandered their natural wealth, achieving little in terms of development. They are just about as poor and miserable as their less bountiful neighbors. In fact, there is increasingly compelling evidence and logic showing that natural resource wealth (most notably oil) produced from economic enclaves generates incentive structures that undermine economic development.[12] Only one African country with mineral wealth (diamonds) has managed it effectively for development, Botswana. Only two African countries, Botswana and Mauritius, have achieved a relatively good development performance in the past three decades. Not coincidentally, these are the only two African countries that have been continuously democratic since independence.

It is difficult to make a case for the economic benefits of democracy by comparing only two small countries with the other 46 in Africa. Still, the data not only show that Botswana and Mauritius have had dramatically better development performance then the rest. They also suggest that the African countries that democratized during the 1990s made some development progress during the decade while the lingering semidemocracies and autocracies continued to slide backwards.[13] It is too soon to know if democracies will continue to outperform autocracies on the continent. Uganda has made significant development progress under a regime that has been only semidemocratic at best. And the HIV/AIDS pandemic is already beginning to register a staggering negative impact on life expectancy and other aspects of human development throughout Southern Africa, which contains the continent's largest concentration of democracies, including Botswana and South Africa, which are being ravaged by the disease. Yet, as Gyimah-Boadi trenchantly argues, the HIV/AIDS crisis exposes in sharp relief the shortcomings of governance even in the formally democratic countries of Africa, while the crucial elements of democracy—openness, civic organization, political empowerment (particularly of women)—are proving to be vital tools for combating the plague.[14]

Evidence on the link between democracy and development is not only coming from Africa. Roll and Talbott found that among the most significant factors in explaining variations in per capita national income during the 1990s were several different measures of freedom, including political rights, civil liberties, press freedom, and property rights, each of which "has an independent, strong, and positive influence on country income."[15] More strikingly, they found that there is clearly a causal effect of democracy on economic growth, as "democratic events" (transitions to democracy or increases in freedom) "have been followed by rather dramatic increases in GNIpc [gross national income per capita]," which tend to accelerate further over time if a country sustains the democratic trend, while antidemocratic events are followed by declines in economic growth.[16] Comparing the 176 most democratic leaders and the 179 most autocratic leaders since 1952, Bueno de Mesquita and his colleagues found that the average democratic leader produced a real annual economic growth rate of 3.04 percent, compared to 1.78 percent for the average autocrat.[17] Within Africa, Eifert finds "a large and robust relationship" between political openness and economic growth, both across African countries and over time. "The difference in political openness between the most democratic and the least democratic African state is associated with a growth gap of over 4.5 percentage points per year."[18] Globally, democracy has had a discernible effect over the past half-century in reducing infant mortality, even when controlling for other developmental factors such as per capita income.[19] And when broadening the analysis to consider a wider range of governance variables (including "voice and accountability" and rule of law), Kaufmann and his colleagues in the World Bank find "a strong positive causal relationship from improved governance to better development outcomes."[20]

One reason why Africa continues to lag so far behind economically is that it lags well behind in governance as well. In the latest survey of perceptions of global corruption, only 17 African countries are assessed, but 12 of these 17 are among the most corrupt half of the world's states (the other five African states in the survey are all democracies, and relatively liberal ones at that).[21] Among the major regions of the world, only the Middle East is clearly worse in terms of democracy and freedom. Only about two in every five every African governments are accountable to their people through the most minimal instrument of free, fair, and competitive national elections. And of these 19 or so democracies (at the end of 2002), only about five can be said to be liberal, in terms of allowing extensive civil and political freedom. Certainly, freedom has improved and democracy has expanded dramatically in Africa since 1990, but the promise of a "second liberation" across the continent has stalled, and where political freedom is most abused so are economic and social development as well.

There is no disputing the fact that a few autocracies, mainly in East Asia, have achieved rapid economic growth over the past few decades. But African countries lack the unique historical circumstances (greater cultural coherence, an ideological external threat) that facilitated the East Asian miracles under authoritarian rule. As several scholars have noted, autocracies have a much wider range of variation in development performance, from stunning growth to staggering disaster, including mass famine. Democracies do not have famines, and generally they avoid developmental disaster because when people are able to monitor the performance of their leaders and to turn them out in free and fair elections, leaders must perform to some extent or they will be held accountable.[22] When a Mobutu or Idi Amin or Sani Abacha can loot his country and murder his compatriots with abandon, there is no check on predation. Resources bleed out of the country and production withers. Conflict and instability grow, further weakening already porous and fragile states, and making entire regions "no-go" zones for investment.

The fundamental new insight that is reshaping the political economy of development is in fact a very old one. Governance matters. The nature and quality of governance, and the types of policies that governments choose, have a huge impact—apparently, the decisive one—in shaping how economies perform, and whether and how rapidly people will escape from mass poverty. As William Easterly writes, "Bad governments ... can kill growth."[23] And that is exactly what has happened in Africa. Growth requires that people reduce present consumption in return for greater income in the future. Where government policies and actions discourage investment in the future—through policies and practices that generate high inflation, high black market premiums, negative real interest rates, high budget deficits, restrictions on free trade, rotten public services, and massive corruption—investors and producers run for cover.[24] Indeed, Easterly has found that "Africa's higher government budget deficits, higher financial repression, and higher black market premium explain about half of the growth difference between East Asia and Africa over the past three decades."[25] If Africa's economic policies had been as liberal on average as East Asia's, African per capita income on average would be about $2,000 higher (in 1989 U.S. dollars).[26]

The partial understanding that economic policies would have to change if investors and producers were to be given the right incentives led to the wave of economic stabilization and structural adjustment pressures on African states in the 1980s and 1990s. As Nicolas van de Walle shows, under pressure from the donors, the majority of African states did much to stabilize their economies over the past two decades, particularly recently, in the 1990s.[27] But this progress has been halting, uneven, tentative, and partial. At the same time, stabilization has also further squeezed public investment budgets, while public infrastructure has continued to decay. Some liberalization of prices and regulations has occurred, but African states have not had the will or ability to implement the sweeping transformation of economic structures and policies that is needed. Again, as van de Walle shows, much of the old racket remains, as the state still obstructs and intervenes in ways that privilege the few over the many. And invariably, the few who benefit are those in state office or with some connection to it.[28]

Beyond the very partial implementation of economic reform lies the pervasive problem of corruption in Africa, which, as Sahr Kpundeh argues, is profoundly antidevelopmental.[29] Corruption can be dressed up analytically in a variety of terms, but it is basically a process in which the powerful (those with control over or access to the state) use their power illicitly to accumulate wealth without generating much of anything for the society in return. This "urge to steal everything not bolted to the floor is the most obvious growth-killing incentive."[30] It discourages private investment, distorts resource allocations, deforms policies, proliferates regulations, swells budget deficits, enervates institutions, diverts resources from productive (wealth-generating) activity, and squanders large amounts of resources. Funds that could go to educate and inoculate children, pave roads, build markets, dig wells, generate electricity, and otherwise provide an overall enabling environment for growth instead wind up in overseas bank accounts and real estate, financing luxury purchases for already wealthy individuals. Worse still, officials often waste even more money purchasing weapons and building structures the country doesn't need (and likely will never use) in order to generate an opportunity for kickbacks. A 2002 report prepared for the African Union estimates that corruption costs the continent $148 billion annually.[31] That is well over a quarter of the continent's entire gross domestic product.

As van de Walle explains, politics in the typical African country still remains deeply stuck in the "logic of neopatrimonialism."[32] State incumbents at all levels use their power and office to appropriate resources for themselves, and their families, cronies, clients, and kin.[33] State offices are distributed with the expectation and understanding that their incumbents will use them to accumulate wealth.[34] Corrupt resources flow up and down chains of clientage in a vast cascading drain upon public wealth and honest effort. Corruption in these countries is not an aberration. It is the way the system works, the way people acquire power and wealth, and the way officials retain power and expand wealth. At its most extreme, locally or nationally, the state is little more than a criminal racket, and the police and organized crime may be one and the same.

For the several dozen African countries that are caught more or less in this corrupt, neopatrimonial logic, there is no commitment to the larger public good and no confidence in the future. Every actor is motivated by the desire to get what can be gotten now, by any possible means. Communities as well seek immediate government jobs and favors, in a zero-sum struggle over a stagnant and potentially fleeting stock of resources. Thus, there is no respect for law, and no rule of law. The judicial system is politicized and routinely suborned, or so demoralized and starved of resources that it cannot prosecute corrupt conduct in public and private life with any kind of energy and regularity. Governmental decisions and transactions are deliberately opaque in order to hide their corrupt nature and evade embarrassing disclosures. Information about how government works and how contracts are awarded is simply unavailable. Exposure of corrupt deeds typically brings little more than embarrassment because the rule of law does not function to constrain or punish the behavior of public officials. Power is heavily centralized and institutions of scrutiny and accountability function only on paper, or episodically, to punish the more marginal miscreants or the rivals of the truly powerful. Lacking a sense of public purpose, discipline, and esprit de corps, the civil service, police, customs, and other public institutions function poorly and corruptly. Salaries are meager because the country is poor, taxes are not collected, corruption is expected, and government payrolls are bloated with the ranks of political clients and fictitious workers. Corruption is rife at the bottom of the governance system because that is the climate that is set at the top, and because government workers cannot live on the salaries they are paid.

In fact, institutions in such a society are a facade. The police do not enforce the law. Judges do not decide the law. Customs officials do not inspect the goods. Manufacturers do not produce, bankers do not invest, borrowers do not repay, and contracts do not get enforced. Any actor with discretionary power is a rent-seeker. Every transaction is twisted to immediate advantage.

In such circumstances, state elites may be feared (and envied) for their sweeping and unaccountable power, but the state as an institution is weak and porous. By every one of Huntington's criteria of institutionaliza-tion—coherence, complexity, autonomy, and adaptability[35]—the African neopatrimonial state appears as a shallow, brittle, highly personalized set of structures, captured by narrow (and typically, ethnically exclusive) elites for their own ends, lacking a larger sense of autonomous purpose and mission.

This is why the worst instances of plunder and neopatrimonial rule col-lapse completely into state failure and civil war. Indeed, most of the 35 African civil wars that Stephen Stedman and Terrence Lyons chronicle took place in contexts of highly authoritarian and abusive governance.[36] This includes all the recent "textbook" instances of state collapse—Somalia, Liberia, Sierra Leone, and the Democratic Republic of the Congo (the former Zaire). All four of the "repeat offenders" in suffering civil wars— Burundi, Chad, Uganda, and Zaire—have been notable for their extreme lack of democracy, and no African civil war has broken out in a truly dem-ocratic political system. Indeed, as Stedman and Lyons note, the same predatory quest for control of resources that has been dragging down African states internally has also contributed to regionalizing these conflicts, as corrupt governments seek the spoils of war in neighboring countries.

For a long time, Africa's leaders and official institutions blamed these woes and failures on the legacies of colonialism and the injustices of the inter-national system. Increasingly, however, Africans are recognizing that the core of the problem now lies in the defects of their own institutions of governance and the distorted incentives they generate. The 2003 *African Development Report* is strikingly reflective of this new spirit of candor, and thus merits quoting at some length:

> More than four decades of independence for many countries should have been enough time to sort out the colonial legacies and move forward. Thus, Africa needs to look at itself—especially the nature of political power and governance institutions. In most African countries, the economy is still dominated by the state—with the state as major provider of formal employment, contracts, and patronage while parties are regionally and ethnically based. And politics in most of these coun-tries is such that victor assumes a "winner-takes-all" form with respect

to wealth and resources, patronage, and the prestige and prerogatives of office. If there is lack of transparency and accountability in governance, inadequate checks and balances, non-adherence to the rule of law, absence of credible and peaceful means to change or replace leadership, or lack of respect for human rights, political control becomes excessively important and the stakes dangerously high.[37]

These dynamics, the ADB argues, have been a major factor behind the plethora of armed conflicts in Africa, which, in addition to claiming several million lives over the past decade, displaced 12 million people into refugee status by 2000, 40 percent of the world total.[38]

If Africans are to achieve peace, progress, and human dignity, they must get better governance, with democracy and a rule of law. But transforming governance will also require fundamental changes in the way the external world relates to Africa.

The continuing aid addiction

Corruption is the bane of development and democracy in Africa. Yet the donor agencies were slow to recognize it as a fundamental problem, and even when they began to do so in the 1990s, the money kept rolling in to the coffers of most corrupt, decadent, unaccountable African states. Particularly in the early 1990s, pressure for better, more accountable governance did heighten the financial squeeze on bankrupt African states and led to a number of transitions from authoritarian rule, beginning in Benin in 1990. A number of African countries, such as Sudan, Somalia, and Kenya (until its dramatic breakthrough to electoral democracy in December 2002), saw their aid receipts decline significantly during the 1990s. But for most African states, the money has kept rolling in. By the year 2000, development assistance had begun to gravitate somewhat more to the democracies of Africa, which averaged higher per capita aid receipts than the nondemocracies. But a number of highly authoritarian and corrupt governments, in countries such as Cameroon, Angola, Eritrea, Guinea, and Mauritania, received levels of aid equaling or even well exceeding the African average of $20 per capita. Almost all the authoritarian regimes, including those under international pressure for bad governance (such as Kenya and Zimbabwe), received aid well above the global average ($11 per capita) that year for low and middle-income countries. Even most of the democracies receiving aid have yet to overcome the neopatrimonial style of politics, as they still suffer from extensive corruption and a weak rule of law.[39]

Thus, aid has so far had only a very limited and tentative impact in improving governance. And it is not just the aid recipients that are addicted. It is the donors, too, who need to offer aid in order to justify being an aid institution; who evaluate and promote their aid officers on the basis of their ability to push allocated aid dollars out the door; and who believe that they have a humanitarian obligation to help all countries, even where it is clear that aid is doing no real good—or even more harm than good.

In fact, the overall structure of Africa's current aid dependence *is* doing more harm than good, for it facilitates and reproduces the patterns of corrupt, neopatrimonial governance that obstruct development. Venal, abusive rulers need a flow of resources from somewhere in order to pay off their networks of supporters and cronies, accumulate personal wealth, maintain at least minimal control over a coercive apparatus, and thus survive in power. They cannot get much of these resources from the tax revenues of their citizens, because they do not have the legitimacy and their decrepit state does not have the capacity to raise much revenue from taxation. If their countries (like Cameroon, Angola, and Nigeria) have oil, or other geographically concentrated mineral wealth (diamonds, gold, copper, and so on) that can be mined, they may derive the necessary income from mining rents (both the official taxes on corporate revenues and the unofficial bribes). As Leonard and Straus note, agricultural production on large corporate estates can also generate a "rentier" economy that does not "depend on widespread productivity" and tax revenue.[40] Strikingly, foreign aid can play a functionally similar role, producing a kind of pseudoenclave economy. Whether the money derives from mineral rents or foreign aid, ruling elites get autonomous sources of revenue that disrupt the bonds of accountability between the rulers and the ruled. In either case, the state does not have to function effectively or responsibly or transparently in order to get the lifeblood of its existence, revenue. In either case, state elites get "a steady stream of lucrative, easily cashed 'rents' (taxes and bribes) that can be quickly dispersed to clients and personal networks, ... while doing nothing to build the institutions or incentives that would discourage" corruption and clientelism.[41] In either case, elites are freed from the need to build and maintain broader domestic bases of support, which would require better, more open and public-spirited governance.

African political systems based on the corrupt distribution of patronage (which includes, to a lesser degree, even most of Africa's democracies) are thus addicted to aid (even several of the oil states, such as Cameroon and Angola, now heavily depend on it). And the donors are addicted to providing the aid—partly out of bureaucratic inertia, partly out of misplaced idealism and guilt, and partly out of the need to keep recycling unpayable African debts. Unless this mutual addiction is overcome, Africa will not move onto the path of sustainable development. For development will only happen when governance fundamentally improves—when African state officials at all levels become truly accountable to their publics, and when state resources come to be used to advance the overall welfare of the society, rather than that of a narrow clan of beneficiaries. Controlling corruption and generating accountability, participation, and a true rule of law are not simply one set among a number of diverse requirements for development in Africa. These conditions of good governance form the essential prerequisite for Africa's emergence out of its entrenched, degrading, seemingly intractable poverty. And they can be generated. The situation is far from hopeless, for as demonstrated by Bratton and Mattes, African people do understand and value democracy and oppose authoritarian alternatives.[42] Moreover, as Gyimah-Boadi shows, African civil societies have been organizing and mobilizing—despite significant handicaps and obstacles—for freedom, democracy, and better governance.[43]

If Africa is going to attain better governance, the push for it will have to come from within. The popular and civil society aspirations for better governance are evident. But the problem now is that in most African states, the incentives for elites to yield to these pressures from below are weak, because African state elites depend so little on their own people for the resources they need to operate. Until the donors embrace and interact with popular demands for justice, accountability, and good governance, most elites (including those elected in superficially competitive contests) are not going to permit (much less actively construct) the kinds of independent and vigorous institutions of horizontal accountability that will foster better governance. We know what these are—autonomous courts, prosecutors, and legal aid systems; countercorruption and audit agencies; ombudsman's and human rights commissions, central banks, and so on.[44] Increasingly, international donor agencies stand ready (and able) to assist in the construction and institutional development of these agencies of accountability. But the political will to get them up and effectively running is extremely weak.

The core challenge for African development is this: How can the political will for fundamental governance reform be generated?

The stalled African renaissance

African leaders are keenly aware that their legitimacy has badly eroded at home and abroad. The more serious and public-spirited among them know that something must be done to improve governance if there is to be any hope of healing the continent's bleeding sores of poverty, disease, and violent conflict. Others at least concede that some gesture toward reform is needed. In this spirit of criticism and reflection, the Organization of African Unity (OAU) resolved in July 2001 to transform itself the following year into a new African Union (AU), which held its first summit in Durban, South Africa, one year later. The hope of many was that the AU would take a tougher, more direct approach to the problems of poverty, conflict, and bad governance on the continent than had the OAU, which was "hindered in its activities by internal conflict and self-serving heads of state."[45] Yet it is difficult to see how a new body, made up of the very same heads of state—and initially proposed by one of the worst dictators on the continent, Libya's Moammar Al Qaddafi (who has been plying his fellow African leaders with all sorts of personal "gifts")—can transcend the limits of the old structure. The AU intends to have a pan-African parliament, an

African court of justice, new continental economic institutions, and harmonized policies. Its founding objectives included promoting not only peace and security on the continent, but also "democratic principles and institutions, popular participation and good governance."[46] Yet when the new organization faced its first test, in confronting the blatantly rigged 2002 presidential elections in Zimbabwe and the subsequent deepening political and humanitarian crisis in that country, it failed to act.

The hopes for an African "renaissance" (as South Africa's President Thabo Mbeki has termed it) now rest heavily with the New Partnership for Africa's Development (NEPAD), which envisions fundamental reforms of policy and governance on the African side in exchange for significant new infusions of development assistance from the multilateral and bilateral donors. Initiated in 2001 (with Thabo Mbeki and Nigeria's President Olusegun Obasanjo playing prominent roles), NEPAD embodies an affirmation by African leaders and their governments that they have a duty to eradicate poverty and pursue sustainable development, and it establishes 7 percent annual economic growth as a target toward that end. In a break with the statism of the past, NEPAD recognizes that the private sector must be the engine of growth in Africa, and that a major task of the government is therefore to stimulate the development of the private sector. It concedes that Africans must take ownership of their own future, and it identifies peace, democracy, and good governance as preconditions for reducing poverty. Under NEPAD, African leaders have agreed not only to broad economic and social development goals—revitalizing education and health care, maintaining macroeconomic stability, making financial markets transparent and orderly—but also to promoting and protecting democracy, human rights, and accountability. They further pledge to combat the proliferation of small arms, strengthen mechanisms for conflict resolution and prevention, and promote the provision of public goods such as water, transportation, energy, and other infrastructure within the region and the various subregions of Africa. Toward these ends, NEPAD promises to use official development assistance more transparently and effectively, in a partnership of mutual accountability between African states and aid donors. At their annual summit in 2002, the leaders of the G8 (industrialized democracies), meeting with representatives of the European Union and several prominent African leaders, welcomed and endorsed NEPAD and pledged to deepen their partnerships with African countries that are committed to implementing NEPAD. Subsequently, donors announced increases in development assistance to Africa for the first time in many years. Also in 2002, the United Nations formally endorsed NEPAD as the framework for international (including UN) engagement with Africa.

At the level of rhetoric and objectives, NEPAD is an important step forward. But its success will depend on implementation, and that is where postindependence Africa has repeatedly faltered in the past. To prevent a repeat of past failures, NEPAD provides for a new African Peer Review

Mechanism (APRM), which will review the institutions and policies of individual African governments in order to identify strengths and weaknesses and propose strategies for overcoming the latter.

At the second assembly of the AU, in Mozambique in July 2003, Nigerian President Obasanjo, chair of the NEPAD Heads of State and Government Implementation Committee, announced that 15 African countries (out of 53) had so far agreed to the peer review mechanism, and that an initial panel of "eminent persons" had been appointed for the purpose of developing the mechanism. Peer reviews were to begin in the second half of 2003.[47] The formal architecture is moving forward, but there is little in the recent or distant past to suggest that African leaders—most of whom themselves are drenched in the very problems of corrupt, neopatrimonial, patronage politics that NEPAD is supposed to combat—are prepared to allow blunt and probing evaluations of their own and their fellow governments' performance.

There are two major criticisms of NEPAD. One comes from the political and intellectual left in Africa, such as the Dakar-based think tank CODESRIA, which sees the initiative as abandoning previous development action plans, too accepting of the neoliberal economic framework, and too deferential to international capital, which they regard as an agent of a hostile international economic system.[48] In this view, which clings to the discredited statist approaches of the past, NEPAD is just another surrender to the neocolonial forces of globalization. The other critique, which comes from below, in civil society (and overlaps in some instances with the first), challenges NEPAD "for being elitist and top-down in its approach, having been drawn up by a few Heads of State, and virtually excluding civil society in its preparation."[49]

While it registers valid concerns about the plight of Africa and the lack of popular participation in these policy processes, the first critique, advancing the tired and discredited arguments of dependency theory, is a recipe for the continued marginalization and immiseration of Africa. However, the second line of criticism speaks to the biggest flaw in NEPAD, its detachment from the nongovernmental forces in Africa that have been the most prominent and consistent advocates for democratic and good-governance reforms. By mid-2003, Africans still did not know what the NEPAD peer review standards would be.[50] But civil society advocates for good governance are clear in insisting that evaluation committees must be composed not only of government appointees, but also parliamentary representatives (including from the opposition), ombudsmen, officials of countercorruption agencies, and representatives from NGOs, think tanks, and the private sector. Unless these broader societal forces are given a prominent role both in the policy direction of NEPAD and, in particular, in the peer review process, African governments will pat one another on the back and turn away from confronting the fundamental and deeply rooted perversions of governance that represent the core obstacle to achieving the NEPAD goals.

Then, NEPAD will just degenerate into a sad iteration of the previous aid failures: African states will pretend to improve their governance and the donors will pretend to reward them for it.[51]

The donor countries say they want a new approach, and NEPAD's explicit concern to promote democratic good governance and assess performance is partly a response to donor pressure. But it does not go nearly far enough. The idea of linking development assistance to better governance is one whose time has finally arrived. African leaders and governments acknowledge in principle the need for it. Many African civil society organizations are demanding it. But if linkage is to be effective and meaningful, it must be more than an idea, and more than a mechanism that African leaders "enforce" upon themselves in a closed and collegial process. Monitoring of performance must be broad, and from multiple sources. The G8 and other donors must then really link aid levels to performance, independently assessed, and not allow misplaced guilt, idealism, or flowery rhetoric to substitute for acute analysis and clear standards. All of this brings us back to the fundamental question of how the political will for genuine—not cosmetic—governance reforms can be generated.

A new deal for African development

Africa needs a truly new bargain: debt relief for democracy and development for good governance. Under such a new deal for African development, African governments would not merely hold each other accountable; they would be monitored, evaluated, and held accountable by the international community, and by their own people working closely in coordination with the donor agencies. The political will for fundamental governance reform is not going to come from "peer" review among African governments. The incentives to fudge and dissemble are simply too powerful. The political costs of ripping up entrenched clientelistic networks and closing off the channels and practices of corrupt patronage are just too great. The habit of covering for and excusing each other's failings is too engrained. African leaders will embrace fundamental reform only when they have no choice—when the costs of bad governance become too great, because the international community denies bad rulers the external resources with which to govern and the international, social, and financial access with which to enjoy the good life. Generating the political will for reform requires manipulating the incentive structure that ruling elites confront.

"Political will" is the commitment of a country's rulers to undertake and see through to implementation a particular policy course. At its most resilient, political will here involves a broad consensus among ruling elites, across parties and sectors of government, in favor of democratic and good governance reforms. But consensus is always imperfect, and will is most important at the top levels of government (among major political leaders and senior civil servants). There, political will must be robust and sincere.

That is, reform leaders must be committed not only to undertake actions to achieve reform objectives, but also "to sustain the costs of those actions over time."[52]

Such political will is generated from three directions: from *below*, from *within*, and from *outside*. Organized pressure from *below*, in civil society, plays an essential role in persuading ruling elites of the need for institutional reforms to improve the quality of governance. There may also be some reform-minded elements *within* the government and the ruling party or coalition who, whether for pragmatic or normative reasons, have come to see the need for reform (but are reluctant to act in isolation). Finally, *external* actors in the international community often tip the balance through persuasive engagement with the rulers and the society and by extending tangible benefits for improved governance and penalties for recalcitrance.

International assistance can help to develop the first two forms of pressure, and in fact has done so in a number of countries in the past decade. When political will for systemic reform is clearly lacking, the principal thing that foreign assistance can do on the political front is to strengthen constituencies for reform in civil society, including NGOs, interest groups, think tanks, and the mass media. Assistance can enhance these actors' understanding of key reform issues, their knowledge of other country experiences, their coordination with one another, their capacity to analyze and advocate specific institutional and policy reforms, and their mobilization of support and understanding in society. Sometimes international donors must redirect their democratic governance assistance programs away from the central government when political will falls sharply. But then they must be prepared to resume engagement with state actors when political will revives with the election of a different ruling party or coalition, or a change of heart or calculus on the part of existing leaders. Often political will appears more patchy and ambiguous. In that case, the best strategy is to work with those elements of the government in particular agencies or ministries that seem serious about improving governance, while seeking to enhance demand for reform within the society.

A key lesson from international efforts to stimulate governance reform is that fundamental reform is only sustainable when there is a "home-grown" initiative for it. If changes in policies and institutions are promised merely in response to international pressures, they will not be seriously and consistently implemented. "Imported or imposed initiative confronts the perennial problem of needing to build commitment and ownership; and there is always the question of whether espousals of willingness to pursue reform are genuine or not."[53] International engagement, therefore, does not succeed if it simply compels a government to sign on the dotted line of some package of dictated reforms, as has frequently been the case with International Monetary Fund (IMF) assistance packages. Its goal must be deeper and more procedurally democratic: to generate public awareness and debate, and to induce government leaders to sit down with opposition and societal forces to fashion a package of reforms that is unique to and owned by the country.

The vigor and depth of the political will to reform can then be assessed by several additional criteria. First, to what extent have (self-proclaimed) reformers undertaken a rigorous analysis of the problem and used it "to design a technically adequate and politically feasible reform program" that rises to the scale of the challenge? Second, to what extent have reformers mobilized political and societal support for their initiatives broad enough to overcome the resistance of threatened interests (and how sustained are these efforts to rally support)? Third, to what extent are reformers seeking changes in laws and institutions and allocations of human and financial resources that hold promise of effecting real change? In the case of controlling corruption, this would include, for example, laws to monitor and punish corrupt conduct and an anticorruption agency with the authority and staff to enforce them. These issues must be assessed through review mechanisms that broadly include civil society and international observers, not just government-chosen elites. They must then periodically use the above criteria "to track the evolution of political will over time" and to feed that assessment back into the reform implementation process.[54]

Successful international engagement must shift from *conditionality* to *selectivity* in foreign assistance. Traditionally in international lending, for example, conditionality has been "*ex ante* in the sense that governments promise to change policies in return for aid." As a result, "reforms are 'owned' by the donors."[55] This is why they have failed, and why "conditionality" is now such a widely discredited concept. A better approach is to dispense aid selectively to reward and deepen, and thus preserve and consolidate, reforms that have already begun to be implemented by the country, according to its own design. Selectivity focuses aid on good performers—countries that have reasonably good policies and institutions—and on assisting reform movements that are seriously under way, by governments and societies that have taken responsibility for the design of their own policies and institutions.[56] Where governance is bad, international assistance should focus on trying to strengthen civil society actors that are pressing for democratic and good governance reforms, while delivering humanitarian and health assistance directly via donor action or through civil society, bypassing the corrupt state.

It takes patience, intelligence, coherence, consistency, and dexterity for external actors to help generate authentic, "home-grown" political will for improved governance. Toward this crucial end, the following principles should guide the development assistance policies and allocations of international development donors.[57]

1   Overall levels of international development assistance must be linked more clearly to a country's development performance, and to demonstrations of political will for reform and good governance.

2   Good performers must be tangibly rewarded. Africa needs more "carrots" to encourage reform by predictably and meaningfully rewarding it when it has already occurred. When political leaders demonstrate respect for democratic procedures and freedoms, and a willingness to undertake and see through difficult political and economic reforms, they should benefit with steady increases in official development assistance. In addition, good performers—principally, democracies that are getting serious about controlling corruption and strengthening the rule of law—should be rewarded in other tangible ways: with debt relief, incentives for foreign investment (including publicity about their good governance), and trade liberalization.

3   Rewards must be granted for demonstrated performance, not for promises that may be repeatedly made and broken. The only way to exit from the chronic "cat and mouse" game of international conditionality is to make increases in development assistance and other economic rewards contingent on what governments actually do (and keep doing), not what they say they will do. As much as possible, rewards should be structured to lock into place the institutions and practices of democracy and good governance. For example, the European Union requires that democracy and respect for human rights be institutionalized before a country can be considered for admission. A similar standard should be adopted before African states receive the enhanced aid flows of the NEPAD process, and before they are given free trade access to the markets of industrialized countries. And there should be clear and credible procedures for suspending countries that depart from this standard.

4   Permanent debt relief for the highly indebted poor countries (HIPCs) should also be linked to the quality of governance. Comprehensive relief (retiring most or all of a country's external debt) should only be granted to countries that have demonstrated a basic commitment to good governance by allowing a free press and civil society, an independent judiciary, and a serious countercorruption commission. Even in these cases, the debt should not be relieved in one fell swoop. Rather, debt service payments should be suspended and the existing stock of debt retired incrementally (for example, at 10–20 percent per year). This would generate ongoing incentives for adhering to good governance. After five or ten years of good governance, the country would have permanently retired its external debt and the institutions of democracy and accountability would have begun to sink roots.

5   In the absence of any political commitment to democratic and good governance reforms, international donors (bilateral and multilateral) should suspend most governmental assistance and work only with nongovernmental actors. The only exceptions to this suspension should be humanitarian relief, regional infrastructure, and responses to global public health threats, and even in these areas reliance on the poorly performing state to deliver aid should be minimized.

Development assistance to chronically badly governed countries should be administered through and to nongovernmental actors. And beyond humanitarian and public health assistance, aid to chronic poor performers should mainly aim to empower civil society in an effort to change the regime or otherwise dramatically improve governance. Corrupt and repressive rulers must learn that they will pay a heavy international price for their bad governance. They will forfeit material resources and become more isolated diplomatically. For this approach to be truly effective, it must have substantial consequences.

6 The donor countries should also impose targeted sanctions on particularly corrupt, repressive, and irresponsible ruling elites, as well as their families and cronies. Such ruling elites should be prevented from traveling to, investing in, or schooling their children in the donor countries (including the European Union, the U.S., Canada, Japan, and Australia), and in any other countries that will cooperate in this quest for better governance. The banking systems and legal institutions of all countries that want to be recognized as respecting the rule of law globally should be required to cooperate vigorously in tracking down and recovering assets accumulated through corruption, bribery, and theft.

7 The bilateral donors need to coordinate pressure on truly bad, recalcitrant governments. Reductions in aid from one or two donors will not have much impact in changing the calculations of political leaders if their governments continue to receive levels of funding from the other donors. Witness the continuing high levels of aid to several Francophone dictatorships, such as Togo and Cameroon. Leadership calculations will be most likely to change, and to be translated into action, when those leaders perceive a relatively coherent message from the universe of international donors.

8 A greater proportion of international development assistance should be devoted to developing the institutions of democracy and good governance. In intractable cases, the most important thing donors can do to aid development is help to generate the demand for democracy and better governance by strengthening the capacity and reform commitment of NGOs, interest groups, religious bodies, social movements, mass media, universities, and think tanks. For in the absence of minimally decent governance, efforts to work with state institutions to improve health, education, or agricultural productivity will be enervated by corruption, waste, and incompetence. In struggling democracies, and more generally, improvements in governance enhance reform efforts, and investments in better governance are likely to yield more numerous, immediate, and powerful multiplier effects. Whatever progress is made on governance will almost certainly have a positive impact on other sectors, enabling given levels of sectoral assistance to go further. Probably no other dimension of foreign assistance yields so many synergies and such good development value per dollar.

9   Where committed reformers can be identified within the state, donors should work with them. If pockets of political will for reform exist within the state, donors should identify those opportunities and try to strengthen the hand of reform-oriented ministers, agency heads, and provincial governors through specific democracy and governance (DG) assistance programs. "Assistance can be provided to reformers to help identify key winners and losers, develop coalition building and mobilization strategies, and design publicity campaigns."[58] Often, reform majorities or nodes of reformers can be found in some branches of the state outside the executive, such as the legislature, the judicial system, and other agencies of horizontal accountability that may be deprived of resources and authority. Even when reformers lack the power today to implement far-reaching change, enhancing their training and technical capacity may enable them to enlarge public constituencies for reform. Such assistance may also represent an investment in the future, when electoral alternation or some other political shift gives reformers real power.

10 State capacity must be generally enhanced, but it makes no sense to try to strengthen the technical capacity and administrative ability of state structures that lack the political will to govern responsibly. Building effective state structures—and hence the ability to deliver on heightened societal demands and expectations—must become a major strategic objective of development assistance, but it cannot be pursued until state leaders are serious about governance. Expensive investments to improve the infrastructure and strengthen the technical capacity of bureaucracies, judiciaries, and legislatures will be largely wasted if there is no political will to use enhanced capabilities for more honest, responsive, and accountable governance.

11 The global private sector should be encouraged to accelerate its efforts to incorporate judgments about the quality and transparency of governance into its decisions on private capital flows. Support for Transparency International and other global anticorruption efforts should be institutionalized to continue pressing this agenda. An important priority is improving the comparative measurement of the quality of governance and then widely publicizing the results, so that investors will be encouraged to invest in countries that are governing well and adopting promising institutional and policy reforms. Credible (independent) and publicly disseminated measurement of governance is particularly important for smaller, more peripheral developing countries, about which investors are slower to find reliable information. Donors might also accelerate private capital flows to better-governed countries through incentives to invest in such countries (for example, through the U.S. Overseas Private Investment Corporation, and through the negotiation of free trade agreements).

12 International donors must strengthen the global rule of law, particularly the capacity to track down and close off corrupt flows of money in the international banking system. The donors must work to institutionalize rigorous global standards and procedures for the rapid identification and recovery of corruptly acquired assets. They should work vigorously to ensure enforcement of the new Organisation for Economic Co-operation and Development (OECD) convention against bribery. The same anti-money laundering tools that are being used to fight the wars on terrorism and drug trafficking can be enlarged into a broader war on international criminality and corruption.

13 The advanced industrial countries should work vigorously to negotiate an end to agricultural subsidies that impede African access to their markets. The estimated $300 billion that rich countries pay their farmers in subsidies constitute one of the biggest obstacles to development in Africa. By stimulating overproduction and dumping of many crops on world markets, they prevent African (and other developing country) farmers from competing fairly. For example, with US cotton growers able to dump cotton cheaply on world markets due to subsidies of $3 billion per year from the US government, four of Africa's poorest countries (Benin, Mali, Chad, and Burkina Faso) lose a quarter of a billion dollars annually in exports.[59] Negotiating an end to these subsidies, through a generous stance in the current round of the World Trade Organization negotiations, and then mobilizing the political will in rich countries to face down special interests and implement the policy, is one way to benefit all of Africa (even the poorest and most poorly governed states) through market forces, by strengthening the returns to productive activity.[60]

All sorts of arguments can and have been levied against a governance-led strategy of development assistance. First, critics contend that it risks plunging badly governed countries over the abyss into chaos and state failure. But that is where these countries are headed with aid flowing in a business-as-usual fashion. Zimbabwe and Côte d'Ivoire are classic recent cases in point. Only a radically different approach can pull countries out of the gradual descent into deepening praetorianism, violence, and stagnation. The conservative approach—just back stability—condemns Africans to indefinite misery. A second, related critique sees the above strategy as hard-hearted, punishing African people for the sins of their governments. But the statistics tell a different story. Hundreds of billions of dollars of aid later, most Africans remain desperately poor. Only where aid has been received in a context of democracy and good governance has it made dramatic progress in reducing mass poverty. Only when there is some degree of transparency and responsibility in governance does the aid really reach the people. Tying active forms of developmental assistance—aid, debt relief, and special trade preferences (see below)—to better governance can help to transform the structure of incentives that shape politics and governance in Africa. At the same time, broadly removing unfair trade barriers within the rich countries can enable African producers to benefit from world markets, even in the absence of any targeted assistance.

A third criticism sees the above approach as, in one respect, not radical enough. Some would like to simply do away with aid altogether and force African states to depend on the taxes of their people and the assessments of international investors about which environments are market-friendly. A more sympathetic and creative approach, proposed by David Leonard and Scott Straus, would dramatically reduce development assistance to Africa, while also writing off all (or most) of Africa's external debt burdens. Under their proposal, general budgetary support for African countries would end, but targeted assistance for humanitarian problems, such as health and refugees, would continue.[61] They criticize my appeal to link debt relief to democracy and good governance, arguing that conditionality has not been effective in Africa, and that "both debt and aid force African elites to be accountable to the international system, not to domestic populations."[62] But selectivity is fundamentally different than conditionality. It rewards countries for what they are already doing, not for what they promise to do. And as proposed here, it would *precisely* compel African rulers to be accountable and responsive to their own people as a prerequisite for permanent and comprehensive debt relief, as well as most official development assistance.

In fact, involvement of the African people themselves is crucial to the success of this approach. Only in a context of openness, accountability, popular participation, and debate can genuinely indigenous ownership of the necessary policies and institutions emerge. World Bank and other donor policies (such as the HIPCs) debt relief program, or the multidonor budget support for country poverty reduction strategies) have begun to articulate some of the above kinds of governance-related standards and concerns. However, these programs still tend to treat governance as an adjunct concern—relevant, worth mentioning, but not fundamental to sustainable poverty reduction. And the broader society is not adequately involved in the search for a viable strategy for development. Development assistance strategies must emphasize governance processes at least as much as policy outcomes if they are going to be effective.

Can it be done?

I believe it is possible to construct a truly new structure of incentives for African rulers. But it is going to require a "tough love" approach—tough in that it will deny most corrupt ruling elites (those who do not have access to substantial mineral wealth) the resources they need to operate their neopatrimonial systems, and compassionate in that it will provide rulers committed to democracy and accountability with the kinds of resources—for public infrastructure, health care, education, and improved agricultural productivity—that will yield highly tangible improvements in popular well-being. Rulers who opt for good governance will thus find a different set of rewards. They will win reelection because they "deliver the goods" for their people. When they leave power, they will be honored and respected by their own people, and by the international community, rather than treated as criminals, thieves, and pariahs. Their children and grandchildren will grow up in a country that is economically prosperous and at peace. Their political successors will not need an army of bodyguards in order to campaign for office, and a fistful of cash for the electoral officer in order to win. They will be free to travel abroad, even welcomed when they do so, rather than having to worry about evading warrants from international courts.

To work, both parts of this strategy must be vigorously and coherently pursued—by all the major donors acting in concert. Corrupt, abusive, recalcitrant dictators must be stigmatized, isolated, and pressured from all sides—including by their fellow African leaders. Democratic rulers who are serious about controlling corruption and governing responsibly must get the infusion of resources early on to develop the human and physical capital that will then attract investment capital.

In addition, the donors must reform themselves institutionally and operationally. The corruption that blights development in Africa is not only in the recipient governments and societies. It is also in the international corporations that pay the bribes, and almost never face prosecution in their own countries (despite the OECD requirement that the paying of foreign bribes be made a criminal offense). And it can be found within the administration and contracting of the donor projects as well. Beyond gross corruption, and much more common among the principal donors, are other wasteful and counterproductive practices, such as the lavish spending on expatriate experts, and the tying of aid to the purchase of products and services from corporations based in the donor country.[63] Political leaders in the donor countries need to summon the political will to face down their own domestic actors that want to capture overseas aid dollars to advance their own corporate or bureaucratic interests. If the donors are serious about promoting development, they need to allow themselves to be monitored and held accountable. They need to invest much more in understanding the countries and contexts in which they operate, and in being able to monitor and evaluate developmental performance. At the same time, while monitoring carefully to ensure that aid is spent *for* development, they need to give recipient states and societies more leeway in how to use the aid to advance development. One vehicle for doing so might be to channel some aid through national development funds that are administered by autonomous, respected trustees who are separated from patronage politics; that are focused on specific sectors (such as agriculture, health, and education); and that award various types of grants and loans by reviewing competitive proposals from both governments and civil societies.[64]

There are some promising bilateral donor reforms on the horizon. In 2002, President Bush announced a new aid initiative, the Millennium Challenge Account (MCA), which would allocate a new pool of development assistance to a limited number of low and lower-middle income countries on the basis of three criteria: governing justly (which includes political freedom, control of corruption, and the rule of law); investing in people (through health and education); and encouraging economic freedom (in pursuing market-friendly economic policies). The Bush Administration has pledged to increase funding for the MCA to $5 billion within three years of its creation, which would represent a roughly 50 percent increase in U.S. development assistance, and "a near doubling in the amount of aid that focuses strictly on development objectives."[65] The attraction of the MCA is not only that it will selectively reward and support countries with better governance and more developmental purpose, but that its goals are developmental (poverty elimination and economic growth), its country selection process is transparent, and its method of aid distribution involves extensive country participation (both by governmental agencies and by civil society groups) in the design and implementation of funded projects and programs.[66]

There are serious problems and pitfalls with the MCA proposal: the potential for a bureaucratic turf war between the proposed autonomous Millennium Challenge Corporation and the existing U.S. Agency for International Development (USAID), the potential for the selection criteria to be politicized and manipulated to reward political clients of the United States, the envisioned expansion of the program by 2006 to middle-income countries (weakening the focus on the poor), and the possibility that the poorest countries could be disqualified by a rigid and formulaic application of the policy criteria. This is why some sympathetic observers have recommended that the MCA be administered by a multilateral institution like the World Bank or the African Development Bank that would be less likely to skew country selection with nondevelopmental (geopolitical) considerations.[67] One can also question the very limited emphasis on good (accountable, honest, democratic) governance, which is only one of three criteria, and which only requires countries to be above the median (for all eligible countries) on half of the six indicators (including control of corruption).[68] Still, these defects are correctable, and if the MCA is administered objectively and intelligently, it could represent precisely the shift toward selectivity that would begin to foster and reward better governance in Africa (and elsewhere around the world). "With clear criteria and substantial sums of money with enticing terms, the MCA could create incentives for governments to improve economic policies and governance, while helping strong performers sustain growth and improve investment climates."[69]

Even if the MCA fulfills its lofty potential and provides a new model for dispensing international development assistance, this will only be a start. A deeper and more thoroughgoing reform of aid will be needed, not only rewarding good performers but also cutting off bad ones and enhancing governance assistance to countries that come near to qualifying and appear ready for reform. Debt relief must be similarly linked to performance. And substantial reform is needed on the part of the industrialized countries in providing Africa market access, beyond just eliminating the most egregious obstacle, agricultural subsidies. An important initiative in this regard is the Africa Growth and Opportunity Act (AGOA), passed by the U.S. Congress in June 2000. In eliminating U.S. duties on textile imports from eligible African countries, AGOA has generated significant inflows of foreign investment and new jobs in the dozen or so African countries that qualified in the first two years, most notably Madagascar. Significantly, AGOA establishes conditions that African countries must meet in order to obtain preferential tariff treatment. These include a market economy, political pluralism and the rule of law, countercorruption efforts, policies to reduce poverty, and protection of human and worker rights. Yet, in December 2002, President Bush certified for eligibility a total of 38 Sub-Saharan African countries, excluding only ten and including such blatantly repressive and corrupt governments as those in Cameroon, Chad, the DRC (former Zaire), Mauritania, and Eritrea. Such certification makes a mockery of the standards and sets a poor precedent for the future. Another problem is that AGOA is set to expire in 2008, which could undermine the nascent progress toward labor-intensive industrialization of the participating African countries.

More recently, in June 2003, a private U.S.-based Commission on Capital Flows to Africa released a report recommending "A Ten-Year Strategy for Increasing Capital Flows to Africa."[70] Its proposals included a 10-year extension of AGOA beyond its expiration date in 2008; the negotiation of a free trade agreement with the Southern African Customs Union, followed by other subregional free trade agreements, and culminating in 10 years in a free trade agreement between the U.S. and all of Africa; a ten-year moratorium on taxation of repatriated earnings from new investments by U.S. companies in Africa; and the publication of "best practices" for African governments seeking to increase foreign direct investment. These are the kind of bold ideas that are needed to jumpstart development in Africa, but boldness and generosity must be matched by tough standards, which are lacking in the proposal. Like increased aid and debt relief, the benefits of truly free trade should be reserved for those countries that demonstrate a serious commitment to free, open, and accountable governance.

We are at a formative moment in the long, sad relationship between Africa and the West. More African countries are governed democratically today than ever before. If most are still not governed well, public pressures and international expectations are at least moving in the right direction. Today there is a chance—a real chance—to generate an entirely new set of incentives for political actors in Africa, to govern constitutionally, responsibly, and effectively. Today, there is a real chance to win the kinds of institutional reforms that will truly empower parliaments, courts, and civil societies, control corruption, and strengthen states. But all of this depends on leaders mustering the political will to embrace and permit enormously difficult governance reforms. That will not happen through an indiscriminate flow of new benefits to African states, good and bad. Generosity and compassion, in the absence of clear standards, will do Africa little good.

African civil societies and governments must join with one another and with the international community to monitor and enforce their governance obligations under NEPAD—and, for that matter, the Universal Declaration of Human Rights. Only if governance is really transformed will Africa emerge from its needlessly protracted rut of poverty, conflict, and despair.

Notes

This chapter benefited from the research assistance of Benn Eifert and the very helpful comments of E. Gyimah-Boadi and Nicolas van de Walle.

1 Originally published as "Promoting Real Reform in Africa," in *Democratic Reform in Africa: The Quality of Progress*, E. Gyimah-Boadi, ed. (Boulder, CO: Lynne Rienner Publishers, 2004), 263–292.
2 This figure and Table 14.1 have been updated for the purposes of this publication.
3 The UNDP's Human Development Index, which ranges from a low of 0 to a high of 1, measures overall levels of human development in a country relative to other countries in the world, using three indicators: life expectancy at birth, knowledge (with adult literacy weighted two-thirds and the combined school enrollment ratios one-third), and gross domestic product per capita in purchasing power parity dollars. See United Nations Development Programme, *Human Development Report: Millennium Development Goals: A Compact Among Nations to End Human Poverty* (New York: Oxford University Press, 2003), 341.
4 Ibid., table 3, 47; African Development Bank, *African Development Report 2003: Globalization and African Development* (Oxford: Oxford University Press, 2003), 255.
5 Temporarily, Eastern Europe and Central Asia had higher average per capita foreign aid receipts in 2000 than Africa ($23 vs. $20). But since independence, Africa has received much more per capita than any other region.
6 Nicolas Van de Walle, *African Economies and the Politics of Permanent Crisis 1979– 99* (New York: Cambridge University Press, 2001), 220. In some countries, aid "reached staggering levels—for five African states, aid represented at least one-fifth of gross national product (GNP) at some point in the 1990s, and in one year it stood at 42 percent in Mozambique," according to David Leonard and Scott Straus, *Africa's Stalled Development: International Causes and Cures* (Boulder, CO: Lynne Rienner, 2003), 13.
7 Leonard and Straus, *Africa's Stalled Development*, 26, table 2.1.
8 See the relevant data in tables 1 and 4 of the appendix of the *World Development Report 2002: Building Institutions for Markets* (New York: Oxford University Press, 2002), 233 and 239. Africa's ratio of 166 percent compared to 132 percent for South Asia, 41 percent for Eastern Europe, 7 percent for Latin America, and 365 percent for the Middle East and North Africa.
9 Leonard and Straus, *Africa's Stalled Development*, 28.
10 Van de Walle, *African Economies*, 222.
11 William Easterly, *The Elusive Quest for Growth: Economic Adventures and Misadventures in the Tropics* (Cambridge, MA: MIT Press, 2001), 22–44.

12 Terry Lyn Karl, *The Paradox of Plenty: Oil Booms and Petro-States* (Berkeley: University of California Press, 1997); Leonard and Straus, *Africa's Stalled Development.*

13 See tables 1.1 and 1.2 in E. Gyimah-Boadi, "Africa: The Quality of Political Reform," in E. Gyimah-Boadi, ed., *Democratic Reform in Africa: The Quality of Progress* (Boulder, CO: Lynne Rienner Publishers, 2004), 16–17. This argument was later (after the initial publication of this article) established with more systematic and convincing empirical evidence by Steven Radelet, *Emerging Africa: How 17 Countries are Leading the Way* (Washington, DC: Center for Global Development, 2010).

14 Gyimah-Boadi, "Africa: The Quality of Political Reform," 18–19.

15 Richard Roll and John R. Talbott, "Political Freedom, Economic Liberty, and Prosperity," *Journal of Democracy* 14 (July 2003): 79.

16 Ibid., 82.

17 Bruce Bueno de Mesquita, James D. Morrow, Randolf Siverson and Alistair Smith, "Political Competition and Economic Growth" *Journal of Democracy* 12 (January 2001), 65.

18 Benn Eifert, "Political Equality and the Performance of African Economies 1972–99" (Senior honors thesis, Department of Economics, Stanford University, 2003), 2. The relationship was tested for African countries during the period 1972–1999.

19 Thomas Zweifel and Patricio Navia, "Democracy, Dictatorship and Infant Mortality," *Journal of Democracy* 11 (April 2000): 99–114; Patricio Navia and Thomas Zweifel, "Democracy Dictatorship and Infant Mortality Revisited," *Journal of Democracy* 14 (July 2003): 90–103.

20 Daniel Kaufmann, Aart Kraay, and Pablo Zoido-Lobaton, "Governance Matters" Policy Research Working Paper no. 2196 (World Bank, October 1999), 15. Each of their six governance dimensions has a large and significant positive effect on per capita incomes and a large, significant negative effect on infant mortality. For example, "a one standard deviation improvement in governance leads to between a 2.5-fold (in the case of voice and accountability) and a 4-fold (in the case of political stability and violence) increase in per capita income" (ibid.).

21 Transparency International, *Global Corruption Report 2003* (London: Profile Books, 2003), 264–265.

22 Amartya Sen, *Development as Freedom* (New York: Alfred A. Knopf, 1999); Adam Przeworski, Michael E. Alvarez, Jose Antonio Cheibub, and Fernando Limongi, *Democracy and Development: Political Institutions and Well-Being in the World, 1950– 90* (Cambridge: Cambridge University Press, 2000), ch. 3.

23 Easterly, *The Elusive Quest for Growth,* 217.

24 Ibid.

25 Ibid., 237.

26 Ibid.

27 Nicolas van de Walle, "Economic Reform: Patterns and Constraints," in Gyimah-Boadi, *Democratic Reform in Africa,* 29–64.

28 Ibid. For further documentation and analysis of these trends, see also Van de Walle, *African Economies.*

29 Sahr Kpundeh, "Corruption and Corruption Control," in Gyimah-Boadi, *Democratic Reform in Africa,* 121–140.

30 Easterly, *The Elusive Quest for Growth,* 241.

31 African Development Bank, *African Development Report 2003: Globalization and African Development* (Oxford: Oxford University Press, 2003), 42.

32 Van de Walle, "Economic Reform," 44.

33 The recognition that state power in Africa has been the basis for class formation and personal wealth accumulation, thereby destabilizing and distorting politics

and governance, is one of the most widely established in the literature on post-colonial African politics. See for example Richard Sklar, *Nigerian Political Parties: Power in an Emergent African Nation* (Princeton, NJ: Princeton University Press, 1963) and Sklar, "Nigerian Politics in Perspective" *Government and Opposition* 5 (May 1967): 1–11. See also Larry Diamond *Class, Ethnicity, and Democracy in Nigeria: The Failure of the First Republic* (London: Macmillan, 1988) and more recently on neopatrimonialism, Michael Bratton and Nicholas van de Walle, *Democratic Experiments in Africa: Regime Transitions in Comparative Perspective* (New York: Cambridge University Press, 1997).

34 Richard Joseph, *Democracy and Prebendal Politics in Nigeria: The Rise and Fall of the Second Republic* (Cambridge: Cambridge University Press, 1987).

35 Samuel P. Huntington, *Political Order in Changing Societies* (New Haven, CT: Yale University Press, 1968), 12–24.

36 Stephen John Stedman and Terrence Lyons, "Conflict in Africa," in Gyimah-Boadi, *Democratic Reform in Africa*, 141–158.

37 African Development Bank, *African Development Report 2003*, 38.

38 Ibid., 39.

39 This is suggested by the rankings on the Corruption Perceptions Index published by Transparency International, although it is an imprecise and only very suggestive instrument based on a number of subjective surveys.

40 Leonard and Straus, *Africa's Stalled Development*, 13.

41 Ibid., 17. For a similar style of argument, showing how political systems with narrow winning coalitions (like those that prevail generally in autocratic and closed regimes) generate incentives for the provision of private, not public, goods, see Bueno de Mesquita et al., "Political Competition and Economic Growth."

42 Michael Bratton and Robert Mattes, "What 'The People' Say About Reforms," in Gyimah-Doadi, ed., *Democratic Reform in Africa*.

43 E. Gyimah-Boadi, "Civil Society and Democratic Development," in Gyimah-Boadi, *Democratic Reform in Africa*, 99–120.

44 Andreas Schedler, "Conceptualizing Accountability" in Andreas Schedler, Larry Diamond and Marc F. Plattner, eds, *The Self-Restraining State: Power and Accountability in New Democracies* (Boulder, CO: Lynne Rienner, 1999); Larry Diamond, "Building a System of Comprehensive Accountability to Control Corruption" in *Nigeria's Struggle for Democracy and Good Governance: A Festschrift for Oyeleye Oyediran*, ed. with Adigun A. B. Agbaje and Ebere Onwuiwe (Ibadan: Ibadan University Press, 2004).

45 African Development Bank, *African Development Report 2003*, 249.

46 Ibid., 251.

47 Progress Report of H.E. Olusegun Obasanjo, President of Nigeria and Chairperson of the NEPAD Heads of State and Government Implementation Committee, to the Second Ordinary Session of the Assembly of the Heads of State and Government of the African Union, Mozambique, July 10–12, 2003, accessed at www.avmedia.at/cgiscript/csNews/news_upload/NEPAD_2dCORE_2dDOCUMENTS_2edb.ProgressReportof.pdf.

48 See the "Declaration Africa's Development Challenges" of the CODESRI-Third World Network/Africa Conference in Accra, April 23–26, 2002, www.radi-afrique.org/nepad/docs/codesria.pdf.

49 African Development Bank, *African Development Report 2003*, 255. For a selection of early civil society critiques, see www.web.net/~iccaf/debtsap/nepad.htm#ngo.

50 African Development Bank, *African Development Report 2003*, 224 identifies an excellent set of good governance criteria, including government transparency, simplicity of procedures, seriously fighting corruption, holding offending officials responsible, individual and press freedom, independence of the legal system, competitive procurement, and efficiency in public service delivery.

51 The latter phrase was suggested to me by Nicolas van de Walle (private communication).

52 Derick W. Brinkerhoff, "Identifying and Assessing Political Will for Anti-Corruption Efforts," Working paper no. 13, Implementing Policy Change Project, USAID, January 1999, 3. See also Brinkerhoff, "Assessing Political Will for Anti-Corruption Efforts: An Analytic Framework," *Public Administration and Development* 20 (2000): 242.

53 Brinkerhoff, "Identifying and Assessing Political Will for Anti-Corruption Efforts," 3.

54 Brinkerhoff, "Assessing Political Will for Anti-Corruption Efforts," 249.

55 Paul Collier, "Learning from Failure: The International Finance Institutions as Agencies of Restraint in Africa" in Andreas Schedler, Larry Diamond and Marc F. Plattner, eds. *The Self Restraining State: Power and Accountability in New Democracies* (Boulder, CO: Lynne Rienner, 1999), 322.

56 Collier also calls this conditionality "as an agency of restraint" (ibid., 327).

57 I have previously proposed these as principles to guide U.S. foreign aid. Most of these recommendations appear (in slightly different form) in chapter 1 of *Foreign Aid in the National Interest* (Washington, DC: USAID 2002), and some of the above analysis is also reproduced from my chapter in that report.

58 Brinkerhoff, "Assessing Political Will for Anti-Corruption Efforts," 249.

59 See http://news.bbc.co.uk/2/hi/business/3099596.stm.

60 Global trade negotiations broke down acrimoniously in Cancún, Mexico, in September 2003. Developing country delegates charged that the rich countries were unwilling to reduce their agricultural subsidies, while the rich countries said the poor were unwilling to allow greater access to foreign investors and other improvements in market access.

61 Leonard and Straus, *Africa's Stalled Development,* 31–35.

62 Ibid., 128, note 40.

63 USAID is also hampered by extremely ponderous personnel and procurement regulations and a host of Congressional stipulations "earmarking" funding for very specific purposes. Steven Radelet proposes that this "morass" of rules and regulations be eliminated wholesale and that the legal and administrative architecture of U.S. foreign assistance be completely redesigned in his article "Bush and Foreign Aid," *Foreign Affairs* 82 (2003): 104–117.

64 This model has been proposed by Goran Hyden in "Aid and Developmentalism in Southern Africa" in Steven W. Hook, ed., *Foreign Aid Towards the Millennium* (Boulder, CO: Lynne Rienner, 1996), 202–204.

65 Steven Radelet, "The Millennium Challenge Account: Testimony for the House International Relations Committee," March 6, 2003, 1. Unfortunately, pressures on the U.S. federal budget, as a result of recession, tax cuts, and the war in Iraq, make it unlikely that the $5 billion increase will be realized within the three-year time frame originally envisioned, and at this writing it is not clear what, if any, funding the U.S. Congress will allocate for the 2004 fiscal year, when the program was to have been initiated.

66 Ibid., 2.

67 Nicholas Van de Walle, "A Comment on the MCA Proposal," Center for Global Development, January 9, 2003. Available online at www.cgdev.org/briefs/van-dewalle_20030109.pdf.

68 In fact, the very standard of simply being "above the median" can be quite weak, given that most low-income countries are very corrupt and poorly governed. Eventually, it could also become quite perverse, if a large number of countries are motivated to dramatically improve their governance and development policies. A better approach would be to require certain absolute institutional conditions, such as judicial independence and an autonomous corruption

control apparatus of some kind, verified by an international commission of neutral experts. Moreover, as Radelet notes in "The Millennium Challenge Account," the statistical data on levels of corruption are too unreliable to serve as a decisive criterion. I also believe that no country that badly abuses human rights and press freedom should qualify, and this requires more than one measure in order to enhance the reliability and legitimacy of a potentially fateful judgment.

69 Lael Brainard, Carol Graham, Nigel Purvis, Steven Radelet and Gayle E. Smith, *The Other Ward: Global Poverty and the Millennium Challenge Account* (Washington, DC: Brookings Institution, 2003), 4.

70 See www.uneca.org/eca_resources/Press_Releases/2003_pressreleases/Media Advisory0403.htm.

15 Petroleum to the people

Africa's coming resource curse— and how to avoid it[1]

With Jack Mosbacher

In October 2011, the United States Department of Justice filed a motion to seize a cliff-top home in Malibu, California. The 16-acre property towers over its neighbors, with a palm-lined driveway leading to a plaster-and-tile mansion overlooking the Pacific Ocean. Situated in the heart of one of America's most expensive neighborhoods, this $30 million estate includes a swimming pool, a tennis court, and a four-hole golf course. In its complaint, the Justice Department also set its sights on high-performance speedboats worth $2 million, over two dozen exotic cars (including a $2 million Maserati and eight Ferraris), and $3.2 million in Michael Jackson memorabilia—in total, assets equaling approximately $71 million.[2] What made these extravagant possessions all the more remarkable was that they belonged to a government worker from a small African country who was making an official salary of about $80,000 a year: Teodoro Nguema Obiang Mangue, the oldest son of and heir apparent to Teodoro Obiang Nguema Mbasogo, the long-time president of Equatorial Guinea.

Home to over one billion barrels of oil reserves, Equatorial Guinea has exported as many as 400,000 barrels of oil a day since 1995, a bonanza that has made the country wealthier, in terms of GDP per capita, than France, Japan, and the United Kingdom. Little of this wealth, however, has helped the vast majority of Equatorial Guinea's 700,000 people: today, three out of every four Equatoguineans live on less than $2 a day, and infant mortality rates have actually increased slightly since oil was first discovered there. The president's family members and other elites connected to the Obiang regime, meanwhile, have prospered.

As a result, Equatorial Guinea has become a textbook example of the so-called resource curse, a global phenomenon in which vast natural resource wealth leads to rapacious corruption, decimated governance, and chronic underdevelopment. Worse still, for the last three decades the Obiang family was able to trade and travel freely around the world, until the Justice Department finally raided the younger Obiang's home on the charge that he had used his position and influence to acquire illicit wealth. The United States' recent crackdown is laudable, but the family's ability to travel and conduct business in the United States and around the world for so long highlights the gaps in the architecture of international accountability and justice. Equatorial Guinea's story yields many foreboding lessons, but none more obvious than this: oil-rich developing countries that want to avoid the resource curse cannot wait for the international system to fight corruption for them.

Equatorial Guinea's example will become increasingly relevant over the next decade as a massive wave of new oil and gas discoveries transforms Africa's economic and political landscape. Over the next ten years, new technologies will allow oil producers to extract billions of barrels of exportable oil from the East African Rift Valley and offshore in West Africa's Gulf of Guinea. If current estimates are even close to accurate, trillions of dollars in oil revenue will ultimately descend on a dozen African countries that have never before experienced such influxes. In East Africa, that list will likely include Ethiopia, Kenya, Uganda, Tanzania, Malawi, and Mauritius; in West Africa, it will probably include Gambia, Ghana, Liberia, São Tomé and Principe, Senegal, and Sierra Leone. (Niger is another possibility, but we do not include it in our calculations here.) And this windfall would come on top of the enormous oil revenues that still-poor Sub-Saharan African countries such as Nigeria, Angola, Sudan, Gabon, and Chad have been earning for decades, as well as the new oil revenues that Ghana is beginning to accrue. All told, within a decade a third or more of African countries may derive the majority of their export earnings from oil and gas.

Oil booms poison the prospects for development in poor countries. The surge of easy money fuels inflation, fans waste and massive corruption, distorts exchange rates, undermines the competitiveness of traditional export sectors like agriculture, and preempts the growth of manufacturing. Moreover, as oil prices fluctuate on world markets, oil-rich countries can suddenly become cash-poor when booms go bust (since poor countries rarely save any of these revenue bonanzas). Oil booms are also bad news for democracy and the rule of law. In fact, not a single developing country that derives the bulk of its export earnings from oil and gas is a democracy. Rather than fostering an entrepreneurial middle class, oil wealth, when controlled by the government, stifles the emergence of an independent business class and swells the power of the state vis-à-vis civil society.[3]

In Africa, then, where one-party dominance or outright authoritarian rule prevails, as in Ethiopia, Uganda, Tanzania, and Gambia, oil wealth will further entrench it. And where democracy is struggling to sink roots— as in Senegal, Liberia, Sierra Leone, Kenya, and Malawi—it could easily overwhelm weak state institutions. Even Ghana, the most liberal and stable democracy in West Africa, could fall victim to the problem of oil revenues. The country now exports fewer than 100,000 barrels a day, but that figure is estimated to soar to as much as half a million barrels a day by 2015.

If used wisely, this influx of capital has the potential to fund path-breaking improvements in physical infrastructure and human well-being. But if state officials, enabled by the absence of meaningful institutions of transparency and accountability, manage to divert the oil revenues for themselves, then the new wealth will serve only to further consolidate the power and inflate the personal fortunes of the ruling elites. There is no reason to expect that newly rich oil producers in Africa will meet a fate much different from that of Nigeria, Angola, Sudan, and Equatorial Guinea, all of which rank in the bottom fifth of all countries in terms of bribery and corruption.

Unless, that is, African governments embrace a radical policy approach: handing a large share of the new revenues directly to the people as taxable income. The influx of funds from new oil discoveries will be so large that if it is properly managed, it could catapult developing countries into genuine economic and social development. By taking control of revenues out of the hands of the political elite and restoring the link between citizens and their public officials, this oil-to-cash strategy offers the best hope for tomorrow's oil-rich African nations to avoid the resource curse that has befallen so many of yesterday's.

The cause of the curse

For a long time, those who studied economic development assumed that valuable natural resources were a blessing—that, as scholar Norton Ginsburg wrote in 1957, "the possession of a sizable and diversified natural resource endowment is a major advantage to any country embarking upon a period of rapid economic growth."[4] Since the 1980s, however, experts have come to the consensus that the opposite is true. In fact, the economies of resource-rich countries have performed far worse than their resource-poor neighbors, and increases in natural resource wealth are strongly correlated with greater corruption, authoritarianism, political and economic instability, and civil war.[5]

The root cause of the curse is the divergent effect that resource wealth has on the incentives of citizens and public officials. When unearned income—or "rents," as economists say—replaces taxes as the main source of government funding, the social contract between a population and its government is severed. In well-functioning states (especially democracies), citizens consent to be taxed in exchange for public services and protection. Since the government relies on tax revenues for its very existence, taxation becomes the binding force of accountability between public officials and their constituents: public servants are incentivized to meet the public's expectations, because the population at large is the most direct and important stakeholder in the government's functions. As direct investors, citizens also have a powerful interest in seeing that their taxes are used properly and efficiently.

It follows that the introduction of nontax revenue—from foreign aid or the sale of valuable natural resources, for example—reduces a government's reliance on revenue from its people and thus weakens the incentive to serve them. In the absence of the bonds of scrutiny and accountability that taxation forges, the external rents that fall into state coffers are not seen as belonging to the people, but are up for grabs by the luckiest, the best connected, or the most brazen. Corruption, patronage, and rent-seeking flourish. Elites grow rich; everyone else grows dependent, cynical, and detached.

The result is that oil states do not generate public goods for development but private and political goods instead. When state revenue seems to just gush up from the ground as free money, and when resource rents displace taxation as the main source of government revenue, political elites have incentives to focus on the private accumulation of wealth and limit distribution of it to their political support networks. They have little reason to use this public treasure to deliver roads, schools, boreholes, fertilizers, clinics, medicines, and so on. Meanwhile, the people have incentives to plead and compete for whatever crumbs may fall from the political table.

These political dynamics already tend to impede progress in all low-income countries. They become insurmountable traps in ones where state revenue is largely derived from external rents, especially a massive flow of oil revenue. Yet that is exactly what many African countries will likely soon experience.

Africa's coming oil bonanza

In the next decade, thanks to innovations in exploration and extraction technology, oil producers will be able to profitably tap areas in Africa where reserves have long been suspected to lie. Thirteen African nations are likely to become new high-level oil exporters. Although estimates of oil reserves and exporting capacity are notoriously volatile, it is possible that more than 25 billion barrels of oil will become available for export in Africa over the next decade—enough to increase export earnings many times over in some countries and revolutionize the social well-being of over one billion Africans.

These new sources of oil are highly concentrated in two geographic areas: to the west, offshore in the Atlantic Ocean and the Gulf of Guinea, and to the east, in the Rift Valley running through much of East Africa. Oil is not new to the Gulf of Guinea.[6] With major long-term exporters such as Nigeria and Equatorial Guinea, the area has been exporting as much as three million barrels of oil a day for over five decades. A period of unprecedented regional stability, however, has allowed for a new wave of investment in the exploration and production of previously untapped deepwater oil sources. In the past five years, commercial-quality oil sources have been found in or off the coast of Senegal, the Gambia, Sierra Leone, Liberia, Ghana, and São Tomé and Principe. Although the estimates of recoverable oil reserves vary greatly by country (four billion barrels in São Tomé and Principe, two billion in Ghana, 1.5 billion in Senegal and Liberia, and one billion in the Gambia), and while these estimates vary in their certainty, what is clear is that each country has enough exportable oil to transform its politics and economy.

In East Africa, tectonic plates have been splitting apart for millennia, creating a massive rift that runs for roughly 3,500 kilometers long and up to 150 kilometers wide. As the plates have diverged, deep-seated plumes of magma have expelled oil into reservoir sands. Recent technological advances, such as extended reach drilling and new long-distance imaging technology, have made extraction of oil from these sands more economically efficient for oil companies. Meanwhile, relative regional stability over the past decade has taken much of the financial risk out of long-term investment. As in West Africa, the estimates of reserves vary. But the best estimates available suggest that roughly nine billion new barrels of recoverable oil and gas could be found in the Rift Valley within the next decade: 3.5 billion barrels in Uganda, up to three billion in Kenya and Tanzania, and at least half a billion in Ethiopia.

At current prices, the new sources of oil and gas could inject close to $3 trillion into the economies of some of Africa's poorest and least developed nations.[7] Consider this: the total annual GDP of the 13 future exporters in 2011 was $163 billion. If $3 trillion flows to these countries from oil over a period of 30–50 years, then the total annual increase in economic output would amount to $60 to $100 billion—an increase of over one-third (and much more if oil prices rise).

These future African oil exporters already rely heavily on another rent in the developing world: international assistance. Each of these governments already derives at least a quarter of operating revenues from foreign aid; several of them, including Uganda, Sierra Leone, Malawi, Liberia, and Ethiopia, derive over half of their income from it. Given current rates of economic growth, it is possible that every future African oil state (with the possible exception of Ghana) will derive more than half of its total revenue from some form of nontax income, whether it be oil or foreign aid. Historically, aid has generally come without conditions, although that has changed somewhat in the last decade or two. For African elites who want to use state revenue as they wish, the beauty of new oil revenues is that they come with no conditions at all.

For every dollar that the 13 governments in Table 15.1 currently receive from the taxation of their citizens, an additional $1.40 is received from foreign aid rents. With the infusion of oil and gas into their economies, these countries are projected to receive an estimated average of $11.30 in external rents for every $1 earned from taxes.[8] If we control for the distortion of huge per capita revenues in tiny countries (Gambia and São Tomé and Principe), *the ratio of external rents to domestic taxation is still expected to nearly triple*, from a median ratio of roughly one-to-one to three-to-one. Put differently, this will mean that the median new oil producer will be nearly as dependent on oil and aid as the continent's most famous victims of the resource curse, Angola, Nigeria, and Chad.

External rents are likely to begin to ravage a state's incentive structure when they significantly outstrip taxation—say, by a factor of two or more.

Table 15.1 Ratio of foreign aid and oil to tax revenue in Africa's future oil exporters

Future oil exporter	Current ratio of foreign aid to taxes	Ratio of projected oil to taxes	Ratio of rents (aid + projected oil) to taxes
Ethiopia	1.7:1	0.8:1	2.8:1
Gambia	1.2:1	17.8:1	19.1:1
Ghana	0.2:1	0.3:1	0.6:1
Kenya	0.2:1	0.8:1	0.8:1
Liberia	6.1:1	7.2:1	13.3:1
Malawi	2.1:1	4.8:1	6.9:1
Mauritius	0.07:1	0.9:1	0.9:1
Niger	1.2:1	1.8:1	3.1:1
São Tomé and Principe	0.7:1	79.0:1	79.7:1
Senegal	0.3:1	0.6:1	0.9:1
Sierra Leone	2.0:1	7.3:1	9.3:1
Tanzania	1.1:1	1.3:1	2.2:1
Uganda	2.8:1	5.2:1	7.5:1
Average	1.4:1	9.8:1	11.3:1
Median	1.2:1	1.8:1	3.1:1

Table 15.2 Ratio of foreign aid and oil to tax revenue in Africa's current oil exporters

Current oil exporter	Ratio of foreign aid to taxes	Ratio of oil to taxes	Ratio of rents (aid + oil) to taxes
Angola	0.02:1	4.0:1	4.0:1
Cameroon	0.2:1	0.3:1	0.5:1
Chad	0.8:1	3.4:1	4.2:1
Congo, Dem. Rep. of	2:1	2.7:1	4.1:1
Congo, Republic of	1.1:1	4.0:1	5.1:1
Côte d'Ivoire	0.4:1	0.1:1	0.5:1
Equatorial Guinea	0.05:1	3.7:1	3.7:1
Gabon	0.3:1	7.8:1	7.8:1
Nigeria	0.3:1	4:1	4.3:1
South Africa	0.01:1	0.01:1	0.02:1
Sudan and South Sudan	0.8:1	1:1	1.8:1
Average	0.8:1	2.7:1	3.46:1
Median	0.4:1	2.7:1	4.0:1

That is already the case in some heavily aid-dependent countries, such as Uganda, Liberia, Sierra Leone, and Malawi. With the expected surge in oil income, these countries will see their revenue structures distorted to degrees even beyond Nigeria, Angola, and Chad. Even countries with more balanced revenue structures, such as Ethiopia and Tanzania, will experience major swings, with their ratios of rents to taxes likely soaring above the two-to-one ratio.

Although several countries in Africa have made great strides in improving governance over the past decade, no continent has more obviously displayed the sad drama of the resource curse: Africa's oil-rich states have become strikingly more corrupt than their resource-poor neighbors. According to the Worldwide Governance Indicators compiled annually by the World Bank, Africa's current oil exporters rank in the bottom global quintile in their relative ability to control corruption, formulate and implement effective policies, regulate private sector development, and enforce the rule of law. Conversely, Africa's future exporters currently well outpace the regional average in these percentile rankings. Unless a new approach is tried, oil will drag the future exporters down to the miserable governance levels of the current ones.

To date, no African country has been able to keep oil money from being largely usurped and misused by the powerful. Every one of the 12 major African oil exporters currently falls into the bottom half of the UN Human Development Index (Table 15.3). According to the World Bank, more than a tenth of all children born into oil-rich African countries die before the age of 5, double the average of other developing regions. If Africa is the worst governed continent in the world, its oil states are the worst of the worst.

Oil to cash

At the heart of the resource curse lie weak institutions that fail to prevent public officials from exercising discretion over the revenue from oil and other external rents. Experts have traditionally recommended solving that problem by focusing on instilling transparency and accountability. If only

Table 15.3 Percentile scores on World Bank governance measures

Category	Current exporters	Future exporters	African average
Control of corruption	14	36	32
Government effectiveness	13	36	27
Regulatory quality	19	41	30
Rule of law	15	37	29

Source: World Bank – World Governance Indicators

the people knew how much oil revenue their government was receiving and how the money was spent, the thinking went, they could hold their leaders accountable at the ballot box. And so the International Monetary Fund and the World Bank began making increasing the transparency of resource revenue a condition for multilateral aid. Global initiatives such as Publish What You Pay, which advocates for fiscal transparency by having governments declare all money received for the rights to natural resources, and the Extractive Industries Transparency Initiative, a standard that creates a public–private partnership for transparency and accountability in resource-rich nations, have brought external pressure to bear on governments receiving income from natural resources.

These transparency initiatives are vital to promoting good governance in resource-rich developing countries, and they should be extended to the new oil producers. But transparency initiatives alone are not nearly adequate to the task. Resource flows are complex, with countless steps in the process from the time oil is discovered, then extracted from the ground, sold on the international market, transferred as revenue to government accounts, and then spent by officials. Efforts to expose how revenues are accrued and dispersed have not worked as well as expected because, as the scholar Todd Moss has written, they "only shed light on one link in the long chain from oil in the ground to development outcomes."[9] Although transparency is an integral piece of any country's pursuit of effective and honest governance, transparency alone fails to reverse the underlying incentives afflicting oil-rich countries.

Given that reality, it is time to try a new policy approach, one that could drastically alter these incentives: the direct distribution of a portion of oil revenues directly to citizens as taxable income. In practical terms, this scheme would work as follows. When a government received revenue from oil and gas exports, a certain predetermined proportion of it (ideally, at least 50 percent) would immediately be distributed directly into the bank accounts of the country's citizens. Then, the government would treat those distributed revenues as income and tax some of it back. Each country can adjust the rate of taxation to effect the transfer of only that amount of cash that professional economic analysis determines can be absorbed by the average poor family without fueling inflation or distorting incentives.

The "oil to cash" approach has been engineered by a team of scholars at the Center for Global Development (including Todd Moss, Nancy Birdsall, Arvind Subramania, Alan Gelb, and Alexandra Gillies), who contend that it attacks the fundamental causes of the resource curse. The direct distribution of oil revenues as taxable income would create a broad and active constituency of citizens who were directly affected by the government's management of their resources, in place of the often passive populations of corrupt, resource-cursed states. In a single step, it would build a broad domestic tax base—a fundamental piece of any modern, well-governed state. Moreover, immediately taxing back the income through explicit

deductions from the transfers would make citizens aware of the fiscal relationship, strengthening ties of accountability between officials who control
the state and the people whose money they are spending. Citizens would
come to realize that it is indeed their money that the state is spending.[10]

To many, the concept of direct cash transfers of oil dollars seems like a
well-intentioned but utterly infeasible option. For starters, one might ask,
how can countries that lack a modern banking sector or even a national
identification system be expected to implement a cash transfer program?
The answer is that many already have. Moss has estimated that as of 2009,
some 60 developing countries, including Botswana, Brazil, India, Mexico,
and Panama, have made regular direct transfer payments to approximately
170 million people. That success owes to recent advancements in affordable
and reliable personal identification technologies, using biometric identifiers
such as fingerprints and facial and retinal recognition. Gelb estimates that
as many as 450 million people in developing countries have had their biometric data catalogued. Although governments will need to invest in systems
that allow them to properly and transparently transfer money into citizens'
accounts, technology in the area of electronic banking is making this process continuously cheaper and logistically feasible.[11] Africa has experienced
an explosive growth in mobile phone subscriptions, estimated at now over
800 million, which, even allowing for multiple subscriptions, means the
majority of Africans now have access to mobile phones. Moreover, mobile
banking platforms, such as Kenya's M-Pesa, are proliferating.[12]

The greatest obstacle to oil-to-cash programs, of course, is political. Why,
many wonder, would any politician ever willingly give up control of oil
money? Indeed, in developing countries, control over natural resource revenues fuels the patrimonial ties and patronage networks that keep leaders
in power. And it is true that an autocrat is very unlikely to give up this vast
opportunity to accumulate wealth and perpetuate his rule.

But nine of the 13 future oil exporters are democracies, and therein lies
the hope for these revenue-distribution systems. In these countries, competitive elections with uncertain outcomes determine who rules. In some of
these countries, democracy may well expire in the fever of sudden riches.
But in others, a broad coalition of forces in civil society and politics could
compel rulers to implement some kind of oil-to-cash model, or else vote
into office an opposition party that has pledged to do so. It is hard to imagine a more compelling opposition platform than the distribution of at least
some share of natural resource revenues directly to the long-impoverished
people who are the real legitimate owners of the country and its resources.
Public opinion survey data from the African Barometer show that Africans
are more aware of their rights and more demanding of democracy than
social science theories traditionally assumed about the poor in developing
countries. Moreover, African civil societies are becoming better organized
and more assertive, and with the growth of new technologies of communication (including community FM radio stations) a more vigorous public

sphere is emerging. Once African publics understand the possibilities of oil to cash, they may seize upon it with a vengeance. At that point, it will not be easy for elected leaders to insist that the state monopolize these revenue bonanzas—unless they rig elections and repress protests. Desecrating democracy to corner this wealth may be a tempting strategy, but it is one with huge risks, including being toppled from power and punished. Some democratically elected leaders could opt instead to become public (and international) heroes by embracing reform.

The prospects for preempting the oil curse are unfortunately much worse in Africa's authoritarian states, for they lack the mechanisms of political competition and the scope for civic voice and pressure that could induce reform. But despite the dangers of challenging autocrats, public demands for reform may rise as corruption and misrule deepen. Such a scenario is not unthinkable, for example, in Uganda, where, after nearly three decades of Yoweri Museveni's presidency, the signs of governance rot are proliferating. It is also possible to imagine an autocratic leader (even conceivably Museveni) embracing at least a limited oil-to-cash reform to burnish his sagging legitimacy. After all, if presidents and ruling parties give some of the new bonanza back to the people, that still leaves quite a lot of state revenue for them to manage. Yet even a partial reform would begin to change the relationship between citizens and the state and create a new incentive for the public to monitor their rulers' handling of the oil wealth.

A radical approach

Nobody knows exactly how much oil will be pulled from the ground of Africa's new oil exporters over the next decade. Current projections made by governments and oil exploration companies might be overly optimistic, or perhaps the current period of relative political stability in Africa will end, scaring off investment in oil infrastructure.

Regardless, oil will shape Africa's future more than ever before. Some groups and individuals will find themselves much wealthier in the next decade. The choice Africa's governments and people have to make is whether the winners will be, as before, well-connected elites, or whether the pattern can be broken and a new premise can be embraced: that a country's natural resources belong not to the state but to the people.

Admittedly, oil-to-cash is an unwieldy and largely untested initiative. But in an area where every conventional approach has failed, only a radical departure is likely to succeed. The biggest mistake Africa's new oil producers can make, a mistake that several are already making, is to assume that their country is different: that through good leadership, better statecraft, or incremental improvements in their legal systems, they can avoid the resource curse. The stakes are simply too high for anything but a radical new approach.

Notes

1 Originally published as Larry Diamond and Jack Mosbacher, "Petroleum to the People: Africa's Coming Resource Curse, and How to Avoid It," *Foreign Affairs* 92(5) (September/October 2013), 86–98.

2 *Filthy Rich*, CNBC Investigators, broadcast July 2, 2012. See www.cnbc.com/id/47864304/US_Increases_Pressure_on_039Filthy_Rich039_African_Regime.

3 Neena Rai and Jenny Gross, "Ghanaian Oil Surge Could Spell Trouble for Cocoa," *Wall Street Journal*, September 5, 2012, http://online.wsj.com/article/SB10000872396390443686004577633080263468336.html.

4 Norton Ginsburg, as cited in Andrew Rosser, "The Political Economy of the Resource Curse: A Literature Survey," Working Paper 268 for the Institute of Development Studies (2006), 7.

5 R. M. Auty, *Abundance and Economic Development* (Oxford: Oxford University Press, 2001); Thorvaldur Gylfason, "Natural Resources and Economic Growth: What Is the Connection?" CESifo Working Paper No. 530 (August 2001); Michael L. Ross, "Does Oil Hinder Democracy?" *World Politics* 53 (April 2001): 325–361; Paul Collier and Anke Hoeffler, "Greed and Grievance in Civil War," World Bank (November 2000).

6 Ricardo Soares de Oliveira, *Oil and Politics in the Gulf of Guinea* (New York: Columbia University Press, 2007).

7 This will be particularly if oil prices remain over $100 per barrel. In February 2013, the Brent Crude Oil Index listed the price of oil at $113.70 per barrel.

8 We drew these estimates from the most recent and credible existing sources from host countries and oil exploration companies, and we applied a blanket 60:40 take ratio for governments and oil companies.

9 Todd Moss, "Oil to Cash: Fighting the Resource Curse through Cash Transfers," Center for Global Development Working Paper 237, January 2011, p. 2. See www.cgdev.org/files/1424714_file_Oil2Cash_primer_FINAL.pdf.

10 Alexandra Gillies, "Giving Money Away? The Politics of Direct Distribution in Resource-Rich States," CGD Working Paper 231, November 2010. See www.cgdev.org/files/1424574_file_Gillies_The_Politics_of_DD_FINAL.pdf.

11 Alan Gelb and Caroline Decker, "Cash at Your Fingertips: Biometric Technology for Transfers in Resource-Rich Countries," CGD Working Paper 253, June 2011, p. 2. See www.cgdev.org/files/1425165_file_Gelb_Decker_biometric_FINAL.pdf.

12 Natasha Lomas, "ABI: Africa's Mobile Market to Pass 80% Subscriber Penetration in Q1 Next Year." See http://techcrunch.com/2012/11/28/abi-africas-mobile-market-to-pass-80-subscriber-penetration-in-q1-next-year-13-9-of-global-cellular-market-by-2017.

Part III

In search of democracy in Asia

16 The coming wave of East Asian democracy[1]

If there is going to be a big new lift to global democratic prospects in this decade, the region from which it will emanate is most likely to be East Asia. With the eruption of mass movements for democratic change throughout the Arab world in 2011, hopeful analysts of global democratic prospects have focused attention on the Middle East. Three Arab autocracies (Tunisia, Egypt, and Libya) have fallen in 2011. At least two more (Yemen and Syria) also seem destined for demise soon, and pressures for real democratic change figure to mount in Morocco, Jordan, Palestine, and perhaps Kuwait, and to persist in Bahrain. Yet among these and other countries in the Middle East (including Iraq and Iran), only Tunisia has a good chance of becoming a democracy in the relatively near future. Aspirations for more democratic and accountable government run deep throughout the Middle East, and for years to come the region will be a lively and contested terrain of possibilities for regime evolution. But if a new regional wave of transitions to democracy unfolds in the next five to ten years, it is more likely to come from East Asia—a region that has been strangely neglected in recent thinking about the near-term prospects for expansion of democracy. And East Asia is also better positioned to increase the number of liberal and sustainable democracies.

Unlike the Arab world, East Asia already has a critical mass of democracies. Forty percent of East Asian states (seven of the 17) are democracies, a proportion slightly higher than in South Asia or Sub-Saharan Africa, though dramatically lower than in Latin America or Central and Eastern Europe, where most states are democracies. As a result of the third wave of global democratization, East Asia has gone from being the cradle and locus of "developmental authoritarianism," with Japan as its lone democracy— and a long-standing one-party dominant system at that—to at least a mixed and progressing set of systems. Today, Japan, South Korea, and Taiwan are all consolidated liberal democracies. East Timor, Indonesia, Mongolia, and the Philippines are at least electoral democracies with some resilience.

Moreover, as I will explain, there are now significant prospects for democratic change in a number of the region's remaining authoritarian regimes. Thailand is progressing back towards democracy; Malaysia and Singapore show signs of entering a period of democratic transition; Burma, to the surprise of many, is liberalizing politically for the first time in 20 years; and China faces a looming crisis of authoritarianism that will generate a new opportunity for democratic transition in the next two decades (and possibly much sooner). Moreover, all of this has been happening during a five-year period when democracy has been in recession globally.

The democracies of East Asia

There are three democracies in East Asia today that rank among the stable liberal democracies of the industrialized world: Japan, South Korea, and Taiwan. They are not without stiff economic and political challenges and large numbers of disenchanted citizens who in surveys express only tepid support for democracy. Yet in each of these countries, overwhelming majorities of citizens reject authoritarian regime options while voicing reasonably robust support for broadly liberal values such as the rule of law, freedom of expression, and judicial independence.[2] Comparative data on political rights, civil liberties, and the quality of governance confirm that these are liberal democracies, though they could become better, more liberal ones by deepening the rule of law and civil liberties and improving mechanisms of accountability and transparency to control corruption and political favoritism.

East Asia's merely electoral democracies have further to go towards deepening and consolidating democracy, of course. Mongolia scores relatively well in Freedom House ratings of political rights and civil liberties, but in this phenomenally mineral-rich country, the judiciary remains underdeveloped, the rule of law is weak, and corruption remains a grave problem, widely recognized by the public. Indonesia's democratic performance over the past decade has been much better than what many experts on that country might have expected. The Philippines has returned to democracy with the 2010 election, in which Benigno Aquino won the presidency. Yet semifeudal elites retain a strong hold on the politics of many Philippine provinces and constituencies and their presence in the country's Congress has so far largely blocked basic reform. In the World Bank's annual governance ratings, Indonesia and the Philippines rank in the bottom quartile of all countries in corruption control and not much better (the bottom third) in rule of law. In 2010, among big (mainly G20) emerging-market democracies such as Argentina, Bangladesh, Brazil, India, Mexico, South Africa, and Turkey, only Bangladesh did worse on these two governance indicators.[3]

In each of these three electoral democracies—Mongolia, Indonesia, and the Philippines—at least three-quarters of citizens agree that "Democracy may have its problems, but it is still the best form of government." In each, likewise, only about half the public is satisfied with the way democracy is working, but majorities believe that democracy remains capable of solving the country's problems. One possible reason for this faith in democracy is suggested by the wide majorities in each country (up to 76 percent in

Mongolia and 80 percent in the Philippines) who say that they believe the people retain the power to change the government through elections.[4]

Prospects for further democratization

It is by now widely appreciated that Singapore is by any standard a massive anomaly. As we see in Table 16.1, Singapore is far richer today than any major third-wave countries were when they made their transitions to democracy (this includes Spain and Greece, which do not appear in the table). Singapore is the most economically developed nondemocracy in the history of the world. But Singapore is changing, and this change will probably accelerate when the founding generation of leaders, particularly Lee Kuan Yew (who turned 88 in September 2011), passes from the scene. In the May 2011 parliamentary elections, the ruling People's Action Party (PAP) recorded its weakest electoral performance since independence in 1965, winning "only" 60 percent of the vote. Although the PAP still won (yet again) well over 90 percent of parliamentary seats thanks to a highly rigged electoral system, the opposition Workers' Party broke through for the first time to win a five-seat group constituency, and a total of six seats overall—a record for the Singaporean opposition. While a postelection survey failed to reveal a general increase in support for greater political pluralism since the last elections (in 2006), the expressed preference for a more competitive political system did increase dramatically in the youngest age cohort (those aged from 21 to 29), shooting up from 30 to 44 percent.[5] If Singapore remains in the grip of a half-century-long single-party hegemony, that hegemony now seems to be entering a more vulnerable phase, as opposition parties find new energy and backing, as young people flock to social media to express themselves more openly, as independent media crop up online to provide a fuller range of news and opinions, and as the ruling party feels compelled to ease censorship and other controls. Singapore, in other words, has already joined the ranks of the world's "competitive authoritarian" regimes—the class of autocracies among which democratic transitions are most likely to happen.[6]

Singapore's exceptionalism is widely known. Less well known is that Malaysia now also has a higher per capita income than most third-wave countries did when they made their transitions to democracy. In fact, among the prominent cases in the Table, only Taiwan had a higher per capita income than Malaysia when it completed its democratic transition. Moreover, Malaysia's score on the UNDP's Human Development Index— which, in measuring not only per capita income but also levels of health and education, is arguably a truer measure of development—is now significantly higher than the levels in Brazil, Chile, Mexico, and even Hungary, Poland, and Ukraine when they made their respective transitions to democracy. From the standpoint of modernization theory, then, Malaysia is also ripe for a democratic transition.

Table 16.1 Development levels and democratic transitions

Country	Year of transition	GDP per capita, PPP$ (in 2009 international dollars)	HDI score (year of transition)
Turkey	1984	6,316	—
Brazil	1985	7,596	0.687
Philippines	1986	2,250	—
South Korea	1988	9,086	—
Pakistan	1988	1,722	—
Hungary	1990	12,979	0.692
Poland	1990	8,376	0.683
Chile	1990	6,896	0.675
Bangladesh	1991	748	0.186
Thailand	1992	4,732	0.685
South Africa	1994	7,235	0.716
Taiwan	1996	19,938	—
Indonesia	1999	2,666	0.681
Mexico	2000	12,662	0.698
Ghana	2000	1,653	0.431
Ukraine	2005	6,037	0.696
Current Asia			
Singapore		56,522	0.866
Malaysia		14,670	0.761
Thailand		8,505	0.682
China		7,519	0.687
Vietnam		3,134	0.593
Laos		2,436	0.524
Burma		1,256	0.483

Notes: GDP per capita and Human Development Index (HDI) scores in the bottom part of the table are for the years 2010 and 2011, respectively. All GDP per capita figures have been transformed into the value of constant 2009 dollar values using the GDP deflator.

Sources: For HDI, see http://hdrstats.undp.org/en/tables/default.html; for GDP per capita, see www.imf.org/external/pubs.

For more than a decade, Malaysia's competitive authoritarian regime has faced a much more serious challenge than anything Singapore has so far seen. As the opposition has gained in unity, credibility, and mobilizing power, the long-ruling United Malays National Organization (UMNO) feels under increasing threat. Much of what is driving change in Malaysia is not only exhaustion with half a century of rule by one party (formally through a ruling coalition), but also a much better educated and more pluralistic society, with the attendant growth in independent organizations and the intense and innovative use of social media (including one of the most influential online newspapers in the world, *Malaysiakini*).

Alarmed by the upheavals that began sweeping the Arab world at the end of 2010, Malaysia's Prime Minister Najib Razak pledged to appoint a broad committee to review the country's electoral system and recommend reforms, and then vowed to repeal the draconian Internal Security Act. Many opposition and civil society leaders, however, saw these promises as empty, citing Razak's push to enact stiff new security laws in place of the old ones. After winning control of five of the 13 states in 2008, opposition forces are poised to do better in the next elections, which could come in 2012. The new opposition alliance, Pakatan Rakyat, is gaining momentum, and the regime's renewed effort to destroy former deputy prime minister Anwar Ibrahim with trumped-up charges of homosexual misconduct seems even less credible than when the ploy was first tried some years ago. To be sure, Malaysia's authoritarian establishment still has a lot of resources, but Razak's proposed reforms now seem "too little too late," as "cynicism still pervades the country."[7] A transition to democracy could happen any time in the coming years through the familiar instrument that has brought it about in other competitive authoritarian regimes: the electoral process.

Thailand is less developed than Malaysia, but also has far more democratic experience and now, once again, more freedom and pluralism. Although Thais remain deeply polarized between a camp that backs ousted premier Thaksin Shinawatra and one that clusters around the institution of the monarchy, national elections are highly competitive and seem to meet the "free and fair" standard of electoral democracy. With the decisive opposition victory of the new Pheu Thai Party (led by Thaksin's sister Yingluck Shinawatra) in the May 2011 parliamentary elections, the political force that the military deposed in the 2006 coup has returned, and Thailand has apparently become once again an electoral democracy. Yet it faces a rocky road ahead, as the stabilizing presence of long-reigning King Bhumibol (b. 1927) draws toward a close. If the end result is a weaker monarchy (and military), this might ultimately help to ease the country's intense polarization and create a more mature and securely institutionalized politics. The military seems to have learned from the political turbulence and polarization of the last decade that its own direct intervention will not solve the country's political problems. Though it clearly preferred the incumbent Democrat Party, the military made a point of declaring its neutrality in the recent election. If the 2006 military coup does prove to be the last in Thailand's history, democracy will sink firmer roots over the coming decade as modernization further raises incomes and education. Already, Thailand has a per capita income and human-development score roughly equivalent to those of Poland when it made its transition to democracy around 1990 (see Table 16.1).

It is not only Southeast Asia's wealthier countries that are experiencing the winds of democratic change. As Burma's iconic democratic leader Aung San Suu Kyi has recently acknowledged, that country's political opening, launched in 2008 amid widespread skepticism with many voters abstaining from a constitutional referendum, suddenly seems quite serious. Labor unions have been legalized, Internet censorship has been eased, and a number of political prisoners have been freed. Now, Suu Kyi's National League for Democracy (which won the aborted 1990 elections) is preparing to register for and run in parliamentary by-elections to be held probably later in 2012. As has happened with other authoritarian regimes that opted to liberalize politically, Burma's authoritarian rulers seem to have been influenced by democratic developments elsewhere in the world, as well as by the prospective economic benefits—chiefly flowing from closer integration with the global economy—that political liberalization might bring. As an advisor to Burma's President Thein Sein noted in December 2011, "The president was convinced about the global situation; he saw where the global stream was heading."[8]

The coming change in China

Per capita income in China is still little more than half of what it is in Malaysia, but it has been rising rapidly and now approaches the level that South Korea could boast at the time of its democratic transition in 1987–1988. In fact, by IMF projections, China could surpass that level—about US$9,000 in 2009 purchasing power parity (PPP) dollars—by next year. In 1996, Henry Rowen predicted on the basis of data and projections regarding economic development that China would become what Freedom House would call a "partly free" country by 2015, and a "free" one (with political-rights and civil-liberties scores as good as those of India or Indonesia today) by 2025.[9] More recently, Rowen affirmed that analysis, estimating that even if China's growth in GDP per capita slowed to 5 percent annually starting in 2015, it would have by 2025 a per capita income roughly equivalent to that of Argentina's in 2007 (about $15,000 in current PPP dollars—which is roughly where Malaysia is today).[10] And if China's growth in per capita income were to slow immediately to 6 percent annually, it would still reach $13,000 in current PPP dollars before 2020—the level of Hungary in 1990 and Mexico in 2000 when they transitioned to democracy.

It is not only modernization—the spread of democratic values and capacities in tandem with rising incomes and information—that is feeding the escalating pressure for democratic change in China. As Yun-han Chu notes, the growing density of ties between mainland China and Taiwan—including direct access (through travel and satellite television) to political news from the highly competitive and even raucous democracy that is Taiwan—is serving as an additional stimulant to the growth of democratic norms and aspirations in China.[11] The irony of communist

China's relentless push for closer integration with Taiwan is that it may well begin to generate political convergence—but not in the way that the communist leaders imagined.

Rowen's projections were a bit mechanical in assuming that economic growth would necessarily drive *gradual* political change toward democracy in China. Instead, it seems increasingly likely that political change in China will be sudden and disruptive. The Communist Party leadership still shows no sign of embarking on a path of serious political liberalization that might gradually lead to electoral democracy, as their counterparts in Taiwan's then-dominant Nationalist Party did several decades ago. Instead, the rulers in Beijing are gripped by a fear of ending up like the USSR's Mikhail Gorbachev, who launched a process of political opening in hopes of improving and refurbishing Soviet communist rule only to see it crumble and the Soviet Union itself fall onto the ash heap of history. Torn by intense divisions within their own ranks and weakened by the draining away of power and energy from the center to the provinces and a congeries of increasingly divergent lower-level authorities, China's political leaders seem as frozen and feckless on the grand question of long-term political reform as they are brisk and decisive in making daily decisions on spending and investments.

As Francis Fukuyama has argued, the one flaw in the otherwise impressive institutionalization of Chinese communist rule is its lack of adaptability.[12] For a regime whose specialty is producing rapid economic change, such rigidity is a potentially fatal defect. With every month or year that ticks by while corruption, routine abuses of power, and stifling constraints on expression go unchecked, citizens' frustration mounts. Already, protests erupt with ominous frequency across tens of thousands of Chinese localities every year, while subversive and democratic ideas, images, and allusions proliferate online, despite the best efforts of 50,000 Internet police to keep Chinese cyberspace free of "harmful content." As Minxin Pei has been arguing for some time, the strength of the authoritarian regime in China is increasingly an illusion, and its resilience may not last much longer.[13] As frustration with corruption, collusion, criminality, and constraints on free expression rise, so do the possibilities for a sudden crisis to turn into a political catastrophe for the Chinese Communist Party (CCP).

Beyond the ongoing frustrations with censorship, insider dealing, abuse of power, environmental degradation, and other outrages that can only be protested by antisystem activity of one sort or another, there are, as Fukuyama notes, the big looming social and economic challenges that China faces as the consequences of its one-child policy make themselves felt in a rapidly aging (and disproportionately male) population.[14] Jack Goldstone reports that China's labor force stopped growing in 2010 and has begun shrinking half a percent a year, which "will, by itself, knock 2.2 percentage points off China's annual economic growth potential." Urbanization, a key driver of productivity increases, is also slowing dramatically, and the growth of education "has clearly reached a limit," as the number of college graduates has expanded faster than the ability of the economy—even as it faces labor shortages in blue-collar industries—to generate good white-collar jobs.[15]

The Chinese economy will have to pay for rapidly rising wages and cope with industrial labor shortages even as it comes under pressure to finance pension, welfare, and healthcare benefits for the massive slice of the populace that is now moving toward retirement. Moreover, as it manages all this, China will need to address growing frustration among college graduates who cannot find jobs to match their expectations. If the suspected bubbles in the real-estate and financial markets burst as these twin generational challenges are gathering force, political stability in the world's most populous country may well become no more than a memory.

Increasingly, the CCP faces the classic contradiction that troubles all modernizing authoritarian regimes. The Party cannot rule without continuing to deliver rapid economic development and rising living standards—to fail at this would invite not gradual loss of power but a sudden and probably lethal crisis. To the extent that the CCP succeeds, however, it generates the very forces—an educated, demanding middle class and a stubbornly independent civil society—that will one day decisively mobilize to demand democracy and end CCP rule for good. The CCP, in other words, is damned if it does not, and damned if it does. The only basis for its political legitimacy and popular acceptance is its ability to generate steadily improving standards of living, but these will be its undoing.

For some time, I suspected that Henry Rowen's projections were a bit optimistic, and that China's democratic moment, while foreseeable, was still 25–30 years away. Now, as the need for a more open, accountable, and law-based regime becomes as obvious as the current leaders' inability to bring one about, I suspect that the end of CCP rule will come much sooner, quite possibly within the next ten years. Unfortunately, a sudden collapse of the communist system could give rise, at least for a while, to a much more dangerous form of authoritarian rule, perhaps led by a nationalistic military looking for trouble abroad in order to unify the nation at home. But this would likely represent only a temporary solution, for the military is incapable of governing a rapidly modernizing, deeply networked, middle-class country facing complex economic and social challenges.

Whatever the specific scenario of change, this much is clear: China cannot keep moving forward to the per capita income, educational, and informational levels of a middle-income country without experiencing the pressures for democratic change that Korea and Taiwan did more than two decades ago. Those pressures are rising palpably now in Singapore and Malaysia. They will gather momentum in Vietnam as it follows in China's path of transformational (even if not quite as rapid) economic development. In Thailand, continuing modernization over the next decade will change society in ways that will make democracy easier to sustain. In short, within a generation or so, I think it is reasonable to expect that most of East Asia will be democratic. And no regional transformation will have more profound consequences for democratic prospects globally.

Notes

1 Originally published as "The Coming Wave of East Asian Democracy," *Journal of Democracy* 23 (January 2012): 5–13.
2 See for example Yun-han Chu, Larry Diamond, Andrew J. Nathan, and Doh Chull Shin, *How East Asians View Democracy* (New York: Columbia University Press, 2008), and various reports of the Asian Barometer, www.asianbarometer.org.
3 "Worldwide Governance Indicators," the World Bank Group, 2011, http://info. worldbank.org/governance/wgi/sc_country.asp. Indonesia and the Philippines were rated in the 27th and 22nd percentiles, respectively, on control of corruption and the 31st and 24th percentiles, respectively, on rule of law. South Korea, by contrast, was scored in the 69th and 81st percentiles on these two measures.
4 Data is from Round III of the Asian Barometer.
5 "IPS Post-Election Survey 2011," Institute for Policy-Studies, Singapore. My thanks to Tan Ern Ser for sharing a copy of the summary findings.
6 Stephan Ortmann, "Singapore: Authoritarian But Newly Competitive," *Journal of Democracy* 22 (October 2011): 153–164.
7 Ooi Kee Beng, "In Malaysia, Reforms Take a Staggered Path," *Today Online*, December 3, 2011, www.todayonline.com/Commentary/EDC111203-0000021/ In-Malaysia,-reforms-take-a-staggered-path.
8 "In Myanmar, Government Reforms Win Over Some Skeptics," *New York Times*, November 30, 2011.
9 Henry S. Rowen, "The Short March: China's Road to Democracy," *National Interest* 45 (Fall 1996): 61–70.
10 Henry S. Rowen, "When Will the Chinese People Be Free?" *Journal of Democracy* 18 (July 2007): 38–52.
11 Yun-Han Chu, "China and East Asian Democracy: The Taiwan Factor," *Journal of Democracy* 23 (January 2012): 42–56.
12 Francis Fukuyama, "China and East Asian Democracy: The Patterns of History," *Journal of Democracy* 23 (January 2012): 14–26.
13 Minxin Pei, "China and East Asian Democracy: The Patterns of History," *Journal of Democracy* 23 (January 2012): 27–41.
14 Fukuyama, "The Patterns of History."
15 Jack A. Goldstone, "Rise of the TIMBIs," *Foreign Policy*, December 2, 2011, available at www.foreignpolicy.com/articles/2011/12/02/rise_of_the_timbis?page=0,1.

17 Why China's democratic transition will differ from Taiwan's[1]

If China is headed toward democracy, one possible path it might take would be to replicate (more or less) the logic, pace, and sequence of political transition in the first Chinese democracy, Taiwan. Will this be the case? I think not. There are many lessons to be learned from comparing the social, cultural, and political dynamics of democratic transition in Taiwan with the way those same variables are operating in China today. But as we see in the book I edited with Bruce Gilley (from which this chapter is drawn), there are also limits to the comparison.[2]

There are, to be sure, some striking similarities between the two political systems. To begin with the obvious, both societies share a common language, culture, and history, and as Gilley notes, both political systems have their origins in the revolutionary politics of early twentieth-century China.[3] Both evolved and adapted under new forms of authoritarian rule after profound political traumas—for Taiwan, the retreat of the KMT (Kuomintang, or Nationalist Party) to the island after its 1949 defeat by the Chinese Communist Party in the civil war; for China, the mass bloodshed, political turmoil, and revolutionary upheaval of Mao Tse-tung's years. Following those periods of political turmoil, each system was launched into a remarkable period of rapid economic growth that transformed society in Taiwan and is in the process of doing so in China. Rapid economic development had in Taiwan and is having in China today many of the effects predicted by modernization theory: the growth of civil society and social and intellectual pluralism, and the emergence of more liberal values, which place more of an emphasis on freedom and personal autonomy. These changes generated powerful internal pressures in Taiwan for democratic change, and they are beginning to do so in China, despite the continuing freeze on large-scale institutional reform ever since the pro-democracy demonstrations of 1989 almost brought down Communist Party rule.

However, the differences between Taiwan's transition (as it occurred) and China's transition (as I predict it) are more decisive than the similarities. To appreciate this, I suggest taking a different slice in time than the economic development trajectory (1951–1986 in Taiwan, 1977–2012 in China) that Gilley examines.[4] If we wish to understand the effects of socioeconomic development on politics, we have to factor in a generational lag of about 20 years. This requires us to compare the quarter century of political change in Taiwan—from the beginning of the U.S. tilt toward China in 1971 to the holding of Taiwan's first direct presidential election, in 1996, which completed the transition to democracy—with a similar period of change in China's history. Following the same logic of generational delay, I will date that period from the start of China's economic growth boom, in 1997, to the as yet unknowable situation in 2022.

To appreciate what lessons Taiwan's experience may hold for China's future, we must not only compare the internal dynamics of these two systems in these two different periods, but also the global context that each confronted, or, in the case of China, will confront. Here, I argue, we need to compare a relatively small and insecure society that needed to democratize to refashion its international legitimacy and maintain the support of its most vital ally, the United States, with a rising global power that finds itself in tension (and potentially some day at war) with the United States. The two situations could not be more different, and as I will explain, these are far from the only dimensions of difference in historical context and the international environment surrounding the democratization of Taiwan, 1971–1996, and the political evolution of China during the early decades of the twenty-first century. These differences do not imply that China will not become a democracy. But they do imply that China's transition to democracy will take longer, be driven by somewhat different logics, and will be more fraught with internal and, potentially, international peril than was Taiwan's.

A tale of two modernizations

The most striking parallel between Taiwan and China is the nearly identical profile of the growth trajectories in per capita income of the two systems, separated by a 26-year lag in time.[5] China has so far replicated, virtually identically, the soaring ascent in per capita income achieved by Taiwan during more than a quarter century from 1951. During this period, Taiwan's per capita income increased more than eightfold, from roughly $1,000 (in constant year 2000 purchasing power parity dollars) to nearly $8,500 in 1986. By 1996, when the transition to democracy was completed, Taiwan's per capita income had nearly doubled again, to about $16,000.[6] By 2004, Gilley shows, China's per capita income of $5,333 was almost precisely that of Taiwan in 1978. If China maintains this pace (which was Taiwan's torrid pace in the miracle years of the 1970s and 1980s), it will reach Taiwan's 1986 level of per capita income in the year 2012.[7]

How does this look from a broader comparative perspective? If we examine per capita income denominated in international prices according to purchasing power parity (PPP) dollars, rather than nominal dollars, then we see that China has already entered what Samuel Huntington called the "zone of transition," that is the range of economic development levels in which transitions to democracy are more likely to take place. According to the World Bank, China's per capita gross democratic product (in constant year 2000 PPP dollars) had reached $6,621 by 2006. That is slightly higher than the level ($6,515) at which Brazil made a transition to democracy in 1985, and not much below the levels of Korea during its democratic transition year (1987, $7,420) and of Chile when it voted to end the Pinochet dictatorship (1989, $7,041).[8] Moreover, Henry S. Rowen predicts that even with a more realistic projection of future economic growth for China—slowing from the 8.5 percent annual rate of increase in per capita income over the last decade to 7 percent annual over the next one—China will reach a per capita income of $8,600 (again in year 2000 PPP dollars) by 2015.[9] Rowen anticipates that with slower workforce expansion (as the one-child-family generation matures) and China's "expected approach toward convergence with the world's leading developed economies," growth in per capita income may slow further toward an annual rate of about 5 percent starting in 2015, bringing per capita income to about $12,000 (in year 2000 dollars) by 2025. Projected against average international trends in the relationship between economic development and freedom, Rowen predicts that China will move into the "partly free" category of Freedom House by 2015 and will become a "free" country, or in other words, clearly a democracy, by 2025.[10] If growth is faster, China's democratization would happen sooner. Of course, as I will explain below, things could go badly wrong, and China's economic growth could implode in a financial, environmental, or political crisis. Then, a different type of transitional logic would take hold. But if the momentum of economic development is largely sustained, China will be within a generation about as rich as Taiwan was *when it completed its democratic evolution.*

It is vital to look beyond the aggregate income figures to consider the social impact of growth. One of the principal means by which economic development has fostered democratization—in Taiwan, Korea, Spain, Chile, and many other societies—is by raising levels of education and information, thereby creating a much more aware and empowered citizenry. In this respect, China—surprisingly for a "socialist" country—has lagged somewhat. "In 2000, the country's entire over-25 population had only an average of 5.74 years of schooling," which fell between the averages for all developing countries (4.89) and for the East and the Pacific (6.50).[11] But with the pace of educational expansion, Rowen projects an increase in this figure to an average of eight years of formal schooling by 2025. In 2004, China's combined gross enrollment ratio for education at all levels (primary, secondary, and tertiary) was only 70 percent, behind, for example, the Philippines at 82 percent, Brazil at 86 percent, and South Africa at 77 percent.[12] This is primarily due to a much lower rate of secondary school enrollments (74 percent of the age group in 2004) as compared to other such countries (which range from 82 percent in the Philippines to 100 percent in Brazil).[13] But nine of every ten Chinese are literate today, and educational access is rapidly expanding. "Between 1999 and 2005, post-secondary admissions tripled, reaching five million during the latter year. Currently China has about twenty million people with higher degrees; by 2020 there will be more than a hundred million."[14]

There are other signs of the social empowerment that follows from rapid economic growth. By 2004, there were 258 cellular phone subscribers for every 1,000 people and an estimated 140 million Chinese Internet users (including some 34 million Chinese bloggers).[15] By 2009, the estimated number of Internet users had more than doubled in five years, to some 300 million.[16] Life expectancy has risen to 72 years, nearly the equal of countries with much higher human development levels. In the 25 years following Deng Xiaoping's accession to power in 1978—when per capita income in China increased sevenfold and some 250 million people were lifted out of poverty[17]—the number of newspaper copies tripled, and the number of book titles published increased 11-fold. Today there is more than one color TV set for every two households, where in 1978 only three homes in every 1,000 had a TV of any kind.[18] As a result of the dizzying pace of market reform and expansion over the past two decades, China's rulers now have to contend with a much larger, more resourceful, and better net-worked civil society than existed during the democratic uprising in 1989.[19] With the boom in newspapers, books, televisions, and computers, "China is now awash with information that would have been considered seditious as recently as the early 1990s."[20] The number of NGOs officially registered with the government has risen from 4,500 in 1988 to over 300,000 in 2006, and some estimate the actual number at ten times that.[21]

As Yun-han Chu shows, there is early evidence that economic and social modernization is being accompanied, as it was in Taiwan and has been in so many other developing societies, by democratic value change.[22] Between 1993 and 2002, levels of support for democratic values increased signifi-cantly in Mainland China, even though they remained well below the levels in Hong Kong and Taiwan. For example, the percentage of Chinese agree-ing with the statement, "Government leaders are like the head of family, we should all follow their decisions," fell from 73 to 53 percent; those will-ing to let "morally upright leaders ... decide everything" fell from 70 to 47 percent; those saying judges should accept instruction from the execu-tive branch in deciding important cases fell from 64 to 45 percent; and those thinking the government should decide whether certain ideas should be allowed to circulate in society fell from 56 to 46 percent—all in the space of just a decade. By 2002, these levels of rejection of authoritarian values were not much different from Taiwan in the mid-1980s, shortly before it began its democratic transition.[23] In fact, as Chu's data show, the percent-age of Mainland Chinese in 2002 who were unwilling to let morally upright leaders decide everything (43 percent) exceeded the figure for Taiwan in 1993 (37 percent). Moreover, we see from Chu's analysis that authori-tarian value orientations are significantly associated with rural vs. urban residence, with older generations, and most of all with low levels of education. The more highly educated Chinese, and the younger and more urban Chinese, are significantly more democratic in their value orientations. As China continues to become more educated and more urban, and as the younger generations socialized after the 1949 revolution and after the Cultural Revolution replace the older generations, democratic value orientations can be expected to increase markedly—precisely as modernization theory would predict, as Chu affirms, and has happened in Taiwan (as well as Korea). It is even possible that the pace of democratic value change in China could accelerate in the coming years as the country becomes more interconnected internally and more intensely wired to rest of the world via cell phones, the Internet, and travel.

The dark side of China's development path

All of this assumes, however, that China will continue, albeit possibly at a somewhat less torrid pace, its extraordinary economic development, and that its benefits will be reasonably broadly distributed. There are many reasons to expect that China, with the world's largest market and financial reserves, and with a new generation of more skillful policy technocrats at the helm of government and the economy, will do so. But there are also reasons to question this scenario of continuity, and thus the assumption that Taiwan's relatively smooth rise to modernity will be replicated in China. Any social science projection of China's developmental future must at least consider the possibility that deepening contradictions in China's model of growth are not sustainable, and that even the current, better educated, more pragmatic and skillful generation of Communist Party leaders cannot manage them much longer without democratizing changes in China's system of government that they have so far demonstrated little willingness to entertain. For some analysts of contemporary China, like Minxin Pei, the party and the state lie at the core of the problem (to a much greater degree than was the case in Taiwan, where, as I will shortly explain, there was significantly more political reform going on much earlier in the economic development process). Pei sees China's authoritarian regime not any longer as "developmental" but as a "decentralized predatory state" in which "the individual interests of its agents"—to cash in on the boom while it lasts and to get rich as quickly as possible by any means—are slowly dismantling political stability. The result is unsustainable economic growth, "achieved at the expense of rising inequality, underinvestment in human capital, damage to the environment, and pervasive official corruption."[24]

Many cities and counties have seen organized crime gain control of business with such collusion and protection from the authorities that they have become "local mafia states."[25] Local rulers prey on poor peasants, levying illegal taxes and fees and then selling off their land for lucrative developments.[26] A 2006 government report "claimed that over 60 percent of recent land acquisitions for construction were illegal."[27] In September 2006, "the country's top auditor warned that looting and misuse of government-held property were wrecking the value of many assets and constituted the biggest threat facing the nation."[28] There have been some high-profile crackdowns, but these have been selective—to neutralize rivals—and fail to address the vast scale of the crisis. Pei and other critics predict that the system will be unable to correct itself in more than superficial ways; sooner or later it will succumb to "the self-destructive dynamics found in nearly all autocracies: low political accountability, unresponsiveness, collusion and corruption."[29] Like previous Chinese dynasties, the Communist regime could lose its "mandate of heaven" as pathologies of bad governance reach critical mass. Crime, corruption, cronyism, bank fraud, local tyranny, national unresponsiveness, and a host of other ills threaten the stability of Communist Party rule more than can be described here. The dramatic rise in economic inequality, to levels that now "rival some of the most skewed countries in Latin America or Africa," could increasingly undermine social stability and in particular the legitimacy of Communist rule, not only locally but also at the center.[30] The gap is widening fast between income strata and between cities and the countryside. With development lagging and unemployment soaring in the rural areas, young men have moved to the cities and constitute a huge pool of rootless migrants, ready to be mobilized in protest. "At any given moment, there are over 120 million rural migrant workers roaming the streets of Chinese cities looking for jobs."[31]

Sustained underinvestment in health and education, which makes the country vulnerable to pandemics like AIDS and avian flu or outbreaks like the SARS crisis of 2003, has deprived the poor of even the limited access to health care they enjoyed under (real) communism. Chronic disease is exploding, with reported cases of HIV increasing by 30 percent in 2006 while hepatitis affects 10 percent of the population.[32] A third of China's land is severely eroded; a third of China's 33,000 dams (including 100 large ones) "are deemed 'defective;'" and three-quarters of its lakes and half its length of rivers have been polluted. The results are spreading deserts (to the edge of Beijing), crippling pollution, and devastating floods.[33] Then there is the state of road and workplace safety: over 100,000 road fatalities in 2002, 100,000 illnesses in a year from rat poison seeping into the human environment, and a level of mining deaths 13 times that of India.[34] Any one of these ills, not to mention the complex interaction of them, could explode into crisis in the coming decade—or what Gilley calls "metastatic crisis," when dysfunction spreads beyond its initial boundaries to affect other functions and the country as a whole.[35]

These statistics tell a different story of China's modernization, one that cannot continue to progress indefinitely. In this story, China suffers increasingly systemic drags on its sustainability that Taiwan did not have to contend with, and that China lacks the institutional means or the will to correct. It is certainly conceivable that, in the coming decade, these pathologies will inhibit economic growth, intensify popular discontent, and further grind down the legitimacy and capacity of the state until a specific crisis metastasizes into something systemic. Pei does not anticipate the fall of communism any time soon. Rather, the system could remain "trapped in prolonged economic and political stagnation" before it ultimately collapses "in the political equivalent of a bank run" if it is not fundamentally reformed first.[36] Another possibility is that economic growth could continue, but with widening inequality, corruption, and injustice, until "the radicalization of the poor" reaches truly explosive dimensions and political change comes through an upsurge of social protests or a crisis catalyzing a nationwide wave of protests more intense and possibly more violent than in 1989.[37]

If Pei and other critics are right that political change in China is not going to be evolutionary (as in Taiwan), with more or less steady growth, but rather abrupt and disruptive, in the face of some large-scale social, economic, or environmental crisis that ultimately becomes political, there are two directions in which this could lead. One, which Pei believes is just as likely as anything else, is a new form of authoritarianism, possibly a nationalist right-wing one, to hold the country together. The other, which Bruce Gilley envisions in his provocative book, *China's Democratic Future*, is a transition to democracy.

If the scenario of social and political crisis does unfold, then China's political fate—movement to dictatorship or democracy or some hybrid regime—will not be determined solely by internal events and forces. It will also depend on the regional and international environment in which China finds itself at the time. These are only some of the dimensions on which China's situation today is quite different from that which Taiwan faced in the 1970s, 80s, and early 90s. I consider first other contrasting features of the two cases internally, and then turn to the markedly different international and historical contexts.

How China today differs from Taiwan historically

China today differs dramatically from the historical example of Taiwan in some obvious ways. Perhaps the most obvious is scale: China's population today is more than 60 times that of Taiwan's during its transition. Almost all of its provinces are much larger than Taiwan's. Indeed, about nine of China's provinces have three times the population of Taiwan, equaling or exceeding the populations of sizable European countries like Britain, France, and Italy (at roughly 60 million each). Sichuan province has a population of over 80 million people, Henan and Shandong provinces over 90 million. Even most smaller Chinese provinces, like Fujian, just across the strait from Taiwan, are larger (in the case of Fujian, about 50 percent larger) than Taiwan in population.[38] Physically as well, China dwarfs Taiwan, with a land mass (of 9.3 million square kilometers) more than 250 times the size of Taiwan. Indeed, at about the time Taiwan completed its transition, when it still commonly referred to itself as "The Republic of China" and made reference to its being a part of (and the legitimate government of) China as a whole, the official yearbook of the Republic of China acknowledged that "Taiwan is the smallest province of the Republic of China."[39]

Scale matters politically. During several decades of limited political competition, and especially during the ten-year process of transition from 1986 to 1996, Taiwan's ruling party was able to penetrate down more effectively to the local level and maintain more confident command of the process because of Taiwan's relatively small size geographically and demographically. Of course, the Chinese Communist regime represents one of the world's biggest historical experiments in centralized administrative control and ideological and political penetration of a very large territory.[40] But, while the Beijing leadership still exercises effective authority over China's vast continental territory, it is not the kind of monolithic and ideological control of Mao's era. Increasingly, there are vast differences among the provinces (particularly between the coastal provinces and the interior) in income levels and political outlook, and the implementation of central governmental initiatives, like village elections, varies widely not only across provinces but within them. Although China is much more ethnically homogeneous than was the former Soviet Union, representing (for the most part) a country of long historical standing rather than the recently crafted and hence much more brittle empire of the Soviet Union, China's political leaders worry about losing control. With so many provinces having populations larger than most nations (other than China, there are only 21 countries in the world with populations over 60 million), many of China's provinces have more ability to contemplate and wrest governing autonomy from the center than do the units of most other countries.[41] And it is much more difficult for the central authorities in Beijing to know reliably what is really going on at so many local levels. The authorities in Taiwan never had to confront such scale as they loosened central government control, phased in competitive local elections, and then tolerated the rise of an opposition party during their transition to democracy.

A second enormous difference has to do with the timing and pace of introducing competitive elections. This happened from very early on in the establishment of the KMT regime on Taiwan, virtually from the beginning of its retreat to Taiwan after its defeat on the mainland in 1949.[42] In this case, the ethnic and political cleavage between the mainlander émigrés and the local Taiwanese created an imperative for legitimation of KMT rule and incorporation of local leaders, which the KMT leadership—unable to afford a second political calamity—recognized. Moreover, these elections conferred some real power to govern and manage developmental resources—at the township and county levels from 1950, and at the level of Taiwan's provincial assembly from 1951. Over the subsequent four decades, even in the absence of an opposition party, these elections were surprisingly competitive for an authoritarian regime, with the opposition (prior to the start of the transition in 1986) winning between 30 and 40 percent of the votes and between 10 and 30 percent of the seats. The process was not free of coercion and control, but it did begin to institutionalize real political competition over meaningful levels of authority from an early date. Nothing like this has happened in China; there, the only level of political authority where electoral competition has been introduced systematically (and yet unevenly) has been the village, a tiny microlevel that is largely powerless.

This difference has enormous political consequences for the likely transition trajectories of the two systems. Taiwan was able to, and indeed driven to, negotiate a gradual "soft landing" to real democracy, in part because of the intricate web of pressures and reassurances generated by several decades of local elections. On the one hand, as Cheng and Lin note, these created a growing cadre of ruling party leaders (increasingly from the native Taiwanese majority) who "came to rely more and more on voters' voices than on the party's internal disciplinary and auditing units," who broke free earlier of the party ideology, and who generated what they call "'trickling up' pressure for the ruling party to expand the scope of electoral competition."[43] Over time, these locally legitimated party elites were recruited to positions of greater authority at the center and helped provide further impetus for the transition. Although the members of China's new generation of party elites are also less ideological and better managers, they owe their positions to the party, not the people, and thus lack the incentive to press for a continuous expansion of the scope of electoral competition that prevailed in Taiwan. This is a major reason why competitive elections in China remain stuck at the largely inconsequential level of the village, and why the prospect of real electoral competition at the county level—not to mention the provincial one—remains a distant dream. Coming back to the problem of scale, it is also hard to imagine how a province of 40–90 million people could stage, as Taiwan province did for decades, competitive elections without competing parties to organize the competition. The impetus to form at least underground opposition parties to structure the choice and signal the voters would become more compelling as well as more threatening to the Chinese Communist Party.

There was also a strong element of reassurance or political confidence building in the repeated practice of competitive elections over several decades in Taiwan. The KMT leaders developed a strong political machine and a confidence that they could continue to win elections, even with the legalization of opposition parties and the democratization of the key levers of central government power between 1986 and 1996. By 1986, the KMT had more than three decades of experience in contesting (and for the most part winning) local elections, and about a decade of experience in contesting limited but gradually more competitive elections for the central legislative authority. Thus, Cheng and Lin inform us, "local elections eventually made inter-party competition more imaginable and less repulsive to the KMT leaders."[44] As the opposition committed to playing by these rules, each side experienced what Dankwart Rustow calls "habituation," in which the norms, procedures, and expectations of democracy (or in this case, initially, an increasingly competitive authoritarian system) gradually become internalized among contending political actors, so that these politicians placed their faith in and learned to conform instinctively to the rules of the game.[45] Part of this process involves the growth of trust among competing political actors, as each side gains confidence that the victory of the other will not mean its elimination or victimization, and thus what Robert Dahl calls a "system of mutual security" takes hold between government and opposition.[46] Although the process was far from perfect or smooth, something like these changes in political norms and expectations were able to unfold over several decades in Taiwan, beginning at a very early point in its economic development. By contrast, as China races out of poverty toward Taiwan's mid-1980s development level, nothing like this process of political contestation and confidence building between ruling party cadres and at least loosely organized opposition forces *has even begun.*

Of course, one should not dismiss altogether the significance of China's experiment over the last two decades with competitive village elections, which, as Cheng and Lin observe, have gone reasonably far toward institutionalization, and have seen the defeat of a fairly high percentage of incumbents (e.g., over 40 percent) in at least some provinces.[47] There is even a certain parallel with Taiwan, in which the model and momentum of competitive village elections have encouraged a "trickling up" to the township level, for election of the township head and in some cases the township party committee and secretary. But this has been trickling up at a snail's pace, still limited and experimental. The village committee remains a largely powerless, policy-implementation body, under the thumb of the township authorities, while even the township is well below the level (relative to authority at the center) at which Taiwan had permitted electoral competition decades before its transition. Moreover, a crucial missing element, as Cheng and Lin stress, is the promise of eventual multiparty democracy, which bound the KMT to a democratic reform agenda at some point but which the CCP has so far steadfastly eschewed. In this respect, as Gilley notes, the ideological and institutional difference between the two settings—the authoritarian pluralist regime in Taiwan under the KMT versus the (still) communist regime in China—should not be minimized.[48]

Finally, it is worth noting another striking difference between the two internal settings of Taiwan historically and China today. During the 1970s and 1980s, Taiwan was reaching the stage of an industrialized country with a relatively egalitarian growth pattern (like other East Asian Tigers, such as Singapore and Korea). It is true that during the 1980s, income inequality widened in Taiwan, from a Gini coefficient of 0.277 in 1980 to 0.303 in 1988, with a majority of Taiwanese listing the gap between rich and poor as a serious social problem.[49] But in China today, inequality is already considerably worse, with the Gini coefficient estimated at somewhere between 0.45 and 0.50, and possibly even higher.[50] Moreover, this more extreme level of inequality than Taiwan ever experienced during its political evolution or transition comes in a communist country which has trumpeted an ideology of equality, with the party as the proclaimed defender of mass popular interests, for six decades. It also comes in a context of more visible and extreme corruption and misrule than was evident in Taiwan during its transition. Thus, the longer the Chinese Communist Party waits to open up political power to electoral competition at higher levels, the more it risks an unraveling of its authority, since its cadres have less experience at competing in elections and more burdens of social and economic problems than did the KMT cadres in Taiwan.[51]

The international contexts

The international context of the early Cold War and the Communist threat across the strait was hardly conducive to democratization in Taiwan.[52] But beginning in the late 1970s and accelerating in the 1980s through the completion of the transition in 1996, that context changed dramatically. Taiwan's top leaders—first Chiang Ching-kuo and then Lee Teng-hui— came to recognize that democratization was vital to Taiwan's quest for continued geopolitical and military support from the United States, and thus literally to its survival. It is important to recall that when Chiang Ching-kuo made the decision to initiate the political transition in 1986 and then tolerated the formation of an opposition party, East Asia was seized with democratic ferment. In February 1986, the Philippine "people power" revolution toppled the dictatorship of Ferdinand Marcos through peaceful mobilization after a stolen election. The 1980s had been a time of rising student, worker, and other civil society mobilization against military rule in South Korea, and in 1987 (when martial law was formally lifted in Taiwan), the Korean military dictator, Chun Doo Hwan, was forced to yield to massive public pressure and allow a direct popular election for his presidential successor. In both cases, timely pressure from the United States helped to foster a peaceful transition to democracy, and both the Reagan Administration and the U.S. Congress were becoming increasingly active in pushing to advance human rights and democracy abroad. Not long after Chiang Ching-kuo died in 1988, Thailand crossed the murky line from a military-dominated semidemocracy to an electoral democracy when Chatichai Choonhavan became the first elected member of parliament to become prime minister since the breakdown of the country's previous democratic experiment in 1976. Also in 1988, the Pakistani military dictator, General Zia ul-Haq died (or, some believe, was assassinated) in a plane crash, and there quickly followed a transition to electoral democracy that brought the democracy advocate and opposition party leader, Benazir Bhutto, to power as prime minister.

During the 1980s, most Latin American countries were also making or had already made transitions to democracy. Between the beginning of the "third wave of democratization" in 1974 and 1988, the number of democracies in the world increased by more than 50 percent, from 40 to 67, and the proportion of democracies in the world rose from 27 to 40 percent. Then in 1989, the Berlin Wall fell, communism collapsed in Eastern Europe—and nearly so in China itself—and a second burst of the third wave erupted. Between 1989 (as political liberalization was gathering steam in Taiwan) and 1996 (when Taiwan's transition to democracy was completed by Lee Teng-hui's reelection as president in a direct popular contest), the number of democracies worldwide exploded, from 67 to 118, and the proportion of democracies in the world increased from about two-fifths to three-fifths of all states.[53]

In other words, Taiwan made its transition to democracy during a unique moment in world history, probably the most rapid expansion in the number and proportion of democracies we will ever see within the period of a single decade. China, by contrast, is unlikely to benefit from such a democratic global zeitgeist. By 1996, the expansion of democracy in the world had leveled off. Although more countries in the world subsequently became democratic, and overall levels of freedom rose for another decade, the proportion of democracies in the world essentially remained static. Moreover, a new burst of democratic breakthroughs in the near future will be more difficult and unlikely, for several reasons. First, most of the most fertile countries for democratization from a developmental standpoint have already made transitions. Second, the majority of the remaining authoritarian regimes are hard cases, because of very low levels of development and/or unfavorable regional contexts (especially in the Middle East). Third, the difficulties surrounding the U.S. interventions in Iraq and Afghanistan, combined with the increased self-confidence and resolve of authoritarian states such as Russia, China, Iran, Egypt, Kazakhstan, and Venezuela (many of which are major oil exporters at a time of high oil prices) have generated an authoritarian backlash against democratic mobilization and democracy promotion. This, in turn, makes it more difficult for civil societies and political oppositions to adopt the techniques that led to democratic breakthroughs in the 1990s and early 2000s (in the so-called "color revolutions"). Cooperation among authoritarian states (for example in the Shanghai Cooperation Organization that draws together Russia, China, and many Central Asian dictatorships) further diminishes the prospects. Add to this the new cold war that has emerged in the form of a U.S.-led "global war on terror," and the difficulties of many of the new democracies in controlling corruption, achieving broad economic development, improving political institutions, and therefore consolidating democracy, and there emerges a much less favorable global context for democracy in the world.

Indeed, China may have more of an effect on global democratic trends than vice versa. Whether new global momentum gathers for the expansion of democracy in the world will depend in no small measure on whether China itself liberalizes and eventually democratizes politically. Certainly no development in Asia would more powerfully tip the odds in favor of democratization in authoritarian countries as disparate as Burma, Vietnam, Singapore, and Malaysia than a breakthrough to electoral democracy in China. In contrast to Taiwan, then, China will be much more of a shaper than a receiver of regional and global political pressures and demonstration effects.

There is one ironic twist to this generalization.[54] One of the few regional or global actors with the potential to affect significantly whether and how mainland China moves to democracy is Taiwan itself. Should the island continue to be gripped by political deadlock, enmity, and rising nationalist pressure for Taiwan independence, this would likely dampen Chinese enthusiasm for democracy at the level of societal norms and aspirations, as well as elite political intentions. Worse still, political polarization and renewed moves by some future government in Taiwan to legally separate from China and further press out the boundaries of Taiwan's separate identity could feed an intense nationalist reaction in China. In a context of political crisis, these developments could provide grounds for reactionary forces in China to mobilize popular sentiment and tilt a future moment of possible democratic transition toward a right-wing military or nationalist dictatorship. By contrast, should Taiwan's politics stabilize and its leaders sustain a policy of pragmatism and normalization of economic and social ties with Beijing, then the political balance in China could well be tilted toward a more positive view of democracy. In this scenario, growing experience with and observation of Taiwan's democracy would generate much more compelling diffusion and demonstration effects. Probably no external event would redound more favorably for democratization in China than a political accommodation between Beijing and Taipei, a prospect that was at least nudged forward by the election of Ma Ying-jeou to the presidency of Taiwan in 2008.

There is one potential additional parallel, however, between Taiwan and China, and it is an extension of the one causal driver that is most likely to affect democratization in each system in a similar fashion: economic development. One aspect of economic development that helped to generate pressure for democratic change in Taiwan, by accelerating normative change and the growth of civil society, was the large number of social scientists, businessmen, economists, technocrats, lawyers, and ultimately politicians who were trained in the United States. This training abroad, particularly in law and the social sciences, heavily disposed them to "Western democratic ideals."[55] More generally, the density of social and economic ties between Taiwan and the West, especially Taiwan and the U.S., gradually helped to shape the view in Taiwan that it could not become a fully modern country and a member of the club of advanced industrial countries without becoming a democracy.

Will Chinese political and social elites begin to think in a similar way as their country becomes increasingly rich, educated, and powerful? There is no guarantee; Singapore continues to defy the odds (though I do not believe it will do so indefinitely), and both Taiwan and Korea would have been more likely to remain authoritarian if they had the geopolitical weight to become global models in their own right. Increasingly, China will have that power. But it will also have, even if it is alongside booming growth, a vexing tangle of social, environmental, and governance problems that cannot be addressed unless the country allows much more individual and media freedom, social and political pluralism, transparency and judicial independence, and more competition for power than it has so far. In other words, as development creates a more and more educated and resourceful society, but with deeper and deeper contradictions, China's leaders will have to accommodate democratic evolution in order to keep the system stable. The natural instinct will be to institute more economic and social freedom, judicial professionalism, and effective, accountable governance, but in the absence of real political competition: in other words, Singapore. But much as they might wish to make a soft landing to the Singaporean system as a long-term (if not permanent) way of governing, China is too large and diverse, its political rulers are too corrupt, and its problems are too deep for those very limited reforms to suffice. For one thing, as China moves in that direction, toward what the Chinese political scientist Pan Wei has termed (and advocated) as a "consultative rule of law regime," people will not rest content with the limited political freedom and space granted to them.[56] They will demand more freedom and more pluralism, partly because their political values and aspirations will have changed so much, and partly because they will see that the only way to contain corruption in China at this point is to enable the people to replace their leaders in free, fair, and competitive elections.

In China, there will be no natural resting place, no enduring equilibrium for this process of governance reform short of democracy itself. This is why the Chinese Communist leaders sit on the horns of a dilemma. If they do not open up the political system and move toward democracy, they risk popular discontent exploding at some point as a more politically restless, resourceful, and assertive populace demands more freedom and more accountable government, while governance problems mount. If they do gradually introduce political competition at successively higher levels of authority, while also expanding the scope for dissent and criticism, then they risk seeing the Communist Party grip on power erode and eventually slip away—and possibly faster than happened in Taiwan. For as Bruce Gilley has written:

> the CCP [of the current era] is not the KMT [of Taiwan's democratizing era]. The power of the CCP ... has weakened considerably in the post-Mao era. While it remains a dominant force when compared to society as a whole, it is probably not dominant enough to successfully carry out a phased political transition.[57]

At some point, then, China's Communist rulers may be forced to pick their poison. They may be confronted with three options. One would be to begin democratization and try to negotiate guarantees of their political and financial interests before it is too late, knowing that this process of opening could well bring their downfall from power. The second would be to sit tight and hope for the best (which would mean kicking the political problems down the road to the next generation of leaders). But delaying reform runs a different risk: "Regimes that waited too long saw their rulers dragged from their offices and shot in the head."[58] The third would be to divert attention by using or manufacturing a crisis with the West, perhaps over Taiwan, to recover some temporary legitimacy for the regime and mobilize people behind it with nationalist fervor.

The third option is of course the most dangerous—for Taiwan, for the United States, for the world, and not least, for China. Whether that becomes a serious option will depend in large measure on the environment China faces regionally and internationally—whether Taiwan seeks accommodation or independence; whether the world can avoid a protracted global recession and cooperate to address the mounting shortages of energy, water, and other resources; and whether the United States can draw China into a new era of global partnership, as what Deputy Secretary of State Robert Zoellick termed in 2005 "a stakeholder that shares responsibility" for managing common economic and security challenges, such as trade, terrorism, and nuclear proliferation.[59] Doing so means that the U.S. must walk a fine line between respect for China's dignity and sovereignty as a rising great power, and resistance to its efforts to defend or entrench authoritarian regimes in Asia and around the world. It means standing up rhetorically for principles of human rights and the rule of law in China, and working patiently in private with Chinese leaders to keep human rights on the agenda, while recognizing that American leverage over China is extremely limited. Probably the most important thing that the United States can do is to create a benign environment for the tremendous developmental changes that China is undergoing to work their own autonomous effects in generating democratic change.

China today is dramatically different from Taiwan, then and now. Its path and pace of regime transformation will not follow Taiwan's. But many of the political and normative consequences of economic development will be the same. And if new generations of Chinese political leaders, technocrats, entrepreneurs, intellectuals, and artists can be vigorously and yet respectfully engaged, the political outcome will, sooner or later, likely be the same as in Taiwan: some form of genuine democracy.

Notes

1 Originally published as "Why China's Democratic Transition Will Differ From Taiwan's," in Bruce Gilley and Larry Diamond, eds, *Political Change in China: Comparisons with Taiwan* (Boulder, CO: Lynne Rienner Publishers, 2008), 243–257.

2 Gilley and Diamond, *Political Change in China.*
3 Bruce Gilley, "Comparing and Rethinking Political Change in China and Taiwan," in Gilley and Diamond, *Political Change in China,* 1–27.
4 Ibid.
5 Ibid., 6.
6 All of these figures, cited by Gilley (ibid.) are drawn from Alan Heston, Robert Summers and Bettina Aten, Penn World Table Version 6.2, Center for International Comparisons of Production, Income and Prices at the University of Pennsylvania, September 2006, http://pwt.econ.upenn.edu/php_site/pwt_index.php.
7 And subsequent to the publication of this article, that is precisely what happened. By 2012, China's per capita GDP had grown to $10,950 in PPP current dollars, which is equivalent to $8,527 in year 2000 dollars. See http://data.worldbank.org/indicator/NY.GDP.PCAP.PP.CD.
8 In his book *The Third Wave: Global Democratization in the Late Twentieth Century* (Norman: University of Oklahoma Press, 1991), table 2.1, p. 62, Samuel P. Huntington calculated the most likely zone of transition as those countries with a 1976 per capita GNP of $1,000 to $3,000, which would be roughly $2,500 to $7,400 in nominal year-2000 dollars. Between 1974 and 1990, 16 of the 21 nondemocratic countries in that income group democratized or liberalized politically, and five other states in that group were already democracies. It is difficult to transform that category from nominal into international prices because the latter figures must be computed for every country individually. The gap between China's nominal GDP per capita in 2004, $1,323, and the same figure in PPP dollars, $5,493, is much greater (about four to one) than the disparity for Brazil ($3,337 vs. $6,515) or Korea ($5,291 vs. $7,420) during their transition years (1985 and 1987 respectively). So while China in its nominal dollar per capita income is not yet in the prime of Huntington's zone of transition, when the figure is computed more realistically in international prices, it is roughly equivalent to Brazil's per capita income and so has clearly entered the "zone of transition."
9 This would be $10,000 in year 2006 PPP dollars, as Rowen reported it in "When Will the Chinese People Be Free?" *Journal of Democracy* 18 (July 2007): 39.
10 Ibid., 38–49.
11 Ibid., 41.
12 United Nations Development Programme (UNDP), *Human Development Report 2006* (New York: UNDP, 2006), table 1, 284–285.
13 World Bank, World Development Indicators Online, https://publications.worldbank.org/subscriptions/WDI.
14 Rowen, "When Will the Chinese People Be Free?" 41.
15 The cellular phone figure is from UNDP, *Human Development Report 2006,* table 13, 328. The latest figure on Internet use is from U.S. Department of State, *Country Reports on Human Rights Practices, 2006,* section 2a. The data on the estimated number of bloggers comes from Tony Saich, "China in 2006: Focus on Social Development," *Asian Survey* 47 (January–February 2007): 35.
16 Juliet Ye, "With Another Rise in Users, China Pads Its Global Internet Lead," *Wall Street Journal* Digital Network, *China RealTime Report,* January 13, 2009, http://blogs.wsj.com/chinarealtime/2009/01/13/with-another-rise-in-users-china-pads-its-global-internet-lead/tab/article.
17 According to UNDP statistics. Ying Ma, "China's Stubborn Anti-Democracy," *Policy Review* 141 (February–March 2007), www.hoover.org/publications/policyreview/5513661.html, p. 4 of online version.

18 Minxin Pei, *China's Trapped Transition: The Limits of Developmental Autocracy* (Cambridge, MA: Harvard University Press, 2006), 2.
19 Bruce Gilley, *China's Democratic Future: How It Will Happen and Where It Will Lead* (New York: Columbia University Press, 2004), chapter 4, 60–94.
20 Ibid., 73.
21 Ying Ma, "China's Stubborn Anti-Democracy," 6.
22 Yun-han Chu, "The Evolution of Political Values," in Gilley and Diamond, *Political Change in China*, 27–48.
23 Gilley, *China's Democratic Future*, 69; Larry Diamond, *Developing Democracy: Toward Consolidation* (Baltimore, MD: Johns Hopkins University Press, 1999), table 5.7, 189.
24 Pei, *China's Trapped Transition*, 209.
25 Ibid.,161–165. As in the U.S. and Europe, favored sectors for the mafia include real estate, transportation, and construction.
26 Ibid., 189, 191–196. The party itself reported a total of 87,000 "mass incidents" in 2005, an increase of over 6 percent from the year before. Tony Saich, "China in 2006: Focus on Social Development," *Asian Survey* 47 (January–February 2007): 35.
27 The figure rose to 90 percent in some cities. Saich, "China in 2006," p. 38.
28 Ibid., 39.
29 Pei, *China's Trapped Transition*, 208.
30 Gilley, *China's Democratic Future*, 38.
31 Ying Ma, "China's Stubborn Anti-Democracy," p. 5 of online version.
32 Harry Harding, "China: Think Again!" *Foreign Policy* 159 (March–April 2007).
33 Pei, *China's Trapped Transition*, 175–176. The data on dams is from Gilley, *China's Democratic Future*, 103. In 1975, he reports, twin dams burst in Henan Province, killing an estimated 300,000 people. No catastrophe on anything approaching such a scale could be covered up today in China, even with the level of state control of the Internet and other media. For similar views anticipating that profound governance crises will cripple and probably bring down Communist Party rule in the next two decades, see Shaoguang Wang, "The Problem of State Weakness," *Journal of Democracy* 14 (January 2003): 36–42, and Guogang Wu, "Why the Regime is Decaying and Headed for Crisis," Paper presented to the Conference on Democratization in Greater China, Center on Democracy, Development, and the Rule of Law, Stanford University, October 20–21, 2006. Both Wang and Wu are skeptical, however, that crisis generated by state decay will lead to democracy.
34 Pei, *China's Trapped Transition*, 170. See also An Chen, "China's Changing of the Guard: The New Inequality," *Journal of Democracy* 14 (January 2003): 51–59.
35 Gilly, *China's Democratic Future*, 103.
36 Pei, *China's Trapped Transition*, 210–212.
37 An Chen, "The New Inequality."
38 "Chinese Cities and Provinces," ChinaToday.com, www.chinatoday.com/city/a. htm.
39 That is no longer true since Hainan Island became a province in April 1988, but the ROC government at the time did not recognize that move. *The Republic of China Yearbook, 1997* (Taipei: Government Information Office, Republic of China, 1997), 3.
40 Tun-jen Cheng and Gang Lin, "Competitive Elections," in Gilley and Diamond, *Political Change in China*, 161–184.
41 If China broke apart into separate countries based on its provinces, nine of its provinces would be among the 30 most populous countries in the world.
42 Cheng and Lin, "Competitive Elections." For a comprehensive treatment of the gradual rise of democracy in Taiwan, see Linda Chao and Ramon H. Myers, *The*

First Chinese Democracy: Political Life in the Republic of China on Taiwan (Baltimore, MD: Johns Hopkins University Press, 1998).

43 Cheng and Lin, "Competitive Elections," 165 and 166.

44 Ibid., 167.

45 Dankwart A. Rustow, "Transitions to Democracy: Toward a Dynamic Model," *Comparative Politics* 2(3) (April 1970): 337–363.

46 Robert A. Dahl, *Polyarchy: Participation and Opposition* (New Haven, CT: Yale University Press, 1971), 16.

47 Cheng and Lin, "Competitive Elections."

48 Bruce Gilley, "Taiwan's Democratic Transition: A Model for China?" in Gilley and Diamond, *Political Change in China*, 215–242.

49 Hai-yan Chu, "Taiwanese Society in Transition: Reconciling Confucianism and Pluralism," in Murray Rubenstein, ed., *The Other Taiwan: 1945 to the Present* (Armonk, NY: M. E. Sharpe, 1994), 91–92. The Gini coefficient varies from 0 to 1, with 0 being most equal (indicating everyone having the same income) to 1 being most unequal (indicating control of all income by one individual).

50 Saich, "China in 2006," 40. But Gilley (*China's Democratic Future*, 38) cites some sources indicating that it may be as high as 0.60, making it one of the most unequal in the world. Saich cites official sources as reporting the urban-rural income gap at 3.22 to 1 in 2005.

51 While the KMT had the burden of a party that was identified with a privileged and historically resented ethnic minority, even that changed when Lee Teng-hui assumed the leadership of the party and the presidency in the late 1980s.

52 For a thoughtful analysis of the comparative international contexts, see Jacques deLisle, "International Pressures and Domestic Pushback," in Gilley and Diamond, *Political Change in China*, 185–211.

53 Larry Diamond, *The Spirit of Democracy: The Struggle to Build Free Societies throughout the World* (New York: Times Books, 2008), chapter 2, and appendix table 1.

54 DeLisle, "International Pressures and Domestic Pushback."

55 Tun-jen Cheng, "Democratizing the Quasi-Leninist Regime in Taiwan," *World Politics* 41(4) (1989): 483.

56 For Pan Wei's influential essay and responses to it, including mine, see Suisheng Zhao, *Debating Political Reform in China: Rule of Law vs. Democratization* (Armonk, NY: M. E. Sharpe, 2006).

57 Gilley, *China's Democratic Future*, 100.

58 Ibid., 99.

59 Robert Zoellick, "Whither China: From Membership to Responsibility?" Remarks to the National Committee on U.S.–China Relations, September 21, 2005, http://usinfo.state.gov/eap/Archive/2005/Sep/22-290478.html.

18 Hong Kong's democratic prospects[1]

Eleven years after the establishment of the Hong Kong Special Administrative Region, the great unresolved question about Hong Kong's future remains the nature of its political system. And the more specific question in Hong Kong—as in most of the world's political systems that are nondemocratic—is whether the society is ready for democracy, and whether, when, and how it can achieve democracy, even if it is in most cultural, economic, and social senses more than "ready" for it.

In 2004, the National People's Congress (NPC) in Beijing determined that Hong Kong was "not yet ready" for full democratic government, and on this basis rejected appeals for full universal suffrage to directly elect the chief executive in 2007 and the Legislative Council (LegCo) in 2008. This it had the legal right to do under one interpretation of the Basic Law, which establishes "selection of the chief executive by universal suffrage" ("upon nomination by a broadly representative nominating committee") as only an "ultimate aim" subject to the "actual situation in the HKSAR" and "in accordance with the principle of gradual and orderly progress."[2] In December 2007, as I discuss below, the Standing Committee of the NPC (the NPCSC) kicked the democratization of Hong Kong further down the road, setting 2017 and 2020 as the earliest dates by which universal suffrage for the chief executive and the LegCo, respectively, could be achieved, and leaving a number of questions of the democraticness even of these somewhat distant elections still unanswered.

My first purpose here is to assess, from the standpoint of comparative democratic theory, the claim that Hong Kong is "not yet ready" for democracy, even the somewhat constrained level of democracy that might initially be permitted under the Basic Law. I will show that, from a comparative standpoint, it is impossible to find a basis for claiming that Hong Kong is "not yet ready" for democracy, other than the obvious fact that its desired political evolution into a democracy is liable to the constitutional veto of a larger political entity that is "not yet ready" to have it become a democracy and fears the subversive implications that Hong Kong's democratization would generate for the stability of its own authoritarian rule. I will then go on to weigh the real problem, which is political and therefore concerns the possible mode of transition and manipulation of the balance of power and fear.

Is Hong Kong ready for democracy?

Since the "third wave" of democracy began in 1974, well over 90 countries have undergone transitions to democracy. Some of these new democracies have broken down, but most have not. As a result, about 120 states today—or roughly three in every five independent states—are democracies. This means that they can choose and replace their leaders in free, fair, and competitive elections, with universal suffrage, and that those elections confer real power and authority to govern on those parties and individuals that get elected. It also means that there is sufficient freedom of expression and organization so that political parties, interests, and movements can compete in a serious (even if not purely fair) manner in between and in the run-up to elections. It does not necessarily mean that there is a strong rule of law, effective control of corruption, genuine checks and balances, sound macroeconomic management, and thus good governance. Electoral democracy can exist (at least for a time) in a context of bad governance, but it is very hard to get comprehensively good governance, with a genuine rule of law, in the absence of electoral democracy. Indeed, vertical accountability—the ability of citizens to speak freely, hold their leaders accountable, and make them responsive to broad popular preferences—is such an important element of good governance that it is really not possible to get fully good governance without democracy. (Thus even the World Bank Institute identifies political "voice and accountability" as one of its six dimensions of good governance.)

There are several ways to look at the question of whether Hong Kong is "ready" for democracy. One way is to look at the conditions that sustain democracy and ask whether there would be a good prospect of sustaining democracy if it were installed. Another way is to examine the political culture of the society—the prevailing attitudes and values—to determine whether there is a strong societal desire for democracy. This can also serve the first approach, since a preponderance of democratic attitudes and values is certainly one highly favorable condition for democracy. A third way is to look at the larger geopolitical context and ask whether power relations outside the system's control will permit it to become a democracy. It is this third angle that is the most problematic and hence that I will focus on the most, in the context of pondering *how* Hong Kong might become a democracy.

The conditions for democracy

If we examine the principal structural conditions for democracy, the claim that Hong Kong is not intrinsically ready for democracy becomes (from a sociological standpoint) untenable. One of the most durable conditions for democracy, and still one of the better ways of predicting whether a democracy will survive, is the level of economic development. No democracy has ever broken down at a level higher than what Argentina had in 1975—about $9,300 in 2004 purchasing power parity (PPP) dollars. Hong Kong's current per capita income is now about *four times* higher than that—far, far beyond the threshold of economic development that appears to provide immunity from democratic breakdown.[3] In fact, if we look at the broader (and I think more meaningful) indicator of socioeconomic development, the UNDP's latest Human Development Index, Hong Kong ranked twenty-first in the world in 2005—just behind the UK, New Zealand, and Italy, and ahead of Israel, Greece, Korea, and even Germany.[4] Hong Kong's level of socioeconomic development (by this measure) is higher than every one of the new Central and East European democracies that have been admitted into the European Union in this decade, and higher as well than a number of other now stable democracies, including South Korea (hereafter, Korea), Portugal, Chile, Uruguay, and Costa Rica. In all, it has a higher level of development than 100 existing electoral democracies in the world. And it is the richest and most developed society in history that is not governed by an electoral democracy. (Singapore is the only other one that comes close, and from a developmental perspective, it is also an extraordinary anomaly).

Most societies that have experienced transitions to democracy as a result of economic development and the attendant transformation of values and social structure have done so at levels of economic development far below Hong Kong's today. For example, when Korea made its transition to democracy in 1987, its per capita income (in 2004 PPP dollars) was about $8,500—less than a quarter of Hong Kong's current per capita gross national income. When their democratic transitions began, Taiwan (in 1987) was a little higher than Korea, and Chile (in 1989) was somewhat lower. When the dictator Francisco Franco died in 1975 and a transition to democracy began, Spain's per capita income (in 2004 PPP dollars) was $13,000, putting it in the ranks of more developed countries.[5] But all of these levels of development were much lower (by a factor of several times) than Hong Kong's. There is no precedent in world history for such a developed society still needing to make a transition to electoral democracy.

It is worth emphasizing other features of contemporary Hong Kong that social scientists would consider highly favorable to democratic success and stability. Hong Kong is not deeply divided along ethnic or identity lines. In fact, the deepest division in the society is a political one, on the question of electoral democracy itself. But political (or economic, that is class) divisions are always easier to negotiate and manage than identity divisions.

In addition to a highly developed economy, Hong Kong also has a strong rule of law and highly developed state structures. Scholars of democratization and political development, going back to Samuel Huntington and forward to Juan Linz and Alfred Stephan, and most recently Francis Fukuyama, have emphasized the importance for democracy of an effective state (including a professional civil service) that is able to control violence, manage the economy, and administer public services efficiently and transparently. By these counts, Hong Kong is one of the readiest systems in the world for democracy. In the latest World Bank Institute ("Governance Matters") measurements, it ranks in the 89th percentile in terms of political stability, 94th in government effectiveness (in terms of the quality and neutrality of the civil service and the quality of policy formulation), 90th percentile in the rule of law, 93rd in corruption control, and 100th in regulatory quality, meaning, by the methodology of the World Bank, that Hong Kong is the best in the world at formulating "policies and regulations that permit and promote private sector development" (see Figure 18.1). Moreover, Hong Kong's relative standing on each of these measures has steadily improved since the initiation of the SAR in 1997, and on some measures quite dramatically. Only on the measure of "voice and account-ability" does Hong Kong lag well behind other societies (especially other economically developed systems), scoring in 2006 in the 65th percentile.

It is possible to argue that Hong Kong is doing so well *because* it is not a democracy, and that introducing electoral democracy will only mess up these exceptional governance scores. There are three possible rejoinders to this serious objection. First, this is quite a different argument than the claim—which I believe I have shown here to be untenable—that Hong Kong is not developmentally ready for democracy. Second, there is no evidence that governance generally deteriorates following a transition to democracy. In the systems most similar to Hong Kong in development and culture, Korea and Taiwan, we see a mixed picture: Since the governance measures began to be compiled in 1996, Korea has generally improved or maintained its scores on the different measures of governance, under a democratic system, while Taiwan has shown a more uneven pattern, due in particular to the corruption scandals and political polarization under the DPP govern-ment of President Chen Shui-bian. But precisely because it is a democracy, Taiwan achieved dramatic electoral alternation in the March 2008 presi-dential election, and I believe this will result in significant improvement in some of its governance indicators. Moreover, while opponents of the democratization of Hong Kong may cite the poor record of Chen Shui-bian's government in stimulating Taiwan nationalism, populism, political division, and instability as justification for deferring democracy, Hong Kong is a lot more like Korea than Taiwan in its underlying cleavage structure. Also, its state structures are today much stronger and less politicized than Taiwan's were under the one-party rule of the KMT in 1996. More globally, one can point to better rates of economic growth and patterns of govern-ance in the democracies than the dictatorships of Africa, and sustained or improved governance in some of Latin America's emerging democra-cies, such as Chile, Uruguay, and (to a lesser extent) Mexico over the last decade.

The third response to the intrinsic claim for the superiority of nondemo-cratic rule is that it is really for the people of a society, not its self-appointed (or externally chosen) rulers to decide what kind of political system is best

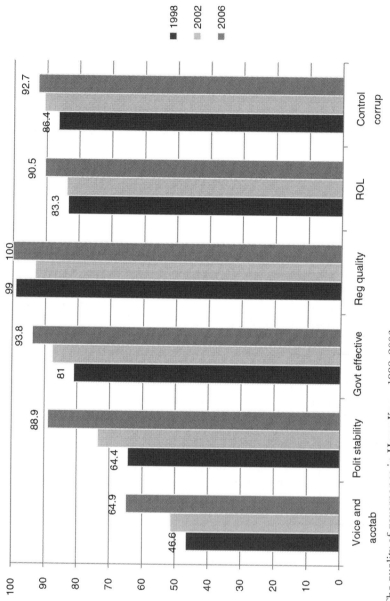

Figure 18.1 The quality of governance in Hong Kong, 1998–2006

for them, and how to weigh competing values. If there is a risk of diminished governance in some arenas as a result of better governance in others (more voice and accountability, for example), then the people ought to assess the risk and weigh what they value most. But here, too, if we look at political values in Hong Kong, we see that they are substantially democratic. When surveyed at the end of 2001 by the Asian Barometer, residents of Hong Kong showed some of the highest levels of rejection of authoritarian regime options of seven East Asian political systems surveyed (including also Korea, Taiwan, Japan, Mongolia, Thailand, and the Philippines). Explicit commitment to democracy lagged behind the established democracies of Asia, but this was still expressed by a majority of the population. And on most measures of political values in Hong Kong, substantial majorities expressed a democratic tendency: for example, 90 percent agreed that people with little or no education should have as much say in politics as those with high education; 69 percent disagreed that "the government should decide whether certain ideas should be allowed to be discussed in society"; and two-thirds also rejected the notion that "government leaders are the like the head of a family; we should all follow their decisions."[6] Moreover, education, income, and youth are all strongly positively associated with democratic value orientations in Hong Kong.[7] Thus, as the society becomes richer and better educated, and as generational change works its way through the society, the desire for democratic modes of governance is likely to grow. If we compare Taiwan and Hong Kong, we find that on most clusters of democratic values, the mass public in Hong Kong is as democratic as that in Taiwan, and Hong Kong elites also compare favorably to their peers in Taiwan. Not surprisingly, supporters of pro-democracy political forces in Hong Kong manifested more pro-democratic values than did citizens who support pro-China political forces, but the differences are not large, especially at the mass level.[8]

Models and constraints of transition

It should be clear, then, that the limits to democratization in Hong Kong do not derive from its intrinsic "lack of readiness" for democracy. By comparative or theoretical calculation examining the level of socioeconomic development, the cultural cleavages in the society, the level of state capacity and effectiveness, the rule of law, and the attitudes and values of the people, Hong Kong seems about as "ready" to receive and sustain democracy as any society that has become democratic in recent decades.

There is one major problem. Unlike *any* other of these societies that has become democratic, Hong Kong seeks to do so as a semiautonomous unit of governance within a larger nondemocratic system. And not just a "nondemocratic system," but a highly authoritarian regime which has none of the features of democracy that Hong Kong has enjoyed for some time—a multiparty political system; free and fair, multiparty elections for at least a portion of the system-wide legislature; and relatively high levels of civil liberties, including press freedom, freedom of association, and freedom of speech. It is important for objective observers to be analytically clear, even if parties to the controversy must take strident or stylized positions to mobilize their followings, reassure their allies, or tiptoe past uncomfortable realities. The big constraining reality is that Hong Kong's transition to democracy can, under the Basic Law, be blocked indefinitely by Beijing while it claims that the Hong Kong SAR is still "not yet ready" for full democracy, and that "gradual and orderly progress" means whatever pace of very incremental evolution Beijing will allow, "in light of the actual situation," as the Beijing authorities frame and interpret it. To be sure, indefinite postponement of full democracy by Beijing would be inconsistent with the spirit of the Basic Law, at least, and specifically articles 45 and 68, which proclaim democratic election of the chief executive and the Legislative Council "by universal suffrage" as "the ultimate aim." As one Hong Kong democrat privately observed to me, "Constitutional power unconstitutionally exercised is but force under a different name. Of course, there is no legal remedy in China against such an abuse by the highest organ of state power, but that does not give it a legal right to do so."

Beyond the constitutional veto power of the Beijing authorities at any moment in time is the fact that powerful segments of the administrative and business elite in Hong Kong have been willing to go along with and support—indeed have welcomed—Beijing's go-slow approach, and thus the Beijing veto is not purely an external imposition but enjoys some vocal and potent internal support within Hong Kong itself. Hong Kong democrats must find a way to address and alleviate the anxieties of these critical, weighty constituencies within Hong Kong.

The basic political problem in Hong Kong today is that pro-Beijing forces are unwilling to concede that Hong Kong is in every sense but one long since "ready for democracy," while pro-democracy forces have failed to recognize that in the sense of the political and constitutional balance of power and authority, Beijing can block the SAR's transition to democracy indefinitely (if they wish, beyond 2017 and 2020, and quite possibly for decades, or at least until China itself becomes a democracy). Unless Hong Kong pro-democracy forces figure out a way to change the current polarized power game that finds democrats on one side demanding democracy now—that is universal suffrage in the next rounds of elections (2012)— while pro-Beijing forces take a variety of go-slower approaches (which, even in the best light, leave ambiguous just how democratic Hong Kong would be allowed to be by 2020), the transition to genuine democracy will continue to be deferred or diluted (again, unless the political system for the rest of China undergoes significant democratization).

There are basically three models of transition to democracy, as Samuel P. Huntington explained in his famous work *The Third Wave.*[9] One model is imposition from above—what Huntington calls *transformation*—by an authoritarian regime that is holding most of the cards. This was essentially the mode of transition in Taiwan, Mexico, Spain, and Brazil. The opposite mode, *replacement*, occurs much more infrequently, when an authoritarian regime loses its resolve or the commitment of its support base (particularly in the military) as a result of a dramatic failure, such as defeat in war (Argentina and Greece), the flight of its people (East Germany), the inability to pay its soldiers and civil servants (Benin), or some kind of military (Portugal) or electoral revolution. The latter mode has occurred in the Philippines in 1986 and more recently with the "color revolutions" in Serbia, Georgia, and Ukraine. In these circumstances, regimes miscalculated, thinking they could rig or prevail in manipulated elections, and democratic forces outlasted and outmaneuvered them. The third mechanism is a negotiated transition, what Huntington calls *transplacement*, between an authoritarian regime that remains too powerful to be pushed out and a democratic opposition that has become too mobilized and resourceful to be suppressed without costs that the regime does not wish to (or cannot) bear. Such negotiated transitions between regime and opposition have been the norm, characterizing the transitions in Korea, much of Central America, Uruguay, Poland, Czechoslovakia, Mongolia, and South Africa. (There is also a fourth mode—foreign intervention to overthrow the dictatorship, as in Grenada and Panama—but no Hong Kong democrat seriously contemplates that).[10]

My premise here is that the only way a transition to democracy is going to happen in Hong Kong is through a negotiated bargain. The Communist regime in Beijing has no interest in initiating or imposing it; that is usually an option taken either because the ruling elite judges that it needs to extricate itself from power or more often because values have changed over time and the regime leaders come to believe that democracy is best for their country. China's political leaders will only initiate or enthusiastically oblige a true democratic transition in Hong Kong if they have resolved to implement it throughout the Chinese political system. That may happen, but it is not on the political horizon in China, and so for the coming 10–20 years, at least, Hong Kong will only break the constitutional stalemate and achieve universal suffrage for a fully democratically elected parliament and a *democratically elected* chief executive if China's Communist Party leaders agree. And they will only agree if they think their critical interests and those of their allies in the industrial, commercial, and financial sectors have been reasonably respected and protected.

This point may seem obvious, but I do not think its implications have been fully pondered and grasped by Hong Kong pro-democracy forces. They are in a weak position politically. In other situations where democratic civil societies and opposition parties pressed forward transitions to democracy, authoritarian regimes were weak or on the defensive, and usually under significant international pressure to democratize or at least liberalize. None of that is the case today, either with the larger political system of

China or with the specific regime in Hong Kong. It would be nice if democrats of the world would unite and demand that Hong Kong be allowed to become a democracy, but the world's democratic governments and societies cannot even agree on whether and how to press China to: improve its own still very repressive human rights situation; stop condoning genocide in Darfur; stop supporting and enabling the brutal dictatorship in Burma; and so on. Since Hong Kong does not have a human rights emergency as in Darfur or Burma, and does not suffer the kinds of systemic constraints on freedom and egregious violations of civil liberties that other citizens of the PRC suffer, the world does not feel much urgency in pressing for democracy in Hong Kong. Sadly, the people of Hong Kong are on their own.

Thus, unless political forces in Hong Kong find a way to bridge their differences and agree on a compromise plan and timetable for democratic transition, the situation is likely to remain stuck short of democracy for a very long time, possibly even well beyond 2017 or 2020, for three reasons. First, the December NPCSC decision permitted but did not mandate universal suffrage by 2017 and 2020 respectively. The lack of a firm commitment (indicated by the use of the word "may" rather than "will" or "must") is (understandably) a major issue for the democratic opposition in Hong Kong, and seriously handicaps it in future negotiations. Second, the (tentative, permissive) commitment in 2017 is to "universal suffrage" for election of the chief executive. Universal suffrage is of course one component of a democratic, free, and fair election, but not the only component. In addition to many other requirements that could be noted,[11] democratic elections require open and free access to the ballot on the part of potential competing candidates and parties. More than anything else, that is what remains indefinitely in doubt in Hong Kong. Given that the decision to implement universal suffrage must happen by consensus, and under the Basic Law, one is left to presume that Beijing and establishment forces in Hong Kong will insist upon retention of some kind of nominating committee (probably similar in composition to the current election committee) to vet candidates that will be allowed to stand for the position of chief executive. Unless some kind of consensus can be fashioned on this question, and on the electoral system for a fully, directly elected LegCo, and on the transitional arrangements until 2017–2020, hopes for democratic change could be frustrated for much longer.

Thus, the real dialogue that is needed now is serious negotiations between pro-democracy and pro-China forces within Hong Kong to find common ground. There is a parallel to the negotiated democratic transitions that O'Donnell and Schmitter discuss in their seminal work, *Transitions from Authoritarian Rule*. They argue that all transitions in the 1970s and 1980s began with a split in the regime between hard-liners and soft-liners, which was then widened and exploited by intensified mobilization by democratic civil society and opposition forces, and then pushed forward to democratic transition when the moderates (soft-liners) on the regime side and their counterparts on the pro-democracy side sat down and negotiated with one another. This was often a complex and delicate game, in which opposition mobilization could generate sufficient alarm on the part of the regime to realize that it had to find a way out, while moderate opposition willing-ness to talk—and, crucially, the capacity of moderate opposition leaders to wind down mobilization at crucial moments, to command their civic follow-ings—led to successful negotiations for democratic transition.[12]

It is important to stress that typically, democratic forces initially won at the bargaining table—in Poland, in Chile, in South Africa—less than they would have gotten if the authoritarian regimes had just collapsed, as they did in Argentina, Greece, and the Philippines. Instead, the democrats had to settle for transitional periods and in some cases lengthy periods in which certain "authoritarian enclaves" or prerogatives (for example, for the military in Chile) were preserved. It is quite likely that a constitutional bargain in Hong Kong will preserve less than fully democratic practices for some transitional (hopefully not long) period of time. This is already apparent from the insist-ence on 2017 and 2020 as the earliest possible dates for universal suffrage, and is implicit as well in the mechanism for electing a chief executive. But against a longer (really, only moderately long) sweep of history, these aspects of deferred democratic gratification proved to be fairly temporary in these other cases. South Africa's majority party only had to put up with mandated power-sharing for five years. In Chile, the military's prerogatives and insulated powers lasted longer, but have gradually given way as democratic governments became stronger and more self-confident, and as the society (including some of the old support base for General Augusto Pinochet) shifted more emphati-cally in favor of modern, real, unconstrained democracy.

Implications for a negotiated transition in Hong Kong

Morally, any democrat in the world must feel great sympathy for those in Hong Kong who have demanded universal suffrage and full democracy in 2007 and 2008—or at least by 2012. From the perspective as well of empiri-cal democratic theories of the conditions for democracy, that achievement seems long overdue, and anything less seems patently unnecessary and unfair. But from the standpoint of the comparative politics of transition, Hong Kong democrats appear to lack a favorable tactical situation to achieve their goal. Unless they broaden their coalition, they could be mak-ing this demand and losing out for several more electoral cycles to come. Sometimes, democrats must swallow hard and compromise for something less than what is morally due to them but more than they can otherwise achieve by civic mobilization and moral appeals alone.

There are obvious points for compromise, and they involve two sets of issues: the timetable for achieving full universal suffrage, and the structure of the democratic system that would result. The broad lessons from other democratic transitions—to the extent they are applicable—suggest the fol-lowing points.

First, pro-democracy forces will be more effective in pressing for a genuine transition to democracy to the extent that they can unite in a strong, coherent political and civic coalition that is capable of negotiating with pro-Beijing or "pro-system" forces, including the government of the HKSAR.

Second, if pro-democracy forces cannot unite for negotiations, a breakthrough might nevertheless be facilitated if a prestigious and politically weighty subset of the pro-democracy camp were to opt for pragmatic negotiations with their moderate and compromise-seeking counterparts on the pro-Beijing side.

Third, it will help if pro-democracy forces demonstrate from time to time the capacity to mobilize large numbers of demonstrators and other expressions of mass popular sentiment for democratic change, but the moderate bloc must exercise the moral authority and political discipline to cease mobilization as well as ignite it.

Fourth, the near-term tactical goal must be the achievement of an internal agreement in Hong Kong among the major political players: the pro-democracy forces, the pro-Beijing political forces (including leading elements of the business community), and the government. Only if the major actors in Hong Kong come to a compromise agreement on the timing and structure of a democratic transition are the Beijing authorities likely to judge that "actual political conditions" have evolved to the point where Hong Kong is "ready" for democracy.

Fifth, pro-democracy forces probably have no choice at this point but to accept in principle the dates of 2017 and 2020, and focus on the key issues of what the interim electoral arrangements will look like in 2012 and (for the LegCo) 2016, and how the universal suffrage elections will be structured from 2017 and 2020 on.

Sixth, democrats would do well to focus on practical initiatives to get from the current system to full democracy. In a policy essay before the December 2007 NPC decision on Hong Kong's constitutional development, former Secretary for Security Regina Ip proposed incremental steps for opening up the election of the chief executive. She proposed direct election of the chief executive in 2012 among candidates nominated by a Nominating Committee that would involve a very considerable expansion in the size (and electoral base) of the current Election Committee for Chief Executive (to 1,800 members), and some threshold of support needed from the Nomination Committee in order for a candidate to contest for election (10 percent overall and in each of the four sectors of the Election Committee). Her fallback or compromise position (in the event full universal suffrage for the chief executive could not be obtained in 2012) was to expand the current Election Committee in 2012, and then make it a nominating committee in 2017 for choosing candidates for the universal suffrage election. Pro-democracy forces object that such requirements for nomination could give any one functional sector a veto to block the candidacy of a pro-democracy candidate for chief executive, but her proposal could serve as a basis for negotiation among diverse camps in Hong Kong. For example, an expanded Election Committee for 2012 could be better than the current one. And it could also be a bridge to a more democratic future. If such an expanded committee were retained for the first direct chief executive election, in 2017, it might help to build broad confidence in the process, after which its role would be gradually relaxed or abandoned entirely. The key is that democrats must stress that any continued restrictive use of a nomination committee departs from democratic principles and norms and can only be acceptable as a transitional confidence-building arrangement, with a clear date for its termination (or its transformation into a merely nominal procedure).

Seventh, creative thinking is needed for the mode of transition to a fully, directly elected LegCo as well. A variety of institutional options should be tabled and discussed, both publicly and in private negotiations among the major political forces in Hong Kong. Prior to the December NPCSC decision, Regina Ip proposed to increase the size of the body from 60 to 80 members in 2012, if a fully, directly elected LegCo could not be achieved by that year. The additional 20 seats would be elected by universal suffrage from PR lists (proportional representation) put forward by political parties or groups of candidates. This would increase the percentage of democratically elected seats to a clear majority and would then give way in 2016 to a democratic mixed system of fully universal suffrage (like that in many established and new democracies). Under this permanent system, the functional constituencies would disappear and half of the 80 LegCo seats would be elected from the geographical constituencies and half from the party or group lists (contesting Hong Kong-wide).

It appears that Beijing is adamant about preserving the 50–50 split of functional and geographical constituency seats in the LegCo until 2020. But there could be other ways of moving gradually, through the 2012 and 2016 elections, to a fully democratically elected legislature in 2020. This could involve, as Professor Kin-man Chan of the Chinese University of Hong Kong has proposed, starting in 2012 to alter the nature and representativeness of the functional constituencies.[13] Some are also proposing to add ten more LegCo seats and have the five new functional constituency seats represent very broad constituencies. The proposed step that would move the furthest in a democratic direction, it appears, would be to draw these five additional functional constituency seats from among the existing elected district council members. Chi-Keung Choy has built on this by also recommending that, in the subsequent two LegCo elections, functionally similar constituencies be merged and progressively enlarged, with 18 of the proposed 35 functional constituency seats being drawn from one large "District Council" constituency (using the preferential system of the single transferable vote).[14] These are practical and innovative ideas worthy at least of a hearing. The larger strategic principle for transition is this: Negotiations between different camps in Hong Kong could essentially trade incremental reforms up to 2020 and a definite commitment to full universal suffrage for LegCo elections in 2020 in exchange for acceptance of that delayed date, consensus behind the timetable, and thus enhanced "governability" in Hong Kong affairs between the current moment and 2020.

We return, however, to the core problem, which is that Hong Kong democrats appear at the moment to be in a structurally weak bargaining position, which is further weakened by their own divisions. Their ability to bargain for a clear commitment to democratic transition (rather than partial or pseudodemocracy) would be enhanced by three things. First, they need to unite as much as possible around a practical strategy for negotiation. Second, they need to augment their political and thus negotiating power by winning more of the seats that are realistically available to them and mobilizing broader civic support and consciousness. And third, they need to reach out to more conservative and pro-Beijing political forces, build trust, and explore practical possibilities for achieving consensus on these transitional arrangements.

Hong Kong does have one advantage, if political forces are smart enough and flexible enough to seize it. Differences over timing and increments of power are easier to settle, if competing parties and factions put aside their pride and fixed positions and agree to bargain, than are deeper-seated, more symbolic and emotive differences over identity. In this respect, Taiwan has faced in the last decade a seemingly more intractable problem than Hong Kong. Yet even in Taiwan, a corner has been turned, with the 2008 election victory of Ma Ying-jeou, toward reconciliation and moderation on this dangerous issue. If a much more deeply divided Taiwan can make progress on such an explosive issue, then Hong Kong should be able to do so as well. There are many ways of "splitting the difference" between a democratic transition date of now or the next election, versus in five years, twelve years, or some indefinite and constantly receding future horizon. There are many ways of allocating seats through different electoral methods and among different groups in society. Hong Kong, in other words, is at a point in its political and economic development when it should be possible for people of imagination and good will to strike a viable constitutional bargain.

Such a bargain is more conceivable now than five years ago precisely because there are political forces that have the trust and respect of Beijing and who are sincerely looking for a way to move Hong Kong to democracy. This is a new and critical development. These new political forces are not agents of the Beijing authorities, but Beijing is watching closely how their ideas and proposals fare. If the political battle lines continue to be drawn starkly into two camps—real democracy now or never—while creative transitional proposals are spurned, Hong Kong is likely to remain mired in its stalemate. If Beijing sees that political forces are reaching across previously polarized lines to come to a flexible common ground that delivers eventual democracy while offering established interests reasonable grounds of confidence, it might draw the conclusion that "gradual and orderly progress" has indeed taken place in Hong Kong, and that "the actual situation" in the HKSAR has finally reached a point where a firm commitment can be made to a timetable for democratic transition. If that is truly to be a transition to democracy, the timetable must involve not just prospective or permissive—but definite—dates on the foreseeable horizon. And it must guarantee not only full, universal suffrage for the election of the legislature and the executive, but—sooner or later—the right of all political parties to contest for the position of chief executive.

Notes

1 Originally published in full as "A Comparative Perspective on Hong Kong Democratization: Prospects Toward 2017/2020," in Ming K. Chan, ed., *China's Hong Kong Transformed: Retrospect and Prospects* (Hong Kong: University of Hong Kong Press, 2008), 315–333. An earlier slightly shorter version was published as "Prospects for Democratization in Hong Kong: A Comparative Perspective," in Carola McGiffert and James T. H. Tang, *Hong Kong on the Move: 10 Years as the HKSAR* (Washington, DC: Center for Strategic and International Studies, 2008), 3–17. First presented to the conference, "Hong Kong on the Move: American and Hong Kong Perspectives on the First Ten Years of the HKSAR," sponsored by the Center for Strategic and International Studies and the Hong Kong's Washington Economic and Trade Office, October 22, 2007, Washington, DC.

2 Article 45 of The Basic Law of the Hong Kong Special Administrative Region of the People's Republic of China, www.info.gov.hk/basic_law/fulltext.

3 Hong Kong's 2006 per capita gross national income (GNI) is $38,200. World Bank Indicators Online. See http://data.worldbank.org/indicator/NT.GDP.PCAP.CD?page=1.

4 United Nations Development Programme, *Human Development Report 2007–2008* (New York: UNDP, 2007), 2229, table 1.

5 These comparisons and other domestic drivers of democratization are considered in greater detail in Larry Diamond, *The Spirit of Democracy: The Struggle to Build Free Societies Throughout the World* (New York: Times Books, 2008), ch. 4.

6 Andrew J. Nathan, "Political Culture and Diffuse Regime Support," Asian Barometer Working Paper No. 43, 2007, tables 1a and 4a, www.asianbarometer.org/newenglish/publications/workingpapers/no.43.pdf.

7 Ibid., table 5, 31.

8 Alfred Ko-wei Hu, "Attitudes Toward Democracy Between Mass Publics and Elites in Taiwan and Hong Kong," Working Paper No. 9, Asian Barometer, 2003, www.asianbarometer.org/newenglish/publications/workingpapers/no.9.pdf.

9 Samuel P. Huntington, *The Third Wave: Democratization in the Late Twentieth Century* (Norman: University of Oklahoma Press, 1991).

10 Ibid., ch. 4, 109–163. On negotiated transitions, see also Guillermo O'Donnell and Philippe Schmitter, *Transitions from Authoritarian Rule: Tentative Conclusions about Uncertain Democracies* (Baltimore, MD: Johns Hopkins University Press, 1986).

11 See Diamond, *The Spirit of Democracy*, 24–25, and Jorgen Elklit and Palle Svensson, "What Makes Elections Free and Fair?" *Journal of Democracy* 8 (July 1997): 32–46.

12 O'Donnell and Schmitter, *Transitions from Authoritarian Rule*.

13 Kin-man Chan, "Shixian puxuan hongyuan sanfang reng xu nuli" ("Tripartite Efforts are still needed to Achieve the Noble Goal of Universal Suffrage"), *Ming Pao*, January 8, 2008.
14 Kin-man Chan, "Min wang zheng gai fang'an chuyi" ("My Humble Opinion on the *Min Wang* Constitutional Package," *Ming Pao*, April 24, 2008.

19 Indonesia's place in global democracy[1]

Indonesia has been a latecomer to democracy during the historic "third wave" of global democratization. It was not until a quarter-century into this wave—in 1999—that Indonesia became an electoral democracy. By then, the third wave of democracy had essentially crested, though levels of freedom in the world continued to improve for some years thereafter. The other transitions in East Asia had already occurred (the Philippines' in 1986, South Korea's in 1987, Taiwan's from 1987 to 1996, and Mongolia's in the early 1990s). By the time Taiwan completed its transition in 1996, Indonesia seemed as unwaveringly authoritarian as it had ever been during the three-decade period of Suharto's authoritarian "New Order."

Oddly, it has been in this recent period of global democratic stagnation and recession that Indonesia has emerged and developed as a democracy. During its first full decade of democracy, Indonesia has become in many ways a surprising political success story. This progress stands in marked contrast to a number of other large and strategically significant developing countries that saw democracy erode in the same period, such as Nigeria, Venezuela, the Philippines, Thailand, Pakistan, and Bangladesh. Today, Indonesia is not only a reasonably stable democracy—with no obvious threats or potent antidemocratic challengers on the horizon—but it is even in some respects a relatively liberal democracy, with reasonably fair elections and extensive freedoms of press and association. It remains, as it has been for decades, in the bottom half of countries on all measures of the quality of governance, but it has made significant improvements on most of these in the last decade. And its public exhibits one of the most robust profiles of support for democracy and liberal values, and trust in public institutions, of any of East Asia's democracies. This, I argue, is an impressive record of progress, but still only a partial one. If Indonesia's democracy is to become truly "consolidated," and hence stable for the long run, it must become a higher-quality democracy, in particular one that makes much more dramatic progress in reducing corruption, providing a rule of law, and modernizing and professionalizing the overall architecture of the state.

This chapter proceeds as follows. First, I evaluate Indonesian democracy's relative performance in socioeconomic development during its first decade, then its political performance on indicators of democracy and governance. The following section looks in depth at public opinion data from the second wave of the Asian Barometer to compare Indonesians' attitudes and values toward democracy with those of publics from the other emerging democracies of East and Southeast Asia (South Korea, Taiwan, the Philippines, Thailand, and Mongolia). Finally, in conclusion, I weigh the meaning of these and related trends and analyses for the future of democracy in Indonesia.

The relative performance of Indonesian democracy: socioeconomic development

How has Indonesia's democracy done in its first decade? I assess Indonesia not against the lowest standard—democracies that have broken down or seem at imminent risk of doing so—but rather by comparing Indonesia with two sets of reference groups. One is a set of other large and significant emerging-market democracies (outside East Asia): Argentina, Bangladesh, Brazil, Ghana, India, Mexico, South Africa, and Turkey. The list is somewhat arbitrary but captures size and strategic importance (or in the case of Ghana, the best performer among the new democracies of Africa). The other set contains the other five countries in East Asia that are or have recently been democracies: South Korea, Taiwan, Thailand, the Philippines, and Mongolia. One way to judge how Indonesia's democracy has done in the last decade is to compare its performance on a number of measures of development, governance, and democracy with these two reference groups.

On the measures of social and economic development, Indonesia's performance as a new democracy has been reasonably good relative to other emerging-market democracies around the world. Its average GDP growth rate for the period 1999–2008 (4.76 percent) has been better than its emerging-market peers in Figure 19.1 (save India and Bangladesh, which were starting from much lower levels). During the decade 1995–2006 (admittedly, not fully overlapping with the era of democracy), it also recorded around a 10 percent improvement in its Human Development Index Score, which is quite respectable in comparative terms (see Figure 19.2). Its annual population growth rate during 2000–2007 was at a level (1.4 percent) reflective of an economy and society where improved health, education, and job opportunities for women are reducing fertility. Its adult literacy rate at 91 percent is well above the average of 79.6 percent for the emerging-market set, and even slightly exceeds that for much richer democracies like Brazil (89.6 percent), South Africa (87.6 percent), and Turkey (88.1 percent). In the mortality rate for children under 5, Indonesia, with a figure of 31 deaths per 1000 births in

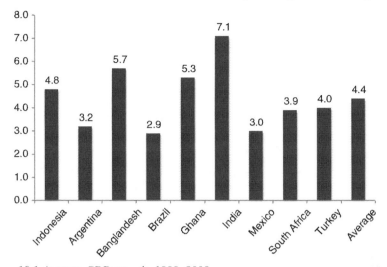

Figure 19.1 Average GDP growth, 1999–2008

2000, outperforms much richer Mexico with a rate of 35 deaths per 1000 deaths, let alone poorer countries like India (72) and Bangladesh (61). Underlying such positive social outcomes is the fact that Indonesia has a much better income distribution than all its richer peers among the emerging-market democracies, with a Gini coefficient well below those of Argentina, Brazil, Mexico, South Africa, and Turkey. Some of this is a legacy of the authoritarian period, but it does appear that socioeconomic progress has continued under the period of democracy—which, after all, inherited an economy that had been badly shocked by the 1997 financial crisis. Of course, if we compare within East Asia, Indonesia's performance on most social indicators lags well behind the now developed economies of South Korea and Taiwan (for instance, the child mortality rate is only 5 per 1000 births in South Korea, compared to 31 in Indonesia). But relative to the Philippines (which is now about the same level of per capita income) and Thailand (which is twice as rich as Indonesia), Indonesia performs well. It has improved its Human Development Index twice as fast as the Philippines (4.8 percent) and slightly faster than Thailand (9 percent). It has brought its population growth and child mortality rates down much faster than the Philippines. And its income is much better distributed than either of those countries.

Indonesia's relative performance in democracy and governance

Indonesia has also done surprisingly well in terms of democracy and governance. Let us examine first its scores on political rights and civil liberties,

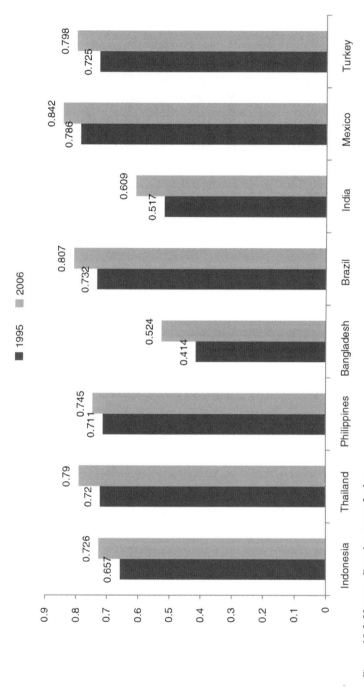

Figure 19.2 Human Development Index

as measured annually by Freedom House, which awards a score of 1 for most free and 7 for least free on each scale. Indonesia's freedom scores have steadily improved over time, from a score of 6 on political rights and 4 on civil liberties during the 1998 transitional year to 4 and 4 in 1999, 3 and 4 during 2000–2005, and 2 and 3 during 2006–2009 (Table 19.1). This reflects significant improvements in the climate of freedom, rule of law, and political competition, even from the early years of Indonesia's democratic decade, and in essence confirms other assessments that democracy has moved forward politically under the presidency of Susilo Bambang Yudhoyono (SBY). As a result, Indonesia has been rated as a "free" country since 2006.

As we see in Table 19.2, Indonesia's freedom scores in recent years have been on a par with India and Mexico, and better than Turkey's. And its democratic progress during the last decade stands in stark contrast to the Philippines and Thailand, where freedom (and democracy) have deteriorated sharply in the last decade. Over this decade, in terms of democratic vitality and quality, and on some more general measures of governance as well, Indonesia has "traded places" with these other two Southeast Asian countries, an outcome that few if any observers of the region anticipated during the early to mid-1990s.

Yet on other measures of governance, Indonesia still has considerable distance to go; outstripping countries like Bangladesh and the Philippines is not exactly cause for celebration. The bottom rows in Table 19.2 examine Indonesia's performance on several other dimensions of governance as measured annually by the World Bank (I have combined two of the measures, government effectiveness and regulatory quality, into a single average measure of "state quality").[2] By these more complex measures, the quality of political development in Indonesia has not progressed to nearly as high a level as the Freedom House ratings of political rights and civil liberties would suggest. Indonesia's percentile score on voice and accountability stood in 2008 at only 44.2—better than Turkey, the Philippines, Thailand, and Bangladesh, but well behind the other emerging-market democracies, which ranged from 50 to 67.

The next rows in Table 19.2 assess state quality, as an average of two percentile scores: government effectiveness (the quality of public services and policy formulation, the independence and capacity of the civil service) and regulatory quality ("the ability of the government to provide sound policies and regulations that ... promote private sector development"). Here, as

Table 19.1 Trends in Indonesia's Freedom House scores (political rights, civil liberties)

Indicators	1997	1998	1999	2000–05	2006–09
Score: political rights, civil liberties	7, 5	6, 4	4, 4	3, 4	2, 3

Table 19.2 Comparative measures of democratic and governance indicators in emerging democracies

Indicator	Indonesia	Thailand	Philippines	India	Bangladesh	Argentina	Brazil	Mexico	South Africa	Turkey
FH scores, PR and CL, 1998	6, 4	3, 3	2, 3	2, 4	2, 4	2, 3	3, 4	3, 4	1, 2	4, 5
FH 2008	2, 3	6, 4	4, 3	2, 3	5, 4	2, 2	2, 2	2, 3	2, 2	3, 3
WB voice 1998	16.3	61.1	60.6	58.2	41.8	55.3	55.8	47.1	73.6	29.8
Voice 2008	44.2	32.2	41.3	58.7	30.8	57.2	61.1	50.5	67.8	41.8
WB state quality: avg govt effectiveness & regulatory quality, 1998	29.2	57.7	54.9	43.2	27.6	66.4	57.0	64.5	70.3	59.8
WB state quality 2008	46.4	59.4	53.4	50.3	21.8	38.4	56.3	63.2	73.5	60.8
WB ROL 1998	23.8	65.7	52.9	60.5	21.9	57.1	46.2	37.1	58.1	53.8
WB ROL 2008	28.7	54.1	39.7	56.5	27.3	32.1	46.4	29.7	56	55.5
WB control corruption 1998	9.2	57.8	41.3	45.6	25.2	53.9	58.7	35.9	71.8	51
WB control corruption 2008	31.4	43	26.1	44.4	10.6	40.1	58.5	49.8	65.2	60.4

Source: World Bank, "Governance Matters 2009: Worldwide Governance Indicators, 1996–2008," interactive website, accessed September 2009, http://info. worldbank.org/governance/wgi/index.asp.

on other items (I will return to this point shortly), Indonesia has improved considerably since its transition to democracy. Whereas in 1998 it was just about at the bottom of this comparison set of emerging-market democracies, by 2008, it was at least doing more respectably, close to India, and better than Bangladesh and Argentina.

It is on the rule of law (which measures not only the independence and effectiveness of the police and courts but the quality of contract enforcement and property rights as well) that Indonesia still lags furthest behind. Its percentile score has improved little since 1998, and trails very far behind even some other emerging-market countries that are poorer (Ghana, not shown here, and India) or face horrible legacies of crime and state violence (South Africa). Here, even the Philippines (at 39.7) and Thailand (at 54.1) score well ahead of Indonesia (28.7).

In 1998, Indonesia was in the bottom 10 percent (9.2) of countries in the world in its effectiveness in control of corruption. None of Indonesia's peers among emerging-market democracies scored nearly so miserably then on this measure. A decade later, Indonesia is still—according to this index—very corrupt, as anyone who reads the almost daily revelations in Indonesia's press of new corruption scandals involving parliamentarians, police officers, prosecutors, and other senior officials would know. It has at least escaped the bottom quartile of countries (scoring now at 31.4), but it still lags behind the other emerging-market democracies in Table 19.2, except for Bangladesh and the Philippines.

The above presents a mixed picture of Indonesia's political progress in the past decade. It has taken long strides toward freedom but less so in the quality of governance. Its level of state capacity in economic and administrative affairs is about middling now, but it is still plagued by extensive corruption and a weak rule of law. Yet, when we look at change over time, the picture becomes more impressive. According to the World Bank, Indonesia has made significant progress on virtually every one of the six indicators of governance since 1998. For example, on voice and accountability its score has jumped from 16.3 in 1998 to 44.2 in 2008, on government effectiveness it has jumped from 19.4 to 47.4, control of corruption from 9.2 to 31.7, and even rule of law has increased from 23.8 to 28.7.[3] In some cases this has been steady progress, in some cases there was significant progress only after a dip in performance between 1998 and 2003, reflecting some of the drift and even chaos of the early transition.[4] These positive changes also doubtlessly reflect institutional reforms taken by Indonesia during its first decade of democratic transition, and the establishment of new government bodies, such as the powerful Corruption Eradication Commission (KPK), designed to improve governance.

The picture becomes rather more dramatic, and more positive, when we compare Indonesia's progress on some of the governance scores over the last decade with that of other countries around the world. On voice and accountability, Indonesia's improvement in score (of 0.9 on a point scale range from 2.5 to –2.5) was one of the top five records of improvement in the world (trailing only Ghana, Niger, Sierra Leone, and Serbia).[5] On government effectiveness, Indonesia's gain during this decade (0.56 points) ranked 13th in the world in terms of improvement. And in control of corruption, Indonesia's improvement (0.51 points) was eighth best in the world. Also striking about this record of globally pace-setting improvement on three of the six governance indicators is that Indonesia is one of the few "normal" countries to appear repeatedly on these lists of "most improved." Generally, the ones that frequently show up are the states that are recovering from violent conflict, civil war, or state collapse—places like Serbia, Iraq, Rwanda, Liberia, and Sierra Leone. Similarly strong relative improvement is visible in most other fields of governance measured by the World Bank. In these areas Indonesia improved its percentile rank more than most of its emerging-market peers, which improved more modestly, remained at roughly their previous levels, or declined.

In sum, Indonesia has made quite significant progress in democracy and governance over the last decade. It is not only a much freer country than it was in 1998, or even than in its very early years of democracy, it is also at least a somewhat better governed country on every one of the World Bank's measures of governance. Few countries in the past decade have made more progress in improving the quality of governance than Indonesia (and most of the others were completely failed states). Yet much remains to be done, if the expert ratings behind these statistics are to be believed. Indonesia remains in the bottom third of countries in the world in terms of both corruption and rule of law, and its average level of state quality, while having improved a lot, is still in the bottom of half. If Indonesia is to institutionalize liberal democracy, and probably if it is to launch into the higher rates of economic growth of which it is capable, it will have to do much more to improve the quality of its governance.

How Indonesians and other East Asians view democracy

Indonesia's democratic prospects become even more hopeful when we examine what its people actually think. Doing so is vital to understanding the depth and durability of democracy in Indonesia for two reasons. First, democracy is about popular sovereignty, and one cannot gain adequate purchase on the quality of democracy without knowing how its people evaluate the extent and performance of democracy in their country. And second, democratic stability depends heavily on robust public support for democracy. To measure progress toward the consolidation of democracy, we must know the extent to which its citizens regard it as legitimate—a better form of government than any other they can imagine. The only way we can know the extent to which people value and support their democratic institutions (or even perceive them as democratic) is to ask them, by scientifically surveying a representative sample of the voting-age public. This is what the Asian Barometer does. Indonesia was one of six emerging East Asian democracies surveyed systematically by the Asian Barometer during 2006.[6] The Barometer, drawing national, random samples of the voting-age population, asked a large number of standardized questions about people's attitudes and values toward democracy and their evaluations of their own governments, enabling meaningful and revealing comparisons among these countries.

Let us first examine how East Asians evaluate the extent of democracy in their country and to what extent they want their country to be democratic now. Each of these questions is evaluated by showing the respondent a card with a 10-point scale, with 1 being the least democratic and 10 the most democratic. Relative to other East Asians, Indonesians evaluated their democracy quite highly, at an average level of 7.0 on the 10-point scale. Only Thais placed their democracy higher (but ironically, their democracy was displaced by a military coup in September 2006, just a few months after the survey was conducted). And Indonesians said they want a strongly democratic country, placing their desire at an average level of 8.5, as high as South Korea, higher than Taiwan, and slightly outpaced again by Thailand (here though Mongolia was off the charts in first place; see Table 19.3).

Several more demanding and complex measures of support for democracy show similar depth and vigor of democratic attitudes in Indonesia. The Asian Barometer constructed a scale of five individual measures of support for democracy.[7] Figure 19.3 presents the mean levels of agreement with these five items (summarized as "support for democracy"), along with overall satisfaction with the way that democracy is working in the country. Interestingly, the emerging democracies of Indonesia, Thailand, and Mongolia (but not the Philippines) show higher levels of support for democracy on these measures used by the Asian Barometer than do South Korea and Taiwan. As we will see, the picture changes when we measure democratic tendencies differently, but it is nevertheless striking. (We, the scholars in the Asian Barometer survey, believe the difference is due to two factors: citizens in the more highly educated democracies of East Asia are more critical because of their higher levels of knowledge and information, and they compare their current democracy to previous authoritarian

Table 19.3 Perceived extent and desire for democracy, average scores

	Indonesia	*Korea*	*Taiwan*	*Thailand*	*Philippines*	*Mongolia*
Perceived extent of democracy	7.0	6.7	7.0	7.5	5.6	6.7
Desire for democracy	8.5	8.5	8.1	8.8	7.4	9.5

Source: Asian Barometer Wave 2. Scores can range from 1 to 10.

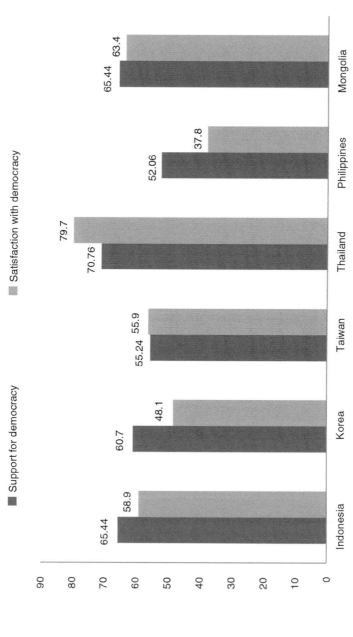

Figure 19.3 Support for and satisfaction with democracy

regimes that were quite successful in delivering economic development.) Indonesians show robust levels of support for democracy on four of the five measures. Only when democracy is pitted against economic development as a choice or priority do Indonesians waiver in large numbers, with only 21 percent saying that they believe that democracy is equally or more important than democracy (but similarly low figures were found almost everywhere in the region).

Indonesians are (or at least were in 2006) also reasonably satisfied with "the way democracy is working in our country." Nearly three in five Indonesians expressed strong or at least some satisfaction, again only exceeded by Thailand and Mongolia. This is encouraging because democratic satisfaction may help to sustain higher levels of support for democracy and discourage the temptation to search for authoritarian alternatives. It is a sign of "performance" legitimacy, and democracy is probably on its strongest legs when it enjoys support both as an intrinsic value and instrumentally, based on what is judged to be good performance.

The problem with explicit support for democracy is that it is not clear what people have in mind when the word "democracy" is mentioned. And in this day and age, there is a certain general social desirability attached to the word. Thus the Asian Barometer also seeks to get at the depth of democratic commitment in two other ways. One is to pose authoritarian alternatives and see how consistently citizens reject them. We asked respondents whether they agreed or disagreed with each of three statements: That the army should come in to govern the country; that only one political party should be allowed to contest and hold office; and that "We should get rid of parliament and elections and have a strong leader decide things." After a dozen years of examining public opinion survey data in new democracies, I have come to believe that the percentage of the population rejecting all three of these alternatives is one of the most important indicators of the depth of commitment to democracy. And here, now not surprisingly, we see something of a reverse pattern: The strongest levels of democratic support are in South Korea and Taiwan, where respectively 77 and 69 percent of the samples reject all three authoritarian options. But a majority also does so in Indonesia (56 percent) compared with much lower levels in the Philippines and Mongolia (see Figure 19.4).

The other way to examine the depth of democratic commitment is to pose a series of questions that test support for liberal values, such as civic pluralism, freedom of speech, judicial independence, popular sovereignty, and checks and balances. The Asian Barometer has constructed and tested a seven-item scale of liberal values that performs well in scale tests of coherence and reliability. It asks respondents to agree or disagree with statements such as "Government leaders are like the head of a family; we should all follow their decisions," "If the government is constantly checked [i.e. monitored and supervised] by the legislature, it cannot possibly accomplish great things," and "If people have too many ways of thinking, society

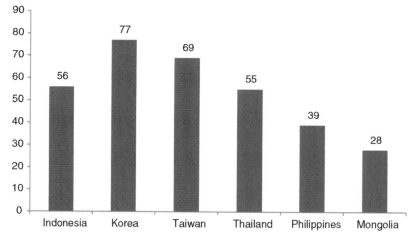

Figure 19.4 Rejection of authoritarianism

will be chaotic."[8] This is a high bar for exhibiting democratic commitment, because a liberal orientation requires disagreeing with each of the seven statements posed.[9] Nevertheless, the average level of support for liberal values in Indonesia is roughly 47 percent (Figure 19.5). I regard this as the single most striking comparative statistic, because the average level of liberal values is not much lower than in Taiwan and South Korea (52 and 55 percent, respectively), and these are much more developed, educated, and globally integrated societies. On this measure of liberal values, Thailand, the Philippines, and Mongolia all place much lower (none over 40 percent). Clearly, Indonesians are not just supporting democracy out of some vague preference for elections or popular government. For example, 57 percent of Indonesians disagree that judges should accept the view of the executive branch when deciding important cases; 52 percent disagree that if the society has morally upright leaders "we can let them decide everything." In addition, though it is not technically part of the "liberal values" battery, 68 percent of Indonesians *disagree* that it is alright for the government "to disregard the law in order to deal with a difficult situation." This is the same solid majority as in Taiwan and much higher than in Thailand and Mongolia. Figure 19.5 compares Indonesia with its East Asian peers on this latter item and on the liberal values scale.

To complete the portrait of public support for liberal democracy, the Asian Barometer has assembled the respondents from each country into four groups based on their levels of support for democracy and for liberal values. Consistent Democrats are above the mean for East Asia in levels of support both for democracy and for liberal values. Critical Democrats support liberal values but are below the mean on support for democracy. Superficial Democrats support democracy but are below on the mean on liberal values. And Non-Democrats are below the mean on both scales.[10] It

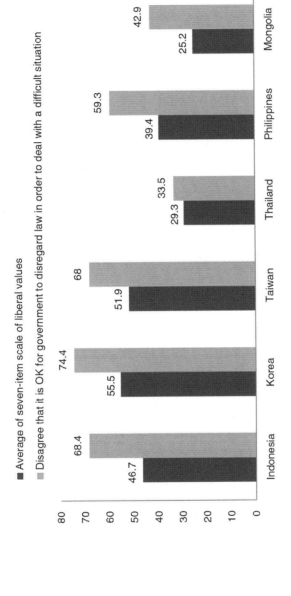

■ Average of seven-item scale of liberal values

▨ Disagree that it is OK for government to disregard law in order to deal with a difficult situation

Figure 19.5 Support for liberal values

will come as a surprise to many readers (as it did to many of us in the Asian Barometer project) that Indonesia has the highest percentage of Consistent Democrats (38 percent) of *any* of the six East Asian democracies (or quasi-democracies). Only South Korea is also over 30 percent (Figure 19.6). In South Korea and Taiwan, where highly educated publics reject authoritarian options but are more wary of democracy and democratic parties and politicians, the modal category is by contrast Critical Democrats (who represent 40–45 percent of each sample). By contrast, Superficial Democrats are the modal category in Thailand and Mongolia (50 and 59 percent respectively), while Non-Democrats now represent the modal category in the Philippines (40 percent), showing how far that society has fallen in democratic practice and spirit. If one were to imagine an ideal step pattern in the categories, it would be Consistent Democrats as the largest category, followed by Critical Democrats, Superficial Democrats, and then Non-Democrats (ideally at a fairly low level). Only Indonesia among the six countries exhibits precisely this pattern. While further research is clearly needed to explore the correlates and causal dynamics of these attitudinal and value patterns in Indonesia, and to determine their evolution and resilience over time, it appears that there is a broad normative foundation in society for the progress that Indonesia's democracy has made in the last decade. Whether this is a response to democratic improvement or a cause of it is not clear, and we should be wary of inferring too much from one survey. But the picture that emerges is certainly an encouraging one.

Finally, let us examine comparative levels of trust in political institutions. We asked respondents how much trust they had in a variety of political and state institutions ("a great deal of trust," "quite a lot," "not very much," or "none at all.") Those answering "a great deal" or "quite a lot" are counted as trusting a particular institution. None of the six East Asian countries exhibits higher levels of trust in political institutions, on average, than Indonesia (at 62 percent; Figure 19.7).[11] Save for Thailand, average levels of trust in political and government institutions are much lower in the other countries, and only about half or less in South Korea and Taiwan—where publics tend to be liberal but also deeply skeptical and rather disaffected. In much of the rest of the democratic world, particularly in Latin America and the postcommunist countries, as well as South Korea and Taiwan, one is hard-pressed to find even a quarter of the public saying they trust political parties and parliament. In Indonesia, 42 percent trust parties and 59 percent parliament.[12] About two-thirds of Indonesians in 2006 said they trust the national government—the highest figure among the East Asian countries (and perhaps one advance indicator of why SBY stood such a good chance of being reelected as president in 2009 on the first ballot).

To summarize, then, Indonesians are not only superficially supportive of "democracy," they also manifest support for liberal values to a degree that we would not predict from their country's level of economic development. Indonesians' strong support for democracy *and* for liberal democratic

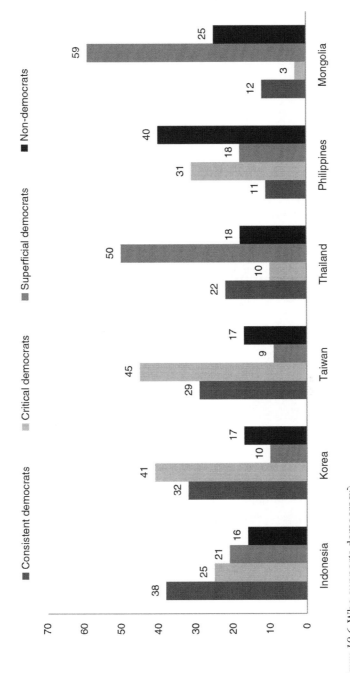

Figure 19.6 Who supports democracy?

Legend: ■ Consistent democrats ■ Critical democrats ■ Superficial democrats ■ Non-democrats

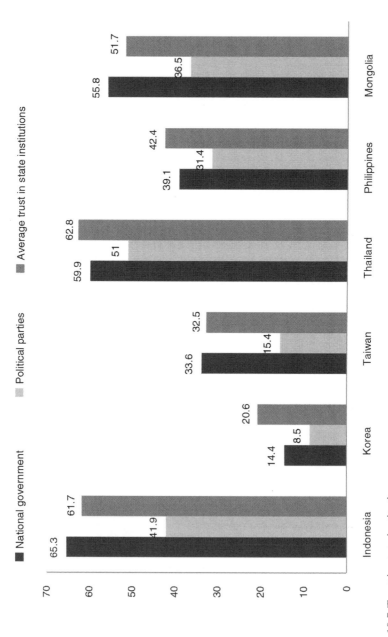

Figure 19.7 Trust in state institutions

values also powerfully contradicts arguments that posit a fundamental contradiction between Islam and democracy, or between Islam and values such as tolerance, due process, and individual rights. Indonesians also show quite a lot of trust in the political and administrative institutions of their democracy, and they judge that their political system is already fairly democratic. Thus, they are more satisfied with the way democracy is working in their country than are most publics in East Asia or elsewhere in the developing world.

To widen the comparative optic, we can briefly compare a few of these attitudes and values in Indonesia with identical questions asked in 2008 in Latin American and Sub-Saharan Africa. In Latin America in 2008, only 37 percent on average (and about the same percent in Brazil) said they were satisfied with the way democracy is working.[13] In Mexico, the figure was 23 percent—compared to 59 percent in Indonesia in 2006. While Indonesians put their democracy now at 7.0 on the 10-point scale, Latin Americans put theirs at only 5.8 on average (in Brazil the average is 6.0). While 64 percent of Indonesians say democracy is preferable to any other form of government, only 47 percent of Brazilians do (and 57 percent of all Latin Americans, on average). Only 30–32 percent of Latin Americans trust parties and parliament, compared to the levels of 42 and 59 percent found in Indonesia in 2006.

In the most recent Afrobarometer, conducted in 2008, the average level of preference for democracy was higher than in Indonesia (70 percent compared to 64 percent). But Indonesia's level was not much lower than South Africa's (67 percent), and the average level of satisfaction with democracy in Indonesia, 59 percent, was substantially higher than in Africa on average (49 percent), though Ghana's was much higher (80 percent). Indonesians were also slightly more inclined to reject military rule (62 percent) than Africans overall (despite having experienced rapid economic development during most of the period they lived under it), but this level was lower than in South Africa (67 percent) or Ghana (78 percent). Ghana shows that democratic support and satisfaction can realistically range higher than it does in Indonesia, even (or perhaps, especially) in a country with lower levels of income and education.

Overall, these levels of public attitudes and values toward democracy in Indonesia not only appear encouraging in isolation, but even more so when compared with a variety of relevant reference groups. But more detailed analysis is needed to determine who among Indonesians (in terms of class, regional, and religious characteristics) supports democracy and who is ambivalent or rejecting of it. And much more time is needed to determine how resilient these orientations will be, and how much they depend on the relatively good performance, economically and politically, that Indonesia's democracy has experienced, especially (so far) under the presidency of SBY.

Conclusion: is Indonesian democracy consolidating or consolidated?

This chapter has given a largely encouraging portrait of Indonesia's democratic growth and performance in its first decade. Between 1998 and 2009, Indonesia became a relatively free country and a more vigorous, stable, and legitimate democracy than probably most sympathetic observers dared hope when the decades-old autocracy came crashing down in 1998. As we have seen, Indonesia has made appreciable progress on a large number of measures of both governance and socioeconomic development during its first full decade of democracy. Moreover, its people seem to recognize and appreciate that performance, as they are by and large satisfied with the way democracy works in their country and trusting and supportive of its institutions. If we look comparatively, Indonesia still lags well behind the more democratically institutionalized and economically developed emerging-market countries in the quality of its governance, but it has improved faster than most, and has levels of support for democracy and liberal democratic values that compare favorably with most of its East Asian peers.

It is comforting to know that the quality of and public support for democracy in Indonesia is improving more, and in some respects appears more resilient, than in other developing countries to which Indonesia might be compared. But in the end, Indonesian democracy will succeed or fail on its own terms, not simply because it is not doing as badly as some other emerging-market democracies. The most important question is whether democracy in Indonesia is really here to stay. Is it consolidated? Has democracy so clearly become "the only game in town" that its reversal is unthinkable?

Despite clear progress over the last decade, democracy in Indonesia still appears vulnerable to reversal. It is possible, as Liddle and Mujani have recently done, to apply the three-dimensional typology of Juan Linz and Alfred Stepan—attitudes, behaviors, and constitutional commitment—and conclude that Indonesian democracy is essentially consolidated because:

1 "No significant political group currently threatens to overthrow democracy or to separate from the Indonesian nation-state"[14] (the behavioral dimension);
2 there is, attitudinally, pretty substantial and steady mass support for democracy as the best form of government; and
3 key political and social actors are committed to solving their disputes and pursuing their interests nonviolently, through the constitutional process.[15]

But as they note, there remain significant (and not fully known or understood) levels of political violence in Indonesia, and it is not clear to what extent Islamist parties and movements that favor a sharia state fully accept the democratic constitutional order, even though both Islamist phenomena are currently in decline. While "the oldest self-declared Islamist party," the Partai Persatuan Pembangunan (United Development Party), declined from 11 to 8 to 7 percent of the parliamentary vote over the three democratic national elections, the more militant PKS improved from 2 to 7 to 8 percent.[16] Yet, encouragingly, their combined support has remained stable at 13–15 percent, and the PKS has yet to top 10 percent (moreover there is a live debate about the extent to which the PKS is adapting to, and being domesticated by, democratic politics).[17] More worrisome may be the level of behavioral, attitudinal, and constitutional commitment to democracy among key elites who retain the ability to diminish or reverse democracy in Indonesia. This could still be the case with the military—although its prerogatives and political role have clearly been diluted over the course of Indonesia's democratic transition—and with former high-ranking military officers like the two unsuccessful vice-presidential candidates in 2009, Prabowo Subianto (PDIP) and Wiranto (Golkar).[18]

A democracy has not really crossed the threshold of consolidation until it has become *enduringly* "the only game in town." For this to happen, commitments to democratic norms and behaviors must not only reach a high critical mass among the mass public, they must also encompass all elites and organizations that have the potential to disrupt the system. This means that powerful actors must become either unconditionally committed to democracy and its rules and restraints or so marginal that they can no longer threaten the system. While the evidence from 2004 to 2009 is encouraging, we cannot really assess these trends without the passage of more time, and in particular without knowing the extent to which democratic progress has been dependent on a skillful and restrained leader like SBY or can carry on without him. It will also be important to track public opinion and value indicators over time to assess their resilience. I have argued elsewhere that at the level of mass public support, 70 percent seems to be a critical threshold of democratic consolidation.[19] Ideally, this should be assessed not by a single indicator but by multiple ones, perhaps especially by rejection of all authoritarian alternatives.

I have argued that there is a strong causal association between the quality of democracy and the stability or consolidation of democracy.[20] In the first presidential term of SBY, 2004–2009, Indonesia has improved its performance on a number of indicators of governance, but the levels of corruption and rule of law remain an obstacle to genuine consolidation.

The consolidation of democracy overall tends also to be associated with the consolidation of specific democratic institutions, not least the party system. Here one could see hope in the growth of SBY's Partai Demokrat to become the largest party in parliament, but still it only has a quarter of the seats, while seven other parties also have at least 5 percent of the seats. Comparative experience tells us that the combination of presidentialism and such a high number of relevant parties (due to a purely PR electoral system) is an unstable one for democracy. Further aggregation of the party system, perhaps by adopting a mixed electoral system (for example, in which half of the seats would be filled from single-member districts), while also democratizing parties and deepening their popular roots would both contribute to democratic consolidation. It would help as well if Indonesian parties were developing some stable institutional bases of support in society, beyond the individual personalities and networks of their leaders.[21] But around the world, this is not an easy thing for democratic parties to do when they are born into a media-saturated age. On the other hand, the country now is largely free of the most common sources of destabilizing political polarization, in that "most Indonesian voters do not give high priority to religious and ethnic group demands."[22]

The most formidable challenge for consolidating democracy involves the rule of law. Levels of corruption must continue to be brought down. The independence, training, and integrity of the judiciary must be strengthened. The nascent anticorruption institutions, particularly the KPK, must be defended against the inevitable assaults on their vitality and efficacy by vested interests who feel threatened by any serious pursuit of public integrity. Access to justice by ordinary Indonesians must be improved. And the capacity, professionalism, and political neutrality of the police and security forces must be enhanced. If these things happen, levels of political violence figure to diminish even further.

To conclude, if we apply absolute (theoretically derived) standards, rather than merely "grade on a curve," Indonesian democracy is progressing, but not nearly as well as the comparative data sometimes suggest. If democracy is really to become "the only game in town," it must continue to become a better—more accountable, transparent, lawful, inclusive, fair, and responsive—democracy for ordinary Indonesians.

Notes

I am very grateful to Aayush Man Sakya for his outstanding research assistance in preparing most of the tables and figures for this paper.

1 Originally published as "Indonesia's Place in Global Democracy," in Edward Aspinall and Marcus Mietzner, eds, *Problems of Democratisation in Indonesia: Elections, Institutions and Society* (Singapore: Institute of Southeast Asian Studies, 2010), 21–49. This is an abbreviated and edited version of the original.

2 These measures are compiled quite differently than those of Freedom House, even for the dimension of "voice and accountability," a composite measure of freedom to participate in selecting the government, and freedom of expression, association, and media. Rather than using one set of expert assessments, as Freedom House does, the World Bank governance indicators average a number of different sources: various expert ratings, political risk analyses, surveys of domestic firms, public opinion surveys, and the perceptions of country analysts at the major multilateral development banks. Daniel Kaufmann, Art Kraay, and Massimo Mastruzzi, "Governance Matters VIII: Aggregate and Individual Governance Indicators, 1996–2008," Policy Research Working Paper 4978, The World Bank, June 2009, 7.

3 World Bank, "Governance Matters 2009: Worldwide Governance Indicators, 1996–2008," http://info.worldbank.org/governance/wgi/index.asp (accessed September 2009).

4 Its score on the World Bank's political stability measure fell from 10.1 in 1998 to 3.8 in 2003, suggesting Indonesia was one of the most unstable places in the world, but it has climbed back up from that brink, and in 2008 stood at 15.8.

5 Kaufmann et al., "Governance Matters VIII," table 5, 33. The authors also note that we may have considerable confidence in the reliability of this verdict of improvement, since almost all of the component measures point in the same direction.

6 Indonesia was surveyed in November 2006, the Philippines actually in November–December 2005, and the other four countries in between. See www. asianbarometer.org/newenglish/Introduction/Surveytimetable.htm.

7 These items were: desire for democracy (again on the 10-point scale, but here simply the percentage of the public picking a figure of six or higher); the belief that "democracy is suitable for our country" (again as measured by a score of six or higher on the 10 point scale); an affirmative answer to the question of whether the respondent believes democracy can be effective in "solving the problems of the country"; the belief that "democracy is always preferable" (in contrast to two other options—that "sometimes authoritarian rule can be preferable" or that "it doesn't matter"); and the response that democracy is either more important than economic development or "equally important" when asked to choose between the two goals.

8 The other statements are: "Government should decide whether certain ideas should be allowed to be discussed in society," "Harmony of the community will be disrupted if people organize into lots of groups," "When judges decide important they should accept the view of the executive branches," and "If we have political leaders who are morally upright, we can let them decide everything."

9 Public opinion survey researchers have long noted a somewhat greater tendency for respondents to agree with any random statement than to disagree, perhaps because some respondents instinctively want to be polite or agreeable in response to the survey researcher, even though the instructions stress that there is no "right" answer to any question. Thus, posing illiberal statements that respondents must disagree with represents a strong test of liberal values.

10 This framework, a significant conceptual and methodological advance in the study of democratic legitimacy, was developed by Yun-han Chu and Min-hua Huang, "A Typological Analysis of Democratic Legitimacy," paper presented to the World Congress of Political Science, International Political Science Association, Santiago, Chile, July 12–16, 2009.

11 Thailand was effectively tied for the average at 63 percent, but in the wake of the coup and the intense polarization of Thai politics, this figure has probably declined sharply in Thailand.

12 It should be noted, however, that surveys conducted by some domestic polling organizations in Indonesia show widely varying results on similar questions.

13 The average I report here for Latin America is the average of the mean percentage level in each country. The country scores may be found in Corporacion Latinobarometro, *2008 Report*, www.latinobarometro.org.

14 R. William Liddle and Saiful Mujani, "Indonesian Democracy: From Transition to Consolidation," in Mirjam Kuenkler and Alfred Stepan, eds, *Democracy and Islam in Indonesia* (New York: Columbia University Press, 2013): 25.

15 Ibid., 43.

16 Ibid., 30–31 and for the full electoral trends, see Saiful Mujani and R. William Liddle, "Voters and the New Indonesian Democracy," presented to the 27th Indonesia Update Conference, The Australian National University, October 9–10, 2009.

17 See Anthony Bubalo, Greg Fealy, and Whit Mason, *Zealous Democrats: Islamism and Democracy in Egypt, Indonesia and Turkey* (Sydney: Lowy Institute for International Policy, 2008).

18 For the role of the military in the democratic transition—and the continuing obstacles to military reform—see Marcus Mietzner, *Military Politics, Islam and the State in Indonesia: From Turbulent Transition to Democratic Consolidation* (Singapore: Institute of Southeast Asian Affairs, 2009).

19 Larry Diamond, *Developing Democracy: Toward Consolidation* (Baltimore, MD: Johns Hopkins University Press, 1999), ch. 5.

20 Ibid., ch. 3.

21 Mujuni and Liddle judge that this is not happening: that electoral volatility remains high and the roots of parties shallow, in "Voters and the New Indonesian Democracy," 33.

22 Ibid., 31.

20 Burma's political opening[1]

Burma today is in the midst of what will likely be a drawn-out game of political transition. It is going *from* a highly authoritarian military regime *to* something else. It is by no means clear that this will be a transition to democracy—or that the long-ruling military intends genuine democracy to be the destination. Indeed, even the current nature of the regime—whether it still reflects "military rule"—is in dispute. The core feature of all political transitions is uncertainty. As Guillermo O'Donnell, Philippe Schmitter, and Laurence Whitehead have observed, when countries move from one regime type to another, the rules are "in constant flux" and "are usually arduously contested." Thus, in all transitions, at least two types of contests proceed simultaneously. One is the substantive competition over power and policy outcomes. The other is the constitutional struggle "to define rules and procedures whose configuration will determine likely winners and losers in the future."[2]

There are also political struggles within each of the competing camps. Almost invariably, authoritarian regimes in transition are divided between "hard-liners," who either do not want to relinquish the spoils of power or who viscerally fear and unconditionally reject democracy, and "soft-liners," who have been part of the authoritarian regime (and perhaps are even parties to its repression), but who have become persuaded that the regime must open up, allow greater civic freedom, and "make use … of some degree or some form of electoral legitimation."[3] As Mary Callahan's essay on Burma's military shows, this is a highly salient cleavage in Burma today, and one that could set back the transition if it is not managed artfully.[4]

In transitions away from authoritarian rule, the intraregime cleavage between hard- and soft-liners finds its mirror image in the opposition's likely split between moderate and militant elements. Moderates may be passionately committed to democracy, and they may have sacrificed much in the struggle for it, but they understand the need to negotiate with the authoritarian rulers in order to bring about a transition to democracy. Militants are not inclined to compromise, but rather seek to use strikes, demonstrations, and other forms of mass mobilization to compel the autocrats to transfer power more or less unconditionally. Where the authoritarian regime is in crisis, as a result of defeat in war, fiscal distress, or a general meltdown of its authority, it may have no option other than to hand over power on the opposition's terms. However, "no transition can be forced purely by the opponents against a regime which maintains the cohesion, capacity, and disposition to apply repression."[5]

Whatever its inner splits and liberalizing intentions, Burma's authoritarian regime—with the Tatmadaw (military) at its core—still has the cohesion and coercive readiness to guard what it sees as its vital interests. Many political prisoners remain in jail; fierce fighting persists in some ethnic-minority states; and it is unclear how far anyone can go in challenging the regime without harsh consequences. So if there is to be a transition to democracy, it will have to be a negotiated one, in which regime soft-liners and more pragmatic and flexible leaders of the democratic opposition come together to agree on new rules.

Transition pacts are by their nature difficult and often painful compromises. "At the core of a pact lies a negotiated compromise under which actors agree to forgo or underutilize their capacity to harm each other by extending guarantees not to threaten each other's corporate autonomies or vital interests."[6] A core reason for making a pact is to build what Robert Dahl called a "system of mutual security" between the government and its opponents, in which each side comes to recognize that the costs of repressing the other are greater than the costs of toleration. This system emerges when oppositionists gain enough power to make it costly for the regime to repress them, and when both (or all) political sides are sufficiently able to narrow their differences and accumulate trust so that they can be confident that if the other comes to (or retains) power their most vital interests will not be decimated.[7]

The more issues that pile up to be resolved, the trickier and more complex transitions become. Inevitably, there is a struggle over policy and interests, and a struggle over the rules of the game. But there may also be simultaneous struggles over the structure of the economy, the role of the armed forces, and the nature and boundaries of the state. In Burma, all these issues are on the table. This means that pulling off a successful democratic transition there will be harder than what we have seen in Southern Europe and Latin America over the last four decades and at least as hard as what South Africa went through, even if easier than Iraq's exceptionally wrenching, violent, and still uncertain transition following the fall of Saddam Hussein.

Fortunately, Burma does have a functioning state. While that state's coherence and authority have been challenged by more than half a century of waxing and waning ethnic insurgencies—to say nothing of drug traffickers and other organized criminals—in the border regions, Burma has a central government with some ability to make its writ run over most of the national space. It is not emerging from state collapse or full-scale civil war, even if the state's capacity to deliver basic public services has been decimated by decades of misrule and sanctions. But Burma confronts the imperative of simultaneous transitions on several other fronts: from authoritarianism to democracy, from military to civilian rule, from a closed and monopolistic to an open and competitive economy, and from an ethnically fractured state to a more viable and coherent union. Moreover, it lacks a number of the conditions associated with successful democratization, such as prior experience with democracy, a sizable middle class, a strong civil society, a unified political opposition, widespread access to modern information and communications technology, and a regional context conducive to democracy.

Burma does have some things going for it. These include an extraordinary democratic leader with broad moral authority in Aung San Suu Kyi; a passionate aspiration for democracy on the part of a society that has risen up repeatedly and courageously to demand it, most recently in the 2007 Saffron Revolution; an emerging civil society that is now blossoming with programs to educate, mobilize, and prepare citizens for democratic self-rule; and the dominance within the authoritarian government of soft-liners who now appear to have a compelling mix of strategic incentives to sustain political reform.[8]

By virtue of the transition timetable that the military has imposed though its 2008 constitution, Burma has one other advantage: time. National parliamentary elections are not due again until around November 2015. This means there are three more years to address the formidable structural and institutional problems that stand in the way of successful democratization. Let us look at the key challenges—relating especially to questions of political process, constitutional structure, and means of handling ethnic conflict—that Burma will have to meet during this time.

Renegotiating the rules

Any hope for democratic change in Burma must confront the hard realities of the constitution that the military imposed in 2008. The document was officially adopted via a May 2008 referendum widely condemned as a mockery of democracy. Although opposition groups had loudly urged a boycott or a "no" vote, the regime absurdly claimed 98 percent turnout and a 92 percent "yes" vote despite the mass devastation that Cyclone Nargis had wrought just a short time before polling day. The new constitution then opened the door to a process of political reform that few observers at the time expected, but that still severely limits how far the opening can go. Careful examination of the 2008 Constitution's provisions suggests an intent to set up a competitive authoritarian regime in which the military will remain a dominant veto player in politics, even if its favored party fares poorly in future elections.

If the political transition is to lead to democracy, numerous provisions of the 2008 Constitution will have to change. These onerous provisions are listed in Box 20.1.

Box 20.1 **Where the 2008 Constitution needs reform**

- Articles 109(b) and 141(b), which give the Commander-in-Chief (C-in-C) of the Defense Services—a uniformed, active-duty military officer—the right to appoint a quarter of the members of each house of parliament.

- Article 232(b), which requires the president to appoint the ministers of Defense, Home Affairs, and Border Affairs from lists of nominees (which can include serving military officers) provided by the C-in-C.

- Article 201, which appears to ensure that the military will have at least six seats on the powerful 11-member National Defense and Security Council.

- Article 59, which effectively disqualifies Aung San Suu Kyi from the presidency because she was married to a foreigner and her sons have citizenship in another country.

- Article 60, which establishes a cumbersome process for electing the president by means of an electoral college comprising the two houses of parliament, including all the military-appointed MPs. (This provision also effectively gives the military MPs—assuming they vote as a bloc—the power to choose one of the three vice-presidents, one of whom is then made president by the whole electoral college.)

- Article 40(c), which authorizes the C-in-C "to take over and exercise State sovereign power in accord with the provisions of this Constitution" under a broad set of vague conditions: "If there arises a state of emergency that could cause disintegration of the Union, disintegration of national solidarity and loss of sovereign power or attempts by wrongful forcible means such as insurgency or violence." Chapter XI gives the president power to declare a state of emergency "after coordinating" with the C-in-C and other top officers. The president must also "submit the matter" to parliament, but taken together, these extensive provisions for declaring a state of emergency have the air of a license to return to military rule and suspend basic rights if things seem to be going too far.

- Article 20(b), which gives the Defense Services "the right to independently administer and adjudicate all affairs of the armed forces," thus insulating the military from any civilian control or oversight (particularly if, in some future government, the executive and legislative branches are not dominated by former military officers).

- Chapter VIII on Fundamental Rights, which guarantees civil liberties only to the extent that they are "not contrary to the laws, enacted for Union security, prevalence of law and order, community peace and tranquility or public order and morality"—a very broad set of exceptions.

Although it is indirectly elected, the presidency is a powerful position under the new constitution, as the president not only heads the executive branch but also names the electoral commission. But with a majority on the National Defense and Security Council, the Tatmadaw will retain enormous power even if the president is someone from outside its ranks. And with 25 percent of the seats in parliament, the military can block any constitutional amendment, which will need the support of 75 percent of the members of parliament.

Burma's democrats thus face an acute and urgent structural dilemma. If they play by the rules of the current constitution, they *could*—if elections are as free and fair as they were the April 2012 parliamentary by-elections—win the vast majority of seats in both houses of parliament. And then they could elect the president, but not (by the current provisions) Aung San Suu Kyi. Yet at that point they would still be saddled with a deeply defective "democracy" whose institutional rules could be amended only if some military MPs broke ranks—an unlikely act made even more difficult by the military high command's retention of the right to replace any military-nominated MP at will.

If the 2008 Constitution goes unrevised, Burma could find itself stuck indefinitely with a hybrid system—part democratic, part military-dominated, and intrinsically prone to instability stemming from the irreconcilable tension between those two competing sources of authority. Or, given the potentially prominent role of the military-dominated National Defense and Security Council in declaring a state of emergency, the new electoral regime might fall victim to renewed military intervention should a democratic president go too far for the military's taste in trying to establish civilian supremacy and the rule of law.

Hence near-term prospects for democracy in Burma depend heavily on whether constitutional amendments can be negotiated and adopted in advance of the 2015 elections. There is a deal to be had on political rules and structures, for two major reasons. First, the regime needs democratic forces, particularly the largest opposition party, Suu Kyi's National League for Democracy (NLD), to go along in order to stage credible national elections in 2015. Only a credible vote will allow the regime to claim that it has made the shift to a "normal" constitutional regime and thus get remaining U.S. and international sanctions lifted.

Moreover, the regime is beginning to realize—as are most of the ethnic-minority parties and the smaller (mainly NLD spinoff) democratic parties—that the current first-past-the-post (FPTP) electoral system is in no one's interest except the NLD's. As Min Zin and Brian Joseph note, FPTP is likely to hand the NLD a super-landslide not unlike that of May 1990, when NLD candidates totaled about 60 percent of the vote and got 81 percent of the seats while the military's party got about a fifth of the vote but only 2 percent of the seats.[9] Even the NLD should be wary of FPTP because, as 1990 showed, too big a win can rouse a backlash that will cost it everything: The military stepped in that year and annulled the results, driving much of the NLD leadership into exile.

The search for a viable pact

On general principles, it is not good for democracy to have any party—even one that professes deep commitment to democratic ideals—enjoying an enduringly lopsided edge over all rivals. In similar circumstances in the South Africa of 1990, a newly freed Nelson Mandela and a newly unbanned African National Congress (ANC) quickly came to grasp that their own interests would be best served by guaranteeing other groups, especially the ruling white minority, representation in parliament roughly proportionate to their vote share. In the actual constitutional negotiations themselves, moreover, the ANC went further and gave guarantees not only to whites but also to other minority groups and the Zulu-based Inkatha Freedom Party. After an initial round of failed negotiations in 1991–1992, the apartheid regime, led by President F. W. de Klerk, and the ANC, led by Mandela, agreed to press on toward compromise. In November 1993, they agreed on an interim constitution that provided for a transitional power-sharing period under a government of national unity. Any party winning 20 percent or more of the vote in the founding election (held on April 27, 1994) would be entitled to nominate an executive deputy president, and each party was allowed to nominate one cabinet minister for every 5 percent of the vote that it won. Other provisions, such as the continuation of public servants and even hard-line military officers in their posts, also reflected the broad nature of the pact that was negotiated.[10] In the end, the ruling National Party barely won 20 percent of the vote and President de Klerk assumed the position of deputy president under the new president, Nelson Mandela.

What is crucially instructive about the South African case is not only the usefulness of power-sharing during transitions, but also the explicitly *temporary* nature of this power-sharing. The National Party sought early on to lock in long-term constitutional guarantees of power-sharing and minority vetoes, not unlike the veto powers that the Tatmadaw in Burma has given itself in that country's 2008 Constitution. But the white minority party lacked the power to impose its will indefinitely. In the words of a leading ANC strategist, it may have been "necessary to share power for a while and meet de Klerk halfway," but this could not be allowed to "block permanently any future advance towards a nonracial [democracy]."[11] The power-sharing provisions were dropped in the 1996 Constitution, which took full effect after the 1999 elections. Other provisions to help reassure the white minority and ease the way to a new political order remained, however. These included an amnesty (granted through the truth and reconciliation process) for acts of political violence, guaranteed pensions, generous severance packages for bureaucrats who were eased out, and a commitment to respect existing property rights.

It is unlikely that Burma's military regime will agree to a wholesale rewriting of the 2008 Constitution. But amending key provisions could achieve an effect similar to South Africa's interim constitution: power-sharing with "sunset clauses." Having repeatedly seen the military crush democratic hopes, many in the opposition are ready for compromise. Among these pragmatists are not only the small democratic parties that agreed to contest the 2010 elections on the regime's terms, but also Aung San Suu Kyi herself, her party, the pro-democratic ethnic-minority parties, and many leaders of the "Four Eights" generation associated with the pro-democracy upsurge that began on August 8, 1988. In negotiations, complexity can be an advantage. Having many issues to resolve means that there will be many ways to horse-trade and strike compromises.

The search for a viable pact must begin by identifying the core interests of each constituency. In particular, the military needs guarantees that its autonomy will be respected, its members will not be prosecuted, and its wealth will not be confiscated. And Burmese democrats need to know that the country is on a clear path to genuine democracy, even if there are limits for a period of time. It is possible to imagine a pact, for example, that would phase out the military-appointed MPs after one term, as was done in Indonesia in 2004.[12] The military's right to nominate three cabinet ministers might also be phased out after a term, while other problematic parts of the constitution could be amended before 2015. In exchange, the military and its cronies might receive amnesty for past crimes, security for their assets (however corruptly acquired), and preservation of their institutional autonomy.

The regime could also obtain a consensus agreement to switch the electoral system to proportional representation (PR), though in the case of a geographically complex and predominantly rural country such as Burma, it will be important to preserve bonds of electoral accountability and responsiveness between specific geographic constituencies and their respective MPs. Probably the best way to do this would be with some version of the German (two-ballot) system, which is fully proportional but which elects half the seats from single-member districts, and then gives each party an additional number of seats from its PR list so that its overall representation is proportional to its vote share.[13] (The one change that I would recommend is a much lower electoral threshold than Germany's 5 percent barrier. Burma has small, ethnic minorities and fledgling democratic parties that ought not to be locked out of the legislature by a too-high threshold.)

If such a scenario were to unfold, one of the most difficult issues would probably involve the military's demand for institutional autonomy and an ongoing "leading role" in national political life. From the standpoint of normative democratic theory, Burma's democrats would be completely justified in seeking clear constitutional provisions mandating civilian supremacy over the military. But given the balance of power, it is hard to imagine the military agreeing to such an immediate, radical restructuring of its prerogatives. The urgent early imperative is to get the military out of politics and government, and to shrink back its mission "to a relatively more limited set of 'professional' responsibilities that involve defending the constitution and the territory," as Mary Callahan characterizes the stated goal of top Tatmadaw commander, Vice Senior General Min Aung Hlaing.[14] For a country emerging from half a century of military rule, that would be a huge step forward, and even that would require time to take effect.

In Brazil, which experienced only two decades of military rule before its transition to democracy was completed in 1985, "the Brazilian military entered the New Republic with a sense of their legitimate role ... that entail[ed] deep, permanent involvement in managing conflict in the polity."[15] As Alfred Stepan argues in his seminal work on civil–military relations, change in such entrenched role conceptions and power relations will not happen overnight. Civilians must gain knowledge and influence in matters of military and national-security policy. "The democratic leadership of the state" must implement "a well conceived, *politically led* strategy toward the military," and a new generation of military leaders must come to see its own institutional interests as being served by a new, more limited role for the military that restores its internal hierarchy and discipline, modernizes its capabilities, and elevates its professionalism.[16]

Managing ethnic conflict

In terms of national identity, Burma is among the most deeply divided transitional countries that anyone has seen since the "third wave" began in 1974. Up to a third of Burma's estimated 54 million people are outside the Burman majority, sharing neither its language nor its ethnic identity. More than 100 minorities—including the Shan, the Karen, the Karenni, the Chin, the Kachin, the Mon, and the Rakhine—live mainly on the geographic periphery of Burma, in borderlands rich in natural resources such as timber and gems. Since independence in 1948, they have had a history of violent conflict with the center in what has amounted to a decades-long, intermittent civil war. In some of these areas, fighting still rages. For decades, the military has been trying to defeat ethnic insurgencies and control resources found in minority areas.

Although it gestures toward devolution, the 2008 Constitution remains highly unitary whereas Burma's minorities want federalism. Only a broad shift away from the current overcentralized form of government can offer hope of lasting peace and genuine integration. It would seem that Burma needs something like what Aung San Suu Kyi called for in 2010, a "second Panglong Agreement" like the one that her father Aung San, modern Burma's founder, signed in 1947 with leaders of the Shan, Chin, and Kachin minorities. The Panglong accord established the basis for a Union of Burma in which frontier minority groups would enjoy "full autonomy in internal administration" and even the right to secede after ten years of national independence. But Panglong did not specify these groups' autonomous powers and rights, and the rise of secessionism in the late 1950s was a key factor in the military's takeover of power.[17] It is difficult to imagine a successful Burmese transition that does not resolve the persistent structural problem regarding the nature of the union.

As Juan J. Linz and Alfred Stepan have written, "In a democratic transition, two potentially explosive questions are unavoidable: Who is a citizen of the state? And how are the rules of citizenship defined? A democracy requires a definition of the *demos*."[18] A multinational state such as Burma cannot quickly, peacefully, and democratically become a nation-state. Rather, like India, its better prospect is to become a "state-nation"—that is, a state made up of many nationality groups in which the central state "nonetheless still manages to engender strong identification and loyalty from [its] citizens."[19]

In a state-nation, the central government and the dominant ethnic group recognize that they cannot impose a single exclusive linguistic and cultural identity upon all the people and territory of the country. Instead, they encourage "multiple but complementary" identities through institutions such as asymmetrical federalism, or at least some significant devolution of power down to subnational units dominated by various minority ethnic groups. These institutional arrangements must recognize each group's right to its own language and culture, while obtaining commitment to membership in the state-nation.[20]

A viable democracy would require Burma to become in some form or degree a "state-nation," similar in many respects to India, with its asymmetrical federalism and ample provisions for cultural autonomy. The current constitution does not go nearly far enough to ensure devolution of power. Although legislation could probably go a long way toward granting the states and regions significant powers and responsibilities, the constitution gives the national president the right to appoint the chief minister of each region or state (technically, regional legislatures can reject such nominees, but only under hard-to-meet conditions). Fully elected subnational government, with some meaningful authority over local development, resources, and culture, seems a *sine qua non* for democratic stability. In return for such restructuring, Burma's ethnic minorities would have to commit fully to permanent membership in the Union and drop secessionism for good.

The moment for pact-making

If the 2015 elections are to produce a viable democracy, rather than a repeat of the 1990 calamity or a deeply resented and unstable semi-authoritarian regime, Burma has a lot of political work to do in the next two years. The good news is that national elections are still three years away. The worrisome news is that the hardest political work of the transition—the negotiation of political pacts—has not yet begun. Neither is there a clear sense among democratic forces of the urgent need for these negotiations, or a strategy for entering and pressing them. Intensive negotiations are needed to forge a complex, interlocking set of compromise agreements between the regime and the democratic opposition, the civilians and the military, the major opposition party (the NLD) and its lesser rivals, and the majority Burmans and the various minorities. Fortunately, there appears to be a rapport and mutual respect between President Thein Sein and Aung San Suu Kyi. But dialogue is not a substitute for negotiations, and even a leader as esteemed and heroic as Suu Kyi cannot negotiate alone on behalf of such a diverse array of forces in politics and society.

Whether Burma gets to democracy in 2015, or at least manages to place itself clearly and consensually on the road to democracy, will heavily depend on what happens over the next two years. Democrats in Burma must use this time to forge a structure of compromises and a system of mutual security that can allow democratization to proceed. Politics needs to go from a zero-sum to a positive-sum game, and each major group in both the regime and the opposition needs to see that it has a clear stake in a democratic future.

Before opposition forces can effectively engage the regime in negotiations, they must engage one another. They must craft a more unified, politically coherent, and tactically coordinated front to present to the regime, even as they rally society behind their common vision of a democratic future. Clearly, the democrats must and will be led by Aung San Suu Kyi in these negotiations. But as she revives and modernizes her own party, she must reach out across partisan, ethnic, and generational lines to forge a broad opposition front. And while some of the most sensitive negotiations must be carried on delicately—indeed, often very personally, and in secret—in order to build trust, there also needs to emerge a broader and more structured negotiating framework.

The challenge, to be sure, appears daunting. But there is a new and more hopeful mood in Burma today. Neither the regime nor the opposition wants to see another painful implosion of political reform, for each side is now more acutely aware than it was in 1990 of what it has to lose from such a reversal. And if one looks at other transitions such as South Africa's 20 years ago, similar portraits of daunting, almost impossible challenges appear. Analysts of democratic success and failure rightly give great weight to underlying circumstances. But within those constraints, people do make history, and this great drama is now in the hands of Burma's regime and opposition leaders. Success or failure is up to them.

Notes

1 Originally published as "Burma's Political Opening," *Journal of Democracy* 23 (October 2012): 135–146.
2 Guillermo O'Donnell, Philippe C. Schmitter, and Laurence Whitehead, *Transitions from Authoritarian Rule: Comparative Perspectives* (Baltimore, MD: Johns Hopkins University Press, 1986), 6.
3 Ibid., 16.

4 Mary Callahan, "The Opening in Burma: The Generals Loosen their Grip," *Journal of Democracy* 23 (October 2012): 120–131.
5 O'Donnell et al., *Transitions from Authoritarian Rule,* 21.
6 Ibid., 38.
7 Robert A. Dahl, *Polyarchy: Participation and Opposition* (New Haven, CT: Yale University Press, 1971), 15–16, 36–37.
8 For more, see the cluster of articles on the theme of "The Opening in Burma" in *Journal of Democracy* 23 (October 2012).
9 Min Zin and Brian Joseph, "The Opening of Burma: The Democrats' Opportunity," *Journal of Democracy* 23 (October 2012): 104–119.
10 Steven Friedman, "South Africa: Divided in a Special Way," in Larry Diamond, Juan J. Linz, and Seymour Martin Lipset, eds, *Politics in Developing Countries: Comparing Experiences with Democracy* (Boulder, CO: Lynne Rienner, 1996), 549–550; Ian Spears, "Africa: The Limits of Power-Sharing," *Journal of Democracy* 13 (July 2002): 126.
11 Vincent Maphai, "A Season for Power-Sharing," *Journal of Democracy* 7 (January 1996): 71.
12 However, the proportion of appointed military and police members of Indonesia's parliament during the first five-year term of the new democracy (1999–2004) was much smaller than in Burma, less than 10 percent (38 of the 500 seats).
13 Germans cast two ballots, one for district representative and one for the party list, but it is the latter that determines the overall share of the vote each party will have in parliament. Germany's PR lists are state lists, which might also be a good idea for a country as big as Burma. The key is to avoid the disastrous situation of South Africa, in which opting for a fully proportional system drawn from provincial and national lists left the country with no meaningful geographic ties between voters and representatives.
14 Callahan, "The Generals Loosen their Grip," 128.
15 Alfred Stepan, *Rethinking Military Politics: Brazil and the Southern Cone* (Princeton, NJ: Princeton University Press, 1988), 131.
16 Ibid., 142.
17 Michael Lwin, "Ending Myanmar's Civil War," *Al Jazeera English* (February 13, 2012), www.aljazeera.com/indepth/opinion/2012/02/20122494825985895.html.
18 Juan J. Linz and Alfred Stepan, *Problems of Democratic Transition and Consolidation: Southern Europe, South America, and Post-Communist Europe* (Baltimore, MD: Johns Hopkins University Press, 1996), 28.
19 Ibid., 34.
20 Alfred Stepan, Juan J. Linz, and Yogendra Yadav, "The Rise of 'State-Nations,'" *Journal of Democracy* 21 (July 2010): 50–68; and Stepan, Linz, and Yadav, *Crafting State-Nations: India and Other Multinational Democracies* (Baltimore, MD: Johns Hopkins University Press, 2011). It should be stressed that in Burma, as in India, there are other minorities living within each of the states where this or that ethnic minority predominates (thus probably a third or more of the people living in Shan State are non-Shans, for instance). It should go without saying that in any new arrangement, the rights of *all* (and not merely the rights of a local majority) must be secured.

Part IV

Promoting democracy

Policy implications

21 Empowering the poor

What does democracy have to do with it?[1]

Morally and analytically, there is no more vexing phenomenon than the persistence of mass poverty. Over the past half-century, remarkable gains have been made in reducing infant mortality, extending life expectancy, raising levels of income and education, and reducing the incidence of severe diseases.[2] Huge investments of analytical work, empirical research, and development assistance have been made in the quest to eliminate, or at least dramatically reduce, absolute poverty, which leaves an individual to survive on less than $2 or even $1 per day. Yet absolute poverty persists on a mass scale throughout much of what has been termed, rather euphemistically, the "developing" world. Why?

The perspective adopted here is that the obstacles to the elimination of poverty are heavily, if not fundamentally, political. This is not to deny that poverty is, by definition, an economic phenomenon, resulting from inadequate income with which to live a minimally dignified and decent life and inadequate assets (human, financial, and infrastructural) with which to generate such incomes. Neither is it to neglect the many ways in which social norms and relations structure and reproduce poverty. It is merely to acknowledge that transforming these economic and social realities requires, in large measure, policy responses by the state to empower the poor.

Empowerment implies providing the poor with assets—education, health care, credit, potable water, electricity, roads—that enable them to be productive. It also requires an enabling environment for poverty reduction, including a transparent and efficient state bureaucracy, a fair and accessible justice system, and protection for their property rights.[3] When the poor are able to nourish themselves and protect their health, raise their skills, educate their children, finance their productive activities, transport their crops and goods to markets, register their property and enterprises, and protect their rights without discrimination, they are well capable of producing their way out of poverty.

However, in every nation where much of the population remains trapped in absolute poverty, circumstances conspire to prevent the poor from doing these things. These circumstances are invariably political, in that they involve powerful actors at various levels of society and the political system who benefit from a "disabling environment" for the poor and use their power to perpetuate it. This privileged and quite often predatory elite is typically a tiny minority. Logically, one would expect that democracy—a political system that includes regular, free, and fair elections in which the people choose their rulers—should empower the poor majority to constrain these powerful elites by choosing leaders, parties, and policies that favor poverty reduction.

Yet, as many analyses have shown,[4] many democracies do a lackluster or only mediocre job of reducing poverty. Of course, sustainable poverty reduction requires overall economic growth, and to the extent that a poor economy suffers a drop in international trade or other shocks, it may experience a recession through no real fault of its own. But shocks are by definition temporary. The long-term persistence of high levels of absolute poverty in a given society is logically attributable to systemic conditions. And these conditions, I would argue, emanate to some considerable extent from bad governance.

The first section of this chapter offers a theory of failed development—which is to say, persistent poverty—based on the nature of governance. The second section explores the ambiguous relationship between democracy and development, explaining why democracy *in principle* should help empower the poor and promote development. Briefly reviewing the cross-national empirical evidence on this question, it explains why democracy often does not help development much, and why the enduring reduction of poverty requires a broader context of good governance beyond the narrow electoral arena. The third section discusses two priorities for achieving democracy at the national level: free and fair elections, and democratization of political parties. The final section offers concluding reflections.

The political roots of development failure

The deepest root cause of persistent mass poverty is not a lack of resources or international isolation. Rather, it is a lack of good governance—the inability or unwillingness of those in power to apply public resources effectively to generate public goods.[5] Both good and bad governance have striking effects on a country's ability to empower the poor and move out of poverty.

Good governance and development

Good governance has several dimensions. One is the *capacity* of the state to function in the service of the public good. Effective functioning requires knowledge of the policies and rules that best serve the public good, and hence training of state officials to that end. It requires a professional civil service with a set of norms and structures that promote fidelity to public rules and duties, in part by rewarding those who perform well in their roles.

This relates intimately to the second dimension of good governance, *commitment to the public good*. Where does this commitment come from? It may be generated by dedicated and charismatic leadership. Or it may derive from a cultural ethic that appreciates—and a structure of institutional incentives that rewards—disciplined service to the nation or the general community over the use of office for private benefit. Or it may, in part, be induced by the structure of political incentives (domestic and international) that leaders confront. In every modern society, however, this commitment must, at a minimum, be reinforced by institutions that punish betrayals of the public trust.

A third dimension of good governance is *transparency*, the openness of state conduct to the scrutiny of other state actors and of the public. Transparency is closely related to *accountability*. Governing agents are more likely to be responsible when they must answer for their conduct to the society in general and to other specific institutions that monitor their behavior and can impose sanctions upon them. Effective oversight requires open flows of information, and hence transparency, so that monitors can discover facts and mobilize evidence. This requires a system of government in which different institutions hold one another accountable, compelling them to justify their actions. Power is thus constrained, bound not only "by legal constraints but also by the logic of public reasoning."[6]

Transparency and accountability are bound up with a fourth dimension of good governance, the *rule of law*. Governance can only be good and effective when it is restrained by the law, when the law is applied equally to the mighty and the meek, and when there are professional, independent authorities to enforce the law in a neutral, predictable fashion.

A fifth dimension of good governance consists of mechanisms of *participation* and dialogue that enable the public to provide input to the policy process, to correct mistakes in policy design and implementation, and to promote social inclusion. Policies will be more likely to be stable and sustainable when they enjoy popular understanding and support. This requires some means for distinct organized interests, and for historically marginalized groups such as women and minorities, to have input into governmental decisions and some means of protesting policies and actions that harm their interests.

Finally, when good governance functions in the above five ways, it also breeds *social capital* in the form of networks and associations that draw people together in relations of trust, reciprocity, and voluntary cooperation for common ends. Social capital not only fosters the expansion of investment and commerce, embedded in relations of trust and predictability, it also breeds the civic spirit, participation, and respect for law that are crucial foundations of political development and good governance. In other words, it generates a political culture of responsible citizenship.

In many respects, then, good governance constitutes a "virtuous cycle" in which several elements reinforce one another to advance the public good.[7] Conceptualized in this way, good governance promotes broad-based development, and thus poverty reduction. By generating and defending broad commitment to the public welfare, it increases the likelihood that public resources will be used to generate public goods that raise the general quality of life. When government itself is transparent and disciplined in its commitment to the public good, it provides credible signals to the rest of society about what types of behaviors are expected. In providing a fair means for the resolution of disputes, the rule of law generates an enabling environment for economic growth and some means for attenuating inequality. In incorporating groups that historically have been confined to the margins of society, good governance mitigates social conflict and harnesses the full range of talent and resources in the society. In fostering the accumulation of social capital, good governance cultivates trust (in individuals and in government), cooperation, compliance with the law, and confidence in the future.

Bad governance and the persistence of poverty

Countries that have failed to realize their development potential in the past half century have invariably suffered yawning deficits of good governance. Why is bad governance such a pervasive and profound obstacle to development? Just as good governance promotes the accumulation of financial, physical, social, and political capital, bad governance inhibits or drains away that accumulation.

Consider the archetypical badly governed country. Corruption is endemic throughout the system of government at every level. Public infrastructure decays or is never built because the resources for it are diverted to private ends. Decisions on public expenditures are tilted toward unproductive investments—sophisticated weapons, white-elephant construction projects—that can deliver large kickbacks to the civilian officials and military officers who award them. Schools are not built or maintained, clinics are not stocked and staffed, and roads are not repaired because the funds are squandered or stolen. Businesses cannot get licenses to operate and small producers cannot get title to their land because it would take half a year and a small fortune to navigate the shoals of a bloated, corrupt state bureaucracy. Every interaction with the state—to obtain a building permit, register a marriage or a death, report a crime, or receive a vaccination—exacts its petty, unofficial price.

In such a context of rotten governance, individuals seek governmental positions in order to collect rents and accumulate personal wealth—to convert public resources into private goods. Governmental decisions and transactions are deliberately opaque in order to hide their corrupt nature, but exposure of corrupt deeds typically brings little more than embarrassment because the rule of law does not function to constrain or punish the behavior of public officials. Power is heavily centralized and institutions of scrutiny and accountability function only on paper, or episodically, to punish the more marginal miscreants or the rivals of the truly powerful. Corruption is also rife at the bottom of the governance system because that is the climate that is set at the top, and because government workers cannot live on the salaries they are paid.

Institutions of political participation may or may not exist in this venal environment, but if they do, the government is not responsive to them. Instead, political participation cleaves society vertically, typically along ethnic lines, into competing chains of patron–client relations that all mobilize for one purpose: to get control of public resources so that they can convert them into private goods. In such a society, violent conflict is also rife, or never far from the surface, because ordinary people are exploited and desperate, rights are routinely abused, and communities are mutually resentful of any perceived advantage of the other in a zero-sum game. The only way to generate truly sustainable development in this context is to bring about a fundamental transformation in the nature and quality of governance. Granted, the ways people think and behave must change. But individual behavior is not the largest or quickest point of leverage. Such changes can only be effective if the social environment of incentives and expectations is transformed. That in turn requires a shift toward more responsible, professional, open, and accountable governance. In particular, it requires specific and well-functioning institutions of democracy, horizontal accountability, and the rule of law.

The relationship between democracy and development

The relationship between democracy and economic development has been the focus of intensive research and theorizing for decades. For a time, particularly during the 1970s and 1980s, the fashionable argument was that economic growth in lower-income countries might be better served by a period of "developmental dictatorship."[8] However, the weight of theory and evidence is now swinging behind the benefits of empowerment, and thus democracy, for development in general, and for lifting up the poor in particular. To do so, however, democracy must extend beyond occasional elections to provide real accountability and access to power.

The empowering benefits of democracy

Poverty is not just a lack of resources. It is also a lack of voice and political power that would enable the poor to articulate and defend their interests. Because they are poor, ill-clothed, and "backward," they are treated in an abrupt, contemptuous, and even humiliating manner by public officials (including the police), who identify psychologically with the upper strata and/or sell their services and decisions to those who can pay for them. Because they are poor, illiterate, and unorganized, poor people lack access to justice, and thus cannot demand transparency or challenge abuses in the courts. All of this renders them utterly vulnerable to exploitation by the powerful.[9]

In principle, democracy should provide a corrective, empowering the poor in the following ways. First, when competitive elections are truly free and fair, they serve as an instrument to remove corrupt, unresponsive, or ineffectual leaders. They thus provide an incentive for leaders to govern more effectively in the public interest, and to attend to the needs and concerns of the poor majority. Second, democracy provides nonelectoral means for the poor to articulate and defend their interests, and to participate in the making of public policy—through nongovernmental organizations (NGOs), informal associations, community-based organizations, interest groups, social movements, and the mass media. Third, democracy enables all these actors in civil society, as well as elected representatives at various levels of government, to monitor the conduct of public officials and to seek redress in the courts and administrative forums. With such participation and debate, the poor are more likely to feel some sense of ownership of the resulting policies, which they perceive can help them craft their way out of poverty. But all of this depends not just on democracy, but also on freedom.

Does democracy promote development?

The empirical evidence about the relationship between democracy and development is ambiguous. We do know that there is a much higher incidence of stable democracy among higher-income countries, and that globally, democracy is highly correlated with development. This is at least in part because rich countries are much more likely to sustain democracies than poor ones.[10] Going back to Lipset,[11] and before him to Aristotle, it has been a basic tenet of political science that democracy is more viable in relatively prosperous, middle-class societies. But do democracies grow more rapidly—and eliminate poverty more effectively—than authoritarian regimes?

This question is more difficult to answer, and the statistical evidence is contradictory and ambiguous. Overall, two reviews of the literature in the early 1990s concluded that there was no clear and consistent relationship.[12] For Inkeles and Sirowy, the evidence seemed to suggest that "political democracy does not widely and directly facilitate rapid economic growth, net of other factors."[13] However, Roll and Talbott, using cross-sectional data from 1995 through 1999, found that 80 percent of the variance in per capita national income could be explained by nine separate influences that heavily involved factors of governance, such as political rights, civil liberties, and property rights.[14] Moreover, with a highly innovative time-series design, they also found that following political regime changes, democracies did perform clearly better in terms of economic growth than dictatorships.

To understand the relationship, we need to disaggregate countries and time periods. One reason that democracy often does not appear in statistical analyses to have a clear positive relationship to economic growth may be the strong growth performance of the "East Asian tigers"—the Republic of Korea, Taiwan, Singapore, and Hong Kong—under authoritarian rule, particularly in the 1960s and 1970s. More recently, Thailand has begun rapid economic growth under authoritarian, or semiauthoritarian, rule, and Malaysia has grown rapidly under semiauthoritarian rule. China started the process of economic reform and opening earlier than India, and has outstripped it in growth performance, though India has improved markedly in recent years.

Before deriving policy conclusions, one needs to ask: How replicable is the East Asian historical experience, or was it somewhat unique to place and time? A case can be made that the "tigers" were able to impose a strong sense of self-restraint and discipline—to limit predatory corruption—both for cultural reasons and because they faced an existential threat from the spread of communism and the growing power of China. They realized that in order to survive, they had to deliver development. Moreover, they had or they crafted a degree of national solidarity that was conducive to viewing the development process as a collective national enterprise for the public good. In the cases of Korea, Taiwan, and Thailand, huge amounts of U.S. aid early on also made a difference.

In Africa and Central Asia, there is no such pressure for good governance to ensure regime survival that ruling elites readily recognize. Societies are deeply divided along ethnic, clan, religious, and regional lines, leading each group to see the state as something to be captured for its own benefit rather than for the overall "national" good. Thus, authoritarian rule in these circumstances is unlikely to generate economic development, and certainly not with the broad distribution that reduces poverty. Rather, it facilitates the domination of one group or coalition over others, and an extractive, predatory attitude toward governance. In these circumstances, a benevolent, development-oriented leader or ruling party is unlikely to emerge. And if, as in Uganda, such a leadership does emerge, its commitment to good governance will eventually fray if it is not disciplined by the instruments of vertical and horizontal accountability that democracy provides.

Authoritarian rule, particularly of a prolonged or indefinite nature, therefore offers poor prospects for sustained poverty reduction in the countries that still suffer from mass poverty. However, democracy does not provide any guarantee of better performance. Much depends on the type and degree of democracy.

The limits of (purely) electoral democracy

There are several reasons why democracy often fails to do much to empower the poor. These derive not from the intrinsic limitations of democracy as a political system, but rather from the fact that democracy often functions in a limited, shallow, and illiberal fashion. Of course, many regimes that claim to be democracies are instead "pseudodemocracies" or "electoral authoritarian regimes" (see Chapter 8). These regimes have many of the superficial features of democracy, in particular, regular electoral competition between different political parties. But their elections are not completely free and fair, and therefore it is not possible to defeat the ruling party through normal electoral means. To the extent that the ruling party knows it can rig itself back into power, a key mechanism of vertical accountability and democratic responsiveness breaks down.

Where elections are free and fair, the poor stand a better chance of effecting poverty-reducing changes in budget priorities, policies, and institutions—but even then, the chance is not always that much better. Electoral democracy may be diminished in several respects that impede its potential for poverty alleviation and empowerment. First, the arena of electoral competition may be distorted by corruption, so that while the polling is not grossly rigged on voting day, parties and candidates obtain the resources to compete through the sale of political decisions and influence. Such corruption in party and campaign finance diminishes the need of political competitors, particularly incumbents, to be responsive to the majority of their constituents and gives them a shortcut to electoral victory.

Related to this are two characteristic problems with political parties, having to do with the lack of internal democracy and transparency. Where parties are opaque, autocratic, hierarchical, and dominated by a single leader or small circle, they are less effective at representing a broad range of interests, and may wind up imposing candidates on constituencies. Second, such parties tend to be extremely vertically organized, not only inside the party leadership structure but also at every level in a cascading pyramid of patron-client relations. They seek to "represent" impoverished constituencies by mobilizing them along ethnic, religious, or other cultural lines, by distributing state jobs to loyal followers, and by distributing a dollop of cheap goods around election time in place of any real policy response to poverty. In the narrow sense, such a system may be democratic, but it may lead either to individual political machines entrenching themselves in different districts, towns, and states, or to a succession of largely corrupt and exploitative governments.

Democracy should provide alternative, nonelectoral means to check and reverse bad governance. These come through the activities of civil society and of institutions of horizontal accountability—the courts, parliamentary oversight, audit and countercorruption agencies, ombudsmen, human rights commissions, and so on. But when democracy is illiberal and hollow, these institutions also fail to function effectively. Some democracies allow for true electoral competition, but nevertheless have very weak rule of law, with extensive abuse of citizen rights by the police and government officials. Civil society organizations may not be free to organize, and the press may not be free to report, investigate, and criticize. Or civil society may be dominated by NGOs that are externally funded and driven, led by the educated middle class, and only faintly sensitive (at best) to the frustrations and needs of the poor.[15]

These deficiencies of democracy do not only stem from abusive or "delegative" democracy at the national level.[16] Just as often, they stem from the weakness of the state—its inability to break local power monopolies, discipline local police forces, protect the weak and vulnerable, and enforce accountability and the rule of law—at all levels of public life. In large federal democracies such as India, Brazil, and Nigeria, it is in fact the state and local governments, and the local political bosses, who are responsible for the worst abuses of human rights, which invariably harm mainly the poor. A growing body of evidence suggests that one of the chief problems for development is that the state is lacking in capacity and authority.[17] In important respects, it can be said that rural people, and poor people generally, are "undergoverned."[18]

Reforming governance at the national level

There is a good reason why development assistance still focuses largely on nations and national state structures. True, some states have collapsed, and we are seeing alternatives to the classic Westphalian state structure in such places as Somalia. But for the most part, national states persist as the framework for governance and as indispensable facilitators of economic growth and poverty reduction. If we are going to witness large reductions in poverty, it will only be because states themselves become more capable, effective, open, accountable, responsive, honest, and just. Clearly, the improvement of governance cannot only happen at the center, and indeed cannot involve only formal state structures at any level. But improving the quality of governance at the national level is a *fundamental condition* for reducing poverty "from the bottom up."

Although the rigid divide between donor activities for economic development and those for democracy assistance is beginning to soften, it persists. There is still a tendency to view donor assistance for economic development—and particularly poverty reduction—as social, economic, and technical, in other words, as nonpolitical. This may be the biggest mistake in efforts to relieve poverty. After a half-century of international development assistance, the persistence of poverty is not for want of effort, resources, and international goodwill, though we could use more of all of these. It is not primarily a failing of technical understanding, though we can always do with more of that, too. It is certainly not a consequence of fate. Poverty persists because of power disparities. At every level of organized life, the powerful attempt to prey on the weak and disorganized (and not only in low-income countries). Two principal forces contain this predation: open and competitive markets, and resourceful and authoritative states, the latter preventing and correcting market distortions through democracy and the rule of law. Unless these forces are brought to bear to level accumulated power disparities, poverty will be reproduced from generation to generation.

In designing democratic and other governance institutions, the social, economic, and historical context is important to bear in mind.

However, certain broad, generic features of governance will work to promote development, empowerment, social justice, and poverty alleviation. One obvious priority is to strengthen the overall training, capacity, and professionalism of state bureaucrats, including their technical understanding of economic policies that promote development. With specific respect to the elements of democratic good governance, two priorities are elaborated in more detail below: free and fair elections, and democratic political parties.

Free and fair elections

If elections are to be an instrument for registering citizen preferences and holding public officials accountable, they must be free and fair—and thus neutrally and professionally administered. As with other aspects of governance, those who seek shortcuts to power and privilege will subvert elections unless there are strong rules and institutions to prevent it. Electoral administration consists of a daunting range of tasks, any of which may be compromised by fraud or ineptitude. These include registering voters; publishing and distributing voter lists; registering and qualifying parties and candidates; establishing and enforcing rules on campaigning and campaign finance; ensuring the security of campaigners, voters, and the polling stations; administering the polls during voting; counting the ballots; reporting, collating, and announcing the results; investigating and adjudicating complaints; and certifying the results.[19] This set of tasks requires a professional and permanent administration that is able to administer competently and regulate impartially, and that is not subject to direction or manipulation by incumbent officials or the ruling party.

Democratic political parties

Where governance is bad in democracies and quasi-democracies, political parties are invariably a major part of the problem. Quite often they are corrupt, insular, internally undemocratic, detached from societal interests, and ineffective in addressing the country's problems.

Yet in a modern society, democracy cannot function without political parties. They structure electoral competition, organize government, and recruit leaders. And even if parties are only one among many vehicles for stimulating political participation and representing interests, they remain essential to the overall functioning of democracy.[20]

Development assistance must meet the challenge of helping democratic political parties to become more capable and mature as organizations, more internally competitive and transparent, and more externally responsive and accountable. Toward this end, party assistance programs should focus on three traditional objectives:

1   *Organizational development:* Helping parties to research issues, assess public opinion, develop policies and platforms, craft long-term strategies, build professional staffs, recruit members, raise funds, and manage resources.
2   *Electoral mobilization:* Helping parties to select and train candidates, craft campaign messages, manage campaign organizations, improve communication skills, contact voters, identify and mobilize supporters, and mobilize women and youth.
3   *Governance:* Helping parties to function effectively as a legislative caucus, constitute a government or opposition (including at the regional and local levels), forge coalitions, reform electoral laws, and monitor elections through poll watching.

In addition, two innovative arenas merit more emphasis in the coming years:

4   *Internal democratization:* Helping parties to develop more democratic and transparent means of selecting candidates (such as through primaries and caucuses), choosing leaders, making decisions, formulating policies, and eliciting member participation.[21]
5   *Reforming party and campaign finance:* Helping party, legislative, governmental, and civil society actors to identify alternative rules and systems for reporting and monitoring financial donations to parties and campaigns, auditing party accounts, providing public funding to parties and campaigns, and widening the access of all political parties to the electronic mass media. Also: helping parties to promote higher standards of ethical conduct among their leaders, candidates, and members, and helping civil society actors and electoral administrations to develop better technical means to monitor party and campaign finance.

Political parties will not be strengthened by party assistance alone. Interest groups and NGOs can be supported in efforts to forge channels of communication and working relations with political parties. Civil society activists can be given training if they opt to enter the arena of party and electoral politics. One of the crucial challenges of improving party politics is recruiting better-educated and more public-spirited actors into the process.

Concluding reflection

There is growing evidence, including from within the World Bank itself, that governance matters. And there is growing recognition in development assistance circles that poverty reduction and empowerment of the poor require broad improvements in governance. Yet policy and practice lag well behind understanding. International donors remain reluctant to violate too blatantly international norms of sovereignty, and there is a powerful tendency for political conditionality to give way to gestures at compliance.

Yet if poverty is, to a considerable degree, a political phenomenon, then a *serious* effort to reduce, once and for all, the structural conditions of mass poverty is also a political action. There is no getting around it. Is the world ready for the scope of *political* intervention that will be needed to build democracy, promote freedom, increase accountability, empower the poor, and thereby truly reduce poverty?

Notes

1 Originally published as "Empowering the Poor: What Does Democracy Have to Do with It?" in *Measuring Empowerment: Cross Disciplinary Perspectives*, Deepa Narayan, ed. (Washington, DC: World Bank, 2005), 403–425. This is an abbreviated and edited version of the original.

2 USAID (United States Agency for International Development), *Foreign Aid in the National Interest* (Washington, DC: USAID, 2003), www.usaid.gov/fani.

3 Deepa Narayan, ed. *Empowerment and Poverty Reduction: A Sourcebook* (Washington, DC: World Bank, 2002).

4 Ashutosh Varshney, "Why Have Poor Democracies Not Eliminated Poverty?" *Asian Survey* 40(5) (2000).

5 Public goods benefit the entire community. They are "nonexcludable" in consumption: in other words, the consumption of such goods by one person does not reduce the amount available to others, and they are available to all (even those who do not pay). An example of a pure public good is national security, which is available to all citizens of a country simultaneously. There are also some quasi-public goods, access to which may not necessarily be nonexcludable. Examples include physical infrastructure (sanitation, potable water, electric power, telecommunications, public transport), and social, economic, and political infrastructure (schools, clinics, markets, courts, a neutral and capable state bureaucracy).

6 Andreas Schedler, "Conceptualizing Accountability" in *The Self-Restraining State: Power and Accountability in New Democracies*, Andreas Schedler, Larry Diamond, and Marc F. Plattner, eds (Boulder, CO: Lynne Rienner, 1999), 15.

7 Robert D. Putnam, *Making Democracy Work: Civic Traditions in Modern Italy* (Princeton, NJ: Princeton University Press, 1993), 167–176.

8 Samuel P. Huntingdon, and Joan Nelson, *No Easy Choice* (Cambridge, MA: Harvard University Press, 1976).

9 For evidence, see Deepa Narayan, with Raj Patel, Kai Schafft, Anne Rademacher, and Sarah Koch-Schulte, *Voices of the Poor: Can Anyone Hear Us?* (New York: Oxford University Press for the World Bank, 2000).

10 Adam Przeworski, Michael E. Alvarez, Jose Antonio Cheibub, and Fernando Limongi, *Democracy and Development: Political Institutions and Well-Being in the World, 1950–90* (Cambridge: Cambridge University Press, 2000).

11 Seymour Martin Lipset, "Some Social Requisites of Democracy," *American Political Science Review* 53 (March 1959): 69–105.

12 Alex Inkeles and Larry Sirowy, "The Effects of Democracy on Economic Growth and Inequality: A Review," in *On Measuring Democracy: Its Consequences and Concomitants*, Alex Inkeles, ed. (New Brunswick, NJ: Transaction, 1991), 125–156; Adam Przeworski and Fernando Limongi, "Political Regimes and Economic Growth," *Journal of Economic Perspectives* 7(3) (1993): 51–70.

13 Inkeles and Sirowy, "The Effects of Democracy on Economic Growth and Inequality: A Review," 149; Przeworski and Limongi, "Political Regimes and Economic Growth."

14 Richard Roll and John R. Talbott, "Political Freedom, Economic Liberty, and Prosperity," *Journal of Democracy* 14 (July 2003): 75–89.

15 Marina Ottaway and Thomas Carothers, "Toward Civil Society Realism," in *Funding Virtue: Civil Society Aid and Democracy Promotion*, Ottaway and Carothers, eds. (Washington, DC: Carnegie Endowment for International Peace, 2000), 293–310.

16 Guillermo O'Donnell, "Delegative Democracy," *Journal of Democracy* 5 (January 1994): 55–69.

17 Richard Joseph, "Africa: States in Crisis," *Journal of Democracy* 14 (July 2003): 159–170.

18 S. R. Osmani, "Participatory Governance, People's Empowerment and Poverty Reduction" in UNDP/SEPED Conference Paper Series 7, United Nations Development Programme, Social Development and Poverty Elimination Division, New York, 4.

19 Robert A. Pastor, "A Brief History of Electoral Commissions" in *The Self-Restraining State: Power and Accountability in New Democracies,* Andreas Schedler, Larry Diamond, and Marc F. Plattner, eds. (Boulder, CO: Lynne Rienner, 1999), 77–78.

20 Larry Diamond and Richard Gunther, eds, *Political Parties and Democracy* (Baltimore, MD: Johns Hopkins University Press, 2001), 7–9; USAID, *USAID Political Party Development Assistance,* Technical Publication Series PN-ACR-216 (Washington, DC: USAID Office of Democracy and Governance, 1999), 7–8.

21 While most political parties in emerging democracies need to become more internally democratic, there is a tradeoff between internal democracy and party coherence. For example, if there is no role for the central party leadership in candidate selection, a party may lack unity of purpose, programmatic or ideological coherence, and organizational discipline.

22 Promoting democracy in postconflict and failed states[1]

As we move into the fourth decade since the great wave of global democratic expansion began in 1974, the task of promoting democracy faces a deepening set of challenges and contradictions. These revolve around two interrelated facts. First, as the number of democracies has increased, the task of promoting democratic transitions and consolidation has become more difficult, because the countries with the economic, social, historical, and geographic conditions most conducive to democracy have already installed (and in many cases, largely consolidated) democracy. Second, and related to this, many of the tough cases that remain are so not simply because they lack the classic facilitating conditions for democracy—more developed levels of per capita income, civil society, independent mass media, political parties, mass democratic attitudes and values, and so on—but because they lack as well the more basic conditions of a viable political order. Before a country can have a democratic state, it must first have a state—a set of political institutions that exercise authority over a territory, make and execute policies, extract and distribute revenue, produce public goods, and maintain order by wielding an effective monopoly over the means of violence. As Samuel Huntington observed in the opening sentence of his classic, *Political Order in Changing Societies*, "The most important political distinction among countries concerns not their form of government but their degree of government."[2] While this sentence (and really, the book itself) does not do justice to the importance of freedom and democracy for good governance, it does orient us to the fundamental importance of a coherent, capable state. It is an insight that has been coming back vigorously into the literatures on both democracy building and state building in recent years.[3] The daunting reality of the contemporary world is that perhaps two dozen states either lack this most basic foundation for building democracy, as a result of state collapse in war, or are fragile and at risk of collapse. This includes not only the countries that have descended into or are trying to emerge from violent conflict but also others that are chronically besieged or at serious risk of collapse due to rising levels of civil violence.

Failed or acutely failing states pose distinctive problems for democracy promotion. In these states, the challenge is not only (or in some cases, even at all) to pressure authoritarian state leaders to surrender power, but rather to figure out how to regenerate legitimate power in the first place. The imperative is not only to empower citizens and their independent organizations but also to endow state institutions with resources, training, organization, and a sense of a common mission.

Within this broad context, there are three distinct types of cases. First are the postconflict states that are emerging (or trying to emerge) from a period of external, or more commonly civil, war. Many of these countries have been in Africa—South Africa, Mozambique, Liberia, Sierra Leone, and Somalia. Some have been in Latin America (Nicaragua, El Salvador, indeed, much of Central America), in Asia (for example, Cambodia and one hopes now Sri Lanka), and in the Middle East (Lebanon, Algeria, and now Iraq). Second are the countries that are in the midst of civil war or ongoing violent conflict, where central state authority has largely collapsed, as in the Democratic Republic of the Congo. And third are the states that, while not yet gripped with large-scale internal violence, are at severe risk of it because of weak or weakening state authority and capacity, high levels of crime and privatized violence, and increasing polarization of domestic politics (as in Nigeria).

Each of these three types of cases requires specific kinds of strategies for democracy promotion. Obviously, the first imperative for states suffering civil war is to end it, and here international mediation, intervention, and peace implementation (as well as the more conventional forms of peacekeeping) have a vital role to play. There is a large and distinct literature on this set of challenges, and I will only address it as it bears on the challenge of democracy promotion in these settings.[4] In addition to all the usual types of efforts to build democratic civil societies, public values, political parties, and governmental institutions, weak, feckless, and failing states require focused efforts to get at the sources of state failure, which frequently have to do with ethnic domination and injustice and endemic political corruption. Obviously, state institutions in this class of cases need to be strengthened in their skill and resource levels across the board, but this is generally not possible unless a new structure of incentives is institutionalized to foster commitment to the state and the country—the public interest—rather than to the advancement of individuals and their families, patronage networks, parties, and tribes. This is one of the most pervasive challenges of economic and political development assistance, and as I have addressed this extensively elsewhere,[5] I will touch on it only briefly as it bears on the class of postconflict states, which will be the subject of the rest of this chapter. Mainly I examine here the distinctive problems confronting the building of democracy in postconflict states, and the lessons that can be derived from recent experiences, particularly in Iraq. I use Iraq as a kind of critical case here because the American-led intervention and postconflict reconstruction violated every one of the lessons that were available from previous international postconflict reconstruction efforts, and thus Iraq exposes in vivid relief both the validity of these lessons and the potentially catastrophic consequences of ignoring them.[6]

The distinctive features of postconflict states

Democracy promotion in postconflict states begins with the problem of order. By definition, there has been violent conflict. In some instances (such as El Salvador, Nicaragua, Rhodesia/Zimbabwe, South Africa, Cambodia, and Liberia), a peace agreement (often internationally mediated) may restore the authority of the state over its territory and implement peaceful means for sharing power or regulating the competition for power. One of the distinctive features of postconflict state building in the past two decades has been the increasing reliance on formal democratic mechanisms, particularly elections, to determine who will rule after violent conflict. In other instances, either the preexisting state has completely collapsed, so that there is no overarching indigenous political authority left, or the authority of the state has shrunk back to only a portion of the territory over which it exercises international legal sovereignty. A vacuum of power is always filled, one way or another.

In the absence of an effective state, there are basically three possibilities. If there has been a civil war and a rebel force has ultimately triumphed, then the vacuum may be filled (gradually or even very rapidly) by the rebellious army and political movement as it establishes control over the state. However, this is highly unlikely to lead to democracy, as the triumph of violent insurgencies usually leads to the replacement of one form of autocracy with another (the American Revolution being a striking exception). Second, there may simply be a patchwork of warlords and armies, with either no real central state (as in Somalia) or only a very weak one, as in Afghanistan. In this situation, the conflict does not really end, but may wax and wane in decentralized fashion, as in Afghanistan today. The third possibility is that an international actor or coalition of actors steps in to constitute temporary authority politically and militarily. This may be an individual country, a coalition, an individual country under the thin veneer of a coalition (essentially the case in Iraq with the American administration after the fall of Saddam Hussein in 2003), or the United Nations acting through the formal architecture of a UN postconflict mission, as in the UN Transitional Administration in East Timor (UNTAET) from 1999 to 2002.

Whatever the specific form of the postconflict effort to build democracy, one thing must be stressed above all others: no order, no democracy. Democracy cannot be viable (and neither can it really be meaningful) in a context where violence or the threat of violence is pervasive and suffuses the political calculations and fears of groups and individuals. Thus, the promotion of democracy in postconflict situations cannot succeed without the rebuilding of order in these contexts, and the tasks of democracy building and of peace implementation are inseparable. It is possible to implement peace without democracy, but it is not possible to build democracy without peace (and in fact, peace will be better and deeper with democracy). More generally, we can specify six distinct challenges of political reconstruction in a postconflict setting:

1 rebuilding the capacity of the shattered state, including its means of providing order and security (the army, police, and intelligence);
2 controlling and demobilizing alternative sources of violence in the hands of nonstate actors, such as religious and party militias, warlords, and other private armies;
3 reducing the structural incentives to violence through the design of political institutions—and ultimately a new constitution, arrived at through broad public consultation and debate—that give a real stake in the system to each group that is willing to play by the rules of the democratic game;
4 developing the political and social institutions of democracy in the state and civil society;
5 administering the postconflict nation; and finally,
6 designing and implementing a plan for transition to a new, self-sustaining, and democratic political order.

These six tasks overlap in their temporal sequencing, often become highly compressed in time, and encompass a number of contradictions. It is, in part, the failure to acknowledge and somehow mitigate these tensions that accounts for the failure to build a sustainable democracy in these circumstances.

First is the tension between order and freedom. The postconflict state needs an authoritative and capable public security establishment. But building up the police (and probably some kind of conventional armed forces) is in tension with the goal of empowering and privileging civilian political actors. The new state must have an internal monopoly on the means of violence and the legitimate use of force, but this must be constructed carefully, with mechanisms and norms of civilian supremacy, so as not to create a new, antidemocratic military Frankenstein. It takes time to build the norms of deference to civilian control and respect for human rights and the rule of law, yet time is precisely what the reviving state does not have a great deal of. Moreover, the new security apparatus may face terrorists, warlords, and other violent spoilers whose brutal threats to the incipient new order can be easily seen to justify abridgements of due process and other restraints.

A second tension pits the imperatives of postconflict democracy building against postconflict administration and stabilization. The goal may be to establish democracy, but in a postconflict setting it may be some time before free, fair, and meaningful elections can be organized. Thus, for some interim period, an unelected authority has to administer the country. Who? The best solution, it would seem, is a transitional government in which the former combatants or (as in Afghanistan) a wide range of disparate and hostile forces share power by some agreed-upon formula until democratic elections can be organized. However, it is difficult to broker such agreements in the midst of violent conflict or state collapse, and "The instability of post-settlement constitution-building in Cambodia and Angola serves as a warning about the potential brittleness of formal power-sharing institutions."[7] A frequent model has been international intervention of both a military and political nature, with the international authority providing both a stabilization force to secure the country and a transitional authority to rule the country, or at least to help referee the political situation, until a new constitution can be written and elections can be held for a new permanent government. Herein emerges the dilemma. A nondemocratic (often in many respects quasi-colonial) power is asked to establish a democratic form of government.

The dilemma may be reduced when the international transitional authority "has been empowered primarily to hold an election and then withdraw" according to a defined and fairly imminent timetable (as with the 18-month UN Transitional Authority in Cambodia, UNTAC).[8] It becomes more serious when the international authority is tasked with both administering the country and preparing it for sovereign democracy, with no specific end date, as was initially the case in Iraq and has been the case for quite some years now in Bosnia and Kosovo. The scale of operation and formal scope of authority also matter a great deal. In East Timor, the mandate and resources of the UN gave it effective governing authority over the territory for more than two years, while the UN mission in Afghanistan operated with a much lighter footprint, involving only "a fraction of UNTAET's staff and budget ... in a country perhaps forty times the size and thirty times the population of East Timor."[9] The heavy footprint worked in East Timor, but those conditions (a situation of new nationhood emerging; support and acceptance from the local population; international consensus; and, therefore, broad domestic and international legitimacy) are likely to prove rather unique in the contemporary era. Gerald Knaus and Marcus Cox argue that the European Union's mission in Bosnia and the UN Interim Administration Mission in Kosovo (UNMIK) have failed to build democracy in these two territories because they have ruled them as protectorates through a model of "authoritarian state building." While this has achieved some degree of stabilization, it has not cultivated the tools, incentives, and culture of democratic self-governance, but instead has run roughshod over local resistance. By contrast, in dealing with candidate member states, the EU has worked with local institutions, "giving them the capacity and the incentive to become active forces for development."[10]

Knaus and Cox offer a compelling critique of the Bosnia and Kosovo interventions. But these territories are certainly not Poland and Hungary, nor even Bulgaria and Romania. The problem is that the more a post-conflict situation is dominated by undemocratic leaders, parties, and movements, and by overriding ethnic or political divisions among them, the more a "light footprint" by the international community may leave only a light impact at best. A transitional administration must be strong enough to control, contain, and face down undemocratic elements, especially if they are armed and violent, and yet "light" enough to allow—and indeed cultivate—the emergence of local initiative and control that fosters democratic self-governance. This may not be an impossible combination, but in the worst postconflict situations, it is a formidably difficult one.

Related to this is the third dilemma, involving time again. If the mission, or at least one important objective, of transitional administration is to promote democracy, then this requires the holding of free and fair elections. However, if elections are to be truly free and fair (and democratically meaningful), there must be time to prepare them properly: time to construct electoral administration and disperse its offices and resources throughout the country; time to devise an electoral system that can provide the right kinds of incentives to restrain and transcend conflict; time to provide conditions of reasonable physical security for campaigns and voters; and time to register and educate voters, organize election monitoring, train political parties and candidates, and enable them to build their organizations and mobilize support. Again, during this time, some nonelected authority has to rule. If that authority is international, the longer it rules, the more it risks a legitimacy crisis with the public it is trying to prepare for democracy and falling into the model of "authoritarian state building." If that authority is domestic, a protracted period of interim rule may enable the unelected political forces to entrench themselves in power, generating a severely "unlevel" playing field for the elections when they do come.

Ill-timed and ill-prepared elections do not produce democracy, or even political stability, after conflict. Instead, they may only enhance the power of actors who mobilize coercion, fear, and prejudice, thereby reviving autocracy and even precipitating large-scale violent strife. In Angola in 1992, in Bosnia in 1996, and in Liberia in 1997, rushed elections set back the prospects for democracy and, in Angola and Liberia, they paved the way for renewed civil war.[11] There are compelling reasons, based on logic and recent historical experience, for deferring national elections until militias have been demobilized, new moderate parties trained and assisted, electoral infrastructure created, and democratic media and ideas generated.

In a context of shattered political order, truly free and fair elections take a long time to prepare, for they require not only a neutral and skillful administrative infrastructure but also an informed citizenry, organized parties, and a political climate largely free of coercion and violence. In many postconflict settings, especially where the state has collapsed or there is no previous history of democratic elections, that would seem to require an extended process of institution building in the state, polity, and society over perhaps five to ten years, or certainly much longer than the two or three years that typically intervene between the end of conflict and the holding of national elections.

It would have been better in the abstract for postwar Iraq if national elections could have been deferred for at least five to seven years. However, the reality was that there was no way of constituting legitimate authority for very long in the interim, particularly with the country's most important spiritual leader demanding elections for a national parliament as soon as possible. Often then, postconflict administrations must seek a difficult balance between the need for speed to get to a legitimate (elected) government and the need for time to prepare decent democratic elections (see below).

The fourth contradiction emerges out of two competing visions of post-conflict stabilization, one deeper, longer-term, and more costly, the other easier to secure but far more vulnerable to failure. There is a temptation in a country that has been torn by war to reach for a false sense of peace because it is quicker and easier to obtain—to defer indefinitely the hard challenge of disarmament and demobilization and, in effect, let different armed groups keep their arms and armies in exchange for implicit prom-ises or hopes of fealty to the new democratic order. This happened with the first false start at peace in Sierra Leone, which sought to draw in the war-lord Foday Sankoh, and with the failed attempts at disarmament in Angola, which led to the resumption of civil war. It happened quite dramatically in Iraq after the fall of Saddam Hussein, and has been a major factor behind the subsequent rising levels of violence.

Implementing a more thoroughgoing stabilization—in which alterna-tive sources of violence outside the state are systematically demobilized—is time-consuming, financially expensive, and potentially costly in lives as well. Indeed, it is one of the ironies of a postconflict situation that the new authority may have to wage new armed conflict in order to create the conditions for a more organic and sustainable peace. Such a genuine and democratic peace often requires a comprehensive "DDR" plan for the dis-armament, demobilization, and reintegration (into society, and, selectively, into the new police and army) of various nonstate armed forces. DDR plans require much money, preparation, organization, and monitoring. If they are going to succeed, they also need sufficient military power to forcibly disarm those groups ("spoilers") that will not voluntarily sign up, and thus to ensure the compliance of those groups that have made commitments to demobilize and disarm. If stability in the transitional period is secured with international troops, they usually are not large enough in number and robust enough in their rules of engagement to take on this task.

Like other dimensions of postconflict democracy promotion, there is no one standard model or formula for the control of violence. Social and cultural (and political) realities may require a concession that allows the citizens to keep small arms, but Joanna Spear argues that there is a com-mon imperative to demobilize (disband) large-scale military or paramilitary formations outside the state, and this requires considerable political will and skill, knowledge of the specific environment, and often financial and military resources.[12] Another irony is that, if international military force must be mobilized to demobilize private militias and violent challengers to the new democratic order, these foreign troops may also become part of the problem, in that their presence can provoke resistance, particularly if they kill local combatants, and more especially if they become undisciplined and themselves violate individual rights and the laws of war. This has become a big part of the problem in Iraq, where American troops have been both a bulwark of security and a lightning rod for nationalist resistance and insecurity, but it has also been evident in some African cases, such as the intervention of the Economic Community of West African States Cease-Fire Monitoring Group (ECOMOG) in Liberia.[13]

To summarize, in a way: When we mention the term democracy promotion or democracy building, we tend to think of a fairly conventional set of tasks—helping to develop political parties, civil society organizations, representative and legal institutions, and so on. All of these are important. Indeed, all of the things that need to be done to promote and develop democracy in a historically authoritarian setting must be done in a postauthoritarian, postconflict setting. However, postconflict settings are distinctive in terms of the roles of violence, order, and "stateness." If these challenges are not met, all the others—political, legal, societal, and economic—will fail. This was a problem that the American occupation of Iraq never adequately grasped. Consequently, the ambitious conceptual plans for political, civic, and economic reconstruction could never really be implemented because of the widespread violence. To a lesser degree, Afghanistan faces the same problem today.

Some (tentative) general lessons and guidelines

Postconflict situations vary considerably in their dynamics and distributions of power, and in the hierarchy of challenges they face. Probably the single greatest lesson to be learned from previous efforts at stabilization and democratization of conflict-ridden states is that there is no one lesson or model. Just as generals always fight the last war, so do nation builders always apply the model of the last postconflict mission, or of some earlier historical model that may be quite a limited fit. For example, the late UN administrator Sergio Vieira de Mello brought to the new UN mission in East Timor the same basic model he had used in Kosovo—only to find that it did not fit.[14] The American occupation of Iraq, under the sweeping authority of the Coalition Provisional Authority, seems to have been inspired to some extent by the last major American occupation of a country, Douglas MacArthur's postwar administration of Japan, despite the profound differences in the political, sociological, geopolitical, and historical conditions of those two occupations. Understanding the context is crucial.

Still, there are some lessons from recent postconflict democracy-building and stabilization experiences that appear to be generally relevant. I begin by formalizing the first imperative that was just mentioned.

1 *Understand the local context in its historical, cultural, political, and sociological dimensions*

While this is generally important for assisting democratic development in *any* context, it is especially vital in the wake of violent conflict or state failure, because state collapse generates conditions that are very unfavorable to the development of democracy and that often require not just democratic assistance but also a much more massive and wide-ranging set of international commitments (see below). Thus, in postconflict settings, the scope of international intervention is likely to be far greater (if there is to be any chance for democratic success), and the margin for error is at the same time much less. Inadequate understanding of the local context—including such vital issues as political leaders and alliances, historical trends and grievances, religious, ethnic and subethnic divisions, the sources of legal and illicit revenue, and the structure and loyalties of private militias—can be crippling.

The problem is made worse by the fact that many of the countries whose states are emerging from conflict or collapse are poorly understood by Western governments or by actors in the international community. This is partly because extremely closed countries such as Iraq under Saddam and Afghanistan under the Taliban are difficult for Western social scientists to visit and research, and for Western intelligence agents to penetrate. As for smaller, troubled states such as Somalia or Liberia, until they collapse and create problems for regional and international order, their lack of size and strategic importance tends to result in their being shortchanged in analytic attention. War, and before it a long period of brutal misrule or social disintegration, make many failed and failing states difficult to study. War may also alter many of the structural parameters (political leadership, ethnic divisions, and alliances) that had previously been understood by academic, diplomatic, and intelligence experts.

Thus, a serious effort to promote democracy in a postconflict state must begin early on with a fairly intensive and comprehensive mobilization and integration of existing country knowledge from all sources, private and public, governmental and nongovernmental, academic and operational. Next, any international mission should be advised on the ground, on an ongoing basis, by some number of leading experts on the country—not just political scientists, but ideally historians and anthropologists (as well as economists when they have acquired some expertise on the country). These experts should be drawn from across the available resources in the international community, not just from one country. The failure of the United States to mobilize and more fully utilize expert knowledge of Iraq from the beginning was an important contributing factor to the bumbling, ineffectual character of its occupation.

2 *Mobilize and commit adequate military and financial resources*

This is probably the most difficult lesson to apply, because all resources are scarce, and it is very difficult to get the primary national and multilateral actors in the international community to commit the military force necessary to truly stabilize a country where the state, and with it civil order, has broken down over an extended period of time. For one thing, it is financially costly. For another, it is risky in that countries contributing forces may suffer casualties, and their leaders may then pay a high political price. Finally, deployable military force is a far more finite resource than money alone. The UN Secretary General's High-level Panel on Threats, Challenges and Change noted that with 60,000 UN peacekeepers deployed in 16 missions around the world by the end of 2004, and more likely to be committed soon to other war-torn African states, the world is running out of available forces for peacekeeping and peace enforcement. (The panel did not mention the military engagement of the American-led coalition in Iraq, since it is not a UN mission, but even 150,000 troops have not been able to stabilize that country over more than three years, and it is clear that the United States, with the best military in the world, is already feeling the strain on its own sustainable military capacities.) As the UN panel's report makes clear, significantly more international peacekeeping/enforcement forces must be made available, along with "sufficient transport and logistic capabilities to move and supply those who are available ... The developed states have particular responsibilities here, and should do more to transform their existing force capacities into suitable contingents for peace operations." Currently, the armed forces of many of these countries have outmoded, cold war-era structures, "with less than 10 percent of soldiers in uniform available for active deployment at any given time."[15]

Sometimes, it takes many troops to create the enabling environment for democracy building and national reconstruction, because the situation confronting international actors is not truly one of "postconflict." War in its conventional form may have ended, but order has been shattered, violence continues, and armed groups stand ready to use violence and intimidation to enhance their political position or to undermine the implementation of any peace agreement that does not meet all of their key demands (the latter marking them as "spoilers").[16] One of the two greatest obstacles to the democratization of postwar Iraq has been the lack of adequate force for stabilization of the country after the end of formal hostilities (with the collapse of Saddam Hussein's Baathist regime). As I and others have argued repeatedly, this was not due to lack of advance warning of what could be expected during the "postwar" period, but rather to a stubborn, blinding refusal on the part of Secretary of Defense Donald Rumsfeld and other key Pentagon and Administration officials, including President Bush himself, to heed the experts on postconflict stabilization and on Iraq (including the senior command of the United States Army, which sought an invasion and stabilization force of several hundred thousand troops, or at least twice as large as what has been utilized).[17]

The Army's initial request for troops in Iraq was much more in line with the ratio of foreign troops to domestic population of the international interventions in Bosnia and Kosovo, which if replicated in Iraq would have meant an initial international force of 460,000–500,000 troops.[18] Pentagon planners probably worried about the capacity of the United States to mobilize such a large force, and about the resulting casualties. But the RAND study, led by James Dobbins—who had served in the previous decade as U.S. special envoy for the postconflict missions in Bosnia, Kosovo, Haiti, Somalia, and Afghanistan—concluded: "There appears to be an inverse correlation between the size of the stabilization force and the level of risk. The higher the proportion of stabilizing troops, the lower the number of casualties suffered and inflicted."[19]

Being able to mobilize adequate resources for postconflict stabilization and (democratic) reconstruction requires three further imperatives. First, the actors who would intervene must assess the difficulty of the mission and the prospects for success. Stephen Stedman and his colleagues, in the most systematic and comprehensive study to date of peace implementation efforts, identified three factors in particular that are "most commonly associated with a difficult environment." These are first, the likelihood of spoilers, especially total spoilers; second, neighboring states hostile to the peace agreement (or the new, democratic postconflict political order); and third, "spoils—valuable, easily tradable commodities."[20] The difficulty of peace implementation also increases with five additional factors that emerged as important: the number of warring parties, the absence of a (noncoerced) peace agreement before intervention, a collapsed state, the number of combatants in the conflict, and demands for secession.[21]

Iraq, in this regard, was completely off the charts in terms of difficulty— virtually all of the above eight unfavorable conditions specified by Downs and Stedman were strongly present. Analysts warned that a violent insurgency (consisting of dedicated spoilers) would emerge in the postwar situation, especially if there were a prolonged occupation. It was clear that neighboring states, particularly Syria and Iran, would be hostile to the construction of democracy and would try to sabotage it—as, indeed, they have tried to do. The insurgency has consisted of a number of different elements with different interests, and there are various other armed militias in the mix as well. Oil looms large, the state has collapsed, there is no peace agreement, there is a fair number of armed combatants (though not in terms of formal armies), and there is powerful Kurdish sentiment for secession (along with periodic threats from Kurdish elites).

The more difficult the (post)conflict situation, the more successful implementation of peace requires an accurate estimate of the difficulties involved and the resources—and sacrifices—that will be required, as well as a powerful state willing to bear at least a considerable share of those risks and costs.[22] Facing down spoilers and stabilizing a war-torn country where peace must really be imposed, not simply kept, requires the commitment of a major international or at least regional power, which views stabilization in its own vital strategic interests. This means not just an international organization (such as the UN) or loose international coalition, but at least one powerful state. After surveying the bloodied landscape of peace implementation, Stedman found: "All too often in the 1990s international and regional organizations were sent to implement peace agreements in extremely challenging environments where no major state possessed a security interest. When implementers were challenged, the missions failed, usually with catastrophic consequences."[23]

The lessons learned from failed peace implementation efforts are sobering. If the international actors that are intervening to implement peace—and democracy can be meaningful and viable only in a context of peace—do not judge the difficulty wisely, and are not willing to commit adequate resources, they will likely fail. And since failure entails a tragic loss of lives and resources, and can discourage future interventions (even ones that are more likely to succeed), it is better not to intervene than to do so with a level of resources and commitment that makes failure quite likely. This generates a third lesson, about the international circumstances that will more likely call forth the necessary resources.

3 Establish international legitimacy and active support for the postconflict intervention

Such an intervention will more likely raise and sustain the necessary resources and commitment if there is a shared sense of importance and commitment in the international community, ideally formalized by a United Nations Security Council mandate. As the difficulty of the challenge rises, the need for a powerful state to take a vital interest in the mission increases, but that alone will probably not be enough to generate success unless there is significant international participation. This is not only because of the need to distribute and share the burdens, but also because of the imperatives of legitimacy internally in the country, which require that the intervention not be seen as (and truly, not be) the imperial action of another powerful state.

4 Generate legitimacy and trust within the postconflict country

No international reconstruction effort can succeed without some degree of acceptance and cooperation—and eventually support and positive engagement—from the people of the failed state. If the local population has no trust in the initial international administration and its intentions, the intervention can become the target of popular wrath, and will then need to spend most of its military (and administrative) energies defending *itself* rather than rebuilding the country and its political and social order.

In the final page of an impressively wise and learned book on postconflict state building, Simon Chesterman writes: "Modern trusteeships demand, above all, trust on the part of local actors. Earning and keeping that trust requires a level of understanding, sensitivity, and respect for local traditions and political aspirations that has often been lacking in international administration."[24] Unfortunately, the occupation of Iraq lacked these qualities, and the Iraqi people knew it.

Chesterman advises that, when the United Nations and other international actors come "to exercise state-like functions, they must not lose sight of their limited mandate to hold that sovereign power in trust for the population that will ultimately claim it."[25] This requires a balancing of international trusteeship or imperial functions with a distinctly nonimperial attitude and a clear and early specification of an acceptable timetable for the restoration of full sovereignty. The humiliating features of an extended, all-out occupation should be avoided as much as possible. In fact, whenever possible, the better course will be to avoid international occupation altogether and organize a broad-based national conference to choose an interim government, as was done in Afghanistan following the fall of the Taliban.

Some theorists and practitioners have been searching for a formula for international intervention to democratize failed states that stops short of full-scale imperial rule (whether by one nation or many). One possible approach is through some form of "shared sovereignty."[26] However, these formulas are viable precisely because they build not only on the de jure sovereignty of a state, but also on that state's retention of de facto sovereignty over most conventional aspects of policy. One could speculate that such formal abridgements of sovereignty would be more likely to be palatable if they were negotiated with international institutions or multilateral actors rather than a single powerful state.

Shared sovereignty is for the longer run, when failed states have begun to revive. In the nearer term, only international military intervention in some form—or the fairly rapid (and often brutal) victory of one side or another—can fill the vacuum left behind when a state has collapsed and a country is in or at the edge of or just emerging from chaos and civil war. Force must be used, or at least effectively deployed and exhibited, to restore order. Military occupation does not legitimate itself, however, but needs to be paired with a clear indication, from the very beginning, "as to how a temporary military occupation is to begin the process of transferring political control to local hands."[27] Such a framework should limit the political occupation not only in time, but in scope as well, allowing for the occupier, or the peace implementation force, to be held accountable. Such mechanisms of accountability can "encourage the emergence of an indigenous human rights and rule of law culture as well as improve the day-to-day governance of the territory," while also stemming the accumulation of local resentment and frustration.[28] (Two huge mistakes of the American occupation of Iraq were the establishment of an indefinite occupation with no clear timetable initially for the return of sovereignty, and the prevention of any means by which the occupying authorities could be questioned, scrutinized, and themselves held accountable.)

5 Hold local elections first

International interventions that seek to construct democracy after conflict must balance the tension between domination for the sake of implanting democracy and withdrawal in the name of democracy. The two competing temptations are:

1 to transform the country's institutions and values through an extended and penetrating occupation (*à la* British colonial rule); and
2 to hold elections and get out as soon as possible.

A key question is always how long international rule can be viable. In the case of Iraq, the answer—readily apparent from the history of Iraqi resistance to British colonial imposition in the 1920s, and from the profound and widespread suspicion among Iraqis of U.S. motives—was "not long." The failure to establish early on a date for national elections to choose a constitutional assembly became a major bone of contention between the U.S.-led occupation and the most revered religious and moral leader in Iraq, Ayatollah Sistani.

The pressure for rapid national elections might have been contained better if the United States had not constructed a full-blown occupation, but rather transferred power back to Iraqis quickly through a broad-based national conference with UN assistance, and if the international authorities in Iraq had allowed local elections to take place fairly soon. Even when the Coalition Provisional Authority (CPA) did organize at least indirect elections for provincial and local councils, it then undermined their authority by failing to give them meaningful resources and authority. This violated Chesterman's general guideline that executive authority should be devolved to local actors as soon as practical, and that "once power is transferred to local hands, whether at the municipal or national level, local actors should be able to exercise that power meaningfully, constrained only by the rule of law."[29]

In general, there is a strong logic to holding local elections before national ones, and as soon as practicable. Dobbins and his RAND coauthors find that holding local elections first "provides an opportunity for new local leaders to emerge and gain experience and for political parties to build a support base."[30] That could well have happened in Iraq if local elections had been allowed to proceed during 2003, and if some meaningful scope of authority and resources had been devolved to the newly elected bodies.

Then, the United States would have faced a broader, more diverse, and more legitimate array of Iraqi interlocutors, and the elected local bodies could have provided one basis for selecting an interim government.

6   Promote knowledge of institutional choices for democracy, and of democratic principles and norms

Postconflict societies are generally weak in knowledge of the institutional options for structuring democracy to manage ethnic and other group conflict, to protect individual and group rights, and to generate incentives for moderation in political behavior. The choice in Iraq's first election (in January 2005) of a national-list proportional representation system that was highly likely to reinforce ethnic and sectarian solidarities was only the latest example of this (the choice was made not just by Iraqi officials but by an experienced UN expert!). In the polarized debate on Iraqi federalism, each side (for example, the Sunnis completely opposed to federalism, the Kurds and some Shia in favor of a highly decentralized form) has proceeded with limited awareness of the lessons from experiences of other countries. Any effort to promote democracy in this setting has to involve the dissemination of knowledge about the likely effects of different institutional designs, with some detail and sophistication for political elites, but in simpler terms for the mass population as well. Assisting the formation and development of research institutes and NGOs that promote understanding of institutional designs to manage ethnic conflict and respectful debate on constitutional options for political reconstruction should be an early priority for democratic assistance. So should efforts by various types of NGOs and state institutions to educate the public about democratic norms, principles, and values. A mass civic education campaign must make people aware of their rights, train them in the arts of active citizenship, and lead them to hear, tolerate, and respect opposing views and interests.

7   Disperse economic reconstruction funds and democratic assistance as widely as possible

Both for the effectiveness and speed of economic revival, and for the building of local trust and acceptance, there is a compelling need to decentralize relief and reconstruction efforts, as well as democratic civic assistance, as much as possible. The more the international administration and private donors work with and through local partners, the more likely that economic reconstruction and democracy-building efforts will be directed toward the most urgent needs, and the better the prospect for the accumulation of political trust and cooperation with the overall transition project. The more reconstruction efforts are centralized in international aid or occupation missions, the more attempts at democratization will tend to neglect one of the biggest threats to postconflict stabilization: "high unemployment that affects a large majority of the population in the first years after war."[31]

In Iraq, as in Bosnia and so many other postconflict cases, there was a particularly compelling need for the creation of jobs. This need could have been met more rapidly if the repair and reconstruction contracts had been channeled more extensively through a wide range of local Iraqi contractors, instead of through the big U.S. corporations. Decentralization and rapid impact require dispersing some operational and spending authority to lower-level international officials who are resident in different cities and provinces, who get to know the local social and political contexts, and who can therefore distribute the funds to a much larger number of small, indigenous contractors and employees. It may make it more difficult to obtain the kinds of receipts that permit auditing. It may be more conducive to corruption—though corruption was hardly contained in the centralized operation in Iraq. Difficult choices must be made. However, in the hard and urgent circumstances of a postconflict situation, there is a case to be made for decentralized dispersal of small contracts and grants, along with early efforts, gathering as much information as possible, to evaluate performance. As Anne Ellen Henderson concludes based on the Iraqi reconstruction experience, "Reform and reconstruction initiatives imposed from above—whether by an occupying power or a centralized regime—are vulnerable to failure because they create so few empowered owners with the capacity and desire to ensure their implementation. Diffusing authority over reconstruction is cumbersome and time-consuming, but it can strengthen accountability and stimulate recovery in the long term."[32]

There is a particularly urgent need to diffuse sustainable employment opportunities, particularly ones beyond the temporary and somewhat distorting servicing of the international aid community itself. New jobs in labor-intensive rehabilitation of the economy and infrastructure, as well as in agriculture, industry, mine-clearing, and the new security forces, can help to reintegrate militia fighters and former combatants into society, promote reconciliation between previously (or still) warring parties, and give people livelihoods, thereby promoting their commitment to the new political order and their faith in the future, while at the same time rebuilding the country's physical infrastructure, health services, and educational system.[33]

8   Promote local participation, and proceed with humility and respect for the opinions of the people in whose interest the intervention is supposedly staged

There is, or certainly can be, a large dose of arrogance in any effort at international assistance, including democracy promotion. The danger of arrogance, or fatal conceit grows with the weakness, poverty, and urgency of need of the recipient state—up to the point where that state has failed altogether and is more or less helpless. Such ambitious international intervention cannot succeed, and the institutions it establishes cannot be viable, unless there is some sense of participation and ownership on the part of the people in the state being reconstructed. This is why holding local elections as early as possible is very important. It is why it is so vital to engage local partners, as extensively as possible, in postconflict relief and economic reconstruction. And it is why the process of constitution making must be democratic and broadly participatory, not merely through the election of a constituent assembly or a constitutional referendum (or ideally, both), but through the involvement of the widest possible range of stakeholders in the substantive discussions and procedural planning, and through the organization of an extensive national dialogue on constitutional issues and principles. This is one of the major findings of the process of creating a permanent constitution in 19 transitional countries, "most of which have emerged from armed conflict in the last three decades" (such as Bosnia, East Timor, Liberia, Nicaragua, and South Africa). One of the study leaders, Jamal Benomar, concludes: "Constitutions produced without transparency and adequate public participation will lack legitimacy."[34] And illegitimate constitutions augur poorly for future stability.

9   Institutionalize the capacity for effective intervention and democracy promotion in postconflict settings

The UN Secretary General's High-level Panel has offered a number of promising and ambitious suggestions for enhancing and institutionalizing capacity in the UN and the international system. Prominent among these is the establishment of a Peace-building Commission (with a significant permanent support staff) to identify countries at risk of state failure and intervene early to prevent it; to assist the transition from conflict to peace (and one hopes to democracy, though the panel does not mention this); "and in particular to marshal and sustain the efforts of the international community in postconflict peacebuilding over whatever period may be necessary."[35] In addition, the panel recommends that member states "strongly support" the efforts of the UN's Department of Peacekeeping Operations to facilitate more rapid deployment by enhancing strategic stockpiles and standby arrangements for peacekeeping deployment, and it proposes to strengthen, and, in essence, shake up and professionalize the UN Secretariat.[36]

Fortunately, the establishment of the UN Peace-building Commission is now under way. However, the United States needs to strengthen its own efforts for coordinated, effective, and rapid deployment into postconflict settings based on the studied absorption of lessons from previous experiences. The best way to do so, I believe, would be by creating a cabinet-level Department of International Development and Reconstruction, building on the core of USAID and incorporating as well the State Department's Office of the Coordinator for Reconstruction and Stabilization. A specialized department would provide a permanent, institutionalized standing capacity to land on the ground quickly after conflict and (in concert with local actors and a wide range of other international donors) help the country reconstruct itself politically, economically, and socially. This requires specific training and skills and a substantial professional and reserve corps of civilian experts. These assets would not be well situated in the Departments of State or Defense, which have as their purposes, respectively, the conduct of diplomacy and the conduct of war—not the rebuilding of war-torn or collapsed states. A separate cabinet department would better enable the United States to build a coherent administrative and reconstruction capacity, much readier to deploy, with a mix of experiences and language capabilities and close working relations with other government departments and agencies.[37]

Conclusion

The remarkable growth of democracy in the last three decades—reaching nearly all major cultural zones and over a third of the world's poorest countries—suggests that every country can become a democracy eventually. No country is ruled out because of its history, culture, or social structure. Yet, not any country can become a democracy at any particular moment, and certainly not quickly. Failed states pose among the most difficult challenges for democratization. Sometimes democratization—assisted heavily from the outside—will be an indispensable means for the restoration of order, as in South Africa and Nicaragua. Sometimes, as in Cambodia, the international community will claim to be promoting democracy, when it does not have the stomach or resources for the fight. Even then, the international intervention may leave behind fragments of hope for political pluralism, and at least a less thoroughgoing authoritarianism than what otherwise might have emerged. Authoritarian states do not become democracies just because they hold elections in which opposition parties compete and win some seats. Still, in granting some space for opposition and dissent, they are often preferable to the harder authoritarian alternative, and leave open the possibility of eventual democratization.[38]

It would be better if, in countries such as Cambodia, the international community would summon the resources and the will to promote and insist upon true democracy. However, the hard truth is that we lack in the international community today the finances, the troops, the political will—and probably also the knowledge—to promote democracy successfully in the most forbidding cases. In all likelihood, Iraq will bear out this sad truth once again. In these circumstances, it is possible that we are better off having tried, even if half-heartedly, to build democracy, while winding up with a partially democratic system—a country at least struggling in the "gray zone"—than we would have been if we had just resigned ourselves to dictatorship from the start. Nevertheless, the people who suffer under new forms of oppression—however much they fall short of genocide, absolute dictatorship, or civil war—still wish for something better politically. At a minimum, we owe it to them to remain engaged, morally, rhetorically, diplomatically, and with concrete programs for democracy assistance, once the failed state has begun to take shape on less than democratic grounds.

It is not inevitable that we will fail to promote democracy, even in the hard cases. When we do, we should not regard that as the end of the story. If a new authoritarian state emerges, the struggle to promote democracy resumes, on more familiar if incremental terms. The tragedy, however, is that once a new authoritarian regime consolidates its grip, as Hun Sen and his Cambodian People's Party have done in Cambodia,[39] it may be very difficult to dislodge, particularly if it has authoritarian neighbors and defenders. For all their challenges and vulnerabilities, postconflict countries do provide an arena of considerable fluidity for building a more democratic state and society.

Notes

1 Originally published as "Promoting Democracy in Post-Conflict and Failed States," *Taiwan Journal of Democracy* 2 (December 2006): 93–116.
2 Samuel P. Huntington, *Political Order in Changing Societies* (New Haven, CT: Yale University Press, 1968), 1.
3 See, for example, Juan J. Linz and Alfred Stepan, *Problems of Democratic Transition and Consolidation* (Baltimore, MD: Johns Hopkins University Press, 1996), and Francis Fukuyama, *State Building: Governance and World Order in the 21st Century* (Ithaca, NY: Cornell University Press, 2004).
4 Perhaps the definitive work to date on this subject is Stephen John Stedman, Donald Rothchild and Elizabeth M. Cousens, eds, *Ending Civil Wars: The Implementation of Peace Agreements* (Boulder, CO: Lynne Rienner Publishers, 2002).
5 Larry Diamond, *Foreign Aid in the National Interest: Promoting Freedom, Security, and Opportunity* (Washington, DC: USAID, 2002): ch. 1, www.usaid.gov/fani; Diamond, "Promoting Real Reform in Africa," in *Democratic Reform in Africa: The Quality of Progress*, ed. E. Gyimah-Boadi (Boulder, CO: Lynne Rienner, 2004): 263–292; and Diamond, "Building a System of Comprehensive Accountability to Control Corruption," in Adigun Agbaje, Larry Diamond, and Ebere Onwudiwe, *Nigeria's Struggle for Democracy and Good Governance: A Festschrift for Oyeleye Oyediran* (Ibadan, Nigeria: University of Ibadan Press, 2004): 221–242. See also Diamond, "Democracy, Development and Good Governance: The Inseparable Links," First Annual Democracy and Governance Lecture, Center for Democratic Development, Accra, Ghana, March 1, 2005, https://web.stanford.edu/~ldiamond/papers/CDD_lecture_05.htm.
6 For more extensive discussion of the American occupation experience in Iraq and its legendary mistakes, see Larry Diamond, *Squandered Victory: The American Occupation and the Bungled Effort to Bring Democracy to Iraq* (New York: Times Books, 2005).
7 Donald Rothchild, "Settlement Terms and Postagreement Stability," in Stedman et al., *Ending Civil Wars*, 122.
8 Simon Chesterman, *You, the People: The United Nations, Transitional Administration, and State-Building* (Oxford: Oxford University Press, 2004), 72–73.
9 Ibid., 97.
10 Gerald Knaus and Marcus Cox, "Building Democracy after Conflict: The 'Helsinki Moment' in Southeastern Europe," *Journal of Democracy* 16 (January 2005): 49.

11 Stedman et al., *Ending Civil Wars*. See, in particular, Terrence Lyons, "The Role of Postsettlement Elections," 215–236.

12 Joanna Spear, "Disarmament and Demobilization," in Stedman et al., *Ending Civil Wars*, 141–182.

13 Adekeye Adebayo, "Liberia: A Warlord's Peace," in *Ending Civil Wars*, 599–630.

14 Chesterman, *You the People*, 63.

15 *A More Secure World: Our Shared Responsibility*, Report of the High-level Panel on Threats, Challenges, and Change (New York: United Nations, 2004), 69, par. 216.

16 Stephen John Stedman, "Introduction," in Stedman et al., *Ending Civil Wars*, 9, 11–14. Stedman reserves the term "spoiler" for leaders and factions who use violence to undermine a signed peace agreement, but I believe the term can usefully be applied as well to any postconflict situation where there is broad domestic participation in the effort to stabilize and rebuild the country but some armed groups use violence to undermine the process for strategic gain. In either case, a judgment must be made (following Stedman's model) as to whether the violent actor in question is a "total spoiler" who "sees power as indivisible" and seeks to conquer it all, or merely a tactical, "greedy" spoiler who utilizes violence to obtain more power and resources (ibid., 12–13). The effort to stabilize Iraq has been bloodily undermined by both total and tactical spoiler forces, and one of the great political failings of the United States has been its inability to separate the latter from the former and to draw them into the political process with a judicious mix of assurances and inducements.

17 Diamond, *Squandered Victory*, ch. 10.

18 James Dobbins et al., *America's Role in Nation-Building: From Germany to Iraq* (Santa Monica, CA: RAND, 2003), 198.

19 Ibid., 165–166.

20 Stedman, "Introduction," 3. See also George Downs and Stephen Stedman, "Evaluation Issues in Peace Implementation," in Stedman et al., *Ending Civil Wars*, 43–69. With regard to commodities, diamonds and timber are much more easily tradable than oil, but oil provides a huge incentive for a potential spoiler group to seek substantial or total control over the area producing it, especially if the oil lies in their traditional area of ethnic and political dominance. In general, the more rents that flow to the new state from tradable commodities or even huge foreign aid flows, the greater the stakes in controlling the state.

21 Downs and Stedman, "Evaluation Issues," 55–57.

22 Ibid.

23 Stedman, "Introduction," 3.

24 Chesterman, *You the People*, 257.

25 Ibid.

26 Stephen Krasner, "Building Democracy after Conflict: The Case for Shared Sovereignty," *Journal of Democracy* 16 (January 2005): 69–83.

27 Chesterman, *You the People*, 153.

28 Ibid.

29 Ibid., 243.

30 Dobbins et al., *America's Role in Nation-Building*, 154.

31 Susan Woodward, "Economic Priorities for Successful Peace Implementation," in Stedman et al., *Ending Civil Wars*, 201.

32 Anne Ellen Henderson, "The Coalition Provisional Authority's Experience with Economic Reconstruction in Iraq: Lessons Identified," United States Institute of Peace, Special Report No. 138, April 2005, 1.

33 Bertine Kamphuis, "Economic Policy for Building Peace," in *Post Conflict Development: Meeting New Challenges*, ed. Gerd Junne and Willemijn Verkoren (Boulder, CO: Lynne Rienner Publishers, 2005), 187–193.

34 Jamal Benomar, "Constitution-Making after Conflict: Lessons for Iraq," *Journal of Democracy* 15 (April 2004): 89. The study was a joint project of the United Nations Development Program and the United States Institute of Peace.

35 *A More Secure World*, 84, par. 164.

36 Ibid., 69, 91–92.

37 As I envision it, the Department would also incorporate traditional development assistance work now done by USAID and would give the U.S. the ability to engage and coordinate among other donors with the same cabinet-level representation that many other industrialized democracies have for their international cooperation and development work.

38 See the cluster of essays on the theme of "Elections without Democracy" in the *Journal of Democracy* 13 (April 2002): 21–80.

39 Duncan McCargo, "Cambodia: Getting Away with Authoritarianism," *Journal of Democracy* 16 (October 2005): 98–112.

23 Promoting democracy
Enduring tensions and new opportunities[1]

Since the founding of the American Republic, the U.S. has been torn between two quite different visions of how it should relate to other countries. One approach sees the world as it is—an intrinsically anarchic and amoral collection of states seeking to expand their power and influence in the world. In this unsentimental conception of a dangerous, conflict-ridden world—where (to paraphrase the nineteenth-century English statesman Lord Palmerston) "nations have no permanent friends or allies, only … permanent interests"—the guiding foreign policy priorities for the U.S. are the safety of its citizens, the security of its borders, the extension of its power, and the advancement of its economic interests in trade, investment, and natural resources. Not surprisingly, this approach to foreign policy has come broadly to be known as the "realist" school, though realism has contained within it sharply different tendencies, from isolationism to a strong propensity for interest-driven intervention. In the early decades of American independence, when the U.S. was still a relatively new and fragile nation, its basic tenet was caution about alliances and "foreign entanglements." Thus, in 1821, President John Quincy Adams proclaimed that America's principle "gift to mankind" was its repeated affirmation of democratic principles. The U.S., he said, had been wise to abstain from "interference in the concerns of others, even when conflict has been for principles to which she clings." He added, in terms that would have a deep impact on twentieth century advocates of realist restraint in global affairs, like Hans Morgenthau and George Kennan:

> Wherever the standard of freedom and Independence has been or shall be unfurled, there will [America's] heart, her benedictions and her prayers be. But she goes not abroad, in search of monsters to destroy. She is the well-wisher to the freedom and independence of all. She is the champion and vindicator only of her own.[2]

An alternative strain of thinking in American foreign policy has insisted that the ideals of the American Revolution and its founding Declaration must somehow shape and inform the way the U.S. relates to other countries in the world. Its first full expression came in the Presidency of Woodrow Wilson, who believed that it was America's moral obligation and vital interest to shape the rest of the world in the image of its own values of freedom and democracy—that (as the historian of American foreign policy, Walter Russell Mead, has characterized it), "the U.S. has the right and the duty to change the rest of the world's behavior."[3] Out of this Wilsonian conception sprang not only America's military engagement in World War I, and Wilson's pursuit of a League of Nations, but a recurrent American concern with the nature of government in other countries around the world that would find prominent expression in the presidencies of FDR, Truman, Kennedy, Carter, and Reagan. This approach became labeled the "idealist" school in American foreign policy, though idealism always coexisted with (and not infrequently was trumped by) frequent concessions to geostrategic realities.

If the early American realists were isolationists in their caution about foreign entanglements, their more modern-day successors understood that America's territorial expansion and economic rise inevitably gave it global interests that required robust alliances, partnerships of convenience, coercive actions, and even long-term military deployments around the world. This more muscular and ambitious worldview first emerged full-blown in the foreign policy of Theodore Roosevelt and then reached its apogee during the Cold War struggle to check Soviet expansionism and communist revolutions. Its most consummate practitioners were Henry Kissinger and Richard Nixon. Other American presidents during this era, including Dwight Eisenhower and Lyndon Johnson, also privileged the defense of American power over the advancement of American ideals, and were even willing to use American power to oust elected leaders or block popular aspirations when they seemed to conflict with American interests. After each of these periods of foreign policy realism, however, there came a correction. Kennedy's Alliance for Progress, and his rhetorical embrace of freedom and socioeconomic reform, renewed an emphasis on idealism after President Eisenhower and his Secretary of State, John Foster Dulles, had emphasized containing communism and advancing American economic interests. After the supremely "realist" years of the Nixon–Ford era, Jimmy Carter launched a new and lasting emphasis on human rights in American foreign policy. It succeeded in pressuring a number of Latin American dictatorships to return power to elected civilians, but critics charged that it also paved the way for anti-American revolutions in Iran and Nicaragua.

Ronald Reagan came into power criticizing Jimmy Carter's naivety in undermining American allies and interests, yet he wound up going much further, making the promotion of democracy an elevating purpose of American foreign policy. Reagan not only challenged communism as a system, but he ultimately pressed for democratic transitions among American allies—the Philippines, Korea, and Chile. Both Carter and Reagan permanently changed American foreign policy by establishing new and lasting institutions to press for democracy and human rights. Although he was considered a realist, George Herbert Walker Bush then further institutionalized democracy promotion by making it a major purpose in American foreign aid, and by crafting an ambitious strategy of diplomacy and aid to solidify the emerging democracies of Central and Eastern Europe. During the subsequent presidencies of Bill Clinton, George W. Bush, and Barack Obama, the weight given to democracy promotion in American foreign policy has shifted back and forth, in rhetoric and in practice. But these shifts have always occurred within the boundaries of broad agreement among foreign policy elites that the U.S. should spend at least some resources and diplomatic capital working to advance and defend democracy around the world. And strikingly, each of the last five American presidents, from Reagan to Obama, has over the course of his presidency given more emphasis to democracy promotion than he did in the early stages of his presidency.[4]

If public opinion polls are to be believed, the American people are much more skeptical about the value of promoting democracy abroad than are the country's elected leaders and foreign policy practitioners. Since 2001, Pew surveys have found democracy promotion finishing last in the public's list of priorities for American foreign policy, well behind such "realist" concerns as protecting American jobs, protecting the U.S. from terrorism, and reducing dependence on imported energy (though in reality, the first and last are much more the province of domestic than foreign policy). Between September 2001 and May 2011, the percentage of Americans listing democracy promotion as a foreign policy priority fell steadily from 29 to 13 percent, and the proportion listing promotion of human rights also slipped from 29 to 24 percent.[5]

Is democracy promotion in the American national interest?

Is it in the national interest of the U.S. to promote freedom and democracy in other countries? Any answer to this question must first raise several others: What do we mean by "promoting" democracy—what methods count, and are all methods equally acceptable? Should we distinguish among countries, or different types of countries? Is it possible that promoting democracy may be more in the American interest in some places—and at some times—than in others? And if it is *an* interest of the U.S. to promote democracy, does this mean it must be *the* central interest, trumping other items on the agenda or diffusely shaping every aspect of policy? Moreover, how does one factor in the temporal dimension to thinking about the national interest? If Americans have a long-term interest in fostering democracy, but doing so carries risks in the short run, which point on the time horizon should prevail? And how do all these considerations change in an era when the world—including the community of democracies—is becoming increasingly multipolar?

There are many reasons to think that the U.S. should "keep its nose out of other people's business," at least in terms of how states are governed internally. To begin with, a strict reading of the norms of sovereignty, as codified by the Peace of Westphalia in 1648, grants each state not only territorial integrity but also the exclusive right to determine its own policies and governmental structures within its territory. From this has come the principle of "nonintervention" in the internal affairs of other states, which was elevated to a nearly sacred status during the immediate post-World War II era of decolonization and has been written into the charter of the World Bank (the IBRD) and other international structures. When states invite international assistance for their efforts to administer free and fair elections, build independent judiciaries, and construct and deepen other structures of democracy, that is one thing. But when other democracies provide assistance to independent organizations, human right activists, critical media, and opposition movements that are trying to change a state's form of government from authoritarianism to democracy, this is a form of intervention, however peaceful the means and idealistic the motivation.

There are, of course, possible real costs to the U.S. of promoting democracy, including financial costs. But the entire budget for "core," nonsecurity U.S. international affairs—in essence, diplomacy and aid, outside of elevated contingency operations in places like Iraq and Afghanistan, as well as all U.S. support for international organizations like the UN—was only slightly over $50 billion in 2012.[6] That is just 1.7 percent of the entire federal budget (far exceeded by the $671 billion requested for the Pentagon in the 2012 fiscal year), and total funding for all democracy and governance assistance programs (not including economic assistance) probably does not exceed $2 billion—considerably less than a tenth of a percent of the overall budget.[7] In short, if a case is to be made for *not* promoting democracy, it is difficult to make it on fiscal grounds.

Neither is it convincing to argue any longer that democracy is mainly a "Western" concept, unsuitable for and largely unwanted by non-Western peoples and cultures. As we saw in Chapter 4, for some two decades now, the majority of the world's states have been democracies, and there is at least a critical mass of democracies in every region of the world except the Middle East—which has at least seen the emergence of the first genuine democracy in the Arab world (Tunisia). Some Muslim-majority states, such as Indonesia and Senegal, have made noteworthy progress in developing and institutionalizing democracy (and Turkey and Bangladesh seemed to be doing so until they slipped back more recently, as is noted in Chapter 4). Moreover, public opinion surveys show clear majorities of the public in each cultural zone preferring democracy as the best form of government. In short, democracy has become a universal value, with broad appeal in every region of the world and with no global rival as an ideal form of government.[8]

The more sophisticated objections come in two forms. One is that the world is still a dangerous and essentially anarchic place, where "real" security and economic interests must trump the moral concern to see the triumph of democracy and human rights. It would be nice if Saudi Arabia and China were democracies, but securing trade and financial relationships with these countries is more important. Similarly, the U.S. needs Russian cooperation on strategic arms reduction, and in containing nuclear arms proliferation, Islamic terrorism, and the spread of Iranian influence, more than it needs Russia to be a democracy. By the same token, moderate and friendly Arab autocracies, the argument goes, have kept at least a cold peace with Israel and a broader stability in the Middle East region, which accounts for nearly half of world oil reserves and supplies more than a third of the world's oil exports. Moreover, they have been reliable sources of cooperation in the war on terror, even if the U.S. has had to look the other way while they torture suspects handed over to them. Indeed, since September 11, 2001, there has been a tendency to work with any regime, no matter how repressive, so long as it presents itself as an ally in the battle against terrorism, just as the U.S. allied during the Cold War with any dictatorship that was willing to cooperate in the struggle to contain Soviet and communist expansion. Common to both approaches has been a simplistic, monolithic view of the threat and a failure to think clearly about the long-term costs of embracing illegitimate regimes.[9]

A second objection asserts a bias for modesty and restraint in the conduct of foreign affairs, doubting that the U.S. knows enough—about other countries or the underlying dynamics of development—to intervene intelligently and responsibly to advance democracy, and suggesting that such intervention often is clumsy, ill-considered, and resented for its pretentious and overbearing moralism. Too often, these realists insist, an initial intention to do political "good" in places like Vietnam and Iraq ends up in horrific miscalculation and costly and debilitating (if not downright immoral) entanglements. When arms are taken up in the cause of advancing freedom, the line between democracy promotion and imperialism can become blurry—or crossed. Thus, in making the case for "ethical realism," Anatol Lieven and John Hulsman lean heavily on the writings of Hans Morgenthau and George F. Kennan to urge a foreign policy based on prudence, caution, and humility—"including humility concerning our ability to understand the outside world, foresee the future, and plan accordingly."[10] By this realist reckoning, democracy is a difficult thing to achieve. Each country must find its own path and pace, and America should instead pursue more limited "ethical" goals of peace and development while also privileging its security and economic interests. Some realist critics often add that inordinate amounts of money and manpower get devoted to building democracy and peace in the world's hardest cases, like Afghanistan, Iraq, Haiti, and Somalia, which are likely to remain mired in conflict and autocracy no matter what the U.S. does.

The case for promoting democracy is in part moral—that democracies do a much better job of protecting human rights, and that peoples have a right to determine their own future democratically—but it proceeds as well on fiercely practical grounds. Democracies do not fight wars with one another; in fact, no two genuine, liberal democracies have ever done so, and all of America's enemies in war have been highly authoritarian regimes. Today, the principal threats to American security—whether from terrorism or from potential military adventurism or cyberwarfare—all come from the world's remaining authoritarian regimes, such as Iran, North Korea, Russia, and China, or from states like Somalia and Yemen that have collapsed or decayed because of authoritarian rule. Democracies make better trading partners because they are more likely to prosper and to play by fair rules, as they are more "likely to develop fair and effective legal systems."[11] This same regard for law makes democracies more likely to honor their international treaty obligations. And they make more reliable allies because their commitments are grounded in and ultimately sustained by public opinion; "democracies are like pyramids standing on their bases."[12] By contrast, the international posture of autocracies rests on the personal interests of the autocrat, and when he dies, changes course, or is overthrown, American interests can get burned.[13] Much of the Cold War history of America's engagement with the Third World is a story of heavy investments in authoritarian client regimes—in places like China, Vietnam, Iran, Nicaragua, Haiti, and Zaire—eventually going down the drain due to revolution or state collapse.[14] Moreover, once democracy takes root in a country, the U.S. is relieved from having to worry about responding to famine, genocide, and humanitarian emergency (though certainly not poverty). These are uniquely phenomena of authoritarian regimes, and state failure is also the product of authoritarian abuse. As the spread of democracy in Europe and Latin America has demonstrated over the last two decades, a zone of democracy is also a zone of peace and security.

Short-term vs. long-term interests

To argue that every country can and should immediately become a democracy flies in the face of history and evidence. Numerous transitions have floundered because of a rush to hold national elections too quickly. And in other instances, the sudden downfall of a tyrant can unleash civil war or a new form of tyranny if there is not time for an array of new political forces to organize, establish support bases, and generate a pluralistic and tolerant political landscape. Depending on the social order and recent historical circumstances, it can take time to build a viable democracy. But that time is probably measured in years, not decades. The opposite argument—that it took the U.S. 200 years to become a democracy and so Uganda or Azerbaijan needs the same amount of time—is equally silly, and a transparent excuse for indefinite, predatory autocracy. Even many poor countries with few of the presumed developmental requisites for democracy, such as a strong middle class and high levels of education and income, have managed to implement at least the rudiments of democracy rather quickly and sustainably.

Means and instruments of democracy promotion

Much of the debate about "democracy promotion" in American foreign policy involves those with opposing views making assumptions and talking past one another. When many Americans see the words "promoting democracy," they think: "imposing democracy." Yet the people and organizations that work to advance and strengthen democracy around the world think of "democracy promotion" mainly as "democracy assistance." Moreover, they understand that to be effective it must be done in partnership with local actors and in response to their stated needs. In truth, there is a very wide range of instruments available to the U.S. to extend democracy in the world and help it become more effective and viable. Whether one thinks "democracy promotion" is a worthwhile purpose for the foreign policy of the United States (or of other democracies) may depend not only on the priority one thinks it should be given in competition with other foreign policy goals but also on the means that are used.

Force

At the extreme end of the range of instruments for promoting democracy is imposing it by force. Particularly in the wake of the 2003 U.S. military invasion of Iraq, followed by a quasi-colonial, U.S.-led, foreign occupation of the country, many Americans imagine coercion and imposition when they think of democracy promotion. President George W. Bush made the decision to invade Iraq on the basis of national security concerns. However, in the run-up to the war, and even more so in its aftermath (when weapons of mass destruction were not found), many hawks inside and outside the Bush Administration also justified the intervention by insisting that it could enable Iraq to emerge as a free (and pro-American) democracy, and a source of democratic diffusion throughout the Arab world.

For more than a year, from May 2003 to June 2004 (the period of formal occupation under the Coalition Provisional Authority), the U.S. led a complex and extremely ambitious "nation building" effort that had as one of its principal aims developing the political institutions, civic structures, and values of democracy. Promoting a democratic transformation of Iraq was not only embraced as a means of legitimating the American occupation, but reflected deeply held convictions on the part of President Bush and many in his administration, as memorably expressed in Bush's second inaugural address:

America's vital interests and our deepest beliefs are now one ... So it is the policy of the U.S. to seek and support the growth of democratic movements and institutions in every nation and culture, with the ultimate goal of ending tyranny in our world.

To be sure, President Bush went on to add immediately:

This is not primarily the task of arms ... America will not impose our own style of government on the unwilling. Our goal instead is to help others find their own voice, attain their own freedom, and make their own way.

But the far-reaching mission that was the Coalition Provisional Authority in Iraq, and the enormous, high-profile investment of American lives, talent, and treasure, along with the rapid emergence of a virulent anti-American and antidemocratic insurgency, gave credence to the view that the American project of transforming Iraq into a democracy had a good bit of the character of imposition.[15]

In the wake of the Bush presidency, "democracy promotion" was a "policy badly damaged from its prior association with the war in Iraq and with forcible regime change more generally."[16] As a result, the new Obama Administration downplayed it as a goal or theme in its new foreign policy. President Obama failed to mention it during his first inaugural address, and Secretary of State Hillary Clinton also glaringly omitted "democracy" from the other "three Ds of U.S. international engagement—diplomacy, defense, and development."[17] Instead the Obama Administration focused on engagement, believing that it would be more effective than the "cold shoulder" of the past and make autocratic regimes more receptive to tough messages on democracy and human rights issues going forward.[18] This "step back" from the aggressiveness of the Bush Administration returned the U.S. to familiar footing, but it opened the Obama Administration to criticism that it had overcorrected for the mistakes of its predecessor. As time went on, Obama would become more outspoken in support of freedom and democracy, particularly after the eruption of the "Arab Spring."

In recent decades, no major current of American foreign policy thinking has advocated using force in order to promote democracy as the main or highest objective. From Iraq and Afghanistan in the last decade back to the most ambitious American ventures in democratic transformation—in Germany and Japan at the end of World War II—national security has always been the principal driver of American decisions to wage all-out war. To be sure, some other American (and international) military interventions—Somalia, Haiti, and Bosnia in the 1990s, and Libya in early 2011—were motivated by humanitarian imperatives (or the intersection of humanitarian and geopolitical concerns) rather than by "hard" security calculations of imminent danger or harm to the United States. But in virtually all of these interventions, the effort to stand up and strengthen democratic institutions became an important part of the postwar nation-building effort. Moreover, this has not just been an American impulse to make democracy the form of government left behind. Increasingly, democratization has been a major theme of United Nations' nation-building missions in war-torn countries like El Salvador, Mozambique, Sierra Leone, and East Timor. And despite the legendary tensions between the American administrator of the Coalition Provisional Authority in Iraq, Ambassador L. Paul Bremer III, and the UN mission there, the goal of reconstructing the Iraqi state on democratic foundations was one that the UN and the U.S. shared.[19] As is evident from the previous chapter, postconflict states present some of the most challenging circumstances for promoting democracy because they lack many of the conditions that make democracy sustainable. International democracy promotion in these circumstances is not bereft of at least partial success stories, including El Salvador, Mozambique, Liberia, Sierra Leone, and East Timor. But the more broken the state, the more "nation building" is an immensely challenging, expensive, and protracted exercise. Moreover, the evidence shows that regime transitions are much more likely to give birth to democracy, and democracy is much more likely to persist and gain in quality if the struggle for democracy occurs mainly through nonviolent means.[20] Thus, if the goal is success in promoting democracy, violence is the least promising tool for achieving it.

Diplomacy

American power and influence is in decline, but the U.S. is still by far the most powerful country in the world. Beyond its military, it has numerous other instruments—diplomacy, aid conditionality, and sanctions—to pressure states to democratize, to respect human rights, or to govern more democratically. These instruments are also available to other democracies, and some of them can be most effectively applied by regional or international democratic coalitions or international organizations.

Diplomacy is the most common and conventional means by which states try to influence other states. But even when a powerful state like the U.S. appeals privately to a foreign government or leader to enact democratic reforms, or issues a diplomatic démarche formally protesting the undemocratic actions or stances of the foreign government and requesting specific democratic reforms or guarantees, autocratic leaders do not yield simply because they are persuaded by the moral or practical logic. Rather, underlying the diplomatic message is at least the implication that relations with the U.S. could be damaged if the regime clings to its repressive ways. When threats of consequences become explicit, then the diplomatic effort to nudge a regime toward democratic reform has escalated from pure diplomacy to the use of aid conditionality and the possible implementation of sanctions.

Diplomatic pressure works to open up autocratic regimes or to edge them forward to democracy when the U.S. and other democracies have leverage over those regimes because of the density of economic, social, and cultural ties. Linkages that render authoritarian states vulnerable to external pressure include economic ties (trade, investment, and credit), security ties (treaties and guarantees), and social ties (tourism, immigration, overseas education, elite exchanges, international NGO and church networks, and Western media penetration). Strong linkages forge cultural bonds that help rally democratic societies and parliaments to lobby for the defense of human rights and democracy, as seen with pressure on the Clinton Administration to move against the Haitian military dictatorship in 1994 and the "extensive Hungarian lobbying" of the European Union to press Romania and Slovakia to improve the treatment of their Hungarian minorities.[21]

At the same time, international linkages can make critical social and political constituencies within authoritarian countries either more committed to democracy or more sensitive to Western pressures, generating a more subtle form of democracy promotion. Ties to the West induced elites both "to reform authoritarian parties from within (as in Croatia, Mexico, and Taiwan)" and "to defect to the opposition (as in Slovakia and, to a lesser extent, in Romania during the mid-1990s)."[22] After Western countries "forced severance of [Taiwan's] formal ties" and revoked Taiwan's UN membership in order to warm relations with mainland China, Taiwan's elites saw that democratic reform might provide a means to renew the sympathy and support of the American public and other Western democracies.[23] The desire to be accepted as a partner among industrial nations also contributed to the democratic transitions in South Korea as it prepared to host and risked losing the 1988 Olympics, and in Chile as it prepared for the 1988 plebiscite on whether to extend Pinochet's dictatorship. In these contexts, U.S. and international criticism of authoritarian rule bred a sense of isolation and a desire to be regarded with respect by the industrialized democracies.[24] But where ties are less intimate, for example in the former Soviet Union and much of Africa, Western pressure to democratize has been less consequential.

Leverage, too, depends on the power of the authoritarian state, and thus, mighty states like China and the Soviet Union (and subsequently, Russia) have found it easy to slough off American criticisms of their repressive practices. Moreover, successive U.S. administrations have backed away from an initial impulse to confront China on its human rights record, realizing how little leverage the U.S. has and worrying about the consequences for American efforts to obtain China's cooperation on other foreign policy goals. Many authoritarian regimes in the world—Saudi Arabia, Iran, Azerbaijan, Kazakhstan, Venezuela, Angola, and Nigeria under military rule—have been relatively immune from international democratic pressure because oil gives them an independent source of steady, or even staggering, revenue. And geopolitics may also powerfully affect foreign policy calculations. The U.S. has historically been nearly silent about the highly undemocratic nature of Saudi Arabia because of the latter's pivotal importance as a counter to Iran in the Gulf region and as the largest reserve supplier of oil in world markets. Thus, when Saudi Arabia made it clear in 2011 that the preservation of Bahrain's embattled al-Khalifa monarchy was one of its vital interests, and then deployed its own troops to help crush pro-democracy demonstrators in that small neighboring island state, the Obama Administration meekly muted its criticisms and focused its energies on supporting democratic change elsewhere in the region. Similarly, Kazakhstan's oil and gas wealth, its long border with Russia, and its value as part of the Northern Distribution Network in providing an alternate route of supply for American military forces in Afghanistan have all given that former Soviet Republic significant leverage with the U.S., again leading to a muting of American criticisms of political repression.

As noted earlier, strategic interests often led the U.S. to compromise its democratic principles in order to forge mutually supportive relations with dictatorships during the Cold War. This realist practice subsided after the fall of the Soviet Union but resumed after the September 11 terrorist attacks, when a new group of authoritarian "frontline" states in the war on terror—Pakistan, Egypt, Saudi Arabia, Kazakhstan, Kyrgyzstan, and Uzbekistan—became more critical to U.S. strategic interests. Even before September 11, "Pakistan's status as a nuclear power hostile to India, with ties to the Taliban regime in Afghanistan and fundamentalist factions gaining ground at home," led the Clinton Administration to temper its response to the October 1999 military coup.[25] In recognition of Peruvian president Alberto Fujimori's support for the war on drugs, the Clinton Administration maintained military cooperation and attended his third-term inauguration despite describing Fujimori's fraud-ridden 2000 election as "invalid." In the fall of 2005, the U.S. backed away from its appeals for free and fair parliamentary elections in Azerbaijan and accepted a blatantly fraudulent outcome.[26] In April 2010, President George W. Bush granted President Ilham Aliyev an official White House visit. So much for the promise in his second Inaugural Address "to all who live in tyranny" that "when you stand up for your liberty, we will stand with you."

Yet when the U.S. is motivated to exert diplomatic pressure on authoritarian allies, it can make a difference, either in helping to generate space for political opposition and dissent, or in tipping the balance at a critical transitional moment. By publicly documenting and denouncing human rights abuses in Latin America, and then coupling these denunciations with reductions in military and economic aid, the Carter Administration contained repression, narrowed the options for military autocrats, and accelerated momentum for democratic change in the region. When the Dominican military stopped the presidential election vote count in 1978 in the face of an apparent opposition victory, swift and vigorous warnings from President Carter, Secretary of State Cyrus Vance, American embassy officials, and the commander in chief of the U.S. Southern Command succeeded in pressuring the Dominican military to allow the opposition candidate to take office, thus effecting a transition to democracy. Vigorous, explicit diplomatic messages from the Reagan Administration, which artfully coordinated public actions and private appeals, dissuaded Ferdinand Marcos in the Philippines in 1986 and Chun Doo Hwan in South Korea in 1987 from forcibly suppressing pro-democracy protests and helped induce them to allow a democratic transition to unfold. And a more extended strategy succeeded in encouraging a process of democratic change in Chile and discouraging military dictator August Pinochet from thwarting the electoral process. Although President George W. Bush in his final two years backed away from pressuring Arab authoritarian regimes after Islamist parties and movements made alarming gains in Egypt, Lebanon, and Palestine, his public appeals for democracy in the Middle East encouraged opposition movements and helped persuade President Mubarak to open up political space and allow a contested presidential election in 2005. The resulting political liberalization was partial and short-lived, but it stimulated political aspirations and the growth of opposition networks and skills in ways that would ultimately contribute to the downfall of Mubarak in the February 2011 revolution.

Diplomats on the ground, from the U.S. (and other democracies), also have many tools at their disposal to support and advance struggles for democracy.[27] Their reporting back to Washington and other capitals may help to catalyze the use of stronger tools to pressure for democracy. Embassy officials representing democracies may extend their cloak of diplomatic immunity to prevent punitive state violence against dissidents by merely showing up at the scene of protests, demonstrations, and imminent arrests. Or they may give hope, inspiration, and legitimacy to democratic opposition forces by publicly meeting with them and hearing their concerns, monitoring their trials and imprisonments, observing elections, speaking out for democratic principles, and visiting communities victimized by state violence (as U.S. Ambassador Robert Ford did in Syria until he had to be evacuated in early 2012). They may save dissidents from arrest by granting them asylum. The expanding practice of public diplomacy represents American society to the host society through a variety of public appeals, exchanges, and programs that project democratic models, values, and experiences and give ideas and moral support to democratic forces. And increasingly, diplomats from democracies may help to provide or facilitate more concrete forms of democracy assistance and technical advice.

Sanctions and aid conditionality

When efforts at moral or rational persuasion fail, democracies can increase the pressure by manipulating harder interests. This involves threatening or actually moving to impose costs on a country—and/or its key ruling elites—for violations of international norms of democracy and human rights. The range of tools here includes economic sanctions—reduction or suspension of aid and trade ties; diplomatic sanctions, such as the downgrading of diplomatic, cultural, and symbolic ties; military sanctions, such as the suspension of military aid, cooperation, and weapons sales, pursuit of a wider ban on arms sales to the country, and cutoffs of access to military-related technology; and aid conditionality. Whereas sanctions are punitive—imposing penalties for bad conduct—aid conditionality offers positive inducements of new flows of economic assistance if a country meets objective standards of democracy and good governance.

The academic literature is generally skeptical on the efficacy of international sanctions as a tool for inducing changes in the behavior of states. Sanctions only work when they can generate significant and sustained pain among powerful constituencies in the target country. The realization that trade sanctions just were not going to move a country as big and powerful as China to liberalize politically persuaded the Clinton Administration to lift its conditioning of "Most Favored Nation" trading status on human rights in 1994. Typically, sanctioned and isolated states find ways to adapt by developing home-grown alternatives to products they can no longer buy, by simply passing off the costs of sanctions on to their long-suffering populations while blaming the international community for national hardships, and by cultivating or deepening alternative ties and suppliers of resources, technology, and geopolitical support. This explains why pariah regimes like North Korea, Burma, Zimbabwe, and Iran have been able to survive tough international sanctions imposed by the U.S. and other democracies. In these cases, the relative dearth of linkages to the U.S. has greatly limited American leverage in inflicting pain on the regimes and reshaping behavior. And the regimes have been sustained by the tolerance or support of friendly neighbors, like China and Russia, and in some cases by their own sources of mineral wealth. Yet, historical experience shows the corrosive impact of poor economic performance on authoritarian regimes may be cumulative, generating a growing vulnerability that may not be visibly apparent. This may help to explain why the Burmese military finally opted to allow a significant political opening of the country in 2011.

On the other hand, where ties to the U.S. have been strong, sanctions have had an effect in moving regimes toward democratic concessions. Carter's human rights policy toward Latin America had an effect precisely because it coupled moral denunciations with reductions in economic and military aid. Years of stiffening economic sanctions from the U.S. and Europe, as well as disinvestment by private corporations and institutions, gradually ratcheted up the pressure on the apartheid regime and the white population in South Africa during the 1980s. For some time, South Africa adapted by becoming more self-sufficient, but when gold prices declined and domestic debt and inflation escalated, the result was a "protracted recession, capital flight, and a profound sense of isolation ... Whites began to realize that unless they came to terms with the political demands of the black population, the economic noose would not loosen."[28] In the early 1990s, the freezing or suspension of Western aid forced countries like Benin, Kenya, and Malawi to open up and hold competitive, multiparty elections. In short, country-specific sanctions can work when major powers cooperate, when there is extensive linkage, and when domestic pressures converge.

Increasingly, as the sanctions weapon gets refined from a blunt instrument to a range of more targeted and precise tools of punishment, stigmatization, and deterrence, sanctions are becoming more credible and effective in shaping the behavior of authoritarian elites. Targeted sanctions on regime elites, including travel bans and asset freezes, can get the attention of venal rulers who may be more prepared to see their countries suffer than themselves. "The warning by senior U.S. diplomats that the U.S. Government would freeze personal off-shore assets of Ukrainian officials in the event of government repression had considerable restraining impact on potentially violent behavior."[29]

The logic of conditioning economic assistance on democracy (or progress toward it) is relatively recent. While there had been individual country episodes of conditionality prior to 2000, these generally were much more often linked (by World Bank and IMF negotiating teams) to a country's economic reform policies, and typically were linked to promises of future reforms rather than offered as rewards for prior behavior. With the initiation in 2002 of a new development assistance vehicle, the Millennium Challenge Account (MCA), the Bush Administration brought the principle of conditionality to a new level. The semiautonomous implementing agency, the Millennium Challenge Corporation (the MCC), rewards developing countries for demonstrated performance in democracy, just governance, and economic freedom and entrepreneurship, ranking countries on a set of 22 indicators. Countries that rank highly qualify for substantial new grants of aid, which must be negotiated with the MCC in contracts for specific developmental programs. While the MCA has only been funded at a fraction of its promise (falling well short of the anticipated goal of $5 billion annually), it has negotiated quite significant compacts for developmental assistance with a number of developing democracies, such as El Salvador, Mongolia, the Philippines, Ghana, and Malawi. The amounts of the compacts typically run into the hundreds of millions of dollars, providing a tangible incentive to achieve and maintain standards of democracy and good governance. And the willingness to suspend countries, such as Nicaragua, when they veer away from democracy also reinforces the conditionality mechanism. Unfortunately, some of the recipients, like Armenia and Jordan, are clearly not democracies, while others, like Tanzania, are at best ambiguous in their adherence to democratic norms.[30] However, in 2011, the MCC, which administers the grants and judges eligibility, modified the requirements to require that eligible countries score above an absolute threshold on either political rights or civil liberties (as measured annually by Freedom House).[31] Whether this most ambitious experiment to date in aid conditionality succeeds over time in promoting democracy will depend first on whether democracies like Ghana achieve more vigorous economic development with this and other aid flows; second, to what extent the political conditions are sufficiently well-monitored and enforced so that elected leaders perceive real costs in trying to diminish or undermine democracy; and third, whether the selection criteria are in fact tightened so that obviously authoritarian regimes do not continue to be selected. One encouraging trend is that several of the countries that have recently been granted more limited aid under the "threshold program" to try to raise them up to qualifying standards are emerging democracies, like Liberia and East Timor, where a sizable flow of politically conditional aid might help to lock in democratic commitments while advancing the economic conditions for sustainable democracy.

Democracy assistance

In most countries where democracy is absent or insecure, U.S. and other international efforts to encourage it proceed quietly and incrementally, far out of the glare of major media, through quotidian efforts of assistance to strengthen democratic institutions, reform governance, develop independent organizations and media, build democratic culture, monitor democratic elections, and train and support democratic forces in civil society.

Since 1983, the lead American organization for providing this assistance has been the National Endowment for Democracy (NED) and its four core grantees: the international institutes of the two U.S. political parties (the National Democratic Institute, NDI, and the International Republic Institute, IRI), the Center for International Private Enterprise (CIPE), and the Free Trade Union Institute (FTUI, now the Solidarity Center). These five organizations are publicly funded in their grants and programs by annual Congressional appropriations, supplemented in the latter four cases with significant grants and contracts from the U.S. Agency for International Development (USAID). Although it began with very small annual budgets (under $20 million), NED gave critical aid to democratic movements in Poland, Nicaragua, and Chile. Probably its greatest success story was in Poland, where FTUI transferred substantial assistance to the Solidarity trade union to support its education, publishing, and human rights projects. NED and its affiliates also contributed to peaceful democracy transitions in the Philippines, Namibia, Haiti, Zambia, and South Africa, in part by funding election monitoring efforts and helping to organize international election observing teams. In retrospect, each of these efforts has an air of inevitability to it, but at the time, the odds against successful transitions were long, and the combined assistance efforts of NED, other American donors, and

NGOs and aid organizations of other democracies crucially helped to make political breakthroughs possible.

Repeatedly over the last two decades, U.S. and international assistance for independent media, free elections, and civic organizations have made significant, if not always immediate, contributions to democratic change. For example:

- Funding, training, and technical assistance have helped deploy tens of thousands of domestic vote monitors in dozens of transitional countries. Aid enabled many of these groups to organize parallel vote tabulations—independent "quick counts" of the vote—to deter vote fraud in countless instances and to expose it and reverse it in such famous cases as the Philippines in 1986 and then Serbia, Georgia, and Ukraine in the color revolutions of the early 2000s.

- International election observer missions—with American NGOs like NDI, IRI, and the Carter Center playing leading roles—have helped to enhance the credibility and legitimacy of elections in many new and tense circumstances, such as South Korea in 1987, Bulgaria in 1990, and Ghana and the Dominican Republic in 1996; and to mediate bitter disputes over the electoral process in countries like Nicaragua, El Salvador, Albania, and Cambodia.

- Political parties reflecting diverse societal interests have received training and advice on how to develop membership bases, volunteer networks, campaign organizations, local branches, fundraising, public opinion polling, issue research, policy platforms, media messages, constituency relations, and democratic methods of choosing their leaders and candidates and involving members. Some of this has come during election campaigns, but much of it is ongoing organization building, helping parties to govern and legislate, to recruit and campaign, and to involve women and youth.[32]

- Grants from NED, USAID, local American embassies, other American NGOs like the Soros Foundation, the Asia Foundation, and Freedom House, as well as private foundations and other international donors have facilitated the growth and greater impact of civil societies pressing for democracy and accountability. This has included not only independent media and think tanks but groups devoted to human rights, anticorruption, political reform, voter education, election monitoring, environmental defense, community development, consumer protection, and the rights of women, youth, minorities, and the disabled. Aid has also gone to more traditional interest groups—such as trade unions and business chambers—to help them represent their interests and democratically pursue economic and social reforms.

- Grants and programs funded by USAID have also helped to build the governmental institutions of democracy by strengthening the autonomy, capacity, professionalism, and resources of the parliament and its committee structure, the judicial system, local government, and independent bodies that administer elections, monitor corruption, and regulate the economy.

Since the 1990s, the scope of political assistance has widened with the inclusion of parallel or integrated efforts to improve the quality of governance, particularly in terms of state efficiency, transparency, and accountability. Funding to improve governance became so prevalent that "almost all major donors added governance programs to their portfolios in the second half of the 1990s."[33] Governance is not the same thing as democracy; it can be improved even in the absence of competitive, free and fair elections. But aid agencies are increasingly realizing that improving governance not only invigorates development but also is vital to sustaining and deepening democracy. The central insight, as noted repeatedly in this book, is that democracy requires not just a limited state but also a state with the capacity and integrity to deliver the essential things people everywhere expect of government: order, justice, public health and education, social protection, physical infrastructure, and an enabling environment for economic growth. Enhancing governance—and in particular, combating the entrenched dynamics of corruption and clientelism that gut the quality of governance—is notoriously difficult, because it runs up against deep structures of power and privilege that have developed over decades, if not centuries, and that represent the real underlying logic of how a society works. Thus, governance—or better, "democracy and governance" (DG)—programs have learned that progress requires a highly contextualized analysis of these deep power relations and the economic interests underlying them. Then, Carothers and de Gramont argue, reform requires not the rigid application of some idealized "best practice" but rather a "best fit" approach that takes into consideration local factors and cultural mores and accepts that progress will be eclectic and incremental.[34] Donors, they find, are also learning other important insights: that helping to generate informed citizen demand for better governance is as important as working on the "supply" side; that working at the local level and with informal institutions is crucial; and that "aiding governance effectively requires development agencies to rethink their own internal governance."[35]

Of course, not all democracy and governance aid is effective. Reforming state institutions is notoriously difficult. Inappropriate institutional models may be too ambitious or expensive to function in poor countries. Large amounts of aid to modernize parliaments, courts, and other government agencies may amount to little if political leaders lack the will to allow these institutions to function democratically and check the abuse of power. Some civil society recipients are only superficially committed to democratic goals, or they are openly corrupt opportunists who set up BRINGOS ("briefcase NGOs") and GONGOs ("government-organized NGOs," that is, fronts and apologists for authoritarian regimes). Others are simply wasteful or ineffectual. Critics of this aid worry that civil society becomes too dependent on foreign donors—without explaining how independent pro-democracy groups and media could raise the funds to function viably in relatively poor countries, or those where an autocratic state dominates and co-opts the private business sector. Election observation has a checkered record. Strategic calculations may lead international election observers to pull their punches before declaring that a fraudulent election has been stolen and illegitimate. They may also soften the U.S. government's resolve to support democratic opposition forces challenging pro-American autocrats, although NED makes its grants entirely independent of the State Department or White House.

Even where these forms of political assistance crucially contribute to democratic breakthroughs or tangibly help fledgling democratic institutions to gain strength and credibility, they always do so in a supporting role. There is general consensus among scholars and practitioners that democracy assistance cannot substitute for the "courage, energy, skills, and legitimacy" of a country's own pro-democracy groups and leaders.[36] The most careful and dispassionate scholar of U.S. democracy assistance efforts, Thomas Carothers, concludes (not surprisingly) that these forms of aid have the most visibly positive effects where there are already present at least moderately favorable conditions for democratic change, such as sincere and effective democrats, divided autocrats, and higher levels of economic and educational development. Nevertheless, where democracy assistance is "properly designed and implemented," by proceeding from sensitive knowledge of the local political terrain and then endeavoring to monitor grants carefully over time, it can "help broaden and deepen democratic reforms" in new democracies and sustain civic awareness, democratic hope, and independent information and organization in authoritarian regimes.[37]

Thus, if democracy assistance does not in and of itself work miracles, it does occasionally help miraculous democratic breakthroughs to occur, and over time it helps to build the civic and political foundations of enduringly free societies. Given the relatively modest total amounts the U.S. government spends on these forms of assistance annually, this is no small achievement. In fact, when these political aid flows were assessed (for the years 1990–2003) by an independent team of social scientists, they found the effects were clearly and consistently positive, but only modest because individual country levels of assistance were modest (about two to four million dollars on average). Larger levels of democracy assistance appear to yield larger impacts; each additional million dollars of democracy assistance increases the "normal" rate of expected improvement in democracy scores by 50 percent.[38] The findings—unprecedented for their empirical depth and statistical precision and sophistication—justify the authors' conclusions that overall levels of democracy assistance should be increased, and that democracy assistance should be sustained in countries even after they have reached what has heretofore been considered a "satisfactory" stage of democratic development.

The "graduation" myth

One of the biggest mistakes the global democracy promotion community has made over the last 30 years is to cross too many countries off the list of democracy assistance recipients too quickly. Once the transition is completed and a new democracy lifts off in a middle-income country, the development community has too often assumed that it can take care of itself. Or we believe that 10 or 20 years of democratic assistance and engagement should be enough. In short, the democracy promotion community assumes that countries should "graduate" into peaceful independence after an unspecified amount of time and aid.

The foundations of a secure liberal democracy—a strong and capable state; a genuine rule of law, buttressed by a neutral and capable judiciary; effective institutions of horizontal accountability; competent and honest local administration; a pluralistic and resourceful civil society; a culture of tolerance, vigilance, and civic responsibility—do not get constructed overnight. Many of them emerge gradually with economic development. In more mature economies, they can develop more quickly. But even many of the countries listed by the World Bank as "upper middle income" remain well within the danger zone of democratic decay—as were Russia and Venezuela a decade and a half ago. The list of upper middle income countries includes Argentina, which is going through a profound economic and political crisis; Turkey, where the AKP has become a hegemonic party, the press functions in a state of fear, and the opposition parties are in disarray; Romania, an EU country where endemic corruption continues to undermine the health of democracy and governance; South Africa, where a corrupt leadership exhibits visibly declining commitment to the rule of law and liberal values; Thailand, which is now in the grip of a nasty military dictatorship that is not at the moment behaving as if it is transitional; Libya, which had a revolutionary uprising against Qaddafi, and then a state collapse; and Tunisia, which could become the one success story of the Arab Spring, but still faces serious political, economic, and security challenges.

A long-term strategic approach to promoting democracy would make the following resolution: Once a country (and especially a middle-income country) achieves or renews democracy, the democracy promotion community is going to do everything possible to help consolidate and lock it into place for the long run. For instance, we cannot turn our backs on new, fragile transitional governments when they appeal for security assistance, as we did with Libya after the fall of Qaddafi. We should be approaching the new democratically elected Tunisian government to ask it what it needs. What can we do to help revive the economy and rejuvenate flows of tourism and investment in Tunisia? Beyond our existing programs of party training, election observation, and other assistance, what can we do to support new civil society monitoring and training initiatives, to strengthen independent journalism and policy think tanks, to advance democratic civic education in the schools and the media, to support women's groups, student groups, human rights groups, and many other initiatives to build a culture and civic infrastructure to sustain democracy?

The counterarguments to this approach are myriad. There is only so much money. How are we going to help people who have nothing—no financial resources, no protection for their human rights, and little or no democracy—if we dilute the available democracy assistance resources by devoting some of them to countries that are, comparatively, much better off.

First, we must not view the pool of democracy promotion resources as fixed. It may be that total resources for international engagement or international development are fixed. But we need to rethink where the greatest leverage to advance and secure transformative development will lie. We need to set the clear goal of achieving and locking in development success stories. And that requires good governance, and ultimately democratic governance.

Second, we need to take a fresh look at the allocation of democracy and governance assistance resources across our different country programs, instruments and organizations. Are some more cost-effective than others? What are the most effective instruments for developing state institutions, or by contrast civil society organizations? Do we have sufficient instruments to assist the birth of new independent media, which can often involve large start-up costs? What is the proper role of for-profit implementing partners? Why can't we transfer resources from wasteful, pointless, and even counterproductive democracy and governance programs—like the ones Melinda Haring has identified in Azerbaijan[39]—to more promising countries and sectors.

Third, the issue is not just the countries we work in, but the constraints and mentalities we bring. We should always monitor and evaluate flows of assistance. But where democratic civil society organizations have accumulated a long track record of effective monitoring, civic education, issue analysis, policy reform and civic advocacy, they should become candidates to receive new forms and levels of funding that are not tied to endless cycles of project grants. Rather, they should become candidates for block grants to cover their core operations and work to fight corruption and defend and improve democracy. Too many civil society organizations spend inordinate amounts of time constantly writing grant proposals for specific projects even when their work, their judgment, and their capacity to deliver are well known.

In sum, democracy is not an endpoint. It is a process, one that ebbs and flows, and one that must be nurtured and consolidated beyond its initial onset. Only by resisting fatuous assumptions of "graduation" can we help to give new democracies the resilience to withstand pressures for rollback and decay.

Promoting democracy more effectively

A compelling case can be made that a more democratic world is not just an intrinsically better and more humane world, but also a safer, less stressful, and more predictable and secure world for the U.S and other democracies. But even if that is so, how does one get from here to there? The U.S. might well be more secure if democracy really took hold in Egypt and Pakistan, but what about the risks and costs along the way? How much short-term stability is the U.S. willing to sacrifice for long-term gain, and how grave are the transitional risks—not just of a hostile government coming to power, but of political order imploding altogether? And even if these risks are tolerable in many places, what about others—like Saudi Arabia—where the stakes are enormous and so are the dangers of a rapid rush to popular sovereignty? Then there are the questions of means. If America has the interest, does it have the capacity and means? Or should it draw the line at certain types of means?

Promoting democracy can never be the sole purpose of American foreign policy, and at times it will clearly recede as the U.S. pursues urgent and seemingly competing national security concerns. But too often the U.S. has traded short-term gains in stability or economic advantage at the price of long-term costs to its national interest. When autocrats like the Shah of Iran, Somoza in Nicaragua, Duvalier in Haiti, Mobutu in Zaire, and Siad Barre in Somalia fell from power, they left chaos or anti-American revolutions in their wake. Pressing for open, accountable, responsive, and legitimate government—in other words, democracy—is in the American national interest, even if the means, volume, and pace must vary across countries and over time.

One of the attractions of democracy assistance is that it offers some scope for the U.S. to square the difficult circle and have its relations with autocracies proceed on dual tracks when necessary. On one track (the most visible), formal diplomatic ties and aid flows—at the extreme, the two billion dollars a year (more recently down to about $1.7 billion) that went to the authoritarian regime of Egyptian President Hosni Mubarak—can sustain cooperative relations with autocrats the U.S. may not like but judges it needs strategically. On the other track, democracy assistance can provide hope, training, and resources to pro-democracy forces in civil society and the political opposition, while American diplomats can monitor and protest the worst abuses and reaffirm American values. The problem with this approach, however, is that when the U.S. perceives a strategic need to embrace a dictator, it gives the latter leverage. And since autocrats under challenge are locked in an existential struggle for survival—where failure could mean not simply retreat into a plush retirement, but sudden death, humiliating exile, or imprisonment and prosecution for past crimes—they will fight furiously to remain in power.

Historically, the U.S. has retreated too quickly from this authoritarian counterpressure, underestimating its own leverage and overestimating the leverage and options of autocratic actors like Mubarak or the Pakistani military. Getting the balance right is a delicate and high-stakes challenge, in which American foreign policymakers must wrestle not only with the conflict between ideals and interests, but with a conflict between competing interests and rival scenarios of disaster for the American interest. Moreover, one of the things that recipients of democracy assistance most often and loudly complain about is precisely the lack of coordination and consistency between the civic aid they receive from the U.S.—which they appreciate and even depend upon—and the "high politics" of diplomacy and government-to-government aid, which too often rewards and reinforces the very authoritarian regime they are trying to displace.

A few years ago, the World Movement for Democracy—a global network of democratic civil society activists, thinkers, practitioners, and assistance organizations—conducted an online survey of nearly 1,500 leaders of organizations that received democracy assistance between 2008 and 2010.[40] This was supplemented by qualitative case studies of democracy assistance, including field interviews with numerous recipients (totaling another 600-plus confidential interviews across 19 countries).[41] The key results of these two pathbreaking studies convey a revealing picture of global democracy assistance and some clear directions for improvement:

1 International democracy assistance (primarily the bilateral forms of aid from the U.S. and European countries) has not done too badly in the view of democracy recipients, but it can do better and needs to do better in the face of the new challenges and difficulties being imposed by authoritarian regimes, and it must meet the greater demand for accountability and results from taxpayers in the donor countries.

2 Accountability must work both ways. Democracy aid donors are used to requiring their recipients to report and be accountable on a regular basis for the funds they receive. But the donors must themselves be accountable internally and to their domestic and international constituencies.

3 The U.S., the EU, and the big individual European states need to achieve greater integration and consistency between their democracy assistance efforts and their practice of diplomacy and geopolitics (including through governmental aid flows and military and intelligence alliances). There will inevitably be tensions, but the different actors and instruments of American foreign policy must become better aligned—and directed by the President—to resist authoritarian regressions and press for sustained democratic reform, at least at some pace. For many civil society activists struggling at great personal risk for democracy, international pressure on their authoritarian governments to abandon or liberalize laws that restrict their freedom to organize—or even criminalize their receipt of foreign assistance—and to allow greater freedom of expression is more important than the flow of funding.

4 Civil society recipients must confront the contradictions in their own complaints: on the one hand, they want the donors to achieve more accountability and transparency in aid flows, and to terminate support for corrupt, co-opted, or ineffectual organizations. But on the other hand, they want less rigid and burdensome reporting requirements for themselves. Here, new innovations in Internet and mobile phone technology (such as the new web-based platform, Envaya[42]) may enable civil society recipients, particularly those with weak technical and administrative capacity, to report to donors more regularly on their work and expenditures without unduly straining their time and organizational resources.

5 Civil society actors passionately want and deserve more freedom to use democracy assistance funds for projects and goals they identify, rather than in response to priorities and models imposed from the outside. While NED in particular tries to be responsive to locally determined needs, big bureaucratic foreign aid agencies like USAID tend to operate by establishing goals for democracy and governance and then seeking proposals to fund them.[43]

6 Civil society actors nearly universally complain that too much foreign assistance is channeled through American (and other Western) NGOs and providers, causing a lot of leakage and inefficiency in the use of funds. This has been a particular challenge for USAID as it has suffered radical reductions in its career staffing over the last few decades, pushing it to a heavy dependence on contractors (many of them for-profit corporations) to implement its programs through "indefinite quantity contracts."

7 Donors need to be prepared to sustain long-term commitments to civil society actors who have proven over time, and continue to demonstrate, effectiveness in advancing democratic goals. In particular, proven organizations need long-term commitments of core funding to enable them to become institutionalized. While it makes sense to try to generate incentives for local revenue generation, in reality there are few opportunities for NGOs in developing countries—even those in many middle-income countries—to raise funds domestically without compromising their political autonomy and democracy-building focus and resolve. While the appeal of recipients for greater consistency and constancy in funding and priorities may appear self-serving, it also calls attention to the need for sustained partnerships with effective pro-democracy actors (particularly independent organizations, think tanks, and media).

8 In a few countries, the important and worthy principle of transparency in democracy assistance clashes with the need of indigenous groups for discretion and protection in the face of escalating regime assaults on civil society. A growing challenge has been the passage of various repressive laws that ban the receipt of external financial assistance by civil society organizations. Donor agencies need to find creative ways to

protect embattled civil society groups, and democratic donor governments need to press back diplomatically against authoritarian regimes when they use the laws, the police, and the tax authorities to oppress independent organizations working peacefully and honestly for democratic change.

9 Democracy donors, including diplomatic and aid agency staff, need to get out of the capitals more to listen to a wider range of views, and to empower a broader range of civil society actors, including smaller and more informal organizations and networks that represent indigenous and other underserved communities.

10 Donors—especially bilateral aid agencies—need to be willing to take more risks to support challenging groups in civil society rather than caving in to pressure from the host state. In general, friendly authoritarian states should not be granted a veto over which groups in civil society the U.S. assists in an effort to advance democracy and good governance. Where U.S. strategic relations with authoritarian states make it unrealistic, or authoritarian practices make it impossible, for USAID or the U.S. embassy to support pro-democracy groups, funding for that purpose should be transferred to NED or other nongovernmental channels.

11 Civil society recipients need to improve their own internal governance structures to become more transparent and democratic, and donors need to monitor these practices. Some NGOs that receive international support to promote democracy and good governance reforms suffer themselves from a lack of internal democracy and accountability, and are dominated by one or a few leaders. A condition for sustained core funding of NGOs should be internal governance reforms to promote healthy and sustainable organizations.

12 Donors would do well to collaborate and coordinate better with one another to share information on programs, grants, and the performance of grantees; to harmonize their reporting requirements so that NGOs with limited administrative capacity are not unduly strained; and to discuss their norms, goals, and best practices so that the field as a whole can learn and advance.

Much more can and should also be done to reorganize foreign aid around the incentive-based approach of the MCA. Indeed the entire U.S. Foreign Assistance program has become a hopeless jumble of Congressional earmarks and partial objectives that rob aid administrators of the flexibility they need to look at countries holistically and with fresh eyes. The most important question that should be asked in allocating aid and designing country strategies is, "How can the U.S. encourage coherent and sustained progress toward just development?" That means not just economic growth or better health for the next year or two, but more open, accountable, and effective institutions in the state and civil society for the long run.

In an increasingly multipolar world, the United States must also work more often and more closely with other democracies—including the emerging-market democracies—to advance and assist democratic development. Thomas Carothers and Richard Youngs argue that emerging democratic regional powers like Brazil, India, South Africa, Indonesia, and Turkey could "serve as powerful examples of the universal appeal of democracy," countering the pull of nondemocratic models popularized by China and Russia.[44] President Obama should "urge these rising democratic powers to join Western efforts to support democracy and human rights around the world."[45] Indeed, it should now be a major objective of U.S. and European foreign policy to draw these rising democratic powers into a new era of multilateral efforts to encourage and support democracy. However, these emerging-market democracies remain suspicious of the motives of Western powers, wary of interventionist approaches, and sensitive about issues of sovereignty. Thus, they will need to be drawn in through incremental and cautious steps. Carothers and Youngs advise: first, "emphasize low-visibility, sustained endeavors, not high-visibility, short-term impact gestures";[46] second, "keep an open mind with regard to different and potentially clashing approaches on international democracy support";[47] and third, "emphasize nongovernmental rather than governmental approaches and links."[48]

The Open Government Partnership (OGP) is a hopeful example of how a sincere effort to engage the new democratic powers can pay off. Launched in September 2011 and co-chaired by the U.S. and Brazil, its eight founding members include four other emerging-market democracies: Indonesia, Mexico, the Philippines, and South Africa. Each member had to commit, in a far-reaching declaration, to expand access to public information, to increase civic participation, to implement high standards of ethical integrity for public officials, and to "increase access to new technologies for openness and accountability."[49] Because of their commitment to transparency and accountability, member nations have become an attractive target for aid. Many other countries have noticed this, as well as the significant signaling benefits membership provides, and are thus aspiring to join.

Finally, the U.S. can gain a lot in terms of legitimacy and effectiveness by working to defend and advance democracy as often as possible through regional organizations, like NATO and the Organization of American States (OAS), through international organizations like the UN, and through broad multilateral networks like the Community of Democracies and the Open Government Partnership. Over the last two decades, the UN has emerged as a significant player in democracy promotion, assuming critical roles in assisting the organization of democratic elections and in helping to resolve violent conflict through democratic mechanisms. Today, the United Nations Development Programme (UNDP) is one of the largest international providers of democratic governance assistance, with a budget of about $1.4 billion for that purpose in 2005, including support for about a third of the parliaments in the developing world.[50] While the Community of

Democracies has been mainly a symbolic and occasional gathering of states since its founding in 2000, it is now beginning to develop a more effective governing structure, a more robust voice for defending against assaults on democracy, and means (such as through cooperative democracy partnerships) to provide tangible forms of governance assistance to new and troubled democracies.[51] Having as members of the CD Governing Council not just other established democracies, like Canada, Japan, and a number from Europe, but emerging democracies like India, Korea, Mongolia, Mexico, Chile, Mali, and South Africa, in itself sends a significant message about the growing global legitimacy of democracy.

In a world of ongoing security threats—terrorism, narcotrafficking, and proliferation of weapons of mass destruction, to name a few—and of new threats such as cyberwarfare and China's expanding military power and strategic ambitions, promoting freedom and democracy will sometimes recede in priority and visibility. But it should always be an important foreign policy objective. The states that gravely threaten international security are all autocracies, or at least illiberal and weak democracies urgently in need of strengthening. Ultimately, nothing will better advance the security and prosperity of the U.S. and its democratic allies than the gradual movement of the entire world toward more, and more liberal, democracy.

Notes

1 Earlier versions of this chapter were published as "Promoting Democracy, Foreign Policy Imperative?" *Great Decisions 2012*, Foreign Policy Association, September 2011; and as "Promoting Democracy," in Peter Berkowitz, ed., *Renewing the American Constitutional Tradition* (Stanford, CA: Hoover Institution Press, 2013). A portion was also drawn from, "Chasing Away the Democracy Blues," *Foreign Policy*, October 24, 2014, http://foreignpolicy.com/2014/10/24/chasing-away-the-democracy-blues/, which was based on my keynote address to the conference "Does Democracy Matter?" cosponsored by the Foreign Policy Research Institute and the Kennan Institute in Washington, DC, on October 20, 2014.

2 Address by Secretary of State John Quincy Adams to the U.S. House of Representatives, July 4, 1821. www.fff.org/comment/AdamsPolicy.asp.

3 Walter Russell Mead, *Special Providence: American Foreign Policy and How it Changed the World* (New York: Routledge, 2002), 138.

4 However, since the original publication of this essay toward the end of Obama's first term, this has seemed distinctly less true of President Obama, who has privileged other priorities over democracy promotion.

5 Pew Research Center for the People and the Press, June 10, 2011, http://pewresearch.org/pubs/2020/poll-american-attitudes-foreign-poilcy-middle-east-israel-palestine-obama.

6 U.S. Global Leadership Coalition, International Affairs Budget Update, February 4, 2011, www.usglc.org/wp-content/uploads/2011/02/Budget-Analysis.pdf.

7 I say probably because it is impossible to isolate and sum up all the parts of the budget that legitimately constitute democracy and governance assistance. Many expenditures have dual or multiple purposes and one could debate the extent to which they serve the purpose of promoting democracy and better governance.

8 Larry Diamond, *The Spirit of Democracy: The Struggle to Build Free Societies Throughout the World* (New York: Times Books, 2008).

9 Bruce W. Jentleson, "Beware the Duck Test," *Washington Quarterly* 34 (Summer, 2011): 142.

10 Anatol Lieven and John Hulsman, *Ethical Realism: A Vision for America's Role in the World* (New York: Pantheon, 2006), 67.

11 Mead, *Special Providence*, 163.

12 Ibid.

13 Michael McFaul, *Advancing Democracy Abroad: Why We Should and How We Can* (Lanham, MD: Rowman and Littlefield, and Stanford, CA: Hoover Institution Press, 2010), 98–102.

14 Hilton L. Root, *Alliance Curse: How America Lost the Third World* (Washington, DC: Brookings Institution, 2008). See also McFaul, *Advancing Democracy Abroad*.

15 Larry Diamond, *Squandered Victory: The American Occupation and the Bungled Effort to Bring Democracy to Iraq* (New York: Times Books, 2005).

16 Thomas Carothers, *Democracy Policy Under Obama: Revitalization or Retreat?* (Washington, DC: Carnegie Endowment for International Peace, 2012), 5.

17 Ibid., 9.

18 Ibid., 11.

19 James Dobbins et al., *The UN's Role in Nation-Building: Form the Congo to Iraq* (Santa Monica, CA: RAND Corporation, 2005); and Dobbins et al., *America's Role in Nation-Building: From Germany to Iraq* (Santa Monica, CA: RAND Corporation, 2003).

20 Adrian Karatnycky and Peter Ackerman, *How Freedom Is Won: From Civic Struggle to Durable Democracy* (New York: Freedom House, 2005), http://old.freedomhouse.org/template.cfm?page=383&report=29.

21 Steven Levitsky and Lucan Way, "International Linkage and Democratization," *Journal of Democracy* 16 (July 2005): 24.

22 Ibid.

23 Tun-jen Cheng, "Democratizing the Quasi-Leninist Regime in Taiwan," *World Politics* 41 (July 1989) 484.

24 On this effect in Chile late in Pinochet's rule, see George P. Shultz, *Turmoil and Triumph: My Years as Secretary of State* (New York: Charles Scribner's Sons, 1993), 972 and 974.

25 Robert G. Herman and Theodore J. Piccone, eds, *Defending Democracy: A Global Survey of Foreign Policy Trends, 1992–2002* (Washington, DC: Democracy Coalition Project, 2002), 214.

26 Valerie Bunce and Sharon Wolchik, "Azerbaijan's 2005 Parliamentary Elections: A Failed Attempt at Democratic Transition," Working Paper, Center on Democracy, Development, and the Rule of Law, September 2008, http://iis-db.stanford.edu/pubs/22230/No_89_BunceVolchikAzerbaijan.pdf._

27 See Council for a Community of Democracies, *A Diplomat's Handbook for Democracy Development Support*, second edition (Washington, DC: Council for a Community of Democracies, 2010), especially chapter 3. http://diplomatshandbook.org/pdf/Diplomats_Handbook.pdf.

28 All quotes from Pauline H. Baker, "South Africa's Future: A Turbulent Transition," *Journal of Democracy* 1 (Fall 1990), 8–9.

29 Council of a Community of Democracies, *A Diplomat's Handbook*, 27.

30 This was the case for some time with Senegal as well, but then it returned to being a vigorous democracy with electoral alternation in 2012.

31 "Report on the Criteria and Methodology for Determining the Eligibility of Candidate Countries for Millennium Challenge Account Assistance in FY 2012," Millennium Challenge Corporate, September 2011, https://www.mcc.gov/documents/reports/report-2011001066201-fy12-selection-criteria.pdf, 6.

32 Thomas Carothers, *Confronting the Weakest Link: Aiding Political Parties in New Democracies* (Washington, DC: Carnegie Endowment for International Peace, 2006).

33 Thomas Carothers and Diane de Gramont, *Aiding Governance in Developing Countries: Progress Amid Uncertainties* (Washington, DC: Carnegie Endowment for International Peace, November 2011), 4.

34 Ibid., 10–12.

35 Ibid., 1.

36 Thomas Carothers, *Aiding Democracy Abroad: The Learning Curve* (Washington, DC: The Carnegie Endowment for International Peace, 1999), 307.

37 Ibid., 308.

38 Steven E. Finkel, Aníbal Pérez-Liñán, and Mitchell Seligson, "Effects of U.S. Foreign Assistance on Democracy Building: Results of a Cross-National Quantitative Study," Final report to USAID, January 12, 2006, 83, www.usaid. gov/our_work/democracy_and_governance/publications/pdfs/impact_of_ democracy_assistance.pdf.

39 Melinda Haring, "Reforming the Democracy Bureaucracy," *Foreign Policy*, June 3, 2013, http://foreignpolicy.com/2013/06/03/reforming-the-democracy-bureaucracy.

40 Joel D. Barkan, *Perceptions of Democracy Assistance: Findings from a Survey of Recipients* (Washington, DC: World Movement for Democracy, 2011), www.wmd. org/documents/Perceptions_final_report.pdf.

41 Richard Youngs, "How to Revitalise Democracy Assistance: Recipients' Views," FRIDE Working Paper 100, June 2010, www.fride.org/publication/777/ how-to-revitalise-democracy-assistance:-recipients%27views.

42 See http://envaya.org.

43 To be fair, the USAID practice for guiding its democracy and governance aid strategy in a country is to periodically conduct an assessment of needs and possibilities that relies heavily on interviews with relevant actors and analysis of political and economic interests to determine priorities from the ground up.

44 Thomas Carothers and Richard Youngs, *Looking for Help: Will Rising Democracies Become International Democracy Supporters?* (Washington, DC: Carnegie Endowment for International Peace, July 2011), 1, 3.

45 Ibid.

46 Ibid., 20.

47 Ibid., 22.

48 Ibid., 24.

49 "Open Government Declaration," September, 2011, www.opengovpartnership. org/open-government-declaration.

50 Diamond, *The Spirit of Democracy*, 128.

51 See www.community-democracies.org.

Appendix

Classification of regimes at the end of 2014

Liberal democracies have an average score of 1 to 2 on the Freedom House scales of Political Rights and Civil Liberties, while electoral democracies have an average score greater than 2.

Liberal democracy FH 1–2.0	Electoral democracy, FH>2.0	Competitive authoritarian	Electoral (hegemonic) authoritarian	Politically closed authoritarian
Western Europe (24 states)				
United States (1, 1)				
Canada (1, 1)				
Australia (1, 1)				
New Zealand (1, 1)				
Postcommunist Europe (29)				
Czech Republic (1, 1)	Montenegro (3, 2)	Armenia (5, 4)	Kazakhstan (6, 5)	Turkmenistan (7, 7)
Estonia (1, 1)	Albania (3, 3)	Kyrgyzstan (5, 5)	Azerbaijan (6, 6)	Uzbekistan (7, 7)
Lithuania (1, 1)	Georgia (3, 3)		Russia (6, 6)	
Poland (1, 1)	Moldova (3, 3)		Tajikistan (6, 6)	
Slovakia (1, 1)	Ukraine (3, 3)		Belarus (7, 6)	
Slovenia (1, 1)	Bosnia-Herz. (4, 3)			
Croatia (1, 2)	Macedonia (4, 3)			
Bulgaria (2, 2)	Kosovo (4, 4)			

Liberal democracy FH 1–2.0	Electoral democracy, FH>2.0	Competitive authoritarian	Electoral (hegemonic) authoritarian	Politically closed authoritarian
Hungary (2, 2)				
Latvia (2, 2)				
Romania (2, 2)				
Serbia (2, 2)				

Latin America and the Caribbean (33)

Liberal democracy FH 1–2.0	Electoral democracy, FH>2.0	Competitive authoritarian	Electoral (hegemonic) authoritarian	Politically closed authoritarian
Chile (1, 1)	Dominican Republic (2, 3)	Nicaragua (4, 3)		Cuba (7, 6)
Costa Rica (1, 1)	El Salvador (2, 3)	Haiti (5, 5)		
Uruguay (1, 1)	Guyana (2, 3)	Venezuela (5, 5)		
Argentina (2, 2)	Jamaica (2, 3)			
Brazil (2, 2)	Peru (2, 3)			
Panama (2, 2)	Bolivia (3, 3)			
Suriname (2, 2)	Ecuador (3, 3)			
Trinidad & Tobago (2, 2)	Mexico (3, 3)			
Caribbean states with pop <1 million 6[1] (1, 1) 2[2] (2, 2) 1[3] (2, 2)	Paraguay (3, 3) Colombia (3, 4) Guatemala (3, 4)			
	Honduras (4, 4)			

1 Bahamas, Barbados, Dominica, St. Kitts & Nevis, St. Lucia, St. Vincent & Grenadines
2 Belize and Grenada
3 Antigua & Barbuda

Liberal democracy FH 1–2.0	Electoral democracy, FH>2.0	Competitive authoritarian	Electoral (hegemonic) authoritarian	Politically closed authoritarian
Asia (E, SE, & S) (25)				
Japan (1, 1)	India (2, 3)	Bangladesh (4, 4)	Singapore (4, 4)	Brunei (6, 5)
Mongolia (1, 2)	Indonesia (2, 4)	Malaysia (4, 4)	Cambodia (6, 5)	Thailand (6, 5)
Taiwan (1, 2)	Philippines (3, 3)	Sri Lanka (5, 5)	Afghanistan (6, 6)	Vietnam (7, 5)
South Korea (2, 2)	Bhutan (3, 4)		Burma (6, 6)	China (7, 6)
	East Timor (3, 4)			Laos (7, 6)
	Maldives (4, 4)			North Korea (7, 7)
	Nepal (4, 4)			
	Pakistan (4, 5)			
Pacific islands (12)				
5[1] (1, 1) Naru (1, 2) Samoa (1, 2) Tonga (2, 2) Vanuatu (2, 2)	Solomon Islands (3, 3) Fiji (3, 4) Papua New Guinea (4, 3)			

1 Kiribati, Marshall Islands, Micronesia, Palau, Tuvalu

Liberal democracy FH 1–2.0	Electoral democracy, FH>2.0	Competitive authoritarian	Electoral (hegemonic) authoritarian	Politically closed authoritarian
Africa (Sub-Sahara) (48)				
Cape Verde (1, 1)	Lesotho (2, 3)	Tanzania (3, 3)	Togo (4, 4)	Swaziland (7, 5)
Ghana (1, 2)	Botswana (3, 2)	Mozambique (4, 3)	Guinea (5, 5)	Chad (7, 6)
Mauritius (1, 2)	Seychelles (3, 3)	Kenya (4, 4)	Zimbabwe (5, 6)	South Sudan (7, 6)
Benin (2, 2)	Sierra Leone (3, 3)	Nigeria (4, 5)	Burkina Faso (6, 3)	Central African Rep. (7, 7)
Namibia (2, 2)	Comoros (3, 4)	Côte d'Ivoire (5, 4)	Angola (6, 5)	Equatorial Guinea (7, 7)
São Tomé & Principe (2, 2)	Liberia (3, 4)	Mali (5, 4)	Burundi (6, 5)	Eritrea (7, 7)
Senegal (2, 2)	Malawi (3, 4)	Guinea-Bissau (5, 5)	Congo, Rep. (6, 5)	Somalia (7, 7)
South Africa (2, 2)	Niger (3, 4)		Djibouti (6, 5)	Sudan (7, 7)
	Zambia (3, 4)		Gabon (6, 5)	
	Madagascar (4, 4)		Mauritania (6, 5)	
			Uganda (6, 5)	
			Cameroon (6, 6)	
			Congo, DRC (6, 6)	
			Ethiopia (6, 6)	
			Rwanda (6, 6)	
Middle East-North Africa (19)				
Israel (1, 2)	Tunisia (1, 3)	Turkey (3, 4)	Kuwait (5, 5)	Oman (6, 5)
		Lebanon (5, 4)	Algeria (6, 5)	Qatar (6, 5)
		Morocco (5, 4)	Egypt (6, 5)	United Arab Emirates (6, 6)
			Jordan (6, 5)	Bahrain (7, 6)
			Iran (6, 6)	Saudi Arabia (7, 7)
			Iraq (6, 6)	Syria (7, 7)
			Libya (6, 6)	
			Yemen (6, 6)	

Principal source: Freedom House, Freedom in the World Survey, www.freedomhouse.org.

Index

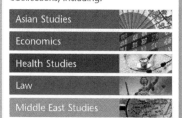

Made in the USA
Middletown, DE
16 August 2021